STRATEGIES FOR PUBLIC MANAGEMENT REFORM

RESEARCH IN PUBLIC POLICY ANALYSIS AND MANAGEMENT

Series Editor: Lawrence R. Jones

Recent Volumes:

Volumes 1–10:	Research in Public Policy Analysis and Management
Volumes 11A & B:	Learning from International Public Management Reform – Edited by Lawrence R. Jones, James Guthrie and Peter Steane
Volume 12:	The Transformative Power of Dialogue – Edited by Nancy C. Roberts

RESEARCH IN PUBLIC POLICY ANALYSIS AND
MANAGEMENT   VOLUME 13

STRATEGIES FOR PUBLIC MANAGEMENT REFORM

EDITED BY

LAWRENCE R. JONES

Naval Postgraduate School, CA, USA

KUNO SCHEDLER

University of St. Gallen, Switzerland

and

RICCARDO MUSSARI

University of Siena, Italy

2004

ELSEVIER
JAI

Amsterdam – Boston – Heidelberg – London – New York – Oxford
Paris – San Diego – San Francisco – Singapore – Sydney – Tokyo

ELSEVIER B.V.
Sara Burgerhartstraat 25
P.O. Box 211
1000 AE Amsterdam
The Netherlands

ELSEVIER Inc.
525 B Street, Suite 1900
San Diego
CA 92101-4495
USA

**ELSEVIER Ltd
The Boulevard, Langford
Lane, Kidlington
Oxford OX5 1GB
UK**

ELSEVIER Ltd
84 Theobalds Road
London
WC1X 8RR
UK

© 2004 Elsevier Ltd. All rights reserved.

This work is protected under copyright by Elsevier Ltd, and the following terms and conditions apply to its use:

Photocopying
Single photocopies of single chapters may be made for personal use as allowed by national copyright laws. Permission of the Publisher and payment of a fee is required for all other photocopying, including multiple or systematic copying, copying for advertising or promotional purposes, resale, and all forms of document delivery. Special rates are available for educational institutions that wish to make photocopies for non-profit educational classroom use.

Permissions may be sought directly from Elsevier's Rights Department in Oxford, UK; phone: (+44) 1865 843830, fax: (+44) 1865 853333, e-mail: permissions@elsevier.com. Requests may also be completed on-line via the Elsevier homepage (http://www.elsevier.com/locate/permissions).

In the USA, users may clear permissions and make payments through the Copyright Clearance Center, Inc., 222 Rosewood Drive, Danvers, MA 01923, USA; phone: (+1) (978) 7508400, fax: (+1) (978) 7504744, and in the UK through the Copyright Licensing Agency Rapid Clearance Service (CLARCS), 90 Tottenham Court Road, London W1P 0LP, UK; phone: (+44) 20 7631 5555; fax: (+44) 20 7631 5500. Other countries may have a local reprographic rights agency for payments.

Derivative Works
Tables of contents may be reproduced for internal circulation, but permission of the Publisher is required for external resale or distribution of such material. Permission of the Publisher is required for all other derivative works, including compilations and translations.

Electronic Storage or Usage
Permission of the Publisher is required to store or use electronically any material contained in this work, including any chapter or part of a chapter.

Except as outlined above, no part of this work may be reproduced, stored in a retrieval system or transmitted in any form or by any means, electronic, mechanical, photocopying, recording or otherwise, without prior written permission of the Publisher.
Address permissions requests to: Elsevier's Rights Department, at the fax and e-mail addresses noted above.

Notice
No responsibility is assumed by the Publisher for any injury and/or damage to persons or property as a matter of products liability, negligence or otherwise, or from any use or operation of any methods, products, instructions or ideas contained in the material herein. Because of rapid advances in the medical sciences, in particular, independent verification of diagnoses and drug dosages should be made.

First edition 2004

British Library Cataloguing in Publication Data
A catalogue record is available from the British Library.

ISBN: 0-7623-1031-6
ISSN: 0723-1318

∞ The paper used in this publication meets the requirements of ANSI/NISO Z39.48-1992 (Permanence of Paper). Printed in The Netherlands.

CONTENTS

LIST OF CONTRIBUTORS ix

PREFACE AND ACKNOWLEDGMENTS xi

1. ASSESSMENT OF PUBLIC MANAGEMENT REFORM
   AND STRATEGY
   Kuno Schedler, Lawrence R. Jones and Riccardo Mussari 1

   PART I: ACCOUNTABILITY, DECENTRALIZATION, AND DELEGATION STRATEGIES

2. RETHINKING ACCOUNTABILITY IN EDUCATION:
   HOW SHOULD WHO HOLD WHOM ACCOUNTABLE
   FOR WHAT?
   Robert D. Behn 19

3. DEVELOPMENT OF CONTRACTING IN
   INFRASTRUCTURE INVESTMENT IN THE U.K.: THE
   PRIVATE FINANCE INITIATIVE IN THE NATIONAL
   HEALTH SERVICE
   Jane Broadbent, Jas Gill and Richard Laughlin 55

4. STAKEHOLDER THEORY, PARTNERSHIPS AND
   ALLIANCES IN THE HEALTH CARE SECTOR OF THE
   U.K. AND SCOTLAND
   Alexander Murdock 85

5. STRATEGIES FOR HEALTH CARE REFORM
   IMPLEMENTATION IN SOUTHERN ITALY
   Marco Meneguzzo, Valentina Mele and Angelo Tanese 105

PART II: INFORMATION TECHNOLOGY AND MANAGEMENT CONTROL STRATEGIES

6. MANAGING THE E-GOVERNMENT ORGANIZATION
   Kuno Schedler and Bernhard Schmidt   133

7. REFORM OF PUBLIC MANAGEMENT THROUGH ICT: INTERFACE, ACCOUNTABILITY AND TRANSPARENCY
   Hiroko Kudo   153

8. RISK, REFORM AND ORGANIZATIONAL CULTURE: THE CASE OF IRS TAX SYSTEMS MODERNIZATION
   Barry Bozeman   175

9. MANAGEMENT CONTROL REFORM IN THE PUBLIC SECTOR: CONTRASTING THE USA AND ITALY
   Lawrence R. Jones and Riccardo Mussari   205

PART III: ANTI-CORRUPTION STRATEGIES

10. POLITICAL CORRUPTION: ESTABLISHING THE PARAMETERS
    Peter deLeon and Mark T. Green   229

11. SUPPLY-SIDE CONTROL OF CORRUPTION: THE U.S. FOREIGN CORRUPT PRACTICES ACT AND THE OECD CONVENTION
    Masako N. Darrough   259

12. COPING WITH CORRUPTION IN ALBANIAN PUBLIC ADMINISTRATION AND BUSINESS
    Denita Cepiku   285

13. REDUCING CORRUPTION IN POST-COMMUNIST
    COUNTRIES
    Alexander Kotchegura   *325*

PART IV: PERFORMANCE ASSESSMENT AND MANAGEMENT STRATEGIES

14. A CONCEPTUAL FRAMEWORK AND
    METHODOLOGICAL GUIDE FOR RESEARCH ON
    PUBLIC MANAGEMENT POLICY CHANGE IN THE
    LATIN AMERICAN REGION
    *Michael Barzelay, Francisco Gaetani, Juan Carlos
    Cortázar Velarde and Guillermo Cejudo*   *349*

15. DEVELOPING PERFORMANCE INDICATORS AND
    MEASUREMENT SYSTEMS IN PUBLIC INSTITUTIONS
    Kuno Schedler   *371*

16. EVALUATION OF NEW PUBLIC MANAGEMENT
    REFORMS IN SWITZERLAND: EMPIRICAL RESULTS
    AND REFLECTIONS ON METHODOLOGY
    Stefan Rieder and Luzia Lehmann   *395*

17. MEASURING AND MANAGING FOR PERFORMANCE:
    LESSONS FROM AUSTRALIA
    Bill Ryan   *415*

PART V: TRENDS IN REFORM STRATEGY

18. ASSESSING PUBLIC MANAGEMENT REFORM
    STRATEGY IN AN INTERNATIONAL CONTEXT
    Lawrence R. Jones and Donald F. Kettl   *453*

SUBJECT INDEX   *475*

LIST OF CONTRIBUTORS

Michael Barzelay	London School of Economics, London, UK
Robert D. Behn	Harvard University, Cambridge, MA, USA
Barry Bozeman	Georgia Tech, Atlanta, GA, USA
Jane Broadbent	Royal Holloway University of London, Surrey, UK
Guillermo Cejudo	Federal Electoral Institute, Mexico City, Mexico
Denita Cepiku	University of Rome "Tor Vergata", Rome, Italy
Masako N. Darrough	Baruch College, New York, NY, USA
Francisco Gaetani	United Nations Development Program, Brasilia, Brazil
Jas Gill	Royal Holloway University of London, London, UK
Mark T. Green	Oregon State University, Corvalis, OR, USA
Peter deLeon	University of Colorado, Denver, USA
Lawrence R. Jones	Naval Postgraduate School, Monterey, CA, USA
Donald F. Kettl	University of Winsconsin-Madison, Madison, WI, USA
Alexander Kotchegura	European Commission, Moscow, Russia
Hiroko Kudo	Waseda University, Tokyo, Japan
Richard Laughlin	King's College, University of London, London, UK
Luzia Lehmann	Interface Institute for Policy Studies, Lucerne, Switzerland

Valentina Mele	Bocconi University, Milan, Italy
Marco Meneguzzo	Tor Vergata University, Rome, Italy
Alexander Murdock	South Bank University Business School, London, UK
Riccardo Mussari	University of Siena, Siena, Italy
Stefan Rieder	Interface Institute for Policy Studies, Lucerne, Switzerland
Bill Ryan	Victoria University of Wellington, Wellington, New Zealand
Kuno Schedler	University of St. Gallen, St. Gallen, Switzerland
Berhard Schmidt	University of St. Gallen, St. Gallen, Switzerland
Angelo Tanese	Pescara University, Pescara, Italy
Juan Carlos Cortázar Velarde	Interamerican Development Bank, Washington, D.C., USA

PREFACE AND ACKNOWLEDGMENTS

So much has been written about public management and administrative reform in the past decade that in developing the approach for this book we wondered whether there was anything new to say. As is the case for most professionals working in our field, we recognize that the topic of New Public Management has been worked over very thoroughly. New public management is no longer "new" and, therefore, we believe in the future it is better to use the words public management change or innovation when speaking and writing about emerging initiatives in the public sector. And, as most in our field also understand, the topics receiving significant attention at present are networking and a set of issues related to what is termed "governance." Research on networking has been on-going since at least the 1970s. Many issues related to networks and networking remain unresolved so that continued dialogue in this area is constructive. Renewed attention to governance (versus government) appears to have emerged in the public management dialogue and literature in the past five years or so.

What do those who focus on the need for renewed emphasis on governance issues mean when they exhort the field to think about this topic? While no claim is made that we capture all of what is intended, it seems to us that a renewed interest in governance concentrates on five issue clusters, each with its own set of imperatives: (a) improved understanding of linkages between politics and administration; (b) the need for improved analysis of stakeholder positioning and preferences in formulating public policy and management execution strategy; (c) analysis to better define network relationships among stakeholders internal and external to government; (d) the necessity for addressing potential and real abridgements of public participation rights and basic principles of democracy; and (e) finding remedies to address the absence of government responsiveness to citizens in policy formation and execution; (f) alternative institutional arrangements for governance of the delivery of services to the public. Furthermore, the governance movement may be viewed as a response to a perceived absence of sufficient attention given to these five issue areas in the drive to devise and implement New Public Management or neo-managerialism in government over the past several decades.

While defenders of NPM may argue that the intent of managerial reform was to improve efficiency and effectiveness within government, thereby making government more responsive to citizen service preferences, few would argue that these objectives have been achieved as a result of world-wide adoption of many of the management policies, procedures and methods advocated by NPM proponents. Proponents of NPM often argue that not enough time has elapsed to thoroughly evaluate NPM implementation. From our view, this is more the truth in some settings than in others. Experience with NPM in New Zealand, for example, is mature enough so that many of the consequences of implementation are relatively well understood. However, in Switzerland it is clear that more time is needed to assess the impact of NPM-oriented reform. In the U.S., there probably is enough evidence to pursue such evaluation but, as of yet, satisfactory empirical analysis has not been presented. However, beyond the issue of evaluation, few defenders of NPM would argue that those who assert the need for improved governance are wrong or misguided in directing attention to problems in this area. One thing that we have learned quite clearly from evaluation of NPM is that little reform takes place beyond reengineering in public organizations (which in most cases has been positive in and of itself) unless political policy makers become interested and take on as part of their mandate a consistent push to put the concepts and practices of NPM into place, and then to monitor and steer its implementation. Thus, the need for improved governance is evident to both supporters and critics of past public management reform.

Given these understandings, our instincts and synthesis of current events in the field of public management indicate that the area most neglected and in need of greater academic and practitioner attention is the issue of strategy, whether viewed from the perspective of management reform implementation, strategic planning, results-oriented management or performance management. Thus, the framework and the works represented in this book address the dimensions of strategy in public management reform from different perspectives including increased demands for accountability, decentralization, devolution, application of information technology, management control, anti-corruption initiatives, and performance assessment and management. Most of the works employ case study methodology as part of their efforts to investigate the presence or absence of strategic intent and approach, and the relative success of various strategies, in venues where reform has been sought as an explicit goal of governments, elected officials and public managers.

We believe the organization of this volume and the works presented offer a valuable perspective on the dynamics of reform in a variety of venues. Our aim is modest in this regard. We hope to contribute to the continuing dialogue over strategy, objectives, management practice, implementation and evaluation of consequences that characterizes research in the field of international public management.

One observation related to this last point is that, as far as we can tell, over the past decade a new sub-discipline has emerged – international public management. With respect to issues deemed worthy of attention in this sub-disciplinary area, there is little or no difference between what is of interest to those who conduct research on domestic reform vs. comparative or international reform. What distinguishes the new sub-discipline is its explicit emphasis on international and comparative research, i.e. a wider content within which to investigate issues of relevance to reform.

What often distinguishes the emergence of new sub-disciplines is the appearance of new outlets for publication. Over the past decade a number of new journals have begun publication of research on or related to management reform in an international and comparative context. Further, a number of existing high-visibility journals are publishing articles that may be viewed to contribute to the relatively new field. The International Public Management Network and its International Public Management Journal and International Public Management Review may have contributed to the emergence of this sub-discipline in some way, but this represent only a small part of a very evident trend across the world landscape. The Chinese blessing "May you live in interesting times" seems to have been realized for many of us who work in the field of international public management. Indeed, never before has there been so much data available from so many contexts upon which to base research on change in public sector management and governance.

In conclusion, we wish to acknowledge the efforts of the authors of the chapters in this book for having brought their works to publishable quality. Most of the chapters in this book evolved from papers presented at the IPMN Siena 2002 Conference convened on June 26–28, 2002. One of these papers, by Jane Broadbent, Jas Gill and Richard Laughlin, won the Naschold Award for best paper of conference. Some of the chapters not presented at the conference were invited contributions from conference participants, in large part resulting from personal interaction at the conference. Several other chapters are included to achieve the topic coverage we deemed necessary to satisfy the design of the book.

In particular, we want to thank the University of Siena, our host Professor Riccardo Mussari and his colleagues and staff, particularly Antonella Casamonti, Alberto Castelnuovo, Dr. Prof. Giuseppe Grossi and Pasquale Ruggiero. We also want to thank the Siena conference organizing committee members that, in addition to the editors of this volume, included Michael Barzelay, Sandford Borins, Elio Borgonovi, Kurt Klaudi Klausen and Fred Thompson. Kuno Schedler chaired the conference committee and, with Riccardo Mussari, shares the credit for the success of the conference. We appreciate their steadfast efforts to make the IPMN conference a success. In addition, we wish to thank Whitney Q. Ning for her significant contribution in editing this volume. Without the initiative and hard work of all of these individuals this book would not have been published. Lastly, we wish to acknowledge the financial contributions made in support of the IPMN Siena 2002 Conference and this book by the Space and Naval Systems Command through sponsorship of the Wagner Chair Professorship at the Naval

Postgraduate School, by the Institute of Public Services and Tourism, University of St. Gallen, the Department of Business and Social Studies and the University of Siena, the Monte dei Paschi di Siena Foundation, and the Italian Ministry for University Scientific and Technological Research.

Lawrence R. Jones, Kuno Schedler and Riccardo Mussari
Editors

1. ASSESSMENT OF PUBLIC MANAGEMENT REFORM AND STRATEGY

Kuno Schedler, Lawrence R. Jones
and Riccardo Mussari

INTRODUCTION: STRATEGIC APPROACHES TO REFORM AND INTEGRATION OF THEMES

This book is organized into five sections. The first four sections are devoted to investigation of the seven different strategies to achieve public management reform delineated in this book. The seven strategies are: (1) increased accountability; (2) decentralization and delegation of authority and responsibility for decision making and management; (3) application of information technology to improve management and responsiveness of governments to citizens; (4) developing and improving management control systems in the public sector; (5) measures to reduce corruption in government, business and society; (6) development and use of performance indicators in public organizations; and (7) integration of performance measurement and management in public organizations. The chapters in each of the five sections address the need for and application of strategy, impediments to implementation, and use cases to support their analysis and conclusions.

The first strategy for implementation of public management reform is to increase accountability. Behn's essay on accountability in education is illustrative of the issues and problems that must be addressed in any policy context to assign accountability among a variety of potential stakeholders. The second strategy of decentralization and delegation is explored in detail by Broadbent, Gill and Laughlin. They demonstrate the complications and unanticipated consequences, potentially positive and negative, that have resulted from installation of the Private Financing Initiative in the health care sector in the United Kingdom. Murdock applies stakeholder theory as an alternative to an NPM-oriented reform model to suggest how operation of the health care system in the U.K. and Scotland might be improved by partnerships, and formation of alliances and increased networking. Meneguzzo, Male and Tenese contribute a critique of NPM and ethics in public management and then derive lessons from the decentralization and delegation within the Southern Italian health care system, with special emphasis on the successful examples excellence centers, networking, informal relationships and entrepreneurship.

The second section on information technology and management control strategies begins with the chapter by Schedler and Schmidt that provides a framework within which management of e-government may be undertaken. Kudo then provides a comprehensive analysis of how application of information technology may improve accountability and transparency of government to citizens. Kudo contrasts the experiences of Italy, Thailand and Indonesia to support her argument. Bozeman then describes and analyzes the risks and organizational culture ramifications related to implementation of new information technology in a case study of the monumental failure of the U.S. Internal Revenue Service tax system modernization initiative. The final chapter in this section investigates improvement of government through implementation of a well-designed management control system. Jones and Mussari explore how management control has been implemented in the U.S. and Italy, including the case of the City of Ravenna. They show, through the cases, why management control system strategy is difficult to implement despite its apparent benefits.

The section on anti-corruption strategy begins with deLeon and Green's framing of the problems that confront reform strategy to provide a structure to understand the issues that must be addressed in battling illegal arrangements within government and between government and the private sector. They also address cultural and social norms as critical variables in the fight against corruption. Darrough explores the strategy of supply-side control of corruption in the case of the U.S. Foreign Corrupt Practices Act and the OECD Convention. She focuses on strategies to control the illegal behavior, including bribery, that multinational corporation sometimes exhibit in their relationships with public officials in foreign country trade and related negotiations. Cepiku follows with a detailed analysis of anti-corruption strategies employed in Albania. She demonstrates the advantages and risks encountered in deployment of a variety of approaches. Kotchegura offers his chapter on corruption and efforts to control it in Central and Eastern European (CEE) nations and countries of the Commonwealth of Independent States (CIS), i.e. former Soviet-controlled countries undergoing significant economic and social transition. As with the case of Albania, Kotchegura's analysis shows how difficult it is to attempt the implementation of a comprehensive regime of anti-corruption controls. Based upon a review of important literature in the field and information from his case examples, he recommends a more incremental or marginal approach wherein governments concentrate effort on high payoff and highly visible targets where success will stimulate the citizenry to resist and reports instances of corruption.

The next section of the book on performance assessment and management strategies begins with a conceptual framework and methodological guide for research on public management policy change in the Latin American region by Michael Barzelay, Francisco Gaetani, Juan Carlos Cortázar Velarde and Guillermo Cejudo. The authors provide methods to improve the methodology of research on public management reform that have been applied successfully in Latin America and are intended to be useful in all contexts. Schedler follows with a well-structured and articulated set of methods for developing performance indicators and measurement systems in public institutions, supported by cases of implementation. Rieder and Lehmann then provide a case-based evaluation of new public management experiments in Switzerland: Noteworthy is that they develop their argument employing empirical testing and analysis and follow their conclusions with comments on a number of critical methodological issues that must be addressed in conduct of such analysis. The final chapter in this section by Bill Ryan explores a wide range of organizational and social issues encountered when attempting to employ a reform strategy based on performance measurement and management. Ryan's grand tour of the issues, grounded in case application in Australia and the state of Queensland, is instructive for all venues.

The last section and chapter in the book by Jones and Kettl assesses and draws conclusions on international trends in public management reform and strategy. More on their analysis and conclusions is provided subsequently in this chapter.

REFLECTIONS ON PUBLIC MANAGEMENT REFORM MODELS

Reform of public management has been in progress for decades in the developed world. Debate over the modernization of government has increased significantly with the emergence of the new public management (NPM). There is an overwhelming amount of literature on NPM that will not be reviewed here, nor will we provide a definition of NPM. Suffice it to say that many elements of NPM have received world-wide acceptance, for better or worse. Many criticisms of "neo-managerialism" seem to us valid, but they risk falling on deaf ears in the practitioner arena as new management methods are implemented in both developed and developing nations. What were a decade ago thought to be new management techniques and methods have become commonplace. Debate over whether NPM has changed the world appears to be moot. NPM has prevailed to the extent that now it is simply part of how public management is defined and practiced (Jones & Thompson, 1999). Thus, as we noted in the Preface to this book, there is little reason to continue to use the term New Public Management because the movement is no longer "new."

In our view there is a roughly defined common strategy for public management reform employed all over the world. Kettl (2000) has termed this as "the global public management revolution." In fact, the majority of reform initiatives worldwide have been undertaken with similar rhetoric and have developed from similar conceptual and theoretical approaches – driven and modified by pragmatic considerations and organizational and cultural circumstance. It has become clear that NPM will continue to represent the reform agenda in selected venues, e.g. Switzerland. However, students of public management reform will discover all kinds of methods around the world in practice, depending on specific perceptions of problems to be solved and methodological appropriateness of various managerial methods (Schedler & Proeller, 2002). And, in all circumstances, they will learn that politics plays a critical role in determining which reforms are chosen for implementation as we would expect in democratic decision making systems, and we may be surprised to learn about in non-democratic settings.

In our view it is unwise to reduce the dialogue on public management reform to critiques of the model and practices of new public management. "Newer than new" public management initiatives (e.g. Pallot, 1997, 1998), including stakeholder models (see Broadbent et al., and Murdock in this volume) must be taken into consideration because reform analysis relative to the criteria of any single model is limited and does not adequately take into account the incremental and evolutionary process of reform. Prominent examples of non-NPM reform approaches beyond stakeholder theory include the introduction of information technology into the service creation and delivery process (electronic government), the renaissance of analysis of the role of politics in reform, and emerging innovations in public governance (Schedler, 2003). From our perspective, NPM was a reform approach built on a collection of models (public choice and agency theory, new institutional economics, etc.) and a wide variety of practices including performance measurement, program evaluation and resource management methods such as program and performance budgeting, management by objectives, mission-driven results-oriented budgeting and other techniques experimented with broadly in the 20th century. In summary, it seems to us that the new public management is a manifestation of a *zeitgeist* that has focused on better management in total – both for the public and the not-for-profit sector. And while many NPM advocates promised their methods would work equally well in the private and public sectors (i.e. management is management regardless of sector), and some techniques including reengineering have satisfied this promise, generalization regarding multiple sector applicability has proven risky.

We acknowledge that the new public management as a conceptual model has lost some credibility among critics in many countries in the 21st century. We would point out that since WWII virtually all reform models seem to have a maximum shelf-life of about a decade. Over the period of a decade, terms and concepts are used, misused and "socialized" by academics, administrators and politicians to the extent that clarity is lost and impact is diminished. New brooms are brought in to sweep at persistent, wicked (Roberts, 2000) and only partially resolved problems – to attack them anew from different angles. This is not to say that the new public management has not produced sustainable impacts. In all countries that have used NPM in a wide range of projects, there remain elements of NPM that have become commonly accepted as part of how public management and reform are defined and implemented. Our point is that much of what scholars have characterized as the *new* public management has become simply *public management*. The key to understanding what is important in reform is likely to be found by defining in various contexts which part of this term is emphasized most – *public* or *management* (Jones & Thompson, 1999, pp. 19–20).

In a broad dialogue among members of the International Public Management Network edited by Jones (2002), Donald Kettl made two valuable points:

- First, public management reform is not going away. He illustrates this with several public management problems that have to be solved by the U.K. and U.S. governments in the present and future regardless of what party and which leaders are elected to serve.
- Second, NPM reforms remind us that all public management reform is about politics. He suggests that we need to pay much more attention to the interaction of political/electoral institutions and administrative institutions and reforms.

THE VALUE OF LEARNING MODELS IN UNDERSTANDING REFORM

Modern public management reforms have in common a focus on the results of government activity. Performance management and measurement have become prominent streams of study within the public management and administration research community. Many countries still aim at creating stronger links between inputs and outcomes or results in the application of various types of control systems.

The maturation of public management projects and the assimilation of methods to practice lead to positive outcomes for academics in that all of these projects and their outcomes are ripe for evaluation. The same claims that reformers make for the public sector as a whole (e.g. movement to an outcomes or results orientation) may be made for specific reform projects. Gone is the time when the NPM offered a "playground" for normative hypothesizing not supported by empirical analysis. We believe that an increase in intellectual investigation emphasizing empirical examination of models of politico-administrative systems is crucial for comprehending the public management reform movement world-wide. However, practical implementation has moved us forward to recognize the many "real-life" obstacles to reform. Limitations in the form of human behavioral patterns, risk aversion in politics and government, and the dynamics of the politics of reform (e.g. promising much but delivering less; claiming victory in absence of supporting data, taking credit for successes but avoiding blame for failures) are difficult to change. In combination with internal bureaucratic politics that resist change of any sort, and divisions in external stakeholder and constituent politics that weaken political resolve, make it difficult to implement any model of reform successfully in any political context, even where there is widespread acceptance of the need for change among elected and appointed officials and major policy stakeholders.

We may observe that the "not in my backyard" (NIMBY) syndrome no longer has much relevance for public management reform. In this light. the chapters in this book assess the process and outcomes of public management reform in a wide variety of contexts. Most authors are sympathetic with public managers in their attempts to implement assessment systems in public sector organizations, although contributors criticize many *status quo* practices.

As a general framework to understand the thrust of the contributions in this book, we may use the management learning feedback loop that forms the basis for what has been termed "the St. Gallen Management model" (Ulrich, 1990) shown in Fig. 1. According to the St. Gallen Management model, management control is a circular activity that starts with a decision process to set objectives and determine actions. Making these actions happen is part of the "setting in motion" or implementation element. During and after implementation, the "check and correct" part of management includes registering actual practice to compare with planned programmatic and budgeted figures. Gap analysis leads to either the adjustment of objectives or the determination of new actions. When this model was designed, the circular nature of management learning was viewed as revolutionary because for so long linear decision making models guided the field. The basic

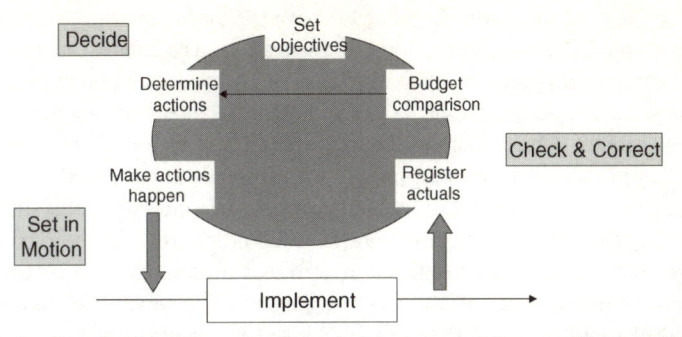

Fig. 1. The Feedback Learning Loop in Management. *Source*: Ulrich (1990).

idea of a feedback learning loop in management is relevant and forms a basis for argumentation in this book. Various strategies of analysis and action designed to obtain specified goals and provide feedback on how better to achieve agreed upon management and policy results are assessed in the works contained in this volume.

Learning is essentially a matter of feedback integration – that has to be organized systematically – and has to be assimilated into the decision making processes of both politicians and public managers.

At the first conference of the International Public Management Network in 1996 in St. Gallen, the learning organization was a primary subject of debate. Reschenthaler and Thompson (1998, p. 59) argued that, "...NPM could help building learning organizations that operate more efficiently and effectively and that also better serve citizens and the public interest." Indeed, the NPM model includes systematic assessment of efficiency and effectiveness indicators (to "register actuals" in the St. Gallen model) that should be used to analyze possible gaps (e.g. in policy and budgets) so as to define either new objectives or actions. This redefinition, combined with a cyclic and continuous assessment process, provides the basis for ongoing learning within management.

Jones and Thompson emphasize the importance of the creating the learning organization as critical to the implementation of public management restructuring, renewal, reinvention, realignment and rethinking (Jones & Thompson, 1999, pp. 203–207). However, recognizing the importance of this approach is far less challenging than is its implementation.

REFORM STRATEGIES

Public management reform in the 21st century will focus on strategies that differ in part or entirely from what has happened in the past. The longer reforms are in place, the more adaptation will occur to move beyond the methods of traditional and "new" public management and administration. The interest of practitioners and researchers will place as much emphasis on institutional and interpersonal relationships as on systems management and control system design. Structures and rules that influence basic human interaction and motivation in the public sector are analyzed in the contemporary public management literature (see for example Pollitt, 2003, pp. 127–149). In fact, under any reform circumstance, strategic decisions have to be made by both managers and politicians – ideally in cooperation – that are motivated by a confluence of different incentives. As explained at the beginning of this chapter, in the works represented in this book we distinguish between seven different strategies divided into four major categories that may be observed in public management reform worldwide. We chose to place the seven strategies into these categories as a way of ordering and linking the works of the authors that comprise this volume. Beyond what we have observed previously, we want to comment further on how and why we have defined these categories as we have in this book.

(1) *Accountability, Decentralization and Delegation Strategies.* It is widely accepted that decentralization and delegation are core management principles (Jones & Thompson, 1999, p. 25) that characterize most contemporary public management reforms. Further, accountability is more critical where authority and responsibility are delegated. Araújo (2002) reports an increase in public institutions (agentification) for the Portuguese central government from 22 in 1974 to 328 in 2000. The reason, he points out, is to improve the coordination and effectiveness of policy implementation. Public institutions, however, are not as independent as they are in other countries. There still remains a direct political control by the minister.

Why is this interesting in our context? To decentralize and to delegate implies that some manager is given a greater room to maneuver. From the public management perspective, this should ideally lead to a closer focus on customer needs, and thus to an increase in effectiveness. Public governance, on the other hand, poses different questions: how is political control guaranteed? How do we avoid public manager motivation exclusively by their own self-interest when implementing public policies? Most often in public management reform, the answer is: if you don't want to retain hierarchical control systems, hold the managers accountable for their results (Jones & Thompson, 1986; McCaffery & Jones, 2001, pp. 321–334; Thompson & Jones, 1986).

(2) *Information Technology and Management Control Strategies:* A different set of structural variables include information and control processes and rules. This approach is a natural response to decentralisation and delegation in that managerial and political leaders want to create and sustain control over their agencies.

Control may be achieved through hierarchy (with significant variation) that may be viewed in the framework of principals and agents, or through other forms of organization. Control may be centralized or delegated, and it may be designated to units or individual managers. In some cases, it may be delegated to other entities and stakeholders including customers, partnering organisations, or citizens. Fountain (2001) points out that the introduction of information technology (IT) may have an impact on structure, but there is no guarantee this will occur. Additionally, due to rejection of new technology there may be an inverse relationship according to Fountain (2001, p. 96): "Organizational, network, and institutional arrangements – and the embeddedness of behavior in them – play key roles in technology enactment."

The introduction of electronic government may be viewed as both a means to different control strategies and a reaction to them. The rigidity or fluidity of structure in general is reflected in control and IT structures, and the behavior of users within organizations. Strategies in this class therefore include managing e-government in public organizations concerned with accountability and transparency, coping with risk and cultural resistance to modernization, and management control process reform.

(3) *Anti-corruption Strategies.* Battling corruption is a significant part of the reform agenda in most nations and particularly in developing countries. Various strategies may be tried and evaluated for their effectiveness. Typically, anti-corruption strategies must include reform of both the public and private sectors, and relationships between the two sectors. Corruption also may be coped with using what can be termed "supply-side controls." Methods for reducing corruption in post-communist countries are of particular interest in this class because of the lessons to be learned for other developing nations.

As indicated in the Global Corruption Report 2003 (Transparency International: www.globalcorruptionreport.org), several aspects of administrative and legal arrangements should be considered. Among these are improving access to information, corporate transparency, uncensored media, freedom of information, and the implementation of electronic government. The latter highlights that management control and anti-corruption strategies are linked as both use new technology as a tool to achieve their specific aims. Bhatnagar (2003) points out that to reduce corruption, some features that lead to greater transparency and accountability need to be consciously built into organizational and system design. "E-government applications must first increase access to information, then ensure that rules are transparent and applied in specific decisions and, finally, build the ability to track decisions and actions to individual civil servants" (2003, p. 25). Authors of selected works in this book demonstrate with that anti-corruption strategies may be assessed similar to other reform strategies.

(4) *Performance Assessment and Management Strategies.* Assessment strategies in this book include the development of a conceptual framework and methodological guide for policy change and application in specific regions (Latin America), developing and applying performance indicators and measurement systems in public institutions, evaluation of new public management reforms using empirical tests (in Switzerland), examining new technologies to measure and manage for performance (in Australia). Managing for results or performance management has become the focus of academics in this decade and characterizes much current practice in governments around the world.

It is interesting to speculate on why each of these strategies is employed, on the relative importance of causal conditions or variables, and on relationships between the strategies depicted in this book. Increased demand for accountability results from many things including a better educated and perhaps wealthier citizenry. However, it also results from financial and managerial wrong-doing, scandals publicized in the media and financial crises in the public sector. Some accountability measures stem from government reform initiatives tied to the political priorities of elected officials. Where a renewed emphasis on governance is present, accountability is an inevitable concern – perhaps the primary concern. And, inevitably, increased accountability is demanded under reform where significant decentralization, delegation and devolution of authority take place, e.g. under NPM.

Information technology as a strategy for reform appears to be driven by government priorities and, of course, the emergence of new technology. The power of new information technology cannot be underestimated as a driver of government reengineering, reinvention and realignment (Jones & Thompson, 1999). However, information technology has to be funded to succeed. In this regard, priority given to investment in information technology is related not just to increased efficiency within government – it is tied to increased demand for accountability, transparency, and requirements for financial responsibility under delegated authority. Information technology strategy also plays a critical role in improving the application of management control strategy. Indeed, without improved information capability it would not be possible to implement the accounting and budget reforms shown to be a vital part of the management control strategy in chapter nine in this book.

Anti-corruption strategies emerge as part of reforms to make governments and businesses operate more equitably, and also as a means for increasing economic efficiency in national and local economies. Anti-corruption initiatives attempt to correct maldistribution of income, wealth, goods and services, and opportunity to accumulate a variety of benefits. All of this is intended to achieve greater social and cultural equity. To the extent that ethics play a role in politics, in Thailand for example, then applying an anti-corruption strategy fits with political priorities. One of the ways to fight corruption is to increase standards and requirements for accountability. Information technology and improved management control both are intended to achieve greater accountability. However, as the authors of the four chapters on anti-corruption strategy in this book demonstrate, the battle against organized crime that permeates business and government must be waged on a socio-cultural basis because traditions of criminal behavior and tolerance of it are deeply rooted in cultural heritage and historical context. Improved application of information technology and better management control systems can be expected to do only so much, and most of what can be achieved through application of these strategies is internal to government. On the other hand, many if not most of the causes of corruption lie outside government in business and society.

Performance assessment, measurement and management strategies clearly are part of the neo-managerial trends of the past several decades rooted in the belief that improved policy analysis, combined with better measurement of performance relative to objectives will enable performance management – leading to achievement of desired results and outcomes. Better analysis, and development and use of performance measures is assisted greatly by new information technology. Performance measurement and management may be used as weapons to fight corruption. And one of the primary objectives of performance measurement is to increase accountability. Also, as with fighting corruption, while installation of performance measurement and management systems may at first seem to be something to be done entirely within government, as the Ryan chapter shows, ability to implement performance management is as much based on changing culture as it is on modifying the internal workings of public organizations. In fact, in assessing the seven strategies depicted in this book, virtually all of them are dependent on cultural change and evolution within and outside of government. Consequently, because cultural change takes place slowly in most instances, reform of the public sector is likely to be only incrementally successful in most venues.

A final comment on why we have cast the reform initiatives detailed in this book under the rubric of strategy. Strategy is defined in the Merriman-Webster on-line dictionary as, "... a careful plan or method; the art of devising or employing plans or stratagems toward a goal; an adaptation or complex of adaptations (as of behavior, metabolism, or structure) that serves or appears to serve an important function in achieving evolutionary success." In our view, all of the approaches to reform included in this book meet these criteria. Each approach entails planning and significant attention to method and application. All approaches are directed to achieve specified goals. Each may be viewed to address the need for adaptation of behavior and structure to achieve evolutionary success. As explained elsewhere (Jones & Thompson, 1999) and as is evident from reading the works in this book, adaptation is a long, slow and incremental process in most settings in which public sector reform has been undertaken.

The main themes of this book fall, in various forms, into the four categories of strategy noted above. These four categories and the seven individual strategies cannot be separated in practice. On the contrary, they are linked through a common objective function – to improve public management and public agency responsiveness to the service demand environment. As noted above, the linkage between control and anti-corruption strategies, for example, is the reformation of structures, processes and rules by using new tools such as IT. Anti-corruption and assessment are linked through the concept of transparency. Control and decentralization/delegation have organizational and procedural reform in common. Decentralization and control enable each other and create a reciprocal need. Delegation and decentralization link with new assessment strategies and the opportunities they create for new forms of control.

In the concluding chapter of this book, Jones and Kettl assess public management reform strategies in an international context. They argue that reform typically is preceded by all sorts of promises, the most common a call for smaller, less interventionist and more decentralized government. We would observe that even with the rapid spread of reforms, they have produced wide diversity in practice, even across countries regarded as models such as New Zealand and the U.K. However, we would point out that there has been little research on what results are produced by various reform strategies. The book attempts to grapple with this deficiency.

Even a preliminary review makes it clear that reforms tend to have promised more than they delivered. The new public management, Jones and Kettl argue, may have some payoffs, but the political constraints and consequences can be significant and unanticipated. A careful review of the reforms in Australia and New Zealand reveals how much we have yet to learn about what worked and why. Jones and Kettl also conclude that public management reform is never finished. Further, they judge that new public management has proven to be a fundamentally different approach to reform. Additionally, they conclude that political reality drives reform more than management efficiency concerns. They note, "Despite the lack of traction from management reform as a political issue it is a puzzle with which elected officials nevertheless feel obliged to wrestle. Management reform has little upside potential but can pose a tremendous downsides threat."

Jones and Kettl also find that despite wide variation in reform strategies, there is a convergence of reforms around general themes. Where new public management has been implemented, reform effort is moving increasingly from restructuring to process reengineering, reinvention and redesign, i.e. implementation. However, many developing nations have different management problems than developed nations and therefore are at different stages of reform. Lastly, the authors point out that the pursuit of the new public management strategy has revealed a mismatch between practice, theory, and instruction. This theme is evident in the findings of the authors of some of the chapters in this book.

REFORMING THE REFORM

What can we learn from the positions taken and conclusions drawn by the authors of the works in this book, and from the evidence they provide? A major lesson is that the reform processes themselves need to be reformed. This is so in part because of the absence of sensitivity to politics within the new public management movement and the managerial reform approach in general. Still, we may ask whether NPM ignored the *primacy of politics*. If so, how is it that the new public management became so attractive to politicians around the world for more than two decades? One reason may be simple: NPM concepts and ideas became associated with the desire for achieving more efficient public management and, as such, it attractive to those who set the political agenda in many nations. Politicians may have been stimulated to grasp onto it in circumstances of fiscal and economic stress. Although beyond this we are not sure how it happened, new public management became politically attractive and found sponsors in influential positions, e.g. the Prime Ministers of New Zealand, Australia, Canada and the United Kingdom, a President and Vice President of the United States of America, the President of Taiwan, leadership in the governments of Switzerland, Austria, Sweden and other Western and Central European countries and selected Asia nations, the mayors and leaders of cities and local governments in the Netherlands, Germany, Scandanavia, Hong Kong, in the U.S. and in numerous other nations, the governors of states in the U.S., premiers of provinces in Canada and leaders of states in Australia. The policies and methods associated with NPM have become so widespread that it has become the paradigm to be challenged, replacing what has been termed "traditional public administration." Perhaps this is the most significant indication of the extent of its adoption.

Experience with politics tells us that no management trend, regardless of its value, stays on the political agenda for long. Therefore, it was foreseeable that NPM would lose attraction at some point, and that like reform programs would be replaced by others – even if only in name rather than method.

Nevertheless, it is important to point out that the new public management elicited a huge (still on-going in many contexts) and world-wide intellectual *par-force* performance by academics and practitioners. Since Weber's analysis of bureaucracy at the beginning of the last century, few if any other organizational models for the public sector have gained as much attention, if not acceptance. We believe that NPM will continue to provide for years to come an optional view or model of public management, an alternative to Weberian bureaucracy and traditional public administration. However, we also believe that implementation of the NPM model needs to be examined and reformed. Evaluation and feedback loops provide the keys to success to promote organizational learning – *but only if we keep alive the dialogue about implementation strategy across the borders of the broad range of disciplines represented in public management.* Complex real world problems seldom if ever can be understood strictly from the lens of single disciplines. Moving forward requires, among other things, academics who are willing and able to sustain an interdisciplinary dialogue intended to define desired methods and outcomes, i.e. solutions to real world problems. This is a trajectory that public management as an academic field needs to achieve.

REFERENCES

Araújo, J. (2002). NPM and the change in Portuguese central government. *International Public Management Journal, 5*(3), 223–236.

Bhatnagar, S. (2003). E-government and access to information. *Transparency International: Global Corruption Report 2003*, pp. 24–32.

Fountain, J. (2001). *Building the virtual state: Information technology and institutional change.* Washington, DC: Brookings.

Jones, L. R., & Thompson, F. (1986). Reform of budget execution control. *Public Budgeting and Finance, 6*(1), 25–41.

Jones, L. R., & Thompson, F. (1999). *Public management: Institutional renewal for the twenty-first century.* Stamford, CT: Elsevier-JAI Press.

Kettl, D. F. (2000). *The global public management revolution: A report on the transformation of governance.* Washington, DC: Brookings.

McCaffery, J. L., & Jones, L. R. (2001). *Budgeting and financial management in the federal government.* Greenwich, CT: Information Age.

Pallot, J. (1997). New public management reform in New Zealand: Financial management and collective strategy in New Zealand. In: L. Jones & K. Schedler (Eds), *Advances in International Comparative Management* (pp. 125–144). Greenwich, CT: JAI Press.

Pallot, J. (1998). Newer than new public management: Financial management the collective strategy phase. *International Public Management Journal, 1*(1), 1–18.

Pollitt, C. (2003). *The essential public manager.* Philadelphia, PA: Open University Press.

Reschenthaler, G. B., & Thompson, F. (1998). Public management and the learning organizaton. *International Public Management Journal, 1*(1), 59–106.

Roberts, N. (2000). Wicked problems and network approaches to resolution. *International Public Management Review, 1*(1), 20–43. www.ipmr.net.

Schedler, K. (2003). . . . and politics? Public management developments in the light of two rationalities. *Public Management Review* (forthcoming).

Schedler, K., & Proeller, I. (2002). The new public management: A perspective from mainland Europe. In: K. McLaughlin, S. Osborne & E. Ferlie (Eds), *New Public Management: Current Trends and Future Prospects*. London: Routledge.

Thompson, F., & Jones, L. R. (1986). Controllership in the public sector. *Journal of Policy Analysis and Management*, 5(3), 47–61.

Ulrich, H. (1990). *Unternehmenspolitik*. Berne: Paul Haupt.

PART I: ACCOUNTABILITY, DECENTRALIZATION, AND DELEGATION STRATEGIES

2. RETHINKING ACCOUNTABILITY IN EDUCATION: HOW SHOULD WHO HOLD WHOM ACCOUNTABLE FOR WHAT?

Robert D. Behn

INTRODUCTION

Everyone wants accountability in education. President Bill Clinton wanted accountability in education. In his 1999 State of the Union address, the President announced "... a plan that for the first time holds states and school districts accountable for progress and rewards them for results." Through his proposed Education Accountability Act, President Clinton sought to insist, "... all states and school districts must turn around their worst-performing schools, or shut them down" (1999, pp. 202–203).

President George W. Bush also wants accountability in education. "Our educators need to get ready for the new accountability era that's coming to our schools," he said (2001b) as he introduced his proposals "to ensure that no child is left behind." The President's proposals (most of which were enacted by Congress in December 2001) sought to create "accountability and high standards." The President's proposal to Congress was designed to "establish a system for how states and school districts will be held accountable for improving student achievement" (Bush, 2001b, pp. 4, 8, 31).

The nation's governors have long wanted accountability in education. As chairman of the National Governors' Association for 1998–1999, Governor Thomas R. Carper of Delaware established a Smarter Kids Task Force, with one of its three major objectives being to "promote accountability." NGA reports that "to ensure that children are receiving the best education possible, the nation's governors are focusing on accountability – from schools, teachers, students, parents, and communities" (Gregovich, 1999a). At NGA's 1999 winter meeting, Governor Tony Knowles of Alaska, co-chair of the accountability component of Carper's task force, told his colleagues that "there is no subject more essential to student achievement than accountability."

School superintendents want accountability in education. As chief executive officer of the Chicago Public Schools, Paul G. Vallas said at the same winter NGA meeting "We are successful in Chicago because we are demanding accountability." Governor George H. Ryan of Illinois echoed these sentiments: "Accountability has made the difference in the Chicago school system." The Chicago Public Schools have a Plan for Systemwide Accountability, an Academic Accountability Council, an Office of Accountability, a Department of Teacher Accountability, and a Chief Accountability Officer.

Yes, everyone wants accountability in education. Presidents want to hold the states and school districts accountable. The governors and state legislators want to hold the districts and schools accountable. School superintendents want to hold principals and teachers accountable. Parents want to hold their children's schools and teachers accountable. Who could possibly be against accountability in education? After all, American schools are certifiably lousy[1] – Bush cited "the low standing of America's test scores amongst industrialized nations in math and science" (2001a) – and it is about time we held someone accountable.

Everyone wants accountability in education – at least everyone who is an accountability holder. And everyone wants to be an accountability holder. Everyone wants to hold someone else accountable. Few, however, want to be an accountability holdee.[2] Our system of accountability for education has two types of people: Either you are an accountability holder, or you are an accountability holdee.

And everyone wants to be an accountability holder so that he or she can get to punish all of the accountability holdees. If an accountability holdee accomplishes something significant, the accountability holders don't do very much. Whenever an accountability holdee makes a mistake, however, the accountability holders get to inflict some punishment upon the miscreant. Our implicit concept of accountability is unidirectional, hierarchical, and adversarial. It requires that there be accountability punishers and accountability punishees.[3]

THE IMPLICIT THEORY OF EDUCATIONAL ACCOUNTABILITY

What exactly is the "theory" behind the current movement to establish accountability in American elementary and secondary education?[4] By that, I mean: What are the implicit and explicit assumptions about what activities are linked to what results? Presumably we want to create a system of educational accountability because it will – somehow – create some improvements.[5] But what improvements? And, more importantly, what somehows? What exactly is the linkage between an accountability system and these improvements? What is this theory of educational accountability?[6]

This question is difficult to answer because there are many different accountability systems and because different people can agree to create a specific accountability system based on quite different theories – on quite different assumptions about the mechanics of the connection between the specific accountability system that they have agreed to create and the improvements, common or different, that they think it will produce.[7]

Nevertheless, the nation, states, and localities are creating accountability systems that are based on several common (if implicit) assumptions:

(1) Schools need to improve.
(2) Schools won't improve unless society creates some mechanism to hold them accountable.[8]
(3) Standardized tests will tell us which districts, schools, and classes most need to improve.
(4) The people who work in the schools should make these improvements, and they need to be motivated to do so.
(5) Explicitly comparing districts and schools (and even teachers and students) using test scores will provide some of the required motivation.
(6) Money and other rewards will provide more of this motivation.
(7) Sanctions and punishments will provide even more of this motivation.

This is the motivational theory of educational accountability (or the motivational component of this theory of accountability): To get the improvements we want out of the schools, we (just) need to motivate them to make those improvements. And this motivational theory of accountability is usually based on a series of carrots and sticks.[9]

For example, President Bush's education proposal emphasized that "the federal government currently does not do enough to reward success and sanction failure in our education system." Thus, to "increase accountability for student performance," the President's "blueprint" contained both carrots and sticks: "States, districts and schools that improve achievement will be rewarded. Failure will be sanctioned." Moreover, creating such accountability would not just be the job of the federal government: "States must develop a system of sanctions and rewards to hold districts and schools accountable for improving academic performance" (Bush, 2001b, pp. 6–7).

But wait, say others, motivation isn't enough. Just because people are motivated to do a better job doesn't mean they can. They need resources. They need the organizational and human capabilities.[10] Thus, the implicit theory behind many accountability systems (or, at least, behind some of the thinking of some of the people who have created these accountability systems) also includes the assumption that poorly performing districts, schools, or teachers (indeed, maybe all districts, schools, and teachers) need help.

Schools Need Resources and Assistance to Create Capabilities Required to Improve

This is the final component of most accountability systems. For example, the Reynolds School District in Oregon complemented its extensive use of performance measures and targets with extensive support, resources, and assistance for schools and teachers (Blum, 2000).

"Most states," reports the NGA, "are focusing on school accountability measures, including public reports of assessment results, rewards for performance, technical assistance for struggling schools, and sanctions for schools that do not improve" (Gregovich, 1999b). Similarly, the Southern Regional Education Board "has identified five policy areas that are crucial parts of a comprehensive school-accountability program: content and student achievement standards; testing [or assessment]; professional development; accountability reporting; and rewards, sanctions, and targeted assistance" (Watts, Gaines & Creech, 1998, p. 1). And, indeed, the education legislation adopted by Congress in December 2001 authorized more money and more flexibility in the use of that money.

But wait, say still others, motivation and capability themselves are not enough either. Before we can do any of this, we need to answer two other basic questions: (1) what do we mean by improvement? and; (2) How will we know when we've got some of it? The answers to these two questions – the first about standards; the second about assessment – are not obvious. Yet, if we are going to hold schools accountable, we need to be able specify what we want the schools to do – what we want to hold them accountable for doing.

Standards

What do we want the schools to do? What is the real purpose of the schools? The most fundamental answer is: We want schools to help children to grow up to be productive workers and responsible citizens. Unfortunately, it is quite difficult to hold schools accountable for doing this: We can't check whether a school has really achieved this purpose until many years (or decades) after its students leave.[11] And, we would find it difficult to develop valid and reliable measures of whether specific students had indeed become productive workers and responsible citizens. (After all, people can be productive and responsible in a wide variety of very different ways, and whether a person is productive or responsible is certainly a subjective judgment.) Moreover, we can never determine how much of any adult's productivity and responsibility should be attributed to his or her schools, church, family, friends, and other institutions or individuals.[12] We want our schools to help to create productive workers and responsible citizens; yet we have absolutely no way to determine whether or not they have helped accomplish this purpose.

Thus, we create surrogate mechanisms for determining whether the schools are doing a good job. Behind all of the systems of educational accountability is the assumption that we know (or, at least, can agree on) what kind of short-term, and medium-term improvements we want the schools to make in students – specifically in students' knowledge and skills.[13] This is the question of standards: What particular forms of knowledge do we want all of the students in all of the districts, in all of the schools, and in all of the classrooms to understand and be able to use?

"Accountability is impotent without standards," U.S. Secretary of Education Roderick Paige told the nation's governor's at their conference in February 2001. Setting high standards and then "holding schools accountable," continued Paige, will improve education performance.

But what standards should we set? What particular skills do we want all the students in all the districts, in all the schools, and in all the classrooms to master and be able to use? Our system of educational accountability is based on the assumption that we can, somehow, develop some mutually agreed upon standards for skills and knowledge.

This might not be such a big assumption. Elementary school students ought to know how to add, subtract, multiply, and divide. To be a productive employee or a responsible citizen in today's world, you have to be able to do some simple math. And, similarly, U.S. students have to be able to read and write in English. Oops. Do they really have to be able to read and write in English? Or is being able to read and write in Spanish or Farsi an acceptable standard? And what should they know about Charles Darwin and evolution? Oops again. Once we move beyond the most basic forms of knowledge (can we all agree that $2 + 2 = 4$?), controversy enters. Accountability holders would have a much easier time creating some kind of accountability system if they could all agree on standards to which the holdees should be held accountable.

Assessments

Also behind all systems of educational accountability is a second assumption: We can determine the level of knowledge and skills mastered by individual students and thus by classes, schools, and districts. What do we want schools to accomplish? This is the question of standards. How will we know if the schools have accomplished it? This is the question of assessment: Can we find or create tests or other assessment tools that really tell us whether a student has, indeed, achieved our standards?[14] In the jargon of education testing, can we create tests that are both valid and reliable? Can we create assessment mechanisms that can, indeed, determine if students know what they are supposed to know? And can we create assessment mechanisms that will produce the same (or similar) results when employed multiple times?

Much of the work on educational accountability is devoted to determining the validity and reliability of various assessment mechanisms.[15] The results aren't always very encouraging. Rogosa analyzed the accuracy of the Stanford Achievement Test, Ninth Edition. He asked: What are the chances that a student is truly at the 50th percentile on nationally normal test will score greater than five percentage points from this score – that is, either below the 45th percentile or above the 55th percentile? His answer: For a ninth-grade student in math: 70%. For a fourth-grade student in reading: 58% (1999, p. 1). For simple forms of factual knowledge, this is not too difficult; for more sophisticated forms of analytical reasoning, it is quite a challenge. Yet, to hold the accountability holdees accountable (under our traditional approach to accountability), the accountability holders need valid and reliable assessment mechanisms. This is the motivation behind much of the research on performance measurement in education: If we could only find the right measures with which to, "hold schools accountable," we would solve the accountability problem. If we, the accountability holders, can identify valid and reliable measures of educational performance, we can collect the right data, determine how well schools are performing, and reward or punish the accountability holdees accordingly.

In many ways, accountability in education has morphed into testing. Annual testing. Of lots of children. As Lorna Earl and Nancy Torrance of the University of Toronto observed: "Testing has become the lever for holding schools accountable for results" (2000, p. 114). That is why Secretary Paige told the nation's governors in February 2001: "We must measure every child every year with good tests."

Indeed, accountability has morphed into high-stakes testing. High stakes for teachers, High stakes for principals. High stakes for superintendents, High states for (some) students. Today, when people talk about the need for more accountability in education, they are talking about – operationally – more testing. "All the governors – across the board – have been champions of testing and accountability," Governor Parris Glendening of Maryland told his colleagues at their August 2001 meeting. To Glendening, it appears, testing and accountability is the same thing.

But let's ignore these two, enormous challenges – the difficulties of agreeing on standards, and the complexities of designing assessments – that can plague any system of educational accountability. Let's assume that a state (or nation or district) can agree on its educational standards – what, exactly, students should know after, say, grades three, six, and eight. And, let's assume that a state (or nation or district) can develop an assessment tool – be it a multiple-choice test, a series of essays and complex problems, or portfolios – that provides a valid and reliable measure of whether individual students do, indeed, know and can employ the educational content specified in the standards. These are two, very large and yet unresolved problems; they cannot be dismissed (Brennan, 2001). Yet, even if these two, very big problems about standards and assessment were, somehow, to miraculously disappear, there would still remain fundamental problems in the design and implementation of any system of educational accountability.

THE CARROTS-AND-STICKS THEORY OF EDUCATIONAL MOTIVATION

When discussing educational accountability, people don't really talk about "carrots and sticks." Sticks just aren't politically correct. We no longer rap student knuckles with rulers or student rears with switches. So we certainly don't want to talk about taking sticks to superintendents, or principals, or teachers. Sticks (and carrots) are out. Accountability is in.

But isn't "accountability" just the politically correct way of saying "carrots and sticks?" Carrots and sticks sounds so crass – so depraved, so cruel. Accountability, in contrast, sounds so neutral – so antiseptic, so fair. And yet, on the cover of Education Week's 1999 special report on educational accountability are the words: "Rewarding Results, Punishing Failure." Sounds like "carrots and sticks."

Behind much of the theory, much of the talk, and many of the details of accountability systems lays an implicit carrot-and-stick theory of human motivation.[16] Of course, it could be that the will is there but the technology is missing.

That is, teachers want to teach, but don't know how. And this isn't because they are dumb. Rather, it could simply be because the technology of teaching is not well developed. As Ogawa and Collom observe, "the causes and effects that comprise schooling and instruction are poorly understood" (2000, p. 210). If only the superintendents, the principals, and the teachers were adequately motivated, we'd get our kids educated. And so, we create carrots and sticks – oops, I'm sorry, rewards and punishments – to motivate educators to do a better job.

The limitations of carrot-and-stick motivation are well known (Kohn, 1993; Levinson, 1973).[17] In contrast, Abraham Maslow's theory of motivation is based on a hierarchy of needs: physiological needs for food; safety needs; love, affection, and belongingness needs; esteem needs (both for self esteem and the esteem of others); and (finally) the need for self-actualization (1943). For individuals who still need to satisfy their physiological or safety needs, financial carrots and sticks can be powerful motivators. And for individuals for who esteem – especially the esteem of others – are particularly important, psychological carrots and sticks may also motivate behavior. Still, the accountability holders who would wield such sticks and dispense such carrots cannot be sure that the behavior that they seek to motivate will be the behavior that they actually do motivate.

In analyzing human motivation to work, Frederick Herzberg (1968; Herzberg et al., 1959, Chap. 12) made a distinction between satisfiers and dissatisfiers – between motivators and demotivators. For example, money, if handled badly, is a dissatisfier, a demotivator. But, if money is handled well, it is not a satisfier or motivator. Rather, money handled well is neutral; it has little impact. Thus, a dissatisfier that is handled badly demotivates; but a dissatisfier that is handled well accomplishes little. In addition to salary, Herzberg found demotivators to include organizational policy and administration, and relations with supervisors. In contrast, he found achievement, recognition, responsibility, and the work itself were motivators – if handled well.

Herzberg described KITA motivation – the stick or "externally imposed attempt by management to 'install a generator' in the employee" – as "a total failure." And so, he reported, was a "positive KITA," or carrot. And, Herzberg noted, although "managerial audiences are quick to see that negative KITA is not motivation," nevertheless, "they are almost unanimous in their judgment that positive KITA is motivation" (1968, pp. 53–54). Yet, as the psychiatrist Harry Levinson writes in his book The Great Jackass Fallacy, in attempting to motivate people with carrots and sticks, we are treating them like jackasses and, thus, should not be surprised when they behave like jackasses (1973).

Still, most systems of educational accountability are based on a carrot-and-stick theory of motivation.[18] Thus, in addition to standards and assessments, the generic accountability system includes ratings and rankings, rewards and punishments.

Schools are rated, ranked, and compared on how well their students do on their assessments. To motivate educators to do a better job, we publish these ratings and rankings. Then, to further motivate them, we reward educators, financially and symbolically, if they do well; and we punish them, again financially and symbolically, if they do poorly.

Yet, in addition to the psychological problems with this reward-and-punishment approach to educational accountability, there are also some practical problems of implementation. For example, why should we assume that an extra $500 or $1000 is a tasty enough carrot to motivate teachers to ratchet up their performance significantly? Suppose a teacher needs an extra $500; which is the more effective and certain way to obtain it? Work harder during the school year to be sure that the students pass their assessment tests? Or work five weekends at the minimum wage at the local mall?[19]

Minnesota rewards its high-school teachers who prove effective in advanced-placement courses (Allen, 1999, p. 1; Bradley, 1999a, p. 50). For every student who takes an AP test and earns a 3, 4 or 5, the teacher receives a bonus – of $25.

Financial Carrots and Sticks

Of the fifty states, 20 have created sanctions that they can impose on schools that are performing poorly. Eighteen states provide rewards to schools that either achieve a high standard or demonstrate significant improvement. Twelve have both carrots and sticks (Meyer et al., 2002, pp. 69, 76–77). In some states, the schools can distribute these carrots among the teachers and staff; in others they can only use them for collective purposes.

For example, both Kentucky and Maryland have created sanctions for low-performing schools combined with financial rewards for schools that make progress – but not for those that merely maintain their past high level of performance. In Kentucky, schools that meet their target of closing the gap between their baseline performance and performance defined as proficient can earn an award that in 1997 averaged approximately $50,000 per school. Approximately 40% of the schools received this award, and most of these schools distributed the money as bonuses to teachers and staff. Under Maryland's "Reward for Success," elementary and middle schools can earn monetary rewards if they have made "substantial and sustained" progress over two years on the state's School Performance Index. Maryland's schools cannot, however, distribute the money to their employees (Kelley et al., 2000, pp. 162–163, 166–167).

Unfortunately, accountability systems can never guarantee that the financial rewards that are distributed this year will be available again next year. After all, no legislature can bind a subsequent legislature to continue distributing rewards. Traditionally, when creating financial motivators for public employees, legislators have been, initially, very enthusiastic. But, as time progresses, the legislators' zeal diminish – at least as measured by the dollars they appropriate for motivation.

For example, Richard King and Judith Mathers of the University of North Colorado studied four of the earliest educational-accountability systems – in South Carolina, Texas, Indiana, and Kentucky – and found (among other things) that three of these states eventually reduced their funding for financial incentives significantly:

- In 1984, South Carolina created the School Incentive Reward Program. For the 1985–1986 school year, the legislature appropriated $6.9 million for these awards (which go to the schools themselves and cannot be used as bonuses for teachers or others). By 1996–1997, however, the legislature had reduced the pool by over 25% to $5 million.
- Also in 1984, Texas created its Successful School Awards Program, and for the 1992–1993 appropriated $20 million, which meant that school awards ranged from $25,000 to $175,000. For 1994–1995, however, the legislature cut the appropriation to $5 million, so that school awards ranged from $250 to $30,000. For 1995–1996 and 1996–1997, it appropriated no funds. (The program was then replaced by a principal performance incentive to award $5,000 to principals whose schools ranked in the top 25%).
- In 1987, Indiana created its School Improvement Award Program with $10.1 million for awards in 1989–1990. By 1996–1997, however, the legislature had cut this appropriation by over two-thirds – down to $3.2 million (King & Mathers, 1997, pp. 151–156).

If teachers, principals and other accountability holdees have reason to believe that the financial rewards may be canceled at any time, how motivating can such carrots be?

What Does Accountability Motivate?

Why do people go into teaching? For the money? Obviously not.[20] So why would we think that using money (particularly an annual bonus of a few hundred or a few thousand dollars) would be the best motivator?[21] Some people are satisfied more quickly by Maslow's need for food and safety. They are willing to live with much lower levels of basic needs than Donald Trump. They have entered teaching because of their need to obtain higher levels on the Maslow scale – companionship, esteem, and self-actualization. Perhaps they are in it for the companionship of teenagers.

Rethinking Accountability in Education 29

Perhaps. Perhaps they are in it for the esteem – though (if this is the case) they have to be in it more for the self-esteem than for the public esteem given how little esteem today's public is willing to accord its teachers. Perhaps they are in it for the opportunity of self-actualization – for the chance to accomplish what they want to accomplish in their own way. If you want to self-actualize with little outside observation or interference, what better occupations to choose than small-business owner, computer hacker, or teacher?

Nevertheless, the public esteem can be important. And, indeed, many of the accountability systems are designed to reward excellent teachers with both more money and more esteem and to punish inadequate teachers with both less money and less esteem. This is one reason why we publish school rankings: to give credit and prestige to the teachers, principles, and others affiliated with outstanding schools; and to, at the same time, embarrass and assign blame to those associated with the low-performing schools. (In 2000, the Connecticut Department of Education decided to publish school tests scores but without combining them into a single, summary measure that could be used to compare schools; however, The Hartford Courant took the state's data, created such an index, and published their results (Archer, 2001, p. 121).) Such rankings can affect teachers' own self esteem, and they will certainly reduce the esteem that teachers earn from parents, colleagues, neighbors, and friends.

Moreover, some educators, it appears, worry more about preventing the negative than gaining the positive. King and Mathers report that "the avoidance of negative publicity and sanctions is a powerful motivator" – particularly for "upwardly mobile principals" (1997, pp. 159, 175). This may well be because a principal's colleagues and friends, neighbors and relatives pay more attention if the school ranks low than if it ranks high. The most significant motivational impact of accountability systems may come from their ability to shame and embarrass educators who work at low-performing schools.

But how does this threat of humiliation affect the behavior of educators? How can superintendents, principals, or teachers respond when publicly labeled by an accountability report as inadequate or a failure? What can they do? They can work harder and smarter. This is the implicit theory behind the accountability system. But this is not the only possible response. The intended incentives that such accountability systems are designed to foster and the resulting incentives that they actually create may not be the same. After all, as Earl and Torrance write, "it is particularly important for policy researchers to routinely investigate the actual consequences of polices that are enacted" (2000, p. 137).

In 1998, Virginia launched its new Standards of Learning tests in mathematics, English, history, and social sciences, which are given every year to students in grades 3, 5, and 8. The real impact of this accountability system won't kick in until the 2006–2007 school year, when a school needs to have 70% of its students pass the test to maintain its accreditation (Portner, 1999). Nevertheless, the tests quickly started motivating behavior. In early 1999, several school districts decided to accept fewer student teachers, fearing that replacing their experienced teachers with student teachers will lower their test scores (Samuels, 1999).

In 1996, North Carolina created its accountability program called the ABCs of Public Education. If a school scores well on the statewide tests, it earns an "exemplary" rating, and its teachers win a performance bonus of up to $1,500. But if a school is rated as "low performing," its teachers don't receive a bonus (and were supposed to take a competency test, although the teachers forced the legislature to postpone such teacher testing) (Manzo, 1999). This testing and rating system has had an impact on teacher behavior though not exclusively in the way that accountability advocates had intended. Previously, some teachers had consciously chosen to work in inner city or other schools with predictably low-scoring students. With the publication of their schools' predictably low ratings, however, these teachers concluded that they were being "punished and being held up to public ridicule," and began to consider returning to suburban schools that have a much easier time earning an "exemplary" rating (Kurtz, 1998).

Agreeing to standards and creating valid and reliable assessments to determine if individual students have achieved these standards is not sufficient to create an accountability system that improves student learning. How the accountability holders deploy the results of those assessments to reward and punish, financially and psychologically, affects how the accountability holdees are motivated – how they change their behavior.

Cheating – Honest and Dishonest

For example, accountability systems can motivate teachers to teach to the test. In recent years, North Carolina has done significantly better on the quadrennial National Assessment of Educational Progress by – in part – teaching to the NAEP test. In the 1990s, North Carolina created its own end-of-the-year tests that employed a format and questions very similar to those of the NAEP. And then, the state used these NAEP clones in its own ABCs accountability system to encourage teachers to teach to this test (Simmons, 1999a, p. 14A).

Is North Carolina's strategy good or bad? As always, the answer is: It all depends. If you think that the NAEP test really captures the important theoretical ideas, analytical concepts, and practical skills that we want students do learn, and if you think that North Carolina is has chosen an appropriately "focused" instructional strategy, you are apt to think this is all to the good. But, if you think that the NAEP test misses many very important ideas, concepts, or skills, or if you think that North Carolina is employing an excessively "narrow" instructional strategy, you will conclude that all this is quite bad.

"In a high-stakes accountability system," notes Robert Meyer of the University of Chicago, "teachers and administrators are likely to respond to the incentive to improve their measured performance by exploiting all existing avenues" (1996, p. 219). Helen Ladd of Duke University worries "whether the undesirable side effects of accountability and incentive systems can be kept to a tolerable level," and suggests that "a balance must be found so financial awards are large enough to change behavior, but not so large that they induce outright cheating" (1996, p. 14). Such "cheating" can be outright dishonesty – such as falsifying test results or giving students the test questions or the answers.[22] I call this "dishonest cheating." Or it can be what I call "honest cheating" – capitalizing on the many available ways (other than actually helping children to become productive employees and responsible citizens) to make sure the scores look better. Teaching to the test is honest cheating. Correcting students' answers is dishonest cheating (Behn, 1998).[23] Meyer lists some of his "avenues" – things that might be called honest cheating – that schools can employ: "create an environment that is relatively inhospitable to academically disadvantaged students, provide course offerings that predominantly address the needs of academically advantaged students, fail to work aggressively to prevent students from dropping out of high school, err on the side of referring 'problem' students to alternative schools, err on the side of classifying students as special education students where the latter are exempt from statewide testing, or make it difficult for low-scoring students to participate in state-wide exams" (1996, p. 219).

Yet, as the accountability holders ratchet up the rewards and penalties that they bestow on the accountability holdees, why should we believe that the holdees – upon examining all of Meyer's "existing avenues" – will respond first by changing their behavior in desired ways and will resort to cheating only as the stakes get higher? Maybe their personal commitment to teaching forces them to try changing their own behavior first – to try teaching harder or teaching smarter. Yet, if they believe that the standards have been set ridiculously high, or if they conclude that the accountability holders have failed to provide them with the necessary resources or support, or if they simply cannot figure out what kind of change in their own behavior will lead to an improvement in the assessments, why won't they resort to cheating first?[24] Moreover, complex – and thus, often obscure – performance measures can prevent a teacher, school, or district from figuring out what it should do to improve. Simple performance measures tend to be biased against low-income communities. Yet, a performance measure that compensates for such socio-economic factors are often complex and, thus, obscure. For example, Clotfelter and Ladd report that "the attempt by Dallas to treat schools fairly has resulted in an incredibly complex methodology that participants view as a black box." Moreover, they observe, this, "lack of transparency could weaken the incentive effects of the program" (1996, pp. 56–57).

Shame, Voice, Exit, and Enter

When threatened with being publicly labeled as a loser, educational systems can take a variety of actions to improve their chances of coming out a winner. Some of these actions might indeed be to work harder and smarter. But some of these actions might involve nothing more than cleverly creating a competitive advantage: Why should we take on any of those green student teachers; why not let another school do the training and pay for it with lower test scores; then, when these student teachers graduate, they'll look at our higher scores, and the best will come work for us?

Similarly, when threatened with being publicly labeled as a loser, individual educators can take a variety of actions to improve their chances of coming out a winner. Some of these actions might indeed be to work harder and smarter. But others might involve nothing more than enhancing their own, personal competitive advantage. Why work for a struggling team, when my seniority lets me sign on with a well-established winner that regularly produces bonuses for its people? Or, why not simply go play an entirely different game in an entirely different league that gives me less hassle, higher prestige, and a bigger income?[25] Note that a university has several options for responding to any effort to impose accountability on its teachers' college. It can improve it (by working harder or smarter). Or, it can exit. If it believes that improving the teachers' college will be very difficult – that is, if it believes that attracting better students will be very difficult – it can choose to put its resources into other lines of business in which it will have a better chance of success. After all, the opportunity cost of improving a teachers' college – in terms of the inability to improve other components of the university – could be very high. Several decades ago, Duke University closed both its nursing school and its education school.

As Albert Hirschman (1970) warned us, people who are unhappy with an organization can respond politically with voice or economically with exit. An individual's voice is, however, less influential than the combined and organized voice of many individuals; thus teachers and principals have formed associations to coordinate their collective voice. The individual, however, may conclude that exit is a much more effective strategy than voice. Why bother complaining – particularly when it is not at all obvious who (even if they were receptive) could act on this complaint.

When faced with the prospect of being publicly shamed by association with a "low-performing" school, how will teachers react? Clearly, they can exit. Teachers with enough seniority can exit to a school with better demographics, a better track record, or simply less bad publicity. Teachers with enough smarts or skills can exit the profession.[26] Indeed, Richard Ingersoll of the University of Pennsylvania argues that the teacher staffing is "a 'revolving door' – where large number of qualified teachers depart their jobs for reasons other than retirement," primarily various forms of "job dissatisfaction" (2001, p. 499). Not only is turnover in teaching higher than in other occupations; Ingersoll estimates that 29% of new teachers leave within three years, 39% within five years (Viadero, 2002, p. 7).

Every year, California needs to recruit 25,000 new teachers (Archer, 1999, p. 20; Sandham, 2001, p. 116). In 1998, to attract fifty excellent teachers, Massachusetts began offering a "signing bonus" of $20,000 spread over four years. Some Texas districts use such bonuses to recruit teachers from Oklahoma (Bradley, 1999b, p. 10). Maryland, Philadelphia, and East Baton Rouge Parish in Louisiana (among others) have added recruitment bonuses (Olson, 2000). Yet why accept the constant turnover; why not concentrate on keeping the existing teachers?

At a time when many are decrying a "teachers' shortage" – the President himself has told us that "over the next decade, America will need more than 2 million new teachers" (Bush, 2002) – should we be employing shame as our most powerful motivator? Imagine a business posting the following employment advertisement: "Come join our company. We put all our new people to work in our lowest performing plants, give them our worst equipment, and require them to employ the raw materials with which it is most difficult to work. And every year, we get the local newspaper to list the plants that are lowest performing on the front page." Who would apply for such a job? And who, if they did, would tell their friends where they worked?

Should we employ shame as our most powerful motivator for principals? Yes, to upwardly mobile principals, avoiding shame may be very important. But schools do need principals, and many districts are having a difficult time recruiting them (Bradley, 1999a, p. 49; Olson, 1999). Who would want to become a school principal? Who would want to become the principal of a low-performing school?[27] Who wants to sign up for an opportunity to be shamed?

Robert Samuelson, Newsweek's economics columnist, explains, "Why I Am Not a Manager." The "drawbacks," he concludes, are many: "resentment from below; pressure from above; loud criticism of failures; silence over successes." Sounds like the drawbacks of being a school principal. But Samuelson isn't writing solely about principals, even though he references their challenge when he describes the accountability demands on any manager:

They're supposed to get results – to maximize profits, improve test scores or whatever. Everyone must 'perform' these days and be 'accountable' (which means being fired, demoted or chewed out if the desired results aren't forthcoming) (1999, p. 47). At least in business, the managers get chewed out in private.

Shame may be an effective motivator for those who choose to remain in the education business. In Florida, the list of "critically low-performing" schools is known as the "list of shame" (White, 1998). But people can make personal, strategic choices. They can exit. Indeed, they have one more strategic choice. They do not ever have to enter.

When developing accountability and motivational strategies for employees – particularly for public employees – we tend to assume that they are conscripts – that they have no choice. In fact, however, public employees are all volunteers. It has been over a quarter of a century since the military has been able conscript to soldiers. Indeed, public employees are all volunteers. They did not have to choose to work for government. They do not have to continue to choose to work for government. Thus, if the shame associated with their association with government becomes too great – if they get chewed out too frequently, too aggressively, and too publicly – they do have another choice. They can exit. They can never even enter.

HOLDING SCHOOLS ACCOUNTABLE: THE INDUSTRIAL MODEL

The contemporary American system of democratic accountability has evolved from the thinking of Woodrow Wilson, Frederick Winslow Taylor, and Max Weber. It emphasizes Wilson's distinction between policy and administration, Taylor's belief in the efficacy of scientific management, and Weber's faith in hierarchical bureaucracies. Thus, the legislature creates policies and assigns to bureaucracies the task of carrying out these policies in the most scientifically efficient way possible (Behn, 2001, Chap. 3). The result is a hierarchical, uni-directional system of accountability:

(1) The state superintendent is accountable for implementing education policy in the state.
(2) The district superintendent is accountable for implementing education policy in the school district.
(3) The school principal is accountable for implementing education policy in the school.

(4) The teacher is accountable for implementing education policy in the classroom (Behn, 2001, pp. 65–66).

Everyone is accountable to someone in the next higher layer in the hierarchy – an example of what Robert Schwartz of the University of Haifa calls, "classical public administration hierarchical accountability systems" (2000, p. 201).

This hierarchical, uni-directional system of accountability is based – if only implicitly – on an industrial model of education: At age five, the raw materials (a.k.a., the children) are delivered to the plant door by their parents; during the next thirteen years, they are processed using a variety of inputs; at high-school graduation, they emerge as finished products.[28] The teachers are the production workers, the principals are the shop foremen, and the superintendents are the plant mangers.[29] Each individual is accountable to his or her boss within this hierarchy. Indeed, this industrial model assumes, the production workers won't do their jobs right unless someone is looking over their shoulders and holding them accountable.[30]

This industrial model of education and of educational accountability is reinforced by the simple use of the words "inputs" and "outputs." Some, for example, might think of kindergarten children as the inputs, and high-school graduates as the outputs.[31] Regardless, however, of which "puts" people label as the "inputs" and which they call the "outputs," they are – if only implicitly – thinking about education as a production process that converts these inputs into outputs. And, anyone who employs this implicit mental model of education needs to make no big logical leap to conclude that the people who run this educational production process, those people who have the job of converting the inputs into outputs, ought to be held accountable.

How should Who Hold Whom Accountable for What?[32] Leithwood and Earl's last question about consequences is, however, narrower that my "how?" I want my "how?" to cover more than rewards and sanctions.

Everyone is thinking about accountability in terms of holding educators accountable. Taxpayers, parents, school-board members, city-council members, district superintendents, state legislators, state superintendents, and governors, even the President – they all want to hold educators accountable. Everyone wants to be an accountability holder. Everyone wants someone else to be the accountability holdee.[33]

But who, exactly, should be this accountability holdee? We debate whom – what size education unit – should be held accountable. The typical effort to create educational accountability, reports Ladd, "starts from the view that the school is the most appropriate unit of accountability." Efforts to hold schools accountable, she argues, "are potentially more productive because they encourage teachers, principals and staff to work together toward a common mission" (1996, p. 11). In contrast, Meyer advocates, "localizing school performance to the most natural unit of accountability – the grade level or classroom." To Meyer, "a specific classroom or grade level" is "the natural unit of accountability in schools" (1996, pp. 214, 221).

But why shouldn't we hold districts accountable?[34] Why shouldn't we hold the school board and city-council members accountable? Why shouldn't we hold state superintendents, state legislators, and governors accountable? Why shouldn't we hold students accountable? Why shouldn't we hold parents and taxpayers accountable? Why shouldn't we hold local business executives, union officials, and other civic leaders accountable? Why do all these people get to be accountability holders? Why can't we think of them as accountability holdees? Reginald Mayo, the superintendent of schools in New Haven, argues that, in addition to the teachers, "other people should be held accountable: parents, businesses, higher education institutions, and the faith community" (Reid, 2001).

Why not hold parents accountable? Education is a co-production process.[35] Parents are at least as important a factor of production as are teachers and schools. It isn't just the school – the principal and teachers – that produces the education that goes into the students' brains. Ever since the release of the "Coleman Report" over thirty years ago, we have understood that parents – more than principals and teachers – contribute the most to their children's learning (Coleman et al., 1966; Leithwood & Jantzi, 1999). And neighbors, peers, mentors, and a variety of civic, social, and religious institutions are other factors of production. Yet, although we are quite prepared to hold teachers and schools accountable, we rarely even entertain the thought of holding anyone else accountable. Why don't we hold parents accountable?

By publishing a school's ranking in the newspaper, the accountability holders seek to reward, punish, and motivate these accountability holdees. But if this is such an effective accountability tool, why don't we publish other rankings, too? We could test children when they enter kindergarten and publish in the newspaper their scores, not next to their names but next to the names of their parents. At the end of each school year, we could publish in the newspaper the names of all the school's parents and how many parent-teacher conferences they attended.

For the 1998–1999 school year, the Washington, DC school system set aside three different days (rather than one) for parent-teacher conferences. And School Superintendent Arlene Ackerman made it clear that she would to hold the schools accountable for getting their parents to attend these conferences: "We're going to be tracking this. And if they [the schools] didn't do it this time, come next time they will" (Strauss, 1998). Indeed, the District's evaluation forms for its school principals included an appraisal of the how well they engage parents in school activities, including these parent-teacher conferences (Ferrechio, 1998).[36]

In some ways, it makes sense to assign to the individual schools the task of getting the parents to come to periodic parent-teacher conferences. After all, the schools have the closest relationships with their parents. The schools are the units that can, most effectively, both publicize these meetings to the parents and make it inviting for the parents to attend. Indeed, some District of Columbia schools did aggressively promote the teacher-parent conferences. Others did little.[37] For the school district, it makes perfect sense to delegate to the individual school – and then to the individual teacher – the task of recruiting, cajoling, motivating, coercing, shaming, or otherwise getting the parents to attend.

But why should the entire burden be on the schools? After all, the school district set the times for the teacher conferences – on Wednesdays from noon to 7:00 p.m. And both parents and teachers complained that these hours were hardly convenient for working parents.[38]

And, apparently, no one thought about also holding the parents accountable. Yet if we believe in rewards and punishments – if we believe in publicly making heroes of people who do their part while publicly shaming others who shirk their obligations – why not employ the same strategy with parents that we use with students and teachers? Why not create a parental report card? We could send this parental report card home with the student. (Don't you believe it would be delivered?) Or we could post a parental report card in the lobby of the school: One column would list the parents who attended the last teacher-parent conference; the other column would list the parents who did not.

Every June, America's schools send their students home with a summer assignment. Often, schools ask their students to read several books over the summer. But why not give parents an assignment? And why not hold them accountable for doing it? Why not ask parents of elementary-school students to read ten books to their children over the summer? And why not ask these parents to somehow report in September on the books they read to their children? Why not ask parents of middle school and high-school students to do a joint history project over the summer? And, why not ask these parents to present a joint parent-child report during the first week of classes in September? Why don't we think of ways to hold parents accountable for their own children's learning?

Teachers, of course, would love to hold parents accountable. In a survey of teachers and parents, Public Agenda found that "teachers say inattentive, lazy students are the most serious problem they face, and they hold parents responsible." When Public Agenda asked teachers how serious they thought various problems were, many of them ranked several problems with parents as very or somewhat serious (see Table 1).

Actually, in Chicago, the United Neighborhood Organization is attempting to hold parents accountable. It convinced thirty schools to distribute parental report

Table 1. Holding Parents and Students Accountable: What Teachers Think.

The Problem	Percent of Teachers Who Thought the Problem was		
	Very Serious (%)	Somewhat Serious (%)	Either Very or Somewhat Serious (%)
Parents who fail to set limits and create structure at home for their kids	36	47	83
Parents who refuse to hold their kids accountable for their behavior and grades	31	50	81
Students who try to get by with doing as little work as possible	26	43	69

Source: Behn (2003), original table.

cards covering such subjects as reading (to their child), homework (checking it), and punctuality (at getting their child to school). But these report cards were ungraded; the parents were asked to grade themselves and then review their grades with their child's teacher (Johnston, 2000).

In New Haven, Superintendent Reginald Mayo is being more aggressive. "I can grade parents," he says. "Why not?" (Zielbauer, 2001). Mayo organized a task force that has prepared a report recommending, among other things, that the school system create a "parent honor roll" for those who fulfill their responsibilities while referring parents who flagrantly fail to help with homework or participate in school activities to the Connecticut Department of Children and Families (Reid, 2001). And New Haven's concept of "shared accountability" contains both "responsibilities" and "performance expectations" for parents that include "95% attendance record for their child" and "attendance at school orientation meetings, parent-teach conferences and parent meetings" (New Haven Public Schools, 2001, p. 17).

Why not hold students accountable? We do, of course. We have long issued student report cards. Now, "report cards" are common throughout society. We issue "report cards" on all sorts of organizations – schools, colleges and universities; hospitals and health maintenance organizations; nursing homes and day-care centers (Gormley & Weimer, 1999) – all in an effort to hold these organizations accountable. But we created the original report cards for students.

Have traditional report cards alone established student accountability? If they had, we would never have developed a problem. Indeed, in many places, student report cards became meaningless. Often, rather than hold students accountable for their grades by holding them back if they failed too many courses, we simply promoted them.

Rethinking Accountability in Education

Now, however, social promotion is out. High-stakes testing is in. Students don't just get a report card. If they don't pass the test, they may not get promoted. If they don't pass the test, they may have to go to summer school to get promoted. It they don't pass the test, they may not receive a high-school diploma.

Across the nation, governors and legislators, superintendents and school board members, business and civic leaders are all decrying social promotion. In a banner headline across the top of the front page, The News and Observer of Raleigh announced: "Death knell sounds for social promotion in N. C. schools." The chairman of the State Board of Education proclaimed, "It's time a diploma means something in North Carolina," while a fifth-grade teacher declared, "I'm glad to see that we are beginning to hold children accountable" (Simmons, 1999b). In South Carolina, the Student Accountability Act of 1998 established "social probation" for students who failed to display the skills required for their grade. Then, if they fail to improve in the following year, they will be held back (Johnston, 1999a).

In Boston, Chicago, New Haven, and elsewhere, students who fail end-of-the-year exams will be required to pass summer-school courses or be held back. And seventeen states require (or will soon require) students to pass an exit exam to receive a high-school diploma (Meyer et al., 2002, pp. 68, 77).[39] Other states reward students with high grades with college scholarships.

Still, it isn't obvious what kind of behavior such a carrot-and-stick accountability system motivates. Students could, of course, decide to work harder and smarter. But they, too, can exit. They can simply drop out – either physically or mentally.[40]

To attack this drop-out problem, to make exit a less desirable option for teenagers, Kentucky, North Carolina, Tennessee, and Virginia have a law: "No Pass, No Drive." To get a learner's permit or driver's license, a student needs to be making sufficient academic progress.[41] Sixteen states have a policy of "No Pass, No Play"; students who fail one or several courses cannot participate in athletics and other student activities (National Association of State Boards of Education, 1999).

Why not hold legislators accountable? Should the board of directors of a firm hold the managers, foremen, and line workers at one of their plants accountable for the plant's production if they don't provide them with adequate resources – if they don't provide high-quality raw materials, appropriate and effective technology, training for employees, and the funds necessary to obtain excellent materials, technology, and staff? This hardly seems fair. Still, we rarely talk about holding the public sector equivalent of a board of directors – the legislature – accountable.

For example, we could rate the chairs of the 99 education committees in the state legislatures in terms of their ability to mobilize and target resources, then rank and publish them in a national newspaper. Or teachers could evaluate their state legislators and publish their findings. For each legislative session, the Delaware

State Education creates a report card that specifies how each legislator voted on key education bills (Miller, 1999), though it no longer posts this report card on its Web site.

The state legislature, school board, and city council provide the resources with which educators must work. They micro-manage the educators. Why don't we hold them accountable?

Why not hold state superintendents accountable? Why not hold their staffs accountable? The state develops the curricula that the schools and teachers must employ. They certify the books that teachers can use. Why don't we hold the state superintendent – and all those curriculum specialists in the state offices – accountable?[42]

Why not hold business executives and other civic leaders accountable? We could rate and publish in the newspaper the names of the top executives of the biggest businesses in a school district based on their firm's overall contribution to education. We could rate the churches for their mentoring programs, for their after-school programs, or for their Saturday tutoring programs. We could publish the scores in the newspaper.

Why not hold citizens accountable? Citizens are the people who, directly or indirectly, choose our educational leaders. They often can approve or reject school bond issues – and sometimes tax increases. Citizens are the individuals who read and joke about the school rankings that are published in the paper. (If people weren't mesmerized by these ratings, newspapers wouldn't put them on the front page.) Why aren't citizens accountable for improving education?

Why not? Why don't we hold parents, or students, or legislators, or governors, or superintendents, or civic leaders – or ourselves – accountable? After all, education is a co-production progress; we all contribute to or detract from the education of our communities' children. And, as Kenneth Leithwood and Lorna Earl of the University of Toronto observe, it is not "legitimate to hold a person solely accountable for expected performances requiring a shared influence" (2000, p. 5).

Why not? Why don't we hold ourselves accountable? Because it is easiest to think about accountability as something we do to others. And the easiest others on whom to focus are the schools, the principals, and the teachers.

CREATING A COMPACT OF MUTUAL, COLLECTIVE RESPONSIBILITY

How should who hold whom accountable for what? Traditionally, the answer is obvious: Superiors hold subordinates accountable for whatever they want by quickly punishing failure and occasionally rewarding success. Indeed, the very phrase we use – "hold people accountable" – clarifies the nature of the relationship. There is an accountability holder and an accountability holdee. And the accountability holdee has no rights and little leverage. The superior holds the subordinate accountable. The superior is the accountability punisher; the subordinate is the accountability punishee. Yet this conventional, uni-directional, hierarchical form of accountability is not the only way to think about enhancing accountability in education.

Accountability could also emerge from an agreement among everyone in what Kevin Kearns of the University of Pittsburgh calls the "accountability environment" (1996). As I have explained in more detail elsewhere (Behn, 2001, Chap. 7) such a "compact of mutual and collective responsibility" would make no hierarchical distinction between accountability holders and accountability holdees. Everyone would be both. Everyone signing on to this compact would also be accepting obligations and responsibilities. Every individual would recognize that he or she is part of a web of responsibility; each member is responsible to all of the others while simultaneously all of others are responsible to him or her.[43]

I make a clearly distinction between the concepts of accountability and responsibility.[44] Someone else imposes accountability on you. But you accept responsibility. You may choose to accept responsibility for what someone else seeks to impose accountability, but no one can force you to accept responsibility.[45] Organizations, argues Kidder, are held together by "webs of voluntary mutual responsibility, the product of many signings-up" (1981, p. 120). All people in an organization have a responsibility to the people above them, the people below them, and to their peers operating at the same level.

With such a responsibility compact, legislative-branch accountability holders would no longer dictate the terms of accountability to executive-branch accountability holdees. Federal accountability holders would no longer dictate the terms of accountability to state accountability holdees. State accountability holders would no longer dictate the terms of accountability to municipal accountability holdees. Rather, each member of the compact would agree to the obligations for which he or she would be responsible. And, no one would attempt to hold others accountable for a failure without first fulfilling his or her own responsibilities.

In this web of mutual responsibility, legislators would accept responsibility not only for creating goals but also for providing schools with the resources necessary to achieve their goals. Further, legislators would accept responsibility for not setting unreasonable deadlines for achieving these goals. Members of the state legislature would also accept responsibility for creating an intelligent macro structure for the state's education system, and the members of the local school board would accept responsibility for creating an intelligent macro structure for the district's education system.[46] In this web of mutual responsibility, the legislative and executive branches would be partners in helping to improve the schools rather than adversaries engaged in the allocation of blame. In this web of mutual responsibility, the feds, the state, the district, the school, the classroom would be a partner along with the taxpayers and the community. Each would be responsible to all of the other members of the compact.

In this web of mutual responsibility, parents would accept responsibility for reading to their children – even to their pre-school children. They would not just be accountable for delivering their five-year-old bundle of raw material to the kindergarten door. They would accept responsibility for preparing their child for kindergarten and for encouraging and working with that child for the next thirteen years. They would accept responsibility for regularly attending teacher-parent conferences and other school activities, for following up on the suggestions offered by teachers, and for following the reasonable requirements of the school. In this web of mutual responsibility, parents would be neither clients nor customers nor accountability holders. They would be partners.[47]

Similarly teachers and parents would be partners. So would states and localities. Indeed, this web of mutual and collective responsibility would need to include legislators, executive-branch officials (both elected and appointed), principals, teachers, parents, business executives, labor officials, and other civic leaders. Each partner would accept that it had a specific responsibility for the education of the children in the partnership's school, community, district, or state.

Such a responsibility compact would create "the sense of collective responsibility" – the "accountability to partners" – that Eugene Bardach of the University of California at Berkeley and Cara Lesser of the Center for Studying Health System Change found among human-service collaboratives. These "collaboratives" are:

Two or more organizations that pool energies and perhaps funds (at least some of which are public) and seek thereby to overcome the fragmentation of services created by a host of current practices and institutional arrangements. For instance, local social services, mental health, education, and juvenile justice agencies might collaborate to serve certain multiproblem families or children.

A collaborative that employees "partnership accountability," report Bardach and Lesser, is "a self-governing community of accountability in which partners hold the collective to account." The "partner agencies are in many senses accountable to one another for competent or even excellent performance, and they use a variety of means to project this sense of accountability" (1996, pp. 198, 204, 206, 222).

Breaking the Accountability Mindset

"Who do I hold accountable?" Parents, reports President Bush, will ask this question when their child fails a reading test. "What went wrong? How come? Where did the system let me down?" (Bush, 2001a). The implication, of course, is that the "system" that let the parents down was the school system.

But maybe what let the parents down weren't the school system but the accountability system. Maybe what went wrong was our system of educational accountability. Maybe we won't really fix our education system until we fix our educational accountability system. Maybe we won't really have an education "system" until we create a sense of mutual responsibility among all of those who can make or withhold a significant contribution to the education of their community's children.

Maybe we need to rethink what we mean by accountability in education. Maybe we need to replace our traditional system of uni-directional, hierarchical, carrot-and-stick accountability with a new compact of mutual and collective responsibility.

To create such a web of mutual and collective responsibility, we must discard as obsolete our conventional concepts of accountability. If we can only think of accountability in terms of superiors and subordinates, then we cannot conceive of a network of partners who agree on what they want to produce, how they will know if they have produced it, and who needs to contribute what to ensure that this co-production process works. If we can only think of accountability in terms of superiors and subordinates, we cannot recognize that separating policy from administration is difficult. If we can only think of accountability in terms of superiors and subordinates, we cannot accept that front-line employees might understand more about the production process than the managers. If we can only think of accountability in terms of superiors and subordinates, we cannot envisage any organizational arrangement other than a hierarchy.

Americans, without even conceiving that there might be an alternative, have created an accountability system for education designed for a very hierarchical production process. Yet, if we conclude that education doesn't quite fit the traditional model of industrial production, we might also conclude that education doesn't fit the traditional model of accountability. If we conclude that the education of our children from kindergarten through high school requires cooperative efforts of teachers, parents, principals, school board members, superintendents, legislators, governors, as well as a variety of citizens, we might also conclude that we need an accountability arrangement that binds these people together as partners so that they feel responsible to each other. And, if we decide to create such a web of collaborative relationships, we need to develop a new theory of accountability in education – one that is based not on institutional rewards and punishments but on a personal sense of responsibility to colleagues and partners.

As Table 2 suggests, a compact of mutual and collective responsibility is a much more complex institution compared with traditional, uni-directional, hierarchical accountability. After all, a sense of personal responsibility cannot be instilled by

Table 2. How Should Who Hold Whom Accountable for What? Two Different Ways of Answering this Accountability Question.

The Question	Traditional, Unit-Directional, Hierarchical Accountability	A Compact of Mutual and Collective Responsibility
How?	With rewards and punishments	By evolving a compact describing the responsibilities of each of its members, fostering personal relationships, and creating informal reporting mechanisms
Who?	The accountability holders (or punishers)	Everyone who is a member of the compact (which ought to include everyone in the accountability environment)
Whom?	The accountability holdees (or punishees)	Everyone who is a member of the compact (which ought to include everyone in the accountability environment)
What?	Standardized test scores	Test scores, graduation rates, parental involvement and whatever else the members of the compact decide

commands and hierarchy. It cannot be coerced by rewards and punishments. It cannot be nourished by labeling people as losers. Individuals will accept and act on a sense of personal responsibility only if they see others acting similarly and if they believe that others will continue to act similarly.

If educators believe citizens and legislators are not providing them with the resources necessary to do their job, they will feel no responsibility to either citizens or legislators. If educators believe that parents are not doing their part, they will feel less responsibility for them (even if they continue to care about their individual children). If educators believe that legislators and state superintendents are hiding behind commands and hierarchy, they will reject the legitimacy of any associated accountability system. If educators believe that the other individuals and institutions in their accountability environment seek only to condemn them publicly for any and all failures, they will simply seek another line of work.

"Who do I hold accountable?" asks the parent of a failing child. "Where did the system let me down?" Maybe, however, this parent really needs to ask: "For what should I accept responsibility?" Maybe this parent really needs to ask: "Where did I let the system down?"

But neither parents nor Presidents will ask these kinds of questions until they rethink what we mean by accountability in education.

NOTES

1. For example, in 1999, on the Third International Mathematics and Science Study (or TIMSS, 1999), a test of eighth-grade students in 38 different nations, U.S. students scored above the international average in Algebra, but below (among others) Bulgaria, the Czech Republic, Slovenia, the Russian Federation, and Hungary (Mullis et al., 2000, p. 98).

2. Various NGA publications note the governors' efforts to "hold schools, teachers, students, and parents accountable" and "to hold teachers and schools responsible for students' achievements" (Gregovich, 1999a, pp. 2–3). To be fair, however, Governor Carper also notes that his "approach will hold students, parents, teachers, schools – and Governors – accountable" (Curran, 1999, p. v).

3. Yes: The official terminology is principals and agents. But this antiseptic language fails to capture how the relationship feels – particularly by the agents. For a more detailed analysis of what we (implicitly) mean by accountability – and by the ubiquitous phrase, "hold people accountable" – see Behn (2001).

4. The "current" movement for accountability in education has actually been around for a while. A quarter of a century ago, for example, one study reported that 30 states had enacted "accountability legislation" (Hawthorne, 1974, p. 2).

5. This article is about accountability for performance – specifically, educational performance. Nevertheless, we should not forget that society also seeks to establish accountability for finances and for fairness (Behn, 2001, pp. 6–14).

6. For a discussion of the linkage between accountability measurement and motivation in education, see Behn (1997).

7. Indeed, accountability and improvement may even be in conflict. Brennan draws attention to "an almost inevitable tension between using a test for instructional improvement and using a test for high-stakes accountability" (2001, p. 14).

8. Schwartz (2000), for example, emphasizes the importance of "external accountability policies" – particularly standards, measurement, monitoring, evaluation, auditing, the public reporting of such measurements, evaluations, and audits, plus rewards and sanctions. He contrasts this with internal, hierarchical, or professional accountability.

9. I am ignoring, of course, another mechanism for motivating improvement: the market. The advocates of vouchers and charter schools argue that the market provides better motivation because it contains more effective carrots and sticks. Ogawa and Collom (2000) argue, however, that most systems designed to hold schools accountable with performance measures implicitly assume a "quasi-market rationale."

10. In education, "organizational" capability includes teachers, teaching skills, curricula, facilities, and educational equipment (from chalk to computers). But there complete

"operational" capability would include parents and others who to the students' education.

11. Lags between treatment and measurement create a generic problem for any effort to use the measures to learn and improve (See Behn, 2002). In education, such lags complicate not just the heroic task of determining whether the schools are yielding – many years later – productive workers and responsible citizens. Such lags even complicate the more traditional effort of evaluating schools using test scores. A recent increase in a school or district's test scores might reflect important improvements in educational practice made several years ago and while masking recent mistakes. Similarly, a decrease in a school or district's scores might stem from significant mistakes made several years ago that have been completely but only recently rectified. Thus, Meyer concludes "the average test score reflect[s] information about school performance that tends to be grossly out of date," which "severely weakens it as an instrument of public accountability. To allow educators to react to assessment results in a timely and responsible fashion, performance indicators must reflect information that is current" (1996, pp. 213–214).

12. Moreover, there is little reason to believe that the influences of these people and institutions are independent and linear rather than synergistic and very non-linear.

13. The link between an individual student's performance on formal tests and that same individual's later functioning as a productive worker and responsible citizen is not the least bit obvious. Most of us, from personal experience or publicized stories, can offer counter examples. Yet, currently, the best we can do is to employ the existing surrogate measures of in-school tests.

14. At the operational level, of course, what counts is not the standards but the assessments. The accountability system will be based on the results of the assessments, regardless of whether the assessment mechanism is connected to the standards or not. Thus, it will be the specifics of the test – not the abstractions of the standards – that will get the attention of teachers. Teachers won't teach to the standards. They will teach of the assessment.

15. Numerous scholars have devoted significant effort to developing and analyzing the validity and reliability of various kinds of assessment tools. See, for example: Meyer (1996), Murnane (1987), Wainer (1993), publications of the National Center for Research, Evaluation, Standards, and Student Testing (CREST), and the RAND Corporation's Center for Research on Evaluation, Standards, and Student Testing, and such journals as Applied Measurement in Education, and Journal of Education Measurement.

16. For example, in its 1999 special report on accountability, Education Week observes: "The assumption seems to be that if performance is the problem, what's missing is the will: Find the right combination of carrots and sticks, and effort and achievement will follow" (Olson, 1999, p. 8).

17. Kentucky and Maryland have both created educational accountability systems but with different structures for their sanctions and financial rewards. In a comparative analysis of these two systems, Kelley and her colleagues observe that "Regarding the effect of the financial incentive, Maryland principals have significantly higher average perceptions than do Kentucky principals that the monetary bonus or award is motivating to teachers." In both states, it appears, the bonus has a positive impact. But look at the question and the possible answers. Over two hundred principals in each state were asked whether they: (1) strongly disagree; (2) disagree; (3) neither agree nor disagree; (4) agree; or (5) strongly agree that "the possibility of a bonus helps me motivate teachers to work towards the accountability goals." For Maryland, the mean score was 2.97 while in Kentucky it was 2.35. That is, at

best, the bonus neither helped nor hindered motivation. The results for three other questions about motivation were similar (Kelly et al., 2000, pp. 184–185, 196).

18. For a discussion of "extrinsic, intrinsic and team-based motivators" applied to education, see King and Mathers (1997, pp. 148–150).

19. The current minimum wage is $5.15 per hour, which means it takes 97 hours to earn $500. Someone can work these 97 hours in five weekends with a four-hour Friday evening shift and two eight-hour shifts on Saturday and Sunday. (In California and Massachusetts, where the minimum wage is $6.75, it would take 74 hours, or just four weekends, to earn $500.) And someone with a teacher's education ought to be able to land a part-time job at something above the minimum wage.

20. If we do identify someone who went into teaching for the money, we have also identified someone who is not smart enough to be a teacher.

21. Bromley does not wish "to discount the profound role of incentives in guiding human behavior." Nevertheless, he concludes "that monetary incentives – at least as economists tend to think of them – may be of equivocal necessity in reforming educational performance, and such incentives are almost certainly insufficient" (1998, p. 46).

22. "We are dealing with the consequences of greater and greater pressure on school administrators to put forth the best performance on schools tests," observes Ken Oden, the county attorney of Travis County, Texas. "That kind of atmosphere is what breeds greater temptation to manipulate ratings for your school" (Johnston, 1999b). On April 6, 1999, Oden convinced a Travis County grand jury to indict both the Austin Independent School District and its deputy superintendent for tampering with government records; on January 8, 2002, he forced the district to plead no contest. District officials had under reported drop-out rates for several schools to prevent them from being classified by the state as "low-performing" and had also modified the identification numbers of some students so that their test scores would not be reported (Jayson, 1999; Kurtz, 1999; Martinez, 2002).

23. George Washington Plunkitt, a leader of Tammany Hall for nearly half a century, made a "distinction between honest graft and dishonest graft." Dishonest graft could earn you a jail sentence. Honest graft was perfectly legal and could make you rich (Riordon, 1963, pp. 3–6). Of course, since Plunkitt's day, we have attempted to convert, via legislation, various forms of honest graft into dishonest graft. Yet, today, honest graft still exists; it is called campaign contributions. Similarly, I distinguish between honest cheating and dishonest cheating. Dishonest cheating can earn you a jail sentence – or a least dismissal from your job. Honest cheating will help your students, your school, your district, and you win at the accountability game without breaking any rules, though it may not help your students grow up to be productive employees or responsible citizens.

24. The typical educational-accountability system reminds me of W. Edwards Deming's "stupid experiment" with the red and white beads. Workers are supposed to "make" white beads from a box containing 800 red and 3,200 white beads. Unfortunately, management (that is, Deming) has failed to provide its workers (volunteers from the audience) with any mechanism for separating the red beads from the white ones; yet management berates its employees for their "failure" (Deming, 1986, pp. 346–354; Walton, 1986, pp. 40–51).

25. Bromley offers a novel suggestion for solving this supply problem: He recommends that "the top ten schools of education raise their admission standards to that required by the schools of business, engineering, and law." This would limit the supply of teachers, thus, he forecasts, "driving up starting salaries – and eventually the salaries of all teachers." And,

he predicts, "it would lead to an increased interest in a career in education among brighter undergraduates" (1998, pp. 61–62).

26. For example, in 1999, Oklahoma needed mathematics teachers. The state had 700 people who are certified to teach math but weren't. They were working elsewhere. In Oklahoma, a college graduate could (then) earn $24,600 as a math teacher or $40,000 to $50,000 as computer specialist (Bradley, 1999b, p. 10).

27. Principals in New York City can increase their salary by $30,000 by moving to the suburbs (Olson, 1999c, p. 21).

28. This industrial metaphor suggests that educational production is a "line operation," which, writes Rosenthal, produces "a high volume of services in rather routine fashion." In reality, however, education is more like a "job shop," which tends "to customize a smaller scale of work" (1989, p. 113). Still, we continue to use a mental model of accountability that suggests we are thinking about education production as a line operation.

29. Inevitably, they will create a few defective products – particularly if some of their raw materials are inferior – but these should be kept to a minimum.

30. Bromley suggests that economists, at least, tend to think about "the school as a firm" and that "the economic literature on the efficiency of public schools starts from the classic production function." Further, he suggests that the implicit use of "this traditional economic model" shapes how we think about what should be done to improve American education (1998, pp. 43–46).

31. Again, however, the outcome that we really want to produce is productive workers and responsible citizens.

32. This single question covers the five accountability questions raised by Leithwood and Earl (2000, p. 2):

> What level of accountability is to be provided? [My "what?"] Who is expected to provide the account? [My "whom?"] To whom is the account owed? [My "who?"] What is to be accounted for? [More of my "what?"] And what are the consequences of providing an account? [My "how?"]

33. At the beginning of the 1999 baseball season, after years of being the accountability holdees, major league baseball players decided to become the accountability holders by publishing a ranking of major-league umpires.

34. Some states seek to hold their districts accountable. In 1999, Mississippi and New Jersey issued report cards on districts but not on schools (though New Jersey now has them for schools). In West Virginia, if one or more schools are failing, the state has the power to take over the whole school district. And Maryland seeks to hold its districts accountable for fixing their failing schools (Keller, 1999, p. 42).

35. The classic example of industrial production is the automobile; after all, Henry Ford invented the assembly line. Nevertheless, automobile production has moved beyond traditional, mass production to something that looks more like co-production. Womack, Jones, and Roos (1990) call this "lean production," with the "company as community" rather than hierarchy and suppliers as partners rather than subordinate vendors. And, rather than impose accountability on their employees and suppliers, lean-production companies create arrangements of mutual responsibility (with mutual reward).

36. In 2001, New Mexico added parental involvement to the accountability criteria used to rate schools (Gewertz, 2002, p. 139).

37. Some schools did post sheets on school bulletin boards on which parents could sign up for a teacher conference, but then did little to inform parents of this system. Moreover, reported The Washington Post, this sign-up system would not work in those schools that "forbid parents from walking their children into the building" (Strauss, 1998).

38. Again, Deming's parable of the red beads seems directly applicable. See Note 25.

39. Arkansas was requiring students to pass a comprehensive exam to graduate from high school, but the high rate of student failure caused it to drop the requirement (Olson, 1999, p. 10).

40. One study of 102 low-achieving students in Chicago found that high-stakes testing motivated a majority of these students to increase in their work significantly but a third of them did little. (Roderick & Engle, 2001).

41. Eighteen states have some kind of "No Pass, No Drive" law. Most, however, only require that students attend school — but they need not demonstrate that they are actually learning anything (Education Commission of the States, 1998).

42. In the fall of 2001, the Illinois Board of Education decided, because of low-test scores, not to renew the contract state superintendent Glenn W. McGee (Stricherz, 2001).

43. Although most of the scholarly literature on accountability in education implicitly employs an accountability relationship that is hierarchical and unidirectional, this is not exclusively the case. For example, Henry (1996) proposes a "community accountability" that is similar to my compact of mutual, collective responsibility. And in an article about accountability in education that explicitly uses the agent concept (and thus implicitly suggests that these agents have principals), Robinson and Timperley report on one "exceptional" school in New Zealand that had created "mutual accountability and shared responsibility for improvement" (2000, p. 78).

44. I am, undoubtedly, pushing the distinction between "accountability" and "responsibility" further than the traditional definitions of these two words may warrant. Webster's New Dictionary of Synonyms lists as synonyms "responsible, answerable, accountable, amenable, and liable." It reports that "responsible, answerable, and accountable are very close... meaning capable of being called upon to answer or make amends to someone for something. Although often used interchangeably they are capable of distinction based on their typical applications." Specifically, it argues: "Accountable is much more positive than responsible or answerable in its suggestions of retributive justice in case of default" (Gove, 1968, p. 690).

45. My concept of accepting responsibility (as opposed to imposing accountability) is similar to the idea of "signing up" as described by Tracy Kidder in The Soul of a New Machine. At Data General, a firm that designed and built microcomputers, engineers were rarely ordered to do things. Rather, they "signed up" to do them. And getting an engineer to sign up was much more effective than an order, because, in signing up, the engineer made a personal commitment to produce the result. Thus, the manager's job was not to give orders but to convince people to sign up: "Nobody had ordered him to do all this. [Middle manager, Carl] Alsing had made the opportunity available, and [engineer Chuck] Holland had signed up" (1981, pp. 63, 160).

46. "Because legislators ought to be accountable for rationalizing the system of delivering publicly financed human services," write Bardach and Lessor, "they should to some degree be accountable to the people who work the system and who know the most about it. It is not enough to say that legislators are accountable to the voters; for the delegate model of representation needs to be supplemented by a trusteeship model

which, properly understood, implies a duty to consider advice from all sources that have a reasonable probability of making a helpful contribution to legislators' performance of the trusteeship function" (1996, p. 220).

47. In the Reynolds School District in Oregon, parents and teachers sign a contract outlining the responsibilities of the school, the parent, and the student. The district also provides parents with information about how to prepare their pre-school children for school (Blum, 2000, p. 104).

REFERENCES

Archer, J. (1999, March 17). New teachers abandon field at higher rate. *Education Week*, *18*(27), 1, 20–21.
Archer, J. (2001, January 11). Connecticut. *Education Week*, *20*(17), 120–121.
Bardach, E., & Lessor, C. (1996, April). Accountability in human services collaboratives – For what? and to whom? *Journal of Public Administration Research and Theory*, *6*(2), 197–224.
Behn, R. D. (1997). Linking measurement and motivation: A challenge for education. *Advances in Educational Administration*, *5*, 15–58.
Behn, R. D. (1998, May/June). Cheating: Honest & dishonest. *The New Public Innovator*, *1*(1), 18–19.
Behn, R. D. (2001). *Rethinking democratic accountability*. Washington, DC: Brookings Institution Press.
Behn, R. D. (2002, forthcoming). Why measure performance: Different purposes require different measures. *Public Administration Review*.
Blum, R. E. (2000, October). Standards-based reform: Can it make a difference for students. *Peabody Journal of Education*, *75*(4), 90–113.
Bradley, A. (1999a, January 11). Zeroing in on teachers. *Education Week*, *18*(17), 46–47, 49–52.
Bradley, A. (1999b, March 26). States' uneven teacher supply complicates staffing of schools. *Education Week*, *18*(26), 2, 10–11.
Brennan, R. L. (2001, Winter). Some problems, pitfalls, and paradoxes in educational measurement. *Educational Measurement: Issues and Practice*, *20*(4), 6–18.
Bromley, D. W. (1998, Fall). Expectations, incentives, and performance in American schools. *DÆDALUS*, *127*(4), 41–66.
Bush, G. W. (2001a). Excerpt from Bush statement announcing start of his education initiative. *The New York Times*, (January 24), A14, see also: http://www.whitehouse.gov/news/releases/2001/01/print/20010123-2.html.
Bush, G. W. (2001b). Communication from the president of the United States transmitting a report for nationwide education reform entitled: No child left behind. House Document 107-34. Washington, DC: U.S. Government Printing Office (January 30).
Bush, G. W. (2002). http://www.whitehouse.gov/news/releases/2002/03/20020302.html.
Clinton, W. J. (1999). Urging nation to 'Aim Higher'. Clinton offers proposals on education, retirement security, health care. *CQ Weekly*, (January 23), 201–207.
Clotfelter, C. T., & Ladd, H. F. (1996). Recognizing and rewarding success in public schools. In: H. F. Ladd (Ed.), *Holding Schools Accountable: Performance-Based Reform in Education*, (pp. 23–63). Washington, DC: Brookings Institution.
Coleman, J. S., Campbell, E. Q., Hobson, C. J., McPartland, J., Mood, A., Weinfeld, F., & York, R. (1966). *Equality of educational opportunity*. Washington, DC: U.S. Government Printing Office.

Curran, B. (1999). *Focusing on results: Toward an education accountability system*. Washington, DC: National Governors' Association.
Deming, W. E. (1986). *Out of crisis*. Cambridge, MA: Center for Advanced Engineering Study, Massachusetts Institute of Technology.
Earl, L., & Torrance, N. (2000, October). Embedding accountability and improvement into large-scale assessment, what difference does it make? *Peabody Journal of Education, 75*(4), 114–141.
Education Commission of the States (1998, September). *States with 'no pass/no drive' restrictions*.
Ferrechio, S. (1998). Parents wanted for conferences: incentives used to lure them. *The Washington Times* (November 16), C3.
Gewertz, C. (2002, January 10). New Mexico. *Education Week, 21*(17), 138–139.
Gormley, W. T., Jr., & Weimer, D. L. (1999). *Organizational report cards*. Cambridge, MA: Harvard University Press.
Gove, P. B. (1968). *Webster's new dictionary of synonyms*. Springfield, MA: G. & C. Merriam Company.
Gregovich, T. (1999a, February 20). *Governors boldly leading the way*. Washington, DC: National Governors' Association.
Gregovich, T. (1999b, February 22). *Nation's governors focus on education accountability*. Washington, DC: National Governors' Association.
Hawthorne, P. (1974). *Legislation by the states: Accountability and assessment in education*. Denver, CO: Cooperative Accountability Project.
Henry, G. T. (1996, September). Community accountability: A theory of information, accountability, and school improvement. *Phi Delta Kappan, 78*(1), 85–91.
Herzberg, F. (1968, January–Feburary). One more time: How do you motivate employees? *Harvard Business Review, 46*(1), 53–62.
Herzberg, F., Mausner, B., & Snyderman, B. B. (1959, 1993). *The motivation to work*. New Brunswick, NJ: Transaction Publishers.
Hirschman, A. O. (1970). *Exit, voice, and loyalty: Responses to decline in firms, organizations, and states*. Cambridge, MA: Harvard University Press.
Ingersoll, R. M. (2001, Fall). Teacher turnover and teacher shortages: An organizational analysis. *American Educational Research Journal, 38*(3), 499–534.
Jayson, S. (1999, April 7). AISD, administrator indicted: District and deputy superintendent face charges in TAAS data manipulation. *The Austin American-Statesman*.
Johnston, R. C. (1999a, January 11). Firm but friendly pressure. *Education Week, 18*(17), 54.
Johnston, R. C. (1999b, March 17). Texas presses districts in alleged test-tampering cases. *Education Week, 18*(27), 22.
Johnston, R. C. (2000, November 8). Chicago parents get report cards on involvement. *Education Week, 20*(10), 1, 20–21.
Keller, B. (1999, January 11). A role for the districts: They can make, or break, accountability. *Education Week, 18*(17), 41–44.
Kelley, C., Conley, S., & Kimball, S. (2000, October). Payment for results: Effects of the Kentucky and Maryland group-based performance award programs. *Peabody Journal of Education, 75*(4), 159–199.
Kidder, T. (1981). *The soul of a new machine*. Boston, MA: Atlantic Monthly Press.
King, R. A., & Mathers, J. K. (1997). Improving schools through performance-based accountability and financial rewards. *Journal of Education Finance, 23*(Fall), 147–176.
Kohn, A. (1993). *Punished by rewards: The trouble with gold stars, incentive plans, A's, praise, and other bribes*. Boston: Houghton Mifflin.

Kurtz, M. (1998). Teachers see disincentive to helping low-rated schools. *The News and Observer* (of Raleigh, N.C.) (February 18), 1A & 9A.

Kurtz, M. (1999). AISD tried to improve dropout rate data: Subpoenaed memos show district's intense effort to avoid 'low-performing' status for Austin school. *The Austin American-Statesman* (April 14), A1.

Ladd, H. F. (Ed.) (1996). Introduction. In: H. F. Ladd (Ed.), *Holding Schools Accountable: Performance-Based Reform in Education*, (pp. 1–19). Washington, DC: Brookings Institution.

Leithwood, K., & Earl, L. (2000, October). Educational accountability effects: An international perspective. *Peabody Journal of Education*, 75(4), 1–18.

Leithwood, K., & Jantzi, D. (1999, December). The relative effects of principal and teacher sources of leadership on student engagement with school. *Educational Administration Quarterly*, 35(Supplemental), 679–706.

Levinson, H. (1973). *The great jackass fallacy*. Boston: Harvard University Graduate School of Business Administration.

Manzo, K. K. (1999, January 11). Seeing a payoff: North Carolina's accountability plan has put the state's troubled schools on the path to reform. *Education Week*, 18(17), 165 & 200.

Martinez, M. M. (2002). District fined for altering test data: Austin school district pleads no contest to tampering with TAAS reports, will pay $5,000. *The Austin American-Statesman*, (January 9), A1.

Maslow, A. H. (1943, July). A theory of human motivation. *Psychological Review*, 50(4), 370–396.

Meyer, L., Orlofsky, G. F., Skinner, R. A., & Spicer, S. (2002, January 10). The state of the States. *Education Week*, 21(17), 68–92.

Meyer, R. H. (1996). Value-added indicators of school performance. In: E. A. Hanushek & D. W. Jorgenson (Eds), *Improving America's Schools: The Role of Incentives*. Washington, DC: National Academy Press.

Miller, B. (1999). Teachers union flexes muscles: When DSEA talks – and it knows the talk – lawmakers listen. *The News Journal*, (of Wilmington, Del.), (March 15), A10.

Mullis, I. V. S., Martin, M. O., Gonzalez, E. J., Gregory, K. D., Garden, R. A., O'Connor, K. M., Chrostowski, S. J., & Smith, T. A. (2000). TIMSS 1999 International mathematics report. Chestnut Hill, MA: Boston College, Lynch School of Education, International Study Center.

Murnane, R. J. (1987, Summer). Improving education indicators and economic indicators: The same problems? *Education Evaluation and Policy Analysis*, 9(2), 101–116.

National Association of State Boards of Education (1999, June). Non pass, no play: Eligibility requirements for extracurricular activities. *Policy Update*, 7(12).

New Haven Public Schools (2001, June 11). *Greater achievement through shared accountability*.

Ogawa, R. T., & Collom, E. (2000, October). Using performance indicators to hold schools accountable: Implicit assumptions and inherent tensions. *Peabody Journal of Education*, 75(4), 200–215.

Olson, L. (1999, March 3). Demand for principals growing, but candidates aren't applying. *Education Week*, 18(25), 1, 20–22.

Olson, L. (2000, January 13). Sweetening the pot. *Education Week*, 19(18), 28–30.

Portner, J. (1999, January 11). Reality strikes: After much debate, Virginia's students start taking the state's new exit exams. *Education Week*, 18(17), 181.

Reid, K. S. (2001). New Haven accountability plan targets parents. *Education Week*, (October 17).

Riordan, W. L. (1963). *Plunkitt of Tammany Hall: A series of very plain talks on very practical politics*. New York: E. P. Dutton.

Robinson, V., & Timperley, H. (2000, October). The link between accountability and improvement: The case of reporting to parents. *Peabody Journal of Education*, 75(4), 66–89.

Roderick, M., & Engle, M. (2001, Fall). The grasshopper and the ant: Motivational responses of low-achieving students to high-stakes testing. *Educational Evaluation and Policy Analysis, 23*(3), 197–227.

Rogosa, D. (1999). *How accurate are the STAR national percentile rank scores for individual students? – An interpretive guide*. Stanford University, August.

Rosenthal, S. R. (1989, Winter). Producing results in government: Moving beyond project management and its limited view of success. *Journal of Policy Analysis and Management, 8*(1), 110–116.

Samuels, C. A. (1999). Some in Va. rejecting student teachers. *The Washington Post*, (February 20), B1 & B7.

Samuelson, R. J. (1999). Why I am not a manager. *Newsweek*, (March 22), 47.

Sandham, J. L. (2001, January 11). California. *Education Week, 20*(17), 115–116.

Schwartz, R. (2000). School accountability – An elusive policy solution: The Israeli experience in comparative perspective. *Journal of Public Policy, 20*(3), 195–218.

Simmons, T. (1999a). Focus on reading pays off. *The News and Observer*, (of Raleigh, N.C.), (March 5), 1A & 14A.

Simmons, T. (1999b). Death knell sounds for social promotion in N.C. schools. *The News and Observer*, (of Raleigh, N.C.), (April 1), 1A & 13A.

Strauss, V. (1998). A school attendance plan for parents. *The Washington Post*, (November 15).

Stricherz, M. (2001, November 28). Getting its wish. *Education Week, 21*(13), 18.

Viadero, D. (2002, April 10). Researcher skewers explanations behind teacher shortage. *Education Week, 21*(30), 7.

Wainer, H. (1993, Spring). Measurement problems. *Journal of Education Measurement, 30*(1), 1–21.

Walton, M. (1986). *The Deming management method*. New York: Dodd, Mead.

Watts, J. A., Gaines, G., & Creech, J. (1998). *Getting results: A fresh look at school accountability*. Atlanta, GA: Southern Regional Education Board.

White, K. A. (1998). Florida's 'List of Shame' shrinks as legislators hail improvement. *Education Week, 17*(35), (May 13).

Womack, J. P., Jones, D. T., & Roos, D. (1990). *The machine that changed the world: The story of lean production*. New York: Rawson Associates.

Zielbauer, P. (2001). In New Haven, report calls for making education everybody's business. *The New York Times* (September 2).

3. DEVELOPMENT OF CONTRACTING IN INFRASTRUCTURE INVESTMENT IN THE U.K.: THE PRIVATE FINANCE INITIATIVE IN THE NATIONAL HEALTH SERVICE

Jane Broadbent, Jas Gill and Richard Laughlin

INTRODUCTION

On-going change in relation to the management of public services has led to the development of many initiatives in the control of day-to-day resources as the New Public Management[1] (Hood, 1991, 1995) continues its reforms. In this context debates about control of capital expenditure have taken a less visible role despite some earlier and influential comment on the area (Perrin, 1978 for example). Perhaps as the flow of ideas for reform in the management of day-to-day activity have waned, recent attention has turned more systematically to the efficient use of capital resources or infrastructure. This has been accompanied by recognition of the poor state of some of the public sector infrastructure. This chapter is concerned with the implications of the changing approaches to the provision of infrastructure is the U.K. National Health Service (NHS). Its particular focus in the Private Finance Initiative (PFI) and the contractual implications this brings into infrastructure development.

The push for efficiency in the NHS has influenced a number of changes in the approach to infrastructure development, initially through the introduction of "capital-charging." This is an accounting device for recognizing the cost of using capital assets. It moves the public sector towards the adoption of the accounting practices of the private sector where depreciation and capital costs are taken into account in the context of calculating profits. This move towards private sector accounting approaches is a trend that has been apparent in the rest of the English-speaking world. However, efficiencies in the use of capital have not seemingly provided sufficient improvement in the state of the public infrastructure. There has been recourse, not just to the practices but also to the resources of the private sector through the introduction of the Private Finance Initiative (PFI). In building linkages to the private sector, PFI advances another of the technologies of NPM in that it extends the use of contractual relationships. It is in this aspect that PFI is a novel policy initiative, since it changes the nature of working relationships in the hospital, moving them from a bureaucratic structure, described by many senior officials as the "NHS family"[2] to a contractual one. Whilst contracting in the NHS is not new, the novelty of the PFI lies in the length of the contracts that are entered into, which can be as long as 60 years.

In analyzing the provision of capital resources in the National Health Service (NHS) in the U.K. this paper will therefore give particular emphasis to the changing contractual relationships that surround the acquisition and use of these resources. Our interest centers on the impact that this different form of provision of capital has on the NHS as an organization. The purpose of the chapter is to extend the literature considering the introduction of contracting in the public sector (cf. Broadbent, Dietrich & Laughlin, 1996). It is driven by questions and concerns about the ramifications of the changes that are occurring. It is also intended to add to the theoretical understanding of the relationships.

Following this introduction, the chapter will comprise four substantive sections and a final discussion and conclusion. First we will review the recent history of capital investment in the NHS, where we illustrate the introduction of contractual relationships. The second substantive section will provide a framework on which to base our analysis of the relationships. We highlight the use of transaction cost economics alongside a critique of this approach (Campbell, 1997) to introduce ideas of relational contracting, which, of necessity, build these contractual relationships in different ways. These issues will be illustrated, in the third and fourth sections, in the context of the contractual relationships generally in the NHS and specifically in the Dartford and Gravesham PFI[3] scheme. Finally, in a concluding section, we will provide a discussion and draw out some implications of this mode of organizing.

THE RECENT HISTORY OF CAPITAL ALLOCATION IN THE NHS: FROM BUREAUCRACY TO CONTRACT

The changing arrangements for developing and controlling capital investment projects in the National Health Service (NHS) from pre-1991 have sought to introduce more control over this area. The motivation for these changes have been well documented and was reflective of and reflected by changes elsewhere in the world (Guthrie, Humphrey & Olsen, 1998). Inherent in those changes was a desire to break down the bureaucratic relationships and introduce some level of competition. The assumption was that competition was good for efficiency and that the introduction of systems of contracting or quasi-contracting was the chosen mode (Broadbent, Dietrich & Laughlin, 1996). In essence, a transition away from bureaucratic to contract type relationships at the operational level was sought, in the context of a strong neo-liberalist thrust that retained control over process.

These changes are reflected in the context of the planning of infrastructure development. Before 1991 what limited capital finance that was available was allocated to the NHS Regions.[4] It was then the responsibility of Regions to allocate this capital fund to District Health Authorities. This was done "... through a system of bidding together with option appraisal of their schemes" (Appleby, 1999, p. 79). Capital amounts were, therefore, allocated rather like revenue amounts – to be consumed within the year of allocation with no thought to future cost or benefit apart from the time when money was allocated. The allocation from any Region to any District Health Authority was undertaken in the context of the bureaucratic structure that ran from the Department of Health down through the service. Once hospitals were built and operational there was no further formal tie between the two bodies in relation to this transaction. Accountability related to the expenditure in the year in question not to amounts allocated in previous years whether of a capital or revenue nature and there was no formal accounting for the "efficiency" of capital asset usage.

This system changed with the introduction of the National Health Service and Community Care Act of 1990, which introduced quasi-contractual relationships. The Act also introduced "capital charging" and "external financing limits" and introduced the "purchaser/provider" split in healthcare provision. District Health Authorities (renamed Health Authorities) and some GP practices (those who chose to be "fundholders") were the new "purchasers" of secondary care from hospital "providers"[5] (which over time all have become NHS Trusts). Hence the notion of a contract or quasi-contract was introduced in the context of the provision of day-to-day services.

NHS Trusts have a unique legal status. They are quasi-independent bodies that, on establishment, took ownership of their land, buildings, plant and equipment. At the same time they incurred "... an interest bearing debt equal to the value of the initial assets" (Working for Patients, White Paper, Working Paper No 1, paragraph 4.4). Trusts were given their assets but were also to be liable to an annual 6% charge on the assets (or more accurately the equivalent debt), to be paid to the NHS Executive. This provided an accounting-led means of considering the "efficiency" of capital asset usage. As many authors have indicated in their analysis of the capital charging system (cf. Heald & Scott, 1995, 1996; Mayston, 1989, 1990; Mellett, 1990; Perrin, 1989) the total cost to the NHS as a whole is nil, as the revenues collected re-circulate into the NHS purse that is then available for distribution. However, individual NHS Trusts incur an additional cost burden of some substance. Individual NHS Trusts recoup their increased costs though the charges they make for the provision of services. In the context of the quasi-contractual relationships that existed at that time the assumption was that those Trusts that do not use their capital assets efficiently would face resistance from their "customers" because their prices would not be competitive.

The strong centralized bureaucratic controls of the capital allocations remained and were reflected in the management of further capital allocations. From 1991, allocation was by the NHS Executive instead of being made through Regions. This allowed the introduction of "external financing limits" as a means of controlling overall borrowing.[6] It should be noted that it was difficult to obtain funding for infrastructure projects, despite the poor state of the NHS estate.

PFI was introduced in 1992, arguably in the first instance as a means by which to avoid public borrowing controls.[7] It provided the possibility of obtaining private finance for public services provision in the context of infrastructure investment (see Broadbent, Haslam & Laughlin, 2000, for more details). PFI gives an on-going provision of facility management services by a private sector contractor, based in infrastructure assets that are owned by them. It has thereby introduced contractual relationships in infrastructure development to the NHS. These are very different contractual controls to those used in the context of such initiatives as competitive tendering that have been common for many years. We will argue below that this new type of contracting affects the internal workings of the hospitals that have previously been organized in a tight bureaucratic structure. As noted in the introduction to the chapter, this structure has led to an often-stated view of the NHS as a "family."

In the context of day to day working relationships, in using private financing as a source of developing the infrastructure, the NHS has created structures that are governed by contracts. Thus, the day-to-day operation of the PFI scheme creates relationships that are very different to the "family" relationships that previously existed in the NHS. PFI involves new partners from the private sector who contract to provide services to the NHS. Instead of building new hospitals and running the services themselves the NHS instead pay a fee for the provision of services in premises provided by the new private sector partners. In essence this provides a substitution of the need for capital expenditure by the payment of increased revenue charges. The nature of the payment for the availability of the "asset based services" will be defined in the contract document that governs the PFI scheme. Equally, the nature of the service quality will be specified, as will any penalties for lack of performance.

It should be recognized that whilst, in the past, contracts have been used to control the provision of facilities management services of various kinds through competitive tendering processes, PFI contracts are very different. The reason for the difference rests in the magnitude and duration of these contracts, typically for over 25–60 years. Was the contract simply for the provision of services, and then the timing could be over a shorter period, as in the previous contracting arrangements. As the PFI projects are associated with schemes that provide premises in which services are delivered, the length of contract has to be longer to ensure the viability of the scheme for the contractor who cannot use the property for other purposes.

Contracts and Control

Relational Contracts

Given that the move to contractual relationships is strongly influenced by a view that this is a way to ensure efficiency, we turn to some of the ideas of contracting to provide a framework for our analysis. The reason for this is that there is a need to understand the underlying assumptions of contracting to understand the implications that they have for the relationships in the NHS. In doing so we will argue that a particular form of contracting, relational contracting, is likely to be more constructive in the context of a long term contract. Campbell and Harris state the matter succinctly when they note that "(E)fficient long-term contractual behavior must be understood as consciously co-operative" (Campbell & Harris, 1993, p. 167).

Campbell (1997) argues that much of the development of classical contract law over the last twenty years has been based on ideas of transaction cost economics. He is critical of this alignment and also of the somewhat crude way in which the two have often been associated, arguing not for a rejection of economic analysis, but for recognition of the limits of economic thinking. His argument is for the adoption of the notion of relational contracting in a manner that does not reject economic thinking but which places transaction costs in the context of their social relations.

Campbell's argument that the neo-classical underpinning of contract law is inappropriate rests on the argument that there has been an inappropriate utilization of transaction cost economics. He turns to the work of Arrow to substantiate his case. Campbell argues that classical contract law relies on the idea of presentation.[8] This means that the goal of a contract is to make the contract reflect all the aspects of the future relationship. What this means is that there is an attempt to agree, at the present time, how any future possibility will be dealt with. It assumes that there is some level of possibility of predicting the future. Campbell points out that this involves an element of risk and the role of the contract is to allocate this risk. He also points to the difficulty of realistically fulfilling these assumptions, implying that this is a particular problem for classical contract law. In turning to the work of Arrow, Campbell finds a framework that he sees as more relevant to the analysis of contracts. This framework still retains the notion of transaction costs. Campbell identifies two elements that he sees as particularly important – strategic or opportunistic behavior and bounded rationality. These are fundamental to transaction cost economics, yet Campbell casts them in ways that are subtly different to their more normal uses.

These factors – strategic behavior and transaction cost economics – are particularly relevant in the context of PFI. Consider first the issue of strategic behavior. PFI is one of the complex contracts that Campbell argues have particular possibilities for strategic behavior. He uses the example of asset-specificity, arguing that where this exists there is a "lock-in" effect for the parties, which can lead to power plays between them. As argued earlier, in PFI there is considerable asset specificity because hospital buildings will not easily be used for other purposes. An environment of rapid technological change attenuates the risk that the premises might become inadequate or redundant before the payback on the building has been received. Consideration of the extent to which provision of medical services has changed over the last twenty years gives some indication of the possibilities here. The problem of predicting whether this will happen leads us to the consideration of Campbell's second issue: bounded rationality. Campbell (1997, p. 313) notes: "Bounded Rationality obviously makes presentation an illusory goal."

Campbell argues that the developments of an ethical, rather than an informational, approach to the organizational theory of the firm can help us to understand how both these matters can be dealt with. His argument is that the reason that firms exist is that they can do things that markets cannot in the context of large-scale complex projects. They allow the possibility of overcoming the residual risk that remains for those making a commitment to an activity in which risk cannot be eliminated or allocated under a contract (Campbell, 1997, p. 316).

This is necessary because presentiation is impossible and this is particularly so in complex contracts. Campbell argues that this has ethical dimensions, which are reflected in the fact that the managerial authority of a firm relies upon the on-going co-operation of individuals within them. Campbell's point is that this allows the consideration of norms, trust and co-operation as part of the debate as to why firms exist. Hence, he recognizes the limit of economic rationality and argues the analysis of contract, even when located in ideas of transaction costs, cannot ignore these limits or the social context in which they are embedded. If this is the case then we can consider the role of the PFI contract as a constitutive element of the social relations and also explore at how the contract is constituted by those relationships. Campbell's argument is that the consideration of social relations has often been ignored and a psychology of utility maximization has been substituted. This has limited the usefulness of many analyses.

The bias towards an economic analysis of law has arguably led to an approach to governance that is unduly market driven. Campbell (1997, p. 325) suggests that "In particular, directly ethical constraints which appeal to (and punish infractions of) norms of mutual self-interest and conscious co-operation must be recognized to be the foundation of solutions to strategic behavior problems."

He argues that if monitoring of behavior ignores or undermines the existing social relations they cannot succeed.

In taking this analysis seriously we can therefore raise questions about the effect of PFI contracts on the social relations that exist in the NHS. In particular we can ask whether the resulting contracts will destroy existing social relations or allow the development of new social relations between the NHS and the private contractors. In a context where the previous relationships have been built through a bureaucratic structure and in the context of strong professional groupings this has the potential to be a sensitive issue. Health professionals are not necessarily sympathetic to an approach that sees the competitive element of market economics as reflective of the social relationships they value and this means there is a need to look at the nature of these contracts and their operation with some care. We need to ask the question as to whether PFI contracts have the capacity to become relational contracts. That is a contract that is geared towards defining the boundaries of the relationship that seeks to clarify a framework in which it can be seen how changes might be dealt with. It is based on notions of regulatory law (Broadbent & Laughlin, 1997; Teubner, 1987) and thus seeks to provide a framework in which social relations can develop autonomously rather than be pre-defined to bring about a particular end.

The Role of Contracts
The discussion above assumes that the contract is important as a descriptor of the relationship. However, we must also question the extent to which contracts actually

regulate exchange relations. In essence, even if a contract exists it may not be the actual or only regulator of the relationship. We turn to the critical exploration of the role of trust relations and co-operation in firms provided by Deakin, Lane and Wilkinson (1997) as a basis on which to develop this issue. Deakin et al. note that socio-legal scholars and transaction cost economics have both contested the importance of the actual contract in the development of the on-going relationship. Thus, it is argued that the actual details of the contract are little used in controlling the on-going relationship. Deakin et al. provide an elaboration of this opinion, and suggest that the role of contract is in fact relevant to the development of trust rather than simply as a descriptor of the relationship between two parties. This is of interest to us because it is echoed in another study (Seal & Vincent-Jones, 1997) that sees accounting processes to act to enable trust in a similar way. Thus, a PFI contract that uses accounting control processes to monitor the day-to-day relationships of the parties may have significant implications for the development of trust relationships. What these studies add to our analysis is an understanding that social relations are important but that they are enabled and inter-relate in complex ways by the contracting process.

Deakin et al. are anxious to move the discussion of the nature of trust beyond its depiction as either embedded in a rational self interest, on the one hand, or as a non-rational element located in social relationships, on the other. In the context of an empirical analysis of contract relations in three different nations Deakin et al. demonstrate the importance of the institutional context for contracting relationships. Acknowledging the importance of co-operation for any level of contracting yet recognizing that this might be problematic as power relationships develop, they note that

> Once the performance of the contract has begun and sunk costs have been incurred, each party is at risk of exploitation by the other (Deakin et al., 1997, p. 107).

As the agreement to a contract does not preclude the existence of either some element of separate interests or differential power, then there has to be some level of trust for any contract to be undertaken and for it to be operable.

Deakin et al. use the work of Sako (1992) to illustrate the complexity of the meaning of trust. Three types of trust are identified. Contractual trust refers to the reliance that the nature of the exchange will be as per expectation and that the contractual terms will be met. For example if the contractor agrees to wash the windows each week then it is to be expected that the windows will be washed at the agreed time. Competence trust refers to a belief that the partner has the relevant skill and expertise to fulfil the requirements of the exchange. Developing the previous example, we trust that the contractor will wash the windows and leave them clean. Goodwill trust provides the belief that the partners will move beyond their original promises to ensure on-going viability of the relationship in circumstances not specified because of the problem of presentation. Thus if new types of staining of windows occur that compromise the washing process and mean that the windows have to be treated with a solvent rather than simply washed, we expect that some negotiation about these new circumstances will be possible. This latter element of trust is different from the first two elements, the former two acting to limit discretion, the latter providing for its existence. Whilst the first two elements are necessary for any contract they are not in themselves sufficient for a relational contract. Arguably a relational contract will have to exist in an environment that allows development of all three elements of trust.

In this connection, Deakin introduces the need for a further type of trust that is related to the "contractual environment"– an institutional or "system" trust (Deakin et al., 1997, p. 110). This can be seen as the institutional structures and the accepted standards of behavior that provide the expectations that bound the nature of the items around which agreements are made. In this environment it is more likely that the parties to a contract will feel confident enough to move to implement goodwill trust.

Deakin et al.'s analysis illustrates the importance of the contractual environment or the institutional context within which individual contracts are made. Whilst there is likely to be a reflexive relationship between the individual and social contexts of contracting, it is important to highlight the extent to which the system trust impacts upon the mix of trust that emerges in the relationship that forms the individual contractual relationship. A consideration of the development of the PFI environment shows how the state has sought to develop system trust. The rather more difficult question to answer at this stage, given that no contracts have been running for more than two years, is whether the contractual regime will allow the development of goodwill trust.

Summary

Bringing together these two strands suggests that if the bureaucratic relationships that have previously characterized the NHS are to be successfully replaced by a contracting regime, the nature of that regime must be carefully constructed. Our argument is that this will require a relational contract. More than that, a relational contract can only develop in an environment in which trust can develop. This means at an institutional level there must be system trust and at an organizational level the capacity to develop goodwill trust.

The view that, at the organizational level, a relational contracting position must be adopted is in some tension with neo-classical approaches to contracting that have taken the view that contracts will provide efficient, comprehensive means for the provision of services. The implications of this will be discussed in the final section of the paper. Relational contracting is an approach that in many ways replicates, in a contractual format, some of the elements of the bureaucratic relationship. This is particularly the case given the long-term nature of the contract. The implications of this will also be returned to in the final discussion. In the next section of the paper consideration will be given to the development of trust at both an institutional and organizational level. This will then be amplified in the following section through an examination of one particular contract and the extent to which it has provided the basis for the foundation for a relational approach.

THE INTRODUCTION OF PFI TO THE NHS: THE INHIBITIONS TO AND CREATION OF SYSTEM TRUST

Some of the events and legislation around the introduction of PFI can be seen as an exercise designed to create an environment of system trust. That this system trust did not exist was evidenced by the initial reluctance to undertake PFI schemes in the NHS. An attempt to deal with this was an early instruction, in 1994, that private finance should be sought for all schemes. This led to considerable activity by hospital trusts with sizeable fees for consultants and accountants hired to assist in the process. Baroness Cumberlege, speaking on 3 June 1997 in the House of Lords, summarized the situation as follows:

> ...71 NHS PFI schemes have been approved since the launch of the scheme, bringing in private sector capital amounting to £626 million. Of these, 43, with a capital value of £317 million, have reached contract Signature State-32 have been completed and 11 are under way.
>
> Larger Schemes are now starting to reach contract signature: the Norfolk and Norwich project, with a capital value of £194 million, was signed in November 1996, although it has yet to reach financial closure.
>
> A further 150 schemes with a total capital value of about £2.1 billion are testing private finance options. They include 22 schemes worth over £10 million each that have got as far as appointing a preferred bidder. Their combined capital value has been some £1.7 billion' (Lords Hansard, 3 June 1997, Column 579).

Baroness Jay of Paddington pointed out in the same debate that this frenetic activity had cost £30 million on "legal and financial advice and other consultancy fees" but then added "... without a single major contract being secured" (Lords Hansard, 3 June 1997, Column 576) (emphasis added). This suggests that despite this attempt to bolster the scheme, system trust was not, at this stage, developed sufficiently to ensure progress on the major schemes. The Conservative

Government had established PFI and there was a feeling it could be abandoned on their removal from power. There was uncertainty about the commitment of the Labor Party to PFI, even though they were committed to exploring partnership working (Brown, Cook & Prescott, 1994).

On taking up government the Labor Party conversion to PFI was rapid. The developments they instigated can be seen as attempts to develop system trust. The new Paymaster General (Geoffrey Robinson) was given overall responsibility for PFI in the new Government. He appointed Malcolm Bates to undertake a speedy and comprehensive review of the PFI. This gave a clear sign of a commitment both to adopt PFI as well as to adapt the approach to provide a solution to the capital shortages in the public sector. Three other immediate actions were taken. First, one week after the general election, on 8th May 1997, Geoffrey Robinson announced that the universal requirement to seek private finance for all capital projects would be abandoned (HM Treasury News Release, 41/97). Second, was a commitment that "clinical services" would be exempt from any private finance arrangements? The third was a commitment, made in the Queen's Speech, to introduce legislation to ". . . free the logjam of privately financed hospital projects" (Independent, 9/5/97). The second and third of these major developments in PFI are particularly important as they provide the foundations of system trust.

The retention of clinical services in the public domain sought to provide legitimacy for the PFI with the general public of the U.K., who value the NHS and the security it provides. Universal care, which is free at the point of delivery, is a fundamental element of the NHS in the U.K. PFI brought with it a fear that this might be one stage in a move to privatization and this in turn brought a fear of undermining the fundamental ethos of free care. Hence, the commitment to retain clinical services in the public sphere sought to relieve this fear. There remained two related elements that clouded the issue; the question as to the nature of "clinical services" and the perceptions, therefore, of what is "PFI-able." The Health Minister, Alan Milburn, acknowledged the problem, promising future attention to this important definitional problem and at the same time demonstrating the extent to which the government has had to fight to legitimate the need for PFI:

> By the end of the year, once the review is complete, we shall have a categorical statement of what may or may not be included in PFI. I do not propose to anticipate the detail of that review, but am pleased to be able to repeat for the benefit of hon. Members an assurance given to my hon. Friend in the other place that pathology and radiology services will be excluded from PFI. I know that there will be other services about which hon. Member will want similar assurances, but I believe strongly that the review should be conducted before conclusions are drawn. Our commitments on pathology and radiology are given in response to specific issues that have been raised during the passage of the Bill, and to act as a signpost for the future' (Commons Hansard, 14 July 1997, Column 81).

Thus, the first element in building system trust was the move to ensure the support of the general community and to seek to demonstrate that the PFI was not meant to undermine the nature of healthcare.

However, this work to legitimate the limits of PFI in the public mind did not relieve the logjam of projects where deals could not be closed. There was a need for the resolution of questions about a number of financial and accounting issues, which can be seen as foundational to the development of the legitimacy of PFI as an activity in a contemporary economy.[9] Therefore, to consolidate the foundations of system trust and ensure that the companies involved would have the confidence to undertake the projects, a number of issues had to be addressed. First, was an issue that related to the risk undertaken by the financial institutions and in which primary legislation was needed? This was to assure the bankers of private sector PFI consortia of the security for their investment in PFI deals. Thus system trust for the financial institutions was consolidated by legislation to reduce the risk to which they are subjects.

This legislation addressed the essential question of to whom the banks providing finance to fund the private sector's investment could have a final call to cover long term leasing costs, if the NHS Trusts should become bankrupt. The Conservative Government passed the NHS (Residual Liabilities) Act in 1996 and committed the Government to pay the debts of a bankrupt NHS Trust, to deal with this possibility. However, a "loophole" was found in the Act and lawyers argued it did not provide the watertight commitment the banks wanted. Despite a further "comfort letter" (Accountancy Age, 9/1/97) from the then Secretary for State for Health (Stephen Dorrell) the banks were still not prepared to release the money and hence agree to the signing of the contracts. As a result a further Bill and Act was deemed to be required to cover this loophole. The new Act which was to "... remove any element of doubt" (Baroness Cumberlege, Lords Hansard, 3 June 1997, column 578) was available before the General Election but was passed by the new Labor Administration even though the bill was "... word for word [that] drafted by the previous government" (Baroness Cumberlege, Lords Hansard, 3 June 1997, column 578). The Act (National Health Service (Private Finance) Act 1997) became law on 14 July 1997 virtually unchanged from its original design by the Conservative Government.

The need for two Acts within a year of each other, that seemed to address similar concerns, rested on the fact that the banks, who are so vital to allow PFI to progress, were unwilling to put forward money without this watertight legal protection. As Alan Milburn (Minister for State for Health) noted the Bill "... is about removing doubt, providing certainty and, above all, getting new hospitals built" (Commons Hansard, 14 July 197, column 155). More directly Baroness Jay of Paddington made plain, "the banks concerned have seen and agreed the wording of the Bill and have made clear that it satisfies all their concerns" (Lords Hansard, 3 June 1997, column 577). Thus, the National Health Service (Private Finance) Act of 1997 was passed to allow PFI contracts to be signed and agreed. It was driven not by health need but by bankers who "... will stump up the cash" (Alan Milburn, Commons Hansard, 14 July 1997, Column 157). The legislation created an environment in which contractual activity could develop. There are now 64 PFI projects worth a total of £7.4 billion. The commitment to these schemes has provided, first, for a foundation and then a consolidation of the system trust that emanates from the existence of a favorable contractual environment.

The consolidation of system trust in the contractual environment of PFI was also affected by ambiguity about its accounting treatment, demonstrating the importance of accounting as a building block in developing trust (Seal & Vincent-Jones, 1997) and as a legitimator. The outcome of debates between the ASB and the Government (including a wide consultation) about the accounting treatment of PFI was rather different to that originally anticipated and the resolution of how to approach it followed a complex discussion (see Broadbent & Laughlin, 2002) for more details). The problem centered upon the question of whether PFI schemes should be "on" or "off" the public balance sheet. Arguably, had the schemes been "on-balance sheet" for the public sector, some of the benefit of the scheme for the state would have been reduced, as borrowing limits would have been affected. Whilst this assertion can be contested, conversations with many parties to PFI make it clear, despite official denials, that individuals were concerned that this might have been the case. This also led to concerns about whether the PFI scheme had a long-term future as a government initiative. Had the accounting rules that were agreed been problematic in relation to the ability of the NHS to provide an off-balance sheet' solution then Trusts would have been left with a problem of affordability. In the year that was taken to negotiate a solution to the accounting problem there was, therefore, a delay in the approval of any new schemes. Thus accounting was fundamental in providing an acceptable "account" of the nature of PFI demonstrating the potential for accounting to affect the way in which things are viewed. The underlying process of PFI remains the same, but the way in which it is accounted for changes the attitudes towards its adoption. In this sense the incident demonstrates the constitutive power of accounting (Hines, 1988) and its potential to act as a legitimator of action (Sikka & Willmott, 1995) as well as a resolver of uncertainty. In the context of this paper it acts as a powerful element in the creation of system trust (or in impeding its development).

Another accounting related element related to the role of the NAO. We have argued elsewhere that the role of the NAO in relation to the legitimization of PFI has been important (Broadbent & Laughlin, 2003). The NAO published a number of value-for-money studies of PFI prior to its investigation of Dartford and Gravesham. Each study reinforced the value for money claims and thus their involvement gave legitimacy to the Initiative. The delay in publication of the National Audit Office (NAO) report on the Dartford and Gravesham PFI project was therefore another factor affecting the building of system trust in relation to the NHS.[10] The contents of this report were seen as important in clarifying concerns about a number of issues including the value for money of the scheme and the NAO view on the robustness of the accounting treatment. Had either of these been subject to criticism this could have undermined the legitimacy of PFI in the eyes of the general public and the business community? Arguably until this uncertainty was resolved system trust was again unsubstantiated. In the event the report published in May 1999 provided a view that the Dartford Scheme was somewhat flawed, but was still value for money. It was therefore legitimate and that legitimacy was provided by the Nag's authoritative support.

This publication of the report, followed by the announcement of the new accounting advice (discussed above) at the end of June 1999 and the release of a Second Bates Report on PFI in July 1999, all provided for on-going business confidence in the continuation of Government commitment to PFI. All these elements acted to dismiss any anxieties and provided reassurance that the PFI would be maintained as an approach to the provision of services and premises in the NHS. Alongside the need to reassure public opinion that their public health care service was not being undermined was a need to reassure the business community of the commitment to PFI. It should be noted that the technologies of accounting were closely implicated in this process. Thus, institutional and system trust was developed in an active way in the early stages of the New Labor Government and many PFI schemes have been launched. Since then, the reflexive relationship between the existence of a contractual environment and the development of schemes has acted to reinforce and extend the possibilities for PFI. In this way system trust has been consolidated and extended and the use of PFI is an established mode of national procurement in the NHS.

However it should be noted that as well as creating a national or societal environment of institutional or system trust, there must also be a local environment of system trust. Thus, an NHS Trust seeking to build a PFI deal, as well as dealing with the private sector, will have to negotiate with its local Health Authority and gain the support of the NHS Executive if it is to build a successful deal. These local dynamics are clearly affected by the societal environment, but it should be recognized that they might also have their own dynamic. Hence many of the NHS Trusts describe the length of time and the extent of the efforts they put into the negotiations with local stakeholders such as their Local Authorities and the local MPs. Clearly successful schemes have negotiated these barriers as well as the national ones.

The provision of property through a different mode creates the need for very different relationships in the general environment, as shown above, that in turn has an impact on organizational relationships. The next section explores how the elements of, competence and goodwill trust are reflected in the contractual relationship at the organizational level.

TRUST AND PFI CONTRACTS AT THE ORGANISATIONAL LEVEL

Generic Issues of Complexity in Contractual Relationships: The Role of Accounting

At the organizational level we highlight two initial issues. The first is that the NHS has to demonstrate that the PFI scheme is both value-for-money (v-f-m) and has effected the relevant risk transfer. This means that the NHS Trusts have to control their activities to ensure that the promised efficiencies are produced. Thus, contractual and competence trust must be demonstrated and the aim will be to use the discipline of the contract to ensure efficiency. This approach fits with the ethos of neo-classical approaches to contracting. Second, the NHS Trusts have to manage their relationship with their institutional partners in the context of ensuring the terms of the contract are being met and at the same time negotiating how to modify them if needed. The need to ensure that modifications can be enabled requires a relational contracting approach so that goodwill trust is created. In essence, the possibility of a contradiction between the broad demands of achieving efficiency and building goodwill is set up.

The detailed outworking of these demands for v-f-m and control are framed by the contract and the documents that operationalize the contract, such as the concession agreement. In general, as well as specifically in Dartford and Gravesham NHS Trust PFI, the contractual documents define the expectations that each party have of the other. Implicit in their signing is an acceptance by each party that they trust the other and can deliver the service required – in the terms used in this paper, that contract trust exists. These documents also define the boundaries of competence trust, thus setting out what each party expects and trusts the other has the ability to be able to undertake. Finally, they frame the arena in which there is the possibility for the development of goodwill trust. The relationships between all these elements is complex and intertwined analytically – as is their outworking in practice.

In the context of this complexity the role of accounting again becomes important as it make visible the relationships between the parties and therefore demonstrates how control is being operationalised. It provides the possibility to demonstrate, though its ability to provide "an account" to each party, the extent to which the terms of the contract are being maintained. Moreover, because it measures the financial elements, it provides a means by which to evidence and measure the notion of value-for-money (v-f-m). In providing financial visibility it also provides the foundation upon which through "goodwill" changes can be negotiated. As such it is an important process that helps in developing the relationship between the parties (Seal & Vincent-Jones, 1997). Thus in operationalising the contract we see a system of monitoring that provides the basis for calculating the payment to the contractors, that has within it a series of penalties for non-achievement of any contractual requirements. It is around these that the notions of contract or competence trust are managed. Equally, here is where goodwill trust is developed as performance and the corresponding payment is judged through negotiation between the contract parties. Thus in Dartford and Gravesham, as will be detailed later in this section, performance cannot fall below 95% without penalty. However, some negotiation may well be possible as it is not always easy to define the more subjective output levels. Hence, the possibility of a penalty if improvement is not achieved in the next month, provides a means by which to motivate future performance. By being lenient in the first instance the Trust managers hoped to build goodwill and mutual commitment to the task.

Contract Complexity: The Structure of Relationships at Dartford and Gravesham NHS Trust

To illustrate how these possibilities are managed operationally at the organizational level we explore the Dartford and Gravesham NHS Trust (the Trust hereafter) PFI contract that achieved financial closure on 30 July 1997. It was the first PFI contract signed and has been subject to an extensive National Audit Office investigation (NAO, 1999), which can be used as illustration of various issues (references in the following will be to NAO, Paragraph...p...). This audit report, coupled with the publicly available "addendum to the full business case" (references in the following will be to ADD, Paragraph...p...) allows considerable public access to material on this PFI contract. In using the Dartford and Gravesham case we shall show some of the key contractual elements, which, at one level, are very specific to that situation, but at another level have applicability to all PFI projects. The purpose of this detail is to demonstrate the ways in which the contractual framework frames the development of these new relationships and enables contractual and competence trust to be demonstrated and goodwill trust to develop (or not).

One major issue that impinges on these matters is the complexity of the contractual framework and the relationships of the parties involved. Figure 1 (ADD: 6) depicts these initial relationships. The Hospital Company (Hospital Company (Darenth) Ltd) (HC hereafter) was a separate created legal entity to manage the PFI project. The HC has entered into two major sub-contracts (or

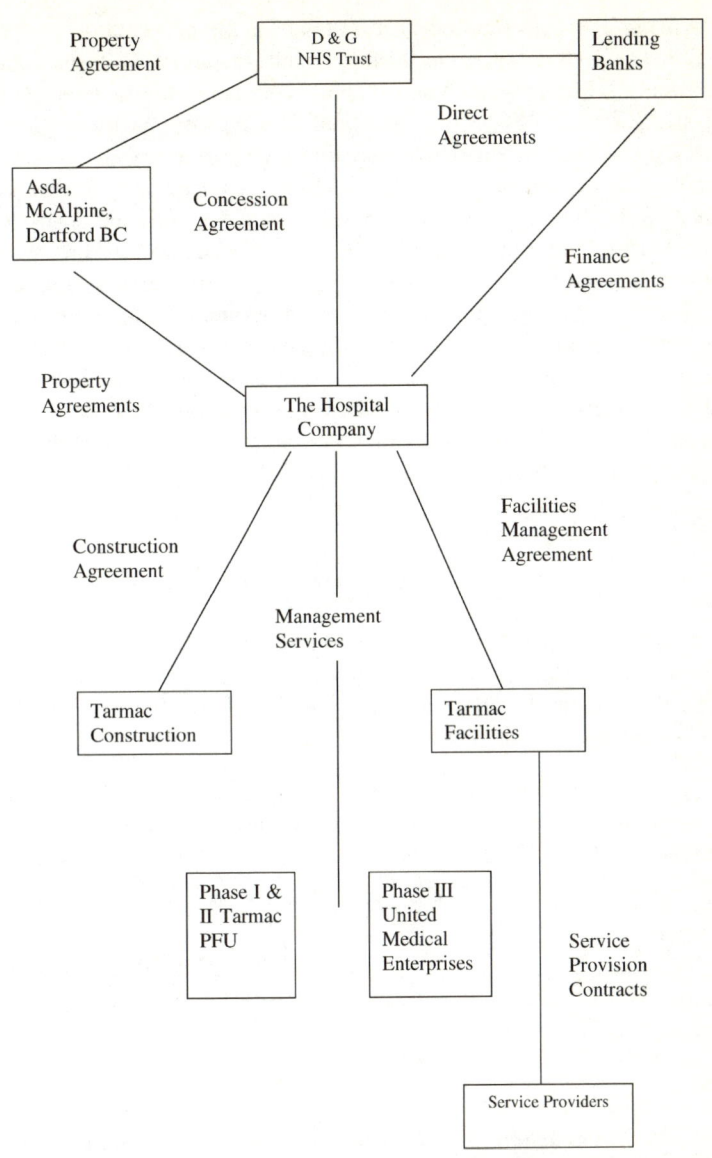

Fig. 1. Contract Framework for Dartford and Gravesham NHS Trust PFI Projects. *Source:* Addendum to the full Business Case, P. 6.

Agreements as they are referred to in Fig. 1) for the provision of construction (from Tarmac Construction), and facilities management (from Tarmac Facilities Management). It has also called on a range of companies to provide management support (from Tarmac PFU initially and finally from United Medical Enterprises). The two sub-contract agreements are largely the responsibility and concern of the HC although as we will see below the Trust has also been party to their content. The Trust has a "Direct Agreement" with the banks who provide finance[11] and a contract of central importance with the HC called a "Concession Agreement." The key issue is the network of contractual and sub-contractual relationships all of that may well be subject to change as parties change their sub-contracting arrangements or sell parts of their operations. This complexity and potential changefulness has the potential to make it difficult to build relationships as well as raising the potential problems of fragmentation of responsibility.[12] Thus the first specific point to highlight in the context of the Dartford and Gravesham contract is the complexity of the contractual relationships.

Building on System Trust

The next issue to highlight in Dartford and Gravesham NHS Trust is that this contract builds on the system trust discussed earlier. Thus, there is a "Direct Agreement" which is the only direct finance-related contract between the Trust and the lending banks, which provides

> ... the banks with step-in-rights exercisable in the event of the Hospital Company's default and other rights which are specific to the banks' lending requirements and which need the Trust's participation or approval (ADD, paragraph 3.4: 5).

Thus the Direct Agreement builds on the societal attempts to develop system trust and provides another element in the range of protection that the banks insisted should be in place before agreeing to lend money to the HC. However, in this way the contract is also dealing with issues of competence: to ensure that there is a competence trust to pay in last resort.

Construction of the Hospital and Trust Relationships

The Concession Agreement provides the key vehicle for defining the contractual agreement between the Trust and the HC and therefore the base for their ongoing relationship. It is a foundation for contractual, competence and goodwill trust:

Development of Contracting in Infrastructure Investment 73

> The heart of the contract structure for the construction of the hospital and its subsequent availability and services, is the Concession Agreement. This is the agreement (to which the Trust and the Hospital Company are parties) by which the Hospital Company is given the necessary rights and placed under the required obligations to build and make the hospital available and provide non-clinical services. It is the document under which the Trust's right to use the hospital arises together with the Hospital Company's entitlement to receive its payments (ADD, Paragraph 3.1: 4).

The Concession Agreement specifies the duration of the contractual relationship. Phases 1 and 2 run from the signing of the Agreement (on 30 July 1997) to the "Services Commencement Date," which is the "first day after the completion of the hospital" (ADD: 8). It "...is intended that Phase 3 (i.e. the period during which The Hospital Company recoups its capital investment by earning revenue from making the hospital available and the performance of the services) will last for 60 years, subject to the parties' rights to terminate after 25 years" (ADD, Paragraph 5: 8). Thus we are dealing with a contract of considerable length.

The Concession Agreement details the scope of the contractual relationships, which comprise property services and facilities services. In the first instance the contract requires the HC "...to design and construct the new hospital to the design agreed by the Trust" (NAO, Paragraph 1.22, p. 21). This phase of the relationship is complex, but relatively short and there is a capacity to judge competence and contractual adherence in a relatively short time.

In Dartford and Gravesham considerable efforts were put into the successful completion of the building on time. PFI contracts, in general, are awarded with an assumption that the contractor has the competence to complete construction on time as building time over-runs were seen as largely responsible for cost over-runs. The Hospital was completed on time and although there was the usual "snagging"[13] the building is functioning and a successful technical evaluation of the building has been completed.

Despite the successful completion, there have been problems with the design and build phase of PFI. Given the argument that PFI would provide superior design, the public expectation has been that the buildings should work well and a good deal of publicity has attended any failures of the buildings. Press coverage at Dartford and Gravesham (and other PFI schemes) has been very critical of this type of failure. This type of publicity has undermined PFI as a means of procurement and the competence of the private sector to "deliver" has been questioned.[14] In this way it has been a countervailing influence on the attempts to build system trust. This has impacted much at the level of the local community.

At the organizational level, goodwill is needed in the context of building the hospital because of problems of presentation and the possible need to change original designs. Rather than provide tight specification of facilities required through standard building notes, design improvement is sought through contracts based only on output specifications. The explicit lack of detailed input specification thus provides some ambiguity as to how a particular facility or service should be delivered. Interpretation of output specifications provides the possibility that goodwill may be required to reach agreement about what is seen as what is good design for purpose.

The boundaries between competence and contractual adherence are blurred and goodwill is likely to be needed to deal with this. In the Dartford and Gravesham scheme, for example, a dispute about the finish of workbenches in a laboratory brought all these matters into play. There was a dispute as to the meaning of terms in the contract (raising questions of contract trust) that the contractor claimed were followed and which had led to the installation of a patterned work surface. This interpretation of the terms of the contract were contested by the Trust who required a plain surface and in essence also thereby questioned the competence of the contractor, as they saw the surface provided as not fit for purpose. In the event and with some goodwill in play, the horizontal working surfaces were replaced but the vertical coverings were retained as installed.

It should be noted that the NHS has considerable experience in commissioning the building of hospitals and the intellectual capital of the individuals in this NHS Trust was of central importance in managing this phase and this relationship. The intellectual capital of the NHS personnel and their consequent skills in working through difficulties with the contractors is based on their detailed understanding of what is required. Without this intellectual capital, the incident noted above would have been a difficult one to be both recognized and settled.

Facilities Management and Contractual Relationships

Moving next to the facilities management and the provision of on going services. In Dartford and Gravesham the HC "... are to provide the Trust with seven facilities management services – building management and maintenance; domestic services, window cleaning and pest control; portering, transport and internal security; linen and laundry; catering; switchboard and telecommunications; and external security and car parking" (NAO, Paragraph 1.23, p. 21).[15] The detailed specification and performance expectations and penalties are contained in the concession agreement in some detail. To provide facilities management services, staff currently employed by the Trust in the seven areas have been transferred to the HC.

The financial elements of the Concession Agreement detail the agreed monthly payments from the Trust to the HC and arrangements for the penalties resulting from reduced service provision.[16] The NAO report details (paragraph 1.25, p. 22) that the monthly payment (in 1996 terms) from the Trust to the HC is £1.32 million (£15.84 million annually) divided into an Availability Payment (of £879,000 per month) "for making the hospital available" and a Performance Related Payment (of £441,000) "for service provision." These are adjusted in line with the Retail Price Index (ADD: 12).

Appendix 5 of the NAO report summarizes the complex rules that apply to deductions for availability and performance.[17] In simple terms the availability of the hospital is assessed every 24 hours and if selected areas are unavailable the Availability Payment will be reduced. The Performance Related Payment for each of the seven service areas are calculated using a scale in which full payment is made when performance reaches a 95% rating, and reductions apply on a sliding scale below that level.

This does not define how availability and performance can be monitored and measured in precise terms. Thus, because the contract itself has not set out the whole detail of the working of the relationship much work has needed to be undertaken to operationalise the framework. Inevitably this relied on the exercise of goodwill trust. For example, the contract gave the NHS Trust the right to define 50% of the facilities management indicators. It is in working through this detail that the foundation of the relationship between the parties has been developed as it involved the parties in more detailed consideration of the nature of the tasks that had been possible at the contract stage. The operational managers themselves were able to debate the detailed nature of the service provision. Relevant performance indicators (PIs) were chosen to monitor the service levels and like all PIs these then become constitutive as well as reflective of performance.

Ongoing monitoring of the contract provides a continuous and reflexive development of contract, competence and goodwill trust. For example, consider the elements relating to cleaning services. One element that is not specified is any penalty for failure in the standard of cleaning in the office space. It follows that this might be seen as an area where contractual trust might be compromised. Some failures in this respect have been noted, and offices have sometimes not been cleaned thoroughly. However, this has not caused any problems to the NHS managers as they recognize that the contractors have an interest in remedying failure in this area. Any on-going failure to perform adequately could be seen by the Trust as providing worries about the competence of the company. The Trust recognizes that this, in itself, provides an incentive to the contractor. The Trust manager concerned indicated he simply calls his opposite number on the telephone and "things are sorted because we have a good relationship."[18] Experience has shown deficiencies have been dealt with quickly and without resort to argument or to arbitration processes, which are the fallback contractual option. This illustrates the complex intertwining of the different streams of trust.

Contracts and the Control of Risk

The allocation of risks between the HC and the Trust was a central concern throughout and a key element in the contract construction and in the pre-decision processes. Risks associated with the Trust's PFI contract and who should bear the costs involved should they occur have been summarized in Appendix 4 of the NAO report. The risks are divided into ten major areas.[19] Within each of these broad-risk categories a number of possibilities are outlined and a cost allocation is specified (between the HC and the Trust) in relation to the potential outcome. For example, in the "design and construction" category, if the "construction lasts longer than expected" or there is a "failure to provide the hospital to specification" then the HC must cover the costs involved.

Because of its centrality the management of risk allocation was a key element in the negotiations for and the formation of wording of the Concession Agreement. The concern to cover as many possibilities and specify who would cover the costs of these, should they occur, permeates the entire Concession Agreement. However, there was a realization of the impossibility to specify all the possible problems and difficulties that might arise in a contract of this length and complexity. This signifies recognition that goodwill trust would have to be implemented in the context of operationalising the contract. Thus, where possible, risks were specified and the costs involved allocated to either the Trust or the HC, but if the totally unexpected happened there was still a set of arbitrating arrangements to ensure that a resolution could be achieved between the parties to the contract. Whilst these provisions might be seen as a substitute for goodwill trust the reality might prove otherwise. It is in neither party's interests to enter expensive arbitration processes when goodwill trust would avoid this. It should be noted that the arbitration process has not been entered into as yet. However, it should be noted that the contracting environment could add a rather adversarial element to the relationship.

A final issue that can be highlighted is that whilst pre-decision the issue of risk assessment was central, post-decision and during the operation of the contract it seems invisible. There has been no attempt on the part of the Trust to seek to evaluate whether the required risk transfer has been achieved. Instead there is an implicit monitoring of the risk transfer. This has been enacted through the monitoring processes that have been designed to ensure that service quality and availability is as required. The implicit assumption is that if the contract is adhered to the risk transfer will be as intended. The post project evaluation required by the NHS relies only on a technical evaluation of build quality. This is an issue that needs further consideration in the context of a broader evaluation of PFI projects.

CONCLUDING COMMENTS

Whilst these examples of the elements of the Dartford and Gravesham contract are not claimed to be exhaustive or fully representative they provide some indication of the way in which the contract sets out the boundaries in which competence trust can be substantiated and in which goodwill trust can be built. They also give some illustration of the way risk definition and allocation occurred in this particular PFI contract.

SOME IMPLICATIONS AND A FINAL DISCUSSION

The recognition of a need to upgrade the capital assets of the NHS has led the U.K. Government to develop the notion of PFI in the NHS, to meet this requirement. This raises a number of issues in the context of a consideration of contracting relationships. It also brings about a number of contradictions.

The extent to which the attempt to ensure this control is successful relies on the degree to which the contract provides the necessary framework. This highlights a central issue for this chapter. In changing the way in which capital assets are provided for the NHS, the state has changed not just the source of the bricks and mortar, but also the whole raft of working relationships within the organization. Instead of these being controlled by a bureaucratic web of rule and regulation they are now controlled by contract.

In essence, instead of the previous bureaucratic relationships, new and extremely complex relationships are being built and pre-defined in the context of the contracting process. In particular, in the context of these long-term contracts, we have argued that the neo-classical view of discrete utility maximizing transactions is unhelpful as it sets up a competitive rather than a co-operative relationship. This may be appropriate if the aim is to extract surplus value for shareholders. It may also be appropriate in the context of seeking to discipline the private sector contractors providing the service, but may be less appropriate for building the long-term relationship needed to make the contract work in the longer term. In particular if presentation is not possible, there is likely to be a need to adjust expectations and obligations to make the contract work in a changing environment. Instead of adopting an adversarial stance, we have argued that there is a need to build trust in these relationships, in and through the contracting process. We would argue that those involved, at different levels, have accepted this and great efforts have been made to create an environment of trust.

Before trust can be developed at the organizational level, it must be built at the societal level and much work has been undertaken to do this through the creation of system trust. Thus, legislative activity was undertaken to pass two legislative instruments to alleviate the worries of bankers as to the security of their investment. Also, there was agreement to an accounting framework to ensure that there were no worries about the balance sheet status of PFI. It was also promised that clinical services would remain in the public sector. Alongside this has been the work of the NAO to study the v-f-m of the schemes, which has given some confidence that v-f-m was possible.

The outcome of these elements to build system trust is that has been a reduction in the overall risk for the private sector partners. The legislative framework, the agreement to the form of the accounting standard, the commitment to retaining clinical services in the public sector and the "endorsement" of the NAO adds to the legitimacy of PFI. This builds its acceptance as a means of procurement and makes it less likely to be discontinued or undermined in the future. The greatest immediate contribution to this reduction of risk is perhaps in the context of the protection offered the private sector in the case of any financial failure of the Trust. The two Acts passed ensure that if the Trust fails the private sector partner will not be left with an asset that cannot be used for other things. Hence, at the macro level, the government has underwritten the potential problems of asset specificity. It should be recognized that this undermines some of the claims that therefore there is in PFI a transfer of risk to the private sector. It may of course substantiate the argument that risk needs to be allocated to those who can most effectively carry it. It highlights the importance of both law and accounting in the construction and monitoring of the risk transfer.

Whilst system trust at the societal level is perhaps a pre-requisite for successful contracting, at the micro, organizational level there is also a need to build goodwill trust at the micro level. We would wish to argue that at this level, the only way that contracting in the long term might successfully be conceptualized is through the idea of relational contracting which recognizes the importance of goodwill trust. This recognizes the difficulties of presentation and acknowledges the need to account for the underlying social relationships in the organizations concerned. The latter are complex in the context of PFI in the NHS. Some of these parties to the PFIs are new people entering a new relationship, not least the managers of the facilities who are managing staff previously working in the NHS and supplying a service to those remaining in the NHS (clinicians for example). Other parties were previously employed to provide a service and remain within it, but are now working for different managers, providing services for their previous colleagues. An embedded set of social relationships exists, but these are now being transformed by the imposition of a contract. Clearly until these relationships become re-institutionalized there is a possibility of great stress. Even without these tensions there is always a possibility of conflict and the industrial relations history of the NHS shows this. However, in a situation where there is a need to re-negotiate the relationship base this tension is likely to increase. This tension is more likely to be difficult in a situation where the values of different parties are challenged and in the context of what is seen to be private sector impingement on the public services this is the case.

Moreover, given that the aim of PFI is to extract efficiencies from the provision of services there is still a strong neo-classical ideology behind the contracting process. This provides a strong adversarial base to the relationship that is likely to be amplified if any of the participants come under pressure. In the case of the NHS this is likely to occur in the context of ensuring that there is efficiency, leading to a need to put pressure on the private sector. In the context of the private sector partner this is likely to be pressure to make returns for shareholders. Contracts have been set in such a way as to seek to ensure that the rights and obligations of the parties are recognized in advance. Nevertheless, presentiation is impossible and for any contract to provide a full framework for relationships is impossible.

Given the fact that contracting provides a mode of operating that exists outside the existing relational structures of the NHS there has already been a need to provide some relational framework within which PFI can work. Our argument is that the existence of system trust is an important precondition for the development of goodwill trust with in a relational contracting mode. System trust at the societal level provides context and the framework for the parties to the contract to recognize the rights and obligations of their own relationship. System trust is important in defining the relationships of both the internal parties to the contract (those who are working together on a day to day level) and the external parties (who provide the finance but are not normally working together daily). Our analysis of the Dartford and Gravesham PFI Contract shows that beyond the general government efforts in providing the institutional or system trust at a macro societal level, the contract has started to develop in such as way as to embed trust organizationally at the micro level. That trust is built not only on contract and competence, but elements of goodwill trust are also developing through the relationships being constructed.

We are not yet able to see how, in the longer term, the environment of societal system trust will frame the internal contractual relationships between the different parties working together. Clearly if we take the argument of Deakin et al. (1997) seriously we also should consider the extent to which the process of contracting has the possibility of developing trust within the system. Once again it is too early in the process of the PFIs to see if this will be the case. Perhaps the whole process of negotiating and closing a deal is about more than formalizing expectations that contractual and competence trust can be met. Put another way, one assumes that if parties were not happy that contractual capability and competence could be achieved then the contract would likely to fail. In that respect the negotiation process itself is also likely to be about building goodwill trust; as the parties to the negotiation build a relationship then social relations emerge. These in turn provide the basis for a relational contract and allow the possibility for goodwill trust to emerge. If parties are seen to have been "fair" in the context of the negotiation then the expectation of "fairness" provides some base for goodwill trust to aid the resolution of issues that were not defined in the original contract. The consolidation of goodwill trust will continue and be tested in the on-going implementation of the contract. Where this may prove to be more difficult is in the context of the situation where those who have negotiated the contract then move on to another post, leaving a new set of people to operationalise their understandings.[20]

As noted above, when the contract is running, the expectations of all parties will be tested on an on-going basis. The complexity of the various relationships will then be important, and the contradictory impetus is inherent. Goodwill for one set of parties may be badwill for others. Deakin et al. also remind us that once a contract is closed then the relative power relationships of the parties becomes important. For example, a very important question for the future is whether the needs of the private sector to provide financial return to their shareholders prove more powerful than the need to maintain goodwill trust within the PFI partnership, Such a question would have been irrelevant prior to the introduction of PFI.

We might also ask whether a relational contract at an operational level can control better than the previous bureaucratic relationships? We can also question whether the relational contracts will, in the longer term, be different to the bureaucracies they replace. To what extent does a contract that runs for 25–60 years simply institutionalize the relationships in the way that a bureaucracy does? Is the need to minimize transaction costs in a long-term contract simply going to lead to the formation de facto, if not de jure, of a set of relationships that are to all intents and purposes bureaucratic? Our on-going work will seek to assess this. In conclusion, all that can be said is that there is much more to learn as the new relationships are operationalised. The political determination to make them work has been demonstrated by the on-going development of legislation to build societal system trust. How the on-going goodwill trust that will be needed to ensure the day to day working of the organisations in question will develop in the context of the diversity of values and the competing financial demands of the various parties remains to be documented.

Finally we should reflect upon the extent to which an initiative that changed the mode of the provision of infrastructure resources was thought through in respect of the impact that it might have at the organizational level. This chapter has argued about the nature of the process that might be necessary to make the long-term PFI contracts work. It has shown how the government has set out an environment at the societal level in which they can build the trust to make PFI work. It has illustrated how a particular contract is addressing the need to build an environment in which the operations can function. It has also commented on the inherent contradictions that are set up in the context of the societal demand for neo-classical efficiency that has driven the approach and the need for long-term working relationships. However, our study has not directly addressed the issue as to whether it is all-worthwhile? The question that remains and can only be answered in the longer term is whether PFI partnerships are in essence better than the bureaucratic structures they replace, or whether they are instead new types of bureaucracies in the making.

NOTES

1. We note the recent debates as to whether New Public Management is a sensible term in the context of a set of issues that are over 20 years old, however, retain the term as it is the one referred to in the literature from which our concerns build.
2. Interviews with successive NHS Financial Directors, with senior officers at regional and hospital trust level has often elicited, without any prompting, the view that the NHS is a "family"-type organization. Whilst this may well be a rhetorical device and less of a reality than a myth, the power of the imagery is important to note and the fact that recourse to this descriptor has been made so frequently is important.
3. Dartford and Gravesham PFI, scheme is the first hospital PFI to be signed. It has had more public exposure than most having been the subject of a value for money audit by the National Audit Office (NAO, 1999).
4. Prior to 1991 three different levels were involved in the management of the secondary (hospital) sector of the NHS. The NHS Executive was, in effect, the head office and then the country was divided into a number of major geographic Regions. Nested within Regions were District Health Authorities who handled healthcare in smaller geographical areas. Each District Health Authority had, within it, a number of hospitals for whom it had responsibility.
5. Note that there has been a further change with the introduction of Primary Care Groups and Trusts in 1999. Our analysis does not seek to address this further change.
6. Appleby (1999, p. 79) provides a full explanation of EFLs.
7. See the Chancellor of the Exchequer, Norman Lamont's, Autumn Statement in 1992.
8. This is an important point in the context of PFI, which rests on the argument that it allocates risks to those who are best able to carry them.
9. That is in a capitalist economy in which there is a need to extract surplus value from on-going business activity.
10. We will look to the organizational implications of this later in the paper.
11. A mixture of agreements finances the HC. These are principally from banks (Deutsche Morgan Grenfell, Rabobank International and the United Bank of Kuwait) but also include external investors (BZW Equity Fund, Innisfree, Tarmac and United Medical Enterprises). Financing was also obtained from once-off sales of land owned by the Trust (sold to Alfred McAlpine, Asda and Dartford Borough Council).

12. The recent debates about the workings of the U.K. rail system have raised concerns about the problems of assigning responsibility in a system which is fragmented in terms of ownership, but has to work as a whole.

13. "Snagging" is the term used in the building industry to refer to the matters that need to be dealt with once the building is completed. These are things that have not been finished satisfactorily or that do not work as intended. It is a phase that would occur with any building be it a large-scale contract or a domestic extension. Clearly the extent of the problems is relevant and the aim should be to reduce any such difficulties.

14. It should be noted that the private sector have always built hospitals and problems about delivery have always occurred but the point here is not to debate that, but to note that the promise of PFI to deliver better quality and better design has not necessarily been perceived to have been provided.

15. However the Trust "... will provide the clinical services of the new hospital" (NAO Paragraph 1.23, p. 21). This institutionalizes the commitment that clinical services would remain in the Public sector, following concerns about the extent to which PFI is privatizing the NHS.

16. Other financial matters concerning the overall value of the project are all to be found in the Outline and Full Business Cases are not considered here.

17. Contained in Clauses 29 and 30 in the Concession Agreement.

18. Interview notes 27th April 2001.

19. Design and Construction, Operation, Legislation/Regulation, Availability, Volume, Technology/Obsolescence, Disposal, Termination, Finance, Employment.

20. Our wider research project suggests that this is often the case with a team breaking up once the contracts are finalized and the scheme moves towards operation.

REFERENCES

Appleby, J. (1999). Financing the NHS. In: *NHS Handbook, 1998–1999*. London: JMH Publishing.

Broadbent, J., & Laughlin, R. (1997). Contracts, competition and accounting in recent legal enactments for the health and education sectors in the UK: An example of juridification at work? In: S. Deakin & J. Michie (Eds), *Socio-Legal Aspects of Contracts and Competition* (pp. 214–254). Oxford: Oxford University Press.

Broadbent, J., & Laughlin, R. (2002). Accounting choices: Technical and political trade-offs and the UK's private finance initiative. *Accounting, Auditing and Accountability Journal, 15*, 622–654.

Broadbent, J., & Laughlin, R. (2003). Control and legitimation in government accountability processes: The private finance initiative in the UK. *Critical Perspectives on Accounting, 14* (1–2), 23–48.

Broadbent, J., Dietrich, M., & Laughlin, R. (1996). The development of principal-agent, contracting and accountability relationships in the public sector: Conceptual and cultural problems. *Critical Perspectives on Accounting, 7*(3), 259–284.

Broadbent, J., Haslam, C., & Laughlin, R. (2000). The origins and operation of the private finance initiative at the organisational level: Some questions to be answered. In: P. Robinson, J. Hawkesworth, J. Broadbent, R. Laughlin & C. Haslam (Eds), *The Private Finance Initiative: Saviour, Villain or Irrelevance?* Working Paper to the Institute of Public Policy Research Commission on Public Private Partnerships.

Brown, G., Cook, R., & Prescott, J. (1994). Financing infrastructure investment: Promoting a partnership between public and private finance joint consultative paper. Prepared for the Labour Finance and Industry Group symposium on Public-Private Finance.

Campbell, D. (1997). The relational constitution of contract and the limits of 'economics': Kenneth Arrow on the social background of markets'. In: S. Deakin & J. Michie (Eds), *Contracts, Co-operation and Competition: Studies in Economics, Management and Law* (pp. 307–338). Oxford: Oxford University Press.

Campbell, D., & Harris, D. (1993). Flexibility in long-term contractual reltionship: The role of co-operation. *Journal of Law and Society*, 20(2), 166–191.

Deakin, S., Lane, C., & Wilkinson, F. (1997). Contract law, trust relations and incentives for co-operation: A comparative study. In: S. Deakin & J. Michie (Eds), *Contracts, Co-operation and Competition: Studies in Economics, Management and Law* (pp. 105–139). Oxford: Oxford University Press.

Guthrie, J., Humphrey, C., & Olsen, O. (Eds) (1998). *Global warning: International financial management changes.* Cappelen Akademisk Forlag.

Heald, D., & Scott, D. A. (1995). Charging for capital in the National Health Service in Scotland. *Financial Accountability and Management*, 11(1), 57–74.

Heald, D., & Scott, D. A. (1996). Assessing capital charging in the National Health Service. *Financial Accountability and Management*, 12(3), 225–244.

Hines, R. (1988). Financial accounting: In communicating reality we construct reality. *Accounting, Organizations and Society*, 13(3), 251–262.

Hood, C. (1991). A public management for all seasons? *Public Administration*, 69(Spring), 3–19.

Hood, C. (1995). The 'New Public Management' in the 1980s: Variations on a theme. *Accounting, Organizations and Society*, 20(3), 93–109.

Mayston, D. (1989). *Capital charging and the management of NHS capital.* York: Centre for Health Economics.

Mayston, D. (1990). Managing capital resources in the NHS. In: A. J. Culyer, A. K. Maynard & J. W. Posnett (Eds), *Competition in Health Care: Reforming the NHS* (pp. 138–177). Basingstoke: Macmillan.

Mellett, H. (1990). Capital Accounting and Charges in the National Health Service after 1991. *Financial Accountability and Management*, 6(4), 262–283.

National Audit Office (1999). *The PFI contract for the New Dartford and Gravesham Hospital HC 423.* London: HMSO.

Perrin, J. (1978). *Management of financial resources in the National Health Service. Royal commission on the National Health Service.* Research paper no.2. London: HMSO.

Perrin, J. (1989). Capital accounting and charging in the National Health Service. *Public Money and Management*, 9(3), 47–50.

Sako, M. (1992). *Prices, quality and trust: Inter-firm relations in Britain and Japan.* Cambridge: Cambridge University Press.

Seal, W., & Vincent-Jones, P. (1997). Accounting and trust in the enabling of long-term relations. *Auditing and Accountability Journal*, 10(3), 406–431.

Sikka, P., & Willmott, H. (1995). The power of Independence: Defending and extending the jurisdiction of accounting in the United Kingdom. *Accounting, Organizations and Society*, 20(6), 547–581.

Teubner, G. (Ed.) (1987). *Juridification of social spheres.* Berlin: Walter de Gruyter the National Audit Office (NAO 1999).

4. STAKEHOLDER THEORY, PARTNERSHIPS AND ALLIANCES IN THE HEALTH CARE SECTOR OF THE U.K. AND SCOTLAND

Alexander Murdock

INTRODUCTION

This chapter explores the potential for the application of stakeholder theory to resolve some paradoxes and dilemmas of NPM where partnership and alliances are concerned. It is argued that stakeholder theory should be further developed and adapted to meet the needs of public sector managers seeking for a "rosetta stone" to negotiate the increasingly complex world which they inhabit. The work will endeavor to bring a practical as well as a theoretical perspective as it draws upon a recent project examining a three way partnership between a third sector organization, local government and the National Health Service in Scotland. The research project utilized both in depth interviews and focus groups with service users and staff. The concept of "public sector bargains" Hood (2000) has some relevance and application to such partnership activity.

New Public Management NPM models and theories have been the subject of a great deal of attention in both the academic and practitioner literature (Ferlie et al., 1996; Hood, 1998; Peters, 1996; Pollitt & Bouckaert, 2000). The debate has also been conducted through a range of journals such as Public Management Review and Public Money and Management. The International Public Management

Journal IPMJ and its associated network of scholars has also emerged as a growing source of international debate.

A number of paradoxes were identified by Hood (Hood, 2000) when considering comparative experience of public service management reform. The paradoxes described by Hood may also be amenable to a different theoretical approach which draws upon a broader theoretical base than "old style public administration." Such an approach is offered by the growing "stakeholder" literature. Stakeholder theory is well established academically with an interesting provenance reaching back into attempts to deal with paradoxes in the "private sector" world of the corporations of the U.S.A. Clarkson (1998). The academic debate has been conducted just as rigorously through the pages of such journals as the Academy of Management Review. As recently as 1999, a whole volume of the Review was devoted to Stakeholder theory (Vol. 24, p. 2). The debate explored the contribution by chiefly American stakeholder theorists such as Donaldson and Preston, Freeman, Jones and Wick. Stakeholder theory attracted proponents from a range of national backgrounds. Juha Nasi (1995), for example, provided a platform that brought together North American and Scandinavian approaches.

The origin and application of stakeholder theory has been explored by the author in work with a Scottish Health Board following devolution. The increase in the number and proximity of political stakeholders was a significant factor (Murdock, 2000). The author has subsequently extended the implications of a stakeholder chapter approach to the Fire Service and to a central government agency (Murdock, 2001a, b).

This chapter will identify and explore the overlap between stakeholder theory and New Public Management NPM where partnerships and alliances are concerned using the data from research on a Scottish partnership. NPM has been presented as four models following (Ferlie et al., 1996). The fourth model Public Service Orientation envisages a move back to user concerns and greater local political accountability. Stakeholder Theory offers the potential to explore the implications of these broader user and political concerns. The chapter will take as its departure the threefold classification of stakeholder theory offered by Donaldson and Preston (1995) and subsequently used by Jones and Wicks (1999).

THE NATURE OF NEW PUBLIC MANAGEMENT

Hood described the rise of New Public Management NPM over 10 years ago in what became a landmark article as "one of the most striking international trends in public administration." At the time he identified the following doctrinal components of NPM:

- "Hands-on professional management" in the public sector;
- Explicit standards and measures of performance;
- Greater emphasis on output controls;
- Shift to disaggregating of units in the public sector;
- Shift to greater competition in the public sector;
- Stress on private sector styles of management practice;
- Stress on greater discipline and parsimony in resource use (Hood, 1991).

The origins of NPM (Hood saw as emerging from new institutional economics on the one hand and "successive waves of business-type managerialism" on the other. Since then NPM has been the subject of much academic debate (Barzelay, 2001; Ferlie et al., 1996; Hood et al., 1998; Minogue, 2000; Pollitt & Bouckaert, 2000). The practitioner aspects have also been explored most notably by Osborne and Gaebler (1992) in the U.S.A. and more practitioners focused, though less well publicized, material has been published in the U.K. (Blundell & Murdock, 1997; Flynn, 2002; Rose & Lawton, 1999). Of the latter Flynn's work is possibly the best known by U.K. practitioners and is now in a 4th Edition – an unusual attribute for a field with a limited text book market.

More recently Hood commented that, "Everyone knows New Public Management is an international or even global phenomenon, that it represents an attempt to correct the shortcomings of traditional public organization in efficiency and service delivery to citizens, and that one of its central themes is to stress the importance of public managers discretionary space or freedom to manage" (Hood, 2000, p. 1).

Gow and Dufour have suggested that, following Kuhn, NPM could be seen as a paradigm change. As such they are following a well established viewpoint that NPM is a reaction against what used to be described as Public Administration (Hood, 1991). They note, "Many governments and scholars believe that NPM is a different and better way than Public Administration (PA) for studying and improving the management of public organizations. Their criticism of PA mainly concerns the fact that it seems unable to explain the reality of public organizations in a context of downsizing or to provide managers with tools to improve their operation. NPM is also different from public policy, of which it is the complement" (Gow & Dufour, 2000, p. 578).

Gow and Dufour pose an interesting question for NPM. Is NPM a paradigm shift and if so at what level? They observe that at the first level the paradigm represents a set of beliefs: "A paradigm governs, in the first instance, not a subject matter but rather a group of practitioners" (Kuhn, 1970, p. 180). At the second level it represents something more than theory alone – it represents a theory which offers a more successful explanation than its predecessors. The third level is that of examples or instances of concrete problem solutions. Gow and Dufour

GRID / GROUP	Low Group	High Group
High Grid	The Fatalist Way	The Hierarchism Way
Low Grid	The Individualist way	The Egalitarian Way

Fig. 1. Four Styles of Public Management Organization. *Source:* Hood (1999, p. 12).

discuss whether it is possible to discern a paradigm for NPM which in effect has substituted for either traditional public administration on the one hand and a straightforward private sector paradigm on the other.

Hood has posited a possible paradigm for the public sector which is capable of operating at a range of levels and between different national entities. He provided a 2 by 2 matrix based upon two factors: GRID and GROUP (Fig. 1).

Hood asserts that, "'Grid' and 'Group' are fundamental to public management" and that if you put them together they will "take us to the heart of much contemporary and historical discussion about how to do public management" (Hood, 1998, p. 8). This is a quite bold assertion which would very possibly be construed as a claim to Group and Grid as the basis for a paradigm for public management in terms of the earlier comments by Gow and Dufour.

Grid represented the difference between accepting government by rule and regulation at one extreme and deciding things on an "ad hoc" basis at the other. The "freedom to manage" which has been part of the management debate in the public sector can be seen as an attempt to move from high to low grid. "Group" on the other hand represents the tension between highly participative forms of governance and delivery of services as opposed to "professional" structures separate from the clientele which they serve.

When these two dimensions are combined according to Hood you get to the "heart of much contemporary and historical discussion about how to do public management" (Hood, 2000). A society with a strong affinity for rules but where a high level of distrust exists, co-operation is rejected, and apathy prevails would, according to Hood, is associated with "fatalist" style of public management. If the rules are present but the society is socially cohesive then the style would be "hierarchist" – something typically found in uniformed organizational structures. With a lesser stress upon rule-dominated behavior low grid the egalitarian style involves a high degree of participation in decision-making where each case is decided on its own merits but through "collective structures" involving government or public sector professionals. An "individualist" approach is where market forces might be seen as appropriate to services with negotiation and bargaining as a way of resolving transaction issues.

THE PARADOXES OF NEW PUBLIC MANAGEMENT

A number of paradoxes were identified by Hood when considering comparative experience of public service management reform.

- In spite of NPM being presented as an international or even global phenomenon there are significant elements of diversity in public sector reforms.

Here Hood is referring to the significant degree of variation found between different countries. The global paradigm of NPM which is implicit in much of the writing has to confront a reality where the same reforms adopted in different countries were in fact due to "different and often contradictory reasons." There were also differences in the speed of adoption of reform. Furthermore, some writers see countries pulling in different directions.

- The issue of what Hood calls the "malade imaginaire" whereby those systems which seemingly had the least need for reform were the first to undertake reform and conversely those most in need of reform were late comers – or resisted it altogether.

Is NPM seen as a remedy to address the deficiencies of previous systems of "old style" public administration? The OECD suggests that competitive international forces have been a driver for change. However, as Hood points out, it is strange that the countries which have adopted NPM are the ones who, in terms of repute and efficiency of their public sector, would seem to be least in need of it. It is reminiscent if the observation that "the poor, who have the most need of money, are the very people who have the least money."

- Even in the most reform focussed countries "managerialism" was often adopted only in part and in an unclear fashion.

The concept of allowing managers space and discretion to deploy resources in order to achieve targets in the style of the private sector has been regarded as a part of NPM. In the mantra of the New Labor Government in the U.K. the phrase has been "... do what works." The implication here has been the "de-politicization" of public services and the separation of "operational and strategic/policy" aspects of the operation of government departments. However this sits uneasily with the emergence of the "regulated state." Elsewhere Hood and his colleagues comment that in the U.K., "Regulation inside U.K. government, when all its forms are taken together, amounts to a large enterprise, approaching, if not exceeding the scale of regulation of the private sector" (Hood, 1998, p. 61). In effect the discretion apparently accorded to managers in the realm of NPM may turn out to be illusory. The manager may be required to operate in a regulatory straightjacket. Indeed the U.K. has seen this in the area of education with the freedom of teachers and education managers becoming the subject of increasing levels of oversight, compliance to standards and inspection regimes.

Hood suggests that these paradoxes can be explained through "public sector bargains" which he uses to mean "any explicit or implicit understanding between senior public servants and other actors in a political system over their duties and entitlements relating to responsibility, autonomy and political identity, and expressed in convention or formal law or a mixture of both" (Hood, 2000, p. 8).

It may further be argued that such bargains not only occur but may be beneficial in terms of enhanced provision of public services. In the public domain services are often contracted by public officials with organizations on behalf of clients or end users. In effect the beneficiary is not the purchaser. This has elsewhere been characterized as the Principal – Agent problem (Arrow, 1985; Ross, 1973). Talking about a welfare situation Monroe described the problem as residing in the fact that "differences of interest and information between the two parties mean that the agent may not always act in the interests of the principal, and the costs and difficulties of selecting an agent and monitoring his performance mean that the principal may not be able to enforce her will on the agent" (Monroe, 1999).

Moore has described the creation of public value as the desire on the part of public managers which equates to the creation of profit in the private sector (Moore, 1995). In conceptualizing this Moore suggests that three key questions might be posed (Moore, 1995, p. 22).

- Whether the purpose is publicly valuable.
- Whether it will be politically or legally supported.
- Whether it is administratively and operationally feasible.

In review of Moore's book, Symes developed this model as a tripartite framework (Symes, 1999, p. 163) (Fig. 2).

The questions and model identify the importance of key groups in the managers' environment. The need to identify and respond to customers and clients in a politically charged setting raises questions as to how managers might identify and work with stakeholders in order to achieve objectives in an environment where it is not easy or may even be impossible to find a generally acceptable measure such as profit. The dilemma for a manager following Moores' approach of "creating public

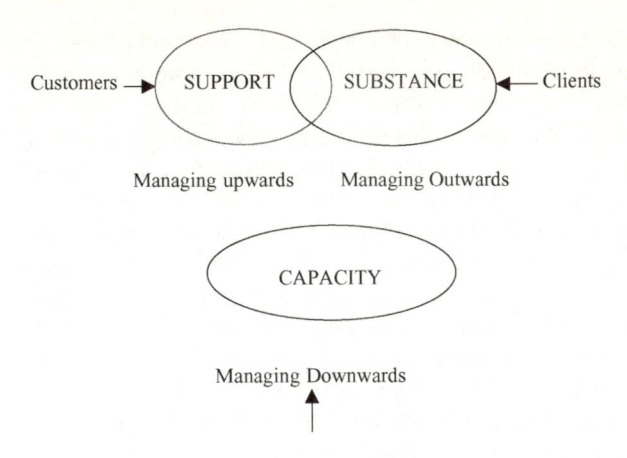

```
      Customers ──▶ ( SUPPORT ( SUBSTANCE )  ◀── Clients

            Managing upwards    Managing Outwards

                    ( CAPACITY )

                    Managing Downwards
                          ▲
                          │
                  Public Sector Organization
```

Fig. 2. Management Environment Framework. *Source:* Author, 2003 (based on Symes, 1999, p. 163).

value" may be to be confronted with several concepts as to what constitutes "public value." The concepts may be incompatible and yet strongly held. As a personal example the author was pressured by a professional team to make a managerial appointment on the basis of race and sex criteria. When an applicant who possessed the desired race and sex attributes was appointed the team then complained fiercely because the person was not also the most highly qualified applicant for the role.

The author believes that to resolve these dilemmas and work with often conflicting objectives a public manager has to find ways of both assessing the perceptions of different groups and also working with such diverse groups to good effect. The stakeholder approach can provide both a theoretical and practical means to do this.

THE STAKEHOLDER LITERATURE

In 1999, the Academy of Management Review devoted much of an issue to examining the state of the literature in stakeholding. In this volume Jones and Wicks set out what they considered to be the current state of research into stakeholder theory. They posit what they consider to be the essential premises of stakeholder theory (Jones & Wicks, 1999). It is useful to examine these in turn:

(1) The corporation has relationships with many constituent groups, i.e. stakeholders that affect and are affected by its decisions.

This premise is drawn from the seminal work by Freeman (1984). Freeman is frequently cited in the literature especially that originating from North America. (Frooman, 1999; Key, 1999; Svendson, 1998). His work is also regarded as important though not perhaps as critical by some European sources (Johnson & Scholes, 2001; Wheeler & Sillianpaa, 1997). Freeman sought to account for the relation between the organization firm and its external environment. His focus was upon commercial organizations and he examined the possibility that non-shareholders might impact upon managerial decision making. He suggested that each company had its own set of discrete stakeholder groups. Some groups would be primary, in that their interests were directly linked to those of the company, and other would be secondary in that their influence was indirect or that they were less directly affected by the activities of the company (Svendsen, 1999).

The interesting questions which Freeman's work gives rise to is the closeness of the relationship, the nature of the influence of the company upon the stakeholder and the stakeholder upon the company. This leads to the second premise of Jones and Wicks:

(2) Stakeholder theory is concerned with the nature of these relationships in terms of both processes and outcomes for the company and for the stakeholders.

Much of the operationalisation of stakeholder theory has appeared in the form of various models which have sought to depict these relationships. Mendelows' mapping model (1991) has become popularized through main stream strategic management texts (Johnson & Scholes, 1999, 2002) and it is hard to imagine a recent MBA student who has not been required to engage in some form of stakeholder mapping exercise. Frooman has sought to explore the concept of stakeholder influence strategies in a more sophisticated fashion through the concepts of power and resource dependence to produce a model of four types of firm-stakeholder relationships (Frooman, 1999). Frooman examined the way in which an environmental pressure group influenced a company StarKist, so that the company in turn prevailed upon its suppliers to change their behavior. The suppliers were foreign tuna fishing fleets and the environmental pressure group wanted them to change their form of fishing practice. They did this by a campaign aimed at the customers of StarKist. The environmental group was not a customer or a significant shareholder of StarKist but felt it had the right as a stakeholder in its activities to take this action. This leads to the third premise about stakeholder theory:

(3) The interests of all legitimate stakeholders have intrinsic value and no set of interests is assumed to dominate the others.

This premise is perhaps more challenging to unpack. It certainly flies in the face of much organizational theory which accords primacy to a particular group whether it be shareholders or to the customer or service user. It begs certain questions such as how does the legitimacy of a stakeholder get established. Can a smoker lay claim to a legitimate interest in being able to smoke even though other stakeholders in the organizational environment are opposed to it? It presumes that stakeholder differences are in some way mediated in a fashion which involves a degree of compromise – or at least acceptance of minority opinion.

Johnson and Scholes express the practical implication succinctly, "Are managers really the honest brokers who weigh the conflicting interests of stakeholder groups? Or are they answerable to one stakeholder – such as shareholders. Or are they, as many authors suggest, the real power behind the throne, constructing strategies to suit their own purposes and managing stakeholder expectations to ensure acceptance of these strategies?" (Johnson & Scholes, 1999, p. 217).

Jones and Wicks (1999) suggest that stakeholder theory might seek to describe behaviors but they view instrumental approaches more favorably – namely that the theory puts up a certain postulates that particular actions may lead to certain outcomes. They suggest various such postulates and outcomes. They note that another approach is to adopt a normative standpoint and suggest what moral obligations stakeholder theory places upon managers. This approach – often explored through the literature on Business and Managerial ethics – purports to furnish a way (or ways?) of answering the dilemma of how to deal with conflicting stakeholder interests.

Jones and Wicks go on to suggest a hybrid theory which brings together the instrumental and normative approaches. This could be achieved by grounding instrumental theory in "morally sound principles." This raises an interesting possibility for extending stakeholder theory into a domain where morally sound principles must reside alongside an expectation or at least acceptance of instrumentality – namely that of state provided health care.

STAKEHOLDING IN HEALTH CARE IN THE U.K.

Health Care represents, in the context of the NHS, a service for the individual citizen of the U.K. or individuals otherwise qualified to receive the service – such as EU citizens. Thus the number of potential stakeholders is enormous. Since the principle of the NHS is a service free to those in need then the recipient is not in effect a purchaser of the service. This makes the NHS what Flynn (1997) describes as a "Type 2 Market." This has some clear implications for stakeholding theory in the NHS. The internal market of separation of purchaser from provider of health care is mirrored in stakeholding terms by the separation of recipient from payment for service.

The internal market was seen by many writers as requiring NHS organizations to "seriously consider their environment, as a failure to do so would adversely affect the viability of those organizations which were not competitive" (Miller & Wilson, 1998, p. 51). Miller and Wilson examined the situation of an NHS Trust whose contract and thus source of funds appeared to be vulnerable. They suggest that this came about because the Trust had adopted a reactive rather than pro-active approach which meant that the stakeholder relationship was being neglected. The research, involved interviewing 12 Trust staff and asking them to list key stakeholders.

Of a maximum of 12 interviewee responses the following stakeholders were identified. Numbers relate to number of interviewees identifying them:

Health authorities	11
Local authorities	11
General practitioners	10
Community health councils	9
Service users	8
Local and voluntary organizations	8
Trust staff	7
Local community	5
MP's	4
Lobbying groups	4
Carers	4
Primary health care teams	3
Universities	3
Other provider units	2
Other professional schools	2
Trust executive	2
Regional health authority	2
GP Fundholders	2

These were the stakeholders identified as more important by more than one respondent. Other stakeholders such as therapy staff, nurses, other care providers, media, and trust management were each named once only.

Miller and Wilson asked respondents to place the various stakeholders on a matrix using the Johnson and Scholes power/dynamism and power/interest matrix. This led them to conclude that Health Authorities, Community Health Councils, General Practitioners, Local Authorities, and Trust staffs were regarded as the most important stakeholders.

The researchers analyzed the reported expectations of the various stakeholders as expressed by respondents and compared these with the researcher's assessment. They concluded that:

> ... although there was considerable consensus as to who the stakeholders are, the interviewees had different perceptions about the power, dynamism, and interest of each stakeholder. The differing perceptions inevitably lead to problems in prioritization which, in turn, exacerbate the difficulties the trust can be expected to experience in formulating its response to the competing claims of its various stakeholders (Miller & Wilson, 1998, p. 57).

Some years earlier Berman Brown and colleagues suggested that there were three main groups of stakeholders in the NHS. These they identified as professional clinicians, managers and patients (Berman Brown et al., 1994). They note that the immediate answer to the question, "Who is the NHS for?" was "the patients who use it" – but then they suggest that "... differing views of how this is to be achieved contribute to a misreading between stakeholders of one another's remit" (Berman Brown et al., 1994, p. 63). They suggest that their three stakeholder groups have differing views of how the purpose of the NHS is to be accomplished. They then went on to assess the views of the different groups and identify the patients as the most dependent and least well informed; the clinicians as powerful and closely linked to the patients and end results and the managers as more remote and more focused on resource efficiency and effectiveness considerations.

Berman Brown et al. consider the impact of the new managerial ethos of the NHS reforms and suggest that both managers and clinicians are more concerned with illness treatment than health promotion. This is fostered by the highly visible nature of the waiting list factor. They observe that:

> An orientation towards health rather than illness would be a profound change for the NHS, but one that may be brought nearer by the rise of the professional manager. To the latter, a particular clinical treatment is only a means to an end, and if allocating resources away from treatment to, say, health education is more efficient at improving overall health, it will seem a rational use of finite resources (Berman Brown et al., 1994, p. 69).

Nwanko and Richardson (1996) stress the importance of a political perspective for an organizational leader. Their article offers some very useful insights for a manager operating in the sort of highly politically charged environment which is characteristic of the NHS. In particular the changes in the Scottish setting make a political awareness an even more critical attribute for an effective manager, as they observe:

> A double-sided political mind-set accedes to the likelihood that some people will be for and some against particular strategic developments. Politically adept leaders seem to carry a cognitive political map into their managerial work. Intuitively and without the need for formal analysis

they understand who, in and around their organizations, have the means and the will either to foster or damage their projects (Nwanko & Richardson, 1996, p. 44).

Nwanko and Richardson suggest a strategy for the politically astute manager to engage in a constructive and effective analysis and strategy implementation cycle with relevant stakeholders. The suggestion that effective managers "intuitively" engage in this may have a considerable basis in the reality of many organizations. However when an organization such as the NHS in Scotland confronts a sudden change in its political environment then the reaction of managers may not have an intuitive template on which to rely. Previously the political levers went but indirectly to Westminster via the more proximate doors of the civil servants. To some extent to Health Ministers based in London, Scotland was probably seen as not possessing the immediacy of health issues nearer to the London media.

A MODEL FOR STAKEHOLDING IN THE CONTEXT OF THE NHS

Strategic Management texts such as Johnson and Scholes (1998) suggest that stakeholder analysis should involve assessing stakeholders in terms of such criteria as:

- power;
- interest;
- predictability.

When a professionally-oriented not for profit public body such as the NHS is concerned we feel that it may be appropriate to open out these criteria to take account of the particular environment within which the NHS Scotland operates. In particular the impact of changes of this environment namely the political changes wrought by devolution, the ending of the internal market and the creation of new relationships and bodies (Tables 1 and 2).

Table 1. Stakeholding Variables: Level of Interest and Power.

Power	Level of Interest	
	Low	High
Low	Minimal effort	Keep informed
High	Keep satisfied	Key players

Source: Author (2003).

Table 2. Stakeholding Variables: Predictability and Power.

Power	Unpredicability	
	Low	High
Low	Few problems	Manageable though uncertain
High	Powerful but known	Greatest risk and opportunity

Source: Author (2003).

It may be suggested that the analysis of stakeholders in this environment could benefit from the following model of stakeholder analysis.

The Nature of Stakeholder Power

Positive vs. Negative
Certain actors in the NHS clearly possess positive power. Thus politicians may allocate extra resources to a particular Health Board and within a Health Board the manager may favor a particular service or department for additional funding More commonly in a large and relatively bureaucratic publicly funded body without an obvious bottom line the power is negative – the power to obstruct or delay.

Understanding the power basis of a stakeholder is clearly critical for the Health Board. Positive power is more easily understood-particularly as it is typically exercised downwards through the provision of funds, the use of performance measures or the operation of contractual arrangements. Negative or countervailing power in the health care setting is less well recognized and understood (Mechanic, 1991).

In the NHS setting a clear example of negative power was the refusal or reluctance to provide information. Under the internal market there were implicit if not explicit financial consequences when a provider failed to furnish information of activities undertaken under a contract. John Harvey Jones graphically uncovered these in the Troubleshooter Series broadcast on television when he assessed the problems of the Bradford Hospital Trust. The Health Authority in Bradford withheld funding from the Trust on the basis that the Trust had not furnished a proper accounting of its activities.

However with the move towards dismantling of the internal market the negative power of the Health Board to withhold funding may be perceived differently by the Trusts with which it deals. The "partnership mantra" implies that the Board is a "conduit" for such funding and "conduits" are not meant to impede the flow.

The move in Scotland towards empowering the Trusts and making the Health Boards more "strategic" and less operational has the potential to change the way

Table 3. Stakeholding Variables: Use of Power and Power I.

Power	Use of Power	
	Negative	Positive
Low	Only a threat in alliance	High alliance potential
High	Change blocker	Key change agent

Source: Author (2003).

in which power is exercised. In particular the financial leverage that the Boards held through control of the purse strings may be weakened with a move towards partnership models and longer duration funding arrangements. The powers of the Boards both in positive and negative terms may be reduced. The model below would predict that this would encourage alliance seeking behavior by the Boards (Table 3).

Direct vs. Indirect Exercise of Power
Stakeholders may exercise power directly and usually openly. This is generally well understood and accepted. Thus the Health Board directly and openly liaises with Local Authorities to produce Health Improvement Plans (HIPs) in accordance with Government requirements. The plenitude of Government directives and official pronouncements give an impression of direct control upon the operation of a Health Board.

However, in a public sector context where there is no clear bottom line such as share price, profit margin or sales it is inevitable that directives are interpreted or mediated. The presence of both national and Scottish government departments creates a complexity of relationships. In a professional collegiate setting the quality orientated bodies which have been set up may prefer to operate obliquely as opposed to the more direct functioning of their contractually focused predecessors. On the other hand the "mantra" of collaboration and partnership may take time to percolate through and replace the culture of the internal market.

The presence of a new set of politicians in the form of Members of the Scottish Parliament has been a factor. Health has been an obvious focus for their activities as it is proportionally a large part of the budget and a key element of devolution. The Scottish Executive has also become involved in Health issues. In areas such as care of the elderly and assessment of health care needs and effectiveness the Scots have parted company with the NHS south of the border.

Overall the pattern of indirect and lower levels of power prior to devolution has thus been replaced by evidence of direct and higher levels of power. The Scots have become "agenda setters." The results of the recent NHS poll by the BBC

Table 4. Stakeholding Variables: Use of Power and Power II.

Power	Use of Power	
	Indirect	Direct
Low	Whispering campaign	"In your face tactic"
High	"Behind the throne influence"	"Agenda setter"

Source: Author (2003).

demonstrated that a key part of the Scottish agenda – free long term care of the elderly – was overwhelmingly prioritized by respondents in both the phone in vote and web vote held on February 20, 2002 (Table 4).

Acting Alone vs. in Alliance With Other Stakeholders
Most people are familiar with the device of the sticks: a Master gives a stick to a disciple and invites the disciple to break it which the disciple does. The Master then gives the disciple a bundle of sticks and the disciple cannot break them. The lesson is of strength in numbers – or in alliance.

In the stakeholding context the analogy is that a weak stakeholder can achieve power through alliance with another stakeholder. The alliance may take several forms.

- Two or more weak stakeholders may join together in order to more effectively press their case.
- A strongly interested but weak stakeholder may prevail upon a stronger but otherwise relatively uninterested stakeholder to champion its cause.
- Two weak stakeholders may agree to support each other in areas where one has an interest but the other has not – or to "take it in turns to be the dominant party."

In a number of public sector settings such stakeholder alliances are familiar phenomena. NOC Local Authorities (No Overall Control) are an obvious example. In order for political impasse to be resolved the political groups must come to an understanding and – usually – engage in some sort of political "horse trading." Health Boards, however, are non-elected bodies and are made up in part of political appointees. Professional clinicians tend to be focused upon the needs of the speciality and "horse trading" may not be an avidly practiced skill.

The work with the Health Board showed that examples of alliances were to be found. In particular there was an example of an agreed policy to site a particular facility for drug users being frustrated by a local politician acting in alliance with the local community and the media (Table 5).

Table 5. Stakeholding Variables: Use of Power and Power III.

Power	Use of Power	
	In Alliance	Alone
Low	"Potential surprise"	"Ineffective protest"
High	Highly effective	"Big hitter"

Source: Author (2003).

Interest Focus

Predictable – Not Predictable
A stakeholder can be considered in terms of how predictable is likely to be their stance on a particular issue. To some extent this is linked to the degree of knowledge and experience of the particular stakeholder. A familiar stakeholder is easier to predict accurately than one who is relatively distant or unknown.

In the context of the changes in the NHS in Scotland this is a key element as familiar stakeholders may have become less predictable due to the "changing environment." New stakeholders are emerging with the requirement to engage in collaborative planning with Local Authorities. New bodies to assess quality and performance of care are set up. Most significantly of all there is a whole new political structure with a Parliament, MP's and a Health Minister. There is often no background of previous experience to draw upon to predict the behavior of these stakeholders. It has to be "learned in the raw." Sometimes it is based upon casual knowledge and rumor related to the individuals concerned.

The Health Boards had to deal with a sudden increase in their political environment. From having distant politicians whose eyes rarely turned northwards they had to confront a complex and active local political environment. Knowledge of local politicians and their particular concerns and interests appeared limited (Table 6).

Table 6. Stakeholder Attitude and Interest.

Individual Interest	Attitude to Issue	
	Favorable	Opposed
Predictable	Nurture as ally	"Disarm" or win over
Unpredictable	Need to assess... and persuade	Need to consult

Source: Author (2003).

Table 7. Stakeholder Interest Types.

Individual Interest	Nature of Interest	
	Specific	General
Favorable	Issue based support	Ally
Opposed	Issue based opposition	Opponent

Source: Author (2003).

Specific or Generic

Stakeholders may have some very specific areas of interest. When these are threatened the stakeholder will become very energetic and vociferous. Otherwise the stakeholder is virtually a "sleeping partner" as far as the Health Board is concerned. Other stakeholders may perceive a broader engagement with the affairs of the Board. If the demeanor of the stakeholder is known then the Board can predict and anticipate or foster particular behaviors by the stakeholder.

An example which emerged strikingly was the relocation of a needle exchange for drug users. The Local Authority had agreed to this and the Health Board was surprised to encounter strong resistance to setting up the needle exchange from a local councilor. It was suggested that this may have been associated with the actual physical location over a local Post Office. Such a location could be predicted to arouse local political sensitivity which the councilor would feel bound to express in a forthright fashion. The generic question of the setting up of a needle exchange was accepted. It was the specific nature of implementation which gave rise to the stakeholder issue (Table 7).

Favorable – Opposed

Stakeholder may be in favor of a particular innovation, service or proposed change to service – or they may be opposed. The oft used phrase is to ask whether the stakeholder is "for it or against it."

A stakeholder who is favorable is obviously likely to be amenable to co-operative strategies and may well be willing to consider some form of alliance to the mutual benefit of both parties. A stakeholder who is opposed may need to be won over either by concession or by some form of trade-off. Alternatively if the stakeholder is not amenable or the situation does not lend itself to such tactics then the likely reaction of the stakeholder has to be assessed. Will the stakeholder be able to singly, or in alliance with others, pose a serious threat? If so how might that threat be countered or neutralized?

This is an area where the skilled politician thrives. The NHS Scotland has "enjoyed" a political distance from Westminster politics in the past. Local

Government politics, due to the structure of the internal market, have possibly represented more of a spectator sport as NHS has not been required to co-operate with local authorities to produce joint plans and agree common strategies.

However with the advent of devolution and a Scottish Parliament and Health minister this has introduced some changes. Members of the Scottish Parliament have been very concerned with local health questions in a way that Westminster MP's were not. The then Scottish Health Minister, Susan Deacon, adopted a highly public profile. The new NHS is also required to collaborate with local councils to produce Health Plans. Where the Health Board has several such councils within its area this poses a complex challenge.

CONCLUSIONS

The paradoxes of new public management noted by Hood may be argued to be relevant to analysis of the NHS in the U.K. and specifically in Scotland. For example, there has been less focus on private sector initiatives and a modernizing agenda in Scotland than in England even though the need for these measures may be greater in Scotland. Indeed there are relatively few PPP/PFI initiatives north of the border. Within one country, the U.K., the differences in speed of adoption of new initiatives in individual parts of the nation are readily apparent.

The key element of NPM – devolution – has, in combination with a different history of public law and institutions, resulted in significant differences in implementation. Scotland may conceivably set some of the agenda for change in the National Health Service south of the border. Although this may be framed to be understood in terms of New Public Management criteria, it may be better illuminated by the stakeholder approach applied herein. The stakeholder environment in Scotland has changed dramatically and the differences in course arising from this are amenable to analysis, explanation, and – possibly – prediction using the stakeholder theory and its associated techniques. New political actors have emerged with the Scottish Parliament; the reduced relevance of London based politicians and public servants in driving change has been accompanied by a re-configuration of local sources of power.

Stakeholder analysis enables public managers and policy makers to make sense of the new landscape. In particular, the health sector that has previously been guided largely by civil servants who looked South of the border for guidance and often for future careers has now become highly sensitive to local political considerations. More questions are asked in the Scottish Parliament presently about health than any other issue.

Adjustments to more local concerns will be challenging and may be very hard for both health professionals and health care managers to make. In a relatively short time, the political environment has become immediate, and often the micro-environment is to the forefront as witness in the example of the needle exchange scheme. Under the former Westminster-based environment the issue would not have been over the sitting of the facility but rather the fact that the budgetary agreement would have been a long, drawn out process involving distant and possibly disinterested parties.

Knowing who your stakeholders are and consulting them appears to be an obvious priority for local managers in the public domain. However identifying the key stakeholder groups and individuals is not a straightforward task and the impact of change is not easy to predict. Potentially affected individuals and groups may not be known to the policy makers or to each other. Therefore, the traditional and formalized consultation mechanisms that policy makers use may elicit limited and sometimes misleading information. The set planning processes beloved in the public sector environment may, by their very nature, favor certain groups over others. When the balance of incentives changes, there are winners and losers; process change and power shifts may not apparent or palatable to many participant stakeholders.

The literature and folklore of public management offers numerous examples of policy failure and of unintended – and often unforeseen – consequences. Stakeholder analysis and mapping techniques can enhance the identification of affected parties and provide knowledge of their interests and their likely reaction to policy changes.

REFERENCES

Arrow, K. J. (1985). The economics of agency. In: J. Pratt & Zeckhauser (Eds), *Principals and Agents: The Structure of Business* (pp. 37–51). Harvard Business School Press.
Barzelay, M. (2001). *The new public management: Improving research and policy dialogue*. Berkeley: University of California Press.
Berman Brown, R., McCartney, S., Bell, L., & Scaggs, S. (1994). Who is the NHS for? *Journal of Management in Medicine*, 8(4), 63.
Blundell, B., & Murdock, A. (1997). *Managing in the public sector*. Butterworth Heinemann.
Clarkson, M. (Ed.) (1998). *The corporation and its stakeholders*. University of Toronto.
Donaldson, T., & Preston, L. (1995). The stakeholder theory of the corporation: Concepts, evidence and implications. *Academy of Management Review*, 20(1), 65–91.
Ferlie, E. et al. (1996). *The new public management in action*. Oxford University Press.
Flynn, N. (2002). *Public sector management*. Prentice-Hall.
Freeman, R. E. (1984). *Strategic management: A stakeholder approach*. Prentice-Hall.
Gow, I., & Dufour, C. (2000). Is the new public management a paradigm? Does it matter? *International Review of Administrative Sciences*, 66(4), 573–597.
Hood, C. (1991, Spring). A public management for all seasons. *Public Administration*, 69(1), 1–19.
Hood, C. (1998). *The art of the state: Culture, rhetoric and public management*. Oxford University Press.

Hood, C. (2000). Paradoxes of public-sector managerialism, old public management and public service bargains. *International Public Management Journal*, *3*(1), 1–22.

Hood, C., Scott, C., James, O., Jones, G., & Travers, A. (1998). Regulation in government: Where new public management meets the audit explosion. *Public Money and Management* (April–June), 61–68.

Johnson, G., & Scholes, K. (Eds) (1999). *Exploring public sector strategy* (5th ed.). Prentice-Hall.

Johnson, G., & Scholes, K. (Eds) (2002). *Exploring public sector strategy* (6th ed.). Prentice-Hall.

Jones, T., & Wicks, A. (1999). Convergent stakeholder theory. *Academy of Management Review*, *24*(2), 206–221.

Kuhn, T. (1970). *The structure of scientific revolutions* (2nd ed.). University of Chicago Press.

Mechanic, D. (1991). Sources of countervailing power in medicine. *Journal of Health Politics, Policy and Law*, *16*, 485–498.

Miller, S., & Wilson, J. (1998, July–September). Perceptions of stakeholding: The case of an NHS trust. *Public Money and Management*, *51*.

Minogue, M. (2000). Should flawed models of public management be exported? Issues and practices. Working Paper No. 15, Institute for Development Policy and Management, University of Manchester.

Monroe, L. (1999). A principal-agent analysis of the family: Implications for the welfare state. Working Paper 58, Institute for Development Policy and Management, University of Manchester.

Moore, M. H. (1995). *Creating public value: Strategic management in government*. Harvard University Press.

Murdock, A. (2000, June). *Developing strategic awareness – Can a new stakeholder approach offer something*? European health care management association annual conference, Sweden.

Murdock, A. (2001a, Summer). Knowing and mapping your stakeholders – Can a stakeholder approach offer something for the fire service? *Fire Command and Management*, *16*(4).

Murdock A. (2001b). No-one loves you baby: The child support agency. In: Johnson & Scholes (Eds), *Exploring Corporate Strategy* (pp. 774–783). Prentice-Hall.

Nasi, J. (1995). *Understanding stakeholder thinking*. LSR Publications, Finland.

Osborne, D., & Gaebler, T. (1992). *Reinventing government: How the entrepreneurial spirit is transforming the public sector*. Addison-Wesley.

Peters, B. G. (1996). *The future of governing*. University of Kansas Press.

Pollitt, C., & Bouckaert, G. (2000). *Public management reform: A comparative analysis*. Oxford University Press.

Ross, S. A. (1973). The economic theory of agency: The principal's problem. *American Economic Review, Papers and Proceedings*, *632*, 134–139.

Rose, A., & Lawton, A. (1999). *Public services management*. Prentice-Hall.

Symes, A. (1999). Review of creating public value. *International Public Management Journal*, *2*(1), 158–167.

5. STRATEGIES FOR HEALTH CARE REFORM IMPLEMENTATION IN SOUTHERN ITALY

Marco Meneguzzo, Valentina Mele and Angelo Tanese

INTRODUCTION

This study focuses on a particular type of public organization characterized by weak boundaries and strong informal relationships, elements that have assisted in driving the reform of an entire national public management system. The case is the Public Healthcare System of the Southern Italy in the period beginning in the early 1990s through the beginning of the new millennium, with particular emphasis on the Sicilian region, selected since it represents an extreme case of informal networks that affect organizational boundaries and governance functions.

This work is intended to contribute to the dialogue on the importance of informal network relationships in the public sector and the impact of managerial reform on these kinds of networks. Thus far, research on public management policy change does not seem to have adequately assessed the role played by informal relationships in halting such reform, in increasing the level of organizational inertia, or even in setting a parallel pattern of change ruled by the internal players. Three main reference fields crowd the academic archive on the subject.

First, we consider the literature on network management, which turns out to underestimate the "informal" component of these organizational constructs. Another reference field for understanding informal relationships in the public sector is managerial leadership, but it failed to provide the greater picture of a systemic phenomenon, being too focused on the heroic achievements of individual leaders. The third set of studies informing the research develops around the concept of ethics in the public sector. Instruments for fostering public ethics in the organizational culture play a major role in the process of managing the informal networks. Yet, one reason it does not provide a satisfactory framework for studying informal relationships in the public sector is that this specific kind of network sometimes acts in a sort of amoral or unethical fashion as a result of self-guidance and evolution. Observation and analysis of the Sicilian Healthcare System, indeed, show the mixed nature of illegitimacy on one hand, and efficient allocation of resources around centers of professional excellence on the other. Therefore, such complex and contradictory organizational cultures are not well assessed by merely looking at public ethics indicators. Further case-oriented research on informal networks in the public sector could tell us more about their functioning logic and mechanisms, and could tackle the problems connected to the implementation of managerial reform in public organizations governed by strong informal relationships.

The public governance paradigm, the focus of several public management studies in the recent years, has emphasized issues such as stakeholders mapping both internal and external to the public administration, and the identification of formal and informal networks which stem from the relationship among stakeholders (Kooiman & Eljassen, 1993). The analysis of public and private (both profit and non-profit) stakeholders, together with the evaluation of the governance mechanisms and interorganizational relationships play a major role in accounting for the successful implementation of public policies. Based on the study of multiple cases we tried to answer two main research questions related to the issue of informal networks within the public sector system as a whole and within the public sector organizations.

To present the work as a business history applied to the public management research field, we first differentiate the features of informal relationships from the features of formal relationships linking public administrations and businesses, such as lobbying, typically falling under the realm of business-government relationships research. Therefore, the first question is: *how to include the "informal" dimension in public management studies*? To approach this question one might consider the impact of such "informal" dimensions of the decision making process, on the connections between politicians and civil servants, on the managerial function, on the performance evaluation and on the progressive introduction of accountability principles in the public sector. Analysis of the healthcare system in Sicily allows one to understand the dynamics that brought the creation of the informal relationships, as well as to evaluate the impact of such informal relationships on the process of strategic and organizational change within the Local Healthcare Units. To answer the question stated above, we have to focus on how public

Table 1. From Public Management to Public Governance.

Environmental Dynamics	Government Role	Public Management Functions	Public Governance Main Problems
Complexity	Decomposition Coordination	Rapresentativeness Selectiveness	Global-Local Consistency
Diversity	Steering Intervention weigthening	Transparency Legitimation	Quality Individual Preferences
Dynamism	Integration Regulation	Learning Effectiveness	Systems dynamics Scenarios

Source: Meneguzzo, 2003, based on Kooiman and van Vliet (1993).

management approaches can be enriched with new, loosely coupled management systems, aimed at governing, coordinating and guiding the informal networks (EFMD, 2001; Jann, 2001).

The second question is: *how to identify the strategies that public organization could and should enforce to leverage the positive impacts, and to control the vicious circles that informal relationships tend to create*? In order to address this question the option of applying new tools for governing and managing the network of informal relationships is considered. Such tools are linked to the new functions required by the introduction and the development of public governance principles, as stated by the "Dutch school" and presented in Table 1 (Kooiman & van Vliet, 1993; Meneguzzo, 2001).

As we present the events in our case, the spread of public governance principles as strategy for governing informal relationships in the healthcare organizations is assessed. Therefore, the third question addressed is: *how* can *the reinforcement of informal relationships among the internal players and the external stakeholders shape the strategic and organizational change of public healthcare organizations to create a better a mix between public organization features and professional organization features?*

To analyze the experience of the public healthcare system a "hybrid" methodology has been chosen. This is based both on the case study approach with a comparative perspective among the healthcare organizations of different local areas, and on the perspective business history approach with a 10-year time frame. Particularly, case-studies have been conducted with the support of the field-analysis, through the analysis of stakeholders, of their expectations and of the available resources (Rebora & Meneguzzo, 1990) and through the cognitive mapping. This work also took into account the policy implementation research field (http://www.inpuma.net). In Fig. 1 we sketch the narrative structure of the experience, according to a framework, introduced by Kingdon and adapted by Barzelay

Previous events

- Growth and Hypertrophy of public Sector
- Deindustrialisation loss of competitivity of economic system
- Weakness of governance and civic community

Contemporaneus events / complex events

- NHS reform of reform 1992
- Local government reform 1990
- North South dualism in public policies implementation

Informal relationship
Center of excellence
Free riding and no boundaries roles

Related events / complex events

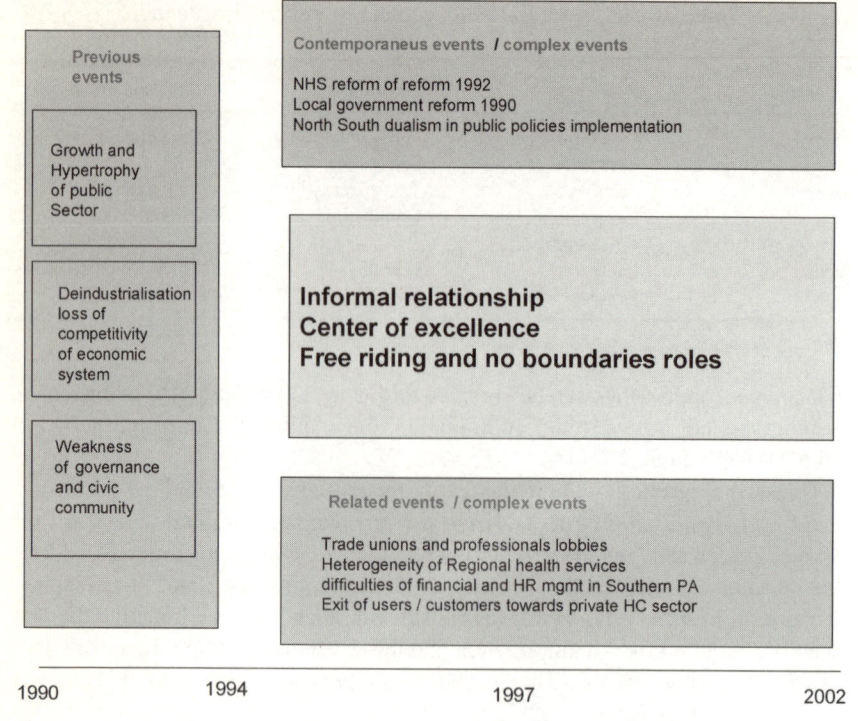

- Trade unions and professionals lobbies
- Heterogeneity of Regional health services
- difficulties of financial and HR mgmt in Southern PA
- Exit of users / customers towards private HC sector

1990 1994 1997 2002

Fig. 1. Narrative Structure of the Experience Studied.

to public management policy change. The framework includes previous events, contemporaneous events and related events, during the time frame 1990–2000.

The following section is intended to provide a description of the events and the institutional features which preceded (previous events) or that proceeded at the same rate (contemporaneous events) as the main episode, mainly related to the Italian public sector reform, at the national and at the Regional level, often characterized by dramatic differences among Regions.

THEORETICAL FRAMEWORK: INSTITUTIONAL AND MANAGERIAL PERFORMANCE IN SOUTHERN ITALIAN PUBLIC ADMINISTRATION

Before considering the main events that determined the development of informal networks in the public sector, it is necessary to consider the reasons that lead to

Institutional performance		CERISDI FORMEZ
Local governance		Organisational and
Community committment		managerial change
At the regional level		in public health care system
		In Southern Italy
Putnam Leonardi		
Nanetti 1985 1991		*Dupuy Thoenig 1992*
		Meneguzzo Del Vecchio 1992

100 Municipalities		Local public
Loss of governance		Policies
governability and		Southern Italy
managerial		Administrive refom
capability		and countereforms
in local governments		
		Cammelli 1988
Cammelli 1989		*Dente 1992 2001*
Rebora 1992		

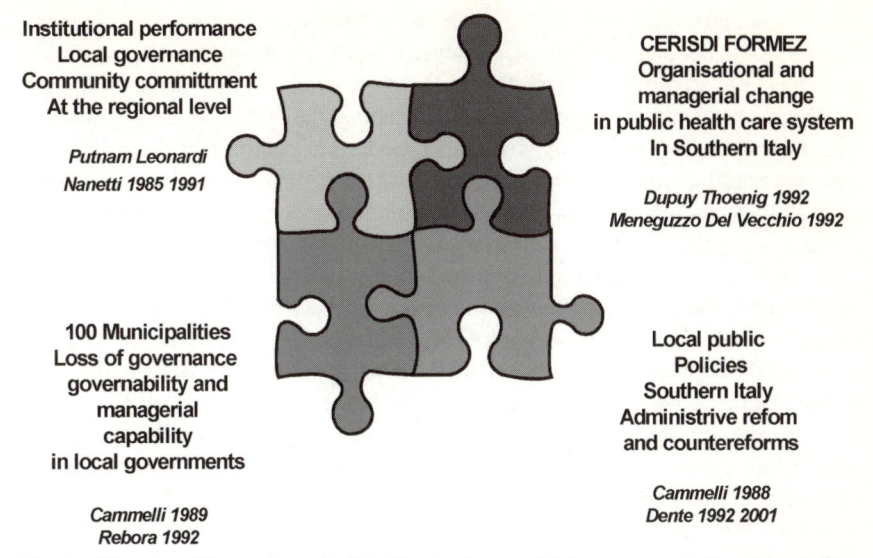

Fig. 2. Mosaic of Research on Public Governance and Management in Southern Italian Public Administration. *Source:* Authors, 2003 based on Putnam, Leonardi and Nanetti (1994).

our choice of the public healthcare system in Italy to define and illustrate our conceptual framework.

The choice of the public healthcare system in Sicily has to be framed in the mosaic of the research on the political, institutional and socio-economic context in Southern Italy. The context of Southern Italy presents peculiarities which can be adopted for interpreting phenomena such as the different speed of modernization processes in the public sector and the obstacles encountered in strengthening new public management and, more recently, public governance, principles. These features have been identified, as shown in Fig. 2, by the contribution of Putnam, Leonardi and Nanetti (1994), that investigated the conditions for creating strong, responsive, effective and representative institutions. These "longitudinal studies" conducted in 1970, 1976, 1981, 1989 on the Italian Regions were aimed at identifying the variables that could explain the regions' different institutional performance.

The research, emblematically termed "Governance and Civic Community," was conducted over a 20-year period through various methods, from direct interviews to political leaders and to the main interest groups, to case-studies of six target regions (ethno-methodological approach), and from the legal analysis and socio-economic planning analysis to the final users opinion poll. The Sicilian case, compared with others of different regional healthcare systems, shows results far below the national average of the level of civic community, interpreted as a synthesis between governance ability, sense of ownership to the local community, and institutional and administrative performance of the regional public sector.

The structural weakness of governance and civic community is an element that preceded the consolidation of informal networks and the rise of free riding paths within the public healthcare system. Another piece of our research mosaic is provided by the studies conducted by Dente on local policies in Southern Italy. This work, on implementation tried to figure out whether there is a capacity differential in the policy implementation processes between Central and Northern regions vs. Southern Regions (Dente, 1992). Indicators of implementation abilities included the financial management of the local governments and of the local public enterprises, the personnel productivity of the local public administrations and the average length of the public procurement procedures. The research also included indicators of final-user oriented services, such as the water cycle, childrens' educational services and waste management.

Dente's conclusions pinpoint the North/South dualism in the political capacity for policy implementation. This may be explained by the lower presence and variety of networks, of a lower availability of information and knowledge management tools, and of a higher level of conflict between different players of the Southern regions compared to the North. Events we considered include North-South dualism in public policy implementation and the hindrances of financial and human resource management in Southern Italian public administrations. A third piece of the research mosaic emphasizes the importance of decision-making, managerial performances and quality of service in the local governments. Extremely interesting is the analysis of Rebora (1993) on the vicious circles that characterize local administration in Southern Italy. Our model was elaborated starting from the analysis of local government reactions in Southern Italy to the public administration reform initiatives that interested in the early 1990s. The model findings were also confirmed by research on the functioning mechanisms of the regional administrations in Sicily (Thoenig, Michaud & Dupuy, 1992). This model emphasizes the features of Southern regions, overwhelmed by administrative formalism and typically unable to detect the needs of their users and, more generally, of the preferences and behavior of various local socio-economic players.

This vicious circle results from the mix between rigid administrative models, only partially improved by the early 1990s reforms, and the social-cultural context they are embedded in, with a low perception of efficiency and productivity values. The prevalence of the tertiary sector, and, particularly, of the public tertiary sector – the main employers in most Southern Italian cities are the municipality and the public hospitals – did not allow the development of professional resources and managerial skills from the industrial sector. In other words, the system missed opportunities for cross-fertilization among public sector, businesses and no profits (Thoenig, Michaud & Dupuy, 1992). This analysis shows a direct link between the growth of public sector coupled with processes of de-industrialization and a consistent decrease of local competitiveness, and other elements such as the diffusion of free riding in the local governments, the strengthening of professional and union lobbying, and, chiefly, the shift of users from the public sector to the private and the non profit sectors.

The modest quality of the delivered public services and the progressive weakening of public administration performance determined the migration of high-level targets of users, a threat that would normally push the administration to change. However, the rigid administrative culture, the scarcity of managerial and professional resources, the weakening of the mission in terms of production and of service towards the community, coupled with the raise of free-riding phenomena all resulted in administrative failure. Also, some players, external and, even more, internal to public administration in Southern Italy, promoted and managed a utilitarian approach to the use of public resources. By strengthening alliances and reciprocal protection agreements, these players enlarged the scope of control over recruitment and procurement. In this regard, the public healthcare system has been a laboratory for the development of free-riding practices, which in some cases led to positive results, such as the case of excellence centers.

Finally, the forth piece of our research design mosaic is the contribution of the CERISDI-FORMEZ[1] (1993) analysis of the features of the Sicily regional healthcare system. As presented in the second section of the chapter, the findings of this research offer an interpretative model not limited to the public healthcare sector or to the case of a single region, but rather that can be generalized to help explain the differential in policy making, policy implementation and administrative capacity of the different Italian public administration systems at regional and local levels. From 1990 to 1992 CERISDI carried out a research project on benchmarking among the Italian regions, *de facto* divided into three sub-systems: Northern, Central and Southern regions. This research focused on the drivers of players and stakeholders, on the obstacles at the local level and on the organizational culture. The methodology included cognitive mapping. The research also focused on the systems of regulation, of functioning and of exchange at the local level.

The project was permanently subject to the auditing of an international scientific committee (see Annex 1) and different teams researched five issues:

- competition system and managerial behavior in the tourism sector;
- socio-economic development of industrial areas (e.g. the Catania industrial pole);

- organizational and managerial change in the local public healthcare sector (Sicily, Apulia and Abruzzo);
- competition system and managerial dynamics in the agriculture and food sector;
- organizational structure and functioning mechanisms of the Regional Directorate for European Union Relations.

The introduction of interpretative models on the functioning mechanisms and principles of the public healthcare system in Southern Italy must be framed with more general considerations. The case of the Sicilian healthcare system, its internal organization with an important role played by the informal actors and informal relations, might look at a first sight like an impenetrable micro-climate with its own equilibrium, rules, functioning mechanisms. Yet, we think its uniqueness should not dissuade us from a deepening the analysis, by framing the Sicilian experience in the ongoing debate about the impact of the administrative reform on the formal and informal relations of its sub-systems. To accomplish this end we considered:

- managerial leadership;
- ethics in the public sector;
- informal networking.

First, an aspect we take into account is the evolution of the role *of public entrepreneurs* and public managers, rethinking the interpretative model of entrepreneurship in government elaborated by Doig and Hargrove (1990). An important point made by this work is the concept of entrepreneurship as focused on turning new ideas into successful business ventures and that this model is *not* well suited to understanding the management challenges of large-scale public enterprise. This work recognizes the role of experimenting, but notes the bulk of the success factors are in the area of the difference of individual leaders in the evolution of substantial public programs over decades. The model conceptualized the role of political executives as entrepreneurs, depending on the two variables "managerial skills" and "commitment to program goals." The combination of low and high scores on the two variables gives birth to different profiles, from administrative survivors to generalist managers, from program zealots to program loyalists (Doig & Hargrove, 1990, pp. 47–67).

What seems to be lacking in the model is the ethical dimension, which should permeate and shape political executive action and also inform the commitment to program goals. The closest mention of ethics is the enthusiasm for the public program – but this downplays and simplifies the role of the ethical dimension.

Still, the value of the Doig and Hargrove approach is confirmed by an analysis by the research group CERISDI of the prevalence of hospital conflict between administrative staff and physicians in Sicily (CERISDI FORMEZ, 1993). This analysis shows that the administrative staff performed bureaucratic management, worked according to logic of exchange in areas such as the recruitment or the systems of career advancement, and was held responsible for effectiveness of selected areas. Such behavior is common among "administrative survivors." On the other hand, the physicians traded a lower hierarchical position with the freedom of pursuing their own pet interests, such as exploiting professional opportunities in the private healthcare sector.

Additionally, the evolution of the concept of *public ethics* is critical to understanding our research approach. From Aristotle onward, thinkers have considered what is ethical, how does ethics relate to other aspects of life and whether there is only one ethic or ethical pluralism and relativism. These issues are part of our research particularly because we are interested in figuring out how to define public ethics according to specific features that conforms to "public" entities, as well as a way to translate public ethic principles into daily managerial decisions and actions of high level and street level bureaucrats in the Italian healthcare system.

This debate on ethics has a long tradition from Aristotle through the discussion of the role of the state and public officials in Locke and Kant, and has recently received a remarkable contribution by Dennis F. Thompson (1990). The main assumption of this work is that, ". . . the conflict between politics and ethics should not be understood in the conventional way: politics as a realm of pure power, governed by prudential prescriptions, and ethics as a realm of pure principle, ruled by moral imperatives" (1990, p. 27). This misconception would underestimate the complexity of our moral and political lives. Specifically, the issue of political ethics seems to be particularly relevant for our study, e.g. do public institutional ethics differ from personal and social group ethics?

There is one tradition of thought that casts the uniqueness of public official ethics, intrinsically linked to the political leadership, e.g. as detailed by Machiavelli. This conception, later modified and adopted by Weber, may be viewed as grounded in the claim that public official's decision making must be virtually beyond ethical limits (it may include the use of violent means) to achieve and enforce the public good. However, Thompson argues, ". . . the more typical moral choices of public officials are much less dramatic than the heroic tradition suggests" (Thompson, 1990, p. 29). The consequences of such demystification in the tautological definition of the character of political ethics turns out to be very relevant for the conceptual basis of this chapter. Public officials and their counterparts in private organizations spend most of the time making marginal choices among policies – typically with mixed moral intent and achieving only incremental change. In our view there should be no single system of ethics and there should be no protective aura around public officials' actions. We must link results and consequences to ethical responsibility.

Thompson notes that public ethical concerns include how we think and we act in relation to something called "the public good" (Thompson, 1990). The public good cannot be defined *a priori*, but must be measured in connection with how we negotiate it among all the other variables, leading to an intellectual and practical discipline that serves the *res publica*. Therefore, there is not one ethics recipe that can be replicated whenever needed, but rather we can adapt and adjust a broad range of intellectual and practical tools that give us the balanced mix of instruments for decision making and implementation. Thompson writes about criteria for making judgements, not particular rules or general theories, "... the criteria should be conceived as a set of factors that citizens as well as officials consider as they deliberate about decisions and policies" (Thompson, 1990). Our model tries to ground the need for accountability of public officials in terms of tools, whether based on education and training or on a system of incentives and punishments, which make public ethics something we can position through the logic of trade-off and of relative weight.

We have to acknowledge the dilemmas deriving from the representative character of the public office, which implies rights and obligations that ordinary citizenship does not share, or at least not to the same degree. The tension between the promotion of general values and of the distinctive values of official duties might not always be solved through a natural syncretistic solution, but rather may tend to identify professional duties as a top priority and, consequently, may cause violation of some "ought to be" shared moral principles. This problem inheres in the representative dimension of the public office known in Italy as "*dirty hands*." Moreover, *dirty hands* are often coupled with the problem of *many hands*, which pertains to the organizational dimension of public office, where players act together to support the decisions and policies of the government. The government can be thus perceived as a whole entity that does not allow ascribing moral responsibility only to the single official.

Finally, our methodology includes the concept of networks. The *network concept* in policy science research dates back at least to the early 1970s. In studies of the bottom-up approaches to management and in the intergovernmental relations literature (e.g. Scharpf et al., 1978), this concept has been used to map relational patterns between organizations to assess the impact of these patterns on policy processes. In these uses of the network approach to policy research, theoretical notions from the study of inter-organizational behavior are influential (Klijn, 1997). On one hand, the perspective builds on an interactive policy approach as an element of political science thought (e.g. Allison, 1971; Cohen, March & Olsen, 1972). On the other hand, insights from inter-organizational theory are applied (Aldrich, 1979; Levine & White, 1961).

The policy network approach focuses on the interactional processes between dependent actors and the complexity of objectives and strategies as a consequence of that interaction. An important element of such analysis is the context in which complex interactions about policy setting takes place. In an attempt to elaborate the institutional context of complex policy-related interactions, network experts have been inspired by the inter-organizational theory. A good example of the bottom-up approach may be found in implementation theory (Hjern & Porter, 1981). The point of the inter-organizational approach is that the environment of organizations consists of other organizations. To survive, an organization requires resources from other organizations, so there is an exchange process among players and a network of mutually dependent actors emerges. The theory gives substantial attention to the links between organizations and to the strategy to influence the exchange process (Aldrich & Whetten, 1981; Levine & White, 1961; Negandhi, 1975). Initially, the network approach was used to analyze complex policy processes in policy sectors (Rhodes, 1997; Wilks & Wright, 1987). In the 1990s, however, a number of new themes emerged in the network literature; including the notion that networks sometimes inhibit policy making while they also offer opportunities to facilitate policy making. This point is important for our study. The emphasis here is on the management of complex processes in networks (Kickert, Klijn & Koppenjan, 1997; Koppenjan, 1993). We give increased attention to the role of actor perceptions when explaining interactions taking place within a network, and we try to detect the influence of concepts grounded in organizational theory (Weick, 1979) and policy science (Rein & Schön, 1992). We draw on critiques of evaluation methods and criteria from a multi-actor perspective, and also investigate the concept of rule (Klijn, 1996; Ostrom, 1986; Ostrom, Gardner & Walker, 1994).

As noted, the network approach may assume that actors are often mutually dependent. Actors cannot achieve their objectives without resources owned by other actors. Interaction patterns among actors emerge around policy issues and resource clusters, and these patterns acquire a certain degree of sustainability because of the limited substitutiveness of resources. Thereby, rules are developed, regulating both actor behavior and resource distribution in the network. This also influences inter-network relations. Resource distribution and rules are gradually shaped through interactions (Giddens, 1984).

Thus, policy networks form a context within which actors act strategically and in which strategic action is confronted by the strategic actions of others. Series of policy-related interactions occur within the network. These series of interactions can be termed "games" (Crozier & Friedberg, 1980; Scharpf, 1997). The position of the players in the individual games is determined by their position in the network and by their strategic actions in the game. During the game, actors operate within the limits of established resources distribution and sets of rules. In addition, they have to operate strategically to handle the given dependence in the game so that they can achieve their own objectives. During this action, they must interpret the existing rules, which typically are ambiguous.

Policy process can therefore be seen as complex games between actors. Each of the actors has their own perception of the nature of the problem, of the optimal solution and of the other actors in the network. They select their strategies based on these perceptions, so that the outcomes of the game are a consequence of the interactions among strategies set by the actors in the network. This concept is crucial to understand our case analysis.

THE SOUTHERN ITALIAN PUBLIC HEALTHCARE SYSTEM: MANAGERIAL REFORM AND ORGANIZATIONAL INERTIA

This part of the chapter defines the characteristics and critical aspects of the refrom of the local public healthcare systems in the Southern Italy – and specifically in Sicily, building on field research conducted in the early 1990s that was updated in the period 2001 to 2003. The field research work focused on the changes that preceded and accompanied the second National Healthcare Reform (1992–1993) in three regions of Southern Italy, namely Sicily, Apulia and Abruzzi. The transformation process in these regions has been compared to the process that took place in some Mid-Northern Italian regions, looking for a link between possible performance differentials and different structural features of the healthcare sub-systems.

Our research focuses on two complex events that represent the main episodes of reform that took place in environment of the public healthcare agencies analyzed in the past 15 years. First, to set the context, we consider the 1992 reform of the National Healthcare System and the reform of the local governments during the 1990s. Then, we lay out our critique of the effects and consequences of failure of reform implementation in the Southern Italian healthcare system. Finally, we relate the second complex event, the emergence of no boundary agents and systems, and provide conclusions about the effects of this phenomenon.

The First Event: National Health Care System and Its Effects

The first complex event was the 1992 Italian National Health System reform introduced corrective measures to the previous reform that, in the late 1970s, established the NHS. The most relevant changes introduced by the 1992 law were the shift from local healthcare units (LHU) to local health agencies, resembling establishment of the Community and Hospital Trust in the United Kingdom NHS, and the empowerment of the Italian Regional governments in the healthcare sector, a move in reversal of the traditional, highly centralized Italian health system.

Before this reform, the 674 local healthcare units were highly complex organizations, due to the different services and markets they were asked to serve, from community care and GPs to tertiary care. Organizational complexity was also given due to the decentralization of the supply structure and, consequently, the service network, and can also be ascribed to the need for balancing clinical autonomy of the staff (typically the physicians) and the organizational rules of the firm. An example is demonstrated by one figure: among the 600,000 employees of the local healthcare units, 100,000 were physicians.

These elements were complicated by patterns of functioning mechanisms common to the Italian public organizations, such as the prevalence of formal rules over quality and results-based management, to the lack of managerial skills and tools, e.g. strategic and economic planning, human resources management, information systems. Among the expectations that the shift from local healthcare units to local healthcare agencies raised, is the reduction of complexity in the healthcare services supply policies. This was expected to work by focusing the activities of the 200 newly established local healthcare agencies (LHA) on core activities such as community care and outpatient services. In fact, the 200 new hospitals, resulting from the merging and downsizing of the healthcare agencies, ended up focusing on inpatient services – but this is only a small part of the story of reform consequences.

The reduction of the executives' roles and the introduction of one CEO, together with the elimination of governmental representatives and local lobbies as a result of the reform of the 1990s was a further element of the simplification of the complex decision-making and organizational structure of the LHUs resulting from the 1970s reforms. It is interesting to note that in the cases analyzed, the introduction of NPM principles in the 1980s and early 1990s did not exert a decisive push on the first complex event – the development of informal networks. Rather, as we demonstrate, such networks resulted from the combined effects of the weak external cohesion and the lack of dynamics that would reinforce internal cohesion.

Given this framework, the research sought to identify the critical variables that assured cohesion in the whole system, comparing Sicily to Northern region LHUs. These cohesion forces are related to policies of the Regional governments and the local authorities, to the behavior of the final users of the medical services, to the strategies of the private competitors and the local governments. On the other hand, the internal cohesion forces concerned the relations between managerial and physician parties, and the strategies put in place by the internal local subjects. The full research methodology and case study is not presented here due to space limitations. What follows are the conclusions based on the case analysis that included the study of both public and private health care facilities and the network relationships throughout the entire healthcare system.

Characteristics of the Southern Italian System: A Synopsis of Conclusions
Analysis of the Sicilian relationship system shows the structural weakness of what were supposed to be cohesive elements. First, the regional Authority does not use self-government and discretion according to healthcare system reform intent, and as a result ascribes the regional institutional level a leading and central planning role. The regional level is not performing that role in a proactive way, stimulating organizational and managerial innovation at the local level, nor at the central level, through a Regional Healthcare Program or a general development project. A critical element of the reformed system was supposed to be the participation of private healthcare providers.

The study of private healthcare reveals a highly concentrated system (50% of hospital beds located in metropolitan areas) providing non-specialized services in a system characterized by:

- The prevalence of family-type businesses that disregard development strategies at the corporate level (e.g. evaluation of make or buy strategies, strategic human resources management);
- The failure to appreciate organizational investments, confiding in the acquired competitive advantage, concerning mostly side aspects of the service (comfort, queues);
- The search for cooperative positions with the public healthcare system through the possibility of financing by the public healthcare system for services provided to citizens by the private structures;
- A lack of entrepreneurship, and low levels of risk taking, coping with greater attention paid to short term return on investment.

Therefore, the private healthcare system does not play the part of a "real" competitor to the public sector, *nor* the part of a synergistic partner in the development of services. What has resulted is an autarchic and collusive (between public and private) system – an almost perfect ecosystem for the development of informal networks.

The study of the healthcare system users showed a remarkable difference in the attitudes of Sicilian and North Italian citizens, mainly regarding expectations of public service and the capability to put up models and mechanisms of representing organizations (advocacy associations). Regarding Sicily, the public service was seen more as a favor or a special consideration of the public organization and less the due satisfaction of a need.

On the other hand, the Sicilian public healthcare organization didn't activate any complaints or information services to citizens or quality improvement projects, started in the early 1990s in most Italian regions (with Citizen Charters, and URP – an institutional communications and marketing specialized unit). Finally, the local authorities (Municipalities and districts/prefectures) contributed to the weakness of the healthcare system. The politically elected bodies are surely interested at building consensus; anyway this depends more on the ability to acquire resources (financing new infrastructures, hiring new staff) and less with the performances.

These dynamics are extremely relevant considering that, in the same time-frame, local government reform had been launched. This reform was aimed at reinforcing strategic, organizational and managerial capacities of provinces and municipalities, as well as at introducing New Public Management approaches, from managerial control to the diffusion of contracting out, contracting in and public private partnership.

The weakness of the external cohesion led the Local Healthcare Agencies to become no boundaries public organizations, characterized by a relationship system that doesn't promotes the development of a coherent institutional environment that halts the momentum of the healthcare agencies change process. On the opposite end, the diverging interests of the actors and the lack of regulatory mechanisms (performance accountability, co-interest of the actors on the quality, evaluation and penalization systems) represented a barrier to innovation and modernization. Furthermore, the lack of converging interests of institutional subjects is coping with strong "centrifuge pressures" inside the organizations.

The lack of internal cohesion concerns, the prevailing centrality of the administrative part of the organization, and the simultaneous weakness of the medical direction all were problems to be faced. It is not, however, the necessary contraposition found in every healthcare organization between administrative attitudes (obey to the norm and formal procedures) and professional ones (clinical autonomy, discretion research, maximization of the resources available). What distinguishes the Sicilian healthcare system is the possibility for the administrative staff to act as a single and powerful gatekeeper of resources in terms of hiring new staff, supervising times and ways of goods and services procurement, and controlling available spending.

Given the extent of the power of the administrative party, the roles of physicians could be "fine-tuned" by administrators in three different ways, accepting, in a first case, a low-level management, without exercising pressure over the administrative sector. In the second option the administrative staff could contract with the physicians the exercise of some flexible interpretation of the rules; this allows the employment of a strong organizational power, finding solutions to problems. In the third option physicians are equipped with the necessary skills and competencies to be self-sufficient without the support of the administrative department.

The centrality of administrative attitudes found in the Sicilian context is strengthened by the external environment with a weak governance role of region and the lack of pressures required for the improvement of the service's quality from local authorities, citizens and private health sector. Besides conflicts between healthcare professionals and administrative bureaucracy, managerial weakness determined an extremely low level of internal cohesion.

The Second Complex Event: Absence of Boundaries and Resultant Effects

The second complex event is the devolution of Italian Healthcare system that resulted from the implementation, over a ten-year period, of important elements of the comprehensive national reforms of the early 1990s. We characterize this event as the development of what we term "no boundaries" public organization that took place in selected public healthcare organizations as one result of the national reforms. A critical part of this story is the emergence and spread of "no boundaries" civil servants. These individuals are subjects inside healthcare organizations that serve important roles in other systems: in the local political system, in trade unions, in private healthcare organizations, in firms supplying goods and services.

These border roles increase the "centrifuge pressures" and the fragmentation of the public healthcare organization (resulting in many sub-organizations and sub-relationship networks carrying special and different interests). However, in some instances, these border subjects are the most dynamic parts of the organization, as they have managerial skills and can employ resources coming from different systems. In presence of organizational weakness, free rider behavior becomes stronger.

Thus, we find examples of chief physicians that increase the medical staff through their trade union membership or other services that have privileged access to technological equipment and are able to develop high specialties in a self-managerial way. These behaviors arise due to the inability to control and contrast the "centrifuge pressures."

Anomalies and Excellence Centers in the Sicilian Public Healthcare System
As mentioned, the presence of a weak institutional context promotes the rise of new managerial forms and the creation of excellence practices. Again, this is about a complex event observed in many realities mutually influenced by informal networks and free riding elements. There are many levels of intervention that

may explain the development of excellence centers in the weak Sicilian healthcare system, including the following:

(1) The capacity to limit the growth of new specialist services inside the hospital to contain the fragmentation pressures and the operative overload; this allows a progressive improvement of the existing medical special fields of activities;
(2) A decrease of the administrative power through the direct assumption of some key functions (equipment procurement process, the management of investment funds, contracting out) by the medical direction; the management procedures performed directly by the medical director, avoided the dependence from the administrative services;
(3) The choice to keep the hospital out of the integration process with other hospitals and local healthcare systems; the CEO was able to limit the interference of local political forces, conserving the institutional and organizational autonomy of the hospital;
(4) The support and promotion of excellence specialized centers inside the hospital, favoring the direct involvement of the physician chief department; instead of limiting managerial autonomy of the physicians, the medical direction has chosen to strengthen hospital power vs. the regional council;
(5) The University's link, organizing seminars and updating the physicians' knowledge, also reinforces their professional identity and improves the hospital's image both inside and outside the local context.

The building of excellence centers indicates how discretion in an informal relationship, combined with the fragmented power of free riders, can result in innovation. The leadership and managerial capacity of the medical system allowed a self-managed and self-organized development of hospitals, in clear contrast with a general non-innovative context.

Our research found other managerial practices that stimulated excellence islands inside the Sicilian healthcare system (e.g. in the Captain and Palermo Hospitals). Common features may be observed in these centers. First, there is the presence of relevant inter-institutional relationships created by single physicians, acting as border role agents. The unit responsible tries to build its own relationship network that goes well beyond the institutional boards of the public healthcare organization, maximizing the free-riding opportunities allowed by the environment. Also accelerated development processes, by knowing how to acquire additional resources, faster and easier than in the traditional procedures (new staff and equipment), and by promoting a virtuous circle with new access to resources. This led to greater development capacity of the units to the detriment of the other medical services, which got less competitive.

Finally, the development of excellence centers does not bring a diffusion of innovation or an emulation process, leading to a general growth of the organization. To the contrary, a passive attitude, not competing for resources and not innovation-oriented, of the other services is highlighted. This is why the excellence units do not find obstacles to their development inside the organization. On the external side, their success depends upon their capacity to build inter-institutional relations that promote access to resources through strategic interlocutors activated on an *ad hoc* basis.

Organization, Network Relationships, Behavior and Innovation

The study of the Sicilian healthcare system in the early 1990s and of the complex events noted leads to some general conclusions concerning the relation between organization features and actor behavior on one hand, and innovation in the development of modernization processes on the other.

The first consideration is the centrality of rent seeking in the context analyzed. The absence of the market and of competitive mechanisms implies for most of the actors the exploitation of present opportunities at the detriment of risk taking. The administrative staff prefers maximizing the discretionary interpretation of norms instead of reorienting its own role and functions to a managerial perspective. The private healthcare system prefers using its competitive edge on the public organization through collusive agreements instead of implementing development processes in the medium term.

Politicians and institutions prefer consensus building on the resources supplied to the system to the detriment of consensus on results. The medical staff employees their own relationship networks instead of becoming part of the organizational development model. In all cases, even the more entrepreneurial ones, individual action and rent seeking prevail on the capacity to implement collective action and development plans.

The institutional mechanisms meant to reduce uncertainty and promote transparency is weak; possible bottom up innovations does not find a structurally prepared system to receive and protect them. This system does not promote entrepreneurial behavior and risk taking. Individuals decode the context on the basis of their own personal standards and experience. Rent seeking is strongly correlated to the way actors consider risks and opportunities. In other words, rent seeking is a way to react to future uncertainty.

The consequence of this process is the progressive lowering of development and efficiency and economic rationale research levels. A systemic economic rationality prevails, coherent with a sub-optimal, strongly inertial development model. In such a system, modernization costs are far higher and time to development much longer. Such a phenomenon is determined by the establishment of behavioral paths that have worked in the past, not searching alternative solutions, even when they should be better referring to costs or quality of the public service.

Third, all processes analyzed evolved through increased fragmentation and a difficult transition to unique model. Who manages the fragmented system? The question is clearly provocative, because the answer is that only the system can manage itself. However, in the case of a system characterized by "centrifugal pressures" and a plurality of external relationship networks driven by diverging interests, any local action tends to reinforce the fragmentation instead of recomposing it. Finally, a system that resists change produces very evident negative externalities and higher implementation costs for the whole society.

CONCLUSIONS: FROM INFORMAL NETWORKS TO NETWORK MANAGEMENT

This concluding section attempts to answer the three questions initially posed in this chapter on how the reinforcement of informal relationships among the internal players and external stakeholders can shape the strategic and organizational reform of public healthcare organizations.

To recapitulate, our first question was: *how to include the "informal" dimension in public management studies*? We have addressed this question by the manner in which we have analyzed the Italian healthcare system in this chapter. Informal variables have been shown to be important to reform. The second question was: *how to identify the strategies that public organization could and should enforce to leverage the positive impacts, and to control the vicious circles that informal relationships tend to create*? The third question was: *how can the reinforcement of informal relationships among the internal players and the external stakeholders shape the strategic and organizational change of public healthcare organizations to create a better mix between public organization features and professional organization features?* We now attempt to answer questions two and three. Also considered in this section is how the introduction and development of new public management approaches attenuated the differences between two main categories of informal relationship, the no-boundaries organizations and the excellence centers.

To address these questions we rely on research reporting the evolution of Italian healthcare systems over a 10-year time frame, concentrating on the Southern Italian healthcare organization case studies initially analyzed by the CERISDI research initiative (1993). We begin by addressing lessons learned from analysis of excellence centers in the Southern Italian healthcare sector, and at the local healthcare agencies that we have characterized as no-boundaries organizations.

Lessons from the Evolution of Excellence Centers

The sixty local healthcare units (of the ninety in existence at the beginning of the reform period) were reduced through the decade of the 1990s to nine macro-healthcare enterprises operating in wider areas defined as *Province* territory. The mergers strengthened the balkanization process, with the passage from LHUs to macro LHAs (Local Healthcare agencies). By receiving staff, hospital and territorial structures from the previous LHUs, such enlarged organizations are forced to face a greater complexity. The excellence centers had completely different development trajectories. For example, the Cervello Hospital in cooperation with the Medical Center of Pittsburgh University started a partnership in 2000 for creating the Mediterranean Institute for Transplant and High Specialization Therapies, which became a pilot project of the Italian National Healthcare System (see the www.ismett.edu).

To understand the links between the reform – the nationally mandated new public management approach of devolution that drove the reforms beginning in the early 1990s – and emergent informal relationships in the Italian healthcare system, we focus on the roles of public leaders and managers based on degree of conformance to a model of entrepreneurship in government. Cross-border roles, no-boundaries organizations and balkanization of the public healthcare administrations – well-known phenomena of the 1990s – created a weakened institutional commitment, and complicated the identification of "zealots" and public program "loyalists" role players. The concentration of zealot and loyalist camps seemed to increase due in great part to the balkanization of the health care system. In summary, we found that the Southern Italian healthcare system to be dominated by characteristic regional organizational values, without much direction and managerial skills, strongly influenced by inter-institutional network management, the socio-political-institutional environment and procedural constraints (see Fig. 3).

Survival is a major value in Southern Italian bureaucratic culture to the extent that administrators/managers are not very interested in taking on cross-border roles. However, they have been positively influenced by the role models of the professional bureaucrats responsible for excellence centers, who generally operate autonomously from the LHAs organization, and the "burogattopardi," who are able to balance the different free-riding strategies, both ones with positive and those with negative impacts on the organization.

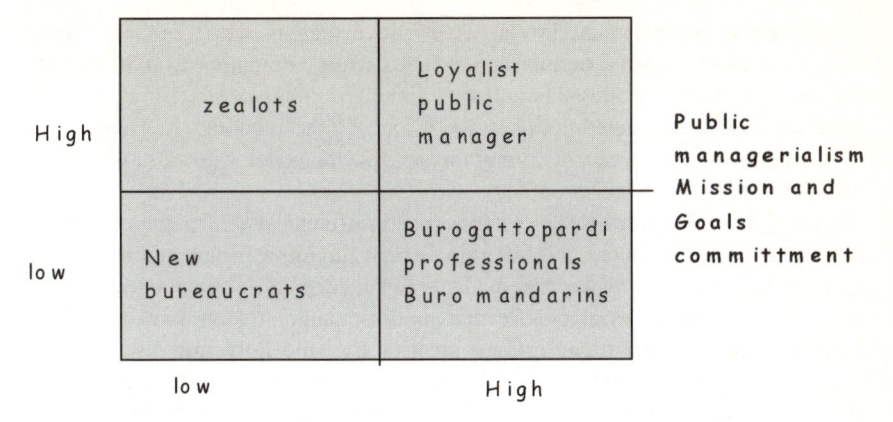

	low	High	
High	zealots	Loyalist public manager	Public managerialism
low	New bureaucrats	Burogattopardi professionals Buro mandarins	Mission and Goals committment

Interistitutional network management
Social political and institutional communications
Exploiting normative and procedural constraints

Fig. 3. Typologies of Managers and Professionals in Public Health Care Organizations. *Source:* Authors, 2003.

Based upon our analysis of case studies we also found that an important contribution to public management and public administration studies may be made through better understanding of informal networks by:

- a more accurate definition of leadership and management roles;
- identification of the relationships between leadership/management roles on one hand and interorganizational/intraorganizational networks on the other.

Another fundamental issue we assessed is how to build and maintain inter-institutional relations to ensure the success of excellence centers through the exploitation of the free-rider behavior and the continuing re-definition of public administration boundaries. The roles of the different players could be structured to facilitate the design and execution of strategies emphasizing the introduction of new public management approaches. Identification of the context and content of such strategies is directly linked to answering the second question posed in this work on the alternatives that might be enforced to exploit potential networking advantages while still governing carefully the critical parts of these informal networks.

One strategy to accomplish the task noted has been to act through managerial re-qualification of public healthcare organizations aimed at increasing the level of internal cohesion and progressively transforming the LHAs into more participative and "unitarian" type organizations. This strategy has required as primary leverage the involvement of what we have termed "zealots" (middle management at the administrative and medical levels) as public managers who "sell" and push reform of the managerial culture and systems while attempting to influence the delimitation of organizational boundaries. Extensive managerial training and ICT development are connected to this strategy. Despite the apparent attractiveness of this strategy, after ten years of trying, this approach has not seemed to work very well in our view.

Case studies show this strategy has induced different dynamics than intended. In local healthcare agencies interested in the merging/networking, and in creating no-boundaries status (Del Vecchio & Cantù Lega, 2001) to exploit the weaknesses of the existing managerial culture that resists change, zealots have interfered with innovation. Some organizations, such as Palermo Polyclinic (a university hospital), have succeeded as no-boundaries organizations despite the presence of selected zealots, through *ad hoc* use of managerial leverage. Such cases are interesting due to their high complexity in terms of functions carried out by their organizations (traditional hospital services plus university training and research), in organizational structure (12 departments including childcare, oncology, neurology and psychiatry, surgery and transplants) and in terms of internal stakeholder membership and participation (e.g. medical and academic professionals).

The no boundary strategy has focused on investing in internal "excellence islands," adopting new managerial systems, and outsourcing ancillary services including those for biomedical technologies. In addition, there was an openness to increased institutional fundraising and creating public/private partnerships to fund information and communication technology and emergency services. The excellence centers made instrumental use of such innovative arrangements to consolidate their position with regards to regional authority and the others institutional stakeholders so as to achieve greater autonomy and control over strategy setting.

Another strategy we identified has focused on the roles played by the mandarins, named here as "burogattopardi." Through their roles as professional bureaucrats, they have operated successfully in applying neo-managerial logic in institutional re-building and organization restructuring, and by exploiting the network management. New managerial systems and the development of new paradigms of public governance, as well as the integration of different cultures and reference disciplines (e.g. human resource management, ethics, philosophy, managerial sciences, economics and law) are illustrative of this second strategy, which indeed is more consistent with the demands of the Italian bureaucratic environment.

Coherence between this second strategy and the context conditions is witnessed in the fact that the primary agencies and managerial training organizations in Southern Italy openly refer to managerial models inspired by network management and network governance (e.g. in CERISDI; ISIDA of Palermo and the Sicilian High Regional School for the Healthcare Sector). This strategy is highly consistent with the dynamics encountered in the NPM-oriented modernization processes operating in the Italian public sector. Indeed, Italy represents an interesting experience in the international panorama in terms of obstacles to implementation of NPM principles through National guidelines. Our success stories of innovation diffusion were found most frequently in local government administrations, and to some extent in the National Healthcare Service.

Thus far, the issues of "innovation-by-law" and of bottom-up managerial reform have been the main themes of NPM research in Italy (Borgonovi & Meneguzzo, 1997). However, this research has not yet fully investigated the issue of the "three Italies," the "one hundred cities" and "North-South administrative dualism." All these cultural and related phenomena reveal great differences in terms of culture, functioning mechanisms and institutional performance of Italian public organizations. So, NPM research may be off to a good start but it has a long way to go to demonstrate significant results.

An evolution cycle of these trends appears to be taking place in Italy with passage from new public management logic to greater emphasis on increasing the capability and integrity of public governance systems, as well as the establishment in numerous local areas not just of better managerial leadership, but also of public entrepreneurship. Such changes have promoted and sustained innovation both in public services delivery and in process management. Moreover, this kind of leadership has succeeded in attracting more external players, such as those from the private sector and third sectors. This and the other strategies reported above provide evidence to answer in part the second and third questions posed in this study.

Finally, what have we found in our examination of cases and strategies regarding ethics in the public sector? The theory of political ethics recognizes the difficulties of identifying individual responsibility for duties exercised for others and with others. We have moved beyond the individualistic definition of ethical responsibility towards a network definition. We found that some network activities appear to break ethical norms by "going around" the established healthcare bureaucracy. Indeed, some successful entrepreneurs also violate social and organizational norms and sometimes even the law to achieve innovation. It seems clear to us based on our research that neither the national nor other levels of government, through the ever-present system of checks and balances, nor the citizens through their monitorial power, can dictate ethics for public healthcare officials. Rather, and this is essentially what we claim for the Sicily healthcare system, "... they should be held responsible for some decisions and policies that result from defective structures, not only those they could have corrected but also some of those that they could not have corrected" (Thompson, 1990, p. 47).

Where ethical standards have been violated, managers should be held accountable. If results are negative, responsibility and blame may be assigned to managers and proper sanctions applied. However, if the results of entrepreneurship are positive then who is to complain beyond those gatekeepers responsible for maintaining the traditional rule-oriented culture? Citizens want better and more services. Service providers want better production attributes, better service to citizens and private benefits, e.g. jobs and income. If these are obtained then the provider community will not complain. They care little about the rules or bureaucratic ethics. However, one problem remains. When networks engage in unethical behavior, who may be held accountable? The easy answer is all of the participants in the network. In reality, this simply does not occur. The characteristics of networks allow virtually all participants to avoid accountability in one way or another. Thus, here we have an area that deserves greater public scrutiny and increased public management research attention.

NOTE

1. In the late 1980s FORMEZ was launched as an operative agency of the Central government with the precise mission of ensuring a professional and permanent training for the Southern public administrations. FORMEZ developed three "excellence schools" of managerial training in the three Southern main metropolitan areas: Naples, Bari and Palermo. CERISDI developed a training program by integrating models of managerial education addressed to business and to the public sector, and by spreading a managerial culture among leaders, in order to enable them to effectively deal with socio-economic environment in which they were embedded.

ACKNOWLEDGMENTS

The authors wish to acknowledge the contribution to this chapter made through editing and rewriting by our colleagues Professors Riccardo Mussari and Lawrence R. Jones.

REFERENCES

CERISDI FORMEZ (1993). *Un modello pedagogico formativo per lo sviluppo manageriale*. Palermo: CERISDI.
Dente, B. (1992). Le politiche locali nel mezzogiorno: Modelli di legittimazione e meccanismi di policy making. Istituto per la ricerca sociale.
Doig, J. W., & Hargrove, E. C. (1990). *Leadership and innovation: Entrepreneurship in government*. John Hopkins Univesity Press.

European Foundation for Management Development: Managing for good governance in the public sector. 16th annual public sector conference Milano 2001.
Jann, W. (2001). *Governance: An issue for Germany*. Potsdam University.
Kickert, W. J. M. et al. (1997). *Managing complex networks*. London: Sage.
Kooiman, J., & van Vliet, M. (1993). Governance and public management. In: K. A. Eljassen & J. Kooiman (Eds), *Managing Public Organizations: Lessons from Contmporary European Experience*. London: Sage.
Meneguzzo, M. (a cura di) (2001). *I network nel settore pubblico*. Milano: EGEA.
Putnam, R., Leonardi, A., & Nanetti, R. Y. (1994). *Making democracy work: Civic traditions in modern Italy*. Princeton University Press.
Rhodes, R. A. W. (1997). *Understanding governance*. Open University Press.
Thompson, D. F. (1990). *Political ethics and public office*. Cambridge, MA: Harvard University Press.

PART II: INFORMATION TECHNOLOGY AND MANAGEMENT CONTROL STRATEGIES

6. MANAGING THE E-GOVERNMENT ORGANIZATION

Kuno Schedler and Bernhard Schmidt

INTRODUCTION

The emergence of electronic government is reaching considerable proportions in the developed world. It would appear that this new reform is consigning everything that went before it to the wastepaper basket of oblivion. This, however, primarily applies to the intensity of the discussions of and the publications about the issue. The concrete results of virtually all empirical studies available on the net show that practical development lags distinctly behind the possibilities of e-government that are being discussed and proclaimed. Kinder (2002) surveys "tele-democracy" (the term he uses for e-government, K. S.) in 31 European cities covering 14 states and shows that progressive city administrations in Europe are early adopters of tele-democracy with a diffusion rate of 72%. He admits, however, that the selection of the cities that were examined displays a considerable bias: it was conducted on the basis of assumed best practice. Moon (2002) looked into the rhetoric and reality of e-government at the municipal level in the United States and concludes that e-government has been adopted by many municipal governments, but remains at an early stage and has not yielded many of the expected outcomes that the rhetoric of e-government has promised.

However, these publications are among the few that have been written by academics to date. A large majority have either been published by governments (thus, for instance, the e-government strategy of the U.S. government, which is of considerable quality; U.S. Executive Office, 2002, or also U.K. Cabinet

Office, 2000) or by consultancy firms, which both have a vital interest in a positive development of e-government (thus, for example, Accenture, 2002; Andersen, 2002; Cap Gemini, Ernst & Young, 2002, and many others). The studies mainly focus on the websites of nations (e.g. Gartner Group, 2001; Jupp, 2000), states (e.g. Deloitte Research, 2000) and communities (Kinder, 2002; Moon, 2002). Supranational organisations, too, are examining the development on the Internet, among them the European Commission (2002) and the United Nations in cooperation with the American Society for Public Administration (2002). The world now has a picture of e-government as encountered by citizens on the Internet, which has been studied and confirmed several times over.

However, little is written about the interrelations between the implementation of e-government and the existing conditions in an administrative organisation although this is likely to be one of the most essential success elements for e-government. Ultimately, the same people who create value for the public in their administration in the traditional manner must now also help support the e-government revolution. In this chapter, we examine the internal and external administrative factors, which are conducive and inhibitive to the development of e-government. We develop a conceptual framework on the basis of existing experiences drawn from administrative reforms. With the help of a broadly based interview among public managers in the German federal government, we show that the elements that we have developed have a direct or indirect influence on the development of e-government. Finally, we deduce further research requirements, as well as consequences for practical project design.

THE CONCEPTUAL FRAMEWORK

The implementation of e-government is a management task that must be assessed in the overall context of an organisation and its environment. For the purposes of this study, we assumed that there are a number of factors, which exert a relevant influence on the implementation of e-government. Our theoretical concept in this respect was similar to that which backs the e-government strategy of the U.S. government (U.S. Executive Office, 2002): the opportunities of e-government result primarily from contact with the citizens, whereas the obstacles are predominantly placed inside the administration. The strategy paper is based on 71 interviews that a task force conducted with more than 150 senior government officials and discovers five barriers for implementation: agency culture, lack of federal architecture, trust, resources, and stakeholder resistance (p. 11). All these factors reappear in our study, but in a slightly different order.

The administrative organisation, which is supposed to introduce e-government, is placed in a more or less problematic environment. The perception of this environment as an obstacle to the implementation by the interviewees has an influence on the status of the development of e-government (Assumption 1). The sub-factors that characterise this environment are described below.

The soft factors of administrative organisation, such as inspiring leadership, trust and motivation, are absolutely central to the implementation of e-government. For this reason, they, too, have an influence on the development status of e-government (Assumption 2).

The third influence factor to be examined is the organisational condition of the unit, which is characterised by various enablers: incentives to change, existing structures and processes, a clear strategy of service orientation, as well as the preparation of the organisation by means of modernisation. The latter was called quality management since this is the term that fits the German situation. These enablers were also thought to have an influence on the development status of e-government (Assumption 3).

The political environment is typical of a public institution. On the basis of many interviews, we were able to assume that political involvement was of significance for the progress of an e-government project (Assumption 4).

Fifthly, it was clear from the start that these variables would probably show correlations but that the influence of the different factors would not necessarily have to be direct. It is conceivable; for instance, those political activities only have an indirect impact on e-government, namely through management activities (enablers). Something similar applies to the problems that can be perceived externally and which may be directly related to the problems that can be seen to result from a lack of soft factors – a comparison between challenges arising from systems in the environment with the possibilities of the organisation's own system. In other words: we suspected that the interviewees only identified a change in the environment as a problem when the soft factors of their own organisations did not appear to have been prepared for them.

Finally, there are many indications that there is a reciprocal influence between an organisation's soft factors and the management activities that lead to enablers. Management activities such as say, the introduction of a quality management system, change perception through the soft factors of a unit, but it can also be expected that managers adapt their activities to the perceived existing soft factors of their units.

This resulted in a theoretical correlation model for e-government implementation as represented in Table 1. This model now had to be checked. Before we move into the empirical part of this paper, we will describe the factors that were used and their substance.

Table 1. Factors for the Examination Model.

Factor Designation	Outline of the Subject Matter. The Interviewees Experience Their Environment in Terms of the Characteristics Described Below
Soft factors SOFTFACT	Personally inspiring leadership Personnel's readiness to assume responsibility Trust within the organisation Motivation of staff Image of the administration
Service orientation (as a proclaimed strategy) SERVIORI	Service orientation as the objective of reform efforts Clear ideas for an improvement of service orientation Service has priority within the eGov reform Ambitious goals exist for the development of the agency
Political involvement POLINVOL	Effects of the political steering level with regard to eGov implementation Identification of the political steering level with the eGov initiative Personal commitment of the political steering level
Project structures PROJSTRU	Supporting structures and processes Optimal distribution of the responsibilities for the realization of eGov Consistent involvement of the administrative management with eGov Integration of staff into the development and design of eGov applications
Quality management QUALMANA	Credible quality standards and success criteria Personnel action in accordance with quality standards Use of modern leadership methods Good cooperation within the unit
Resources (the lack of which is considered an inhibitive factor) RESOURC	High costs, problems with the financing of consultants General budget scarcity High costs of eGov Lack of personnel Lack of technical infrastructure
Incentives INCENTIV	Material incentives Recognition by the management Recognition by colleagues
External inhibitive factors EXTFACT	Security and confidentiality problems Legal barriers Lack of harmonisation with Länder and communities

Table 1. (Continued)

Factor Designation	Outline of the Subject Matter. The Interviewees Experience Their Environment in Terms of the Characteristics Described Below
External partners as a problematic factor EXTPART	Dependence on external partners
	Political preconditions prevent cooperation with external partners Internal administrative resistance to external partners
Market assessment MARKASS	Lack of demand Digital divide
Perceived quality of the reform concept QUALCONC	Uncertainty regarding feasibility Substantial concept deficiencies
Project development PROJDEVE	Duration of the presence of the topic in the organisation Development status in relation to other units of the administration
Internal use of eGov solutions INTUSE	Intensity of the use of existing IT applications (10 items)

Source: Authors (2003).

Management Activities (Enablers)

Schmidt (2003) shows that the management of an administrative unit has a relevant influence on the development of e-government in that it becomes active in three different fields of intervention: strategy, in the sense of setting objectives and the course of the project; the establishment of structures, such as the organisation of structures and processes, but also rules and incentives; and capacity building in the sense of extending the organisation's potential possibilities of action. These activities are not conducted in isolation from each other but should be adapted to each other as finely as possible. It must be the goal of management to act in all these areas in as integral and consistent a manner as possible (also Schedler & Proeller, 2000). As the fourth element in this heuristic model, administrative culture also has an effect on the development of e-government; this, however, can only be established by management to a certain extent. For this study, the factors were not defined according to these intervention areas but according to packages of measures, which are supposed to have an effect on all these areas.

Quality management: to what extent have quality management measures already been implemented and are actually taken seriously by the staff? This factor is regarded as an indication that the organisation has already dealt with elements of modernisation and that it has also reflected on the notion of quality.

Incentives: what is the extent of the incentives for members of staff who are actively committed to change within the framework of e-government? The assumption is that the management will achieve two goals by creating such incentives: firstly, the staff will be motivated by the incentives, and secondly, the management will be emitting a clear signal that it supports the project.

Project structures: to what extent are the structures of the project and of the unit suitable for the implementation of e-government? This is the factor through which the management's activities in the design of the organisation can be integrated into the study.

Service orientation: to what extent is service orientation a relevant component of management strategic statements? Since we assume that during the early implementation stage, e-government primarily aims at an improvement of the services provided for customers, it was mainly against the yardstick of this indicator that the management's strategic activities were assessed and integrated.

Soft Factors

To what extent does a lack soft factors such as motivation, the readiness to assume responsibility, trust, or a type of leadership that is personally experienced as inspiring constitute an obstacle to e-government? It was assumed for the purposes of the interview that in the somewhat bureaucratic administrative culture of the test object, the German federal administration, these soft factors would be unlikely to become an issue before they were discovered to be lacking with regard to the e-government project, thus jeopardising it.

Political Involvement

To what extent is the e-government project supported by the political level of leadership that the interviewees considered being relevant (i.e. as a rule, in their own ministries)? This factor was supposed to determine the particular significance of politics in the case of public institutions that carry out IT projects. Ingraham (1997) examined the role of politicians in the administrative reforms in the United Kingdom, Australia, New Zealand and the United States and discovered that "the role of politics and political leadership is linked to the various models of reform. More comprehensive and strategic efforts require great initial political leadership and will, but incremental efforts require more continuous political involvement." It has remained unclear to us, up to a point; to what extent the e-government reforms in Germany could be described as, "comprehensive and strategic efforts."

If the reverse conclusion can be drawn, namely that clearly recognisable political leadership points to comprehensiveness and strategic significance, then our study might provide indications with regard to this question.

Externals

Finally, we assumed that there was a whole range of external restraints, which could not be influenced by the public managers interviewed. Here, too, the selection was conducted in such a way that the questions referred to such external obstacles to the implementation of e-government in order to make the interviewees more aware of these factors.

Resources: to what extent is a lack of resources an obstacle to the implementation of e-government? Here, the focus was primarily on a lack of finances, a lack of personnel, and on the technical infrastructure.

External inhibitive factors: to what extent are factors inhibitive which, from the administration manager's point of view, must be solved by third parties, such as politics? These are security and confidentiality complexes, legal barriers, and a lack of harmonisation with Länder and communities. The latter are typical of this level of government and constantly present in a federal state such as Germany. Wollmann (2000) and Reichard (2002) point out that Germany has a strongly regulation-oriented administrative culture. Against this background, this factor is likely to have an interesting influence on the German federal administration.

External partners: what effect does (a lack of) cooperation with external partners have on the implementation of e-government? Here, the costs and the quality of cooperation with external consultants were taken into account. Saint-Martin (1998) examined the role played by management consultants during administrative reform in Britain and Canada and discovered that although external consultants have an increasing significance for the design of the post-bureaucratic control model, this still does not result in a uniformity of solutions, from which it may be inferred that public managers' attitude towards consultants is ambivalent: consultants may be necessary, but you do not let them foist standard solutions on you.

Market assessment: to what extent is the e-government market ready for the project in the first place, and what kind of impact does it have on implementation? We assumed that the interviewees would find customer enquiries and the question of the digital divide particularly significant.

Perceived quality of the reform concept: to what extent does the quality of the project constitutes an obstacle to the implementation of e-government? Public managers maintain that project quality cannot be influenced but falls within the competence of the project leaders. These items were therefore integrated into the externals.

EMPIRICAL FINDINGS: THE UNIT EXAMINED

German Federal Administration

This first part of the study design outlines the reasons why the German federal administration was chosen as a research object. In this context, the current e-government initiative BundOnline2005 is described.

The German federal administration with all its ministries and subordinate federal agencies was selected as a research object from a wide range of administrative entities. The main reasons for this are the current intensive efforts made there in the field of e-government. According to the benchmarking of the United Nations and ASPA (2002), Germany occupied sixth place worldwide with regard to e-government development at the time when this study was conducted, i.e. in 2001. It could therefore be assumed that recognisable experiences with the reform process were already in place.

The current BundOnline2005 programme aims to offer all the federal services on-line by the year 2005, while also creating a new form of service quality at the same time (Schily, 2001; Zypries, 2001). Since at present, comparable national initiatives at the highest levels are taking place in many countries, the study acquires a relevance that crosses borders. In the German-speaking area, this includes the Guichet Virtual or Virtual Counter in Switzerland (www.admin.ch) and the Amtshelfer or Official Helper (www.help.gv.at) in Austria. In connection with BundOnline2005, and deserving special mention, is the British e-government initiative "UK-online," which also aims to offer all the services on-line by the year 2005 and which also concentrates on customer orientation (U.K. Cabinet Office, 1999 and 2000, to be accessed through www.uk-online.gov.uk). Initiatives are also being pursued by Canada (www.canada.gc.ca), which intends to be the world leader in the field of e-government by the end of 2003, and by the American government with www.firstgov.gov.

The top administrative level, or for federalist countries the federal level, is playing an important part in the implementation of e-government. Apart from the present international topicality of this issue, this is a further reason why this level deserves a closer look. The top level always sets the pace for development. It provides bearings, and it is a model for subordinate units. If an e-government solution should involve integrated portals in the final stages of its development, then the significance of the top level increases since it must coordinate the integration of subordinate administrative levels. In this context, it sets standards with regard to services and technology. The importance of a jointly coordinated course of action has been recognised. Thus, according to a study by Mies (2000, p. 8), 72% of German cities have called for a national e-government strategy.

However, the service aspect is also relevant to the federal administration. Renner (2002, p. 13) finally identified 376 services which were suitable for provision on the Internet and which were provided by 130 ministries and agencies. They include customs declarations, the approval of pesticides, the allocation of research funds, the granting of patents, the processing of applications, and services provided by the Federal Statistical Office. There are both external and internal customers for these services in all the cases. It therefore makes sense for the federal administration to direct the focus of their reform processes, and particularly of the initiative BundOnline2005, on an improvement of service quality. The federal administration examined in this study includes ministries and all their subordinate agencies, which in turn consist of superior and intermediate government agencies and other institutions.

BundOnline2005 e-Government Initiative

The BundOnline2005 e-government initiative is also directed at the federal administration as a whole. It is still relatively new. In the context of a programme entitled *Aktivierender Staat* or Activating State, the Federal Chancellor announced the initiative on 18 September 2000 with the goal of making all the services capable of provision on the Internet available on-line by 2005. This goal is supposed to be attained by a task force with the name of "Modern State – Modern Administration," which is part of the Federal Ministry of Internal Affairs. At its core, the initiative consists of 18 model projects and the services portal of the Federal Republic (www.bund.de) with the form server, which came on stream in March 2002. The aim is a standardised supply of services, with the focus on user-friendliness and quality. Uniform technical standards are supposed to be developed for this purpose.

An implementation plan was presented in December 2001 (German Ministry of Internal Affairs, 2001). This plan comprises a prioritisation of services in the form of a rollout plan, proposals for the use of technical components and for the determination of the necessary financial resources. It is intended that a central coordination of activities should be insured within the framework of the implementation plan in order to achieve an integrated overall architecture and to increase the efficiency of the programme through the central provision of basic components.

The schedule for the introduction of the services is a function of the time at which the basic components are made available and of the duration of special and specialised applications. More than 60% of the services will thus only go on-line in the years after 2003. At the time of this study, only 21 services were fully available on-line. The overall funding required from the project for the years 2002–2005 amounts to some € 1.65 billion. About 90% of these resources will only be required in the years 2003–2005. In 2005, this will result in recurring costs of € 300 million per annum (German Ministry of Internal Affairs, p. 46). Conversely, it is expected that the system will generate savings to the tune of € 400 million. However, the € 100 million will only be saved if the applications are used adequately (Renner, 2002, p. 13). In purely financial terms, the project does not appear very attractive at this time. Nonetheless, it is making continuous progress, as the fact that a "form server" being opened on schedule has proved.

Random Sample and Returns

In the federal ministries, questionnaires were sent to all the heads of departments and sub-departments, i.e. to ministerial directors and assistant directors, as well as to the heads of the budget, personnel, IT and organisation sections. In the federal administration, questionnaires were sent to the agency heads and their deputies and again to the heads of the budget, personnel, IT and organisation sections. This resulted in a population of 1274 questionnaires to be answered. Of these, 400 were sent to the ministries, and the remaining 874 to the government agencies. These figures constitute the basis for the determination of the return rates. They were the result of an adjustment to the overall number of 1515 questionnaires, which were sent out originally.

The ministries returned 160 questionnaires, which corresponds to a return rate of 40%. Considering the interviewees' status and the long time it took to fill in the questionnaire (about one hour), this result must be regarded as very positive. The return rate from the government agencies is also high: with 407 questionnaires sent back, it amounts to 46.6%. This is remarkable in that, like in the ministries, the questionnaires had been sent to managerial staff, which had not been provided with any incentives apart from the feedback from this study. No follow-up was staged to increase the return rate. Both areas taken together returned 567 questionnaires, which is tantamount to a rate of 44.5% (see also Tables A.1 and A.2 in the Appendix).[1]

The return rate according to institutions amounted to 87.7%, which must be regarded as very good indeed. Twenty out of the 163 agencies that had been contacted did not respond. The return rate thus covers a wide range of authorities. Nonetheless it must be assumed that the agencies that did not respond occupy a particular position with regard to the issue of e-government. Thus a slight bias must be expected, which, however, is unlikely to be of any consequence for the questions under review. After all, our study examines the individual perceptions of those people who are concerned with e-government.

METHODOLOGY

The research design consists of a quantitative, written main part and a qualitative part with a directed interview, which constitutes the substantial basis for the generation of the questionnaires.

In this context, the semi-structured interviews enabled us to make crucial progress in the demarcation of problem areas and the identification of the questions, which were of topical relevance. This is valuable because in the rather new field of research, which is constituted by e-government, only a few valid concepts and constructs have been developed on which research work can be based. In addition, the directed interviews served to test categories for the questionnaires to be drawn up, and to test their range. Moreover, the interviews turned out to be very helpful for the right choice of verbal expression in the questionnaires. At the start-up stage of the interviews, the interviewees were asked questions about current problems, their chances of success, and general experiences. After this beginning, concrete questions were asked according to the interview manual.

The main part of the interview was conducted by regular mail. The questionnaires were designed on the basis of the directed interviews. To begin with, groups of interviewees were established in detail. Then the relevant clusters of issues were defined, and corresponding hypotheses were generated, whose substance is covered by the questionnaires. The questionnaires consisted of direct and indirect questions, depending on individual issues. They largely extend to closed questions with the option "Other." Closed questions were primarily made possible by the extensive analytical work that had been done in advance. Since a number of interviewees are regarded as experts with wide-ranging experience, open categories enabled them to add supplementary information.

In the part that is relevant to this study, the interview exclusively worked with closed questions that could be answered in a five-grade Likert scale. The Likert data are treated as interval-scaled data, as is customary in social sciences. The data were therefore evaluated according to the corresponding method.

Table 2. Factors of the Model.[a]

Factors	α	Items	M	S.D.	Mega-Factors
QUALMANA	0.77	4	2.89	0.64	Management activities (enablers)
INCENTIV	0.69	3	2.28	0.72	
PROJSTRU	0.79	5	2.76	0.73	
SERVIORI	0.77	4	3.51	0.73	
SOFTFACT	0.85	7	2.94	0.74	Soft factors
POLINVOL	0.84	3	3.64	0.77	Political involvement
RESOURC	0.65	5	3.36	0.67	Externals
EXTFACT	0.56	3	3.05	0.74	(Cannot be influenced by management)
MARKASS	0.55	2	2.57	0.85	
EXTPART	0.63	3	2.49	0.68	
QUALCONC	0.72	2	2.92	0.79	
PROJDEVE	0.66	2	3.41	0.92	e-Government implementation
INTUSE	0.81	9	2.69	0.60	(Dependent variable)
EXTCLUST	N/A	N/A	2.93	1.03	

Source: Authors (2003).
[a] Extraction method: principal component analysis; rotation method: Varimax with Kaiser normalisation.

Independent Variables

For the evaluation of the data, the individual items from the questionnaires, which had been subsumed into certain factors, were tested by means of a factor analysis. The factors were named according to the conceptual bases described above. Reliabilities turned out to be good overall (Table 2). Generally, the evaluation was conducted with the statistics software SPSS, as well as with EQS.

Dependent Variable

Development status of e-government in the German federal administration.

To be able to represent the development status of e-government in the German federal administration, we had to carry out a characterisation of the various ministries and agencies. To start with, this was done according to purely organisational features. Depending on the range of services that are provided, the way in which they are provided, and existing contacts, the differences between the institutions are quite considerable in part. For this reason, all the organisations interviewed were asked questions as to the characteristics of these and other influence factors with regard to the development of e-government. A central position was occupied by the grading of the institutions according to the extent of existing e-government applications for the improvement of internal and external service quality. Institutions were graded according to their e-government facilities directed at the outside and according to the utilisation intensity of internal applications.

Having been characterised with regard to activities and contacts with external correspondents, the agencies then had to be graded according to their actual e-government development status. For this purpose, existing measures for external service improvement with the support of electronic media were registered separately from the questionnaire in order to determine a variable that was independent of the interviewees' subjective judgement. In addition to this, the externally directed applications of the first three levels of the most frequently used development grid were examined for each agency: information, communication, and transaction.

Agencies Internet presence was checked on the basis of the information available on the homepage. A distinction was made between basic information and comprehensive information with detailed instructions and explicit offers of help for citizens. Moreover, it was determined whether there were additional features such as multi-lingualism, newsletters and search functions, and whether users were able to register on the page. The availability of information also extends to the possibility of access to electronic archives and documents, and to an increase in transparency.

With regard to communication, it was established whether advice was given, and letters were answered, by e-mail. In addition, it was determined whether form downloads were available for part or the whole range of services. By transaction, we understood the filling-in of forms on-line. On-line orders for information materials were also regarded as a transaction, provided it was not simply carried out by e-mail. Here, too, it was determined whether the offer covered part or the whole range of services. Payment transactions were logged separately.

Apart from these core applications, the agencies were additionally analysed with regard to further services. This concerned the tracking of administrative processes on the Internet, and opinion-forming instruments such as fora and chats or ballot instruments. Questions were asked as to the availability of special offers for private enterprises, such as separate access channels on the homepage and the availability of specific information and contacts. This survey grid was used to examine a total of 18 applications related to external service quality. The number of applications that actually existed was determined for each of the 162 agencies that returned the questionnaire. On the basis of the assumption that the applications were of equal value, the agencies were graded according to this number.[2]

This resulted in a pattern of five groups, each with increasing degrees of intensity. With the help of the interviewees' answers as a control variable, this was used to develop a scale of five with as equal a distribution as possible, which was assumed to be interval-scaled in analogy with a Likert scale. The group characteristics can be outlined as follows:

Authorities of Group 1 do not have any electronic interface to the outside, or only a single website without a great deal of additional information. In individual cases, these authorities can be contacted by e-mail but do not have a website of their own.

Authorities of Group 2 mostly offer a combination of a simple website and communication. Some authorities in this group are slightly further developed: their websites offer more extensive information or very simple form downloads for individual services.

Authorities of Group 3 usually present a comprehensive range of information on their homepage and also offer additional functions. In addition, they often provide access to archives and more extensive download sections. Communication is also possible as a rule; a dedicated contact area has often already been set up for this.

In Group 4, authorities possess all the functions, which are not yet fully available in Group 3. In addition, the authorities in this group frequently offer transactions. Although this chiefly concerns simple orders or forms, the basic prerequisites are in place.

Group 5 offers additional functions such as chats and fora or specific offers for private enterprises.

The application of this grid results in a grading of institutions according to normal frequency distribution. This independent ranking of authorities was allocated to the individual responses, which made it possible for a statistical evaluation to be carried out. In order to be able to have a better view of the development status, two additional assessments by the interviewees were taken into account: the utilisation intensity of internal applications, as well as the relative progress of the project.

For the purpose of assessing utilisation intensity (the INTUSE factor), various internally directed e-government applications were assessed by managerial staff with regard to their utilisation. The result may be described as follows: applications are predominantly used for purposes of communication. On average, communication by e-mail and the transmission of in-house information through an intranet receive the highest rating. Already a significantly lower degree of utilisation was registered for applications such as the Internet as a research instrument, planning instruments, document management and knowledge databases. Applications of the higher development levels of e-government had hardly been used at all. Transactions, advanced training platforms and ballot instruments were not widely used.

Finally, the relative progress of the project (PROJDEVE) was examined on the basis of the interviewees' assessment of the duration of the presence of the topic in their units and of the development status in relation to comparable units. For the later evaluation, these three factors were subsumed in a group of independent variables in order to be able to paint a balanced picture.

RESULTS

As expected, all the independent variables display a highly significant correlation with the dependent variable, i.e. the development status of e-government (correlation analysis in the Appendix Table A.3). However, there are quite big differences in correlation strengths. The strongest correlation is shown by management activities (0.463**), the weakest by externals (−0.156**). For this reason, we were led to suspect that individual factors do not have a direct effect on the dependent variable, but only an indirect one. Following up this suspicion, we examined the interdependencies with a structural equation model based on EQS. In comparison with the theoretical assumptions, some of the results came as a surprise, but were plausible. On the basis of the co-variances of the various factors, the following was found:

Assumption 1, according to which there is a direct nexus between the environment presenting itself as an obstacle and the development status of e-government, must be clearly rejected. No connection of any kind could be proved. It became clear, too, that political involvement does not have any direct influence on the development status of e-government. Assumption 4 must also be rejected. Finally, there was no evidence of a connection between the soft factors and the implementation status (Assumption 2), which would have led to a reliable confirmation of the model in EQS. For this reason, these direct connections were given up.

However, Assumption 3 was confirmed with a high correlation (0.73*), which means that the totality of enablers displays a significant connection with the development status of e-government in a unit. Enablers are the above-mentioned results of preceding management activities in the unit under review. According to the results of this study, the type of management activities that were undertaken in preparation for e-government to make the organisation fit for the impending change are directly decisive.

Assumption 5, which assumes that there is a connection between the factors, was also confirmed. It was shown that there is a significant nexus between political involvement and the enablers, i.e. the management activities (0.36*). This result is perfectly plausible since the interviewees were people in managerial positions in the German federal administration, who naturally always have to keep an eye on supporting their political superiors in their activities. Since politicians, however, are unlikely to interfere directly with the operative business of e-government, their influence on the development status of the project is indirect: they are part of the frame of reference for the management of the administration.

The soft factors display a similarly pronounced correlation. In the EQS model, they are reported with a negative co-variance (−0.39*) since the questions

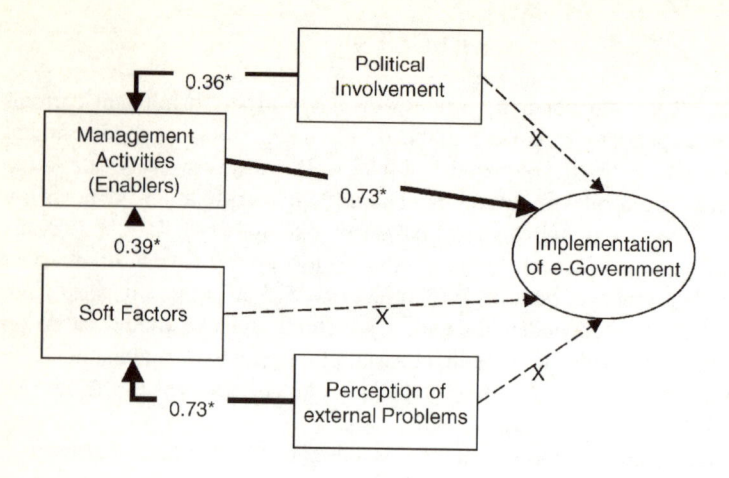

```
         ┌──0.36*──┐ Political
                   │ Involvement
Management ────────┘
Activities
(Enablers)        0.73*
                           Implementation
  ▲ 0.39*                  of e-Government
Soft Factors  ----- X -----
  ▲
  │ 0.73*       Perception of
               external Problems
```

Chi sq.=235.46 P=0.00 CFI=0.91
used software: EQS

Fig. 1. EQS Model with Correlations for e-Government Implementation Status.

concerned a lack of soft factors, which was regarded as an obstacle to e-government implementation. Thus the soft factors are conducive to the development of management activities but have no direct impact on e-government development itself (or rather, a lack of soft factors does not directly inhibit the implementation of e-government). These results come as rather a surprise, but are plausible. By way of a caveat, it must be said, however, that the above cross-sectional data will not allow for a prediction of causalities. The model only refers to the point in time at which the interview was conducted (Fig. 1).

CONCLUSIONS

This study reveals the interconnections as they are experienced subjectively by the public managers interviewed. It contrasts this subjective perception with the development status of e-government in their various organisations, which we verified objectively. The strength of the study is in the broad sweep of interviewees, i.e. public managers in the German federal administration, which at the time of the interview occupied sixth place in the world with respect to the implementation of e-government. On the other hand, it must be considered a weakness that at this point in time, we merely have one (albeit broadly based) set of cross-sectional data, which hardly allow for conclusions to be drawn in respect of impact thrusts. Moreover, the effects on public manager perceptions are limited.

Nonetheless, the available data still clearly indicate that the development status of e-government implementation correlates with all the independently defined mega-factors. However, a direct causal nexus can only be noted between the management activities and the development status of e-government. The other mega-factors would appear to exert their influence indirectly, i.e. through the management activities. In this study, we defined the following activities which a public manager is able to initiate within his organisation: a programme for quality management; the establishment of incentive structures, and particularly non-monetary incentives; the preparation of structures and processes for the implementation of e-government; and a clear shift of the organisation in the direction of service orientation, which we consider to be a strategic activity. All in all, this boils down to increasing organisational fitness for e-government.

How does this prompt a public manager to train his organisation to become fit for e-government? For one thing, his perception of the soft factors in the organisation has a significant influence: commitment on the part of the management, motivation of personnel, and a culture that is well disposed towards technology. The cross-sectional analysis does not reveal, however, to what extent these soft factors were shaped by the management activities themselves. The perception of the soft factors is contrasted with the directly correlated perception of external problems, which cannot be influenced. This combination results in the public managers' subjective assessment of their organisations' ability to solve problems, which evidently provides a crucial stimulus for management activities. As a whole, we gained the impression that public managers who are aware of their role as managers accord correspondingly more weight to these issues and thus exert a positive influence on the implementation of e-government.

Public administration has been markedly hostile to reform for decades. However, e-government may be part of a new reform generation based on technology that has achieved a recognisable degree of success. Future research should thus increasingly focus on factors that are conducive or inhibitive of reform to develop more and better general propositions about the reformability of public administration. In this context, data on the usefulness of league tables about government websites is limited and should be researched.

NOTES

1. These 567 returned questionnaires constitute the random sample ($n = 567$) for the observations that follow below. The n is smaller for certain questions which were not answered by all the interviewees. The overall answer was not removed from the sample because of this. On account of the large size of the questionnaire, this would not have made sense because too much valid information would have been surrendered. Additional

distortions from questions that were not answered need only be expected in individual cases. The influence of a failure to respond will be discussed from case to case.

2. If the applications were to be weighted, this would depend too much on the authorities' task profiles. For this reason, they are not weighted. The grading process thus reflects each institution's skills that may be relevant for an improvement of service quality.

REFERENCES

Accenture (2002). e-Government leadership. URL: http://www.accenture.com/xd/xd.asp?it= enWeb&xd=industries%5Cgovernment%5Cgove_welcome.xml.

Andersen (2002). A usability analysis of selected federal government websites. URL: http://www. andersen.com/resource2.nsf/vAttachLU/US_Fedl_Web_Usability_Study/$File/US_Fedl_Web_ Usability_Study.pdf.

Cap Gemini, Ernst & Young (2002). Webbasierte Untersuchung des elektronischen Service-Angebots der öffentlichen Hand. Ernst & Young. URL: www.de.cgey.com/servlet/PB/show/1005708/ eEurope.pdf.

Deloitte Research (2000). At the dawn of e-government: The citizen as customer: State government approaches to customer service. URL: http://www.deloitte.com/dtt/cda/doc/content/ at_the_dawn_of_egovernment%281%29.pdf.

European Commission (2002). Web-based survey on electronic public services. Results of the second measurement: April. URL: http://europa.eu.int/information_society/eeurope/2002/ documents/CGEY-Report3rdMeasurement.pdf.

Gartner Group (2001). 2002: Government in transition. URL: http://www.gartner.com/ 1_researchanalysis/focus/gov2002.html.

German Ministry of Internal Affairs (2001). BundOnline2005 – Umsetzungsplan für die E-Government-Initiative. Berlin: Bundesministerium des Innern, Stabsstelle Moderner Staat – Moderne Verwaltung.

Ingraham, P. (1997). Play it again, Sam It's still not right: Searching for the right notes in administrative reform. *Public Administration Review, 57*(4), 325–331.

Jupp, V. (2000). Implementing e-government – Rhetoric and reality. URL: http://www.accenture.com/ xdoc/en/industries/government/insightsissue2.pdf.

Kinder, T. (2002). Vote early, vote often? Tele-democracy in European cities. *Public Administration, 80*(3), 557–582.

Mies, H. (2000). E-Government: Eine Modeerscheinung oder digitale Revolution und Zukunft der Städte? Chemnitz: Price Waterhouse Coopers.

Moon, M. J. (2002). The evolution of e-government along municipalitites: Rhetoric or reality? *Public Administration Review, 62*(4), 424–433.

Reichard, C. (2002). Marketization of public services in Germany. *International Public Management Review, 2*(2), 74–82. www.ipmr.net.

Renner, U. (2002). Fahrplan ins virtuelle Amt. *Kommune, 21*(2), 12–13.

Saint-Martin, D. (1998). Management consultants, the state, and the politics of administrative reform in Britain and Canada. *Administration & Society, 30*(5), 533–568.

Schedler, K., & Proeller, I. (2000). New public management. Berne/Stuttgart/Vienna: Paul Haupt.

Schily, O. (2001, February). Auf dem Weg zu einer modernen Verwaltung. BundOnline 2005. Rede auf der Messe. *Effizienter Staat, Berlin*, 5.

Schmidt, B. (2003). e-Government und Servicequalität. Analysen zur Perspektive von IT-anbietern und Verwaltungsführung. Bern/Stuttgart/Vienna: Paul Haupt.
U.K. Cabinet Office (1999). Modernizing government. Modernizing government secretariat. URL: www.cabinet-office.gov.uk/moderngov.
U.K. Cabinet Office (2000). e-Government – A strategic framework for public services in the information age. Modernizing government secretariat, UK cabinet office. URL: www.cabinet-office.gov.uk/moderngov.
United Nations and American Society for Public Administration (2002). Benchmarking e-government: A global perspective. Assessing the progress of the U.N. member states. URL: http://www.unpan.org/e-government/Benchmarking%20E-gov%202001.pdf.
U.S. Executive Office of the President (2002). e-Government strategy. Simplified delivery of services to citizens, Washington, DC: OMB. URL: http://www.whitehouse.gov/omb/inforeg/egovstrategy.pdf.
Wollmann, H. (2000). Local government modernization in Germany between incrementalism and reform waves. *Public Administration*, 78(4), 915–936.
Zypries, B. (2001). Statement für das Forum 2 – e-government – auf dem Kongress OMNI-CARD, 16. January, Berlin.

APPENDIX

Table A.1. Return Rate, Ministries.

Ministries	
Population: public managers in federal ministries	489
Adjustment, including the exclusion of the Federal Ministry of Justice from the population	−89
Population: interviewees in ministries	400
Returns from ministries without Ministry of Justice	160
Return rate from ministries	40.0%

Source: Authors (2003).

Table A.2. Return Rate, Government Agencies.

Government agencies	
Population: public managers in federal government agencies	1026
Adjustment	−152
Population: interviewees in government agencies	874
Returns from government agencies	407
Return rate from government agencies	46.6%

Source: Authors (2003).

Table A.3. Correlation of Mega-Factors (Pearson).

	Management Activities	Soft Factors	Political Involvement	Externals	e-Government Implementation
Management activities	1 $n = 554$				
Soft factors	-0.412^{**} $n = 543$	1			
Political involvement	0.379^{**} $n = 523$	-0.193^{**} $n = 519$	1		
Externals	-0.255^{**} $n = 543$	0.568^{**} $n = 543$	-0.089^{*} $n = 519$	1	
e-Government implementation	0.463^{**} $n = 553$	-0.230^{**} $n = 546$	0.181^{**} $n = 524$	-156^{**} $n = 546$	1 $n = 564$

Source: Authors (2003).
*Correlation is significant at the 0.05 level.
**Correlation is significant at the 0.01 level.

7. REFORM OF PUBLIC MANAGEMENT THROUGH ICT: INTERFACE, ACCOUNTABILITY AND TRANSPARENCY

Hiroko Kudo

INTRODUCTION

Why reform government? The answer to this question varies relative to context and timing. Sometimes reform is stimulated by a shortage of financial resources. Sometimes it is brought on by a change in political power. At other times it may be forced by citizen demand. And, at times it results as a response to corruption and scandal. Moreover, in many cases, more than one of these aspects work together to push forward government reform. This is also why reformers adopt various strategies ranging from institutional reorganization, rationalization of administrative procedures, introduction of new managerial techniques, and more recently, implementation of e-government.

Recent examples of public management reform in different countries and regions demonstrate that the background and contexts of reform have many things in common. For example, member countries of European Union have been implementing public reform policies that include restructuring of government institutions and public organizations, modernization of budgeting process, rationalization of financial policy and its implementation, change of human resource management, renewal of public management and public service delivery, review of public/private

Strategies for Public Management Reform
Research in Public Policy Analysis and Management, Volume 13, 153–174
Copyright © 2004 by Elsevier Ltd.
All rights of reproduction in any form reserved
ISSN: 0723-1318/doi:10.1016/S0723-1318(04)13007-7

partnership, and use of ICT (Information and Communication Technology) to improve managerial process as well as communication better with the citizens. NPM (New Public Management) has become one of the most important conceptual bases for these reforms. Along with NPM comes increased demand and need for accountability and transparency, elements highly requested in European ICT integration. This process can be seen in various public administration reforms of the EU member states (Majocchi, 1997, 1998, 2000).

In the first part of this chapter, Italy is employed as an example of a "typical" case of traditional public management reform. The Italian case is not the most advanced public administration reform among EU member countries; however it shows most of the characteristics of NPM-oriented reform. On the other hand, in Southeast Asian countries, reform of public administration was implemented with similar methodologies but with different targets. In this chapter, Thailand and Indonesia are examined as two cases of e-government-lead public management reform which are different in their characteristics and their techniques from the Italian public administration reform. Asian cases show that their major issue of public administration reform is how to tackle corruption and clean up certain political relationship with public administration. Improving and rationalizing managerial aspects of public administration has second priority. The use of ICT is highly recommended in those plans, because of the need for transparency. In fact, e-procurement, e-bidding, and other uses of ICT for the administrative procedure guarantee the transparency and leave no room for corruption.

In fact in Thailand, the newly instituted Anti Money Laundering Organization (AMLO) is becoming the symbol of the new public management, using ICT and adopting new methodologies, enabling the top priority of tackling the corruption. In Indonesia, different techniques have introduced to its administrative procedure to fight against corruption, to improve transparency in the government and thus, to enable public management reform.

This chapter first introduces three empirical cases; Italy, Thailand, Indonesia, focusing on background of the reforms, major issues and targets of the reforms, paying attention to priority, policy formulation and its implementation process, implemented methodologies, and citizen involvement. The Italian case shows the common characteristics of public sector reforms; the latter two cases represent e-government-oriented public management reforms.

Second, analysis is directed to understand the state of e-government among above-mentioned Asian countries, and a theoretical explanation of information and networks in organizations is provided. Focus is placed on background of policy, major applications and enabled services, issues and priority, impact on public management, management structure of public service delivery (outsourcing, contract out, etc.), relationships such as G to G (government to government), G to B (government to business), G to C (government to citizen), and in particular, use of ICT to tackle corruption. E-government is one of the strategies of public management reform and is widely utilized in Asian countries. General NPM reforms utilize various strategies to manage their public policies. However, e-government is a public policy that directly affects other policies and leads to radical and structural changes. Its characteristics as public policy are different from those of other policies, especially government regulation.

ELEMENTS OF GOVERNMENT REFORM

Restructuring of government institutions and public organizations has become one of the classical methods of reform and widely implemented in many countries. However, recently, reorganization and/or restructuring does not only mean merger among different institutions or rationalization of organizations. It also includes outsourcing and/or privatization of certain function of public institutions, creation of agencies, and introduction of different forms of public-private partnership.

Modernization of budgeting process is another important reform for government and public institutions in general. This reform has been frequently tried and partly implemented in developing countries, where economic and financial transparency, accountability through decision-making process, and prevention of corruption are key issues to be achieved and guaranteed by authorities to get financial support from international organizations and banks (Ateetanan, 2001; Ishak, 2001). Introduction of a more rational accounting systems, including accrual accounting in the public sector, has been combined with public management reform. Kudo (2001c, d, 2002) and Badan Akuntansi Keuangan Negara (2000) relate experiences in pubic finance reform in developing countries. Furthermore, rationalization of financial policy and its implementation has been recognized as a crucial factor for more pragmatic and practical public sector management. Financial policy used to be influenced by the political background of the government and, thus, by ideological stance. However, for more efficient and effective governance, which requires innovation and creativity, pragmatic and strategic policy is needed instead of ideological and political driven measures.

Human resource management is another field that has experienced radical change. In the past, human resource management in the public sector was a product of political compromise under social pressure. Historically, public employment had the function and characteristics of labor policy.

Renewal of public management and public service delivery has become an important trend in public sector reform recently. NPM was introduced into the traditional type of public administration and changed its managerial style with a series of techniques delivered from business management. Customer-oriented and/or outcome-oriented thinking has been introduced in policy making and implementation processes. Reform in public service delivery, affected by these orientations, forced public sector organisations to outsource some functions, privatize its enterprise, and to revise the role of government in accordance with the role of private sector and civil society. Public-Private Partnership (PPP), Public Finance Initiative (PFI), other forms of collaborations became alternatives to traditional government restructuring. This trend is now evolving into the "governance model," i.e. with more emphasis on integrating politics and management rather than relying merely on introduction of new management techniques.

Introduction and use of Information and Communication Technology to improve managerial processes as well as communication to/with the citizens is a key factor for a successful e-government policy. It first developed as a tool for better governance in terms of efficiency in office work, data processing and dissemination. However, now it is recognized as an important tool of communication between government and its stakeholders, providing interface among them. E-government has become one of the most important elements for the public sector reform, as it promises transparency, accountability, and interface with citizens, access to information, and good governance, including prevention of corruption Chan (2001) and Tan (2001) show that Singapore and Malaysia enjoy the leading position in ICT use in government in the Asian region. In fact, when the need for accountability and transparency is highly requested, introduction of e-government is a common strategy.

THE ITALIAN EXPERIENCE WITH PUBLIC SECTOR REFORM

In Italy, the Central-Left coalition government led by the President of the European Union, Prof. Romano Prodi, came into power in 1996 and launched and implemented policy on public administration reform for five years. The reform aimed to restructure government institutions and organizations, rationalizing public corporations, outsourcing public services when needed, improving the managerial capability of the public sector, and reviewing financial and personnel resource allocation. Accountability and transparency became the keywords of the reform, which was the top priority of the government as it was about to join the common currency system of the Union. Different measures were taken to "clean up" political scandals and dark images of corruption and the underground economy. Use of ICT in taxation system (on-line declaration, e-payment in the near future) and in procurement process enables financial rationalization as well as transparency.

Participation of citizens in policy processes became more common, supported and enabled by use of ICT.

After five years of continuous effort, its reform brought significant results not only in the field of public administration in a strict sense, but also to the political sphere in general. Improvement in the quality of public services and policy management is the major achievement, which changed the relationship among stakeholders in public life and restructured the managerial and financial aspects of government.

Political Agenda: Accountability and Transparency

The most crucial issue at 1996 Italian general election was EU integration, and in particular, the introduction of a common currency which was already scheduled. At that time, Italy was one of the countries that were not guaranteed for the first group to enter the Common Currency System, because of its high public debt, inflation, and other economic indicators required as standards for entering the Common Currency (Bernasconi & Marenzi, 1998). In order to achieve the target to be accepted in the first group of EU economic integration, Italy not only needed to restructure its financial, economic policy and institutions, but also public administration and political institutions themselves (Bianchi, 1996, 1997, 1998, 1999, 2000; Bernasconi & Marenzi, 1998; Majocchi, 2000).

Improving accountability and transparency of public institutions was the most crucial issue for the government in order to gain faith from other countries. Political scandals of early 1990s seriously damaged the image of the country toward the international society and the recovery from this negative impression was given the highest priority. The government launched series of reforms of public administration. The technocrat government consisted of professionals of public management, financial policy, governance, social policy and so on. The public administration reform designed and implemented by Franco Bassanini, an administrative science expert and the Minister for Public Function in the Prodi Administration, was aimed to restructure government institutions and organizations to improve their efficiency, rationalizing numerous public corporations, outsourcing public services, improving managerial capability and reviewing financial and personal resource allocation.

Successful reforms in public administration and its transparency affected the political relationship with other government institutions. Decentralization not only improved the managerial skill of local entities and rationalized their financial situation (Arachi & Zanardi, 2000; Fraschini, 1997, 1998, 1999), but also contributed to improve transparency of certain interest stakeholders. The impact of reform forced the political actors to change their behavior and improved relationship between bureaucracy and politics. Political reform was not as advanced as was planned. However, the impact of public sector reform was so significant that it affected Italian politics.

Furthermore, policies to implement ICT became more frequent, first among local governments, then through specific agencies, and lastly among central administrative organs. With the spread of ICT use among the public, it is becoming more and more common to use ICT for public services in general. For example, ICT is used in taxation where it is already possible to do on-line declaration, and e-payment will be possible in the near future. The system improved the speed and cost of transactions and of controlling procedures, as it can be done electronically to a certain extent. E-procurement processes have enabled financial rationalization as well as improvement in transparency. Finally, participation of citizens in the policy process became more common, supported and enabled by the use of ICT.

Restructuring of Government and Managerial Reform

Public administration Reform of the Prodi Administration can be divided into some phases according to the policies and measures taken (Presidenza del Consiglio dei Ministri, Dipartimento della Funzione Pubblica, 2001a). The most crucial issue for the government was financial restructuring. Prodi appointed Vincenzo Visco, a public finance expert, as the Minister of Finance and he started a series of reforms in public finance. His main target was to overcome the problem of high public debt and restructuring the public finance system, focusing on financial decentralization, simplification and modernization of fiscal systems, and privatization and outsourcing of public functions (Bordignon, 1997; Fraschini, 1997, 1998, 1999).

A series of privatisations in the last half decade brought more investment money into the governmental sector. Major public companies, including development agencies and institutions, energy companies, banks and other financial institutions, and transportation companies, all of them at both national and local levels, have been privatized or are on the privatisation track. Privatization has not only brought private money to the public sector, but also changed the management style and thus the efficiency and performance of what were formerly public companies. This change has been influencing markets positively, as the number of competitive actors has been increasing. The energy business has been restructured and now functions more like a market. Financial institutions are now facing reorganization; it is likely they will become more independent in the near future.

Public sector reform promoted by Public Function Minister Bassanini included reorganization of central administrative institutions, revision of their functions, creation of agencies and delegation of functions to them, and outsourcing. Cassese and Galli (1998) and Gambino and Moschella (1998) relate institutional reforms and related policy change, revision of public servant system, introduction of managerial tools in the public sector management. Azzone and Dente (1999) point out the importance of policy evaluation for better governance. Pajno and Torchia (2000) explain managerial aspects in government, simplification of administrative procedure, rationalization of operational process. Arsi, Coronas and De Luca (1998), de Caprariis and Vesperini (1998), Paparo (2001), and Vandelli (1999) relate decentralization and delegation of functions to decentralized institutions. Fossati and Levaggi (2001) also detail the issue of political devolution, information disclosure, and utilization of ICT.

Different managerial tools were introduced such as; policy assessment, analysis of regulation impact. Fossati and Levaggi (2001) also deal with the question of political devolution, performance measurement, policy evaluation, best practice, rewarding by award and prize, customer orientation, customer satisfaction, accrual accounting, and performance based program budgeting. Charters were introduced in most of the former public company turned enterprises to make their missions clearer. In local governments, citizen's charters became more common.

These reform strategies can be classified into two categories according to their tools. The first includes decentralization, delegation of functions, outsourcing, and privatization, aiming at "slimming" the public functions towards a "smaller government." The second is the introduction of e-government, enabling more efficient management of public institutions and better communication with citizen and business. The second is of interest and relevance to this study.

E-government to Improve Communication and Management

E-government projects started in several local governments as experimental tools of communication with citizens, businesses, and other local and national administrations. Some advanced local authorities created community ICT networks including all stakeholders, as well as internal networks for the management of public institutions. They have been trying to improve their decision making process by using the advantage of networks and related ICT tools. New databases and networks, data processing and dissemination, electronic filing systems, documents exchange systems, decision making supporting tools, electronic procurement, electronic declaration and application systems, and other tools have been introduced to enable more efficient, more cost-oriented, more performance based, more user friendly, and more transparent public administration. However after many years since the first experiments, there is still a very small number of municipalities experimenting with ICT tools. Also, in those municipalities with ICT networks, the utilization of networks is often limited to exchange of e-mails and providing one-way information. Only few are successful in constructing two-way and/or multi communication, in realizing transactions, and in utilizing ICT networks for management. The government has been promoting and sustaining the projects of municipalities. However, financial and human resource problems have been keeping local governments from implementing potentially effective experiments. Local political interests are usually against the introduction of ICT and few citizens are keen for this innovation.

In theory, the advantages which should be brought by e-government projects and related tools, should influences not only the managerial aspect of public institutions but also their communication with stakeholders. User friendliness means better communication and more participation of users and/or consumers, that is to say, citizens to the policy-making process of the government and other public institutions. Better communication improves transparency and accountability of public organizations and thus enables democracy. This is considered to be the target of e-democracy.

In order to promote electronic participation, development of local network was and remains the first step and, at the same time, the key issue. Recently, on-line tax declaration and on-line application for permission, licensing, and documents, and also electronic voting and electronic service delivery have been developed and have been to some extent influencing decision making processes. When these are implemented on a wider scale, processes of democracy may change in characteristics. However, in central administration, utilization of ICT is limited to certain policy areas and these single initiatives are without overall coordination.

Information disclosure improves transparency and fairness in this process. In fact, e-government can serve to a certain extent transparency and accountability of administrative and financial systems. ICT has been encouraging a new civil servant system, which is now characterized by political appointees, private contract professionals and managers, part-time workers, tele-workers, contracting-out and so on. The wide variety of workers, planned to be introduced and partly introduced to civil service, can be a strategic tool to enhance new public management. However, there needs to be a certain infrastructure to support the new forms of labor, and e-government is expected to provide this base. At the same time, the characteristics of e-government have influenced human resource management and have been changing informal relationship in organizations. Surveys conducted recently by the Ministry of Public Function show clear evidence of the strong influence of the introduction of ICT on public servants.

When it comes to the relationship between public sector and private sector, especially private enterprises, e-government has been contributing to more efficient and more communicative interfaces. Information and communication technology helped different stakeholders to come to and join the same networks of information and knowledge, thus enabling them to share values and policies. This is now developing towards a "governance model" of public management, as noted. The concept of a "governance model of public administration" or "public governance" derives from the concept of corporative governance, and refers also to policy networks, and includes traditional privatization, PPP, and/or PFI. The "New Governance" and policy network theory are usually the basis of this approach. Rhodes (1997) and others introduced the policy network and "governance" concepts, while "New Governance" is referred to in Salomon (2002) as the tool of "Third Party Government."

The result of all of this reform activity in Italy is some change for the good. However, much is left to be done and cannot be accomplished without better resourcing and organization, particularly at local and regional levels. The national level of government must reform itself; it can do little more than it has already to influence innovation across the nation, except to provide more money in hopes of enabling local reform implementation.

PUBLIC SECTOR REFORM THROUGH E-GOVERNMENT

In this chapter, two cases of e-government policy and its implementation are examined to determine their impact on public sector reform. In some Southeast Asian countries, reforms of public administration are implemented with similar methodologies but with different targets compared to those in EU member countries. Their major issue is how to tackle corruption and clean up certain political relationship within public administration. Improving and rationalizing managerial aspects of public administration has second priority.

Use of ICT is highly desirable in these plans, because of the need for transparency. In fact, e-procurement, e-bidding, and other uses of ICT for administrative procedure improvement increase transparency and leave little room for corruption. In Thailand, for example, the newly instituted Anti-Money Laundering Organization (AMLO) is becoming a symbol of the new public management, using ICT and adopting new methodologies, enabling the top priority of tackling corruption (Ateetanan, 2001). In Indonesia, different techniques have been introduced to administrative procedure to fight against corruption, to improve transparency in the government and thus, to enable public management reform. The first example presented here is the case of Thai government ICT policy and in particular the effort of AMLO, the Anti-Money Laundering Office, which was recently established to tackle the problem of money laundering and thus act against organized criminals. First, the section describes the current situation of Thai government in terms of its ICT policy, e-government policy and projects, and the empirical case of AMLO, focusing on the impact of this agency on other organizations. The second case is Indonesian government ICT policy, in which priority is given to corruption prevention and efficient management in the public sector. Transparency and accountability, which are promised by e-government, are changing the public sector. The focus is on institutional change that was brought on by ICT policy.

ICT POLICY IN THAILAND: THE ANTI-MONEY LAUNDERING OFFICE

There have been numerous major activities and milestones in IT policy in Thailand prior to the e-government project. Among these were: (1) establishment of the NITC (National Information Technology Committee) in March 1992, chaired by the Prime Minister; (2) establishment of UPU (a committee for utilization of information technology in public organization) as an essential item of NITC for promotion of IT in public organizations; (3) a Ministry standard minimum requirement for IT equipment in public organizations in 1996; (4) mandating certain IT training courses for civil servants; (5) launching a School-Net Project in 1997; (6) the regulation of an IT master plan for public organizations; (7) launching the CIO (Chief Information Officer) program; (8) the implementation of a pilot project 'IT Model Office'; (9) conducting research on 'Government Data Structure: GDI'; (10) endorsing the 'Public Data and Information Law' in 1997; (11) drafting Electronics Commerce Laws; (12) launching a Public Sector Administration Reform Plan; (13) the endorsement of the Prime Minister's Office of Regulation of Services of Public Organization; (14) launching regulation on a Document Tracking System; (15) establishment of the Government Information Technology Services Office (GITS); (16) establishment of the Electronic Commerce Resource Center (ECRC); and (17) establishment and implementation of a Software Park Project.

In February 1996, the Thai government approved the first National Information Technology Policy, termed IT2000. IT2000 was initiated and developed by the National Information Technology Committee (NITC) Secretariat. IT2000 identifies three key areas for IT development. These are: (1) National Information Infrastructure: to invest in an equitable information infrastructure; (2) Human Resource Development: to invest in people; and (3) Good Governance: to invest in enhancement of good government services.

From the framework and recommendations put forward in IT2000, the NITC secretariat and NECTEC have initiated and carried out projects to accomplish the goals of IT2000. Some of these initiatives are as follows: (1) School-Net, a national school information action program; (2) Development of Government Information Network (GINet); and (3) Development of legal infrastructure to support application of IT. NITS is responsible for developing and drafting of IT-related laws. IT2000 has provided the framework and guidelines for IT policies and initiatives for the past five years. Meanwhile, the Thai economy and society have evolved enormously, partly as the result of financial crisis in 1997. Globalization as well as international trade agreements also affected the country. Although the principle of IT2000 still prevails to a certain extent, the government has realized that there is a need for a second phase of national IT policy. As a result, NECTEC through the NITC secretariat is carrying out a project on the formulation of national IT policy for the next ten years (2001–2009). IT-2010 is expected to cover the following: (1) overview of development from the global perspective; (2) vision of Thailand in the next 10 years; (3) current position of Thailand, what has been achieved, what remains to be done; and (4) recommendation for policies, measures, and strategies so that the benefits of IT are realized among all sectors in the country. IT-2010 is to serve as a blueprint for the country as it is entering the "knowledge-based economy."

IT-2010 research projects includes the assessment of IT2000, the analysis of current situations in both IT production (the IT industry) and IT consumption in various sectors, and the review of policy development in the country. IT-2010 is not developed in isolation. IT policy needs to take into consideration all developments in the sphere of technology, the economy and society as well. By and large, the future development of the country, as will be specified in the 9th Nation Economic and Social Development Plan, is taken into account. The recent development of the "e-Thailand" initiative is also of particular interest. The core of IT-2010 is arranged into 5 specific areas (Flagships):

- e-Society, covering issues such as the digital divide, quality of life, culture, heath, public participation.
- e-Government, including public service via electronic service delivery, employment, legal infrastructure.
- e-Commerce, with special focus on "e-services" including finance, tourism and IT services, but also including other industries.
- e-Industry, focusing on e-manufacturing and IT-related industries, including issues such as standardization.
- e-Education, including issues of life long learning, computer literacy, human resource development, virtual education.

Regarding the development of the legal infrastructure to support the application of IT, NITC is responsible for development and drafting of six IT-related laws. These are: the Electronic Transactions Bill, the Electronic Signature Bill, the Private Data Protection Law, the Computer Crime Law, the Electronic Funds Transfer Law, and the Universal Access Law.

The e-ASEAN initiative has been encouraging the Thai government to establish an e-Thailand initiative to establish a framework for electronic driven development towards information and services improvement of the country. Ateetanan (2001) points out the connection. The e-government is an inevitably important issue which the government believes will lead to the promotion of good governance and at the same time will create transparency throughout the whole process of delivering public services to citizens.

The Thailand e-government project is multi-agency based. The project scope includes: (1) to coordinate, to facilitate and drive achievements/provisions; (2) a Master Plan, Action Plan, and Strategic Framework for implementing the e-government program; (3) Electronic Services in public agencies; (4) pilot project implementation; (5) suggestions and practical guidelines for reorganization based on construction of e-government; and (6) Standards, Guidelines and Manuals for public agencies in implementing the e-government program. NITC/UPU is the IT Policy body, NECTEC is the core implementation agency, the Bank of Thailand is the Project Sponsor (Governor), and other related public agencies are co-sponsors. The project duration is scheduled from March 2001 to March 2003, with a project budget of B2,080,000.

There are four target tracks for providing electronic services in public agencies:

- Online Information Services: (G2G) (G2C) (G2B).
- Simple Transaction Services: (G2C) (G2B).
- Payment Gateway: (B2G) (C2G).
- E-Procurement: (G2B).

Sample pilot projects in accordance with these four target tracks are:

- Online Information Services: (G2G) (G2C) (G2B), Online Financial Information, Online Social and Economic Information, Online Information for Investment and Industrial linkages.
- Online Simple Transaction Services: (G2C) (G2B), Company Registration Certification, Electronic Business Balance Sheet, Electronic ID Card (Single ID Card), Electronic Counter Service.
- Payment Gateway: (B2G) (C2G), Government Gateway for Fund/Money Transfer from business/citizen to related government agencies in the context of Taxation Revenue, VAT, Income Tax, Custom Duties, Inter-Bank Financial Related Transactions.

- e-Procurement: (G2B), Provision of online information regarding annual procurement in public agencies, including the purchasing process via internet within a limited authorized budget.

As noted, the Anti-Money Laundering Office of Thailand was established to tackle the problem of money laundering and thus to act against organized crime. AMLO was founded to investigate money laundering related transactions and any suspicious transaction through banks and financial institutions, the Land Office, property and asset related transaction from financial institutions, and so forth. It works together with other government agencies in getting information such as census databases immigration databases and Internal Revenue databases to do its job.

The AMLO IT system can be classified into three parts: (1) data input and management, collaborating with other government organizations and their data; (2) data validation in the framework of the AMLO Electronic Reporting System (AERS); and (3) the data analysis. Data preparation is done together with other institutions using the same format and program developed by AMLO. Information is submitted and exchanged through the web. In order to implement this system, coordination among governmental, non-governmental, and financial institutions, both at national and international levels, was needed. This process was much more difficult to complete than the system design and construction. The design criteria of the system include accessibility, reliability, security, scalability, extensibility.

Through AMLO's Electronic Reporting System (AERS), data submission is conducted through the internet and intranet (dial-up), transaction information is managed, data is validated in terms of format and content, and basic data is gathered and examined. This requires not only establishing online interfaces with other government agencies and financial institutions, but also reviewing its offline interface, as well as institutional relationships, and human contacts. AMLO staff has to operate the system to write reports according to the requirements.

For future development, AMLO is now looking for improvement of hardware and software performance, and capability, and also implementing a Customer Information System (CIS) to store account information from banks at AMLO, which will serve to change the system architecture. In order to go further, the government is planning to create an AMLO IT Master Plan which will define the IT structure of the organization and the information flow and organizational relationships among related institutions.

The effort of AMLO shows that through its specific target and mission, it is becoming possible to coordinate institutions of different types and size, not only at the information network level, but also at the organizational and human interface level. It would be a big challenge to coordinate different agencies for more general objectives; however the experience of AMLO shows that an adaptation of IT could lead to overcome much institutional resistance to change.

ICT POLICY IN INDONESIA: GOALS OF TRANSPARENCY AND ACCOUNTABILITY

The ultimate goal of e-government in Indonesia is considered to be good governance itself. This is paraphrased in various government articles and acts on public management reform, and especially on ICT policy. There are three pillars to manage this process: Transparency, Accountability, and Public Participation. E-government will use these as away to reach the broader goals. First, government institutions will realize transparency through interaction and communication; second, government institutions will guarantee accountability through publishing their output and product to stakeholders; last, government institutions will mobilize citizens for deriving information and service.

On April 7, 2000 the Government of Indonesia created the Coordinating Team for Telematika by releasing Presidential Decree Number 50). Telematika" stands for telecommunication, media and information, which means that it includes the tools, the hardware and the content of information technology in all of Indonesian government. E-government is one of the topics covered by the Coordinating Team of Telematika. The team is chaired by the Vice President and consists of Ministers, State ministers, and representatives of numerous entity boards. The mission of the team is: to design Telematika policy in Indonesia, to set priorities to use Telematika, to monitor and control Telematika application, and to coordinate various applications of information technology in Indonesia.

Parallel to the creation of this team, the Government of Indonesia also delivered Presidential Instruction Number 6 in 2001 (April 24) to all heads of Departments, State Departments and Non-departmental Institutions (Boards). There are four elemental factors according to this instruction. These factors are: (1) To apply continuous development and exploitation of Telematika; (2) To facilitate public access to Telematika; (3) To coordinate activities of development and exploitation of Telematika with the Coordinating Team of Telematika in Indonesia; and (4) To report the stages of activity to the President.

There are a number of major concerns in developing and exploring Telematika:

- Background of instruction.
- Telematika to unite the nation and citizen objectives.
- Telematika government efforts to facilitate citizen interaction.

- National Information Infrastructure to enable Government and Private Sector interaction.
- Private sector and business pre-requirements for Government for private sector interaction.
- Technological improvements covering research and development, education, cooperation and rising motivation for Telematika.
- Government on-line, i.e. using e-government.
- Team for Telematika in Indonesia to handle coordination of Telematika.

The Coordinating Team for Telematika in Indonesia introduced actions in four major categories. (1) policy and legal frameworks: telecommunication, information technology, e-commerce, and institutional development; (2) human capital building; (3) infrastructure; and (4) applications for government and for the private sector.

Some interesting aspects about Telematika can be pointed out from the action plan, especially in the section "Application for the government" that relates to the development of e-government. Planning of e-government began in 2001 and government institutions started to prepare their system so that all information could be provided to the public. Free access by the public had to be guaranteed by the beginning of 2002. In the same year, government institutions were also to develop e-procurement, believed to guarantee transparency and thus to serve as an anti-corruption device and to enable efficient financial action. The interaction phase began in 2003 both for public and for government institutions. While focusing on applications for the government, the action also focused on the private sector to support development of information to the public, such as electronic access, internet kiosks and other e-services.

All of these efforts in developing e-government in Indonesia have been made public through web sites. By the end of 2001 there were 293 web sites; 69 units had been categorized as central government, 100 as local government and 29 as central government sub divisions under the government organization category. The development of web sites is not well organized even for central government; most sites begin from sub division and go up to create the Ministry level. From 69 units of central government, there are 35 or 50.72% of all the central government institution web sites that can be accessed by the public. Almost all of the web sites are still in the phase of publishing. However, this effort in constructing web sites is significant for the improvement of accountability and transparency of government institutions.

The Financial and Development Supervisory Board was created in 1983 and modified in 2001. The Board is a non-departmental government institution in the Republic of Indonesian Government. The function of the board according to Presidential Decree Number 103, 2001 is as part of government in financial and development supervision according to the Government Internal Auditor. The ultimate objective of the Board is decreasing corruption and mismanagement in governmental institutions.

In 2001, the Board established a new unit, the "Information System Center," which functions as a coordinating team for Telematika with the Board. Also, the Coordinating Team of Management Information Systems was established. The head of the information system contributes to coordination of all system in the organization. The Board has a local area network with 148 nodes spread to units in the organization to support its operational activities. The web site (www.bpkp.go.id) serves for interaction among all agencies.

The local area network model of the organization reflects the uniqueness of the Board. The network has interchangeable data connections for each deputy (sub-ordinate of the head) and bureau. The Board has 25 regional offices in the capital cities of provinces. Beginning of 1997, the regional offices were connected with e-mail for communication, data transmission and reporting. According to the master plan, in 2004 the Board will release an interchangeable database for all units.

There are some problems in implementing e-government policy despite all this planning and activity:

- Human resources, including leadership, culture, and political will.
  Organizational structures and regulations in government institutions are different from those of the private sector. Almost all the employees begin their careers at lower levels, thus seniority prevails in the public sector. Furthermore, the salary of government institutions is based on regulations which guarantee incremental payment in accordance with career level. Thus employees who reach higher level or position are paid better. Information technology often requires younger persons with adequate higher education backgrounds. However, as these younger civil servants are in lower levels, their salary standard is rather low and thus some IT professionals are less motivated. Strong leadership and/or political initiatives are needed to change this situation.
- Commitment.
  Commitment of top management of government institutions is needed to promote IT development.
- Financial resource and funding.
  When the country fell into economic crisis, this caused government to utilize all possible financial resources to get out of the crisis and to help people with the greatest problems. Almost all funds have been put into emergency priorities, leaving information technology as less important for funding. The IT and related

budget is only 0.10% of the total government budget. This may change as the economy improves.
- Organization.
  There is no formal decree to establish a State Ministry for Communication and Information. However, a new state ministry is expected to coordinate the IT policy of the country.
- Infrastructure and Law.
  Along with law and regulation, IT should be supported by the telecommunications and related infrastructure. However, telephone service is still not diffused in Indonesia. The legal framework and regulations are another crucial problem. The Government has not yet issued any laws and/or regulations concerning IT application.
- Coordination.
  Coordination among government institutions is a crucial matter. Institutions have to coordinate among themselves for data exchange and information systems.
- Standardization.
  Standardization is needed to operate information system in a more efficient way.

How will the nation and government cope with and solve these problems? Based on the experience of other nations, several steps might be taken and some conditions might be considered including: (1) localization; (2) integration of resources; (3) socialization and enforcement of the action plan; (4) designing and redesigning business processes; (5) redesigning business networks; and (6) redefining business objectives. The conditions to be considered include: (1) starting e-government in simpler service area such as product delivery programs, human resource management programs, and asset management programs; (2) simplifying processes and procedures through electronic processing systems; and (3) systematic change in management processes through restructuring and reorganization. Some applications to solve the problems noted are:

- Designing e-government for mandatory institutions.
- Coordination among institutions.
- Cyber laws and related regulations.
- Standardization of systems and implementation.
- Socialization and training of the workforce and citizenry.

Indonesian IT policy and its e-government project show that the efforts attempt to achieve better governance, although there are still technological, legal, and institutional problems to be solved. IT policy is directed toward the prevention of corruption and realization of good governance through the potential of e-government. In fact, e-government has, so far, pointed out a number of institutional problems, including human resource mismanagement, and other political and social issues to be resolved. Still, overall, public sector reform has been accelerated through the e-government project even though it is underfunded.

PUBLIC SECTOR REFORM THROUGH E-GOVERNMENT

As the cases of public sector reform and e-government projects has shown, e-government can play a role in public sector reform. In this chapter, the characteristics of e-government were first examined as a tool for public sector reform. We know well the traditional public policies reform areas including industrial policy, economic development policy, financial policy, social welfare policy, environment policy, risk management policy, research and development policy, investment policy, and so forth. However, e-government, or Info-Communication Technology policy, is rarely considered as a major public policy in reality, partly because of its unique characteristics. What significant differences are present and how do they influence on public policy?

E-government policy has characteristics different from most other public policies. Usually, public policy is characterized by regulatory and/controlling intentions and actions of government towards private sector activities and initiatives. The reason differ from market coordination, consumer protection, to security control. Public policies have been legitimized through "market failure" theory, explaining governmental regulation, control and/or coordination over the private sector. Moreover, traditional public policy tends to be designed and implemented according to single issues to solve specific problems. Thus, much policy development deals initially at least with the contents of policy, not with institutions, procedures, and methods.

To the contrary, e-government policy has unique characteristics different from other public policies. It is, first, overall policy, covering different economic sectors. It deals with the policy making process and the organization and management of government in general. As it influences how to manage institutions, how to decide policies, and how to implement them, it is an area that spans different policy fields.

E-government is, secondly, often a policy aimed to overcome "government failure." Those "government failures," which are considered to be the targets of e-government are inefficiency of public sector management, irrational procedures and/or methods, lack of an outcome orientation, and lack of customer orientation. These "government failures" are considered as problems to be solved through e-government policy, which introduces private sector management tools and/or methods and tries to use these experiences and techniques to overcome the problems typical in public sector. Thus, e-government policy expectations are different from other types of public policy – the demands placed on it are overburdening.

Another important aspect to be stressed is that e-government policy is the only public policy that guarantees its legitimacy with best practices. Usually, traditional public policies are legitimized with participation of stakeholders in the policy making process and its implementation. The reason why e-government and related policies are expected to be legitimized by empirical "best" cases and experiences is not clear. Perhaps this is the result of the halo of technology as a solution to all problems. However, as there is no established model of public governance that includes e-government comprehensively, perhaps a new "governance model" should be examined – to legitimize e-government policy using a broader range of stakeholders.

CONCLUSIONS

E-government policy and projects are presently undertaken in many countries all over the world, bringing a new stage to public sector reform. First, through technological development enabled by e-government, public institutions have been forced to change some of their methods and processes. Managerial skills seem to have improved drastically due to this challenge, affecting human resource management, financial remanagement, decision making processes, operations, service delivery, communication with citizens and business, and evaluation systems.

These products of e-government are in the Thai and Indonesian cases, where ICT policy is considered as a very important strategic policy of government. National, long-term and comprehensive ICT plans and/or strategies have been developed by these governments. Specific institutions were established by political decision to deal with various aspects of e-government implementation. As experiences in these two Asian countries show, institutions and/or committees are driven by high-ranking officials of related ministries and agencies who work to coordinate policy and facilitate the decision making process for implementation.

In this regard, the differences with the Italian case are clear. Although the Italian government issued a series of public management reform bills, e-government and ICT policy was considered as merely a tool of managerial reform and was not given priority relative to other reforms. Furthermore, there was no e-government act in law, no ICT national plan, nor specific institutions created to deal with ICT issues. Absence of a national strategy and a co-ordinating body left the singular and isolated experiments of local governments to move forward alone, not integrated in any strategic process.

NPM has already introduced many new ways of thinking, methods, and skills to public organizations. However, the emphasis on "governance" has brought additional and significant change to government institutions. In fact, e-government policy now is typically aimed not only to introduce new methods and/or skills to the decision making and management processes, but also to revise the process itself to involving many stakeholders that had been somewhat marginalized in NPM-oriented and traditional policy making processes. Because of its technological characteristics, many e-government projects have been accepted rather easily by the existing public management systems, although this has revealed many contradictions in public organizations. For instance, younger ICT experts have been accepted into existing government institutions and have gained certain power to enable institutional change. However, these skill workers often are not paid as well as other employees despite the value of their contributions to reform and innovation. Still, even in Italy, where human resource management in the public sector has been very rigid, the introduction of ICT has influenced the types of employees hired, their work, and their employment contracts.

Secondly, the e-government and ICT policy have affected a wide range of other policies and not just one sector or field of government. This has enabled policy to change government itself, affecting especially human resource management and decision making processes of all related institutions. The changes in government in the two Asian cases show some of the most important impacts of ICT policy. Revision and construction of information systems means revision and restructure of the institutions responsible for these systems. This process has been accelerated by the effort to make systems more user friendly and customer-oriented.

This also means that, thirdly, e-government policy not only has performed a function as a managerial tool, but can supply reason to invest and to reform governmental institutions through construction of new legal and financial frameworks. The last point is shown in the cases of Thailand and Indonesia. For these nations, ICT policy has been an investment policy for the entire economy. With the help of the private sector and using new technology, ICT policy has been designed to overcome many of the typical problems of public institutions, e.g. through networking and co-operation among many players and agents. In case of Italy, however, these dynamics were not present in the ICT policy environment. Best practices in local governments were left out of the overall strategic reform plan and process, and thus e-government was not able to gain the status it achieved in the Asian nations studied.

ACKNOWLEDGMENTS

The author wishes to thank colleagues Professor Kuno Schedler and Professor Lawrence Jones for their assistance in helping to develop this paper, originally presented at the 2002 IPMN Conference in Siena, Italy in June 2002, into publishable form. Also, I wish to express my gratitude to all those who commented on the paper in Siena and elsewhere at other conferences and venues and in redrafting for this book.

REFERENCES

Arachi, G., & Zanardi, A. (2000). Il federalismo fiscale regionale: opportunità e limiti. In: L. Bernardi (a cura di), *La finanza pubblica italiana* (pp. 157–194). Rapporto, Il Mulino.

Arsi, M. Coronas, M. G., & De Luca, P. (a cura di) (1998). L'Italia da semplificare: Procedimenti amministrativi di interesse delle imprese. Il Mulino.

Ateetanan, P. (2001). Country Report Thailand. Paper presented at the 12th International Workshop for Information Policy and Management in the Public Sector 2001.

Azzone, G., & Dente, B. (a cura di) (1999). Valutare per governare, ETAS.

Badan Akuntansi Keuangan Negara (BAKUN) Department Keuangan. R. I. (Indonesia) (2000). Overview of the Government Accounting System for the Central Government. BAKUN.

Bernasconi, M., & Marenzi, A. (1998). Il deficit pubblico al 3%. Linee interpretative del processo di risanamento. In: L. Bernardi (a cura di), *La finanza pubblica italiana* (pp. 85–108).

Bianchi, C. (1996). Tassi di interesse e costo del debito nella prospettiva dell'Unione monetaria europea. In: L. Bernardi (a cura di), *La finanza pubblica italiana* (pp. 57–79). Rapporto, Il Mulino.

Bianchi, C. (1997). Riduzione degli interessi e misure strutturali di finanza pubblica. In: L. Bernardi (a cura di), *La finanza pubblica italiana* (pp. 61–85).

Bianchi, C. (1998). Tassi di interesse, debito e politica monetaria verso l'Euro e oltre. In: L. Bernardi (a cura di), *La finanza pubblica italiana* (pp. 59–84).

Bianchi, C. (1999). Gli obiettivi della Bce, i tassi europei e i vincoli di bilancio. In: L. Bernardi (a cura di), *La finanza pubblica italiana* (pp. 67–95). Il Mulino.

Bianchi, C. (2000). Politica monetaria e riequilibrio dei conti pubblici. In: L. Bernardi (a cura di), *La finanza pubblica italiana* (pp. 71–97).

Bordignon, M. (1997). L'Irap e la riforma delle finanze regionali. In: L. Bernardi (a cura di), *La finanza pubblica italiana* (pp. 137–160).

Cassese, S., & Galli, G. (a cura di) (1998). *L'Italia da semplificare*. Le istituzioni, Il Mulino.

Chan, C. W. (2001). Country Report on e-government. Paper presented at the 12th International Workshop for Information Policy and Management in the Public Sector 2001.

de Caprariis, G., & Vesperini, G. (a cura di) (1998). *L'Italia da semplificare. Le regole e le procedure*. Il Mulino.

Fossati, A., & Levaggi, R. (a cura di) (2001). *Dal decentramento alla devolution*. FrancoAngeli.

Fraschini, A. (1997). La finanza locale: tendenze e riforme. In: L. Bernardi (a cura di), *La finanza pubblica italiana* (pp. 309–328).

Fraschini, A. (1998). Finanza locale e decentramento amministrativo. In: L. Bernardi (a cura di), *La finanza pubblica italiana* (pp. 343–363).

Fraschini, A. (1999). Finanza locale: autonomia e vincoli. In: L. Bernardi (a cura di), *La finanza pubblica italiana* (pp. 211–230).

Ishak, A. W. (2001). Moving toward Indonesian e-government. Article presented at The 12th International Workshop for Information Policy and Management in the Public Sector 2001.

Kudo, H. (2001c). Performance measurement and policy evaluation in Japanese national and local governments. 2nd annual performance in government conference.

Kudo, H. (2001d). *How to manage Public Sector Organizations? – Some reflections from empirical studies*. EIASM Workshop on Performance Measurement and Management Control.

Kudo, H. (2002). Performance measurement for governance: From TQM to strategic management and programme budgeting. In: D. Bräuning & P. Eichhorn (Eds), *Evaluation and Accounting Standards in Public Management* (pp. 94–103). Nomos Verlagsgesellschaft.

Majocchi, A. (1997). Il Patto di stabilità e i vincoli per la politica fiscale. In: L. Bernardi (a cura di), *La finanza pubblica italiana* (pp. 39–60).

Majocchi, A. (1998). La sostenibilità dell'Unione monetaria e il ruolo del bilancio comunitario. In: L. Bernardi (a cura di), *La finanza pubblica italiana* (pp. 37–58).

Majocchi, A. (2000). Le scelte di Maastricht e il futuro dell'Unione economica e monetaria. In: L. Bernardi (a cura di), *La finanza pubblica italiana* (pp. 37–58).

Pajno, A., & Torchia, L. (a cura di) (2000). *La riforma del governo*. Il Mulino.

Paparo, S. (a cura di) (2001). *Semplifichiamo*. Rubbettino.

Presidenza del Consiglio dei Ministri, Dipartimento della Funzione Pubblica (2001a). Cinque anni di riforma della Amministrazione Pubblica Italiana 1996–2001.

Rhodes, R. A. W. (1997). *Understanding governance: Policy networks, governance, reflexivity and accountability*. Open University Press.

Salomon, L. M. (2002). *The tools of government*. The Oxford University Press.

Tan, S. M. (2001). Country Report Malaysia. Paper presented at The 12th International Workshop for Information Policy and Management in the Public Sector 2001.

8. RISK, REFORM AND ORGANIZATIONAL CULTURE: THE CASE OF IRS TAX SYSTEMS MODERNIZATION

Barry Bozeman

INTRODUCTION

One of the most familiar nostrums of the public management reform literature is that public managers must be risk takers (e.g. Gore, 1993). As is so often the case with prescriptions for public management reform, there is much more advice about risk-taking, its merits and demerits, than there is research on its incidence, causes and effects of public management risk-taking. Only a handful of studies have actually provided systematic evidence about public agencies' risk-taking (e.g. Bellante & Link, 1981; Berman & West, 1998; Bozeman & Kingsley, 1998) and some of these studies point to the complexities of conceptualizing and measuring public management risk.

Despite the fact that organizational risk-taking remains a surprisingly uncommon focus for empirical researchers, the conventional wisdom about its significance seems well warranted. Even if risk-taking is not always an unleavened blessing (Berman & West, 1998; Cohen & Eimicke, 1996; King & Roberts, 1992; Schneider, Teske & Mintrom, 1995) the organization's and the public manager's approach to risk often seems a powerful determinant of policy and administrative outcomes. Anecdotal evidence abounds.

Perhaps the most dramatic recent episode underscoring the importance of public agency risk-taking is the case of the Federal Bureau of Investigation (FBI) and the war on terrorism. While the vulnerability of the U.S. to terrorism is clearly a complex issue that goes well beyond the domain of any particular agency or its problems, one former senior official cites a risk averse organizational culture as a major factor:

> Twenty-five years ago, the thought was you had to tame down the FBI... (b)ut in the last 15 years, we have become a very docile; don't take any risks agency, particularly at headquarters. And if you make a mistake and it blows up in your face, then your career is shot, because basically it's one strike and you are out of the FBI. All that has to change (Van Natta & Johnston, 2002).

Some have blamed the FBI's risk averse culture, its "paralytic fear of risk-taking" (Van Natta & Johnston, 2002), as a chief culprit in FBI headquarters' failure to respond to the memorandum written in July 2001 by a Phoenix agent Kenneth J. Williams, a memo urging an investigation of U.S. aviation schools' training of possible terrorists. While this analysis is, perhaps, a bit pat, it is certainly the case that any agency hoping to respond quickly to diverse information cannot succeed with an organizational culture hobbled by a fear of the negative career ramifications attendant to well reasoned risk-taking.

If the case of the FBI and its approach to risk is a recent and particularly dramatic one, there are many well known instances where the organization's "risk culture" (Bozeman & Kingsley, 1998) seems to have played a major role, either for good or ill, in vitally important organizational outcomes. If we define risk culture as managers' perceptions of the organization's propensity to take risks, and of the organizational leaderships' propensity to either reward or punish risk-taking (see Bozeman & Kingsley, 1998), we can understand how these perceptions serve as powerful antecedents to managerial behavior. In many instances, there is some dispute about the positive and negative effects of risk and risk culture, even as there is agreement about their importance. For example, the tragedy of the space shuttle Challenger has been interpreted variously as a case of too much risk, not enough risk, and the wrong sort of risk (Bell & Esch, 1989; Kovach & Render, 1988; Marshall, 1986; Presidential Commission on the Space Shuttle Challenger Accident, 1986; Romzek & Dubnick, 1989; Vaughan, 1996). But even if there is no agreement about the particular role of risk in the Challenger disaster, there is a consensus about its importance.

A WINDOW INTO ORGANIZATION RISK CULTURE: THE IRS AND TAX SYSTEMS MODERNIZATION

This chapter focuses on a public management disaster not nearly as familiar or as heart-wrenching as the Challenger but one that nonetheless cost nearly $8 billion, occupied the time of literally thousands of public managers and consultants, and, most important, directly affected nearly every adult living in the United States. In an attempt to understand the role of risk culture in public management reform, I examine the Internal Revenue Service's (IRS) experience implementing the largest information technology (IT) reform ever undertaken by a U.S. civilian agency. The IRS work in IT reform has been on-going at least since 1989, but I focus specifically on the period 1990–1996, under the phase known as Tax Systems Modernization (TSM). This period is especially interesting inasmuch as it involved one of the greatest investments in federal agency IT ever undertaken, because it was generally viewed as a signal failure, and because one of the chief factors in this failed reform was the agency's "risk culture" (Bozeman & Kingsley, 1998).

In 1989, Tax Systems Modernization began with considerable fanfare. Congress had been told that TSM was likely to cost $4 billion and would not be fully operational until about 2000 and Congress did not blink. By 1996, the program was essentially dismantled and IRS was instructed to go back to the drawing boards. Critics of TSM differ only in the degree of severity of their criticism. Representative Jim Lightfoot, the Iowa Republican who was then chairman of the House appropriations subcommittee overseeing IRS, characterized Tax System Modernization, as "a $4billion fiasco" (Hershey, 1996). Senator Bob Kerrey, co-chair of the National Commission on Restructuring the IRS, observed, "while the world has moved into the wireless age with home banking, ATMs on every corner and stock investing over the Internet, IRS technology has remained stagnant" (Stengel, 1997). But political officials were certainly not alone in their criticism. A National Research Council (1996) study committee on Tax Systems Modernization (established at the behest of the IRS) concluded its five-year study saying, "Technical lapses appear symptomatic of a fundamental management problem plaguing TSM." Perhaps most damning, a long string of GAO reports (see Bozeman, 2002 for summary), ground out year after year, specified scores of technical and managerial shortcomings of IRS' modernization effort.

With so many talented people, both in the IRS and in private sector partner organizations, using so many resources, for so long a time, on so vital a project, how could this happen? Was it the enormity of the task? Was the level of technology renewal simply beyond human ability to manage complexity? Was it because IT is inherently more difficult in government setting? Or was it something about the IRS and its organizational culture and, particularly, its approach to risk? In fact, it seems to have been due to all these factors and more (Bozeman, 2002; National Research Council, 1996), but for one interested in organizational culture and risk-taking this case is interesting because it is so "over-determined." The TSM case provides insights into the ways that risk culture interacts were a congeries of organizational, technological and external political variables to conduce outcomes.

If multiple factors contributed to the demise of TSM, by most all accounts, organizational risk culture was front and center. In particular, the circa 1996 IRS culture was well adapted to a legally dominated view of the world and driven by paper processing but was not well suited to a technologically dominated world view driven by electronic information processing. The IRS failures with IT modernization are of great interest because IRS has talented managers and, in many respects, excellent resources. As we see in this analysis as well as a more detailed companion study (Bozeman, 2002), IRS managers failed by not adapting, by using approaches successful in an environment that no longer existed. A previously effective organizational culture had, by virtue of new technological demands, become an ineffective one. A culture in which risk was reasonably eschewed was not effective for tasks in which risk was an inherent part of effective management performance. Moreover, the TSM case is instructive, among other reasons, because it suggests that the value of managerial risk-taking is contingent. Few of us pine for an IRS that has a swash-buckling, risk-be-damned orientation, but, at the same time, the agency cannot succeed in its technological missions without cultivating certain types and levels of risk.

RESEARCH APPROACH AND ORGANIZATION OF THIS STUDY

This study is a case study, a single case, at least if a project as large in its scope as the IRS technology reform effort can be viewed as a single case. The research draws from the interviews and documents developed in a much larger monograph (Bozeman, 2002). In addition to review of documents and reports, the study is based on interviews with more than 100 key respondents, including, among others, several former IRS commissioners, current and former IRS managers, consultants, Congressional staff, and officials of oversight agencies. With few exceptions (including IRS commissioner Charles Rossotti, who agreed to have his comments in the public domain) I have chosen not to list the individuals interviewed for the study. While I made no promises of confidentiality and anonymity and, perhaps surprisingly, none of the interviewees asked for anonymity, it seemed to me that very little would be gained by identifying interviewees. Thus, while the report includes ample quotations and paraphrases, they are not attributed except, in most instances, by the respondent's role. In the few cases where quotations are attributed to individuals, the source is not my transcripts but quotations from public domain resources.

The interviewing approach I employed is best described as "tailored semi-structured interviewing." While a few themes were common to all interviewees, particular care was given to identifying the particular role, perspective and historical vantage of the interviewee and tailoring questions to the individual. The organization of this report is as follows: in the next section I consider relevant theory and research pertaining to organizational risk and risk culture, with a view to using the literature to help interpret the finding of the case analysis. Then I provide an historical background for IRS efforts in IT reform. With this backdrop I provide a description of the TSM experience. In a next section I analyze the failures of TSM, focusing particularly, but not exclusively on risk culture. In a concluding section I provide a postscript, detailing the IRS' largely successful strategy employed post-TSM and seek to draw conclusions about IRS IT modernization (including post-TSM activities), about the role of risk culture and, finally, some more general implications for technological change and organizational reform.

ORGANIZATIONAL RISK AND "RISK CULTURE"

Public managers are often alleged to be more risk averse than private managers. One argument is that the choice to take employment in the public sector is itself an indicator of risk aversion (Bellante & Link, 1981) and, indeed, there is some evidence that public employees are somewhat more motivated by security concerns than their private sector counterpart; they are also more motivated by public service values and less motivated by pecuniary reward (see Rainey, 1996 for an overview). Other arguments for the risk aversion of public managers relate to the lack of a profit motive and entrepreneurial oversight (Alchian & Demsetz, 1972); structural barriers to risk taking due to checks and balances built into the federal system (Wilson, 1989), alleged the goal ambiguity experienced by public sector managers (Brown, 1970; Nutt & Backoff, 1995) (but see Lan & Rainey, 1992 for an alternative interpretation), and the dampening effects off the public sectors higher levels of red tape in public organizations (Bozeman, 1993, 2000; Scott & Pandey, 2000). In general, the incentive structure one finds in many public agencies is believed to encourage public managers to avoid situations in which they might be blamed for a failure to follow proscribed procedure (Davies, 1981; Wilson, 1989). Taken together, these arguments, some better supported than others, present a view of risk averse public managers and, thus, gives rise to the prescription that greater risk-taking can improve public management performance.

Not everyone is convinced that risk-taking is just what is needed to improve public management. The best known popularizes of public management theory, Osborne and Gaebler (1993, p. xx) argue that public managers need to be more entrepreneurial but this does not necessarily require risk taking. Berman and West (1998) discuss "responsible risk-taking," risk tempered by responsiveness and accountability. A number of researchers suggest that risk-taking and managerial ethics should be closely linked (Light, 1998; Robledo, 1999; Wittmer & Coursey, 1996).

The effort to distinguish entrepreneurship from risk-taking reflects, in part, the negative connotation of public bureaucracy in the United States. Indeed, much of the criticism of reform proposals is based upon concerns that unleashing public managers with entrepreneurial values would damage important democratic (Terry, 1993), legal and structural controls upon managerial behavior (Goodsell, 1993; Moe, 1994).

Studies of public sector entrepreneurs clearly demonstrate patterns of behavior that can only be described as calculated risk-taking (Doig & Hargrove, 1987; Lewis, 1980; Roberts & King, 1996). These studies tend to note the heroic effort required of public sector entrepreneurs in identifying opportunities and forging alliances in an effort to achieve self-identified goals. Efforts to reduce the uncertainty in the environment can resemble campaigns of conquest towards the goal of organizational autonomy (Lewis, 1980). Other studies of reform accept that risk-taking is a part of public entrepreneurship but argues that this can be tempered. For example, Bellone and Goerl (1992) suggest that public entrepreneurial behavior should be accompanied by a civic-regarding ethic that encourages citizen participation.

Private sector research on risk-taking has a different tone and thrust, often having a more situational or contingency approach and focusing as often of perceptions as concrete behaviors (e.g. Fischhoff, Watson & Hope, 1984; Hansson, 1989; MacCrimmon & Wehrung, 1986; Yates & Stone, 1992). Several components of risk-related behaviors have been empirically investigated by psychologists and managers concerned with business organizations. Some of these topics include risk perception and propensity (Bettman, 1973; Sitkin & Weingart, 1995), risk and decision-making (Figenbaum & Thomas, 1988; Janis, 1977; Libby & Fishburn, 1977), and personal characteristics of risk-takers (Jackson & Dutton, 1988; MacCrimmon & Wehrung, 1990; McClelland, 1961; Vlek & Stallen, 1980). While empirical research on risk-taking has grown markedly in the past two decades, none of the best-known studies differentiate systematically between public and private organizations. Those that do exist are somewhat dated (Brown, 1970) and do not directly measure risk-taking associated with a manager's work-life (Bellante & Link, 1981).

The paucity of empirical research on public manager risk-taking is somewhat surprising in light of the growth of the public management literature and, in particular, the recent interest in empirical studies comparing public and private organizations. For example, Knott's (1993) findings that organizations respond to similar internal and external factors rather than simple sector differences may have important implications for our understanding of risk-taking that are, as yet, unexplored.

The chief conceptualization considered in this paper is not risk-taking but "risk culture" (Bozeman & Kingsley, 1998). I am less interested in particular behaviors of public managers, agency heads and public officials than the ways in which perceptions of risk permeate organizational culture.

RISK-TAKING AND ORGANIZATIONAL RISK CULTURE

Two concurrent developments in organization research and theory are an interest in the concept of organization culture (e.g. Schein, 1985) and organizations' propensity to take risk (e.g. MacCrimmon & Wehrung, 1986). While there are many streams in these respective research topics that do not converge, the intersection is considerable. In particular, Deal and Kennedy's (1982) typology of organizational cultures takes organizations' risk-taking propensity as a starting point and, for example, their notion of a process culture depicts a highly formal, bureaucratized organization that is too entangled in its procedures, internal controls and processes to sustain risk. Several other scholars (Baird & Thomas, 1985; Bowman, 1980; Hofstede, 1980), including some dealing with public organizations (Backoff & Nutt, 1988) development theories or typologies of organizational culture or strategy in which risk is among the most significant cultural elements.

I define risk culture as the organizational propensity to take risks as perceived by the managers in the organization. Often it is the perception that creates the culture, even more than any tangible and documented set of decisions or actions taken by organizational actors, because it is the perceptions that provide the cues to acceptable behavior. As Sitkin and Pablo (1992, p. 21) note, organizational members come to view their world through the lens of their organization's culture, which can distort their perceptions of situational risks, sometimes by overemphasizing risks or underemphasizing risk. Top managers and organizational leaders play a particularly important role in influencing perceptions that risk is or is not legitimate and even subtle cues from leaders about their preferences regarding risk can powerfully affect the risk perceptions of other decision makers (Sitkin & Pablo, 1992, p. 22). Thus, if we have knowledge of perceptions of top managers' risk behavior we have insight into perceptions of acceptable behavior concerning risk. It is these perceptions, taken in aggregate, that comprise conceptualize as risk culture. With this background, I turn next to the case of IRS Tax Systems Modernization and the role organizational culture; especially risk culture seems to have played in determining outcomes. Before analyzing TSM, its outcomes and the relation of risk culture, I provide a brief history of IRS' information technology.

THE EARLY HISTORY OF IT AT THE IRS

The automation of tax returns processing has long been a dream of IRS officials. In 1918, IRS Commissioner Dan Roper, using Frederick Taylor-style task measurement and design, found that the name, address, and amount of tax from each taxpayer needed to be recorded at seven different points in processing procedures. He set out to acquire the latest efficiency-promoting technology: mechanical stencils. Similarly, in 1927, David Blair, IRS Commissioner during Calvin Coolidge's administration, purchased sixteen automated folding-and-sorting machines. One of a long line of IRS technophiles, Blair bragged that his new machines were capable of doing the work of three human processors (Davis, 1997, p. 57). The Bureau of Revenue, as the IRS was known before 1953, was not in its early years an organizational behemoth, not even by standards of the day. Before 1800, the U.S. relied chiefly on customs duty for its revenue. In 1850, customs duties yielded $25.6 million whereas the internal revenue produced less than $50,000. This changed dramatically as an income tax helped finance the Civil War. In 1862, the Office of the Commissioner of Internal Revenue included only 3 clerks in the Treasury Building, but after the passage of the Revenue Act of 1862 their number was closer to 4000. This was about the size of the Bureau of Revenue for the next 50 years, with growth spurts occurring predictably during World War I and II. Even as late as fiscal year 1939, the 6.5 million citizens who paid income tax provided only $1 billion in revenue, about the same amount as excise taxes yielded. But by the peak war year of 1945, 48 million taxpayers were paying $19 billion in income tax revenue. Unlike previous wartime spikes, the incomes tax did not recede after World War II (Chommie, 1970, pp. 22–30). In 1952, the Bureau of Revenue underwent a massive reorganization, creating the modern IRS as a geographically distributed organization that was to change relatively little in its structure until the IRS Restructuring and Reform Act of 1998, an act that not only fundamentally changed the organization structure of the IRS but its mission as well.[1]

It was in 1961 that the IRS took its first giant step into the computer age, opening its National Computer Center in Martinsburg, West Virginia, the county seat of Berkeley County, Virginia. The Martinsburg center is the home of the IRS Masterfile on taxpayers, a system vital to the functioning of the IRS, one including information on virtually every taxpayer. In 1961, the computers and software of the Martinsburg center were near state-of-the-art. But by 1989, the beginning of TSM, the Martinsburg computers were antiquated and more at home in the Smithsonian than in one of the most complex information processing organizations in the world. For years, a major challenge to the IRS has been to find ways to improve the Masterfile while at the same time ensuring that the most vital part of the system does not come crashing down.

Risk, Reform and Organizational Culture

There is a prodigious gap between today's IRS operational requirements and its information technology resources. Few organizations, public or private, have a more daunting operational mission than the IRS. The agency's activities are the lifeblood of the federal government. The IRS is responsible for collecting more than $2 trillion in gross revenue each year, more than 95% of the federal government's total revenue. The IRS employs more than 100,000 people to accomplish its mission. Perhaps unsurprising for an agency employing so many accountants and statisticians, the IRS provides a wealth of statistical information about itself. In reviewing the statistical reports issued by the IRS, one cannot help but be impressed by the magnitude of IRS operations. One-study projects that more than 232.5 million tax returns (of all types) were filed in calendar year 2001 and estimates that by 2007, the figure should reach 258 million (Zaffino, 2001, pp. 146–152). The individual income tax form (1040, 1040A, 1040EZ, 1040PC) constitutes the bulk of returns, 130 million in 2001, but not necessarily the bulk of content (since single corporate income tax forms 1120 and 1120S can run to book length).

Information Technology Renewal Efforts Pre-TSM

The need for technology renewal at the IRS seems clear. Today's IRS is perhaps one of the largest organizational information technology users in the world. Among the more than 100,000 full-time and seasonal IRS employees, over 70,000 use computers to deliver services to taxpayers. The IRS installed base (IRS officials no longer use the out of favor term "legacy systems") includes a network of 40 mainframe computers, 871 midrange computers, over 100,000 personal computers (desktop, laptop and PDA), 2779 vendor supplied software products, and over 50 million lines IRS maintained computer code (IRS, 2000b, p. 8). Despite the magnitude of the IRS information technology operation, it has not, even today, managed sweeping IT reforms. Despite the important IT progress the IRS has made in the past decade or so (reviewed subsequently), despite much progress (often overlooked amidst the storm of modernization criticism), the IRS still has not achieved many of its most important IT goals. Even today the IRS continues to have relatively limited interoperability, insufficient integration, and relatively few modernization project successes. Most important, the IRS remains (as we all do) at the mercy of the Martinsburg Masterfile, its computer tapes and its near-retirement (or post-retirement) COBOL programmers. So we return to the question advanced at the beginning: "How could something so important, go so wrong for so long?" Much of the answer to this question requires an understanding no only of recent modernization efforts but also pre-1990 failures.

Since the implementation of the 1961 Martinsburg Center, the IRS has known that regular technology change and renewal would be imperative to its success. But nearly all its renewal programs have, for various reasons, been flawed. The most important thing to know about IRS early modernization efforts is that they largely fell on deaf ears. Computer-based processing went nationwide in 1967 and the IRS computer system was widely viewed as leading the world in automation of tax collection. IT renewal plans were developing at the same time as the system was being brought on-line throughout the nation. The "System of the Seventies" was developed in 1969 and, since the chronology-based title was not so exciting once the 1970s arrived, was soon renamed the Tax Administration System (TAS). This system, the IRS' first major renewal effort, was also the first to fail.

Interestingly, the IRS early modernization efforts were to some extent a casualty of Watergate. In the early 1970s, the IRS spent six years developing a sweeping plan, called the Tax Administration System, projected to cost $649 million and be rolled out in the early 1980s. The proposal went to Congress in September 1976. The timing could hardly have been worse. With Congress still reeling from Watergate, including President Nixon's political use of the IRS to snoop for information about those on his infamous enemies' list, Congress was not eager to enhance the IRS ability to gather and manage information on taxpayers. When in 1977 the Office of Technology Assessment provided a report raising many questions about the privacy and security protections under TAS, the initiative was essentially dead (U.S. Office of Technology Assessment, 1977). Congress simply advised the IRS to replace worn out computers, nothing more.

The next IRS attempt to develop a sweeping IT renewal was the innocuously titled Equipment Replacement and Enhancement Program, later the Equipment Replacement Program (ERP). Congress found this sweeping plan indigestible but provided a modest technology upgrade increment for the IRS budget for a program labeled Service Center Replacement System. In 1983, a comprehensive technology improvement plan was presented to Congress, under the name Tax Systems Redesign (TSR). With a price tag of $225 million, TSR was to be rolled out in 1985. Part of the strategy to get approval for the comprehensive change under TSR was to show gains from the Service Center Replacement System. IRS haste to introduce new technology for the 1985 tax season was in large measure responsible for the infamous 1985 service center "meltdown." This system collapse was an event that lives in infamy but was, at the same time, the chief impetus for congressional support of Tax Systems Modernization (Davis, 1997).

The systems replaced under Service Center Replacement Systems led to the well-publicized episode often labeled the Philadelphia Service Center calamity. Actually, it was even worse than usually portrayed. The story broke in April 1985, after a janitor reported finding unopened and often mangled returns in the bathroom and in wastebaskets outside the Philadelphia Service Center. Of the 109 envelopes recovered, 94 had checks made out to the government, all totaling more than $300,000.

What most people did not know at the time is that the other service centers were experiencing delays and Ludditism equaling the Philadelphia experience. The new systems simply did not work. The result of implementing a poorly tested system was that tax processors could not do their jobs and often panicked. This, in turn, resulted in postponement of return processing at a cost $15.5 million in interest payments on delayed refunds (Dolan, 1993). After receiving angry mail and phone calls from constituents, members of Congress quickly agreed that a technologically inept or backward IRS was not in the nation's interest or their own political self-interest. The response to the service center melt down was an unusually lavish reward for failure. In 1989, Tax Systems Redesign became Tax Systems Modernization, replete with an open checkbook and broad latitude about the design, acquisition and implementation of new IT technology.

INFORMATION TECHNOLOGY AT IRS: FROM "PRE-HISTORY" TO TAX SYSTEMS MODERNIZATION

The Tax Systems Modernization Saga

After the 1985 service center technology meltdown, Lawrence Gibbs, a Washington tax attorney, was appointed IRS commissioner and given a mandate to make the IT systems work. Mr. Gibbs began by soliciting the ideas, opinions and experience of government and corporate executives who had designed or implemented large IT systems. Mr. Gibbs told the New York Times, "we knew we didn't have all the procurement and technical capability in information systems we needed... (w)e were not a bunch of bumbling bureaucrats who just started off not knowing what we were doing" (Broder, 1997). One of the lessons learned from consulting the experts was that it was not sensible to just let a contract and have an industrial group or consortium design and implement the system. According to Mr. Gibbs, the received wisdom was that agency officials should be deeply involved in every aspect of IT renewal, not only because of the unique experience of the IRS in collecting the nation's revenue but also because "you can't just throw this to the outside and have people within the agency buy into it. Even if you bring in state-of-the-art systems, you're going to have difficulty making them work unless people inside accept them" (Broder, 1997).

New Commissioner Fred Goldberg, a tax attorney by training, appointed the first IRS Chief Information Officer, Hank Philcox, an IRS insider who had risen from the ranks after beginning as a revenue agent. In 1990, Commissioner Goldberg approached the National Research Council, asking that the NCR set up a study committee to provide technical and management advice about TSM. The NRC's Computer Science and Telecommunication Board appointed a committee that included, among others, academic researchers from a variety of backgrounds, ranging from computer science to public administration, CEO's who had helped design and implement large IT systems, a privacy lawyer and privacy advocate, a high level union official, a former IRS commissioner, and IT officers from other government agencies.[2] The committee was chaired by Robert Clagett, a member of the National Academy of Engineering, and a retired AT&T technology manager.

The Committee began its operations August 27, 1990, in Washington, DC at the National Academy's Wisconsin Avenue offices. Commissioner Goldberg and Philcox began by introducing the key IRS players and assuring the Committee of the IRS' interest in and receptivity to independent criticism. Among those key players were Mark Cox and Wally Hutton. Cox was the TSM executive in charge of all new projects and Hutton was to person who was to keep the train running, making sure that the existing systems functioned even as they were to be phased out over a ten-year period. In early meetings, the IRS provided drafts of its Design Master Plan, the overall operational plan for developing, integrating and implementing the many projects envisioned under TSM.

In November 1990, Philcox shared the early TSM vision with one of the IRS' major stakeholder groups, professional accountants. In a paper published in The CPA Journal, he noted that TSM operated under a "double imperative-first, that we be clear in our own minds about where we are headed and, second, that we articulate our plans to stakeholders and prove we are serious about incorporating their ideas" (Philcox, 1990). He went on to emphasize the careful planning behind TSM noting that while most of TSM would not be implemented until about 2000, "specific milestones and clear objectives already direct us every step along the way. Already, more than 40 major modernization projects have been identified" (Philcox, 1990). What is especially interesting about that early article, especially in light of the failure of much of TSM and the dismantling of most of the "more than 40 major modernization projects," is Philcox' assessment of the risks. Under a section entitled "What Can Go Wrong?" He began by dismissing some possible threats. Executive turnover was not a problem because TSM "is not the brainchild of any individual IRS Commissioner or Chief Information Officer" and because the approach also "represents the accumulated wisdom of outside experts-private sector information technology specialists, members of Congress with IRS oversight responsibility, General Accounting Office government-wide directives, and an independent review by the National Academy of Sciences" (Philcox, 1990). (Mr. Philcox may have had his rose-colored glasses on here since the private sector information technology specialists were not formally represented at the time, the Congress certainly had no ability to design or evaluate the technical detail of an information system, GAO at that time had very few relevant government-wide IT directives, and the NRC system is to appoint (pro bono) persons who have their own full-time jobs and who meet irregularly and work episodically with NRC staff to craft a usually brief report).

Philcox perceived the chief threats to TMS as factors external to IRS. One threat was the red tape-bound legalistic federal procurement system of 1990, a system designed to procure standard commodities and a system permitting endless challenges from disappointed bidders. A second perceived threat was the annual federal budget cycle and the lack of multi-year capital budget. Finally, Philcox viewed federal personnel constraints as a possible Achilles heel, including the difficulty of paying competitive salaries to persons with technical skills. The 1990 federal personnel system generally based pay rates on number of people supervised rather than technical qualifications for technical jobs.

Once TSM was fully underway, project ideas were developed at a staggering rate. Perhaps even more than the Department of Defense, the IRS has always been enamored of acronyms, so much so that even persons directly involved with system development often do not know the title of the project the acronym represents. During 1990–1992 the acronym machine was well oiled as new TSM projects were stacked one upon the other. Table 1 provides a list of TSM projects and acronyms, not only to suggest the proliferation of projects but also as a glossary for some of the projects that are described below only by their acronym.

As the projects proliferated, so too did the sense that not all was as it should be. One of the first highly public TSM embarrassments occurred with a 1993 General Accounting Office report finding that the IRS could not account for $301 million of TSM expenditures. But the most important problems with TSM had less to do with financial management than technology management.

By 1996, the list of cancelled and endangered projects was piling higher and higher. Cyberfile, an experiment to permit submission of tax returns over the Internet was canceled at a cost of $17.1 million. As the primary plan for moving from paper to electronic forms, the Service Center Recognition/Image Processing Systems (SCRIPS) was one of the cornerstones of TSM. But the technology never came up to standard. After noting that it was not possible to determine exactly how much the IRS had spent on SCRIPS, due to the fact that the IRS "does not have an accurate cost accounting system," the U.S. General Accounting Office estimated in its report that SCRIPS had already cost $145 million, despite no sign of technological viability, and was on track to cost another $140 million. The Corporate Accounts Processing System (CAPS) was meant to create a single integrated database of taxpayer account information. The idea was to resolve corporate issues

Table 1. TSM Projects and Acronyms.

Project Acronym	Project Title
ACI	Automated Criminal Investigation
AICS	Automated Inventory Control System
AUR	Automated Underreporter
CHEX	Check Handling Enhancement Expert System
CASE	Counsel Automated Systems Environment
CFOL	Corporate Files on Line
ELF	Electronic Filing (test project for Cyberfile)
ICS	Integrated Collection System
SCRIPS	Service Center Recognition/Image Processing System
SERP	Service Electronic Research Project
TSIS	Taxpayer Service Integrated System
TIES	Totally Integrated Exam System
CPS	Case Processing System
CMS	Corporate Systems Modernization
CAPS	Corporate Account Processing System
DPS	Document Processing System
EMS	Electronic Management System
WMS	Worldwide Management System
EF	Electronic Filing
MIA	Mirror Image Acquisition
ALSS	Automated Litigation Support System
OCRSR	Optical Character Reader System Replacement
TSAW	Taxpayer Service Advanced Workstation

Source: Author (2003).

immediately via access to the CAPS database. The system was terminated after spending $179 million. The Integrated Case Processing (ICP) system was supposed to permit customer-service representatives to access in one step all the data needed to answer taxpayer questions or resolve problems. It was terminated after spending $44.8 million.

RISK CULTURE AND TSM

One of the most interesting theoretical questions about the IRS case is how an organization can develop a risk culture where people "think they will get shot if they say their project has a problem" while clearly trying, albeit unsuccessfully, to promote openness and even risk. The IRS case shows the ways in which notions of risk are embedded in organizational culture and the importance of one to the other.

Every organization has a culture that is in some respects unique, but the IRS organization culture is unique in many ways and understandably so. Nearly everyone who works for the IRS understands that their neighbors are likely to be either curious about them, revile them, or fear them, sometimes all at the same time. Those working at managerial levels in IRS understand that their life will resemble career military personnel-brief assignments, rotating to a new duty. The mission of the IRS shapes its culture. Dealing with money, secrets and incredible legal complexities requires an unusual set of work skills and perhaps breeds a unique worker. The selection effects for working in IRS surely must be strong. There is no reason to believe that the IRS would attract persons who are strong nonconformist, whose life is governed by creative opportunity, who rebel against authority, or who cannot live within a hierarchy. At the same time, the IRS has never been a sinecure. The jobs are challenging and the facts that managers typically circulate from one functional area to another means those those who want to play it safe have difficulty succeeding. It is a strange mix. Layer on top of this mix a new mandate to become technologically adept, or at least to engage technology, and it is clear that the organization culture is a demanding one where, if we can engage in a bit of dime psychology, people are likely to have cross-cutting demands, to be job-focused and tightly wound. It is not easy to succeed in the IRS.

Not everyone agrees on the nature of the IRS organizational culture but all the interviewees seem to be acutely aware of the impacts of organizational culture and felt that the IRS culture is like no other. One point of widespread agreement is that IRS management-level employees tend to be insular and distrustful of outsiders. If so, this may be a good starting place to look for ways in which organizational culture can affect perceptions and meanings of and can undermine efforts at IT renewal and, generally, organizational change. One interviewee (no longer with the IRS), who came to IRS from another agency, but who had worked with IRS for years and who knew many people in IRS before joining the agency, said he felt like a "stranger in a strange land." When asked if he felt like an outsider when he tried to work closely with others on a particular IT project he responded:

> I'm one of the poster children for that [feeling like an outsider]. I ended up staying there [IRS] for six years and had a really good experience. But there were days when I felt I was in this club where I didn't know the secret handshake (.) I had some credibility coming in the door and I was given some good people to work with and though I was hard on them, they thought I was fair. I don't think IRS is as insular as it used to be but I still had to prove myself. The question is whether someone who was not known to IRS would have to prove themselves more than I.

Why the historical insularity and distrust of outsiders? As one senior executive put it: "For years we didn't recruit outside the service. I'm a 20-year vet [of the IRS] and only recently really one of the families. There's a very military career path. Now we're bringing in people from the outside ... but there is still a lot of suspicion of people recruited from the outside." In many respects the insularity is not difficult to understand. In the first place, working at IRS is a truly thankless task. Very few outside of IRS appreciate its work and many are hostile. Second, the past two decades of experience with outsiders involved in criticizing IRS reforms, including TSM, has not been pleasant. Many have been scapegoated. Interviewees spoke of more than one high level IRS official as "falling on his [her] sword for the Service." The news media have often portrayed the IRS and its employees as incompetent or malevolent. It is not difficult to understand how such and environment can foment distrustfulness and insularity.

Other aspects of IRS organizational culture have reinforced insularity and distrust, pitting one geographical or functional group against another. (Changes in the 1998 IRS reorganization address both these factors). As is the case with many agencies, there is a long-standing animosity between headquarters and field. It is commonplace for IRS managers to scorn the Washington, DC national office while, at the same time, angling to get a plum job there, knowing that it is generally a prerequisite to continued advancement. To some extent, headquarters-fields relations are strained, typically with the "Washington doesn't know what it's like here out in the field" point of view (and the corresponding "why can't those out in the field understand national priorities" point of view). But in some cases problems in communicating management priorities may be owing to dysfunctions not obviously related to culture.

An employee who remains with the IRS and who has been with the agency for many years was asked if he thought there was less insularity and distrust than in the past. His response indicated that this issue was mixed up with communication issues inside IRS: "Are we less insular? Yes and no. Sure, there are many new faces, many from the outside. But if you go down a little into the organization [i.e. below the top management levels] you still find pretty strong resistance to any kind of change. Not much happened in TSM that changes day-to-day life. Modernization hasn't penetrated down. The commissioner has made calls for changes in the grass roots, especially changes in values."

Another IRS IT project member explained how much care his team had taken in developing an IT architecture and physical design for a project to be deployed in the Austin Service Center. The response: "That's nice. Now here is what we are really going to do." IT modernization has taken so long and delivered so little in way of fully functional technologies that many in the field have, essentially, given up on solutions coming from Washington. It is not clear whether this is organizational culture or simply the triumph of experience over optimism.

Many aspects of IRS culture have, at the same time, bad and good sides to them. Sometimes strength can be turned into a weakness. One conspicuous example is the long-standing "can do" attitude that emphasizes local problem solving and performing assigned tasks rather than complaining about them. This attribute often leads to accomplishment and pride in work. The bad side of this is a tendency to suppress dissent and a failure to deliver bad news even when it is clear that doing so may have disastrous results. As mentioned above, this is one of the primary explanations of the 1985 service center melt down.

In an atmosphere of distrust and poor vertical communication, one would predict risk-averse behavior (Bozeman & Kingsley, 1998). The IRS culture does, indeed, seem to inhibit risk taking. It is easy enough to identify some individuals who have taken enormous risks, but usually at great cost and at considerable personal sacrifice. It seems to be the case that the organizational culture does not reward risk. Consider the following: "I remember a conversation with Larry Westfall [TSM-era CIO]. He felt no one really took a chance with his or her best systems on modernization; they were always hedging the bets. The key is to understand what the Philadelphia Service Center disaster meant. It was the genesis for TSM, but it also left an indelible mark on IRS' ability to take a risk with change. It made it very hard for people to take leap of faith to really commit to modernization. But Larry did."

Another former IRS employee, one who worked on IT projects in IRS and other government agencies, felt that risk aversion was, in part, due to the atmosphere created by the nature of Congressional oversight: The Hill bears some of the responsibility; with their legitimate desire for oversight they exacerbated the risk aversion that already exists at IRS. I really think it's unintentional.

One wonders, of course, whether the IRS is any more risk averse than other public agencies or even private firms. With a few notable exceptions, the interviewees describing the risk aversion of the IRS have not worked in other organizations. One consultant interviewed, an individual who has worked on IT projects with the IRS but many other federal agencies, described working with the Federal Aviation Administration on a roughly comparable IT mega-technology project:

At FAA the culture was so risk averse that it was better to do nothing except what is safe. Operations were too risky. Like IRS, they were working with mission critical systems, not much different than the IRS Masterfile. But IRS feels that necessity [to make critical systems work] in their bones. I have so much respect for those folks.

ANATOMY OF IT MANAGEMENT FAILURE: RISK CULTURE AND THE DOCUMENT PROCESSING SYSTEM

One way to get an idea of the ways in which risk culture affected TSM is to focus on a specific TSM project, one of the most important ones. The project that sounded the death knell for TSM was the Document Processing System, a $1.3 billion system to digitize paper tax returns. After spending $284 million of the total cost of the project, the DPS was scrapped. The trial runs indicated that the system was not functioning at an acceptable level and had little promise of accurately capturing sufficient digital image to allow replacement of paper processes.

Like SCRIPS, the Document Processing System was meant to create optical images from paper returns, converting them to a readable format for the agency's computers. DPS was central to the TSM development plan. The idea was that TSM would be an integrated system and that DPS would be one of the chief links. Thus, tax returns would be processed by DPS, by electronic filing (ELF, later Cyberfile) and by telephone filing (TeleFile), and each of these would result in the same form of electronic tax return that would be routed to a central computer. In this format, data could be retrieved according to IRS business needs. The vast majority of IRS forms were to be channeled through the DPS system.

The DPS system included high-speed, non-impact printers, document processing equipment, forms conversion software. The intention was for DPS to read data from 1040 forms and, ultimately, all of the 285 IRS forms. The chief DPS contractor was Lockheed Martin Corporation, but a stable of software and hardware vendors lined up behind the Lockheed Martin prime contractor, including IBM/Pennant and Elixir Technologies Corporation, among others.

The target date for IRS-wide rolls out of DPS was 1996. Instead, that was the year the project was terminated. When DPS was closed down in 1996, IRS Commissioner Margaret Richardson said "given the revised priorities and budget realities for the next several years, the IRS has decided not to invest additional resources in DPS" (Dorobek, 1996, p. 1). The contract with Lockheed Martin was cancelled as a "partial cancellation for convenience," which is another way of saying that considerable negotiations occurred to enable the cancellation, with all parties agreeing that contractor performance was not a factor and that the option remained of re-opening the contract (which, of course, no one contemplated doing).

The chief problem was not changing priorities or cost overruns but the simple fact that DPS did not work. The scanning state-of-the-art did not seem to be up to the IRS need to examine forms that included both handwritten and typewritten information, not to mention notes taped or stuck on. The GAO's Rona Stillman, chief computer scientist, noted "At the time they were closing it (the DPS project) down, they were asking 'which forms should be read? How much of the data should be read?'– Those are questions that should be asked at the beginning, not $280 million into it (Associated Press, 1997)." According to one former IRS official who was intimately involved with DPS, there were two sorts of failures, one technical, the other a failure of managers to see the inevitability of technical failure.

The technology simply wasn't ready. The character recognition was around 50%, so you miss one number you miss them all. For it to be worth the money, it had to have downstream benefits such as seeing the image of tax reforms rather than pulling it. You need to see all the return-margin notes, post-its, etc. If you capture all the data, you can store, generate cases, and have a way to get images distributed. You can have workstations and tools in hands of customer service reps so they can use it.

I asked how this project got so far along if only 50% of the forms material could be read. The answer:

> Right in the middle of DPS [one of the project managers] said we would actually have more keystrokes with DPS than we did before. He even showed us. The big problem was moving paper through the system just like a paper jams in a Xerox machine. [A project manager] went to see a demo and said they have nice pristine returns with no post-it notes or paper clips. They had returns in stacks of 8 at a time and they did it because the machine jams and the block of a hundred has to be rerun, so they were done eight at a time. There was so much pressure keeping the thing going, tacit pressure but still there, people sometimes said they could do it in six months. They couldn't do it but they felt so much pressure. People were not going up the line and airing their bad experiences. It was not a good atmosphere for saying, "my project isn't working." The same thing happens in my shop. We go overboard to tell people we expect them to have problems, create an open atmosphere, but that's tough to people to believe. They think they will get shot if they say their project has a problem. That's what happened in 1985 [with the Service Center breakdown] – they were trying to be good soldiers, got have that "can do" attitude, got to make it work myself. They say, "we are going to fix it, we are going to fix it, we can't fix it." (Unattributed)

The DPS case encapsulates many of the problems IRS has had with IT renewal, especially under the TSM regime. Many factors contributed to failures. The causes are multiple. The nature of the technological task was (and remains) very difficult, as in DPS. The operational benchmarks are not entirely clear, as in DPS. The organizational culture undermines communication, as in DPS. But many of these problems have been resolved and others diminished.

The DPS case is in many ways a touchstone for IRS problems in implementing technological change. The quotation immediately above speaks volumes. This is a statement about risk culture. This is a mismatch between intent ("We go overboard to tell people we expect them to have problems, create an open atmosphere") and perceptions ("They think they will get shot if they say their project has a problem").

The IRS organization culture is a double-edged sword, but one that cut deeply into its ability to succeed with TSM. The very aspects of IRS that had allowed it to solve problems effectively for years- "can-do-don't-complain," rotating management personnel so they get the "big picture" rather than develop management specialization, promoting through the ranks, emphasis on the field and regional decentralization-turned against the IRS with TSM.

POST-TSM (1997–2002): CULTURAL CHANGE, ORGANIZATIONAL REFORM AND TECHNOLOGICAL RENEWAL

The IRS experience with TSM has been a force for revolutionizing the agency. As is so often the case, disaster has chipped away at old assumptions. Since 1997, the IRS has adopted a new, sweeping strategic plan, undergone its most significant reorganization since the early 1950s, and even changed its mission from one focused chiefly on revenue collection to one elevating taxpayer service to the highest of priorities. It has its first IT savvy Commissioner, Charles Rossotti, and has had a succession of CIO's with significant high level IT experience in government or industry. Positive findings from a GAO report (USGAO, 1998) on the IRS' modernization blueprint, one infers that not only is the revolution well under way but that it has a good chance of victory. The IRS now has more technical expertise on top and on tap, it has a prime contract to help it development and implement IT, and it has the confidence of its external political overseers.

What IRS does not yet have is a new, high performing, integrated IT system. Instead, the IRS has undertaken two extreme challenges in place of one. In the words of a GAO report: "The sheer magnitude of undertaking both business and systems modernization will strain IRS' management and staff. Such an ambitious undertaking, along with the need to 'stay in business,' makes the restructuring initiative a high-risk venture that will take years to fully implement" (USGAO, 1999, p. 2).

Indeed, it will take years, probably at least another five or six, fully to implement the restructuring and, in tandem, IT modernization (and both Commissioner Rossotti and GAO officials agree that the two must be undertaken simultaneously). What this implies for the task at hand, the task of analyzing the development, implementation and management of IT mega-technology is that lessons must be distilled not from a completed episode but from a never-ending story. This is perhaps fitting in one sense-IT renewal in any large organization is never completed but evolving. But in another sense the IRS story is not only never-ending but still writing its early chapters. Even today, more than twelve years after the term "Tax Systems Modernization" was developed, very little new, integrated IT technology or systems have been implemented by IRS. Thus, rather than providing an evaluation of post-TSM efforts, this section provides a brief overview of major post-TSM activities. While there have been several important changes during the post-TSM period (1997-present), the ones most important for IT modernization are: (1) the Modernization Blueprint and statutory change; (2) the award of the prime contract; and (3) changes in IT management.

"Modernization," Blueprints, and Statutory Change

The IRS mission was changed not by agency introspection and self-assessment but by statute. The IRS Restructuring and Reform Act of 1998 (RRA) changed the IRS mission from a major focus on compliance to "Provide America's taxpayers top quality service by helping them understand and meet their tax responsibilities and by applying the tax law with integrity and fairness to all."

The IRS has gone from Tax Systems Modernization to Modernization (IRS, 2000c), implying a from-the-ground-up overhaul, starting with the mission statement but reaching nearly every aspect of IRS. According to the RRA, "the Internal Revenue Service shall review and restate its mission to place a greater emphasis on serving the public and meeting taxpayer needs."

One means of achieving the new taxpayer service mission is through a mandated reorganization focusing on taxpayers with similar needs rather than the traditional regional and functional organization. In 1998, the IRS organizational structure was based chiefly on districts (33) and service centers (10), with each taxpayer being served by one of each. These offices were divided into functional units including Examination, Collection, Criminal Investigation, Submissions Processing and Customer Service. These district offices and service centers reported to one of four regional offices and the national office, which also operated three computing centers. The hierarchy included eight levels between the first line managers and the Deputy Commissioner. Under the new structure, first proposed in 1998 and implemented in 1999, there are four divisions, based on taxpayer type and serving integrated functions. These operating divisions include Tax Exempt and Government Entities, Large and Mid-Size Business, Small Business and Self-Employed, and Wage and Investment Income. Two agency wide divisions include Shared Services, focused on facilities and procurement, and Information Systems Services, the new home of IT and directed by the IRS CIO. Interestingly, the Information Systems Services unit includes 7,000 employees, making it larger than the Shared Services unit, larger than any of the remaining functional units (Appeals, Taxpayer Advocate Services, Criminal Investigation) and larger than one of the four operating divisions.

While it is too early to judge the impacts of the reorganization, it is certain that there will be important impacts on information technology. One result is that the IRS (1997) "blueprint" for IT modernization was rendered obsolete. In May 1997, the IRS (1997) released its Blueprint For Technology Modernization, the chief legacy of then-CIO Arthur Gross (who resigned shortly thereafter and was replaced by Paul Cosgrove). This first blueprint included the following principles, based in large measure on recommendations of a 1995 GAO report (U.S. GAO 1995):

- Ensure that the modernized computer system maximizes IRS employees' ability to serve taxpayers.
- Develop a centralized, mainframe computer system that guarantees taxpayer privacy and minimizes cost.
- Fully integrate the central computer with the existing computers and enable all systems to communicate.
- Require that technological improvements be implemented incrementally; that new stages be installed only when previous stages have been proven successful.
- Provide credible estimates of potential cost and deliverables before implementation.

This version of the blueprint included the following requirements:

- A centralized and flexible system that is capable of adapting to constant changes in tax law.
- A computer system that is easy to use and enables IRS employees – customer service representatives and compliance personnel – to access accurate and timely information from one terminal in order to be more productive and offer better service.
- Centralized databases that better analyzes taxpayer records to improve compliance.
- An interactive computer system that will move the IRS to a paperless system, decrease operating costs, and expedites processing of taxpayer returns and refunds.

While there is little in the RRA that explicitly invalidates the earlier blueprint, there are several important differences of emphasis and, as the GAO noted, the fact that the first blueprint was completed eight months before the Commissioner announced the reorganization "raises questions about the modernization blueprint's validity" (USGAO, 1999, p. 7). In Modernizing America's Tax Agency, the document that plots a new course for the agency, IT is featured prominently, both as a cause of past problems and as a solution-in-progress. The current approach is described as follows:

> The approach that the IRS is taking to deal with this monumental task [IT modernization] is to establish an overall architecture for a set of new systems that will accommodate all essential tax administration functions according to modern standards of technology and financial management. Achieving this new system architecture must then be accomplished by defining a sequence of targeted and manageable size projects that meet important and specific needs while, at the same time, working to complete the overall architecture (IRS, 1999, p. 43).

This approach is, indeed, different from that employed in TSM and is more incremental than holistic. It remains to be seen whether the approach will be effective but it certainly seems to fit better with new realities, including an appropriations process that entails more scrutiny. This additional scrutiny is not confined to the IRS. The Information Technology Management Reform Act of 1996 (the Clinger-Cohen Act, S. 1124. Sec. 5126) requires corporate-style capital planning for IT projects. While the financial accountability for IRS IT development seems clearly to have improved, the question of IRS architecture remains controversial. In his barbed commentary after leaving a high level IT post, Dr. Richard Wexelblat quotes Lincoln:

> It is said that Abraham Lincoln once pointed to his dog asleep on the porch and asked his companions, "Gentlemen, if we call a tail a leg, how many legs does a dog have?"
> "Five," they said.
> "No, Gentlemen," he replied, "you are wrong. Calling a tail a leg does not make it one. The dog has but four legs."

And, despite the best of intentions, calling someone who is not an architect an architect does not make him or her one. One becomes an architect through years of training and experience. It takes the ability to extract the general from the specific. It takes the skill to cut through complexity to abstract the essence. It takes the experience to know how to describe the architecture of a complex system in a handful of pages of picture and text, the will to do so, and, most importantly, understanding why you must do so. It also takes the artistry to describe all of this clearly.

It is clear that the IRS has IT architecture and, indeed, it has had several-of a sort. Whether the plans are now ones that can be implemented and will lead to meeting operational requirements remains to be seen. Presently, relatively little new technology being introduced and the effectiveness of IT implementation cannot be determined until there is additional technology in the field. Whether or not there is an "architecture" (an issue that seems to depend on the visual perspective of the beholder), there is an IT blueprint. While the blueprint was developed by PRIME contractor Computer Science Corporation (see next section), it draws upon the one developed in 1997 by then-CIO Arthur Gross. The blueprint takes into account the reorganization of IRS but also new developments in IT technology and needs. The blueprint, unveiled in January 2001, is to serve as a guide, albeit one often readjusted, for the next fifteen years of IT modernization. The components of the revised blueprint include:

- Creating three portals on the IRS Web site to give taxpayers, businesses and internal employees access to tax information.
- Converting tape-based master files to a different database, beginning with the simplest tax returns for the past five years – about 6 million files.

- Giving taxpayers the option of communicating with the IRS via e-mail when there are questions about a tax return.
- Giving taxpayers the authority to give someone power of attorney to communicate with the IRS electronically.

Even now, the IT development is at the beginning stages, but the reorganization has been implemented. While the jury is still out, most of those interviewed for this study felt the Rossotti-led reorganization would prove successful and some felt that it had already led to some positive changes. According to a knowledgeable and experienced consultant to the IRS, "some of the changes developed under TSM actually got implemented with Rossotti's reorganization. The strength now is better management and people, but also better process." A related view from another well informed outsider:

> If you don't look at Masterfile [where there has been little progress], they have done an incredible amount of modernization, very creative and persistent. But they do it in a stove pipe way and its about projects they can manage not about more fundamental change. You get a sense of competition between incremental change and modernization and incremental change always wins.

Is this a criticism? Perhaps it depends upon one's value for incremental change. The TSM approach was certainly not incremental change but wholesale change. With current assets and expectations, incremental change may be the most feasible and realistic.

Has (or will) the reorganization and new approach to modernization changed the IRS culture? Opinions differ. Speaking to one of the hard and fast organizational culture attributes of IRS, hostility between the national office and the field, one long-time IRS veteran, who has served extensively in district offices, the national office and service centers, was reasonably optimistic.

Cultures die-hard. There will always be headquarters chatter, but the way we do business now is different. All the business units are business focused, large and mid sized on large and midsize, wage and investment on wage and investment. From an IT perspective we centralized all resources and so there are no funds to run differently. We have one big organization for IT. It's nice to have core team in one place.

CONCLUSIONS: RISK CULTURE AND IT MODERNIZATION

During the TSM era, the IRS was still laboring with a circa-1950s organization culture that was almost as out of date as the same era's computer technology. What

IRS needed (and is now undergoing) was a cultural revolution, or at least a cultural evolution. If that cultural change does not succeed it seems likely that IT renewal will continue to stall. How important is IT renewal? In 2001, the estimated number of electronic filings was 42.3 million, with the expectation that this number should grow by an average rate of about 12% per year to the year 2007 (Balkvic, 2000). This means that among the 143 million individual tax returns expected to be filed in 2007, 73 million (51%) are expected to be filed electronically. Some of the most important statistics about IRS' tax operations do not relate to time series projections but to big policy changes that render each filing season unique (and, thus, limit the "programmed" aspects of IRS work). For example, just in the 1999 tax season alone, new changes in the tax code changed the expected yield by tens of billions as relatively minor changes were made in the deductibility of student loans, child tax credits, earned income tax credit and capital gains tax (Balkvic, 2000, pp. 191–201). Similarly, the 2001 Bush Administration tax cut and its tax rebate of $500–600 for most taxpayers required a prodigious and not entirely predictable commitment of human and information resources. IRS operations are anything but static.

If it has information systems that are unresponsive and poorly integrated the IRS could collapse under the weight of its contemporary demands. As Commissioner Rossotti notes (after reviewing progress made on several fronts), "even now we still have outmoded technology in Martinsburg, we have not system wide data administration function, no system wide database" (Bozeman, 2002, p. 24).

The IRS current cultural evolution, one carefully managed and planned with their new blueprint (IRS, 2000a), has initiated changes that cannot be fully assessed at this time but which are likely to have major impacts. The shift from region-based management to functional management is extremely important and will have far-reaching consequences. The increased emphasis on service, as compared to revenue collection, is less likely to take hold because it has been imposed by Congress (though through willing top managers) and because the change will be difficult to sustain. And the IRS does not yet seem to have made a major dent in its insularity, though it is well aware of the problem and is taking some steps to address it.

While there are many definitions of organizational culture available in the management literature, one that is both simple and to the point is Trice and Beyer's definition of organizational culture as patterns of shared meaning within an organization (Trice & Beyer, 1993). Edgar Schein (1992), who provides a much more detailed definition of organizational culture, distinguishes among three levels: (1) the most basic assumptions of the organization (e.g. the ways in which one should respond to hierarchical authority); (2) the basic values of the organization (for example, shared ideas about how to interact with persons outside the organization); and (3) the artifacts and creations of the organization (such as administrative handbooks, rituals and ceremonies). While, as Schein points out, there are many different aspects of organizational culture, usually when one uses the term it is just another way of saying "the distinctive or unique features of the organization." If this is what we mean by culture, then the IRS is a particularly "cultured" organization-there are many unique aspects of the IRS that frame its management. I conclude with a set of propositions or "lessons learned" from the IRS experience with IT reform. Each of these relates to issues of risk and organizational culture as these have been enacted at the IRS.

Proposition: Multi-organization management and interdependence requires "soft boundaries." The inability to deal with persons perceived to be at the boundary made it nearly impossible for TSM leaders to quickly integrate needed technical talent, even talent hired by the IRS.

Some of the most fundamental aspects of IRS culture are, at the same time, a blessing and a curse. Moreover, many of these features that have been strengths in the past have worked against the IRS' ability to develop and implement IT, especially during the TSM period. Consider the case of the insularity of the IRS. In some respects, the insularity is the "dark side" of cohesion. The fact that the IRS tends to view employees as (in the words of interviewees) "family," "part of the fraternity," "the secret society," also implies a strong bond among those viewed as insiders. The question often is one of balance. Arguably, the insularity-cohesion dimension of the IRS has not been in balance, certainly not during the TSM years, and this undermines the ability of IRS to work with contractors or even with new employees. Interestingly, it does not seem to play a similar role in the IRS ability to work with outside oversight groups. The GAO, OMB and NRC review committee interviewees all underscored the accessibility of IRS employees and their willingness to engage. The IRS interviewees, by the same token, seemed to have little antipathy to oversight groups, often respecting their contributions.

This seeming inconsistency – the difficulty of accepting new employees and contractors but relative ease of accepting outside groups – is not as strange as it seems. The key is the boundary-setting rules. The oversight groups are outside the boundary and the IRS culture has developed appropriate norms for working with those outside the boundary. But the new employees and contractors are not exactly neither outsiders nor insiders, they are on the boundary, and the IRS culture does not seem to have developed consensual norms about the role of persons on the boundary. Since the boundary lines are not particularly permeable (that is, it is difficult to move from "outsider" to "insider,") the problem is especially acute.

Information technology not only is not the same as other technologies, it may require a different culture than other technical functions. Information technology rewards specialization, adaptability, renewal, and project management skills. Any organization launching mega-projects while failing to assess (or improve) the project management skills of the persons in charge would have a low probability of success.

Proposition: IRS must become a "technology culture." IT mega-technology makes its own cultural demands. Until comparatively recently, no one would have described IRS as a "high tech" organization. But the proportion of de facto high tech organizations in federal government is likely to increase every year as functionality and even organizational survival depend on effective deployment of technology. Moreover, most organizations in the federal government are already "technical," but with a different set of technologies-the technicalities of tax law, or the technicalities of human service delivery, or the technicalities of contacting, budgeting and procurement. Most agencies have rewarded general management and functional management skills and have flourished digging in and mastering a domain rather than by constant renewal and adaptation. This is no longer a good strategy for am organization whose success depends on IT competence.

NOTES

1. Earlier versions of the IRS mission simply emphasized the efficient collection of revenue. The new mission: "Provide America's taxpayers top quality service by helping them understand and meet their tax responsibilities and by applying the tax law with integrity and fairness to all." (IRS [2000A], *Internal Revenue Service Organizational Blueprint*, Document 11052 [Rev.4–2000], Washington, DC: Internal Revenue Service, 2000).

2. The author was a member of the NRC committee on Tax Systems Modernization, both the first committee and a re-appointed committee, serving from 1990 to 1995.

ACKNOWLEDGMENTS

I am grateful to the PriceWaterhouseCoopers Endowment for The Business of Government, who provided funds for this study, and to Columbia University's Center for Science, Policy, and Outcomes for providing office space and resources during my residency in Washington as Distinguished Research Fellow at the Center. Among the many present and past IRS employees who helped me with this study, I am especially grateful to Dennis Szymanski for his role in coordinating interviews and providing material and to Commissioner Charles Rossotti for his assistance and helpful comments on the work. At the Endowment, I am especially grateful to Mark Abramson who provided detailed and very useful comments on an earlier draft. The opinions expressed here are mine and do not necessarily reflect

PricewaterhouseCoopers, the Internal Revenue Service, the Center for Science, Policy, and Outcomes, or any of the individuals consulted during my research. An earlier version of this paper was presented at the International Public Management Network Conference on "The Impact of Managerial Reform on Informal Relationships in the Public Sector," Certosa di Pontignano Siena, Italy 26–28 June 2002.

REFERENCES

Associated Press (1997). IRS struggling to bring agency into digital age. Associated Press story reported April 12. In: *Lubbock Avalanche-Journal*, http://www.lubbockonline.com/news/041397/irs.htm downloaded 8.27.01.

Balkvic, B. (2000). *Individual income tax returns, preliminary data, 1999* (pp. 191–201). Washington, DC: Internal Revenue Service.

Bell, T., & Esch, K. (1989). The Space Shuttle: A case of subjective engineering. *IEEE Spectrum*, June. 42–46.

Bellante, D., & Link, A. N. (1981). Are public sector workers more risk averse than private sector workers? *Industrial and Labor Relations Review*, 34(3), 408–412.

Bellone, C., & Goerl, G. (1992). Reconciling public entrepreneurship and democracy. *Public Administration Review*, 52(2), 130–134.

Bettman, J. R. (1973). Perceived risk and its components: A model and empirical test. *Journal of Market Research*, 10, 184–190.

Bowman, E. H. (1980). A risk/return paradox for strategic management. *Sloan Management Review*, 21(3), 17–31.

Bozeman, B. (1993). A theory of government 'Red Tape'. *Journal of Public Administration Research and Theory*, 3, 273–303.

Bozeman, B. (2002). *Government management of information mega-technology: Lessons from the internal revenue service's tax systems modernization*. Washington, DC: PricewaterhouseCoopers Endowment for the Business of Government.

Bozeman, B., & Kingsley, G. (1998). Risk culture in public and private organizations. *Public Administration Review*, 58(2), 393–407.

Brown, J. S. (1970). Risk propensity in decision making: A comparison of business and public school administrators. *Administrative Science Quarterly*, 15, 473–481.

Chommie, J. (1970). *The internal revenue service*. New York: Praeger Publishers.

Davies, D. G. (1981). Property rights and economic behavior in private and government enterprises: The case of Australia's banking system. In: R. O. Zerbe, Jr. (Ed.), *Research in Law and Economics* (Vol. 3). Greenwich, CN: JAI Press.

Davis, S. (1997). *Unbridled power: Inside the secret culture of the IRS*. New York: Harper Business.

Deal, T. E., & Kennedy, A. A. (1982). *Corporate cultures: The rites and rituals of corporate life*. Reading, MA: Addison-Wesley.

Doig, J. W., & Hargrove, E. C. (Eds) (1987). *Leadership and innovation*. Baltimore: Johns Hopkins University Press.

Dolan, M. P. (1993, March 30). IRS acting commissioner's testimony at ways and means oversight panel hearing on IRS modernization, 93. *Tax Notes Today*, 72–49.

Dorobek, C. (1996, October 21). 800 IT staffers face RIFs under IRS plan. *Government Computer News*.

Figenbaum, A., & Thomas, H. (1988). Attitudes toward risk and the risk-return paradox: Prospect theory explanations. *Academy of Management Journal, 31*, 85–106.

Fischhoff, B., Watson, S. R., & Hope, C. (1984). Defining risk. *Policy Sciences, 17*, 123–139.

Goodsell, C. T. (1993). Reinvent government or rediscover it? *Public Administration Review, 53*, 85–86.

Gore, A. (1993). *Creating a government that works better and costs less: The report of the national performance review.* New York: Plume.

Hansson, S. O. (1989). Dimensions of risk. *Risk Analysis, 9*(1), 107–112.

Hershey, R. (1996, April 15). A technological overhaul of IRS is called a fiasco. *New York Times.*

Hofstede, G. (1980). *Culture's consequences: International differences in work-related values.* London: Sage.

Internal Revenue Service (1997, May). *Blueprint for technology modernization.* Washington: USGPO.

Internal Revenue Service (2000a). *Internal revenue service organizational blueprint.* Document 11052 [Rev.4–2000] Washington, DC: Internal Revenue Service.

Internal Revenue Service (2000b). *Progress report IRS business systems modernization program.* Publication 3701 (Rev. 9–2000), Washington, DC: Internal Revenue Service.

Internal Revenue Service (2000c). *Modernizing America's tax agency.* Publication 3349. Washington, DC: USGPO.

Jackson, S. E., & Dutton, J. E. (1988). Discerning threats and opportunities. *Administrative Science Quarterly, 33*, 370–387.

Knott, J. H. (1993). Comparing public and private management: Cooperative effort and principal-agent relationships. *Journal of Public Administration Research and Theory, 3*(1), 93–119.

Kovach, K., & Render, B. (1988, March). NASA managers and challenger: A profile and possible explanation. *IEEE Engineering Management Review, 16*, 2–6.

Lan, Z., & Rainey, H. G. (1992). Goals, rules, and effectiveness in public, private, and hybrid organizations: More evidence on frequent assertions about evidence. *Journal of Public Administration Research and Theory, 2*, 5–28.

Libby, R., & Fishburn, P. C. (1977). Behavioral models of risk taking in business decisions: A survey and evaluation. *Journal of Accounting, 15*, 272–292.

MacCrimmon, K. R., & Wehrung, D. A. (1986). *Taking risks: The management of uncertainty.* New York: Free Press.

MacCrimmon, K. R., & Wehrung, D. A. (1990). Characteristics of risk taking executives. *Management Science, 36*, 422–435.

McClelland, D.C. (1961). *The achieving society.* Princeton: Van Nostrand.

Marshall, E. (1986). The shuttle record: Risks, achievements. *Science* (14 February), 664–666.

Moe, R. C. (1994). The 'Reinventing Government' exercise: Misinterpreting the problem, misjudging the consequences. *Public Administration Review, 54*(2), 111–122.

National Research Council (1996). *Continued review of tax systems modernization of the internal revenue Service.* Washington, DC: National Academy Press.

Osborne, D., & Gaebler, T. (1993). *Reinventing government: How the entrepreneurial spirit is transforming the public sector.* New York: Penguin Books.

Philcox, H. (1990, November). Modernizing the IRS. *The CPA Journal.*

Presidential Commission on the Space Shuttle Challenger Accident (1986). *Report to the President.* Washington, DC: U.S. Government Printing Office.

Roberts, N. C., & King, P. J. (1996). *Transforming public policy: Dynamics of policy entrepreneurship and innovation.* San Francisco: Jossey-Bass.

Romzek, B., & Dubnick, M. (1989). Accountability in the public sector: Lessons from the Challenger tragedy. *Public Administration Review, 47*, 227–238.

Schein, E. (1985). *Organizational culture and leadership: A dynamic view*. San Francisco: Jossey-Bass.
Schein, E. (1992). *Organizational culture and leadership*. San Francisco: Jossey-Bass.
Schneider, M., Teske, P., & Mintrom, M. (1995). *Public entrepreneurs: Agents for change in American government*. Princeton, NJ: Princeton University Press.
Sitkin, S. B., & Pablo, A. L. (1992). Reconceptualizing the determinants of risk behavior. *Academy of Management Review, 17*, 9–39.
Sitkin, S. B., & Weingart, L. R. (1995). Determinants of risky decision-making behavior: A test of the mediating role of risk perceptions and propensity. *Academy of Management Journal, 38*(6), 1573–1592.
Stengel, R. (1997). An overtaxed IRS. *Time*, April 7.
Terry, L. D. (1993). Why we should abandon the misconceived quest to reconcile public entrepreneurship with democracy. *Public Administration Review, 53*(4), 393–395.
Trice, H., & Beyer, J. (1993). *The cultures of work organizations*. Upper Saddle River, NJ: Prentice-Hall.
U.S. General Accounting Office (1998, February 24). *Tax systems modernization: Blueprint is a good start but not yet sufficiently complete to build or acquire systems*. Washington, DC: GAO/AIMD/GGD-98-54.
U.S. General Accounting Office (1999, April 15). *IRS management: Business and systems modernization pose challenges*. Washington, DC: GAO/GGD/AIMD-99-138.
U.S. Office of Technology Assessment (1977, March). *A preliminary analysis of the IRS tax administration system*. NTIS Order #PB273143.
Van Natta, D., & Johnston, D. (2002). Wary of risk, slow to adapt, FBI stumbles in terror war. *New York Times on the Web*, downloaded June. http://www.nytimes.com/2002/06/02/national/02FBI.html.
Vaughan, D. (1996). *The Challenger launch decision: Risky technology, culture and deviance at NASA*. Chicago: Chicago University Press.
Vlek, C., & Stallen, P. J. (1980). Rational and personal aspects of risk. *Acta Psychologic, 45*, 273–300.
Wilson, J. Q. (1989). *Bureaucracy*. New York: Basic Books.
Wittmer, D., & Coursey, D. (1996). Ethical work climates: Comparing top managers in public and private organizations. *Journal of Public Administration Research and Theory, 6*(4), 559–570.
Yates, J. F., & Stone, E. R. (1992). The risk construct. In: J. F. Yates (Ed.), *Risk-Taking Behavior*. New York: Wiley.
Zaffino, F. (2001). Projections of returns to be filed in calendar years 2000–2007. In: *IRS Statistics of Income Bulletin*, Winter 2000–2001, publication 1136 (Rev. 2–2001), (pp. 146–152). Washington, DC: Internal Revenue Service.

9. MANAGEMENT CONTROL REFORM IN THE PUBLIC SECTOR: CONTRASTING THE USA AND ITALY

Lawrence R. Jones and Riccardo Mussari

INTRODUCTION

This chapter is intended to address efforts to improve management control systems and processes, including budgeting, accounting and reporting, within the context of a responsibility framework in government. The theory of management control is explored and then management control reform in the U.S. federal government is assessed in terms of progress towards meeting the objectives of the theoretical model. Then, the U.S. experience is compared with the efforts to reform management control in Italian local governments.

In public management theory, management control is assumed to be a process for motivating and inspiring people to perform more effectively in the context of working in complex organizations. From this perspective, management control attempts to motivate public managers to serve the policies and purposes of the organizations to which they belong, and to meet the demands and preferences of the citizens and customers they serve. Additionally, management control is a means for correcting performance problems and including inefficient use of resources. Among the initiatives taken to implement management control systems and to control costs is the design of new or reconfigured budgeting, accounting and reporting systems. One approach to redesign is responsibility budgeting and accounting, now widely practiced internationally.

The discipline of management control is based on the presumption that managerial and all behavior of individuals working in organizations is largely self-interested, also a tenet in economics. Goals of management control include increased efficiency and effectiveness, and minimization of agency costs. Three interconnected techniques typically are employed in implementing improved management control systems: (a) performance measurement using internal accounting systems; (b) incentives and disincentives intended to reward or deter particular types of behavior and performance; and (c) methodologies that delineate decision making authority and responsibility within the organization. Bureaucratic organizations define decision authority and responsibility by separating decision control from decision management through the creation of hierarchical structure.

A primary instrument of management control is responsibility budgeting and accounting, implemented through performance related techniques incorporated into budget formulation and execution. Typically, under responsibility budget formulation, organizational policies are formulated into performance and financial targets that correspond to the domains of administrative units and managers. In responsibility budget execution, operations are monitored and managers are evaluated, rewarded and sanctioned relative to achievement of performance targets. Responsibility budgeting thus involves organizational engineering and cost accounting.

Under responsibility budgeting, work is monitored and controlled in administrative units according to mission, function and performance targets. Administrative units and their relationships to each other constitute the administrative structure of the organization. Responsibility budgeting requires decision authority and performance responsibility resulting from decisions to be allocated to individuals who manage units within the organization. This allocation constitutes the organization's responsibility structure, i.e. where responsibility for mission accomplishment is centered. Responsibility budgeting also requires an accounting system to record, measure and evaluate performance information including inputs, costs, transfers, activities, and outputs. This system constitutes the spine of the organization's control structure. Under a fully developed responsibility budgeting and accounting system, administrative units and responsibility centers are coterminous and fully aligned with the organization accounting and control structure, since the information it provides can be used to coordinate unit activities as well as to influence the decisions of responsibility center managers.

The chapter will attempt to extend management control theory and report on progress to implement management control reforms in two nations and at two different levels of government: in the U.S. in the national government and in Italy at the local government level under the authority of enabling national law.

RESPONSIBILITY STRUCTURE FORMULATION

Several basic rules govern organizational design in the responsibility structure formulation. First, organizational strategy should determine structure. Strategy means the pattern of purposes and policies that defines the organization and its missions and that positions it relative to its environment. Single mission organizations thus are intended to be organized along functional lines; multi-mission organizations should be organized along mission lines; multi-mission, multifunction organizations may be organized along mission lines or in matrix structure. Where a matrix organization is large enough to justify an extensive division of labor, responsibility centers should be designated as either mission or support centers, with the latter linked to the former by a system of internal markets and transfer prices.

A second rule is that the organization should be as decentralized as possible. Management theory supports the thesis that the effectiveness of large, complex organizations improves when authority and responsibility are delegated out through the organization (Jones & Thompson, 1999).

Thirdly, authority should not be delegated arbitrarily. Decentralization requires prior clarification of the purpose or function of each administrative unit and responsibility center, procedures for setting objectives and for monitoring and rewarding performance, and an accounting structure that links each responsibility and service center to the goals of the organization as a whole.

As explained elsewhere (Thompson & Jones, 1986), the most significant difference between traditional government budgets and responsibility budgets is that government budgets tend to be highly detailed spending or resource acquisition plans that generally are required to be executed as they are approved. In contrast, operating budgets in the private sector are usually spare of detail, often consisting of no more than a summary of financial targets. One of the originators of responsibility budgeting, General Motors' Alfred P. Sloan, believed that it was inappropriate and unnecessary for top managers at the corporate level to know much about the details of responsibility center operations (Womack, Jones & Roos, 1990, pp. 40–41). If the reporting showed that performance was poor, that meant it was time to induce change in responsibility center management. Responsibility center managers showing consistently good results were promoted and rewarded in other ways.

The notion that responsibility centers should be managed objectively by the numbers from a small corporate headquarters reflects the effort to delegate authority and responsibility outward into the organization. As explained in the OECD report, *Budgeting for Results: Perspectives on Public Expenditure Management* (1995), delegation of authority means giving agency managers the maximum feasible authority needed to make their units productive or, in the alternative, subjecting them to a minimum of constraints. Hence, delegation of authority requires operating budgets to be stripped to the minimum needed to motivate and inspire subordinates. Under responsibility budgeting, the ideal operating budget for each administrative unit/responsibility center contains only one or several performance targets related to corresponding costs to achieve the performance indicated (e.g. a production quota, a unit cost standard, or a profit or return on investment target). It is very important that targets be stated in monetary terms, both to compare the performance of unlike responsibility centers and to keep higher levels of administration away from operating details, thereby discouraging them from "micromanaging" the decisions of responsibility center managers.

THE RESPONSIBILITY FRAMEWORK

Responsibility centers are classified according to two dimensions:

- The integration dimension – i.e. the relationship between responsibility center objectives and the overall purposes and policies of the organization;
- The decentralization dimension – i.e. the amount of authority delegated to responsibility managers, measured in terms of their discretion to acquire and use assets.

On the first dimension, a responsibility center can be either a mission center or a support center, as noted. The output of a mission center contributes directly to organizational objectives or purpose. The output of a support center is an input to another responsibility center in the organization, either another support center or a mission center. On the decentralization dimension, accountants distinguish among four types of responsibility centers based on the authority delegated to responsibility managers to acquire and use assets (Anthony & Young, 1995). Discretionary expense centers, the governmental norm, are found at one extreme and profit and investment centers at the other. A support center may be either an expense center or a profit center. If the latter, its profit is the differences between its costs and its "revenue" from "selling" its services to other responsibility centers. Both profit and investment centers are usually free to make decisions about issues that are significant to the long run performance of the organization.

Discretionary expense centers incur costs. The difference between them and other kinds of responsibility centers is that their managers have no independent authority to acquire assets. Each acquisition must be authorized by the manager's superiors.

In the U.S. federal government system, under detailed line item budgets, acquisitions must be authorized by Congress and signed into law by the President. However, all discretionary expense center managers are accountable for compliance with an asset acquisition plan (an expense budget), whether or not written into law. Once acquisitions have been authorized, discretionary expense center managers are usually given considerable latitude in their deployment and use. In some cases, expense center managers are evaluated in terms of the number and type of activities performed by their center. Where each of the activities performed by the center earns revenue or is assigned notational revenue (*transfer price*) by the organization's controller, these centers are referred to as *revenue centers*. University development offices are frequently revenue centers. Managerial accountants generally believe that unit should be set up as a discretionary expense center only where there is no satisfactory way to match its expenses to final cost objects, as in an accounting department.

In a cost center, the manager is held responsible for producing a stated quantity and/or quality of output at the lowest feasible cost. Someone else within the organization determines the output of a cost center – usually including various quality attributes, especially delivery schedules. Cost center managers are usually free to acquire short term assets (those that are wholly consumed within a performance measurement cycle), to hire temporary or contract personnel, and to manage inventories. In a standard cost center, output levels are determined by requests from other responsibility centers and the manager's budget for each performance measurement cycle may be determined by multiplying actual output by standard cost per unit. Performance is measured against this figure – the difference between actual costs and the standard. In a quasi-profit center, performance is measured by the difference between the notational revenue earned by the center and its costs.

In profit centers, managers are responsible for both revenues and costs. Profit is the difference between revenue and cost. Thus, profit center managers are evaluated in terms of both the revenues their centers earn and the costs they incur. In addition to the authority to acquire short term assets, to hire temporary or contract personnel, and to manage inventories, profit center managers are usually given the authority to make long term hires, set salary and promotion schedules (subject to organization wide standards), organize their units, and acquire long lived assets costing less than some specified amount.

In investment centers, managers are responsible for both profit and the assets used in generating the profit. Thus, an investment center adds more to a manager's scope of responsibility than does a profit center, just as a profit center involves more than a cost center. Investment center managers in the private sector are typically evaluated in terms of return on assets (ROA), i.e. the ratio of profit to assets employed, where the former is expressed as a percentage of the latter. In recent years many have turned to economic value added (EVA), net operating "profit" less an appropriate capital charge, which is a dollar amount rather than a ratio. This change has clear implications for public sector budgeting and accounting to move toward performance reporting, measurement and management, as argued in this chapter.

Finally, under responsibility budgeting, support centers provide services or intermediate goods to other responsibility centers and charge a notational or an actual transfer price, e.g. in the U.S. defense department (see Jones & Thompson, 1999, pp. 52–81). Reasons for transfer pricing within organizations include determining the costs of services provided by one unit to another, establishing and manipulating incentives, and measuring the performance of responsibility centers. Transfer pricing also reveals the internal costs of service decentralization where costs are born to transfer decision rights to others within an organization. When one sub-unit transfers goods, knowledge, skills, etc. to another, both units calculate the cost as a means of revealing their liquid and tangible asset use internally and in external provision of service.

MANAGEMENT CONTRL REFORM IN THE U.S. GOVERNMENT

The federal government of the U.S. accounts for purchases, outlays, and obligations, but it still does not account for consumption. Full value from the application of responsibility budgeting can be obtained only where government adopts a meaningful form of consumption or accrual accounting (measuring the cost of the assets actually consumed producing goods or services). Because the U.S. government does not account for resource consumption, its cost figures are necessarily statistical in nature (i.e. they are not tied to its basic debit and credit bookkeeping/accounting records). Without the discipline that debit and credit provides, these figures are likely to be satisfactory only for illustrative purposes or where a decision maker must make a specific decision and a cost model has been tailored to the decision maker's needs. Another aspect that contrasts current U.S. practice and responsibility budgeting and accounting is that the appropriations process does not employ a separate capital budget. Finally, the existing process segregates every operating cycle to fit the federal fiscal year. Under the fully applied responsibility budgeting and accounting concept, budgeting for operating expenses and capital asset acquisition is separated, and all budgeting is continuous across a multiple year period of time. However, in matrix or networked (versus hierarchical) organizations, the distinction between capital and operating budgets is less necessary, as is the distinction between cost estimation and cost measurement (Otley, Broadbent & Berry, 1995; Tani, 1995).

Responsibility budgeting and accounting has been implemented on a broad scale internationally, e.g. in the United Kingdom in 1982 and modified in 1988 (Lapsley, 1994; Pollitt, 1993), in Australia, Canada, Denmark, Finland, and Sweden. All of these nations have adopted responsibility budgeting and accounting in one form or another. No nation, however, moved as far or as fast with this reform as did New Zealand. Moreover, New Zealand reformers explicitly recognized their debt to the framework of agency theory outlined at the beginning of this chapter (Boston et al., 1996).

Responsibility budgeting and accounting has been attempted in the United States and influenced reform in both the Bush Administration in the period 1988–1992 and the initiatives of the Clinton Administration from 1993 to 2000. Additionally, the content of both the Chief Financial Officers Act of 1990 (CFO Act) and the National Performance Review (NPR) from 1992–2000 called for performance-oriented organizations and mission driven, results oriented budgets (Jones & McCaffery, 1992, 1997; McCaffery & Jones, 2001; OECD, 1995, p. 230). In August 2001 President George W. Bush introduced the management reforms of his administration, among them linking performance to budgets (McCaffery & Jones, 2002). Previously, in 1993 Congress passed the Government Performance and Results Act (GPRA) that requires experimentation with responsibility budgeting and accounting and reporting by all departments and agencies of the federal government under the supervision of the Office of Management and Budget and oversight committees of Congress. In particular, the Defense Management Report Initiatives under Bush and Secretary of Defense Dick Cheney, and the Gore NPR stimulated considerable effort at accounting and financial management reform in the U.S. Department of Defense. Clearly, greater progress was made under Bush (e.g. introduction of reimbursable transaction accounting and budgeting) than during the Clinton – Gore administration, but both successes and failures have resulted from these initiatives (Jones & Thompson, 1999; Thompson & Jones, 1994). It is clear that government-wide progress has not been rapid. As with most large governments, the U.S. federal government has been slow to change (Jones & McCaffery, 1997, 1999; McCaffery & Jones, 2001). The impetus to change presently emanates from a combination of the CFO Act and the GPRA.

The CFO Act requires double-entry bookkeeping and accrual accounting, neither of which are standard practice in the U.S. federal government. To receive a clear audit report from the Inspectors General who perform CFO audits, these accounting changes need to be implemented in federal department and agency accounting systems. However, few federal agencies can comply with either the double-entry or accrual requirements, and there is resistance to investing to do so given that the federal budget and appropriation accounting are done primarily on a single entry and cash basis. Changes in federal appropriation law and congressional appropriation procedures, at minimum, appear to be required to push federal agencies further toward CFO Act compliance.

The GPRA requires strategic planning (SP) and development of performance measures, which has been implemented throughout the government, and linkage between SP and resource planning and budgets, which has been done with varying success. Further, GPRA invited agency experimentation with performance budgets on a voluntary basis, to be evaluated by Congress. To date, the results from these experiments have not persuaded Congress or the President's Office of Management and Budget (OMB) that broad application of performance budgeting, using an agency theory oriented contracting system of the type employed in New Zealand and elsewhere, is worth the effort. Agencies report that their own ability to plan and execute programs, and to justify budgets has been in some instances enhanced as a result of SP and performance measure development (as required by OMB). However, few agencies and no departments in total have the capacities in their accounting systems and procedures that permit accurate and reliable (or in some cases any) linkage between performance or results data and costs or budgets. Consequently, whether reporting costs related to organizational units, functions, accounts and sub-accounts or workload for the CFO Act, or cost performance (e.g. for results) for GPRA, there is little hope for broad-scale success in the medium term for most of the U.S. federal government.

There are additional explanations for this fact. The first is that many participants and observers of the U.S. expenditure process reject the notion that responsibility budgeting and accounting can be reconciled with the American legislative budgetary process. Some even assert that it can be practiced only by unitary governments under the Westminster model, although that claim seems to be contradicted by Swiss and Swedish examples of successful implementation (Arwidi & Samuelson, 1993; Schedler, 1995). While acknowledging that it would not be easy to reconcile responsibility budgeting and accounting with the American legislative process, we do not believe that they are necessarily incompatible (Harr, 1989; Harr & Godfrey, 1991, 1992; Thompson, 1994). If operating budgets were multiple year and funded on the base of what departments and agencies received in their previous year's base, which is how federal budgeting operates for the most part presently only on a one year cycle (Wildavsky, 1964; Wildavsky & Caiden, 2000), then budgets could be linked to whatever performance standards congressional appropriators (and authorizers) would prefer. Good performance would be rewarded and poor performance sanctioned – again, much as it is done presently. Departments and agencies would benefit from a more predictable revenue base, and presumably this stability would be reflected in better service to citizens, although this advantage cannot be predicted accurately.

Capital budgeting under responsibility budgeting would be separate from operating budgets, continuous and responsive to department needs and justification as per the current system. However, persuading members of congress to pass up opportunities for annual "pork rushes" to push pet projects in favor of a more stable, longer-term resource allocation methodology would not be easy, because it is through the annual budget that rewards are provided to loyal and, in some cases, needy constituents. Perhaps the Senate would be more likely to adopt multiple year appropriation because senators are elected for terms of six years, and are often reelected for several terms. On the other hand, members of the House of Representatives serve in two year terms, which means that they have much shorter time horizons within which to provide benefits to supporters. Clearly, multiple year budgeting would be a much harder sell in the House. Still, the reelection rate of members of the House is high, so there is moderate continuity in the business of the lower house of Congress. However, the high rate of reelection is in part attributable to the ability of representatives to demonstrate results from their election quickly. Of course, none of this mitigates against the use of performance measures in budgeting. It only affects incentives toward longer-term or continuous budgeting. And, obviously, little that Congress does with its budget process has anything to do with improving department and agency performance accounting, as demonstrated by the limited results achieved under the CFO Act.

Another, perhaps weaker, explanation for failure of responsibility budgeting and accounting to influence government accounting and budget practices in the United States significantly is that, unlike most other countries, America has large, well-organized associations of government accountants, auditors, budgeters, program analysts, and teachers of government accounting and budgeting. All of these groups have to varying degrees a vested interest in differentiating public from private practice, because that difference gives value to their expertise. Anyone inclined to doubt the significance of this explanation should look carefully at the politics of the Financial Accounting Standards Advisory Board (FASAB), responsible for developing accounting standards for the U.S. federal government, where accountant members did not understand the perspective of appropriation law and the budgetary process and those with experience with appropriations process were frustrated at having to confront a wide range of issues that seemed unresolvable unless appropriation law and procedures were modified, as noted. The standards were completed in 1997, but their success is now under evaluation as departments and agencies attempt to implement the CFO Act, with mixed results. What agencies complain about most, in addition to the absence of financial support for implementation, are the inconsistencies between the standards and the capabilities of the accounting systems, data bases and procedures used by their agencies to perform required tasks in budget formulation and execution, i.e. the same things that irritated "budget-wise" members of FASAB during development of the standards.

RESPONSIBILITY BUDGETING AND ACCOUNTING REFORM IN ITALY

In the past decade the Italian public administration (PA) has been undergoing a renewal process that has redesigned its cultural, organizational, and management arrangement (Jones & Thompson, 1997; Mussari, 1997). Dissatisfaction with performance, observable from both a macroeconomic and an exclusively social standpoint, has acted as a catalyst, fostering the start-up of an intricate reform processes based on a regulatory fabric that has as its main theoretical inspiration new public management (NPM) (Barzelay, 2000; Barzelay & Armajani, 1992; Hood, 1991; Jones & Thompson, 1999; Pollit & Bouckaert, 2000).

In Italy, difficulty with management control in a social and productive is most evident in the expansion of the diseconomies, the public debt, and the substantial incapacity of government systems to assert themselves as a factor of development for the country. Changes in context, together with the community commitments deriving from the European unification process, have fostered the start-up of a widespread, radical transformation process oriented towards the modernization of organizational characteristics.

For a decade Italian PA has been in the centre of a vast renewal process to overcome past weaknesses in bureaucratic organization, processes, and the functioning principles typical of a formal legal cultural that had asserted conformity to the rules as the only criterion for evaluating the worth of the public actions. This has neglected the centrality of the citizen and, above all, the capacity to meet efficiently the needs of the collectivity as the "raison d'être" of the PA (Borgonovi, 1996; Mussari, 1994, 1997).

The study of the crisis of the public system from a managerial perspective has clearly brought to the fore the fact that the primary cause of these difficulties is a substantial misalignment between the conditions of the socio-economic context, the role that the PA has within it, and the logical processes that inspire its organization and functioning.

One of the most noteworthy developments within Italian PA is the local attribution of previously centralized powers and duties. The aim of national legislation is to redefine the relationship between local administration and the administered community so as to strengthen the bond between the inhabitants of a territorial area and their governing body.

An institutional reform project led to a significant constitutional revision resulting in modification of state structure, with a clear federal orientation.

In any case, important legislative initiatives aimed at transferring roles and administrative duties from central to local and regional government have been undertaken during the anticipation of constitutional reform in order to confer greater autonomy. In the context of local government, autonomy may be defined as the possibility, will, and capacity to make decisions, direct activity and deploy resources toward objectives that reflect the values shared by the community. Autonomy confers the ability to make independent decisions and establish strategic and operative objectives along with programs to fulfil them. But autonomy also implies a capacity for lasting survival without artificial intervention, which depends on economic and social evaluations by financiers and consumers of public services (Mussari, 1999; Zangrandi, 1994). An organization is only autonomous when its components are coordinated to afford fulfillment of its basic aims.

Local governments had theoretically been recognized as autonomous in the Italian Constitution (Chapters 5 and 128), but until pertinent legislation was promulgated in 1990 and recent Constitutional renovation (October 2001), autonomy was virtually fictitious. As such, we may consider Italian local government autonomy as a recent initiative yet to be completed. The acknowledgement of local autonomy serves both to belatedly address social embarrassment and to attempt containment of the financial burden resulting from a centralized fiscal system.

It should however be noted that the transfer of duties from the national to the local level has only rarely been justified by verification of a local administration's superior ability to make optimal use of public resources with respect to the national administration. The motivations underlying legislation with such an orientation would seem to be more related to socio-political and financial inspiration than borne out of considerations of a managerial nature (Falcon, 1998).

Decentralization of public-sector decision making should first of all facilitate greater agreement between the supply of locally provided services and the demand expressed by the residents of the geographical areas served by local PA than has thus far been possible. Reform of local government as a manifestation of legislative desire to reestablish a strong link between local governments and the administered community represent an attempt to fill the growing gap between real social needs and the capacity of local authorities to sense them, to "decode," and interpret them so as to respond to them with effective solutions.

Recognition of autonomy may also be justified in terms of the urgent need to totally overhaul Italian public finances. One of the most relevant consequences of autonomy recognition has been a substantial revision of the processes and philosophy used to raise financial resources for daily operations and local government development. The belief that responsibility for spending and responsibility for revenues cannot be separated is finally taking hold. By progressively increasing the quota of earned revenue with respect to transferred revenue from the national government, the effects of local fiscal policy have been refined, alternative forms of financing have been adopted (project financing and bonded loans as opposed to traditional loans) to fund public works, revenue assets have become a significant component of earnings and financial flows, firms furnishing local public services have been privatized (water, gas, waste collection, parking, etc.) and a growing number of products and services require payment of a fee, given that it is no longer possible to expect national or local agencies to fully cover financial and economic losses.

As the mechanisms for generating financial resources have evolved, ways to overcome the distorting effects of a "derived finance" system on monitoring have emerged (Giarda, 1995; Mussari, 1994, 1998). In fact, the mechanisms for allocating centrally distributed funds (based on incremental criteria) encouraged political and bureaucratic groups to refine their "negotiating capabilities" while the economic management of available resources remained unrefined. The immediate consequence of this new resource distribution model was a lack of responsibility attribution to management for its achievements. Results took the form of parameters without relevance for the volume of funding available. Thus, results attainment was not held as an explicit condition for attribution of transferred resources and depended on the conscientiousness of the operators.

In such a context, "success" was based not so much on proven ability to efficiently attain sets of objectives, but rather on succeeding in collecting the greatest possible quantity of funds and in spending these while respecting budget restrictions. Therefore the prestige of an administrator or executive with a corporate assignment or a work group was measured according to ability to collect and spend funds, rather than according to the attainment of objectives. It only follows that a scenario lacking results incentivization should produce political and corporate leaders oblivious to the use of instruments for measuring and monitoring economic performance, especially since formal juridical monitoring was predominant.

As a consequence, material or immaterial incentivization of effective and efficient managerial practices was totally lacking. Promotion among public sector employees was based exclusively on seniority, public executive turnover was practically unheard of, and local governments were unable to attract managers from the private sector. This explains the prevalence of a short-term mentality, the demotion of accounting to a mere formality, the adoption of a financially-based accounting system poorly suited to measure the effects of corporate practices, an emphasis on input rather than on transformation processes, output or the impact of practices, organizational resistance to the adoption of management control and the persistence of traditional forms of auditing.

An important qualifying element of the Italian reforms was the new distinction between politicians and the officials responsible for providing services. Until 1990, spending power was wielded by the Town Executive Board and not by top officials. Consequently, politicians often ended up managing without competence and, in so doing, neglected the role of managers. The absence of coordination among the various functions of the organization generated an impossibility to assign responsibility for the outcome of programs and services. In turn, the relationship between planning, execution and performance could not be clearly specified and this caused a lack of feedback information for managerial and political decision making and, in many respects, for citizens. The solution offered by national legislation to solve the problem was to clearly establish and separate the tasks and the responsibilities of "managers" and politicians.

Of course, rigidly defined roles and duties are feasible only from a theoretical point of view. However it cannot be overlooked that it is always necessary to establish roles, duties and responsibilities in public organizations to avoid overlap and confusion. It must furthermore be noted that the absence of clearly delineated roles for politicians and staff is a commonly cited cause of the current crisis in Italian Public Administration, second only to corruption.

New legislation redistributes decision making power among political office-holders and managers. By law, managers are held to:

(1) manage offices and services according to the criteria and norms established in the statute and regulations of the municipality;
(2) perform all tasks (including the adoption of measures to bind the administration to other organs) which national law and local statutes do not reserve specifically for other organs of the municipality.

Clearly, identifying objectives and performance targets for managers has changed manager attitudes. Most importantly, the widespread use of modern management techniques (including management accounting) has been imposed, and responsibility for results has been attributed. Managers are motivated by performance evaluation not only because it enhances their prestige, but also because it rewards them with a variable monetary bonus linked to their duties and results attainment.

Elected bodies, especially the directly elected mayors, have clearly sensed that their political approval increasingly depends on their proven ability to deliver economic results. Since these results emerge through the work of managers, it is in their interest to generate and steadily monitor them.

We conclude that:

- as the number of people willing to believe political promises decreases, since citizens are tired of and disappointed by ideologies, politicians are obliged to personalize their messages in order to reach all citizens, not just major political groups;
- the form used to communicate political messages no longer holds citizens spellbound, in spite of its effectiveness, due to lack of content;
- citizens now possess a critical conscience, have learned to decode these messages and refuse to passively absorb stimuli;
- the growing presence of reference value makes all trust-based relationships difficult: clarity, honesty and efficient service are what citizens expect from public administrators.

The process of transformation mentioned above has important implications for internal monitoring systems and modifies their objectives, philosophy and instruments. Without full recognition and exertion of autonomy, responsibility cannot be attributed for results in political or managerial bodies. Assigning responsibility for attained performance, and monitoring in general, confirms autonomy and enriches its significance.

Diagnosis of the causes of the PA crisis has indicated the path useful for overcoming it. The reform begun in the early 1990s by action of the Italian Parliament has created new rules for the organization and management of public bodies, pursuing the goal of redesigning the management models to be consistent with the assertion of the result and its optimization as a unit of measurement and the beginning of legitimization of public action. Joint consideration of the interrelations between various sectoral and organizational solutions, management control models, and expected performance has guided and coordinated numerous reform interventions. Many of these dynamics are illustrated in the case study of reform in the City of Ravenna, Italy.

MANAGEMENT CONTROL ORGANIZATION IN THE CITY OF RAVENNA

Management control (MC) reform in the municipal administration of Ravenna is in many ways indicative of reform in Italy. The control system has been restructured on two levels:

- A central structure as part of the staff of the City Manager;
- Nine decentralised units termed "Budget Offices" (BOs).

```
                          ┌──────────┐
                          │  MAYOR   │
                          └────┬─────┘
                               │
                          ┌──────────┐
___ hierarchical subordination │   CITY   │
_ _ functional subordination   │ MANAGER  │
                          └────┬─────┘
                               │         ┌──────────────────────┐
                               ├─────────│ Management Control   │
                               │         │ Central Unit         │
                               │         └──────────┬───────────┘
                          ┌──────────┐              │
                          │ Area …n  │              │
                          └────┬─────┘              ▼
                               │         ┌──────────────────────┐
                               ├─────────│ Budget Office        │
                               │         └──────────────────────┘
        ┌──────────┬───────────┼───────────┬──────────┐
   ┌────────┐ ┌────────┐  ┌────────┐  ┌────────┐
   │Service 1│ │Service 2│ │Service 3│ │Service n│
   └────────┘ └────────┘  └────────┘  └────────┘
```

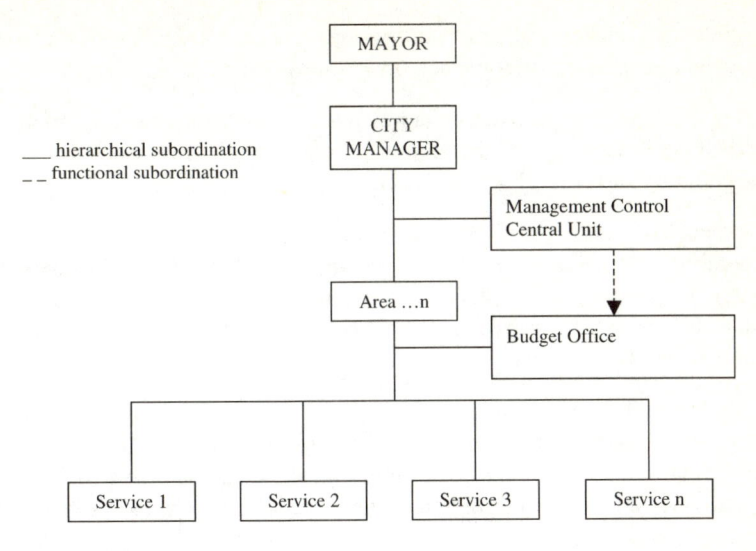

Source: Authors, 2003.

The chart attributes to the central structure the task of furnishing the City Manager with the methodological support necessary for both the preparation of the mandate program and the programs and projects that carry it out, and their updating and checking. The MC organizational unit also supports the BOs in the methodological setting up of the management and operational control aiming for:

(a) the identification of the objectives, the preparation of the budgets for the projects, and the identification of the activities in the various organizational frameworks;
(b) the preparation and updating of the system of efficiency, effectiveness and economy indicators consistent with the administrative need for knowledge;
(c) the preparation and uniform management of:
- a reporting system based on the logic of control by exceptions, by functional framework, and by project;
- an analysis of the differences for the identification of the corrective measures useful for solving the management dysfunction;
- an integrated system of analytic accounting for cost monitoring;
- assistance to and coordination of the budget offices, through periodic meetings, defining methods, indicating the general orientations of the programming logic, preparation of the forms and seeing to the constant training and updating of the personnel employed in the decentralized units;

- the collection and consolidation of the information for drafting summarizing reports and reports useful for space-time comparisons.

The budget office provides the methodological and operational support for the supervisors of the services of the areas with reference to the activities envisaged by the planning and control process, such as:

- costs-benefits analyses and feasibility studies;
- preparation and updating of the intervention sheets and related organization documents (W.B.S. – Gantt diagram – activity matrix – resources);
- monitoring the activities carried out with reference to the objectives assigned to each area and each service.

Each Budget Office has from 3 to 5 employees; the number is established on the basis of the organizational and dimensional complexity of the area. For all employees present in the nine BOs, training and updating courses on MC methods and techniques are organized; therefore these are specifically and professionally prepared personnel.

From a strictly organizational standpoint, a double subordination has been created for the BOs:

- Functional: Under the central MC unit, to guarantee a minimum level of substantial and formal uniformity of the techniques and method and for the coordination of the activities of the various decentralized units;
- Hierarchical: Under the head area manager, for faster legitimization of these offices within the macrostructure and to provide the manager in charge with adequate spaces of autonomy in the definition of the better "consulting" and support relationship between the BO and the organizational units of the areas.

The degree of assimilation of the MC logic, although high as a whole, is heterogeneous and thus different in the nine areas of the administration. It is useful to stress how the existence of the double bond of "subordination" may be, in some organizational contexts, a "limiting factor" since the hierarchical superiority of an area superior who is not MC-oriented may have the upper hand over the functional subordination of the BO under the central MC unit. Nevertheless, the advantages of this arrangement are evident in the identification within each area of a structure with exclusive responsibilities and authority for the MC to allow daily contact with the Services/Organizational Units (OU). Therefore, there is a continuous collaboration useful for the acquisition of a more in-depth knowledge of the internal organization of the area, the activities carried out by the single offices/services, the economic problems and, in general, those of the operational context pertaining to the area.

Considered in its "cultural" implications, the solution adopted makes it evident how MC supports the decision-making processes of the executives and is not viewed as an inspection activity into management activity. In short, the decentralized model makes it possible for the directors to:

- have direct, immediate support for evaluating the validity and degree of attainment of the planned objectives;
- review current programs and prepare future planning;
- verify, with work in progress, the validity and state of implementation of their operational objectives, for the purpose of withdrawing them if they are no longer valid or carrying out any necessary corrective actions;
- for the evaluation unit to have available an informational support that is quantitatively and qualitatively suitable for an advanced evaluation and incentive system for executives and employees.

Improved MC structure for the Service/O. U. and project supervisors permits them to:

- provide the BO with knowledge elements useful for "personalizing" in detail the MC system on the basis of the specific technical-management characteristics of each area and service within it. In other words, the decentralized model stands at a high degree of evolutional complexity that acknowledges the relationship of complementarity of controls with respect to the entire management activity and creates the organizational conditions for the best adjustment of the former to the specificities that the heterogeneity of the various areas produces indirectly on the management responsibilities of the executive. Consider, for example, the difference in importance that efficiency and effectiveness criteria may have within two areas: technical core management functions vs. the policies and social services area;
- plan and manage in a precise and more mindful way the human, instrumental, and financial resources necessary for carrying out institutional activities and projects, avoiding the recourse to non-scientific methods;
- The decentralized model with a central MC unit and nine decentralized BOs within each area guarantees advantages in terms of:
- pervasiveness of the MC within the macrostructure;
- degree of specificity of the system and specialization of the BO compared to the organizational/operational peculiarities of the structures;
- placement of the central unit directly under the City Manager makes it easier to overcome situations of conflict deriving from the double subordination of the BOs.

Adoption of a decentralized organizational configuration, with a BO for each municipal sector, imposes the employment of a higher number of employees.

From an economic standpoint, the consequence of this choice is raising the costs of management planning and control activities, the extent of which may justify doubts on the real economic rationality of the decentralized solution. A valid assessment of the cost-effectiveness of this reform must be done in depth together with the consideration of the following other aspects.

Introduction of the budget offices does not necessarily imply an increase in the total number of employees. Indeed, the implementation of the decentralized model may be the result of an operation of organizational restructuring that has led to the "freeing up" of human resources previously working in other organisational units. The internal mobility of the personnel and the decision to concentrate organizational effort on problems considered of primary importance is a concrete example of a more dynamic management of the resources, i.e. the expression of one of the key principles of MC.

The dimension variable may justify this choice as well. In fact, with the growth of the overall dimensions of the administration, the incisiveness and concrete effectiveness of the Management Control System tend to shrink. This is especially true in administrative contexts where the introduction of private sector like planning and control models is in an initial implementation phase. When these conditions occur, the essential argument in favor of the decentralized model is the necessity to not simply introduce new instruments or techniques, but to endow the executives with a culture consistent with the instruments and techniques upon which MC is based. The adequacy of the human resources to be devoted to MC must be viewed in a medium to long-term perspective.

Also of extreme importance is the strategic-political variable, since the desire to introduce MC may take on, for the institution's top political level, the characteristics of a strategic priority that justifies its cost. Providing a competent structures for MC, not only functionally but professionally also makes it possible to implement continuous training of the center supervisors. In Ravenna, this proved to be effective because it connected to the problems of the distinct, specific administrative units and service activities of City organization.

CONCLUSIONS

There are distinct similarities between the management control reform initiatives in the United States, Italy and other nations. For example, in both the U.S. and Italy, the driving force for implementation of responsibility budgeting and accounting is the legislative branch – the U.S. Congress and the Italian Parliament. In both systems, increased emphasis on delegation of responsibility to managers is a cornerstone of reform and has met with political resistance. In both cases, there is an absence of capacity, in managerial preparation and in the capabilities of accounting systems, to fully implement the changes authorized. In both nations, traditional budget process roles are or will be changed with implementation of reform. In both nations there are technical problems in learning how to define and use performance and results measures to influence decision making. In both the U.S. and Italy, parts of the administrative culture prefer a safer existence with less rather than more responsibility for results. In both nations, the legislative branch has directed elected officials and managers to become more responsive to citizen demands and preferences and to report financial and service results with increased transparency (Jones & McCaffery, 2002).

The changes in management control detailed in this chapter provide some new perspectives on the implementation of responsibility budgeting and accounting. Although problems faced the U.S. have been encountered and resolved to varying degrees in a number of other nations, the means for overcoming barriers to implementation tend to be particular to each nation to a great extent in our view (Jones & Thompson, 1999, pp. 169–171). However, some generalizations seem to be evident.

It is now apparent, as not before, that responsibility budgeting and accounting systems restrict the upward flow of operating information within public organizations – making decentralization and autonomy a necessity and not just an ideal. Responsibility budgeting is essentially a form of internal and external contracting wherein costs of services to meet mission requirements are negotiated. Decision units are then held accountable for execution of their budgets to fulfill the commitments agreed to in the negotiation process. Responsibility budgeting employs explicit contracting between units for the provision of specific services or goods in exchange for financial resources for operation and capital acquisition necessary for production. The distinguishing elements of responsibility budgeting are: (a) the evaluation of units and managers relative to the contract obligations they accept; (b) the use of financial and performance measures to reward accomplishment and sanction failure; and (c) identification and attribution of financial success or failure entirely to managerial decisions and employee performance.

From the perspective of the environments within which public organizations function, in networks and alliances people work in information rich environments. However, access to information is not necessarily symmetrical or equally available to all. Decentralization works in such an environment only where elected officials (e.g. in Congress, the Italian Parliament, or in Italian local governments) and senior management in public organizations attend to executive decision and management functions including strategic planning, organizing, staffing, investment in the intellectual and cultural development of the organization, but refrain from attempts to manage the conduct of operations. This takes practice, self-restraint and a willingness on the part of legislators and senior management to accept the risks of being held accountable by citizens for results that are, to a great extent, determined by public managers and those working for them providing services distanced and insulated by management control delegation from the immediate influence of politics. This is asking a lot, as noted.

For this reason, it may make sense for governments to experiment with responsibility budgeting using pilot projects of the type authorized under the Government Performance and Results Act rather than going quickly to other, more radical, new modes of organization and control. The same may be recommended for Italian local governments. Slow adaptation probably is better that attempts to convert to the new model quickly. One impediment that makes slower transformation almost a necessity is the fact that few managers in government to whom greater delegation of authority and responsibility is to be given under reform have had much experience with this approach, or with New Public Management-oriented devolution of decision making, or decentralization generally. Further, few elected officials and senior executives outside of New Zealand and other nations that have implemented reforms of this nature have much experience with self-restraint and management by results.

The incentives and disincentives implicit in NPM-oriented responsibility budgeting, accounting and management control must be experienced and evaluated in individual institutional contexts. The methods outlined in this chapter must be adapted to the levels of budgeting, accounting and management control sophistication of each organization and level of government in which they are applied. In addition, attention must be paid to the fit of this approach to the political culture of the organization and government in which it is implemented. Leadership and politics make a significant difference in overcoming bureaucratic resistance to change (Johansen, Jones & Thompson, 1997; Jones & McCaffery, 1997; Reschenthaler & Thompson, 1996).

Experience with NPM in other nations teaches that slow, careful and incremental implementation, in contrast to rapid and comprehensive change, is more likely to lead to success in attempts to reform public sector budgeting, accounting and management control practices. Provision of empirical support for this observation is not the purpose of this chapter. However, this has been found to be the case in the United Kingdom, Australia, New Zealand, Sweden, other European nations and elsewhere (Jones & Schedler, 1997). The dynamics of political systems demand that comprehensive reform be given careful scrutiny at both the political and managerial levels of government (Jones et al., 2001). And political preferences with respect to the reform agenda are often short-lived, which dooms reforms that require long periods of time to implement properly. The examples of implementation in the U.S. demonstrate, however, that meaningful change takes decades to accomplish. In contrast, in local government such as Ravenna, Italy, change can take place more rapidly. However, Ravenna is only one municipal example in Italy. Comprehensive responsibility structure and management control reform in the Italian local government context also will take a long period of time to achieve.

ACKNOWLEDGMENTS

The authors wish to acknowledge the contribution to this chapter from work coauthored with our colleague Fred Thompson, Grace and Elmer Goudy Professor of Public Management and Policy, Atkinson Graduate School of Management, Willamette University, Salem, Oregon, USA.

REFERENCES

Anthony, R., & Young, D. (1995). *Management control in nonprofit organizations* (5th ed.). Homewood, IL: Richard D. Irwin.

Arwidi, O., & Samuelson, L. A. (1993). The development of budgetary control in Sweden: A research note. *Management Accounting Research*, 4(2), 93–107.

Barzelay, M. (2000). *The new public management: Improving the research agenda and policy dialogue*. Berkeley, CA: University of California Press.

Barzelay, M., & Armajani, B. (1992). *Breaking through bureaucracy*. Berkeley: University of California Press.

Borgonovi, E. (1996). *Principi e sistemi aziendali per le amministrazioni pubbliche*. Milano: Egea, Milano.

Falcon, G. (1998). *Lo stato autonomista*. Bologna: Il Mulino.

Giarda, P. (1995). *Regioni e federalismo fiscale*. Bologna: Il Mulino.

Harr, D. J. (1989). Productive unit resourcing: A business perspective on government financial management. *Government Accountants Journal* (Summer), 51–57.

Harr, D. J., & Godfrey, J. T. (1991). *Private sector financial performance measures and their applicability to government operations*. Montvale, NJ: National Association of Accountants.

Harr, D. J., & Godfrey, J. T. (1992). The total unit cost approach to government financial management. *Government Accountants Journal* (Winter), 15–24.

Hood, C. (1991). A public management for all seasons? *Public Administration*, 69.

Johansen, C., Jones, L. R., & Thompson, F. (1997). Management and control of budget execution. In: R. Golembiewski & J. Rabin (Eds), *Public Budgeting and Finance* (4th ed., pp. 577–584). New York: Marcel Dekker.

Jones, L. R., Guthrie, J., & Steane, P. (Eds) (2001). *Learning from international public management reform* (Vols. 11A & B). Oxford: JAI Press – Elsevier.

Jones, L. R., & McCaffery, J. L. (1992). Federal financial management reform and the Chief Financial Officers Act. *Public Budgeting and Finance*, 12(4), 75–86.

Jones, L. R., & McCaffery, J. L. (1997). Implementing the Chief Financial Officers Act and the Government Performance and Results Act in the federal government. *Public Budgeting and Finance*, 17(1), 35–55.

Jones, L. R., & Schedler, K. (Eds) (1997). *International perspectives on the new public management.* Stamford, CT: JAI Press.

Jones, L. R., & Thompson, F. (1997). The five Rs of the new public management. In: L. R. Jones & K. Schedler (Eds), *International Perspective on the New Public Management.* Greenwich, CT: JAI Press.

Jones, L. R., & Thompson, F. (1999). *Public management: Institutional renewal for the 21st century.* Stamford, CT: JAI Press – Elsevier.

Lapsley, I. (1994). Responsibility accounting revived? Market reforms and budgetary control. *Management Accounting Research, 5*(3, 4), 337–352.

McCaffery, J. L., & Jones, L. R. (2001). *Budgeting and financial management in the federal government.* Greenwich, CT: Information Age Press.

Mussari, R. (1994). *Il management delle aziende pubbliche.* Padova, Italy: Cedam.

Mussari, R. (1997). Autonomy, responsibility, and new public management in Italy. In: L. R. Jones & K. Schedler (Eds), *International Perspectives on the New Public Management.* Greenwich, CT: JAI Press.

Mussari, R. (1999). *La valutazione dei programmi nelle aziende pubbliche.* Torino: Giappichelli.

OECD (1995). *Budgeting for results: Perspectives on public expenditure management.* Paris: Organization for Economic Co-operation and Development.

Otley, D., Broadbent, J., & Berry, A. (1995). Research in management control: An overview of its development. *British Journal of Management, 6*, 31–44.

Pollitt, C. (1993). *Managerialism and the public services: Cuts or cultural change in the 1990s?* (2nd ed.). Cambridge, MA: Basil Blackwell.

Pollit, C., & Bouckaert, G. (2000). *Public management reform: A comparative analysis.* Oxford: Oxford University Press.

Reschenthaler, G. B., & Thompson, F. (1996). The information revolution and the new public management. *Journal of Public Administration Research and Theory, 6*(1), 125–144.

Schedler, K. (1995). *Ansatze einer wirkungsorientirten verwaltungsfuhrung: Von der idee des new public managements (NPM), zum konkreten gestaltungsmodell.* Bern: Verlag Paul Haupt.

Tani, T. (1995). Interactive control in target cost management. *Management Accounting Research, 6*(4), 401–414.

Thompson, F. (1994). Mission-driven, results-oriented budgeting: Financial administration and the new public management. *Public Budgeting & Finance, 14*(3), 90–105.

Thompson, F., & Jones, L. R. (1986). Controllership in the public sector. *Journal of Policy Analysis and Management, 5*(3), 547–571.

Thompson, F., & Jones, L. R. (1994). Reinventing *the Pentagon: How the new public management can promote institutional renewal.* San Francisco: Jossey-Bass.

Zangrandi, A. (1994). *Autonomia ed economicità nelle aziende pubbliche.* Milano: Giuffrè.

PART III:
ANTI-CORRUPTION STRATEGIES

10. POLITICAL CORRUPTION: ESTABLISHING THE PARAMETERS

Peter deLeon and Mark T. Green

INTRODUCTION

The presence of political corruption possibly predates the historical record. For years, it was viewed as an artifact of political development, a common malignancy that nations would naturally reject as a function of their respective national maturations; this was one of the underlying theses of the American progressive movement. However, this cleansing has been neither as straightforward nor as natural as its proponents would argue. An anti-corruption coalition established in the 1990 under the umbrella of Transparency International (TI) has brought a new light on the world of political corruption. TI annually publishes a Corruption Perception Index that in 2001 ranked over 90 nations in terms of their perceived political corruptions. Peter Eigen, the TI Chairman, observed that "There is no end in sight to the misuse of power by those in public office – and corruption levels are perceived to be as high as ever in both the developed and developing nations" (Transparency International Press Release, 2001).[1]

Anecdotally, cases of corruption continue to intrude onto national agenda. In August 2003, *The Economist* lead editorial asked Italian Prime Minister Silvio Berlusconi to resign for numerous indiscretions, including having his ruling party vote him amnesty while in served as Prime Minister (Anonymous, 2003a); Berlusconi's case was particularly illuminating since he was forced to testify at his own bribery trial (Bruni, 2003a),[2] which he immediately amended by declaring in an interview with the *New York Times* that he was the ultimate defender of Italian freedom (Bruni, 2003a). In France, the former Prime Minister, under President Jacques Chirac, Alain Juppe, has been charged with illegally soliciting funds for their former political party in the mid-1980s (Tabliabue, 2003). Buddy Cianci, the long-time (and often re-elected) mayor of Providence (Rhode Island) was convicted of racketeering and sent to federal prison (Stanton, 2003). Lastly, the collapse of the most recent negotiations of the World Trade Organization (in Cancun, Mexico) floundered (at least in part) on the inability of the developed and less-developed nations (the latter forming a coalition of 21 developing nations) to agree on how (or even if) corruption should be a WTO priority (Anonymous, 2003b). In short, the baleful presence of political corruption continues, today more so than ever.[3]

Within the last few years, the World Bank has focused some of its activities on political corruption, which it viewed as a detriment to the continuation of an orderly and equitable process of economic development in Third and Fourth World nations. Thus, the World Bank has argued for the elimination of political corruption (which it defined as "the abuse of public office for private gain") through the employment of five key elements:

(1) Increasing Political Accountability;
(2) Strengthening Civil Society Participation;
(3) Creating a Competitive Private Sector;
(4) Institutional Restraints on Power; and
(5) Improving Public Sector Management.

This essay considers the potential contribution of the New Public Management (NPM) to address a number of the World Bank's suggestions, specifically, those dealing with political accountability and, of course, improving the management of the public sector. The authors' initial attempt along these lines (deLeon & Green, 2001) posed a similar set of questions, but was only able to address those questions through examples drawn from the American political system. At the time, the argument was made that an examination of the United States' incidents of political corruption would at least test the theory that modernity ameliorates political corruption.[4] We now cast a somewhat wider net, looking at other developed nations as well as the U.S., to ask the central question: what effects would NPM have on the incidents of political corruption across a number of nations?

We need first to pose a number of reservations on this analysis. First, as we have indicated above, we are only addressing political corruption among the economically developed nations, typically those nations within the OECD, and most often within the European/American bloc of nations. While this restriction would undercut any pretensions towards a more general theory of political corruption, the number of additional considerations (e.g. political, social, economic, and cultural) that would have to be entertained to responsibly include the nations of the developing world is simply beyond the scope of the present enterprise. Put in a more positive vein, there is more than ample evident of political corruptions within the developed nations upon which to base the present analysis.

A second, perhaps more of a semantic reservation, is in order. Much of the current literature on political corruption has focused on what many (e.g. Drew, 1999; Etizoni, 1984) might call the 800 pound gorilla – campaign financing. Drew (1999), for one, has termed the conditions surrounding campaign financing as one of the most poisonous elements in contemporary society. But one man's poison is another's elixir, that is, the issue of campaign finance is a highly contentious issue. In the United States, for instance, many, such U.S. Senator Mitch McConnell (R-KY), have strongly suggested that campaign financing is part and parcel of free speech in America and cannot be curtailed; in this, he claims the support of the U.S. Supreme Court in *Buckley v. Valeo* (also, see Burke, 2002). Others (e.g. della Portia & Vannucci, 2002; Golden, 2000) talk to campaign financing as a central contributor to corruption within the Italian political system, and Susan Pharr (2002) argues that it is pivotal to Japanese perceptions of political elections; the French polity suffers similarly, although concern there is somewhat diminished by what Pujas and Rhodes (2002) call a culture of "political hypocricy." There is little doubt that politics and political corruption can and do go hand-in-hand, but until some sort of agreement can be reached on the general permissibility or illegality of such relationships, they need to be treated more as propositions than as definitive evidence.

This essay will briefly presents an overview of research in political corruption as a way of introducing the problem. Next, it sets out the general tenets of NPM and extracts a series of concepts and measurements that, if designed and implemented, should reduce the amount of political corruption. We then offer up a reviews of some relatively recent acts could be described as corruptions, as well as referring to the U.S. cases largely described in our earlier essay (deLeon & Green, 2001). Finally, we will comment on the intersections, with particular focus on both what we have learned and what remains in an NPM research agenda regarding political corruption.

AN ASSESSMENT OF POLITICAL CORRUPTION

Traditionally, public administration and public management (that are, after all, disciplines that traffic in "good government") have viewed corruption as a rare occurrence. The recent conviction of U.S. Congressman James Traficant (D-OH) and his disbarment from the House of Representatives illustrates the "bad apple" syndrome (Clines, 2002; Johnston, 2001). When such a situation occurs, it is typically treated an isolated (usually egregious) issue of public accountability, one in which ethical behavior and education are inevitably portrayed as the ready remedy (Caiden & Caiden, 1977). Alternatively, Quah (1999) has asserted that the solution belongs in a stronger central political authority, with his principal example being his native Singapore. Political science has been much more open in its recognition of political corruption (e.g. Benson et al., 1978; Johnston, 1982) but even here, the empirical literature has been characterized as "not extensive" (Meier & Holbrook, 1992, p. 135) and policy recommendations are murky.[5] Economists have generally have treated corruption as little more than (in their jargon) "side payments," that is, a worrisome but largely inconsequential (as we will see, it is not an especially "expensive") condition.

The important exception is Susan Rose-Ackerman (1978; also, Rose-Ackerman, 1998), who makes two important observations: first, that corruption is most likely to occur at the vital intersection between the public and private sectors, i.e. between public goods and personal gain (also see Johnston, 1982); and second, that corruption can best be described as an inherent, *systemic* activity, as opposed to the insular, case study perspective of public administration scholars. In this latter observation, Rose-Ackerman is in close agreement with sociologist Robert K. Merton (1968), who argues that corruption often serves a manifest, desired social and political function; if the recognized government is unable to provide a good or service (say, dependable policing), there will be occasions for people to engage in "side payments" to obtain the desired articles or services, at times on a systematic basis.

Public policy and public management scholars cannot afford academic detachment of economists and sociologists. We will strongly agree with Rose-Ackerman (1998) and Robert Klitgaard (1988) that if political corruption is found to be "inefficient," i.e. that it somehow distracts from the cost-efficient operations of government, especially in the long-term, then public management must be directly concerned with countering corruption and its costs.

Drawing from these disciplines, let us begin with a basic definition of political corruption, recognizing, with Michael Johnston (1986, p. 379) that "We should not expect to find a sharp distinction between corruption and non-corrupt actions. Instead, we will find fine gradations of judgment, reflecting a variety of equivocations, mitigating circumstances, and attributed motives." Our proposed definition suggests that the typical public administration and economic assumption – that currency lies at the root of political corruption – is incomplete, because alternative means of valued currency or exchange (clan, fame, patriotism, etc.)

can be involved. Thus, we posit our working definition: a co-operative form of unsanctioned, usually condemned policy influence for some type of significant personal gain, in which the currency could be economic, political, or ideological remuneration (deLeon, 1983, p. 25).

The question then poses itself: granted that corruption exists, should public management be concerned with it? Some have suggested that in developing nations, corruption might even serve as a *benevolent* management tool in terms of political recruitment (Nye, 1967). But this recognition extends beyond recruitment activities. For the owner of a diner to give a dough nut to the cop on the beat could easily be construed as a low-level form of bribery, but it might just as justifiably be viewed as a form of direct taxation for a police retainer, services rendered, or maybe as little more than a tip for overtime; similarly, a bribe might be considered a user's fee for overcoming a bureaucratic bottleneck, just another (albeit illegal) business expense, perhaps akin to insurance. Klitgaard (1988, p. 33) captures the idea: "... if the prevailing system is bad, then corruption may be good."

We claim, however, that this arguments is fundamentally wrong on at least two counts. The first addresses economic or opportunity costs. Activities we would consider corrupt (especially if we include illegal drug activities) divert large amounts of resources from the public sector, money that could easily be spent better elsewhere (see Klitgaard, 1988; Rose-Ackerman, 1998). In the U.S. in the 1990s, deLeon (1993, p. 33) "guesstimated," (given that there is no accurate way of "knowing") the "costs" of corruption (particularly if one includes the so-called "victimless crimes" like prostitution) in the tens of billions of dollars; world wide, this estimate could easily run into the low hundreds of billions of dollars, and more if one calculates in the corruption in the public health services (e.g. AIDS vaccines and food distribution services in southern Africa and Southeast Asia). Still, in a world economy that runs into the tens of trillions of dollars, this is hardly a lethal financial wound.

However, a straightforward cost-benefit analysis (assuming for a moment that both costs and benefits could be accurately assessed) of the harm caused by corruption would need to be more than an accounting exercise. It is much more complex because of confounding complications like time frames, the state of specific national economies, and, most centrally, the expectations of a nation's people as they see corruption inequitably sapping their economy and well-being.[6] Writing primarily about Japan and South Korea, Pharr (2002, p. 841) generalizes, "Civic-ness,... is fundamental to social trust and attitudes of cooperation that in turn promote and sustain good government." As political scientists from Almond and Verba (1960) to Frank Fukuyama (1995) to Robert Putnam (2000) remind us, "trust" is the essential national "glue" necessary in any nation building (or maintaining) exercise.

The second concern posits: if corruption is all-but inevitable, simply accept it as a minor cost of democratic governance. The former Prime Minister of Italy, Bettino Craxi, most clearly depicted the "everybody does it" argument (or what sociologists like Merton refer to as the "functionalist" argument) in his 1992 speech to the Italian Chamber of Deputies:

> The political parties have been the body and soul of our democratic structures.... [U]nder the cover of irregular funding to the parties, cases of corruption and extortion have flourished and become intertwined... What needs to be said, and which in any case *everybody knows*, is that the greater part of political funding is irregular or illegal... If the greater part of this is to be considered criminal pure and simple then the greater part of the political system is a criminal system. I do not believe there is anybody in this hall who has had the responsibility for a large organization who can stand up and deny what I have just said. Sooner or later the facts would make a liar of him (Craxi's speech is quoted in della Porta & Vannucci, pp. 717–718; emphases added).[7]

Thus, if corruption is little more than part and parcel of democratic governance and going to happen anyway, why expend valuable resources on something that will happen in any case? In response, we claim that there is little choice (see deLeon, 1993), that "minor" corruptions too often metastasize into larger ones, i.e. the dough nut on the beat segues into a bottle of scotch that seamlessly becomes a protection payment. Moreover, there are too many examples when citizens might have recognized the functional nature of corruption as a latent form of governance, and still found cause to remove its practitioners from positions of authority. Lastly, at its base, corruption is simply inequitable in terms of democratic governance, its accesses, and its citizens, if not in the short run, then surely over the long run (see Kaufman, 1997). When an individual acts as if he somehow personifies government – as might have been the case when former German Chancellor Helmut Kohl solicited funds that remain unaccounted for (see Anonymous, 2002) or the former Foreign Minister of France accepted a bribe from a lobbyist who also happens to be his mistress (Anonymous, 2000) – then the democratic underpinnings and financial assurances of government are potentially at risk. As Klitgaard (1988, p. 42) cautions, "Whereas an occasion act of corruption may be efficient, corruption once systematized and deeply ingrained never is."

Let us assert a few benchmarks. First, most public affairs scholars have recognized the destructive nature of corruption in both political and economic terms. The traffic in corruption fundamentally skews the political process by confusing or substituting private gains for public goods. Public administration scholars propose "remedies" of greater education, higher ethical standards (Frederickson, 1999; Garafolo et al., 1999), higher wages for administrators (in developing nations), or greater centralized authority (Quah, 1999) but these have not proven to be particularly effective. These shortcomings argue for more structural changes. Second, corruption is an important area for continued study, both for its generic activities as well as for the more specific question of how the NPM might ameliorate the condition, especially in light of the World Bank's charge (*supra*: 236). Let us now briefly review the relevant NPM theoretic and applied literatures, focusing on the nexus between the public and private sectors.

EVALUATING THE UNDERPINNINGS OF NEW PUBLIC MANAGEMENT

Many public administration scholars during the 1990s warned about the problems associated with implementing new public management reforms in their respective country's bureaucracy (Lynn, 1998). Their recurrent theme centered an entrepreneurial form of government. George Frederickson (1999) claims that entrepreneurial government will somehow lead to an abuse of administrative powers, an absence of democratic responsibility, and ultimately political corruption. There is little argument that an entrepreneurial government is a conceptual bedrock of NPM in that it is required to make sustainable changes in the managerial ranks. Moreover, it is certainly true that an element of adopted NPM reforms is a certain level of empowered government entrepreneurs capable of making innovative decisions without the usual system of checks and balances.

However, a more complete reading of the NPM texts goes well beyond the reliance of entrepreneurial government (Barzelay & Armajani, 1992; Holmes & Shand, 1995; OECD, 1996; Osborne & Gaebler, 1992; Stokes, 1996). We earlier identified on theoretic and practices bases a number of key features of NPM, as schematically set out in Table 1.

Table 1 reflects such managerial components as accountability, transparency, efficiency, and performance. Certainly, in the minds of NPM scholars such as Barzelay and Armajani (1992) or Kettl (2000), improvements in these areas – that is, not *just* in entreprenuerism – can only enhance public services (see Cohen & Eimicke, 1999).

Taken collectively, NPM principles represent a coherent and interdependent constellation of managerial elements (OECD, 1996; PUMA, 1995, 1996a, b, c, 1997; Uhr, 1999). NPM reforms offer a well-integrated NPM managerial agenda; adopting the values of entrepreneurial government, rule flexibility, and privatization also requires the accompanying functional reforms, such as improved management information systems, performance based monitoring, and enhanced incentive structures. Thus, NPM reforms need to identify and adopt a relatively complete set of NPM principles and functions (Ferris & Graddy, 1997; Frant, 1997; Jones & Thompson, 1999) or risk key gaps. We begin with a short exposition of the theory underlying NPM's functional reforms. To address these matters, we should first address basic theories upon which NPM is based.

Table 1. NPM Characteristics According to Selected Sources.

Barzelay and Armajani (1992)	Osborne and Gaebler (1992)	OECD (1996)	Holmes and Shand (1995)
Shift from the public interest to a focus on results and citizen's value	Catalytic government	Closer focus on results in terms of efficiency, effectiveness and quality service	More strategic or results oriented (efficiency, effectiveness, and service quality) approach to decision making
Shift from efficiency to a focus on quality and value	Community owned government	Replacement of highly centralized hierarchical structures by decentralized management environments where decisions on resource allocation are made closer to the point of delivery	The replacement of highly centralized hierarchical organizational structures with decentralized management environments where decisions on resource allocation and service delivery are take closer the point of delivery, where greater relevant information is available and which provide scope for feedback from clients and other interest groups
Shift from administration to a focus on production	Competitive government	The flexibility to explore alternatives to direct public provision and regulation that might yield more cost-effective policy outcomes	Flexibility to explore alternatives to direct public provision which might provide more cost effective policy outcomes
Shift from control to a focus on winning adherence to norms	Mission driven government	A greater focus on efficiency in the services provided directly by the public sector, involving the establishment of productivity target and the creation of competitive environments within and among the public sector organizations	Focus attention on the matching of authority and responsibility as a key to improving performance, including through such mechanisms as explicit performance contracting

Shift from specifying functions, authority and structures to focus on identifying missions, services, customers and outcomes	Results oriented government	The creation of competitive environments within and between public sector organizations
Shift form justifying costs to a focus on delivering value	Customer driven	The strengthening of strategic capacities at the center to "steer" government to respond to external changes and diverse interest quickly, flexibly and at least cost
Shift from enforcing responsibility to a focus on building accountability	Enterprising government	Greater accountability and transparency through requirements to report results and their full cost
Shift from simply following rules and procedures to a focus on understanding and applying norms, identifying and solving problems, and continuously improving processes	Anticipatory government	Service-wide budgeting and management systems to support and encourage the changes.
Shift from simply operating administrative systems to a focus on separate service from control, expanding customer choice, encouraging collective action, providing incentives, measuring and analyzing results and enriching feedback	Decentralize government	
	Market-oriented government	

Fundamental to an understanding of the NPM practice is the concept of "transaction costs" (see Ménard, 1997; North, 1996; Williamson, 1997; Williamson & Masteen, 1995), which Ferris and Graddy (1997, p. 91) define as "the costs (other than price) associated with carrying out two-sided transactions – that is, the exchange of goods or services from one individual to another with agreed-upon payment for performance. These costs vary with the nature of the transaction and the way it is organized." Basically, transaction cost analysis suggests that successful firms will try to minimize these costs. Nobel Laureate Ronald Coase (1937) had previously argued that organizations were composed by a series of formal and informal contracts that determined by the characteristics of the transaction costs. Typically, the employer would subsume these contracts under one contract, which specified the employer-employer relationship within certain limits (Coase, 1937; Miller, 1992). This relationship later became known as "principal-agent" theory.

The principal-agent relationship is inherently problematic. In Jones and Thompson's (1999, p. 1) words "... (a) the efforts of the agent cannot be perfectly observed; (b) the interests of agent and principal diverge; and (c) agents pursue their own interests, i.e. behave opportunistically." Moreover, at least in theory, there are information asymmetries: the principal has an overview of the firm's objective while the agent has a better view of the day-to-day operation in the immediate sector. And neither actor wishes to reveal his/her information completely, for fear of surrendering her/his comparative (bureaucratic) advantage. Therefore, the practical task of the principal-agent relationship is to justify and respect the two perspectives.

Jones and Thompson (1999) have observed that bureaucratic hierarchical organizations developed specialized rules (codified as "contracts") that outline clearly which activities are allowed and those that are prohibited under a principal-agents regimen, as well as specifying the sanctions for violating the rules. The problem with the rule-based mode of control, however, is that scarce resources (such as human capital) must be expended to monitor the rules instead of allocated toward performance. To address the principal-agent problem, NPM suggests that end results – *not* process – provide clearer, more discerning information regarding the actors' (respective) preferences and thereby leads one to design better incentive systems in the context of the organization. By providing better information to the principal, the agent's activities can monitored, resulting in what economists refer to as "transparency" (Jones & Thompson, 1999). Furthermore, this information can counter the tendency by agents to serve their self-interest or, again, in the language of the economist (and some street gangs), the tendency to "shirk." These capabilities are immensely enhanced by advances in modern management information systems.

The evidence supporting these assertions has a long history of application, albeit in the private sector. Better information systems and incentive structures regarding the principal-agent relationship was a direct result of the rise of industrialization in the early part of the 20th century. Moving from a craftsman production mode to a production system of mass-production assembly line mode (i.e. multiplying the number of contractual relationships) required more accurate systems of monitoring, coordinating, and (in many cases) bargaining, in particular, the evolution of modern cost accounting systems and accrual based accounting. Thus, the employer ("principal") could more easily monitor the activities and performance of workers ("agents") from the perspective of the firm.

There are, of course, noted shortcomings to principal-agents theory when its monitoring activities are applied to the public sector. For instance, labor unions provided a means by which unwieldy individual contracts could be aggregated.[8] There is a growing awareness that principal-agents is a uni-directionable management procedure, in which the principal somehow manages to ride "herd" on the agents (Fischer, 1990). Alternative public management protocols stress such ideas such as a participatory managerial concept, in which agents and principals reach consensual agreements as to goals and missions, a more democratic regimen if you will (deLeon & deLeon, 2002). Furthermore, the public sector is, in many ways, different than its private sector counterpart; for example, Moe (1984) has suggested that the public sector is directed by a multitude (or confusion) of principals such as elected representatives, administrative executives, and a variety of superior-subordinate relationships (e.g. civil service) within the organization itself. In addition, the public and private sectors are often perceived as driven by differing sets of normative concerns; this distinction can most readily be viewed as their respective emphases of "efficiency" vs. "equity" tenets (Okun, 1975). The ultimate "principals" in the public organization are, of course, the citizens themselves and depending on their own policy and program preferences, associated principals and agents can be sent (or receive) a variety of conflicting signals (Ferris & Graddy, 1998). All of these conditions can result in obscured systems of managerial transparency and accountability. These lead, in turn, to different managerial concepts and approaches.

This concern is especially germane with regard to financial matters (e.g. budgeting and accounting) given that the political process has the greatest influence on the management systems (Jones, 1992). Traditionally, public sector budgeting fails to provide a clear picture of program effectiveness. Furthermore, budgeting (Wildavsky, 1964) and even audits (Power, 1993) are primarily driven by politics; any sense of accountability is geared towards politics rather than management. As the record of Government Performance and Results Act (GPRA) points out (Radin, 1998), public sector evaluation is beset by a series of political and methodological compromises that render its precise managerial application problematic. While private sector accounting can be obscured (witness the example of Enron, whose ally was the accounting firm of Arthur Anderson), the opportunities for accounting mischief are easily multiplied in the public sector.

In summary, NPM offers several constructs that would be useful in combating the excesses of political corruption; these include community-owned government, competitive government, mission-driven government, and results-oriented government that is enterprising, anticipatory, and decentralized. Modern accounting and management information systems are necessary adjuncts to these NPM principals. This brief review also indicates some potential oversights:

- while some appreciative nod has been given to the institutional features of an organization, there is little indication as to what are the key organizational variables that would hinder/facilitate the introduction of NPM; that is, all organizations are treated by NPM as roughly isomorphic;
- even though democratic systems are seemingly inferred, there is no direct discussion of the values indicated by that political system; that is, at its basis, NPM appears to be largely indifferent to political ideologies; it should produce laudatory managerial results regardless of its ideological bedrock; and
- potential corruptors are possibly just as versed in the necessary accounting and monitoring procedures as their NPM counterparts and, if they so choose, can potentially counter or avoid them.

With these overviews of both political corruption and NPM in hand, we can now turn to incidents of recent political corruptions to examine how NPM would have addressed them. In conjunction with earlier examples (see deLeon & Green, 2001), we will then consider the potential effects of NPM on corrupt conditions.

STUDY OF NOTEWORTHY CASES OF POLITICAL CORRUPTION

To help understand the capabilities of the NPM to guard against political corruption, we briefly discuss a few recent cases of what many (although surely not all) might view as corrupt actions. While we will later include discussions of national policies relating to campaign finance reforms (e.g. in Italy, the US, France and Germany), in this section we will deal with three specific cases: the so-called "Travelgate" that occurred during the early days of the Clinton Administration in the US; the trials of former German Prime Minister Helmut Kohl; and an account of recent press reporting that indicates pervasive political corruption in France.

Travelgate

The Clinton Presidency did not begin especially well. By April 1992, the Administration was troubled by numerous transitional difficulties. For instance, the newly appointed Attorney-General, Janet Reno, took full responsibility for the FBI attack on the Branch Davidian compound at Waco, Texas, and the resulting conflagration, while the White House did not issue a statement until well after the incident. So it was with particular embarrassment that on May 18, the President was reported in the national press of closing down air traffic at Los Angeles International Airport to have a haircut in Air Force One from Beverly Hills hair stylist Cristophe (usual fee, about $200). The following day, White House Press Secretary Dee Dee Myers announced that seven members of the White House Travel Office – that had the responsibility of arranging commercial (i.e. not on Air Force One) travel arrangements for the White House staff and the attendant press corps when they were traveling with the President – were being terminated. "Travelgate" was thus offered up on the presidential stage, which was to be scripted through at least four separate investigations and a press corps that seeming saw one of its cherished prerogatives threatened.

During the 1992 presidential election, Catherine Cornelius (a distant cousin of the President) had served as Clinton's liaison to World Wide Travel, which was owned by fellow Arkansan Betty Carney. Both wanted to continue working for President Clinton, particularly since World Wide Travel had made a reported profit in excess of over one million dollars during the campaign. Larry Watkins, one of Clinton's principal campaign aides, was the nexus, having once worked for World Wide as well as having been a business associate of Ms Clinton's in Little Rock. Rounding out this cast of central players were two more Arkansans, Harry Thomason and wife, Linda Bloodworth-Thomason, famously (if unofficially) known as "Friends of Bill" (FOB).

In December 31, 1992, Cornelius sent Watkins a memorandum, suggesting that if Clinton were to "privatize" the Travel Office, it would permit him to cut back the size of the staff (Clinton had promised to reduce the size of the White House staff by 25%) and result in better air fares; she also suggested the possibility that World Wide Travel (if chosen) could rebate back to the White House 3.5% of its usual commission, estimated to be approximately $210,000. In a January 26, 1993, memorandum to Watkins, Cornelius proposed that she and a friend assume the operating responsibilities of the Travel Office; thereupon, Watkins had both named as White House assistants. Finally, on February 15, Cornelius wrote Watkins a third memorandum, which again emphasized that the elimination of the Travel Office would result in a more efficient operation (including a reduction of costs), as well as (emphases in original memorandum):

(1) Incoming Clinton Administration More Comfortable and Familiar with this Proven System.
(2) Recommended Staff are More Knowledgeable and Familiar with the Personalities Involved as well as the System; thus, allowing for BETTER SERVICE.

These recommendations clearly inserted a partisan tone to the discussions since the existing Travel Office was staffed with career civil servants who were presumed not to be necessarily friendly with members of the Clinton Administration.

At roughly the same time, Harry Thomason – who, in his FOB position had choreographed the Inauguration and had been accorded a White House pass, complete with office and telephone – asked Press Secretary Myers if the "White House [Travel Office] charter business was subject to competitive bidding" and was referred to Billy Dale, the long-time Director of the Travel Office. Thomason then sent his business partner, Darnell Martens, to speak with Dale about becoming the travel broker for the White House. Dale was neither enthusiastic nor supportive, bluntly telling Martens (as he later recounted in an undated memorandum to Thomason), "... there was no possible combination of price/service under which [you] could earn the White House business and to not waste his time discussing the matter." Martens also indicated to Thomason that the Travel Office had been using a, "Republican-operated charter airline" that he accused of not fully charging the press corps during the 1992 campaign as a way of currying media favor for President Bush, charges the accused firm as well as members of the press denied.

Finally, in early March, Martens indicated to Thomason that he had heard "rumors" about corruption (allegedly, "kickbacks" from the airlines) in the Travel Office. Thomason passed along all of this information to Larry Watkins, who assigned Cornelius to the Travel Office to gather additional information on its operations, with instructions to report back to him by May 15. In the meantime, Thomason brought up during one of his informal conversations with the President what he called "trouble" in the White House Travel Office.

On May 12, Watkins and Cornelius met with Thomason and Martens. Later that day, Watkins and Cornelius met again with Thomason, with White House Deputy Counsel Vincent Foster and Associate Counsel William Kennedy joining them. Cornelius presented what she had observed during her assignment in the Travel Office, but apparently her evidence was insufficient to support charges, so Foster ordered Kennedy to instruct the Federal Bureau of Investigation (FBI) to initiate an immediate investigation of the Travel Office. While the FBI investigators were not initially persuaded with the charges, at the insistence of Kennedy and later Foster – and by the intimation that the "highest levels of the White House" were concerned – the Bureau opened an investigation on May 13. After some prompting by the White House, it became "criminal" in nature, according to a subsequent FBI press release.

Unbeknownst to the FBI, on May 13, Watkins and Foster also set in motion a plan to have the Travel Office audited by a representative of the accounting firm KPMG Peat Marwick, who (by coincidence) was serving in the Vice President's office as part of the Vice President's National Performance Review (NPR). A GAO report later indicated, however, that at this Watkins-Foster meeting, the decision was made to fire the staff of the Travel Office, even though Chief of Staff Mack McLarty insisted that the termination not take place until after the Peat Marwick report was finished, which had not even been started until the morning of May 14. There was still the matter of FBI pending investigation, which the White House had just convinced the FBI of its immediacy.

Foster managed to delay somehow the start of the FBI study until after the Peat Marwick report was completed, no small feat since the FBI had only reluctantly joined the fray. At this point, Watkins chose to brief the First Lady, Hillary Clinton. His notes, later released to the Congressional hearings, quoted her saying "Harry [Thomason] says his people can run things better, save money, etc." In the subsequent GAO study, Ms. Clinton, replying by letter, wrote that she did not remember using those "exact" words.

The Peat Marwick review team worked over the weekend and briefed its draft report to Watkins on the following Monday, May 17, prefaced by the disclaimer:

> Our procedures do not constitute an audit, examination, or review in accordance with standards established by the American Institute of Certified Public Accountants and, therefore, we do not express an opinion or any other form of assurance on the information presented in our report (Peat Marwick, 1998).

Based on the draft, however, Watkins wrote a memorandum to McLarty (with a copy to the First Lady) explaining how the report had provided grounds for firing the entire Travel Office staff, because, he later explained, he believed that the staff worked together "interchangeably."

On the morning of 19 May, Watkins wrote a brief press announcement for Press Secretary Myers, indicating that the Travel Office staff was being released as the result of a "routine review conducted as part of the Vice President's" NPR program; in the background notes, he also mentioned the on-going FBI review. He then met with the staff of the White House Travel Office to inform them that they were all being terminated, based on charges of "mismanagement" alluded to in the Peat Marwick report. They were told to gather their belongings and leave the building immediately. In the meantime, Foster and Kennedy altered Myers' text to exclude the FBI investigation, but, unknown to them, she had already briefed two reporters on the Travel Office dismissal, including the FBI's investigation.

As a result, the FBI criminal investigation was public knowledge literally before the Travel Office staff was aware of its existence.

In retrospect, as Drew (1994) commented, the ensuing "uproar was out of proportion," especially since five of the seven dismissed employees were reinstated to the federal civil service within a week of being fired, assured by the Justice Department that they were neither "targets nor subjects of the pending criminal investigation," and ultimately reassigned. Congress, with the concurrence of the White House, passed an amendment to the 1994 Department of Transportation authorization providing for $150,000 to pay their legal bills. On December 7, 1994, Travel Office Director Dale was indicted by a Federal Grand Jury for mishandling travel reimbursements; he plead innocent the following week; he was acquitted on all charges the following November. Deputy Director Gary Wright was not charged and chose to retire. World Wide Travel served as the White House travel consultant for two days before American Express was awarded the contract on a competitive bid basis. Still, the White House had received such criticism that President Clinton ordered an internal management review of the entire Travelgate incident, which, among other findings, indicated that Myers' briefing on the Travel Office's dismissals was "ill-advised" and that the five of the seven members of the Travel Office had been unfairly impugned. More specifically, it found that

> The abrupt manner of dismissal of the Travel Office employees was unnecessary and insensitive.... All the employees should have had an opportunity to hear the reasons for their termination, especially the allegations of wrongdoing, and should have been afforded an opportunity to respond (*White House Management Review*, 1992).

Comments by the President consistently reflected that he was generally unaware of what had transpired, even after it had become a public issue. He subsequently responded to Travelgate questions during an interview with CBS News reporter Connie Chung on May 27 that it was not, "... handled as well as it should have been. And I said so... [saying] I take responsibility to any mistakes made in the White House and mistakes were made in the way that was handled-absolutely."

While Travelgate probably affected the lives of various individuals, it most centrally affected the institution of the White House and, pivotally, the public's perception of the President and, later, Ms. Clinton. As Drew (1994, p. 179) observed,

> However valid the criticisms of the travel office were, the matter couldn't have been handled worse. The picture that was drawn was of cronyism and looseness with the truth. It apparently didn't occur to anyone that hiring the Little Rock company and putting the cousin – distant or not – in charge wouldn't look particularly good... There was a systemic failure within the White House.

The Scandals of the German CDU

Christian Democrat Helmut Kohl had served as the Chancellor of the Federal Republic of Germany for almost 16 years before being defeated by Social Democrat Gerhard Schröder in 1998. His electoral defeat represented a milestone in post-WW II German and European politics. Kohl had presided over West Germany at the end of the Cold War and, with the collapse of the Berlin Wall, had become known as the "Unification Chancellor." He was in many ways an icon among European statesmen.

In 1999, less than a year after his defeat, during an investigation of possible tax irregularities over a million Deutsch Mark (DM) donation to the Christian Democrat party (CDU) by a Canadian arms dealer, Kohl was forced to admit publicly that he had run a series of "secret accounts" for political contributors. These accounts, clearly outside the purview of German election regulations, were used by Mr. Kohl as "slush funds" for CDU candidates. He later admitted to receiving over two million DMs during the 1990s, and possibly additional millions of DMs during the period of his Chancellorship. Moreover, in Germany, political contributions greater than 20,000 DM are taxed. By not immediately acknowledging them, Kohl had also violated German tax codes. This was, in short, a scandal of the first magnitude, with most observers indicating a case of political corruption (Patterson, 2000).

Kohl later admitted that he had in fact accepted "undisclosed contribution," justifying his position ". . . on the grounds that the funds were needed to strengthen his party's standing among the East German electorate" (Hooper, 2000, p. 2). Kohl refused to divulge the names of the political contributors, because he had "given his word not to," and, simply, that "people came first." Rather, he chose to step down as the CDU's honorary chairman., thus providing some protection from the political fallout to the CDU but sacrificing any chance of political redemption. However, Kohl did continue to sit in the German *Bundestag* (where he could and did claim parliamentary immunity).

Kohl had previously explained in late December that while his acceptance of the funds "may be technically in [the] breach, he has committed no fundamental sin and, in particular, that there were no [political] favors" (Woollacott, 1999, p. 2). Still, rumors immediately surfaced that this was just the tip of the Kohlian iceberg; for instance, it was rumored that French President Francois Mitterand had contributed millions of DM to Kohl in the mid-1980s, even though the charges later proved to be largely unsubstantiated. (These allegations also surfaced in France, in charges brought against President Mitterand by former Foreign Minister Roland Dumas; see below.)

More troubling rumors, however, were disclosed and corroborated. For instance, Kohl's Interior Minister, Manfred Kanther, admitted that the CDU treasury in the state of Hesse "ran a secret Swiss bank account to harbour more than DM 17 million of illicit undisclosed party donations." In addition, Wolfgang Schaüble, Kohl's long-time party deputy and his successor as the CDU leader, confessed that he (Schaüble) had accepted "an illicit DM 100,000 payment from a German arms dealer which was not declared in the party's official audit" (both quotations from Kirschbaum, 2000, p. 2), thus lending greater public credibility to the political corruption charges surrounding the Christian Democrats.

In a not-altogether widely accepted denouement in February 2001, former Chancellor Kohl agreed to pay a fine of 100,000 pounds sterling, in exchange for not having to stand trial or reveal the names of the contributors. Kohl observed that in paying the fine, he would "avoid a lengthy legal process that would be a great burden to him and his family" (Hooper, 2000, p. 1).

But while Kohl may have found some relief from his immediate corruption scandals, the CDU's problems only continued. In April 2002, *The Economist* published an article entitled, "Corruption in Germany: Too Much of It," (Anonymous, 2002), in which the editors listed eight incidents (six, not counting Kohl & Kanther) since 2001, in which state-level CDU functionaries had diverted funds for either party coffers or personal activities. In one case, Hans-Joachim Dörfer, a CDU treasurer in Trier, was sentenced to ten years in prison for embezzling $10 million dollars from a charity.

However, what might easily spell political disaster for the CDU in terms of upcoming elections has been mitigated by the disclosure that five members of Chancellor Schröder's Social Democrats party were also under recent investigation and indictments for various acts of state-level corruption.

Germany's political reputation for liberal democracy, in short, fell under serious challenge, with Peter Eigen (the chairman of Transparency International) being quoted as saying that Germany "is much more corrupt than previously thought" (Anonymous, 2002, p. 45); in the annual TI listings, Germany is ranked only 20th (out of a total of 91) for public honesty. The evidence that has been presented to date covers the political waterfront in Germany, from its highest office (Chancellor) to local politics. If nothing else, it indicates that the lynchpin of the European economy can still be gravely affected by the malfeasance produced by political corruptions.

Recent Political Corruption in France

Political corruption in France brings a very different perspective to an Anglo-American perspective; "crimes of passion" in the United States (witness the impeachment of President Bill Clinton over sexual imbroglios and his unwillingness to own up to them; see Klein, 2002; Rozell & Wilcox, 2000) that would easily result in removal from office and potentially prison terms are often considered as "politics as usual" in France. Indeed, the funeral of former French President Francois Mitterand was openly attended by his wife and children *and* his mistress and their daughter.[9] Still, even under these less stringent rules and a more forgiving electorate (at least regarding *le affaire de coeur*), France has experienced a number of recent political corruptions, or what *The Economist* called "shenanigans" (Anonymous, 2000); in this article, eleven different cases of political corruption are noted.

Perhaps the most noted case was brought against French President Jacques Chirac. While he was Mayor of Paris, he was accused of using over $315,000 of state funds for a personal "slush" fund, which permitted him and his party to travel abroad in luxury between 1992 and 1995 (when he became President). Chirac has explained that "the money was from an official, but secret fund used to pay for covert anti-terrorist activities" (Jeffries, 2001, p. 1).[10] Others have indicated that the Paris has scant access to state funds, especially of this nature. Past that, Chirac has offered no additional material, and cannot be forced to testify since the French Constitution offers immunity to the President of the Republic. The French Supreme Court has upheld this interpretation.

The most involved case deals with the huge French banking firm, *Crédit Lyonnais*, which involves a number of French political and business elites, such as former Finance Ministers Michel Sapin and Edmond Alphadndery as well of *Lyonnais* chairman Jean Peyrelevade (Anonymous, 2001b). Basically, the trouble has to do with the apparent submission of false documents regarding the financial condition of *Crédit Lyonnais* that were supplied to California's insurance regulatory body involving the purchase of Executive Life, a California insurance policy that went bust when its junk bonds collapsed in value in the early 1990s. Evidence has surfaced that *Crédit Lyonnais* management was aware that its submissions were duplicitous. While *Crédit Lyonnais* is a largely privatized bank, the French taxpayer does have some interest in its affairs since the state (under the auspices of the *Banque de France*) rescued it from possible bankruptcy at a cost of roughly $18.5 billion. So this case has caught the French eye as a possible instance of governmental corruption.

Probably the most stereotypical of the French corruption cases involved M. Roland Dumas, former Foreign Minister under President Mitterand, and, more recently, the President of the French Constitutional Council, France's highest court; he had also been a hero of the Resistance as well as a lawyer to Picasso and Chagall. In January 2001, he began his trial on charges of receiving bribes, most notably from his one-time mistress as well as professional lobbyist, Christine Deviers-Joncour. From 1989 to 1993, she was a lobbyist for the French national oil company, *Elf*, with a "limitless" expense account, part of which she shared with M. Dumas, with gifts ranging from very expensive Italian shoes (one pair was estimated to have cost a thousand dollars!) to Greek sculptures (Anonymous, 2001c). Prosecution estimates for the gifts were approximately $9.1 million.

The obvious question was why a state-owned company would lobby a government minister. The answer, if one subscribes to M. Deviers-Jancour's account, is somewhat circuitous but fascinating: *Elf* was lobbying Dumas not on its own behalf, but at the urging of another state-owned company, Thomson-CSF, which was pressing at the time for governmental approval from French authorities to sell six frigates to Taiwan; *quai d'Orsay* was said to be opposed, fearing an adverse reaction from the People's Republic of China. The prosecution estimated that the sale was worth approximately $2.8 billion, while Dumas claimed Mitterand's approval. However, the court said that this particular line of defense was irrelevant to the case at hand.

At their trial, Dumas and Deviers-Jancour were joined by *Elf* defendants Loik De Floch-Prigent and Alfred Sirven (former director of *Elf* and his deputy). In May 2001, Dumas was convicted and sentenced to six months in jail; Deviers-Joncour was also convicted and received three years in prison (with 18 months being suspended); De Floch-Prigent (sentenced to three and a half years) and Sirven were also found guilty.

In June, Dumas was interviewed by correspondents from French newspaper *Le Figaro*, during which he accused former President Mitterand as well as a number of his ministers (including two current ministers) of dealing in kickbacks and bribes. In the interview, he charged that *Elf* had been a long-time "cash cow" to pass illicit funds to state ministers. He also raised the issue of *Elf* purchasing an oil refinery in East Germany, basically as a campaign contribution to German Chancellor Helmut Kohl; he claimed that "Mitterand endorsed the whole [refinery investment] project including the payment of commissions because he thought of France's interests." (In this charge, he was seconded by De Floch-Prigent.) Dumas also suggested that the French justice system was protecting "those still in powers of power . . . I have a few ideas about the system and the people concerned – and the latter know that I know" (both quotations from Graham, 2001, pp. 1–2). At last count, French investigators were looking into these charges.

As in the case of Germany, if these had been the entire body of political corruption in France, things might have settled down. But, as the listing noted in *The Economist* indicates, these case of corruption are only representative of the body of French corruption. Immediately following the Dumas interview in *Le Figaro*, *Business Week*'s International Edition editorialized "Why France's Hands May Never Scrub Clean" (Rossant, 2001). Later that year, viewing the European scene taken as a whole (including Spain and Italy) and the generalized lack of response to the literal outpouring of political corruptions, *Business Week* asked, "Is the Corruption Crusade Over?" (Ewing, 2001). In its most recent rating, TI placed France three notches below Germany, at number 23.

CONCLUSIONS

The juxtaposition of the three previous sections are meant to indicate how and where NPM reforms might most effectively minimize political corruption. Instead of walking our way through the offered examples of corruption, we will overlay them with the basic NPM principals (e.g. transaction cost analysis and principal agents theory), their attending supplements (or programmatic approaches, e.g. community-owned, decentralized government, mission-driven programs, and entrepreneurship), and the necessary workaday components (improved accountability and management information systems). Table 1 has set out many of these concepts. Let us also expand our database slightly by including other well-documented examples (e.g. the Italian patronage system and its relationship to political corruption), as well as some of our earlier examples (deLeon & Green, 2001). This approach results in both an examination of NPM principles and programs as well as leading us to ask some (what public management scholars call) "big questions" (see Behn, 1995; Kirlin, 1996; for illustrations).

We need first to remind ourselves of the working definition of political corruption presented earlier (see Section 2, above, for the supporting exposition):

> ... a co-operative form of unsanctioned, usually condemned policy influence for some type of significant personal gain, in which the currency could be economic, political, or ideological remuneration (deLeon, 1983, p. 25).

It is important to stress that this definition incorporates both economic and non-economic incentives or motivations to engage in political corruption. We also need to re-affirm our recognition (with Rose-Ackerman, 1989; Robert Merton, 1968) as to the *systemic* nature of political corruption.

We also need to observe that all these cases are set in government (read: *large*) bureaucracies; concern over scope, not surprisingly, is one of the underlying NPM tenets, calling for community-based, decentralized government. But this remains a critical observation when discussing the parameters within which the NPM can be most effective. In point of evidence, most governments and their component agencies are large organizations, and even larger when one folds in the relevant private sector organizations; witness the recurrent corruptions found in the U.S. Department of Defense. As public choice theorists have repeatedly cautioned us, government bureaucracies have for years thwarted their downsizing and re-organization as a matter of self-preservation; and, when forced to re-organize, the desired results have not always been realized. Such is the strength of established bureaucracies. In this regard, it was instructive to observe how the George W. Bush administration in the U.S. initially rejected the idea of a new administrative department concerned with domestic security as a response to the September 11th events, opting for a decentralized, flexible, possibly entrepreneurial agency. Then, justifiably abandoning many of those preferences, the Administration turned on an executive dime and demanded Congress create a Cabinet-level Department of Homeland Security (widely advertised as the largest government reorganization in fifty years), aggregating numerous agencies that had very distinct and difference missions. It will be equally interesting to watch how the legislation is amended by a favorably disposed Congress (which still wishes to maintain its own set of oversights), and subsequently to watch the new Department's performance, especially since it is widely suspected that the new Department is underfunded. To return to the main point, however, it seems that corruption is more likely in relatively large *and* unmonitored organizations.

In terms of principal-agents theory, we earlier posited that most of the corruption apparently originated with the principal, that in the case of political corruption, "the onus seems more on the political leadership or appointed administration..., and less on the actions of the 'agents'" (deLeon & Green, 2001, p. 635). The materials covered above, as well as evidence regarding the Italian political system (della Portia & Vannucci, 2002; Golden, 2000; Rhodes, 1997), suggests that political corruption is likely to occur at all levels of government (national, state/province, and municipal), even if the national incidents receive the most attention. Still, we propose that our proposition holds *if* we amend our definition of "principal." In the case of Germany, while we found corrupt actions coming out of the Chancellor's office (both as Chancellor and as the Chair of the CDU), there is little evidence that the Chancellor was instructing state and municipal leaders to act in corrupt manners *as his agents*; in other words, there was no evidence of central coordination. What one might have was a series of decentralized principal-agent relationships with, again, the principals appearing to be more culpable.

Certainly a constant redefinition of principal and agent will result in little more than semantic frustration and ultimate confusion. For example: in the case of Travelgate, was President (or First Lady) Clinton the "principal," or was their nominal "agent," Larry Watkins, the *de facto* "principal" while the Clintons were simply sympathetic bystanders? Or, in the Iran-*contra* affair: was President Reagan the "principal"; if so, he was certainly not the direct source of any orders to Rear Admiral Poindexter or Col. Oliver North. The point, while surely messy, is crucial: if a principal-agent theory to be useful in regards to understanding political corruption, it is necessary to explicate more precisely exactly what is a "principal," an "agent," and the means by which those relationships can be altered.

Again, the observed "decentralization of corruption" does not negate NPM insistence on decentralized government. Kaufman's forest ranger (1960) is a classic example of the benefits that can occur in widely disperse units. Rather, what NMP must do is develop a set of programs so principals at all levels are aware of that corrupt activities will have a negative effect on (i.e. increase) their own transaction costs. Which suggests not only a more aggressive accounting system, but a more complete one as well, that is, a system whose calculus includes both expensive Italian shoes and the assured self-destruction of a prized career in a nation's administration. Even then, however, as utility theorists have endlessly pointed out, each person has a personal and peculiar utility function. Chancellor Kohl knowingly and consciously suffered national disgrace to protect the identities of the CDU contributors, whereas Dumas was willing to name other participants in *Elf*'s "cash cow" activities, whereas Poindexter and North were clearly willing to "fall on their swords" to protect the President (see "Charlemange," 2003).

We earlier posited that "transparency" was only half the struggle in any managerial system. Information theorists, at least since Roberta Wohlstetter (1962), have stressed that the other important half of a message is that responsible officials need to recognize the pertinent information being transmitted and act upon it. One of the constant refrains during the Congressional investigations over the Reagan Administration HUD scandals was that nobody in authority seems to have understood the HUD Inspector-General's reports that outlined Secretary Pierce's improprieties (see deLeon, 1983). Dumas (admittedly not a disinterred party) indicated that many people knew about *Elf* bribes (even being willing to bribe for another firm!), but nobody acted upon it until at least a decade after the fact. The seeming nonchalance in terms of the French citizenry towards corruption is widely noted. *The Economist* has suggested that "It is easy to blame the lack of accountability in a culture whose reflex is to conceal rather than reveal" (Anonymous, 2000, p. 54). We may recall Pujas and Rhodes' (2002, p. 745) reference to France as an example in "political hypocrisy."

There are, to be sure, alternative versions to explanations besides a cultural indifference towards corruption. Polls in Italy and France have both shown a willingness to implement limitations and full disclosure in terms of campaign financing; polls have suggested similar findings in the U.S. More practically, the political devolution in these nations expands the number of people who can now readily see their own opportunities for special opportunities, many legal, a few less so. Moreover, modern political campaigns require greater resources (e.g. advertisements on television), a telling argument when so much of Italian and French political life is based upon the patronage system and its immediate benefits. In the case of Italy, della Porta and Vannucc mince few words:

> The influence of the parties in areas beyond the public administration – from banks and newspapers – has led to an occupation of civil society, further lowing the defences against corruption and mismanagement. The political parties have occupied civil society not in order to realize long-term political programs but to facilitate the extraction of a parasitic rent (della Portia & Vannucci, 2002, p. 732).

If this argument has some validity, then the issue of how the political parties (and, concomitantly, campaign financing) are factored into the equation of reducing political corruption becomes essential. The recent debate over campaign financing reform (the McCain-Feingold Bill) in the U.S. Congress underscores the complexity of this issue, probably across a variety of nations.

NPM proponents make a case for a competitive governments, with the understanding that where politics follows markets (in terms of competition), monopolies are precluded, "prices" are reduced, and, overall, transaction costs are lowered. While we are in general agreement with this hypothesis, we need to indicate at least one crucial reservation. The Italian party system has indeed become more decentralized since the days of the Italian Christian Democrat dominance, but the move to a more competitive party system has resulted in party oligopolies, or what della Portia and Vannucci (2002, p. 792) refer to as a "consociational equilibrium." Under such a regime, patronage is proportionally dispensed as a risk minimization technique rather than a democratic function of voters cast per party. Such behavioral certainly warrants additional examination.

These observations lead us to at least one "big question," namely, the apparent necessity for the highly efficient (and hopefully effective) NPM system to enhance its applicability by incorporating an infusion of what many have termed "new institutionalism" (see March & Olson, 1989) into the corruption equation. As we noted above, institutions (and, in the aggregate, the body politic) can assume a life of their own, one which might not be conducive to an NPM set of protocols. For instance, it is easily apparent that, under present circumstances, New Zealand (through its Ministry of the Treasury) is far more conducive to NPM than France or Italy. In short, NPM cannot rely on the assumption that all polities have a similar political, social, or even economic outlook.

We proposed above that the NPM was basically even handed to the issue of a political ideology, i.e. it would be similarly "efficient" under democratic or authoritarian regimes. Our present research does not permit us to comment on this proposition. Simply, all the polities in our sample are (to greater or less degrees) functioning democracies. We therefore lack the necessary ideological variances necessary to comment on this issue. Still, there is an ethical component to all governmental systems. We observe that NPM is largely predicated on the underlying assumption of economic efficiency and we have seen numerous cases in which officials have opted for high ethical standards that effectively undercut (at least short-term) efficiencies. Robert Gregory, writing from the perspective of the highly successful New Zealand NPM experience, generalizes, "Economistic (*sic*). approaches tend to deny the validity of public interest, but if administrative reforms jeopardize the maintenance of high ethical standards, then it is up to the [NPM] reformers to explain why any such decline ought to be a matter of public indifference" (Gregory, 1999, p. 67).

This observation brings us (albeit a bit indirectly) to a second big NPM question: given that NPM is results-drive and measured, what does it have to say about the means adopted to reach those ends? Which is another way of saying that NPM cannot assume a neutral position on matters pertaining to means; were the means chosen by Chancellor Kohl to protect the CDU acceptable under the German system of government? One suspects not, given the covert nature of the "slush fund" arrangement. Accountability makes a pivotal difference here but the issue is too critical to be left unspecified.

There are several obvious and important ways in which a serious NPM process could reduce political corruption. An accurate and credible accounting system – i.e. transparency – would surely have prevented Chancellor Kohl from establishing a series of CDU secret accounts. But we need, finally, to suggest that the people who engage in political corruption are neither inherently stupid nor powerless; Kohl and Dumas – to say nothing of the bankers who lead the U.S. into the Savings and Loan scandals of the 1980 and the accountants who "cooked" Enron's books – were both sophisticated political analysts and practitioners. Agents and even principals can almost always find ready ways around rules, especially when their own careers are seemingly at risk. This raises again the question of political ethics, an area that public administration scholars keep returning to (e.g. Frederickson, 1999), but the NPM has only addressed in an indirect manner.

This intent of this chapter was less intended to understand every nook and cranny concerning political corruption, and more to appreciate the specific tools that NPM could bring to the struggle to alleviate the incidence of corruption. In this case, it should be clear to all that the general theoretic underpinnings of NPM as well as the programmatic approaches do have a great deal to offer, strengths that we have underplayed. Rather, we have chosen to stress NPM's shortcomings as a means not to undermine NPM but to offer constructive criticism. This essay, then, is not so much an exercise in the on-going "war on corruption" per se but as a means of moving NPM towards a more comprehensive approach to public affairs in general and political corruption in particular.

NOTES

1. In 1997, the Eighth International Anti-Corruption Conference, sponsored by TI, produced the Lima Declaration that pledged an international, multinational effort to eliminate political corruption.

2. Berlusconi's deprivations were heart-felt, as he complained that, "it's a great sacrifice to do what I'm doing... I have a sailboat, but in two years, I've only been on it one day. And I haven't been to my house in Bermuda for two or three years. And the same goes for my house in Portofino" (quoted in Bruni, 2003b, p. A3).

3. A recent check of the World Wide Web using the Googol search engine, keyed on the phrase "political corruption" resulted in over 667,000 entries. In comparison, Googol only registered 183,000 entries when queried on the phrase "erotic literature."

4. Many, including deLeon (1993) and Johnston (1982) have already disputed this explanation.

5. Indeed, Peters and Welch (1978) subtitled their article on political corruption, "If Political Corruption Is in the Mainstream of American Politics, Why Is It Not in the Mainstream of American Political Research?"

6. The *Source Book* published by Transparency International (1999), especially Chapter 3, makes this point with some clarity.

7. This "defense" coincides closely with that offered by the late U.S. Senator Alan Cranston (D-CA), who, in defending his behavior with Charles Keating during the Savings and Loan debacle in the 1980s stated on the floor of the Senate that he was being "singled out" and that all Senators were in jeopardy because "... everybody does it: 'How many of you could rise and declare you've never, ever helped – or agreed to help – a contributor close in time to the solicitation or receipt of a contribution?' I don't believe any of you could say 'never' " (deLeon, 1993, p. 158).

8. This, of course, only transferred the players in the principal-agents relationship, from the managerial "principal" to the "principal" of the union boss; the "agent" remained unchanged.

9. Regarding mistresses and the body politic: The British tabloid *The Sun* quoted French political commentator Francois Froment-Meurice as saying, "France is a kind of a monarchy. It is natural for the king to have his mistresses around, living in the palaces of the republic." Another commentator added: "Nobody cares. We are French. Everybody has affairs. We'd be more worried if our president didn't" (Anonymous, 2001a). Jeffries (2001) addresses another area of Gallic indifference, income tax. He cites a 1996 report that estimated that the cost of French tax evasion is equal to two-thirds of the income tax revenue, and that between one-third and one-half of the population pays no income tax.

10. The present trial of Chirac's aide and former Prime Minister Alain Juppe (and 27 accomplices) indicates that the incidents are far from forgotten (Tabliabue, 2003, p. A8).

ACKNOWLEDGMENTS

This paper was prepared for presentation at the 2002 International Public Network Conference, held at the *Universita degli Studi di Siena*, 27–29 June 2002. We would like to acknowledge the skilled research assistance of Mr. Sean Jones of the University of Colorado, Denver's Graduate School of Public Affairs. Professor deLeon is deeply appreciative of the financial support for this paper given by the International Institute of Business at the University of Colorado, Denver, and its Director, Dr. Donald Stevens.

REFERENCES

Almond, G. A., & Verba, S. (1960). *The civic culture*. Princeton, NJ: Princeton University Press.
Anonymous (2000). Shenanigans in France. *The Economist* (November 4), 53–54.
Anonymous (2001a). Affairs don't shock in France. *The[London] Sun*, October 3. Cited at http://web.lexis-nexis.com/universe/document?_m=a294c44971f88b048d106052eb71.
Anonymous (2001b). Credit Lyonnaise: The curse continues. *The Economist* (January 13), 67–70.
Anonymous (2001c). France: Corruption comes to court. *The Economist* (January 27), 50–51.
Anonymous (2002, April 6). Corruption in Germany: Too much of it. *The Economist*, *363*(8267), 45.
Anonymous (2003a, August 2). Answers please. *The Economist*, *368*(8335), 23–27.
Anonymous (2003b, September 20). The WTO under fire. *The Economist*, *368*(8342), 26–29.
Barzelay, M., & Armajani, B. J. (1992). *Breaking through bureaucracy: A new vision for managing in government*. Berkeley: University of California Press.
Behn, R. D. (1995, July/August). The big questions of public management. *Public Administration Review*, *55*(4), 313–324.
Benson, G. C. S. et al. (1978). *Political corruption in America*. Lexington, MA: DC Heath.
Bruni, F. (2003a). Italian leader in a first, testifies at his own bribery trial. *New York Times* (May 6), A1, A12.
Bruni, F. (2003b). Berlesconi, in a rough week, says only he can save Italy. *New York Times* (May 10), A1, A3.
Burke, T. (2002). Corruption concepts and federal campaign finance law. In: A. J. Heidenheimer & M. Johnston (Eds), *Political Corruption: Concepts & Contexts* (3rd ed., Chap. 34). New Brunswick, NJ: Transaction Publishers.
Caiden, G. E., & Caiden, N. J. (1977, May/June). Administrative corruption. *Public Administration Review*, *37*(3), 295–306.
Charlemange (2003, May 17). Comparative corruption. *The Economist*, *367*(8324), 47.
Clines, F. X. (2002). Ohio congressman is guilty in bribery and kickback case. *New York Times* (April 12), A1, A22.
Coase, R. (1937). The nature of the firm. *Economica*, *4*, 386–405.
Cohen, S., & Eimicke, W. (1999). Is public entrepreneurship ethical? A second look at theory and practice. *Public Integrity*, *1*(1), 54–74.
deLeon, P. (1993). *Thinking about political corruption*. Armonk, NY: M. E. Sharpe.
deLeon, L., & deLeon, P. (2002). The democratic ethos and public management. *Administration & Society*, *34*, 229–250.
deLeon, P., & Green, M. T. (2001). Corruption and the new public management. In: L. Jones, J. Guthrie & P. Steane (Eds), *Learning from International Public Management Reform* (Chap. 31). New York: JAI Press.
della Portia, D., & Vannucci, A. (2002). Corrupt exchanges and the implosion of the Italian party system. In: A. J. Heidenheimer & M. Johnston (Eds), *Political Corruption: Concepts & Contexts* (3rd ed., Chap. 37). New Brunswick, NJ: Transaction Publishers.

Drew, E. (1994). *On the edge: The Clinton Presidency*. New York: Simon & Schuster.
Drew, E. (1999). *The corruption of American politics*. Woodstock, NY: Overlook Press.
Etizoni, A. (1984). *Capital corruption: The new attack on American democracy*. New York: Harcourt, Brace and Jovanovich.
Ewing, J. (2001). Is the corruption crusade over? *Business Week International Edition* (November 26), 32.
Ferris, J. M., & Graddy, E. A. (1997). New public management theory: Lessons from the institutional economics. In: L. R. Jones & K. Schedler (Eds), *International Perspectives on the New Public Management* (pp. 47–62). Greenwich, CT: JAI Press.
Fischer, F. (1990). *Technology and the politics of expertise*. Newbury Park, CA: Sage.
Frant, H. (1997). The new public management and the new political economy: Missing pieces in each other's puzzles. In: L. R. Jones & K. Schedler (Eds), *International Perspectives on the New Public Management* (pp. 24–42). Greenwich, CT: JAI Press.
Frederickson, H. G. (1999, Summer). Public ethics and the new managerialism. *Public Integrity, 1*(3), 265–278.
Fukuyama, F. (1995). *Trust*. New York: Free Press.
Garafolo, C., Geuras, D., Lynch, T., & Lynch, C. (1999, December). Applying virtue ethics to the challenge of corruption. Paper presented to the 5th National Public Management Research Conference, Texas A&M University, College Station, TX.
Golden, M. A. (2000). Political patronage, bureaucracy and corruption in postwar Italy. Presented at the Annual Meeting of the American Political Science Association. Washington, DC.
Graham, R. (2001, June 19). French politics disgraced: Former Foreign Minister claims justice system is protecting those still in positions. *The Financial Times London*. http://web.lexus.nexis.com/universe/document?_m=1449b358e321f91a9052b5e5a2a8e64b.
Gregory, R. J. (1999, January/February). Social capital theory and administrative reform. *Public Administration Review, 59*(1), 63–75.
Hooper, J. (2000, January 19). Towering colossus who fell to earth. [*Manchester*] *Guardian Unlimited*. http://www.guardian.co.uk/germany/article/0,2763,191933,00.html.
Jeffries, S. (2001). France sells its soul for a fistful of francs. *Manchester Guardian Weekly* (July 11). http://web.lexus.nexis.com/universe/document?_m=a294c4497ecdlf88b048dc106052eb71Y.
Johnston, D. (2001). U.S. charges colorful ohio congressman with taking bribes. *New York Times*, 5(May), A1, A-13.
Johnston, M. (1982). *Political corruption and public policy in America*. Monterey, CA: Cole.
Johnston, M. (1986, Spring). Right and wrong in American politics: Popular concepts of corruption. *Polity, 18*(3).
Jones, L. R. (1992). Public budget execution and management control. In: J. Rabin (Ed.), *Handbook of Public Budgeting* (pp. 147–164). New York: Marcel Dekker.
Jones, L. R., & Thompson, F. (1999). *Public management: Institutional renewal for the 21st century*. Stamford, CT: JAI Press.
Kaufman, D. (1997, Summer). Corruption: The facts. *Foreign Policy, 107*, 114–131.
Kaufman, H. (1960). *The forest ranger*. Baltimore, MD: Johns Hopkins Press.
Kettl, D. F. (2000). *The global public management revolution*. Washington, DC: Brookings Institution.
Kirlin, J. J. (1996, September/October). The big questions of public administration. *Public Administration Review, 56*(5), 416–424.
Kirschbaum, E. (2000, August 29). Former Kohl lieutenant stirs German cash row. [*The*] *Manchester Unlimited*. http://www.guardian.co.uk/germany/article/0,2763,360409,00.html.
Klein, J. (2002). *The natural*. New York: Doubleday.

Klitgaard, R. (1988). *Controlling corruption.* Berkeley, CA: University of California Press.
Lynn, L. E., Jr. (1998). A critical analysis of the new public management. *International Public Management Journal, 1*(2), 107–123.
March, J. G., & Olson, J. (1989). *Rediscovering institutions.* New York: Free Press.
Meier, K. J., & Holbrook, T. M. (1992, February). I seen my opportunities and i took 'em: Political corruption in the American States. *Journal of Politics, 54*(1), 133–155.
Ménard, C. (1997). *Transaction cost economics: recent developments.* Cheltenham, UK, Brookfield, VT: Edward Elgar.
Merton, R. K. (1968). *Social theory and social structure.* New York: Free Press.
Miller, G. J. (1992). *Managerial dilemmas: The political economy of hierarchy: The political economy of institutions and decisions.* Cambridge, England: Cambridge University Press.
Moe, T. M. (1984). The new economics of organization. *American Journal of Political Science, 28*(4), 739–777.
North, D. C. (1996). *Institutions, institutional change, and economic performance: The political economy of institutions and decisions.* Cambridge, New York: Cambridge University Press.
Nye, J. S., Jr. (1967, June). Corruption and political development: A cost-benefit analysis. *American Political Science Review, 61*(2), 417–427.
Okun, A. M. (1975). *Equality and efficiency, the big tradeoff.* Washington: Brookings Institution.
Organisation for Economic Co-operation and Development (1996). Public management committee. Integrating people management into public service reform. Paris, Washington, DC: Organisation for Economic Co-operation and Development; OECD Washington Center distributor.
Osborne, D., & Gaebler, T. (1992). *Reinventing government: How the entrepreneurial spirit is transforming the public sector.* Reading, MA: Addison-Wesley.
Patterson, T. (2000). The Kohl scandal: What has happened? [*Manchester*] *Guardian Unlimited*, 21 January. http://www.guardian.co.uk/germany/article/0,2763,191929,00.html.
Peters, J. G., & Welch, S. (1978, September). Political corruption: A search for definition and a theory. *American Political Science Review, 72*(3), 974–984.
Pharr, S. J. (2002). Public trust and corruption in Japan. In: A. J. Heidenheimer & M. Johnston (Eds), *Political Corruption: Concepts & Contexts* (3rd ed., Chap. 43). New Brunswick, NJ: Transaction Publishers.
Power, M. (1993). The politics of financial auditing. *Political Quarterly, 64*(3), 272–285.
Pujas, V., & Rhodes, M. (2002). Party finance and political scandal: Comparing Italy, Spain, and France. In: A. J. Heidenheimer & M. Johnston (Eds), *Political Corruption: Concepts & Contexts* (3rd ed., Chap. 38). New Brunswick, NJ: Transaction Publishers.
PUMA (1997). *Public management committee. Managing government ethics.* Paris: PUMA.
Putnam, R. D. (2000). *Bowling alone.* New York: Simon & Schuster.
Quah, J. S. (1999, November/December). Corruption in Asian countries. *Public Administration Review, 59*(6), 483–494.
Radin, B. A. (1998, July/August). The governmental performance and results act: Hyra-headed monster or flexible management tool? *Public Administration Review, 58*(4), 307–316.
Rhodes, M. (1997). Financing party politics in Italy: A case of systemic corruption. *West European Politics, 20*(1), 54–80.
Rose-Ackerman, S. (1978). *Corruption: A study in political economy.* New York: Academic Press.
Rose-Ackerman, S. (1998). *Corruption and government.* New York: Cambridge University Press.
Rossant, J. (2001). Why France's hands may never scrub clean. *Business Week International Editon* (June 18), 25.

Rozell, M. J., & Wilcox, C. (Eds) (2000). *The Clinton scandals and the future of American Government*. Washington, DC: Georgetown University Press.
Stanton, M. (2003). *The Prince of providence*. New York: Random House.
Tabliabue, J. (2003). Graft trial of ex-Premier opens in Paris. *New York Times* (September 30), A8.
Transparency International (2001). Press release: New index highlights worldwide corruption crisis, says Transparency International. http://www.transparency.org/cpi/2001/cpi2001.html.
Uhr, J. (1999). Institutions of integrity: Balancing values and verification in democratic governance. *Public Integrity*, *1*(1), 94–106.
Williamson, O. E. (1997). *Transaction cost economics: How it works, where it is headed*. Berkeley: Institute of Management Innovation and Organization. University of California, Berkeley.
Williamson, O. E., & Masteen, S. E. (1995). *Transaction cost economics*. Aldershot, UK: Edward Elgar.
Wohlstetter, R. (1962). *Pearl Harbor: Warning and decision*. Palo Alto, CA: Stanford University Press.
Woollacott, M. (1999, December 31). Countries get the sort of corruption they deserve. *Manchester Guardian Unlimited*. http://guardian.co.uk/germany/article/0,2763,191949,00.html.

11. SUPPLY-SIDE CONTROL OF CORRUPTION: THE U.S. FOREIGN CORRUPT PRACTICES ACT AND THE OECD CONVENTION

Masako N. Darrough

1. INTRODUCTION

Corruption is a phenomenon that is ubiquitous, but the extent and the form differ across countries. According to Transparency International, the Corruption Perception Index (CPI) in year 2001 varied from 0.4 to 9.9 (10 is completely corruption free). The average score for the 91 countries surveyed was 4.76 (with a standard deviation of 2.39). Why is there so much cross-country difference? Why are some countries virtually corruption free, but are others fraught with corruption?

Corruption is a complex phenomenon and each country has its own story. Empirical studies, however, have found that certain socioeconomic variables such as GNP per capita, the size of the private sector, and the degree of openness are able to explain much of the cross-country variations. (See Bardhan (1997) and Lambsdorff (1999) for a review.) What emerges from these studies is that it does matter how we organize our society, in particular, political, legal, and economic institutions. North (1999) points out that we collectively structure institutions: in turn they define opportunities and incentives for our choices. These choices ultimately "shape the performance of societies and economies over time."

The term "corruption" is used in many contexts. However defined in a technical sense, by corruption I mean something undesirable from a social perspective. Economists condemn corruption on the ground of efficiency or its adverse impact on social and economic progress. Noonan (1984, p. 703) condemns bribery – a form of corruption – on a moral ground; otherwise "we would live in a world of pure plutocracy where wealth would be the measure of all things . . .." In a corrupt environment, the same jobs might be performed, but the funds that end up in the pockets of officials represent a straight leakage out of the system. Misallocation of scarce resources can take place: the roads built could lead nowhere and contracts may be awarded to contractors who are not the best. Furthermore, corruption undermines public confidence in public officials and the government. Thus, it is generally agreed that corruption undermines the economic and social development of societies. In fact, the World Bank has recently identified corruption "as the single greatest obstacle to economic and social development," since corruption "undermines development by distorting the rules of law and weakening the institutional foundation on which economic growth depends." It is then worthwhile to understand how corruption comes about and examine ways to reduce corrupt practices.

This chapter focuses on a particular form of corruption that involves both the private sector and the public sector. More specifically, it focuses on the role multinational corporations play in dealing with the public officials in foreign countries. The multinational corporations are often accused of "bribing" foreign public officials to conduct business. These officials, in turn, ask for "kickbacks" in awarding contracts. In other words, these companies "supply" and the public officials "demand" corruption. In order to curb corrupt practices of the U.S. multinational corporations, the United States Congress passed the Foreign Corrupt Practices Act (FCPA) in 1977. This Act explicitly criminalizes bribery of foreign officials for the purpose of influencing, retaining, or obtaining business. A similar act ("the OECD Convention") was adopted recently by the OECD members and five additional countries. Thus, these countries are aggressively attempting to control the supply-side of corruption. The FCPA and the OECD Convention also include accounting provisions that require companies to establish and maintain appropriate internal control systems so that corporate funds are not improperly utilized for illegal purposes. Good record keeping and internal control would make it more difficult to conceal such payments.

The primary objective of this chapter is to evaluate the role of internal control in reducing supply-side corruption and identify its limitations. Although good internal control is necessary, I argue that it is not sufficient to ensure proper corporate conduct. Proper corporate conduct is ensured only through social mechanisms that align incentives of corporate members at all levels with those of the society.

Because of their illicit nature, it is difficult to make a precise estimate of the magnitude of bribery payments. The World Bank estimates, however, that 5% of exports to developing countries – $50 to $80 billion per year – go to corrupt officials (Moss, 1997). Other experts estimate that various forms of corruption siphon away "five to thirty percent of all public funds" (Hamra, 2000). Moreover, the customary padding appears to have crept up. In the 1970s, public officials asked 1–5% of the value of the contract, but recently some were asking upwards of 20–30% (Tronnes, 2000). Thus, bribery, like a tariff, significantly increases the cost of a contract (see Clarke & Xu, 2001). But, it is less functional than a tariff. While a tariff in principle can be used for useful social projects, bribery goes into the pockets of officials, who are likely to spend the money on nonproductive luxury goods.

Many forces contribute to corruption. Simply put, corruption exists because there are parties that benefit through an exchange of power for money. The cost of corruption is born by a different party, the general public. The basic conceptual framework I use in this chapter is that of economics, in particular, agency theory. I view the form of corruption analyzed in this chapter as a manifestation of a two-sided agency problem. One side is a private enterprise and the other side is government. For the business agent, the job is first: (1) to get a contract; and then (2) to maximize profit (or his utility). For the public official, the job is to award a contract (for example, to build a power plant, or to supply fighter planes), to award licenses (for example, to import goods), etc. Whatever the job is, it presents an opportunity to the official to extract private gains by abusing the power vested in the public office. The business agent has money and the government agent has power. Money and power can feed each other. For example, Hors (2000, p. 43) describes that under "patrimonialism" in Morocco, access to political power ensures access to economic privileges, while under a patronage-based system in the Philippines, one can buy political power. Are these private gains a "rent" derived from the positions or a form of corruption? Not all opportunistic behaviors are considered corrupt. The same behavior can be viewed either as norm or as corrupt, depending on the context. For example, the distinction between gifts, grease, and graft is often difficult to make. George Washington Plunkitt even came up a concept of honest graft in 1900. Additionally, a set of opportunities in itself does not automatically lead to corruption. Nonetheless, it is argued that making a certain conduct explicitly illegal would influence the choices made by the players in the game.

Although my focus in this chapter is on only one side of the two-sided agencies, even such an analysis presents a challenge. A canonical principal-agent structure with one principal and one agent does not capture the essence of the myriad of players that are involved. Corporate misconduct is not restricted to only one level of corporate hierarchy. Rather, we are dealing with a multi-level hierarchy (the shareholders, the board of directors, the management, the line workers, as well as the external auditor, for example). Furthermore, these corporations operate in a broader socio/political/economic/legal environment. In other words, there are many stakeholders in the game. Exactly how they are related and what roles they should play are questions of how optimally to organize institutions. To evaluate the effectiveness of the supply-side control, the ultimate issue we need to consider is how to arrange various social structures and institutions to align the goals of various constituents of the game.

The accounting provisions on internal control targets only certain levels of agents in the corporate hierarchy but not the top level. Even though management is accountable to the board of directors, the current framework of good internal control does not go far enough to ensure that the wishes of the shareholders are ultimately carried out. Hence, I argue in this chapter that the FCPA and the OECD Convention were not designed to address the issue of corporate governance. Even though these two legislative changes are expected to contribute significantly to curbing bribery, they alone would not be sufficient to prevent corruption at the level of top management. Proper oversight of management conduct requires better corporate governance.

In the next section, I will examine three types of indices that measure different types of corruption. This is done to establish that there is correlation between the overall level of corruption and bribery. In Section 3, I will discuss the FCPA and the OECD Convention. In Section 4, I will first examine the internal control requirement of the legislation and then discuss the limitations of the internal control approach. This discussion will lead to the issues of corporate governance and social institutions in Section 5. The last section offers concluding remarks.

2. MEASURES OF CORRUPTION

Several attempts are made to quantify the level of corruption in each country. Most of the corruption measures synthesize various measures into "corruption indices." Some indices summarize the general level of "perceived" corruption in each country, while others target perceived corruption in more specific spheres. In this section, I focus on three indices that measure corruption in increasingly specific contexts. The three indices are: (1) the Corruption Perception Index (CPI) compiled by Transparency International (TI); (2) the Opacity Index by Pricewater-houseCoopers (PWC); and (3) the Bribe Payers Index (BPI), also by Transparency International. The first index measures the general level of corruption, while the second focuses on transparency in the capital market. The third measures the degree to which corporations are perceived to be willing to pay bribes abroad. For my analysis, each of the three indices has both advantages and disadvantages. The

CPI is more comprehensive, covers more countries, and has the longest time-series data. The Opacity index focuses on the capital market, but covers fewer (35) countries. The BPI is most specific and easiest to interpret, but covers even fewer (21) countries. The Opacity Index has been so far compiled only once, while the BPI has been compiled twice. In the following, I first describe these indices and then examine the degree to which they are correlated.

The CPI is a composite index drawn from different sources to provide data on perceived degree of corruption in various countries. (For more information, visit the website of Transparency International: http://www.transparency.org.) A number of groups are surveyed to express their perception of corruption in different contexts. For example, managers are asked about the extent of corruption in the business environment and the pervasiveness of corruption in the public sector. Transparency International has been publishing the CPI since the early 1980s for a large number of countries. The index can take on values between 0 and 10, with 10 being corruption-free. Not surprisingly, the index for each country has been quite stable over time. For the 54 countries that had indices for most of the time period starting from 1980s to the present, the average CPI is 5.31, the standard deviation is 0.63, and the coefficient of variation is 0.18.[1] Of these countries, only four (Cameroon, Ecuador, Russia and South Africa) increased the index by more than 2, whereas two countries (Egypt and Hungary) slipped by more than 2 over the last two decades. Although TI warns that the indices are not completely comparable across time (due to the changes in sources and methodology), it is safe to say that typically the degree of corrupt practices (or the perception of them) within a country does not change rapidly.

The Opacity Index is concerned with the capital market. PWC defines "opacity" as the "lack of clear, accurate, formal, easily discernible, and widely accepted practices" (the lack of transparency) in the capital markets. Opacity reflects whether the rules of the game are specified, how well they are understood, and followed in the capital markets. In addition, the index is used to measure the effects of opacity on "the cost of capital and foreign direct investment flows worldwide." The primary concern is that opacity imposes significant costs on investors and raises greater "obstacles to the economic progress" of countries. Conversely, greater "transparency across many dimensions of capital markets encourage investor confidence and keep the costs of doing business under control." For example, Lee and Ng (2002) documents that corruption is significant in explaining the cross-country variations in the price-earnings and price-to-book ratios.

The Opacity scores are also based on interviews conducted in the year 2000 with chief financial officers, equity analysts, bankers, and PWC employees in 35 countries. It is a composite index, equally weighing the 5 different areas that affect capital markets: (1) corruption; (2) the legal system; (3) the economic and fiscal policies at the government level; (4) the accounting standards and practices (including corporate governance and information release); and (5) the regulatory regime. The score can range from zero (most transparent) to 150 (most opaque). The best score is given to Singapore (29) and the worst to Russia (84). Note that "corruption" is one of the five areas that are fed into the calculation of the opacity index. It is clear that general corruption is viewed as harmful for the efficient functioning of the capital markets. The compiled Opacity score is then used to quantify the cost of opacity in the form of "risk premium" and "tax-equivalent." Opacity imposes a hidden tax when countries borrow through sovereign bond issuances in international or domestic capital markets.

Transparency International published the second BPI in May 2002, while the first was compiled in 1999. A survey was conducted in 2002 in 15 (14 in 1999) emerging-market countries to measure the propensity of corporations from 21 (19 in 1999) leading exporting countries to "pay bribes to senior public officials." The scores can vary from 0 to 10 (10 represents a virtually corrupt-free exporting country). In 2002, the best score is 8.5 (Australia), while the worst is 3.2 (Russia) with the average being 6.0. These scores highlight considerable differences in the (perception of) willingness of companies to pay bribes in these countries. It is worth noting that the United States, the only country with a history of law that explicitly prohibits bribing of foreign officials, is below average with a score of 5.3. The 2002 survey also included a question on the bribery-propensity of domestic companies in the surveyed countries. It is also interesting to note that the average score for domestic bribery is 1.9, which is lower than that of any of the 21 countries for bribery of foreign officials.

2.1. Correlation Among the Indices

The three indices can be viewed as measures of different facets of the same object (corruption), with increasing specificity moving from the CPI to the Opacity to the BPI. Since these facets are interdependent, the indices are expected to be correlated. Simple correlation using the latest data is presented in the table in the Appendix A. Since these indices do not include the same set of countries, the pair-wise correlation does not necessarily include all the countries for each index. The sample size is indicated in the parentheses. For example, the intersection of the Opacity Index and the BPI turned out to be only 10 countries. However, every country in the BPI and Opacity Index is included in the CPI. In addition to the three indices, I also include the five separate components of the Opacity Index (Corruption, Legal, Economic, Accounting, and Regulatory).

It is evident that all these measures are highly correlated. Since the scale runs in an opposite direction for Opacity, only the absolute values are relevant. The pair-wise correlation between the three indices varies from 0.792 to 0.800. It is reassuring to see that the CPI by Transparency International and Corruption in the Opacity Index are highly correlated with a correlation of 0.899.

Since only 10 countries are included in the BPI, caution is required before generalizing the results. However, these 10 countries do account for a large part of world trade. For the 10 nations included, China, Hong Kong, Italy, Japan, Russia, Singapore, South Korea, Taiwan, the United Kingdom, and the USA, the (perceived level of) overall corruption, opacity, and the propensity to bribe are highly correlated. In addition, for those 34 countries in the Opacity sample, the CPI and Opacity have a correlation of 0.794. That is, transparency in the capital market is closely associated with the general level of corruption. Whether those countries that are not included in the opacity index or the BPI have the same degree of correlation is a question to be answered in the future. Of course, if a particular country had little foreign trade, then the propensity to bribe of foreign officials would be a moot question.

Although correlation does not imply causality, the high level of correlation suggests that curbing bribery can be an effective tool to reduce overall corruption. Thus, the above analysis, albeit crude, lays out an underpinning of the analysis for the rest of the chapter.

3. FOREIGN CORRUPT PRACTICES ACT: ANTIBRIBERY PROVISIONS

This section describes and analyzes the antibribery provisions of the FCPA and the OECD Convention. Both explicitly criminalize "extraterritorial bribery payments," thereby making "supply" of corrupt practices illegal. The FCPA, enacted by the Congress in 1977, uses a two-pronged approach. The more well-known side of the Act (as the title of the Act suggests) makes it "unlawful for a U.S. person, and certain foreign issuers of securities, to make a corrupt payment to a foreign official for the purpose of obtaining or retaining business for or with, or directing business to, any person." The Act was strengthened in 1998 to include foreign firms and persons who take any act "in furtherance of such a corrupt payment while in the United States." The second requires companies whose securities are listed in the United States "to make and keep books and records that accurately and fairly reflect the transactions of the corporation and to devise and maintain an adequate system of internal accounting controls."

3.1. Background

Within the United States, bribery and kickbacks have always been illegal. A myriad of state and federal laws, including RICO, Travel Act, and mail and wire fraud act are applied to such conduct involving both government officials and private persons. No explicit law existed to deal with foreign officials before the FCPA, which was a culmination of scandals such as Watergate and Lockheed. The SEC investigations in the mid-1970s discovered that more than 400 U.S. companies made "questionable or illegal payments" in excess of $300 million to foreign government officials, politicians, and political parties (Gantz, 1998). One U.S. governmental study found that "seventy-seven of ninety-seven responding companies" made "questionable or clearly illegal payments" ranging in size "from $13,349 to $56.7 million over a period of years." In the case of Lockheed Aircraft Corporation, it was found to have paid approximately $202 million of bribe money to politicians, sales agents in the United States, and foreign government officials abroad. In addition to the Nixon campaign, Lockheed paid bribes of substantial amounts to public officials in various foreign countries including the Netherlands, Japan, Italy, Germany, Mexico, Spain, and Greece. This is a corporation that had a $250 million loan guarantee by Congress in 1971 to prevent bankruptcy. Such disclosure of corporate wrongdoing during the Watergate investigation increased the public anger against big companies. A special Watergate prosecutor was selected to investigate and discovered a widespread practice by American multinationals of funneling money through foreign agents to establish unrecorded slush funds for domestic political contributions (in violation of campaign finance law), and to bribe foreign officials to obtain favorable contracts. Thus, the FCPA was enacted in this climate to "bring a halt to the bribery of foreign officials" and "to restore public confidence in the integrity of the American business system." If found guilty, firms and/or individuals can be fined up to $2 million per bribe, imprisoned, barred from future government procurement, or export privileges.

Some thought the FCPA would actually be helpful for U.S. companies. If the FCPA reduces bribery without jeopardizing the likelihood of obtaining business, it could be helpful to companies by reducing business expenses. For example, former Texaco President James Kinnear stated that the FCPA provided "a way to save face while refusing to pay bribes." However, many companies complained that the Act placed them at a disadvantage relative to foreign corporations that were not subject to such a law in their own country. If bribes were the norm for doing business, U.S. firms would have a difficult time competing against foreign firms that are not subject to such a prohibition. Moreover, many countries allowed tax deductibility of bribe payments. For example, fourteen out of 30 OECD member countries recognized bribery payments as legitimate business expenses. A study by the Commerce Department claimed that U.S. companies lost $45 billion of international business in 1994 alone to international competitors that paid bribes (Borrus, 1995).

3.2. The Effect of the FCPA on U.S. Corporations

When firms are not sure if a specific business arrangement is in violation of the Act, they can ask the Department of Justice (DOJ) for an opinion. Although the DOJ's opinion is not binding in subsequent litigation, it is still informative for firms in formulating their business strategies.[2] Between 1980 through 2001, there were 37 such opinions posted on the website of the DOJ (http://www.usdoj.gov/criminal/fraud/fcpa/dojdocb.htm). A perusal of these releases shows a variety of situations. All the releases deal with cleared cases with a statement that "the Department does not presently intend to take an enforcement action with respect to any of the prospective conduct." One such release (No. 95-03) illustrates a typical situation. An American company plans to enter into a joint venture (JV) with foreign entities, one of which is owned by a public official and his relative. The role of these individuals in the JV and their compensation are clearly spelled out to result in a "clean" opinion. In another release (No. 96-2), a U.S. company plans to renew an existing marketing representative agreement with a state-owned enterprise of a foreign country. The request specifies, among other details, the methods of payments and the acknowledgment of familiarity with the FCPA, and includes a statement that the state-enterprise "is not in a position to influence the procurement decisions" of the potential future customers. At a minimum, the very process of requesting an opinion makes companies review the implications of their business arrangements involving foreign officials.

How effective is the FCPA in reducing corrupt behavior? In terms of enforcement, no CEO was ever convicted and between the periods from 1977 to 1988, only 23 cases were prosecuted under the FCPA (Salbu, 1997). Of course such a revelation does not in itself imply that the FCPA was ineffectual. There could have been an effective deterrence. What is clear is that costs of bribery have increased. Some companies have set up formal and rigorous procedures into their "codes of ethics" to "forbid receiving gifts, entertainment, and gratuities from suppliers when a conflict interest would be created thereby..." (Salbu, 1997).

If the FCPA prevents or discourages certain business transactions, one would expect that the impact of the Act is largest where corrupt business practices are common. The negative response on business would be larger, the higher the level of corruption is in a particular foreign country. Empirical evidence is generally consistent with this expectation. Hines (1995) finds evidence that U.S. business activity in corrupt countries showed unusual declines after 1977 and attributes the declines to the FCPA. Wei (1997), on the other hand, finds that although foreign direct investment (FDI) in general is sensitive to corruption, American FDI is no more sensitive than other investors despite the FCPA. After examining the export-market share of U.S. firms before and after the passage of the Act, Beck et al. (1991) conclude that U.S. market share declined: (1) in bribery-prone countries in general; and more specifically (2) in bribery-prone countries where U.S. firms do not have regional advantages (bribery-prone non-Latin American countries). Alesina and Weder (1999) also find that U.S. business is discouraged from doing business in more corrupt countries. In contrast, they find that neither the U.S. nor other countries reduce official aid to more corrupt governments. Of course, there is no explicit law that prohibits giving aid to corrupt governments.

3.3. OECD Convention

Until the late 1990s, the U.S. was the only country that prohibited bribery of foreign public officials. In many other countries, not only was bribery of foreign officials legal but bribery payments were treated as legitimate business expenses. Since the rules of the game were not the same, U.S. corporations were at a disadvantage in competing against foreign corporations. Thus, the amendments to the FCPA (1988) mandated "the President to pursue an international agreement criminalizing foreign bribery through the OECD" as well as other international venues (Tronnes, 2000). Meanwhile, other nations were also becoming concerned with the adverse effect of corruption. Thus, three multinational treaties were signed in the late nineties: in 1996 the Organization of American States (OAS) adopted the Inter-American Convention against Corruption; in 1997 the Council of Europe (EC) adopted the Convention on the Fight against Corruption; and in 1997 the OECD adopted the OECD Convention. Both the OAS and EC Conventions have a wider scope than the OECD Convention in that they cover corruption involving both domestic and foreign officials. Since, neither specifies any provision on internal control, my analysis will focus only on the OECD Convention.

The OECD Convention on Combating Bribery of Foreign Public Officials in International Business Transactions was presented in 1997 and entered "into force" in 1999. Thirty OECD members as well as five additional countries signed the convention. The OECD member countries include Australia, Austria, Belgium, Canada, Czech Republic, Denmark, Finland, France, Germany, Greece, Hungary, Iceland, Ireland, Italy, Japan, Korea, Luxembourg, Mexico, Netherlands, New Zealand, Norway, Poland, Portugal, Slovak Republic, Spain, Sweden, Switzerland, Turkey, United Kingdom, and the United States. Additional five signatory countries are Bulgaria, Brazil, Argentina, Chile, and Slovenia. The OECD considers bribery to be "widespread" and to raise "serious moral and political concerns and distorting international competitive conditions." Similar to the FCPA, the Convention criminalizes bribery of foreign officials and includes accounting provisions. Since the convention is a multilateral treaty, the playing field is finally leveled.

4. INTERNAL CONTROL IN THE FCPA

The second prong of the FCPA does not appear to receive much attention. During the Watergate investigation, a large number of corporations voluntarily disclosed that they made questionable and illegal corporate payments and practices through slush funds and falsification of records. The SEC Report (1976) to the Congress pointed out, "a breakdown in the system of corporate accountability" which was a "matter of concern irrespective of any bribery or questionable payments" and recommended adoption of specific accounting provisions of internal control in the FCPA. It is clear that Congress realized the importance of legislating a systematic approach to corporate accountability.

The FCPA amended Section 13(b) of the Securities Exchange Act of 1934 and codified the accounting control provisions along the line of SAP (Statement of Auditing Procedure) No. 54. Since the accounting control provisions were passed as amendments to the 1934 Act, unlike the antibribery requirement, they apply to all corporations subject to the SEC regulation regardless of whether they are engaged in foreign business. In effect, the FCPA granted the SEC authority over the entire financial management and reporting requirements of SEC registrants (Lacey & George, 1998). The FCPA divides enforcement authority between the Department of Justice for criminal prosecution of antibribery provisions and the SEC for the investigation of civil violations of both the accounting control and antibribery provisions.

The accounting control provisions require: (1) good bookkeeping and disclosure; and (2) maintenance of the internal accounting control system so that:

- Transactions are executed in accordance with management's general or specific authorization.
- Transactions are recorded as necessary: (i) to permit preparation of financial statements in conformity with generally accepted accounting principles or any other criteria applicable to such statements; and (ii) to maintain accountability for assets.
- Access to assets is permitted only in accordance with management's general or specific authorization.

- The recorded accountability for assets is compared with the existing assets at reasonable intervals and appropriate action is taken with respect to any differences.

These provisions were made with an emphasis on transactions and dispositions of assets to prevent valuable assets of a company from being illicitly given away.[3] The books and records should be in "reasonable detail." The immateriality criterion does not apply to bribe payments, since any bribe, however small, would be illegal, although "facilitating payments" are allowed.

Good record keeping is a must for any business. What is significant about the FCPA is that the Act made it a legal requirement. Shortly after the passage of the FCPA, Beresford and Bond (1978) wrote:

> Management's responsibility for maintaining internal control is not new. However subjecting companies and their officers and employees to possible civil liability and criminal prosecution under federal securities laws for not having a sufficient system of internal control is a significant development.... Management must exercise judgment both in determining the steps to be taken and in evaluating the related costs to provide reasonable assurance.... Internal control is a tool used by management in operating the business (Beresford & Bond, 1978, p. 54).

Since the FCPA, the approach and method of internal control have been redefined and refined. In 1987, the Treadway Report (by the National Commission on Fraudulent Financial Reporting) reiterated internal control as a mechanism to prevent fraudulent reporting. The Commission made a number of recommendations and made it clear that the responsibility for reliable financial reporting "resides first and foremost at the corporate level, in particular at the top management level." Top management "sets the tone and establishes the financial reporting environment." Internal control assisted by internal audit is crucial for the purpose. In addition the Commission called for sponsoring organizations to work together to integrate various internal control approaches into an integrated framework. Subsequently, the Committee of Sponsoring organizations (COSO) issued a comprehensive four-volume report on internal control in 1992. The framework integrates five interrelated components (control environment, risk assessment, control activities, information and communication, and monitoring), through which business entities could assess and ensure the effectiveness of their internal control. The central principles of the COSO Report were later codified by the AICPA's Auditing Standards Board in Statement on Auditing Standards (SAS) No. 78 in 1995. In 1991, Internal Research Foundation issued a report on systems audibility and control (SAC), which provides guidance on the usage of information technology. Finally, the Information Systems Audit and Control Foundations incorporated COSO and SAC in 1996 in the report on Control Objectives for Information and Related Technology (COBIT). COBIT is considered as state-of-the-art and is widely adopted by various organizations around the world.

Chapter 8 of the OECD Convention of 1997 also requires signatories to adopt accounting control provisions. Penalties are proposed for "omissions or falsification in respect of company books and accounts for the purpose of bribing foreign public officials or of hiding briberies." Prohibited are off-the-book accounts; the making of inadequately identified transactions; the recording of non-existent expenditures; the entry of liabilities with incorrect identification of their purpose; and the use of false documents. In addition, it requires the disclosure of "facilitation payments."

4.1. Who is Responsible for Internal Control?

The original SAS No. 55 (AU 319.06) defined internal control as "a structure that consists of the policies and procedures" established to provide "reasonable assurance that specific entity objectives will be achieved." Since such a structure could be costly to implement, ultimately "management makes both quantitative and qualitative estimates and judgments in evaluating the cost-benefit relationship" (AU 319.14). Both SAS No. 55 and SAS No. 82 make it clear that internal control is the management responsibility, although SAS No. 82 further requires external auditors to make an assessment of the internal control. More specifically, external auditors assess the risk of fraud on every audit by considering both the internal control system and management's attitude toward controls. Maher, Stickney and Weil (1997) define internal controls as "policies and procedures designed to provide top management with reasonable assurances that actions undertaken by employees will meet the organizational goals." Other textbooks do not even mention internal control at all. The COSO Report, in contrast, defines the responsibility in a broader manner by defining internal control as "a process, effected by an entity's board of directors, management and other personnel" and states that "everyone in an organization has responsibility for internal control," including the management, the board of directors, the internal auditors, and other personnel (i.e. "virtually all employees"). At the same time, the report implies that internal controls are installed as a management tool so that they can "better control the enterprises they run." Internal controls are designed to provide reasonable assurance (to the management and the board of directors) "regarding the achievement of objectives in the following categories: effectiveness and efficiency of operations; reliability of financial reporting; compliance with applicable laws and regulation." Even though the COSO Report holds "everyone" responsible for internal control, the general view in the accounting profession is that it ultimately is the responsibility of top management. A classical textbook in auditing by Carmichael et al. (1996) states, "Management's attitude toward control sets the stage for the attitudes and actions of the entire company.... The control environment sets the tone of an organization.... The purpose of the internal control structure is to prevent or detect errors or irregularities, but absolute prevention or complete detection would be too costly and is probably a practical impossibility" (Carmichael et al., 1996, p. 182).

Thus, internal control is expected to provide only reasonable rather than absolute assurance. If it is practically impossible for management to uncover all errors and irregularities, one would expect that it is impossible for external auditors to discover them especially if management is involved. Management is in a position, if they wish, to "ensure" that internal controls fail. For example, in examining a theoretical model of an auditor's decision to investigate for fraud, Caplan (1999) assumes that management is able to choose the quality of internal control when it has incentives to misreport. He states (1999, p. 101): "Consistent with the practitioner literature, I assume that managers can commit fraud by overriding internal controls, and that audits conducted in accordance with generally accepted auditing standards (GAAS) do not always distinguish between errors and fraud."

What are external auditors supposed to do if they discover fraud? Section 10A of the Private Securities Litigation Reform Act of 1995 ("Auditor Disclosure of Corporate Financial Fraud") explicitly requires them to report to the board of directors and/or the SEC. However, whether the external auditors are responsible for, or even capable of, discovering frauds (especially committed by top management) appears to be a source of never-ending debate in the accounting profession. In fact, all independent auditors' reports of audited annual reports in the U.S. make it clear that the financial statements are "the responsibility of the Company's management." The auditors' "responsibility is to express an opinion" on these financial statements based on "their audits," which, in turn, are carried out in accordance with GAAS and these "audits provide a reasonable basis for opinion." Caplan continues:

> GAAS require auditors to obtain "reasonable assurance" that the financial statements are free of material misstatement, whether caused by error or fraud. However, most audit tests are not designed to detect fraud; auditors typically rely on management's assertions and are not trained to tell when someone is lying or to identify forged or altered documents. SAS No. 82 acknowledges that "because of the characteristics of fraud... a properly planned and performed audit may not detect a material misstatement...." (Appendix B, paragraph 12).

We do not routinely hear about the cases where auditors successfully discover frauds or errors, except when the discrepancies are large enough to cause the firm to issue restatements (Wu, 2002). It is more likely for us to hear about large audit failures, most of which are caused by auditors' inability to detect management fraud. If management is intent on defrauding the other stakeholders, they have perhaps the "best" means to do so. This is not to say that internal control is of secondary importance nor management is intent on defrauding. On the contrary, one cannot overemphasize the importance of internal control as the following two infamous cases illustrate.

4.2. Failures of Internal Control

In a detailed case study, Kane and De Trask (1998) describe two cases, in each of which a single "rogue" trader was able to conceal very large trading losses for a long period. In the case of Baring, the trader brought down a 233-year firm, while in the case of Daiwa, even though the Bank survived, the incident became a major international embarrassment not only to the bank but also to the Japanese government. The authors claim that Baring's "management and British regulators failed in their duty to institute an information and reporting system" to oversee global operation. Basic procedures such as segregation of duties (trading and settlement) and informative accounting standards were not in place. In a subsidiary office of Daiwa in New York, a single trader was able to continue unauthorized trades over 12 years. Once the losses became large, however, top management in Japan got involved in the cover up. Apparently Daiwa had a long history of "misleading U.S. regulators." To make the matter worse, the handling of the whole problem by the Japanese Ministry of Finance was slow and indecisive. Members of Congress registered "deep concern" over the cover-up. In both cases, a better internal control system would have discovered the problem earlier and prevented it from becoming out-of-hand or an international incident. Although Daiwa Bank did not go bankrupt, top executives had to resign and the trader was convicted. The Daiwa shareholders brought a lawsuit against the firm in 1995 and received the largest judgment of $775 million in 2000.

4.3. Management Fraud

Although better internal controls would prevent or discourage fraudulent conduct on the part of employees, it would be more difficult to prevent those at the top level. Eisenberg (1997) provides several examples of infamous fraud cases by management: Archer Daniels Midland, Sumitomo, Prudential, Citibank, and Bankers Trust. In the cases of both Prudential and Bankers Trust, complaints from the internal auditors were ignored by top management. All these firms in the end suffered either legal sanctions and/or large losses.

The recent series of scandals are undermining the investors' confidence in the corporate world. All of them appear to involve management frauds. Although the details may not be known until later, it is difficult to imagine how the malfeasance of such magnitude could have been done without the knowledge and endorsement at the top management level.

Of course, these are well-publicized cases. There may be many more cases that do not surface for the public scrutiny. As Eisenberg points out, internal control is not the right means to limit managerial opportunism, especially if ultimate responsibility for internal control is "vested" in the management. Thus, the ultimate responsibility for internal control would have to be vested in a higher level. This brings us to the next discussion on corporate governance.

5. CORPORATE GOVERNANCE AND ACCOUNTABILITY

The Securities Acts were passed in the Unites States almost 70 years ago. After the stock market crash of 1929 and growing antagonistic sentiments towards big businesses, it was necessary to restore public confidence in the efficacy of competitive capital markets. Underlying is an ideology, according to Merino and Neimark (1982), that a "corporate governance model" should be based on "the image of the stockholder" as "owner." The SEC was entrusted with "the task of ensuring public confidence" in the securities markets and, "by extension, in the credibility of the public philosophy." Through financial disclosure and the proxy provision, Merino and Neimark further argue that the SEC sought to develop a more effective corporate governance model of "shareholder democracy," consisting of: (1) shareholders as owners; and (2) the board of directors, having been elected by shareholders, to represent them to manage the corporation and to monitor or replace management. This model has established the fundamental approach to the equity market in the United States. When there are many shareholders, however, a number of problems arise due to "separation of ownership from control," an issue that has generated a vast amount of academic literature (including agency models, market for corporate control, mergers and acquisitions, corporate governance, among others).

In examining the rise and fall of modern corporations, Jensen (1993) points out that often firms are not able to evolve in an optimal way with the changing economic environment. Jensen attributes this inability to a failure of the corporate "internal control" system. "Substantial data support the proposition that the internal control system of publicly held corporations have generally failed to cause managers to maximize efficiency and value" and "ineffective governance is a major part of the problem with internal control mechanisms." IBM is an example of such a company, according to Jensen, because of its slow adjustment away from its mainframe business following the PC revolution. By "internal control," Jensen clearly implies something very different from the one defined by the accounting profession as well as the FCPA and the OECD Convention. He is addressing the issues that have been recently referred to as "corporate governance." In fact, he defines governance as "the top-level control structure, consisting of the decision rights possessed by the board of directors and the CEO, the procedures or changing them, the size and membership of the board, and the compensation and equity holding of managers and the board" (Jensen, 1993, pp. 51–52).

In terms of corporate hierarchy in the agency relationship, the shareholders represent the first level. The board of directors then represents them. It is the board that is, on behalf of shareholders, responsible for achieving the corporate objectives by providing guidance for corporate strategy and monitoring management. Monitoring management, in turn, involves setting their compensation as well as making promotion and firing decisions. The board is effective only if it is sufficiently independent from management. Board independence usually requires a sufficient number of outsiders, a sufficient time devoted by the members, and access to accurate, relevant and timely information.

In a survey on corporate governance, Shleifer and Vishny (1997) define corporate governance as "the ways in which suppliers of finance to corporations assure themselves of getting a return on their investment." The term is used here to imply a broader concept than how to manage a company. They state that corporate governance mechanisms are "economic and legal institutions that can be altered through political process – sometimes for better." Since these corporations exist in the context of larger social, economic, political and legal environments, the discussion on good governance cannot be restricted only to what goes on within an organization. Transparency (or the lack of opacity) in the capital markets is a necessary ingredient of good corporate governance.

6. OECD PRINCIPLES OF CORPORATE GOVERNANCE

It would be misleading to give an impression that the OECD has ended their effort to promote antibribery with the OECD Convention. In 1999, OECD issued their "Principles of Corporate Governance" to assist member and non-member governments in their efforts to "evaluate and improve the legal, institutional and regulatory framework for corporate governance" and to "provide guidance and suggestions" for various stakeholders in corporate governance.

Since the principles are non-binding, their purpose is to serve as "a reference point." They can be used by "policy makers" in their effort to "develop their legal and regulatory frameworks for corporate governance" in the context of their "own economic, social, legal and cultural circumstances," and "by market participants as they develop their own practices." The principles discuss the rights and fair treatment of various groups of shareholders, the role of various stakeholders, the importance of disclosure and transparency of information, the responsibility of the board, among others. The framework developed should ensure the strategic guidance of the company, the effective monitoring of management by the board, and the board's accountability to the company and the shareholders. In sum, the principles clarify the notion that the board of directors has the ultimate responsibility for governing (not operating on a day-to-day basis) a company.

7. THE ROLE OF AUDITORS

Even though the board is ultimately responsible for corporate governance, what they can do is often limited. Since the board is usually not engaged in its work on a full-time basis, it needs to rely on experts for necessary information, such as the internal auditor and the external auditor. Of course, since internal auditors are employees of the company, there is a built-in conflict in regard to their allegiance. Even though internal auditors might report to the board (or the audit committee of the board) directly, one cannot be sure about their independence from the management. This leads to the role of external auditors. If they are to attest to the "fair representation" of the financial condition of the firm, they need to be able to form their opinion independent of the board and management. Independence of external auditors, then, is crucial in this respect.

Although external auditors cannot be perfect detectives, they do provide an important service of attestation as an independent party. Briloff (2002) claims that "covenant" exists between the accounting profession and society "to assure the effective functioning of capitalism." Whether audit firms are "independent" both in appearance and in fact has been a focus of major debate, however. It is difficult to argue that interests are perfectly aligned between the external audit firm and the owners of the firm, when auditors are paid by the auditee company (i.e. its management) and often provide consulting services to the audit-client firms (again to the management). This is a stark contrast to the arrangement that was common in the first part of the 20th century where auditors were sent and paid by the suppliers of capital from Britain (Knutson, 1994). Research such as DeFond et al. (2002) found no evidence that auditor opinion (defined as their propensity to issue going-concern opinions) is influenced by non-audit service fees. Thus, they conclude that auditor "independence" is not impaired by non-audit fees. Of course, auditor independence is not only a matter of how often they issue going-concern opinions. Empirical research may never resolve the question conclusively.

However, for the opinions of external auditors to be taken seriously by the financial community, both independence in appearance and in fact does matter. One could even claim that, in the case of auditor independence, "form over substance" might apply since the public perception is the key. After all, "credibility" is in the minds of beholder (even though it should be based on the reality).

The recent corporate scandals involving accounting reveals that some firms with the blessing of their auditors have engaged in "creative accounting" stretching the interpretations of GAAP as well as taking advantages of the "rules-based" accounting. This promotes the "check-the-box" mentality – whatever is not in violation of GAAP must be good accounting. Given the rapidly changing business environment coupled with the large stakes involved with financial statement numbers, it would be difficult for standard setters to come up with appropriate "rules" in a timely fashion. Alles (2002) makes an observation that " the FASB simply cannot operate as quickly and flexibly as profit driven managers and financial engineering consultants."

8. REGULATORY AND POLITICAL ENVIRONMENTS: OTHER STAKEHOLDERS

In the United States, accounting standards are developed in the private sector rather than by governmental organizations such as the SEC. The Financial Accounting Standards Board (FASB) is an "independent" body entrusted by the SEC for the task. To ensure independence, all the board members are appointed full-time and are expected to sever all ties from other organizations. Yet, it is impossible for the Board to operate in a political vacuum. Zeff (2002) provides examples of "numerous attempts by industry and other affected parties" both in the U.S. and abroad to pressure standard setters not to impose "an objectionable requirement." The pressure comes from different directions, sometimes directly through business interests and other times indirectly through political legislative bodies. The cases cited include pressures from various groups in the U.S., Australia, U.K., Germany, Italy, Korea and Japan. It appears that good accounting and good business do not always coincide.

To illustrate, consider the treatment of stock options. After lengthy deliberations, the FASB decided not to require expensing of stock options. FASB Statement of Financial Accounting Standards (FAS123) includes the following passage:

> The debate on accounting for stock-based compensation unfortunately became so divisive that it threatened the Board's future working relationship with some of its constituents. Eventually, the nature of the debate threatened the future of accounting standards setting in the private sector.

This is despite the Board's belief that financial statements would be "more relevant and representationally faithful" if stock options are expensed. As a result, the Board specifies expensing as "preferable" and even encourages it, but does not require "recognition" of stock compensation cost.

Examples of political pressures on the FASB are not limited to the case of stock options. In an article published in the New York Times (1/23/02), Granof and Zeff note that some members of Congress pressured the FASB and the SEC to back off from setting tougher standards for financial reporting for the oil industry. In another case, Congress opposed the proposed change in the period of amortization of goodwill. The authors claim that by interfering with the standard setting process, which tries to come up with accounting standards that are to reflect the changing reality of business practices, "Congress paved the way for the current crisis." "Congressional involvement in financial standard-setting has been pure politics, fueled by a system of campaign financing that distorts the pursuit of the nation's legislative agenda."

Clearly, both money and power talk. An insightful summary of how various stakeholders relate to each other and how money might flow between various stakeholders was made by Kinney in his speech at the 2002 American Accounting Association Meetings. A slightly modified version is presented in Appendix B. It is apparent that firms operate in a complex environment and their behavior is influenced by a complex interplay of various forces. Internal control, corporate governance, and regulatory framework need to reinforce each other to promote less corruption.

9. CONCLUSIONS

Although the main focus of this chapter has been on the legislative attempts to curb the supply side of corruption, the discussion has led to broader issues of corporate governance and regulatory environment. Such broadening of scope was necessary since bribery behavior is influenced by economic incentives that are shaped by social, economic and political institutions. The recent debacles starting with Enron painfully illustrate the underlying forces. As the New York Times reported:

> The system of safeguards that was put in place over the years to protect investors and employees from a catastrophic corporate implosion largely failed to detect or address the problems that felled the Enron Corporation, say regulators, investors, business executives and scholars. The breakdown in checks and balances encompassed the company's auditors, lawyers and directors, they say. But it extended to groups monitoring Enron from the outside, like regulators, financial analysts, credit-rating agencies, the media and Congress... In Enron's case, the questions

extend to the political influence wielded by the company. But increasingly the focus has turned to the entire framework of legislation, regulation and self-governance in which it operated (Stevenson & Gerth, 2002, p. 1).

Emerging is a consensus that these debacles represent a "systemic" failure of the systems at all levels: political, regulatory, the board, the management, and the external auditor. Worse yet, it is likely that the systems actually contributed to the ultimate problem. For example, it is alleged that Enron actively campaigned to influence policy legislation.

It appears that the crisis has become serious enough to threaten the ideology of corporate capitalism. Sweeping changes are demanded to restore confidence. Several companies have decided voluntarily to expense stock options. A number of systematic attempts are under way to reform the U.S. corporate governance system. At the federal government level, Sarbanes-Oxley Act of July 2002 includes various new measures that strengthen the oversight of the board of directors and the fiduciary responsibility of CEOs and CFOs. The NYSE and Nasdaq also have new proposals, in the form of listing requirements, to promote more transparency and accountability of the listed companies. Former SEC chairman Levitt (2002, p. 22) said, "Sometimes it takes a crisis to convince the world that the status quo has to change. If there is a silver lining in the past year's accounting disasters, it's that an issue as mundane as auditor independence, which nearly consumed us at the SEC, has finally caught the public imagination."

The FCPA and the OECD Convention will be effective policy tools for combating corruption – specifically, bribery of foreign public officials by corporations from the signatory countries of the OECD Convention. Other multilateral treaties by the OAS and the European Union also help in leveling the field and promoting healthy competition. Competition to obtain and retain business for these would have to take a form other than bribery. Yet, it is clear that their effectiveness will be diminished if other efforts are neglected. Various institutional arrangements need to complement the Convention. After establishing a systematic relation between corruption and institutions, Broadman and Recanatini (2000) conclude:

> ...Our empirical exercise gives some support to our intuition that a well-established market system characterized by clear and transparent rules, fully functioning checks and balances and a healthy competitive environment reduces rent-seeking opportunities and, in turns the incentives for corruption (Broadman & Recanatini, 2000, p. 12).

At least three questions remain unresolved with respect to the FCPA and the OECD Convention. First, do these two legislative acts help resolve the corruption problem in the "bribe-paying" countries, i.e. "domestic" corruption in the signatories of the OECD Convention? My analysis in this chapter suggests that a more systematic approach at all levels is necessary. Internal control is necessary, but not sufficient. The second question is whether and to what extent these legislative attempts help reduce the problem of corruption in the "bribe-taking" countries? The aforementioned Bribe Payers Index points out that the propensity to bribe is higher for the domestic companies. Are these countries interested in reducing domestic corruption? The World Bank states that:

> The harmful effects of corruption are especially severe on the poor, who are hardest hit by economic decline, are most reliant on the provision of public services, and are least capable of paying the extra costs associated with bribery, fraud, and the misappropriation of economic privileges The World Bank (www1.worldbank.org).

If the burden of corruption falls more heavily on the poor, one effective way of reducing corruption is to make the rich feel the pain as well. Facing the OECD Convention, they might switch foreign business partners from those of OECD signatory countries to those from other countries. However, it may be difficult to find such companies since OECD signatory countries account for the majority of world trade. Together, 35 signatory countries can command strong bargaining power. Presumably, it would be more difficult to do honest business in countries where (domestic) corruption is rampant. For the bribe-taking countries, a possibility of reduction in foreign direct investment poses a serious threat to their economic welfare. Various ways to put more direct pressure on the demand-side are available through coordinated actions by governments and international organizations. A private organization such as Transparency International plays an important role in promoting the awareness of corruption issues.

Finally, there remains an extension to the second question: do the FCPA and the OECD Convention reduce the level of corruption in the world indeed? Alternatively, are they just the means to level the playing field for the signatory countries of the OECD Convention? Only time will tell.

NOTES

1. The countries included have increased over time. The earliest CPI available appears to be that for the 1980–1985 period for 54 countries. The next period available is 1988–1992, followed by annual data for 1995–1997, 2000, and 2001.

2. The 1988 Trade Act directed the Attorney General to provide guidance concerning the Department of Justice's enforcement policy with respect to the Foreign Corrupt Practices Act of 1977.

3. Rose-Ackerman (1999) explains the reason why internal control was required as opposed to holding corporations responsible for criminal behavior of the employees. Since most bribes are paid by employees and agents, not by top management, top management might be reluctant to come forward with information on the criminal conduct of their employees if the corporations are "held criminally liable."

REFERENCES

Alesina, A., & Weder, B. (1999). Do corrupt governments receive less foreign aid? NBER Working Paper 108, May.

Alles, M. G. (2002). A management control perspective on financial accounting standards. Working Paper.

Bardhan, P. (1997). Corruption and development: A review of issues. *Journal of Economic Literature*, *35*(September), 1320–1346.

Beck, P. J., Maher, M. W., & Tchoegl, A. E. (1991). The impact of the Foreign Corrupt Practices Act on U.S. exports. *Managerial and Decision Economics*, *12*, 295–303.

Beresford, D. R., & Bond, J. D. (1978). The Foreign Corrupt Practices Act – Its implication to financial management. *Financial Executive* (August), 28–32.

Borrus, A. (1995). A world of greased palms. *Business Week* (November 6).

Briloff, A. J. (2002). Accountancy and society: A covenant desecrated. Prepared Statement for U.S. Senate Committee on Banking, Housing, and Urban Affairs: March 2.

Broadman, H. G., & Recanatini, F. (2000). Seeds of corruption, World Bank. Policy Research Working Paper 2368.

Caplan, D. (1999). Internal controls and the detection of management fraud. *Journal of Accounting Research*, *37*(1, Spring), 101–117.

Carmichael, D. R., Willingham, J. J., & Schaller, C. A. (1996). *Auditing concepts and method* (6th ed.). McGraw-Hill.

Clarke, G. R. G., & Xu, L. C. (2001). Ownership, competition, and corruption: Bribe takers vs. bribe payers. October, Working Paper.

Committee of Sponsoring Organizations of the Treadway Commission (COSO) (1992, May). Internal control – Integrated framework.

DeFond, M. L., Raghunandan, K., & Subramanyam, K. R. (2002). Do non-audit fees impair auditor independence? Evidence form going concern audit opinions. *Journal of Accounting Research*, *40*(4, September), 1247–1275.

Eisenberg, M. A. (1997). Corporate governance: The board of directors and internal control. *Cardozo Law Review* (September/November), 237–264.

Gantz, D. A. (1998). Globalizing sanctions against foreign bribery: The emergence of a new international legal consensus. *Northwestern Journal of International Law & Business*, *18*, 457–497.

Hamra, W. (2000). Bribery in international business transactions and the OECD Conventions: Benefits and limitations. *Business Economics* (October), 33–46.

Hines, J. R., Jr. (1995, September). Forbidden payment foreign bribery and American business after 1977. NBER Working Paper 5266.

Hors, I. (2000). Fighting corruption in the developing countries. *Observer*, *220*(April).

Jensen, M. C. (1993). The modern industrial revolution, exit, and the failure of internal control systems. *Journal of Finance* (July), 831–880.

Kane, E. J., & De Trask, K. (1998). Covering up trading losses: Opportunity-cost accounting as an internal control mechanism. NBER Working Paper 6823.

Kinney, W. R., Jr. (2002). Accounting scholars – Does it matter what we teach them? Speech delivered for the Curriculum Challenge Contest at the 2002 American Accounting Association Meetings.

Knutson, P. H. (1994). In the public interest – Is it enough? *The CPA Journal* (January), 32–34.

Lacey, K. A., & Crutchfield George, B. (1998). Expansion of sec authority into internal corporate governance: The accounting provisions of the Foreign Corrupt Practices Act. *Journal of Transnational Law and Policy* (Spring), 119–155.

Lambsdorff, J. G. (1999). Corruption in empirical research – A review. Transparency International Working Paper.

Lee, C. M., & Ng, D. T. (2002). Corruption and international valuation: Does virtue pay? Working Paper.

Levitt, A., Jr. (2002). *Take on the street: What Wall Street and corporate America don't want you to know. What you can do to fight back.* Random House.

Maher, W. M., Stickney, C., & Weil, R. L. (1997). *Managerial accounting*. Dryden Press.

Merino, B. D., & Neimark, M. D. (1982). Disclosure regulation and public policy: A sociohistorical reappraisal. *Journal of Accounting and Public Policy, 1,* 33–57.

Moss, N. (1997). Who bribes wins. *The European* (December 11), 26–27.

National Commission on Fraudulent Financial Reporting (1987). Report of the National Commission on Fraudulent Financial Reporting.

Noonan, J. T. (1984). *Bribes*. New York: Macmillan.

North, D. (1999). Institutional change: A framework of analysis. Working Paper.

Rose-Ackerman, S. (1999). *Corruption and government: Cause, consequences, and reform*. Cambridge University Press.

Salbu, S. R. (1997). Bribery in the global market: A critical analysis of the Foreign Corrupt Practices Act. *Washington and Lee Law Review, 54,* 229–287.

Securities and Exchange Commission (1976). Report of the Securities and Exchange Commission on Questionable and Illegal Corporate Payments and Practices: Submitted to the Committee on Banking, Housing and Urban Affairs, 94th Congress, Second Session.

Shleifer, A., & Vishny, R. W. (1997). A survey of corporate governance. *Journal of Finance* (June), 737–783.

Stevenson, R., & Gerth, J. (2002). Enron's collapse: The system. *New York Times* (January 20, Section 1), 1.

Tronnes, R. D. (2000). Ensuring uniformity in the implementation of the 1997 OECE convention on combating bribery of foreign public officials in international business transactions. *The Washington International Law Review, 33,* 97–130.

Wei, S.-J. (1997). How taxing is corruption on international investors. NBER Working Paper 6030.

Wu, M. (2002). Earnings restatements: A capital market perspective. Working Paper, New York University.

Zeff, S. (2002). Commentary: Political lobbying on proposed standards: A challenge to the IASB. *Accounting Horizons, 16*(1, March), 43–54.

APPENDIX A

Correlation Between Various Indices

	CPI	Opacity	BPI	Corrupt'n	Legal	Economic	Acctg	Regul'y
CPI	1							
Opacity	−0.794 ($n = 34$)	1						
BPI	0.800 ($n = 22$)	−0.792 ($n = 10$)	1					
Corruption	−0.899	0.850	−0.842	1				
Legal	−0.641	0.878	−0.806	0.669	1			
Economic	−0.721	0.852	−0.751	0.690	0.659	1		
Acctg	−0.490	0.804	−0.496	0.534	0.671	0.566	1	
Regul'y	−0.704	0.908	−0.810	0.769	0.752	0.823	0.599	1

Source: Author (2003).

APPENDIX B

Accounting and Corporate Governance
Show me the Money!

Based on: William Kinney, Jr
"Accounting Scholars- does it matter what we teach them?
Presented at the 2002 AAA Meetings

Source: Author (2003).

12. COPING WITH CORRUPTION IN ALBANIAN PUBLIC ADMINISTRATION AND BUSINESS

Denita Cepiku

INTRODUCTION

The primary aim of this chapter is to offer an overview of corruption and state capture in Albanian public administration and to describe the solutions adopted to fight corruption by the government since 1998. Conflict of interest is a new aspect of concern in the policy agendas. OECD countries have recently adopted some guidelines for managing the phenomenon, which will be then transferred to eastern European countries. Given this novelty, this chapter does not deal directly with conflict of interest situations. Corruption is rarely treated as a management problem, in part because for obvious reasons as data are scarce and also because the literature is thin and tentative, with few theoretical frameworks. Also rare is analysis of how corruption has been or might be reduced. The state of research on corruption is such that there is little inductive theory or statistical evidence about the kinds of policies that work under particular conditions.

This research proceeds on two fronts, theoretical and empirical. At the theoretical level, we extend and adapt to the transition context the model from the literature in the area to study corruption in developing and developed countries. In particular, from review of theoretical contributions we have originated some assumptions, in part confirmed by empirical data. With reference to theory, we reviewed the principal theoretical contributions concerning: (i) causes of corruption in general and with particular reference to public administration in transition economies; and (ii) policy measures implemented by government and public administrations to fight corruption (Hellman et al., 2000; Johnson et al., 1997; Kaufmann et al., 1998b; Klitgaard, 1997, 2000; Mark, 2001; Mussari & Di Torro, 1993; OECD, 2002; Rose-Ackerman, 1997; World Bank, 1997a, 2000c). With reference to empirics, we analyzed surveys at the firm, citizen and public official level that investigate: (i) the causes of corruption in Albanian public administration; and (ii) the anti-corruption plan of the Albanian government (Commission of The European Communities, 2001; ACER, 1998a; Kaufmann et al., 1998a; OECD/CCNM, 1999; Prato, 2000; SELDI, 2001; SPAI, 2000). A comparison between theory and empirical evidence produced answers to the following questions posed in our research:

(1) Are the causes of corruption found in the literature equally present and equally important in the Albanian public sector? Does empirical devidence provide further causes not taken into account in the literature?
(2) Have anti-corruption measures recommended in the literature been adopted by the Albanian government?
(3) The theoretical models claim that an effective strategy for anti-corruption must address the root causes of different forms of corruption to reduce the risk of treating symptoms instead causes. Are anti-corruption efforts in Albania coherent with this position?

Finally, the analysis of the anti-corruption strategy in Albania produced additional questions to which we have tried to provide some early answers in but for which more evidence and further research is needed (Government of Albania, 2000a, 2000b, 2000c, 2000d, 2000e).

(4) Have strategies used to fight corruption and state capture in Albania been effective?
(5) What strategies might in principle prove to be effective in the short and in the longer term?

The chapter proceeds as follows. The next section highlights the principal differences in corruption patterns between transition and developed/developing countries and reviews the literature in search of definitions, causes and effects of corruption as well as policy measures to fight them. Section three focuses on data concerning corruption and state capture in Albania, and its causes and effects. A country and sector background also is provided. Then, we proceed in section four with an analysis of the first Albanian anti-corruption plan (revised in 2000), as well as the second (and current) one. We also try to evaluate the

```
                                    ┌─────────────────────────────┐
    ┌──────────────────────┐    →   │  Causes of corruption in    │
    │  Theoretical level   │        │   transition countries      │         ┌──────────────────────────┐
    └──────────────────────┘        └─────────────────────────────┘         │ Are the causes of corruption │
                                                                            │ found in the literature      │
  • Broadman H.G., Recanatini F. (2001)   ┌─────────────────────────────┐   │ equally present and equally  │
  • OECD/PUMA (2002)                  →   │  Policy measures against    │   │ important in the albanian    │
  • World Bank (1997).                    │  corruption in transition   │   │ public sector?               │
  • Klitgaard R. E. (1988).               │        countries            │   └──────────────────────────┘
                                          └─────────────────────────────┘

                                                                            ┌──────────────────────────┐
                                                                            │ Are the anti-corruption      │
                                          ┌─────────────────────────────┐   │ measures recommended by      │
                                          │  Causes of corruption in    │   │ the literature adopted by the│
    ┌──────────────────────┐          →   │    albanian public          │   │ albanian government?         │
    │  Empirical level     │              │    administration           │   └──────────────────────────┘
    └──────────────────────┘              └─────────────────────────────┘

  • The 1999 Business Environment and                                       ┌──────────────────────────┐
    Enterprise Performance Survey (BEEPS)                                   │ Are anti-corruption efforts  │
    (private firms)                       ┌─────────────────────────────┐   │ in Albania coherent with the │
  • The Vitosha Research based on a   →   │  Policy measures against    │   │ root causes of different     │
    Corruption Monitoring System of       │  corruption in the albanian │   │ forms of corruption?         │
    Coalition 2000 (public opinion, citizens │   public administration   │   └──────────────────────────┘
    and public officials)                 └─────────────────────────────┘
  • ACER and World Bank (1998). Public
    Officials Survey. (public officials)
  • ORT (1997). Household Survey
    (household).
```

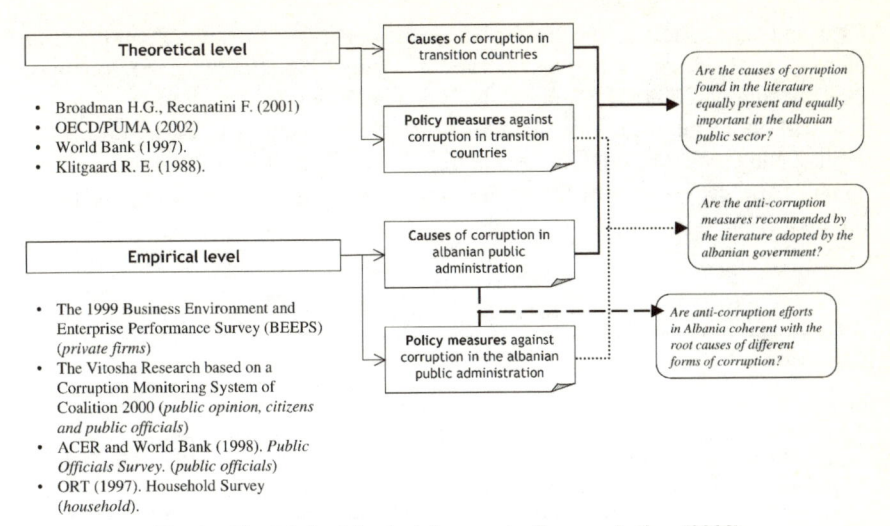

Fig. 1. The Methodological Approach. *Source:* Author (2003).

principal results achieved. The last section offers some concluding remarks and seeks answers to the above questions (Fig. 1).

THEORETICAL FRAMEWORK

In the countries of Central and Eastern Europe, the concurrent processes for developing a market economy, designing new political and social institutions and redistributing social assets have created fertile ground for corruption. The fusion of the state and the economy that characterized the communist system has been replaced in most of the countries by a new order, but one in which the separation of private and public interests has not been adequately defined. The boundaries between state and economy remain murky (Camdessus, 1994; de Melo et al., 1996; Dillinger & Fay, 1999; EBRD, 1998; Exter & Fries, 1998; Feldman & Watson, 2000; Fischer & Gelb, 1991; Fischer & Sahay, 2000; Gelb, 1993; Havrylyshyn & Wolf, 1999; Lenain, 1998; Litwack, 1998; Murphy et al., 1992; Nsouli, 1999; OECD, 1996; Schiavo-Campo, 1994; Tanzi, 1999; World Bank, 1996, 2000a, 2000d, 2002). For many governments throughout the region combating corruption ranks high on the political agenda. "State capture has become not merely a symptom but also a fundamental cause of poor governance" (Hellman & Kaufmann, 2001). The captured economy is trapped in a vicious circle in which the policy and institutional reforms necessary to improve governance are undermined by collusion between powerful firms and state officials who reap substantial private gains from the continuation of weak governance (Allen, 1999; Bale & Dale, 1998; Barzelay, 2001; Hood, 2000; Manning, 2000; Minogue, 2000; Polidano, 1999; Schick, 1998).

It will be useful to provide first some essential definitions of corruption, state capture and conflict of interest used in this chapter. Then we proceed to highlight some of the causes of and the consequences that corruption and state capture provoke (Table 1).

Table 1. Definitions.

Definitions

Corruption
Corruption is commonly defined as *the abuse of public office for private gain* (World Bank, OECD/PUMA, etc.). Another definition of corruption, found in the Webster's Third New International Dictionary, is *inducement (as of a political official) by means of improper considerations (as bribery) to commit a violation of duty.* Klitgaard (1988) gives the following definition: [Corruption = Monopoly + Discretion − Accountability] and draws a distinction between *external corruption, which includes the payment for licit or illicit services and extortion of bribes for refraining from doing harm to the client, and internal corruption, which refers to embezzlement, delays, etc.*

State capture
The tendency by some elite firms and conglomerates to shape illicitly the formation of the state laws, policies and regulations (World Bank, 2000).
Kaufmann defines state capture as *the efforts of firms to shape the laws, policies, and regulations of the state to their own advantage by providing illicit private gains to public officials.*
Broadman and Recanatini (2001) identify state capture with *a particularly harmful form of corruption consisting in the ability of firms to subvert the entire political process to ensure that policies and regulations favorable to their business interests are implemented.*
These definitions underline the basic distinction between corrupt activity, which subverts the implementation of rules, procedures and practices, and state capture which subverts the basic rules of the political system. The World Bank (2000) goes on to suggest distinctions between the types of institutions which are captured (the executive, legislature, judiciary, or independent regulatory agencies), who is doing the capturing (private firms, interest groups, political leaders), and the type of benefits provided to public officials (bribes, equity stakes, informal control rights).

Conflict of interest
A *conflict of interest involves a conflict between the public duty and the private interest of a public official, in which the public official has private-capacity interests which could improperly influence the performance of their official duties and responsibilities* (OECD/PUMA, 2003, forthcoming publication).
Where the private interest has *in facto* compromised the proper performance of public official duties, that specific situation is better regarded as an instance of misconduct or "abuse of office" or even an instance of corruption, rather than as a conflict of interest.

Source: Author (2003).

Table 2. The Corruption Formula I.

Corruption = f (quality of government, quality of political institutions, openness to trade) = $b_1 + b_2$ (GDP) + b_3 (Index of democracy) + b_4 (Imports/GDP).

Source: Broadman and Recanatini (2001).

As emphasized by an increasing literature, corruption affects growth and investment, making its eradication a fundamental challenge for the long-term development of many countries, both developed and developing (Kaufmann, 1994; Mauro, 1995). Given the high costs of corruption, research and policy advice have increasingly focused on identifying the root causes of corruption.

The existing literature on the sources of corruption in developed and developing countries explains corruption by the quality of the government of a country – as reflected by the country's level of economic development – and the quality of the country's political institutions (Ades & Di Tella, 1999; Broadman & Recanatini, 2001; Treisman, 1999). In particular, it is typically hypothesized that incentives for corruption are likely to be lower in countries more economically developed – measured by GDP per capita – and where there are greater democratic political processes and a strong independent press – measured by an index of democracy. In addition, it is usually hypothesized that openness to foreign trade reduces the potential rents of government officials, and, in turn, decreases incentives for corruption. The literature on the determinants of corruption in developed and developing economies generally follows this type of model (Table 2).

However, in the case of transition economies undergoing fundamental changes in basic institutional regimes, this model is likely to be inadequate. In particular, the quality of government in transition economies is likely not to be fully captured by a measure of GDP. Arguably, more than other types of countries, the quality of government in transition economies would seem to be a direct function of the types of basic market institutions. Accordingly, this argues for substituting the various institutional variables described above for GDP per capita. By the same token, the use of a measure of imports as a proxy for openness to foreign trade is also unlikely to be adequate. The linkages between trade and corruption are likely to be affected by activities related to a country's exports as well as to its imports. A better measure of these linkages is an indicator capturing the development and the degree of openness of the overall trade system.

Based on these considerations, Broadman and Recanatini (2001) employ a model different from that specified in the first equation. In particular, as summarized in the next equation, their model employs the following variables: (i) a vector of institutional indicators measuring infrastructure development, entry

Table 3. Corruption Formula II.

Corruption = f (quality of government, quality of political institutions, openness to trade) = $b_1 + b_2$ (Institutional indicators) + b_3 (Index of democracy) + b_4 (Trade system index)

Source: Broadman and Recanatini (2001).

barriers, soft budgets, legal effectiveness, and the bankruptcy regime; (ii) an index of democratic development; and (iii) a trade system index (Table 3).

This is a difficult task because most of the institutional indicators available are correlated with each other. Moreover, some of the institutional indices are likely to be endogenous to corruption: if it is true, for example, that a poorly functioning legal system or an inefficient public administration causes corruption, it may also be the case that widespread corruption prevents the improvement of the legal system and public administration reform. Indeed, this vicious circle reflects accurately the dialectic posed by the problem of state capture that makes implementation of corruption-curbing reforms so challenging. Corruption is most prevalent where there are other forms of institutional inefficiency, such as political instability, bureaucratic red tape, and weak legislative and judicial systems. The truth is that probably all of these weaknesses are intrinsically linked, in the sense that they feed upon each other (for example, red tape makes corruption possible, and corrupt bureaucrats may increase the extent of red tape so they can extract additional bribes) and that getting rid of corruption helps a country overcome other institutional weaknesses, just as reducing other institutional weaknesses helps it curb corruption.

While agreeing with the Broadman and Recanatini model, a second model that highlights the sources of corruption is that of the Public Management Committee of the OECD (OECD/PUMA, 2002). While it is a model reflecting factors contributing to corruption in developed (OECD) countries, in our view it describes better the context of transition economies. The model distinguishes between contributory factors, systemic characteristics and contextual variables. The first include:

- Inadequate compliance with accounting and reporting rules.
- Patronage in appointments.
- Undue influence by major vested interest groups.
- Weak oversight of arm's length public bodies.
- Secretive and unaccountable officials
- Weak internal and external controls.
- Weak safeguards for awarding government contracts.
- Systemic characteristics concern.
- Lobbying and party funding system.
- Incentives and accountability of officials.

- Accounting and reporting standards & compliance.
- Ethical and professional standards amongst officials.
- Senior civil servant system (elite/non-elite, permanent or politically appointed).
- Official information disclosure regime.
- Effectiveness of external invigilators.

Finally, contextual variables relate to the:

- Power of organized labor to resist change.
- Capacity of the legislature to constrain Executive action.
- Balance of power between head of government and ministers.
- Constitutional autonomy of lower levels of government.
- Citizens' interest in and expectations of official behavior.
- Independence/assertiveness of judiciary.
- Political capacity of Executive for hard decisions.

In conclusion, other sources of corruption can be found that are prevalent in transition countries as compared with developed or developing countries (World Bank, 1997b). Indeed, corruption in transition countries has been facilitated by other factors including:

- The rewriting of an unprecedented volume of laws, regulations, and policies.
- The extraordinary redistribution of wealth from the state to the private sector.
- The virtual absence of institutions either within or external to the public sector that could effectively check the abuse of public office during the transition in many countries.
- A distorted policy environment, which creates greater opportunities for public officials to manipulate rules for their own benefit.
- A weak judiciary that is unable to provide a credible threat of punishment when official misconduct is discovered.
- And poor civil service management and low public sector pay.

Corruption has serious effects on public administrations, on firms and on citizens. Klitgaard considers the effects of corruption in four categories: efficiency costs in terms of waste and misallocation, equitable distribution, incentives for rent-seeking and political instability (Klitgaard, 1988). It weakens public service delivery, misdirects public resources, and holds back the growth that is necessary to pull people out of poverty. In countries where the problem is deep-rooted, corruption undermines the driving forces behind reform. New firms are driven into the underground economy. Vital resources are transferred off shore. Foreign investors turn away in frustration. As a result, some countries risk becoming trapped in a vicious circle in which pervasive corruption reduces public revenues, undermines public trust, and weakens the credibility of the state, unless decisive leadership can push through the necessary reforms.

One specific channel through which corruption may harm economic performance is by distorting the composition of government expenditure. Corrupt politicians may be expected to spend more public resources on those items on which it is easier to extract large bribes and keep them secret – for example, items produced in markets where the degree of competition is low and items whose value is difficult to monitor. Corrupt politicians might therefore be more inclined to spend on fighter aircraft and large-scale investment projects than on textbooks and teachers' salaries, even though the latter may promote economic growth to a greater extent than the former. Corruption is thus associated with lower public spending on health and education, which in turn limits opportunities for poor people to invest in their human capital and to participate in markets. At a deeper level, corruption undermines the legitimacy of the state itself and weakens the capacity of the state to provide institutions that support markets (Mauro, 1998).

The costs of state capture and administrative corruption are mutually reinforcing and are themselves influenced by a range of other factors. While increasing private revenues to public officials, corruption tends to have a negative impact on public revenues. A substantial share of administrative corruption is directed towards tax and customs officials, presumably resulting in lower tax and customs payments by firms. Moreover, corruption is closely associated with the unofficial economy, the size of which can have profound fiscal implications in many transition countries. When firms produce for the unofficial economy, they underreport economic activity or avoid the state entirely. This creates competitive advantages that can drive honest competitors out of the market, thereby generating further corruption and fiscal decrease. The reduction of tax revenues reduces the funds available for public services, providing firms with fewer incentives to operate officially. Corruption in procurement, assignment of subsidies, and outright theft leads to an exaggerated flow of funds out of the public coffers. While there is some difference in relation to the causes of corruption, its effects are similar across countries. However, an effective strategy for anti-corruption must be based on an understanding of the root causes of different forms of corruption and their variation. Without it, policymakers run the risk of treating the symptoms without remedying the underlying conditions. In fact, empirical investigation points to the importance of both the design and effective implementation of anti-corruption measures; in other words, it is not enough, for example, to simply enact first class laws if they are not enforced (Broadman & Recanatini, 2001).

Although still in the early stages of development, the experience of anti-corruption programs to date has produced mixed results. Ambitious anti-corruption campaigns in several countries have floundered at the implementation stage. Key structural reforms have been blocked by powerful vested interests. In some cases, politicians have hijacked the anti-corruption agenda and used it to attack their rivals. Governments in the region have tended to prefer strengthening enforcement mechanisms to addressing the structural roots of the problem. One reason for the difficulties has been an overemphasis on technocratic measures in a uniform approach that does not take into account important differences among countries in the power and concentration of vested interests, the capacity of the state, and the channels of accountability between the state and civil society.

The standard advice for combating corruption has traditionally focused on measures to address administrative corruption by reforming public administration and public finance management. But with the increasing recognition that the roots of corruption extend far beyond weaknesses in the capacity of government, the repertoire has been gradually expanding to target broader structural relationships, including the internal organization of the political system, relationships among core state institutions, the interactions between the state and firms, and the relationship between the state and civil society. The fight against corruption in the transition countries has been incorporated into a wider reform agenda combining liberalization and privatization to roll back the state and governance reforms to promote greater transparency and accountability in the state's legal and regulatory framework. PUMA/OECD has defined the concept of an "ethics infrastructure" including eight key elements (OECD/PUMA, 1997): political commitment (politicians should say ethics are important, set an example, and support good conduct with adequate resources); an effective legal framework (laws and regulations which set standards of behavior and enforce them); efficient accountability mechanisms (administrative procedures, audits, agency performance evaluations, consultation and oversight mechanisms); workable codes of conduct (statement of values, roles, responsibilities, obligations, restrictions); professional socialization mechanisms (education and training); supportive public service conditions (fair and equitable treatment, appropriate pay and security); an ethics coordinating body; An active civic society (including a probing media) to act as watchdog over government activities.

As with any set of management tools, the effectiveness of the ethics infrastructure depends on whether it is implemented, understood and applied consistently. Ethics should be linked to public management. If there is too much control, nothing will get done; but if there is too little control the wrong things will get done. A country's ethics management regime should be consistent with its approach to public management in general. It would be inconsistent to marry a strict centralized compliance-based ethics infrastructure with devolved results-based management systems. The following sections provide an overview of corruption and state capture in Albanian public sector and describe the anti-corruption plan.

PUBLIC ADMINISTRATION IN ALBANIA

The Republic of Albania is a country of approximately three million people situated on the Balkan Peninsula. There are three levels of government in Albania: the central, the regional and the local level. Central government comprises the Council of Ministers, the Ministries and other central government bodies. The Albanian public administration has a modest size (Government of Albania, 2001d). In 1998, total employment in Albania's public sector (comprising general government, state enterprises and state farms) was 213,000. Public sector employment, both as a percentage of total population and as percentage of total labor force, has registered a decline since 1993. This reduction has been achieved largely through pro-rata cuts undertaken in the context of government efforts to achieve fiscal stabilization (Fig. 2).

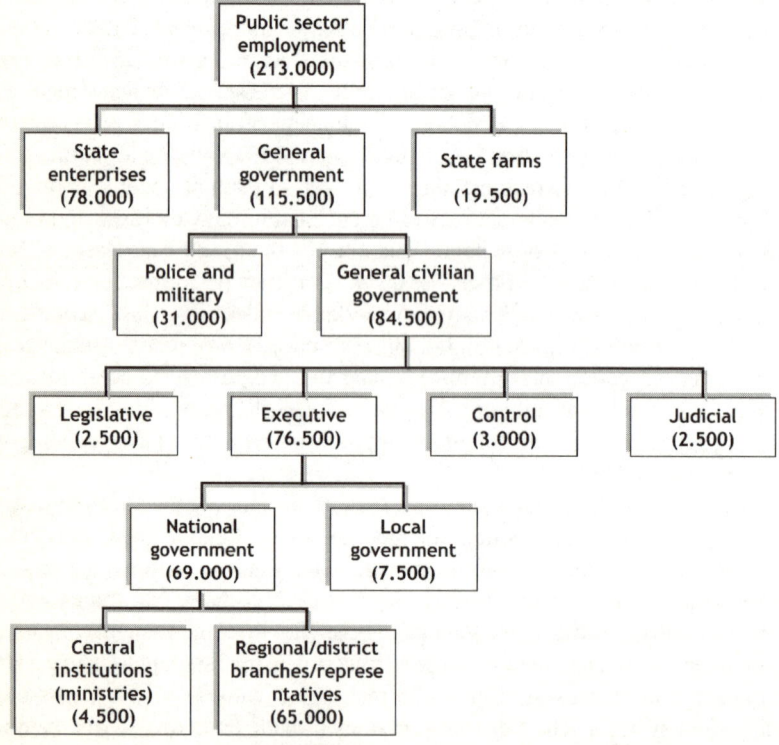

```
                    Public sector
                    employment
                    (213.000)
          ┌─────────────┼─────────────┐
      State         General         State farms
    enterprises    government        (19.500)
     (78.000)      (115.500)
                       │
            ┌──────────┴──────────┐
       Police and          General civilian
        military              government
        (31.000)              (84.500)
                                 │
        ┌──────────┬─────────────┬──────────┐
    Legislative  Executive     Control    Judicial
     (2.500)     (76.500)      (3.000)    (2.500)
                    │
              ┌─────┴─────┐
          National      Local
         government   government
          (69.000)     (7.500)
              │
        ┌─────┴─────┐
     Central      Regional/district
   institutions   branches/represe
   (ministries)     ntatives
     (4.500)        (65.000)
```

Fig. 2. Public Administrations in Albania (1998). *Source:* OECD/SIGMA (1999).

OECD Countries	7,7
Transition economies	6,2
Albania	4,2

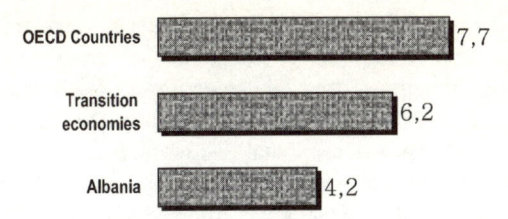

Fig. 3. Public Service Employment (% of Total Population). *Source:* OECD/SIGMA (1999).

Public service employees represent 4.2% of the total population (2001 data). This may be compared with an average of 6.2% for a group of 12 transition economies, and 7.7% for a group of 20 OECD countries. While such comparisons should be approached with caution, they suggest that public service employment in Albania is no longer excessive and that the scope for further reductions is limited. Instead, two other elements should be taken into account: the dominant role of education and health services within the overall public services payroll and the increasing shortages of skilled and professional staff in a number of areas. Staff resources are not distributed appropriately (Fig. 3).

Weaknesses in public administrations and management continue to have an adverse impact on the morale, motivation and performance of public servants (Cepiku, 2002; Government of Albania, 1998; OECD/SIGMA, 1998, 2000; Open Society Foundation for Albania, 2001; Treichel, 2001). Addressing these weaknesses should be part of any anti-corruption strategy. The Department of Public Administration has initiated a program aimed at improving the structure and management of the public service. Local governments were created at the beginning of the process of decentralization in the early 1990s and a number of laws were approved which govern their competencies and authorities. Much of that legal framework has yet to be implemented and the reality is that local governments in Albania have very limited administrative and fiscal autonomy (The Urban Institute, 1998).

In the first years of transition, the focus was mainly on central reforms to build the key institutions based on democratic models as well as on basic economic reforms. As a result there was less attention to local government reforms. The current status of local governments is characterized by general definitions of responsibilities and functions and by a mismatching between responsibilities and the authority to act. Communes and municipalities constitute the basic level of local government. While a commune is usually located in a rural area, the municipality is located in an urban area. Regions are the upper level of local self-government and include several communes and municipalities.

Subdivisions of the regions are the districts. At present, there are 309 communes, 65 municipalities and 36 districts in Albania. Each level performs "exclusive functions," "shared functions" and "delegated functions." The communes and the municipalities have full powers for their exclusive functions, which concern infrastructure and public services, social and cultural functions, local economic development. Communes and municipalities may undertake shared functions, separately or jointly with the central government. Such functions comprise health and education, social assistance, public order, environmental protection, etc. Finally, delegated functions are mandatory (determined by law) and non-mandatory (determined by an agreement between the central and the local government).

Legislation governing local finance in Albania defines two elements of the local government budget: the "conditional" and the "independent" budgets (Law No. 7616 of 30/9/1992). The conditional budget is funded by transfers from the central government and the funds are used for very specific purposes, as determined and allocated by the relevant line Ministries and the Ministry of Finance. Since the conditional budget accounts for 95% of local expenditures in the aggregate, local governments have little financial autonomy and lack the authority to manage their funds in accordance with the best interests of the local community. The legal framework in Albania provides that surplus budget funds derived from locally generated revenues may be carried over to the next budget year. In practice, local governments have never been able to carry over their excess funds to the next budget year. Each year, the Council of Ministers has passed a decision or decree which requires all or some part of local budget surpluses (i.e. those funds not expended by the end of the budget year), sometimes even before the end of the budget year, to be transferred to the state treasury account, regardless of whether they derive from local revenues or from transfers.

The decentralization strategy has included a first phase (2000) with high visible impact on local government, concerning changing in local financing, a package of laws on public property and on local public enterprises. The second stage (2001) addressed some crucial issues linked with the institutional status of local government and local financing. Subsequent phases (2002 and beyond) will address other important issues, which require a longer time frame to be formulated and implemented. The elements of this phase need to complete the legal framework initially developed in previous phases. Some major issues will be the law on urban planning and additional local government functions (education, health, police and civil defense). The current status of local government is a product of the dynamics of the political, economic and social factors of transition, as well as historical, traditional, cultural and social psychology (Fig. 4).

```
                        Centralization
                              |
                              |       ┌─────────────────┐
                              |       │ 2. Local Government │
                              |       │   in 1944 - 1990   │
                              |       └─────────────────┘
   Limited                    |  ┌──────────────────┐                Extended
functions and  ───────────────┼──│ 1. Local Government │───────────  functions and
 competencies                 |  │    in 1924 - 1938   │              competencies
                              |  └──────────────────┘
                    ┌──────────────────┐   ┌──────────────────┐
                    │ 3. Local Government │ │ Local Government │
                    │    in 1991 - 1997   │ │  according to the │
                    └──────────────────┘   │ European Charter for │
                              |            │ Local Self Government │
                              |            └──────────────────┘
                       Decentralization
```

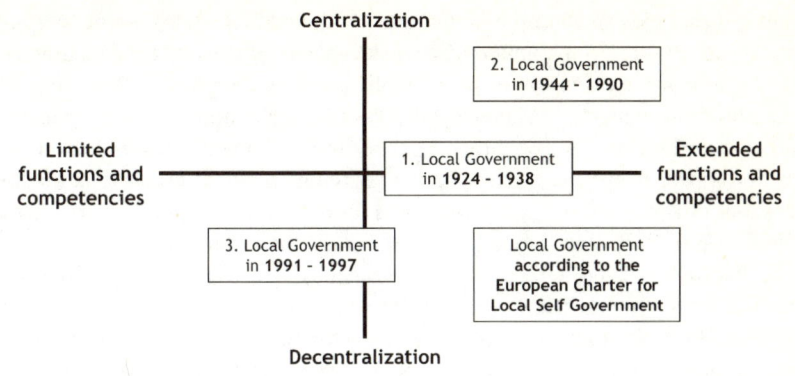

Fig. 4. Scale of Autonomy in Local Government. *Source:* UNDP (1998).

Notwithstanding the two-sided impact of these factors, they have played more of a restraining than a promoting role in the decentralization of power and strengthening of local self-government.

MEASURING CORRUPTION IN ALBANIA

To follow-up the background provided above on the Albanian public administration we examine the presence of corruption and the efforts made to combat it. Figure 5 presents an aggregate index of the impact of state capture and administrative corruption across the transition countries. Both administrative corruption and state capture continue to be serious problems in every country of the region.

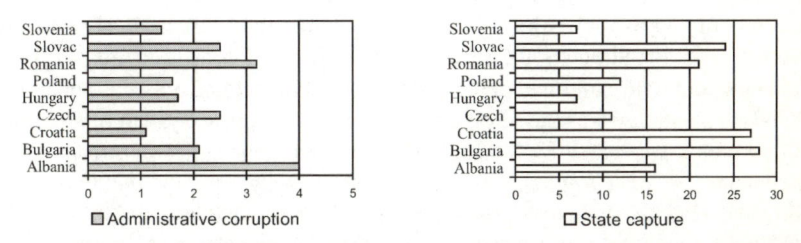

Fig. 5. Administrative Corruption and State Capture in Some Transitional Countries. *Note:* Administrative corruption is measured by bribes as a share of annual revenues, while state capture reflects the share of firms affected by state capture. *Source:* World Bank (2000b).

Albania provides an example of a country with medium state capture and high administrative corruption featured by a weak capacity of existing state institutions, both in terms of the provision of basic public goods and regulatory functions and the existing mechanisms of accountability and control within the state apparatus. State capture by firms is lower than in other transition countries. However, this does not appear to be due to any greater degree of political constraints on state actors, but rather to a less concentrated and less developed economic structure or to the overall lack of state capacity to intervene in the economy.

The instrument used here is the 1999 Business Environment and Enterprise Performance Survey (BEEPS) commissioned jointly by the World Bank and the European Bank for Reconstruction and Development. It is a firm-level survey that interviews more than 3,000 enterprise owners and senior managers in 22 transition countries. It provides new and more robust measures of different forms of corruption across transition countries from the point of view of firms (EBRD/World Bank, 1999). It identified a number of specific activities that fall within the definition of state capture, including: the "sale" of Parliamentary votes and presidential decrees to private interests; the sale of civil and criminal court decisions to private interests; corrupt mishandling of central bank funds; and illegal contributions by private actors to political parties. Firms were asked to assess the direct impact on their business of each of these activities, regardless of whether they engaged in such activities themselves. Thus, capture is measured not by how many firms engage in it, but by the share of firms whose business is directly affected by it.

By investigating the channels through which firms seek to influence the state, the BEEPS survey represents the first attempt to measure some aspects of the incidence of capture across the transition countries, although representing only the problem of capture by firms (as opposed to other individuals or groups).

While the BEEPS survey provided data concerning capture by firms, another survey conducted with the cooperation between Vitosha Research with Center for the Study of Democracy, Albanian Center for Economic Research, Albania, and Forum-Center for Strategic Research and Documentation, Macedonia, explored corruption and state capture as perceived by the public opinion, citizens and public officials. The survey was based on a Corruption Monitoring System of Coalition 2000, which was created by Vitosha Research and is an initial step towards the implementation of a Regional Corruption Monitoring System. Fieldwork was conducted between January 15 and January 25, 2000, and the sample size was 1,002 for Albania, 1,144 for Bulgaria and 1,007 for Macedonia. According to the public opinion in Albania corruption is one of the most important public problems at present (Brunetti, Kisunko & Weder, 1997).

Coping with Corruption in Albanian Public Administration and Business

	Albania Rank	Bulgaria Rank	Macedonia Rank
Political instability	4	8	4
Ethnic problems	9	11	6
Corruption	1	4	7
Low incomes	5	2	2
Crime	2	5	5
Unemployment	3	1	1
Environment	8	9	11
Health Care	6	6	8
High prices	10	10	10
Education	11	7	9
Poverty	7	3	3

Fig. 6. Main Problems Faced by Country. *Source:* Vitosha Research (2000) and Author (2003).

The survey identified attitudes towards corruption of these three countries, measured through different indexes (Figs 6 and 7).

Acceptability in Principle

This index reflects the level of tolerance towards the various corrupt practices. The values reflect the fact that corruption is generally perceived as a morally inadmissible phenomenon. Focusing on Albania, compare to the survey of May 1999 (ACER), according to citizens, now this phenomena is increasingly considered as unacceptable. Anyway looking in detail corruption is mostly perceived as only bribes (cash) while the tolerance for gifts and favours is much bigger (ACER, 2000). This means that the level of understanding of the corruption phenomenon needs still to be improved in the Albanian society.

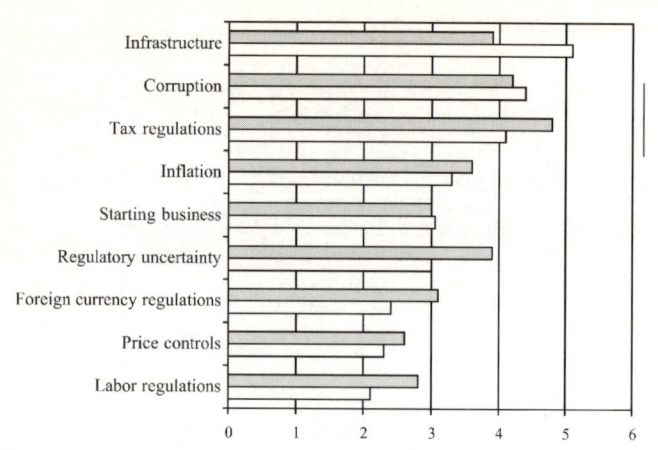

Fig. 7. Obstacles to Doing Business in Transition Economies (1996). *Source:* Vitosha Research (2000) and Author (2003).

Susceptibility to Corruption

The index, which measures the inclination of the citizens to compromise with their principles and values under the pressure of circumstances, has similar values in all of the countries, showing that public opinion in Albania, Bulgaria, and Macedonia demonstrates intolerance towards corrupt practices, and citizens declare their willingness for personal non-involvement in them, despite the pressure of the circumstances.

Corruption Pressure

This index reflects the spread of the attempts of public officials to exert direct or indirect pressure on the citizens of the three countries in order to obtain money, gifts, or services (Fig. 8).

Involvement in Corrupt Practices

This index reflects respondent self-admission of personal involvement in corrupt practices. Obviously, this is a highly sensitive and data are reported anonymously.

Coping with Corruption in Albanian Public Administration and Business 301

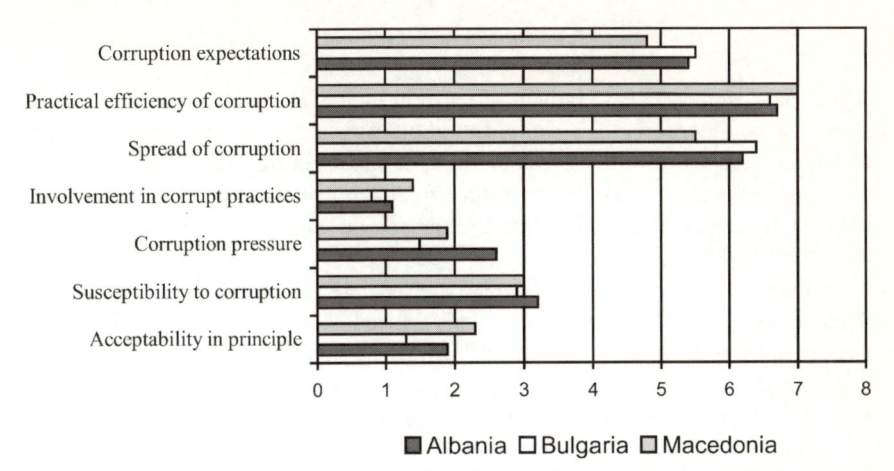

Fig. 8. Attitudes Towards Corruption. *Source:* Corruption Indexes (2000).

Personal Involvement in Corrupt Practices

With reference to Albania, 10% of the respondents declare they have had to pay officials in almost all or most of the cases they have contacted them. Taking into account the fact that not all the respondents have had problems to resolve with public officials (or have not resolved them themselves) this figure is high.

Spread of Corruption

This index registers Albanian, Bulgarian, and Macedonian citizens' estimates of the spread of corrupt practices among public officials. The spread of corruption in the public sector assessed by Albanian citizens is very high. Actually this index is a perception of the public and as such may be affected in time by different events that have to do with corruption in the public sector. Two much commented events in the press lastly are scandals that imply high positions in public administration (Rice Affair and Petrol Affair). Even the fact that corruption is being mentioned in every formal meeting of the government with the representative of foreign governments and organizations as a serious problem for Albania affects this index.

Practical Effectiveness of Corruption

This index shows the likelihood of using corruption to resolve problems. It shows how far the corruption has become a manner of everyday life in the society.

Corruption Expectations

Albanian citizens seems to be very passive in their stand against corruption and have little confidence in their ability to fight it. This is also an expression of their lack of confidence toward success in the fight against corruption. More than half of the respondents (56%) are not optimistic that corruption can be substantially reduced. This lack of confidence is another reason why the success in this field will be difficult to achieve.

Various international comparison survey data sources, as well as each of the Albania-specific in-depth surveys recently carried out, citizen survey (ORT), enterprise and public officials surveys (ACER-World Bank), depict a very consistent and grim picture about the prevalence and costs of corruption in Albania. Related to it, they also suggest that serious institutional weaknesses in the public sector are associated with the high prevalence of corruption, which in turn is having a detrimental impact on socio-economic development in Albania.

All levels of the state administration and justice system have been subject to corruption in the past 10 years. Bribery is most common in customs, taxation, telecommunications, the justice system, police and attorneys' offices, construction permits, and health care service. Another major manifestation of corruption is the payoff needed to secure a post as a customs inspector, tax inspector, judge, natural resource administrator, attorney, policeman, or local government official. This is explained, even by government officials, by the very low wages of state administration and justice system employees (Fig. 9).

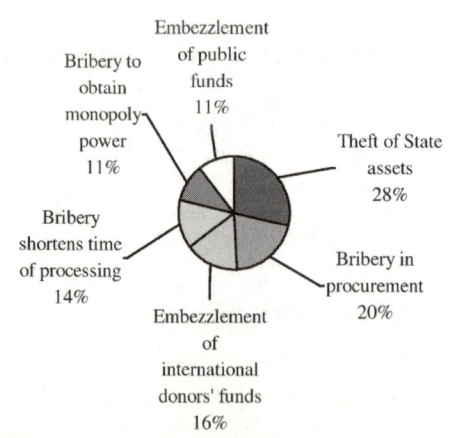

Fig. 9. Common Forms of Corruption in Albania (% of public officials). *Source:* ACER (1998b).

Albania: Common bribes paid by citizens (% of citizens who admit paying bribes).

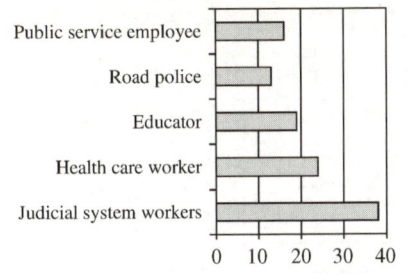

Albania: Bribing in Court (for the 18% of the population who went to Court*).

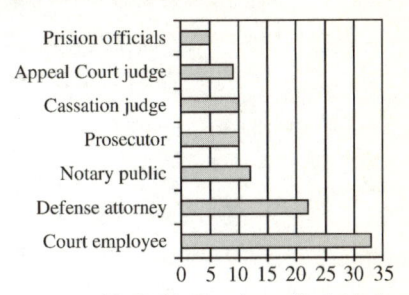

Fig. 10. Bribing Incidence and Location. Percentage of individuals who paid the bribes
Source: ORT (1997).

Albanian corruption is widespread and is generally accepted as an efficient way to solve problems in people's daily activity. Sixty-seven percent of the interviewees who have had problems with various state institutions have solved them through corrupt practices such as soliciting the favor of friends, payments at their initiative, and/or payments required or imposed by officials whose job is to administer these services. More than 50% of the firms that use the following government services admit that bribes are a part of the delivery of the service: Customs and related activities, Telecommunications, Tax and Financial Police, Traffic Police, Judiciary. Corruption in Government procurement remains a key problem. The following figure shows the sources of corruption as recognized by Albanian public officials (Fig. 10).

The quality of public services is considered by households as "very weak." Among lower quality services included are: (in descending order): custom's services; local courts; local attorney's offices; health services; road police; tax offices; local authority for problems of lodging; electrical or water services; telephone services; local police. A strong correlation exists between the quality of services and the "integrity" of institutions. Institutions, which have the weakest quality of services, are the most corrupt and, conversely, institutions that are "less honest" have a strong correlation with those offering lower quality services. This implies that the growth of professionalism in service delivery would bring about directly a reduction in corruption. The institution of complaint is almost non-existent in Albania (Fig. 11).

Higher corruption translates into lower tax collections, yet at the same time is a very significant private tax on enterprises. Almost two-thirds of public elected officials state that a serious anti-corruption program is politically and

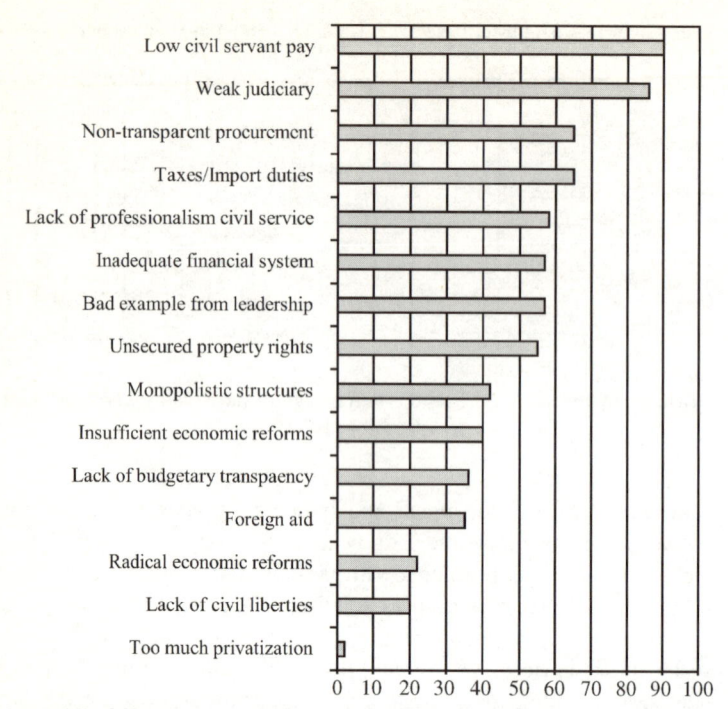

Fig. 11. Public Officials View on Causes of Corruption in Albania. *Source:* ACER (1998b).

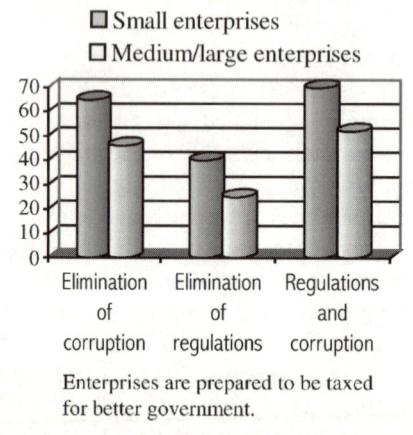

Fig. 12. The Impact of Corruption on Private Firms in Albania: Public Finance Cost of Corruption and Regulations. (% of firms that would pay additional taxes to eliminate corruption and excessive regulation). *Source:* ACER (1998b).

Fig. 13. The Impact of Corruption on Private Firms in Albania: Cost of Corruption and Crime. (% of turnover)*.

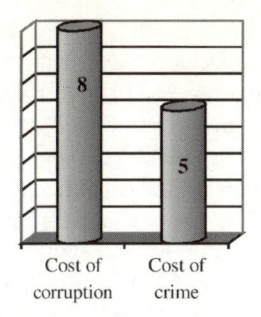

* Frequency of firms facing corruption: 79 %; and crime: 91%.

administratively feasible at present in Albania. But, by contrast, administrative personnel and career public officials are less optimistic. While the incidence of corruption in Albania is still very high at present, its increase appears to be held in check, and the conditions may be ripe for a significant reversal if a decisive action programs is to be implemented in the near future. The next section illustrates the policy measures adopted in the framework of the first Albanian anti-corruption programme (1998–2002) and the results achieved (Figs 12 and 13).

ANTI-CORRUPTION STRATEGY IN ALBANIA

The First Anti-Corruption Action Plan (1998–2002)

Through the decision No. 515, in 1998, the Albanian government was officially committed to fight corruption. An Anti-Corruption Commission was created by the Government Decree No. 72 of January 30, 1998 with the formal objectives:

- to establish a strategy for the organization and direction of the fight against corruption;
- to realize an effective co-ordination of the anti-corruption activities of the state institutions and private sector; and
- to ensure the necessary cooperation with the International Financial Institutions supporting the Government's anti-corruption initiatives.

The review of the anti-corruption plan matrix was instituted in 1999 by the Anti-Corruption Commission and its constituent sector groups. The interagency anti-corruption committee, in its meeting of April 7, 2000 examined the work done by the technical commission, analysed the progress in the fight against corruption and scrutinized the reviewed anti-corruption plan. The conclusion of the review of the anti-corruption plan coincided with the start of the Stability Pact Anti-Corruption Initiative (SPAI) and the presentation by the Albanian government of the status report for the Stabilization and Association Agreement with the European Union. The revised anti-corruption plan takes into account the commitments included in both these documents, serving to reinforcement of the state of law and the institutional fight against corruption. The approval of the Strategy of Institutional Reform of 1999 has defined the main directions of the development of the institutions, which in turn need to have concrete tasks, defined deadlines and suitable methods for measuring results. The main areas of concern of the anti-corruption program were as follows:

The establishment of *a professional civil service* through the implementation of the Law "On the Status of the Civil Servant" and the creation of the Civil Service Commission to ensure objectivity in hiring etc. The management of *Public Finances*, development of supervising functions of auditing (external and internal), and transparent procurement procedures, which was meant to involve computerization and changes in procedures and appeals in the General Directorate of Customs and the General Directorate of Taxes. The strengthening of the *Rule of Law* by means of: (a) professional standards and asset declaration in the judicial system; (b) the adoption of anti-corruption measures in the Sarajevo Compact, 1988 Vienna Convention, Comprehensive money laundering law, Octopus recommendation, Greco mechanism, Criminal Convention on Corruption, Civilian Convention on Corruption; (c) the involvement of state, judicial and customs police; (d) legal framework and professionalism of the High State Control and relations with the General Prosecutor's Office; and (e) ensuring the proper functioning of the new People's Advocate institution. The management of the privatization process and promotion of a *market friendly environment* and integrity in business operations. *Public awareness* through openness to the media and better coordination by designating lead agencies.

Coordination problems were addressed identifying leading bodies (ministries, agencies and others) in each of the areas of concern which are responsible for coordinating activities and initiatives for resolving the identified problem and responsible to the inter-ministerial commission for timely implementation. To this end, objectives were made more concrete and every effort was made to ensure that deadlines were realistic. Other measures not officially included in the anti-corruption which could potentially reduce opportunities for corruption were adopted. Some of important changes in economic policies included:

- Reduction of tariffs and other barriers for international trade.
- Unification of exchange norms and interests defined by market.
- Eliminating enterprises subventions.
- Minimizing state interventions.
- Minimizing the requirements for licenses and other barriers for the new enterprises and investor to enter in the market.
- Demonopolizing and the continuation of the state property privatization.
- Designing and implementation of new proper banking regulations in a transparent process as well as establishing high standards of financial control.

The Minister of State has proposed the establishment of a Triangle-Commission with representatives from the government, General Prosecutor's Office, Civil Society and Media to enhance the transparency and inform the public on the number complaint/denouncements regarding corruptive issues received and forwarded to the prosecution office, in order to protect that any complain or denouncement related to corruption (from different sources) is not being used for political purposes but serves in prosecution from justice bodies. This Commission will also exchange information through confrontation and systematically follow up the number of complaints, criminal allegations of corruption cases and above all inform the public on the outcome results from these discussions through the press or TV (Government of Albania, Council of Ministers, 2003). As a result of the pressure from lending agencies and donor countries, in 2000 the Albanian government established an Anti-Corruption Monitoring Group (ACMG) to ensure the implementation of the Anti-Corruption Plan. The ACMG consists of the Anti-Corruption Monitoring Board and the Anti-Corruption Unit (Fig. 14).

The Anti-Corruption Monitoring Group is a monitoring body designed to support and coordinate the Albanian policy of fighting corruption. Its existence and action are guided among others by the objectives identified by the Stability Pact Anti-Corruption Initiative (see Fig. 15). The objectives of the ACMG Board are to monitor the implementation of the anti-corruption strategy, to promote and support the inter-institutional collaboration and coordination, to counsel and support the institutions included in the Plan as well as to propose preventive activities, to advise the institutions and to report progress to the Government (the Commission and the Council of Ministers), via the Minister of State, who participates in the work of the ACMG Board. The Board examines the implementation of the Action Plan every two months.

The Group is placed under the responsibility of the Minister of State. To ensure work efficiency, the Group is composed of a limited number of permanent members, detached from their ministers and who are specialists in the disciplines

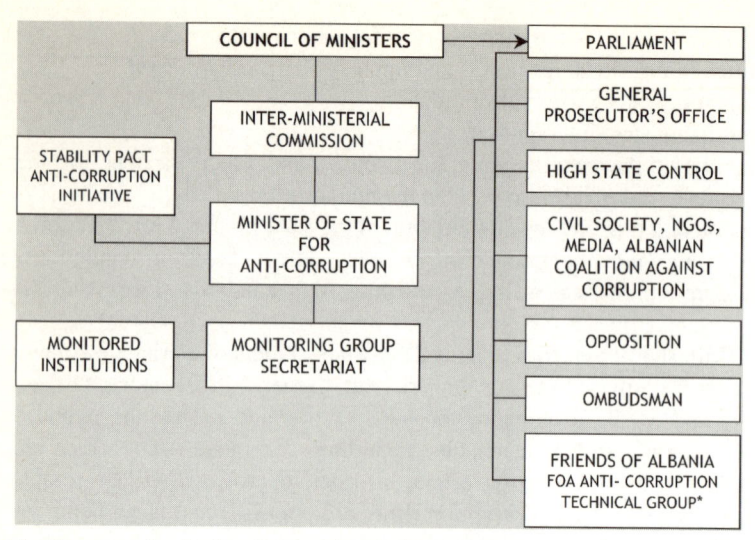

```
                    ┌─────────────────────────┐    ┌─────────────────────┐
                    │  COUNCIL OF MINISTERS   │───▶│     PARLIAMENT      │
                    └────────────┬────────────┘    ├─────────────────────┤
                                 │                 │      GENERAL        │
                    ┌────────────┴────────────┐    │ PROSECUTOR'S OFFICE │
                    │   INTER-MINISTERIAL     │    ├─────────────────────┤
┌──────────────┐    │      COMMISSION         │    │ HIGH STATE CONTROL  │
│ STABILITY    │    └────────────┬────────────┘    ├─────────────────────┤
│ PACT ANTI-   │                 │                 │ CIVIL SOCIETY, NGOs,│
│ CORRUPTION   │    ┌────────────┴────────────┐    │  MEDIA, ALBANIAN    │
│ INITIATIVE   │    │   MINISTER OF STATE     │    │ COALITION AGAINST   │
└──────┬───────┘    │         FOR             │    │     CORRUPTION      │
       │            │    ANTI-CORRUPTION      │    ├─────────────────────┤
       │            └────────────┬────────────┘    │     OPPOSITION      │
┌──────┴───────┐    ┌────────────┴────────────┐    ├─────────────────────┤
│  MONITORED   │    │    MONITORING GROUP     │    │     OMBUDSMAN       │
│ INSTITUTIONS │    │      SECRETARIAT        │    ├─────────────────────┤
└──────────────┘    └─────────────────────────┘    │  FRIENDS OF ALBANIA │
                                                   │  FOA ANTI-CORRUPTION│
                                                   │   TECHNICAL GROUP*  │
                                                   └─────────────────────┘
```

Fig. 14. Structure for the Implementation and Monitoring of the Anti-Corruption Plan. *Note:* The FOA Anti-Corruption Technical Group is composed of EC DEL, WB, COE, OSCE. *Source:* http://www.keshilliministrave.al/shqip/antikorrupsioni/struktura.asp.

covering the fight against corruption and the five pillars of the SPAI Compact. Adequate measures should be adopted in order to insure the independence of the members of the Group and to insure their return after the end of the detachment period. The secretariat of the ACMG is provided by the Anti-Corruption Unit (ACU), comprising six civil servants attached to the Office of the Minister of State. The Unit is composed of a Director and five inspectors (covering areas of public order, public administration, economy/finances, legal affairs/justice, media/civil society and translations). Presently, according to the Law on the Status of Civil Servants, four inspectors have been hired. The Anti-Corruption Unit supports the Board in the monitoring of the situation in Albania and with regard to the implementation of the Action Plan and is also involved in the co-ordination of various bodies concerned as well as in the preparation of measures to increase the impact of the Action Plan. The Anti-Corruption Unit prepares and proposes strategies, methodologies and operational changes of the Plan to the Monitoring Board for approval. Moreover, the Anti-Corruption Unit has an important role with regard to the transparency and public awareness of the anti-corruption strategy and the cooperation with the civil society.

To support the Anti-Corruption Monitoring Group, the Anti-Corruption Unit gathers, processes, and classifies data concerning the corruption situation and the progress of the Action Plan. It prepares regular and ad hoc reports to be

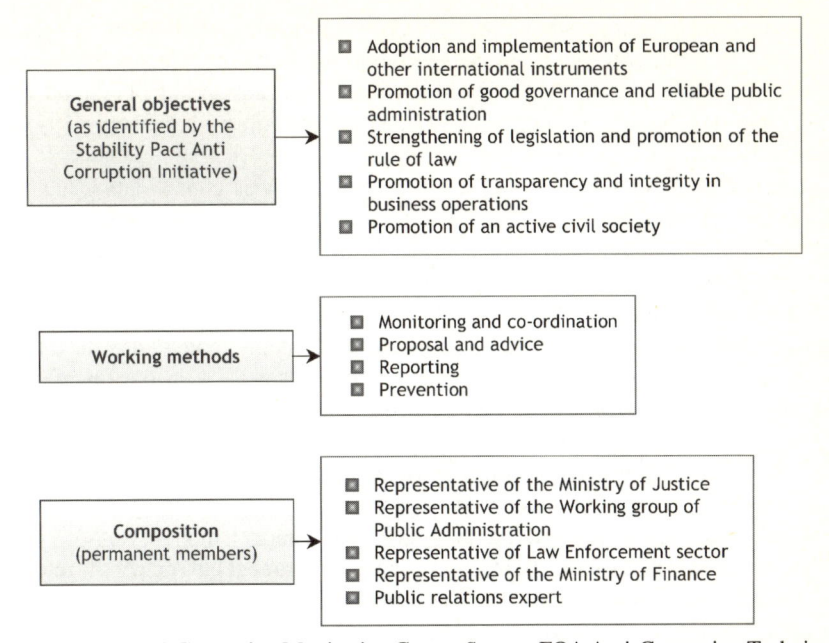

General objectives (as identified by the Stability Pact Anti Corruption Initiative)
- Adoption and implementation of European and other international instruments
- Promotion of good governance and reliable public administration
- Strengthening of legislation and promotion of the rule of law
- Promotion of transparency and integrity in business operations
- Promotion of an active civil society

Working methods
- Monitoring and co-ordination
- Proposal and advice
- Reporting
- Prevention

Composition (permanent members)
- Representative of the Ministry of Justice
- Representative of the Working group of Public Administration
- Representative of Law Enforcement sector
- Representative of the Ministry of Finance
- Public relations expert

Fig. 15. The Anti-Corruption Monitoring Group. *Source:* FOA Anti-Corruption Technical Group (2002).

presented at Anti-Corruption Monitoring Group meetings. In the framework of continuous reforms, the legal basis for the functioning of the Anti Corruption Monitoring Group has continuously been changed. After the approval of the Council of Ministers Decision No. 339, dated 11/07/2002, "On the Action Plan on the Prevention and Fight against Corruption 2002–2003," it became necessary to improve this legal basis and strengthen the Anti Corruption Monitoring Group. The new Order of the Prime Minister No. 252, dated 23/09/2002 reorganized this structure including full membership of the civil society and the business community in the Board of Anti Corruption Monitoring Group.

ACHIEVEMENTS OF THE ACTION PLAN 1998–2002 AND FUTURE DEVELOPMENTS FOR ACTION-PLAN 2002–2003

In August 1998 the World Bank ranked Albania as the most corrupt state in Europe. Almost half of Albanian citizens admitted to pay bribes, while two-thirds of public officials admitted that bribery was a common phenomenon in the country. However, even at this time, corruption did not present a dire issue for Albania in the eyes of the international community. The country had just recovered from the turmoil following the collapse of the pyramids (financial investment schemes in 1997 in which thousands of Albanians lost their savings).

Corruption indices were going down as the state was consolidating and the economy was recovering. In 2000, the World Bank ranked Albania as Europe's seventh-most corrupt country. On June 2001, the European Commission recommended to the European Council the beginning of negotiations for an Agreement of Stabilization and Association with Albania. According to the recommendation, considerable progress had to be made, because although good results have been achieved in the past two years, problems persist, especially in the functioning of the judicial system, all related to widespread corruption. The 1998–1999 Albania's anti-corruption measures brought some good news and a few lessons.

The complete program of reforms, proposed by the first anti-corruption plan, was given in detail, a series of actions the majority of which were expected to achieve obvious results within the first four months. It didn't happen though. Reasons were different. Firstly there was in September 1998 a government fall (one of the reasons that it fell was corruption as well). The Kosovo war and the refugee waves to Albania followed. So, the focus was shifted from the targeted actions. Nevertheless, some changes have already started: society is free to speak about the corruption, its knowledge is wider and there are some responses in community bases. Media is being more targeted, more professional and influential to the corruption scandals.

Business is being recovered after the recent economic and political crises (From 46% not renewed licenses after 1997, in 1998 there were only 29% not renewed). The role of some newly established business associations is getting bigger together with the role of the older association (Chamber of Commences, etc.). Business community representatives are now taking part actively in the policy debate about different issues concerning the business environment (privatization of strategic sectors, capital market development, etc.). Taking into consideration the fact that the business community is feeder and bearer of corruption, it has to be well positioned in the fight against corruption. It should be one of the main actors that should impose this. Another way is the institutionalization of the relations between business organizations and governmental institutions, in order to better attract their opinions and suggestions in the decision making process. They would feel more responsible in preventing the corruptive actions, and more active in the anti-corruption initiative. Some types of corruption are becoming less severe. For instance, firms claim that corruption has fallen slightly during the past couple of years in: enterprise registration, registration of ownership of physical or real property, state banking services and fire and sanitary inspection.

A special point in the budget administration is the administration of judiciary budget. The justice system is identified by several structures in Albania as one of the most corrupted stratum. For this reason it was created even a special department for judiciary budget administration, which is in charge to guarantee a fair and transparency use of expenditures in justice system. It is gradually increasing the independence of the Justice system in Albania. In strengthening tax administration, some good results have been identified. However, because of the high level of corruption in the tax administration, there have been undertaken some further measures such as the: implementation of a strong reform of penalties for non-accomplishing tax dues; establishment of the Administrative Court, which was considered as of great importance because of many concerns in judging the conflicts between tax administration and the taxpayers; strengthening the control on tax officials on how are they implementing the law, as well as undertaking special measures on the people involved in corruptive actions; improving the database and monitoring process of business activities, dealing with import/export as well as sharing the information between tax and custom administrate.

In attempting to increase the professionalism and image of the fiscal inspector, several training courses for tax officials have been developed. The long-term objective is to establish a taxation school, in order to train civil servants in tax administration as well as to change totally the rules for tax inspectors' recruitment. This would have positive effects in tax and custom officials. The government has been active in pursuing a radical judiciary reform, through the execution of law on judiciary administration, the establishment of the structures or the appointment of officers within the courts, responsible for supplying information to the public, the approval of the law on the office for the execution of the court commercial decisions, the review of legislation on advocacy, the improvement of the law on public notary, the law on the attorneys office and the law on judiciary police.

Pursuant to Prime Minister Order No. 252, dated 23/09/2002 item 10, the Anti-Corruption Unit has compiled the achievement records on main areas of public administration reforms; legislation upgrading; managing public finances and controlling devices; urging transparency and integrity on business actions and increasing public awareness; and encouraging an active civil society. In January 2003, the Anti Corruption Unit has prepared *"The annual analysis of 2002 achievements and setbacks in the fight against corruption."* This analysis reflects the observations and analytic assessment of the action plan for the prevention and fight against corruption. Moreover, this analysis includes all activities carried out by the Anti-Corruption Unit for 2002 and describes the main results in terms of: legal framework, specialized structures in the fight against corruption and concrete actions in the fight against corruption (Government of Albania, Council of Ministers, 2003).

Indeed, the first area is prevalent and much remains to be done in the other two areas, especially the third. It is clear that the legislation approximation to international standards has been a priority of the Albanian government. The legal reforms against corruption have had a preventive approach, notably in the public administration area. Nevertheless, the reform is focused on the criminalization of corruptive offences. The Albanian legislation for the general prevention of corruption within public administration (accompanied by numerous bi-laws and codes of conduct or ethics) is considered by many international institutions to be comprehensive and adequate. Moreover, the criminal legislation concerning corruption seems to be satisfactory. It must be noted, however, that the criminalization of corruption is limited to the public sector and that no corporate criminal liability exists.

Regarding the completion of the legislation and the strengthening of the state of law compliant with the European and international legal instruments, special attention has been paid to the ratification of several international conventions. An important work objective will be the adaptation of the domestic legislation in compliance with these conventions. The Decision of the Council of Ministers "For the Admission in the Civil Service" has already been approved. Several decisions have been drafted, such as: Decision draft "for the Establishment and the Functioning of the Public Administration Training Institute and the Training of the Civil Servant"; Decision draft "For the Discipline in the Civil Service"; Guide draft "For the Structure of Job Classification in the Civil Service, the Relevant Methodology and a General Description of the Role of the General Secretariat for this Service"; Other decisions are being drafted for implementing the Law On Civil Service.

The second area of results concerns the establishment of specialized structures in the fight against corruption. Two specific high-level bodies with the overall objective of directing the Albanian National Anti-Corruption Plan have been established, i.e. the Governmental Commission of the Fight against Corruption at Governmental level and the Anti-Corruption Monitoring Group (ACMG) at the highest civil servant level. The work of the latter body particularly aims at coordinating the implementation of the National Anti-Corruption Plan, and thus depends on co-operation from other state bodies. In order to ensure a more efficient cooperation between the different bodies and the multidisciplinary structure (ACMG) and to ensure the continuous report in the ACMG, a network of contact points has been established, i.e., two-three civil servants have been identified in each institution/ministry as interlocutors between their respective institutions and the ACMG.

The last area, the most important to be addressed in order to achieve the desired outcome, refers to concrete actions in the fight against corruption. While the anti-corruption strategy has focused on improving the legal structures and defining functions and responsibilities, the future perspective should be more focused on the implementation of structures and principles and, in particular, on the involvement of civil society. For accurate results in monitoring the Action Plan, the Anti-corruption Unit has drafted and prepared respective Task Charts for all institutions involved in this Action Plan. The task charts contain the present status, progress, obstacles, and success indicators on measures against corruption (including monitoring, prevention, and training), approved in the meeting of the Governmental Commission against Corruption held on November 11, 2002.

In early October, each institution (involved in the Action Plan), has been asked to present to the office of the Minister of State specific reports on the progress by using the Task Charts. The members of the ACMG Board reported by using Task Charts in a meeting of the ACMG Board held in December 2002, which served as a pre-diagnosis of the present status, and presented the problems faced during the implementation of the Action Plan for the Prevention and the Fight Against Corruption. At the end of December 2002, the Anti-Corruption Unit prepared a six Month Macro Report-Inventory of Achievements, which included the main areas of public administration reform, legislation improvement, management of public finances and business operations and enhancing public awareness and encouraging an active civil society. *"The annual analysis of 2002 achievements and setbacks in the fight against corruption"* reports the following achievements in the areas of:

- Public Administration Reform.
- Improvement of Public Finances Management and Audit Mechanisms.
- Increase of Transparency and Integrity in Business Transactions.
- Increase of Public Information and Encouragement of an Active Civil Society.

Public Administration Reform

In 2002, approximately 600 Public Administration civil servants have been trained by the Institute of Public Administration Training. The reform for the system of wages of civil servants in the central administration, of customs employees, INSTAT, Directory of Patents and Trademarks, health care employees holding a university degree and those with secondary education has been completed. The study for the remaining part of the budgetary employees is in process. Among the problems encountered the delay of the draft-law "Rules of Ethics in the Public Administration" deposited for endorsement to the Council of Ministers and the Assembly. In addition, the Draft-Law "On Declaration of the Property, financial obligations, conflict of interest of the public officials and elected officials" is being discussed in the respective Parliamentary commissions.

Some elements of the institutional reform that aim at the legal reinforcement of the institutions and the enlargement of their scope of actions include: the new law on the organization and functioning of Council of Ministers, the law on internal control, the creation of the public administration data registry, the review of the law on the declaration and verification of the wealth of the public officers, the improvement of the law on the High State Control.

Improvement of Public Finances Management and Audit Mechanisms

Increasing the transparency in budget design and execution was an important objective of the first anti-corruption plan. The government has put emphasis on the improvement of the budget planning aiming at a more efficient management of the public finances (Ministry of Economic Cooperation and Trade, 2000). For the first three months of 2000, the realization of the budget revenue has been successful, to the degree of 100%. The income from taxes has increased 105%, which is 7 billion leks (the Albanian currency) more than the same period last year. During this period, the tax administration has collected 11.6 billion leks, or 15% more than projected. This is 50% more than last year's tax collection. The budget design and implementation process has been more transparent to Parliament and media, reporting for some fundamental changes in the budget of 1999, especially in the relations between local and central government. These changes are made in the frame of fiscal decentralization process, which is very important in local government.

Auditing structures in all the ministries and central institutions have been established, and auditing bulletins are published every three months. The disciplinary committee in customs, which is involved in the fight against corruption through implementing duties and delivering disciplinary measures for custom employees, has been established. The Decision of Council of Ministers No. 675, dated 20.12.2002, "For the use of the planned budgetary funds for goods, services and constructions" should minimize the possibility to abuse funds. Implementation of the scheme for bonuses for accomplishments on duty to customs' personnel has served to motivate the staff. The new "Guide for internal audits," regarding the review of methodology, has been published. Among the problems encountered the draft-law "For the internal auditing in the public sector" is still deposited for enactment in the Parliament. The draft law "On the accounting and financial sheets" is being prepared. There are delays in the drafting and approval of standard modules of the Public Procurement.

Increase of Transparency and Integrity in Business Transactions

Transparency in the process of privatization of strategic sectors is accomplished through the publication of all procedures in a web page of the ministry and its continuous updating. Among the included information are: information regarding the history of privatization, further steps; legal and sub-legal acts; matrix of privatization of sectors of special importance. Among the problems encountered the draft-law "For the foreign financing" from the Ministry of Economy has been opposed by the Ministry of Finances with the arguments that the issues treated in the draft-law are part of the Organic Law of Budget.

To ensure the transparency and the integrity of the business operations, the Agency of the Public Procurement has undertaken measures to enforce the monitoring responsibilities from the appropriate institutions all over the territory. The drafted amendment to the Law No. 7971 dated 26.07.1995 "On the Public Procurement" will increase the degree of control over the public procurement and will establish structures to carry out the monitoring of the procurement procedures in a case-by-case fashion. The Agency of Public Procurement will be provided additional competencies to impose sanctions against those who fail to apply and respect the rules of the public procurement. There has also been drafted a decision on some changes to the Decision No. 12, dated 01.01.96 "On the rules of public procurement" and the package of the standard set of bidding document has been developed. The government of Albania was committed to extend full transparency regarding its initiatives within the anti-corruption plan that provides the participation of the public and media in the anti-corruption process, the establishment of specific structures and phone lines within the institutions to provide information to the public, the organization of round tables with the NGO's, the development of public surveys to check the process of transparency within the public services.

Increases in Public Information and Encouragement of an Active Civil Society

To increase the transparency in public services, different institutions publish brochures and bulletins as well as maintain an internet site for information on their activities. By the order of the Prime Minister No. 252 dated 23/09/2002 a member of the Albanian Coalition Against Corruption and one from the Business Community are appointed as permanent members in the Board of Anti-Corruption Monitoring.

In June 2002, the Anti-Corruption Unit has prepared an *ad hoc* study, "On the criminal allegations on corruption activities sent to the Prosecution Office by the Ministries and Central Institutions for 2001 to the first six months of 2002." From this study it resulted that the number of allegations made by different institutions was 241, out of which the ACU has made nine criminal allegations (based on the practices received), the General Directorate of Financial Control in the Ministry of Finance has made five criminal allegations, the General Directorate of Customs has made 29 criminal allegations, the General Directorate of Taxation has made 56 criminal allegations, Ministry of Public Order has made 71 criminal allegations, the Ministry of Local Government and Decentralization has made 22 criminal allegations, etc.

According to the analysis of the statistical data, for a nine months period 2002 (the bulletin on the fourth quarter had not yet been issued at the time of this writing) the number of the subjects recommended to receive disciplinary and administrative measures was 49 and the overall recommended measures are 230. The number of the criminal allegations was eight. In the framework of obligations resulting form the Albanian membership in GRECO, and according to the predetermined calendar, GRECO – Group of States Against Corruption, Council of Europe, evaluated Albania based on a draft-report.

In the final report, Albania was evaluated as follows (Government of Albania, Council of Ministers, 2003): During the last years Albania has taken extensive action against corruption with impressive results. The development of the National Anti-Corruption Plan (the Matrix) and the establishment of the multidisciplinary Anti-Corruption Monitoring Group (ACMG) clearly indicate the strong commitment – at the highest political level – to fight the problem of corruption. There is, in addition, a strong support and assistance provided by the international community.

A reasonably good legal framework (in comparison to the region) is in place and several key institutions for the fight against corruption have been transformed with regard to anti-corruption measures. In brief, Albania has in the first phase, developed legislation and a structure with a potential to deal seriously with the problems of corruption. The implementation of the Anti-Corruption Strategy is constantly monitored and progress in almost all areas of interest has been noticed. In particular, the changes of the national legislation, accession to international treaties and instruments was highlighted, as well as the reforming of existing institutions (judiciary, police, public procurement, etc) and the creation of new bodies, such as the judicial inspectorate at the High Council of Justice. Above all, the very establishment of the anti corruption plan and the machinery for its implementation was highlighted as a great achievement in itself. Virtually all structural and legislative objectives of the initial Anti-Corruption Matrix have been achieved, and Albania is now poised to undertake the difficult task of effectively implementing reform measures.

The report has not been published yet and probably these are only partial recommendations. A simple exercise would be to compare the objectives of the Anti-Corruption Plan 1998–2002 with the results reported by the Anti-Corruption Unit in January 2003; implementation of the civil service law is progressing. However, it is too early to evaluate improvements in terms of more professional civil servants and no attempt to evaluate the impact of training has been made.

Albanian customs has brought in 100% of expected revenue (2000–2001), improving the image of Albania in the eyes of the international financial institutions that were critical of repeated occurrences of fiscal evasion in these offices. Since May 2000, 39 customs employees, including station managers, have been fired. The approval from the Parliament of the Law No. 8449 dated 27.01.99 "On the Customs Code of the Republic of Albania" and the sub-legal acts for its implementation have ensured a satisfactory revenue collection level from the customs administration. They have exceeded the last year's level of collections by 26%. CAM-ALBANIA mission is working closely with the Customs General Directorate to develop a strategy for the customs modernization and the establishment of a general information management system. The Law "On tax procedures in the Republic of Albania" approved and entered force on March 13, 2000, has produced good results in the realization of the tax revenue, through the improvement of procedures related to the tax registration, collection and payment. It would be interesting to monitor the sustainability of the improvements achieved. The third objective, which relates to the adoption of international standards, is placed better than others and ranks high on the government's agenda. The privatization process has become more transparent through the publication of all information online. Finally, public awareness has surely improved. Surprisingly, corruption has been overlooked as a policy question in Albania.

In summary, in a short period of time Albania has developed a reasonably good legislative framework to support an efficient anti-corruption policy. However, there is much to be done at the implementation level. Continuation of anti-corruption measures is critical to achieve any small victory in combating it. It is true that the institutional schemes designed during 1998 should be reviewed, but on the other hand they were never implemented fully as they were designed. Indeed with the exception of some measures the schemes remained in the level of just schemes. It did not penetrate deeper in the structures, which were supposed to implement them. Future developments are planned in the area of anti-corruption. During June 10–11, 2002, the Second National Anti Corruption Conference was organized. The "Revised Anti Corruption Plan 2001–2002" was discussed in the conference and report for the first six moths of 2002 was approved. This analysis identified that the major part of the foreseen measures were accomplished, which resulted in the new project for the Action Plan 2002–2003, taking into consideration suggestions from all public institutions. All changes and suggestions were reflected in the *Second Action-Plan on the prevention and fight against corruption, 2002–2003*, which was adopted by the Conference.

The Government has given particular priority *inter alia* to the following areas in the future implementation (Government of Albania, Council of Ministers, 2003):

- Reform of the civil service, including training.
- Transparency of the privatization process.
- Reform of the public procurement system.
- Reform of the State Police (legal status, etc.).
- Elimination of corruption within the judiciary.
- Information to the public and co-operation with civil society.

CONCLUSIONS

In conclusion, I shall attempt to answer to the questions posed at the beginning of the chapter by comparing the criteria developed from the literature surveyed herein with the Albanian case.

1: *Are the causes of corruption found in the literature equally present and equally important in the Albanian public sector? Do empirics provide further causes not taken into account by the literature?*

Some of the causes of corruption provided by the literature seem to be present and relevant in Albanian public administrations. This is true for:

- Poor human resources management and low public sector pay.
- The absence of basic market institutions.
- Insufficient transparency in the budget and procurement process.
- A weak judiciary unable to provide punishment to corrupt cases.
- The radical distribution of wealth from the state to the private sector.
- A distorted policy environment (bad example from leadership).

While low civil service pay is recognized as the most concerning source of corruption in the Albanian public administrations, other causes equally important in the literature, are not recognized as relevant in the country such as:

- The multiplication in the number of laws and regulation.
- Accounting and reporting standards.
- Power of trade unions to resist change.

On the other hand, at least two causes seem to be important in Albania although being inconsiderate in the literature. They refer to foreign aid and to the high tax levels in the country.

2: *Are anti-corruption measures as recommended by the literature adopted by the Albanian government?*

Anti-corruption measures adopted by the Albanian government concern:

- Changes in the legal framework.
- The creation of specialized structures.
- Civil service reform.
- Management of public finances and audit mechanisms.
- Public awareness.
- Changes in economic policies.

While these tools are all considered by the literature as important components of any anti-corruption strategy, it also states that their effectiveness depends on whether it is linked to public management. This is not the case of Albania where anti-corruption actions have been both formulated and implemented in a top down approach originating from international institutions or central government.

3: *The theoretical models reviewed claim that an effective strategy for anti-corruption must address the root causes of different forms of corruption avoiding the risk of treating instead the symptoms. Are anti-corruption efforts in Albania coherent with this position?*

The most concerning cause of corruption in Albania refers to low civil servant salaries and a weak judiciary. Both are addressed by the first and by the second plan, though insufficiently. Regarding the first one, the reform for the system of wages of civil servants in the central administration, of customs employees, INSTAT, Directory of Patents and Trademarks, health care employees holding a university degree and those with secondary education has been completed. The study for the remaining part of the budgetary employees is in process. It is too early however to draw significant conclusions in relation to this aspect.

Much of economic development, social inclusion and regional stability in the South East Europe region will depend on strengthening of institutions, governance and in consequence lowering the level of corruption. Gradual integration with the European Union will require significantly more mature institutional structures, which are able to satisfy the economic, politic framework conditions of the EU and to implement the *acquis communitaire*.

An anti-corruption strategy in Albania must focus on enhancing state capacity to improve the provision of basic public goods. Priorities should be building the capacity of public administration, developing instruments for financial management, encouraging civil society development. The strategy must be tailored to the particular contours of the country.

Political will to combat corruption is most likely to be driven by external pressures, especially international donors, which can play a decisive role in undertaking the right anti-corruption measures and in building a coalition within a country. The role of donors in the fight against corruption is important in other three areas (Mason, 2001):

- The quality of donor programs in terms of governance.
- The question whether conditionality helps or hinders.
- The extent to which donor assistance undermines institutional capacity and thereby contributes to reducing in the long term the quality of governance in developing countries.

ACKNOWLEDGMENTS

This chapter was prepared for the International Public Management Network Conference, Siena, Italy on 26–28 June 2002. I have incurred a number of intellectual debts in moving from draft to final versions of this work. Marco Meneguzzo, Riccardo Mussari and Michael Barzelay read an earlier draft and provided helpful suggestions for revision. The case of Albania draws in part on a number of sources that cannot be cited. The views expressed herein are solely those of the author.

REFERENCES

ACER (Albanian Centre for Economic Research), The World Bank (1998a, June 30). Enterprise survey. Albania anti-corruption workshop. Tirana.
ACER, The World Bank (1998b, June 30). Public Officials Survey. Albania anti-corruption workshop. Tirana, Albania.
ACER (2000, February). Albanian empirical report. Tirana, Albania. http://www1.oecd.org/daf/SPAIcom/pdf/AlbEmp.pdf.
ACER, World Bank, Kaufmann, D., Pasha, A., Preci, Z., Ryterman, R., & Zoido-Lobaton, P. (1998, June 30). Governance and corruption in Albania: The imperative of institutional reforms, a preliminary empirical inquiry and implications. Albania anti-corruption workshop. Tirana, Albania.
Ades, A., & Di Tella, R. (1999). Rents, competition and corruption. *American Economic Review*, 89(4).
Allen, R. (1999). New public management: Pitfalls for Central and Eastern Europe. *SIGMA Public Management Forum*, V(1).
Bale, M., & Dale, T. (1998, February). Public sector reform in New Zealand and its relevance to developing countries. *The World Bank Research Observer*, 13(1).
Barzelay, M. (2001). *The new public management. Improving research and policy dialogue*. Berkeley: University of California.
Broadman, H. G., & Recanatini, F. (2001). Seeds of corruption: Do market institutions matter? Policy Research Working Chapter 2368, World Bank.
Brunetti, A., Kisunko, G., & Weder, B. (1997). Institutional obstacles for doing business data description and methodology of a worldwide private sector survey. Survey conducted for the WDR.
Camdessus, M. (1994). *Supporting transition in Central and Eastern Europe: An assessment and lessons from the IMF's five years' experience*. International Monetary Fund.

Cepiku, D. (2002). La riforma della pubblica amministrazione in Albania. *Azienda Pubblica: Teoria e problemi di management*, *1*(2), Maggioli Editore.

Commission of The European Communities (2001). Report from the Commission to the Council on the work of the EU/Albania High Level Steering Group, in preparation for the negotiation of a Stabilisation and Association Agreement with Albania, Luxembourg, COM(2001)300 final.

Corruption Indexes (2000, February). Results from the comparative survey in Albania, Bulgaria, and Macedonia. http://www1.oecd.org/daf/nocorruptionweb/pdf/SEEindexe.pdf.

de Melo, M., Cevdet, D., & Gelb, A. (1996). From plan to market: Patterns of transition. *World Bank Economic Review*, *10*(3), 397–424.

Dillinger, W., & Fay, M. (1999). From centralized to decentralized governance. *Finance & Development*, *36*(4), International Monetary Fund.

EBRD (1998). Transition report. European bank for reconstruction and development, London.

EBRD/World Bank (1999). The business environment and enterprise performance survey (BEEPS). Interactive Database. http://www.worldbank.org/wbi/governance/beepsinteractive.htm.

Exter, J., & Fries, S. (1998, September). The post-communist transition: Pattern and prospects. *Finance and Development*, *35*, IMF.

Feldman, R. A., & Watson, C. M. (2000, September). Central Europe: From transition to EU membership. *Finance and Development*, *37*(3), IMF.

Fischer, S., & Gelb, A. (1991). The process of socialist economic transformation. *The Journal of Economic Perspectives*, *5*(4).

Fischer, S., & Sahay, R. (2000, September). Taking stock. *Finance and Development*, *37*(3), IMF.

Gelb, A. (1993). Socialist transformations: Some lessons and implications for assistance. In: *Redefining the Role of the State and the Market in the Development Process*. SIDA, Stockholm.

Government of Albania (1998, October). On the road to stabilisation and development, Tirana.

Government of Albania (2000a, May). Albania: Interim poverty reduction strategy chapter (IPRSP).

Government of Albania (2000b, July). Revised anti-corruption plan. The new planned measures and reforms in the main areas of priority. http://www1.oecd.org/daf/SPAIcom/pdf /ACMeasures.pdf.

Government of Albania (2000c, July 27). Revised anti-corruption plan matrix. http://www1.oecd.org/daf/SPAIcom/pdf/Alb-ACP-Matrix.pdf.

Government of Albania (2000d, July). Anti corruption monitoring group, monitoring mechanism. http://www1.oecd.org/daf/SPAIcom/pdf/ACGroup.pdf.

Government of Albania (2000e, July). Monitoring organigram, proposed structure of the implementation and monitoring of the new anti-corruption plan. http://www1.oecd.org/daf/SPAIcom/pdf/ACPStructure.pdf.

Government of Albania (2001d). MTEF. Technical note on Albanian public administration. Payroll and wagebill Reform.

Government of Albania, Council of Ministers (2003, March). *The annual analysis of 2002 achievements and setbacks in the fight against corruption*. Official unpublished document.

Havrylyshyn, O., & Wolf, T. (1999, June). Determinants of growth in transition countries. *Finance and Development*, *36*(2), IMF.

Hellman, J., Jones, G., & Kaufmann, D. (2000, September). Seize the state, seize the day: State capture, corruption, and influence in transition. World Bank Policy Research Working Chapter 2444. World Bank Institute and EBRD.

Hellman, J., & Kaufmann, D. (2001, September). Confronting the challenge of state capture in transition economies. *Finance & Development*, *38*(3), IMF.

Hood, C. (2000). Paradoxes of public sector managerialism, old public management and public service bargains. *International Public Management Journal*, *4*(1), 1–24.

Johnson, S., Kaufmann, D., & Shleifer, A. (1997, February). The unofficial economy in transition. *The Brookings Review*.

Kaufmann, D. (1994, December). Diminishing returns to administrative controls and the emergence of the unofficial economy. *Economic Policy* (Suppl. 19).

Kaufmann, D. et al. (1998). Governance and corruption in Albania: The imperative of institutional reforms. ACER/World Bank draft.

Kaufmann, D., Pradhan, S., & Ryterman, R. S. (1998, October 7). *New frontiers in diagnosing and combating corruption*. World Bank: Prem Notes Public Sector.

Klitgaard, R. E. (1988). *Controlling corruption*. Berkeley: University of California Press.

Klitgaard, R. E. (1997). Cleaning up and invigorating the civil service. *Public Administration and Development, 17*.

Klitgaard, R. E. (2000, June). Subverting corruption. *Finance and Development, 37*(2), IMF.

Lenain, P. (1998, September). Ten years of transition: A progress report. *Finance and Development, 35*(3), IMF.

Litwack, L. (1998). Economic legality and transition in Eastern Europe. In: AA. VV. (Ed.), *The New Palgrave Economic Dictionary*. London: MacMillan.

Manning, N. (2000). *The new public management and its legacy*. The World Bank Group.

Mark, P. (2001). *Corruption and state capture: An analytical framework*. Department of Politics and International Relations, University of Oxford.

Mason, P. (2001, May 30). The role of donors and IFIs in curbing corruption. Workshop Report to Global Forum II, The Hague.

Mauro, P. (1995, August). Corruption and growth. *Quarterly Journal of Economics*.

Mauro, P. (1998). Corruption and the composition of government expenditure. *Journal of Public Economics, 69*.

Minogue, M. (2000, February). Should flawed models of public management be exported? Issues and practices. Public policy and management working chapter series. Working Chapter 15. Institute for Development Policy and Management, University of Manchester.

Murphy, K., Shleifer, A., & Vishny, R. (1992). The transition to a market economy: Pitfalls of partial reform. *Quarterly Journal of Economics, 107*(3), 889–906.

Mussari, R., & Di Torro, P. (1993). Etica ed efficienza del management pubblico: Un approccio economico aziendale. In: *Azienda Pubblica: Teoria e problemi di management*.

Nsouli, S. M. (1999, June). A decade of transition. An overview of the achievements and challenges. *Finance and Development, 36*(2), IMF.

OECD (1996). On the frontlines of reform. The recent changes in Central and Eastern European administrations. *SIGMA Public Management Forum, II*(1).

OECD (2002). *Anti-corruption measures in South Eastern Europe. Civil society's involvement*. Paris: OECD.

OECD/CCNM, ACER (1999, November 2–3). Albanian experience in anti-corruption process. Second annual meeting of the anti-corruption network for transition economies. Istanbul, Turkey (Non English edition).

OECD/PUMA (1997, February). *Managing government ethics. Puma policy brief. Public management service*. Paris: OECD.

OECD/PUMA (2002). Public sector modernisation: A new agenda. Chapter presented at the 26th Session of PUMA Committee. Paris: OECD.

OECD/PUMA (2003). *Managing conflicts of interest in transition: The Polish experience. Expert group on managing conflicts of interest meeting*. Paris: OECD.

OECD/SIGMA (1998). *Albania. Centre of government profile*. Paris: OECD.

OECD/SIGMA (1999). *Public management profiles of Central and Eastern European countries: Albania*. Paris: OECD.

OECD/SIGMA (2000, September). *Evaluation reports of the Albanian politico-administrative system*. Paris: OECD.

Open Society Foundation for Albania (2001). Public Administration Program. OSFA.

Polidano, C. (1999). The new public management in developing countries. Public Policy and Management Working Chapter 13. Institute for Development Policy and Management, University of Manchester.

Prato, G. (2000). I paradossi latenti della corruzione. Italia e Albania: Due realtà a confronto. *Sviluppo Economico*, 4(1), 115–120, Gennaio – Marzo.

Rose-Ackerman, S. (1997). Corruption and development. Annual World Bank Conference on Development Economics. World Bank, Washington, DC.

Schiavo-Campo, S. (1994). Institutional change and the public sector in transitional economies. World Bank Discussion Chapter NQ 241, Washington.

Schick, A. (1998). *Why most developing countries should not try New Zealand reforms*. World Bank.

SELDI (2001, March). Corruption indexes-regional corruption monitoring in Albania, BiH, Bulgaria, Croatia, Macedonia, Romania and Yugoslavia. South East Legal Development Initiative. http://www.seldi.net/seldi_e.htm.

SPAI (2000, July). Report of the monitoring group. http://www1.oecd.org/daf/SPAIcom/pdf/Alb-ReportMonitGroup.pdf.

Tanzi, V. (1999, June). Transition and the changing role of Government. *Finance and Development*, 36(2), IMF.

The Urban Institute (1998). Assistance in municipal finance reform for Albania. Summary of proceedings and conclusions on workshop 1: Local government responsibilities and expenditures.

Treichel, V. (2001, December). Stabilization policies and structural reforms in Albania Since 1997 – Achievements and remaining challenges. IMF Policy Discussion Chapter.

Treisman, D. (1999). The causes of corruption: A cross-national study. *Journal of Public Economics*.

UNDP (1998, May). Albanian human development report. Tirana.

World Bank (1996). *World development report 1996: From plan to market*. Washington, DC.

World Bank (1997a). *Helping countries combat corruption: The role of the World Bank*. Washington, DC: World Bank.

World Bank (1997b). *World development report 1997: The State in a changing world*. Washington, DC: World Bank.

World Bank (2000a). The need for strong institutions and good governance. In: *The Road to Stability and Prosperity in South Eastern Europe*. A World Bank Regional Strategy Chapter. Washington, DC: World Bank.

World Bank (2000b). *Anticorruption in transition: A contribution to the policy debate*. Washington, DC: World Bank.

World Bank (2000c). *Helping countries combat corruption: Progress at the World Bank since 1997*. Washington, DC: World Bank.

World Bank (2000d). Reforming public institutions and strengthening governance. A World Bank Strategy. Public Sector Group. Washington, DC.

World Bank (2002). Transition. The first ten years. Analysis and Lessons for Eastern Europe and the Former Soviet Union. Washington, DC.

13. REDUCING CORRUPTION IN POST-COMMUNIST COUNTRIES

Alexander Kotchegura

ABSTRACT

International experience in combating corruption allows to relatively easily identify its causes and single out the societies with high levels of corruption in their bureaucracies and private sectors. It is much more difficult to prescribe effective remedies and even more problematic to get new approaches applied in an appropriate and sustained fashion. This is particularly true with respect to the post-communist countries that embarked on the road of transition to a new economic and political reality over a decade ago. Making significant advances along this road has turned out to be much more difficult than expected at the beginning and has revealed risks and obstacles not anticipated. The article explores to what extent the task of containing corruption was on the agenda of public management reforms in these countries, the impact of these reforms on the level of corruption, if any, and seeks to identify more effective approaches for combating corruption in transitional states.

INTRODUCTION

Following the demise of the communist system many CEE (Central and Eastern European) and CIS (Commonwealth of Independent States) countries announced reform of their state administrations. The chapter explores to what extent the task of containing corruption was on the agenda of public management reforms in these countries, the impact of these reforms on the level of corruption, if any, and seeks to identify more effective approaches for combating corruption in transitional states.

International experience in combating corruption shows that it is relatively easy to identify the causes of this "disease" and to single out the societies with high levels of corruption in their bureaucracies and private sectors, whereas it is much more difficult to prescribe effective remedies and even more problematic to get new approaches applied in an appropriate and sustained fashion. This is particularly true with respect to the post-communist countries that embarked on the road of transition to a new economic and political reality over a decade ago. Making significant advances along this road has turned out to be much more difficult than expected at the beginning and has revealed risks and obstacles not anticipated.

From the perspective of this chapter, it is observed that in its many forms corruption exists everywhere – in rich countries and in poor, in the public as well as in the private sectors, and in virtually all regions of the world. What varies among nations and regions are the extent and the prevailing forms of corruption – and also the level of tolerance of society toward this phenomenon. To quote a respected source, "... corruption has been increasing in virtually all kinds of politico-economic system since the 1980s" (Holmes, 1999), and it is commonly recognized that corruption is wide spread in former communist countries. Since late 1980s corruption has grown considerably in dimensions and in the variety of forms it takes, and at present it poses a serious threat to the democratic gains and the advance of public sector reform in these countries.

A recent World Bank study of the corruption in the transitional countries points out that,

> In those countries where the problem is most entrenched corruption undermines the driving forced behind the reform. New firms are driven into the underground economy. Vital resources are siphoned off shore. Foreign investors turn away in frustration. As a result some countries risk of becoming trapped in a vicious circle in which pervasive corruption reduces public revenues, undermines public trust, and weakens the credibility of the state, unless decisive leadership can push through the necessary reforms (World Bank, 2000, p. 24).

Apart from obvious distortion of economic activity, corruption increases inequality and hits the poor hardest either directly or indirectly, e.g. instances of squandered or stolen development loans. As Miller notes, "The state is cheated out of revenue by those who bribe officials, and consequently has to impose greater tax burdens on those who cannot avoid payment by bribing officials and/or let public services, on which the poor in particular depend, collapse" (Miller, 2002).

Furthermore, corruption undermines the rule of law, leads to double ethical standards and results in alienation of citizens from the state. At the same time, examples of successful anti-corruption strategies do exist (some of them are described below) and this fact should encourage developers and managers of future reforms to be consistent and resolute in their efforts in spite of temporary failures and setbacks.

THE ROOTS OF CORRUPTION IN THE TRANSITION COUNTRIES

It appears that corruption has reached new proportions worldwide (e.g. witness the recent scandals in the U.S. corporate environment with Enron, TYCO and other firms), but perhaps this perception is due to more and better media coverage of corruption. After all bad news sells better than good news. In the transition countries, corruption has become generally less risky because it has become institutionalized, leading to increased public cynicism about the power of new governments to stop it. Corruption also has become more cash-oriented to avoid detection and taxation and, as a result of cartel formation and mergers, has become more profitable. In some transition countries corruption is so institutionalized that it has become the norm to the extent that monopoly operation of formerly state-owned enterprises, portfolios and services is a usual phenomenon. As many former government officials, government appointees and civil servants have become involved in management of commercial activities, some of these entities have grown strong enough to define state policy at least in certain areas.

In Russia, for example, rights to operate some monopolies were essentially distributed as political "spoils" during economic transition in the early 1990s to former high ranking government officials and prominent businessmen. This action essentially constrained development of real markets and competition for provision of many services.

EXPLAINING THE PREVALENCE OF CORRUPTION

There are many reasons for the upsurge of corruption in Central and Eastern Europe. The legacy of the past (not only that of the communists – but originating further back in history, e.g. from Austrian-Hungarian empire or tsarist Russia) explains to a considerable extent a long-term departure from ethical standards of good governance, accountability, transparency and the steady movement toward private rent seeking in the bureaucracy, and continuing domination by the state in the economy so typical of the former command structures. This is combined with a deeply rooted bureaucratic mentality of treating citizens as "inferiors." Furthermore, citizens have been conditioned to wait for the state to tell them what to do as producers and consumers, particularly the older generations that grew up under communist regimes.

Economic decline and uncertainty has produced political instability. Poverty and low salaries of civil servants as well as low job security in particular for high-level officials feeds large-scale corruption. At the same time, political and economic instability, along with a lack of clear, stable rules, reduces the planning horizons of market agents and induces them to undertake the risks of unlawful deals with government officeholders in pursuit of beneficial pay-offs.

Shortage of appropriate legislation and, what is more important, poor, if any, enforcement of the existing laws and norms complicates the situation in these nations. Legal reforms fail to meet the rapidly expanding and evolving demand for rules to support and regulate the emerging market economies and civil societies.

Weak and inefficient state bureaucracy of previous regimes aims to survive transition and spares no efforts to insure its self-preservation. Under these conditions the state fails to provide the rule of law and other mandated public inputs and services. Again, legitimate businesses, who are denied officially protection of their rights, seek "special" relations with government officials to stay in operation.

Undeveloped civil society and weakness or lack of democratic traditions is an underlying cause of corruption. Socio-economic crisis leads to common frustration with the inability of the state to perform its basic functions, resulting in even greater alienation of citizens from the government. Low respect for the rule of law undermines attempts to create effective safeguards against corruption.

All of this has created favorable conditions for the emergence or continuation of various types of corruption. Furthermore, these "traditional" stimuli for corruption have been complemented by new opportunities for corrupt behavior that have emerged following collapse of the non-democratic but somewhat effective command-and-control structures in the CEE and CIS countries. The establishment of new political and economic institutions was accompanied by massive redistribution of state assets and thus created favorable conditions for administrative corruption. New horizons for embezzlement and graft opened up with the launch of privatization, lessened control of exports and imports, and the expansion of the shadow economy. In some extreme but far from exceptional cases, state officials sold off state assets to themselves, at prices considerably below what the market would have defined.

For example, it is estimated that in the early 1990s in Russia, approximately 30% of all decisions on privatization were taken in violation of the existing legislation and normative tenets. (INDEM, 1998). Attempts to pass anticorruption laws and have them adequately enforced have been made regularly since 1993 but, so far, with little or no success. The annual damage to the Russian state budget and economy caused by corruption is estimated at around $16 billion (Ustinov, 2001).

The demise of the communist system also meant that the former "master," the communist party, which exercised strict control over conduct of its members and citizens, disappeared, but a new regime, one of democratic institutions, was not strong enough to effectively make the bureaucracy serve the democratic state and the people. While appropriate legislation, control and accountability were virtually absent, resource allocation has remained in the hands of government officials, who in most cases decided on their own which strategic enterprises were to be privatized, the rules for purchasing them, and in some cases who would win new ownership rights – although typically such decisions were made also by political insiders and not only bureaucrats.

In addition, corruption in the post-communist countries has been to a considerable extent generated by old customs and views. Due to the persistent tradition of patronage (inherited from the pre-communist and communist times) the state is still considered by high-ranking officials and citizens as the main actor in resource allocation, and also as a patron dealing with a select clientele. Therefore, many bureaucrats find it difficult to draw a clear line between public and private domains and, consequently, are complicit with corrupt practices.

AN ALGORITHM TO EXPLAIN CORRUPTION AND POTENTIAL CURES

A well-known formula to explain corruption is: $C = M + D - A$ (corruption equals monopoly plus discretion, minus accountability). This formulation adequately reflects the origin of corruption, in particular in post communist states. From the view of Robert Klitgaard, Dean of the Rand Graduate School in the USA and a highly regarded scholar in the field of corruption, "... whether the activity is public, private or non-profit, and whether it is carried out in Ouagadougou or Washington, one will tend to find corruption when an organization or person has a monopoly power over a good or service, has the discretion to decide who will receive it and how much that person will get, and is not accountable" (Klitgaard, 1998, p. 24). In his view combating corruption, therefore, begins with improving public management systems. Monopolies must be reduced, or be carefully regulated. Official discretion must be clarified. Transparency must be enhanced. The probability of getting caught must increase, and the penalties for corruption for both givers and takers must rise.

One may conclude, quite justifiably, that it is easy to declare these objectives, but it is much more difficult to achieve them in practice. This is particularly true, if we consider countries with a relatively high degree of political instability, economic turmoil, undeveloped institutional frameworks and weak civil societies and traditions.

In the end, corruption comes down to two dimensions – people and opportunity. As highlighted at the First Global Forum on Fighting Corruption (February 1999), about 90% of corruptive behavior has everything to do with the opportunity to corrupt. Changing the public mentality also is important. However, these things take time and effort, whereas curtailing opportunity can be achieved in a relatively short period of time and with relatively limited resources. Furthermore, less opportunity produces a different environment. The latter in turn fosters a different mentality in government, business and society. Therefore, the priority objective is to diminish opportunities for corruption through a change in some of the incentives that stimulate it.

There exists a close link between opportunity and patterns of government and governance. Rose-Ackerman explains that the nature of corruption depends both on the organization of government and on the power of individuals. These two elements are rooted in the patterns of government and governance and directly affect the scope of opportunities for corrupt behavior. Patterns of government and governance can be improved, in particular through carefully designed and consistently implemented public management reform. Within the framework of public management reform, opportunities for graft and embezzlement may be dealt with and reduced through enhanced deregulation, transparency and accountability (Rose-Ackerman, 1999). The example of Thailand may be one of success in this regard, but it is too early to tell. The Thai government has institutionalized anti-corruption measures through passage of law, creation of an anti-corruption court and stronger enforcement effort but the results of reform are not yet clear.

Therefore, public management reform offers, "... new modes of action by new sorts of actors, in a joint effort to reveal, destabilize, and subvert corruption" (Klitgaard, 2000, p. 48). This is particularly important in cases when corruption is endemic as in the post-communist CEE and CIS nations.

CORRUPTION AND THE PROMISE OF PUBLIC MANAGEMENT REFORM

In late 1980s and early 1990s of the past century the governments of CEE and CIS countries regarded political and economic reform as their obvious priority and placed this on the top of their agendas. Declarations to launch reform of public management were also made, but in most cases they reflected long-term intentions rather than immediate plans. In those states where such reform was actually undertaken, the process turned out to be fragmentary, incomplete and confined mainly to the adoption (versus enforcement) of a new legislation. In some cases, initiatives were limited to policy statements and strategy reports. The necessity for genuine public management reform, not just cosmetic measures, was realized in most countries later, in the second half of the 1990s. At this time, weaknesses of state institutions became apparent and its impact on slow progress of economic and other reforms in the region was evident. Countries that applied for accession to the European Union were subjected to pressure from Brussels to speed up improvement of their administrative capacities to meet EU standards in this field, and this may have helped to some extent. But, it did little for non-applicants.

The majority of countries in the CEE and CIS regions have adopted new legislation in the areas of public administration roles and standards of ethical behavior for civil servants. However, the laws prove to be of little worth unless there exists a sound mechanism of their enforcement. In illustration, in 1992 the President of the Russian Federation signed a decree, "On fighting corruption in the civil service," which stipulated in particular that every civil servant should regularly submit income and property declarations. It took more than five years and another presidential decree in 1997 before this requirement started to be enforced (INDEM, 1998).

In broad terms, reform of public administration in CEE and CIS countries has achieved little progress to date in addressing such basic issues as developing management and policy making capacity, defining appropriate accountability systems, creating employment conditions capable of attracting highly qualified staff, streamlining relations between politicians and career civil servants, and reducing opportunities for corruption. This is in particular reflected in the reports of the European Commission (1997, 1998, and 1999) on the progress of reforming public administration systems in the country candidates for accession to the EU. These reports described fragmented and politicized administrations, rife with allegations of corruption, underpaid staff and high level of staff turnover in most states.

As a rule, the anticorruption component of reforms was not distinctly articulated in the agendas of the above-mentioned nations, or at best it was confined to improvement of ethical standards of civil servants. During these period there have been numerous anticorruption "campaigns" in CEE and CIS countries launched separate from public management reforms. However, coordination with the latter has been generally weak, or non-existent. Many such campaigns were very ambitious, relied on untested instruments of enforcement in addressing the roots of the problem and usually ended half-way through the implementation stage, producing in the end less than modest results. At the same time even these rather modest attempts to constrain corruption exposed powerful opposition of vested interests. The accumulated experience demonstrates also that anticorruption campaigns frequently are used as an instrument to undermine the positions of political opponents, i.e. these initiatives become part of "politics as usual."

It may be concluded that there has not been a systematic and consistent effort made yet on the part of CEE and CIS governments to challenge expansion of corruption in their countries. As the Global Corruption Report 2001 indicates, "The region's relative success stories in terms of reform advances and openness – Hungary, Poland and Slovenia – have come far in the transition process, witnessing considerable corruption along the way" (Transparency International, 2001).

CITIZEN ATTITUDES TOWARD CORRUPTION

Analysis of the 2001 Corruption Perception Index compiled by Transparency International (see Appendix A), reveals some important facts and lessons. Such countries as Hungary, Slovenia, Poland, considered to be relatively more advanced in implementing public management reform within the former "Soviet block," are placed higher on the list and therefore are assessed to be less infected by corruption compared to their neighbors. The only exception is Estonia, which has the best anti-corruption rating among CEE and CIS states, but has achieved, so far, rather average progress in reforming public administration. This supports the rather obvious conclusion that public management reform is only one of the factors that affects levels of corruption in any country. In the case of Estonia, this may well be the product of the Nordic tradition of relative "immunity" from corruption, reflected also in the high ratings of Finland, Denmark and Sweden. Still, even in Estonia, instances of corruption by police are plentiful, e.g. in "looking the other way" on vice crimes and in corrupt enforcement of automobile traffic.

Another survey on the corruption climate in eleven post-communist countries carried out in 1999 by the Institute of Market Research in Prague resulted in some interesting findings (see Appendix B). The survey actually confirmed that citizens of Central and Eastern European countries are extremely critical of the problem of corruption in their state administrations. An overwhelming majority of respondents believe they live in a corrupt state and that their governments do not want to take effective measures against corruption. At the same time, most people prefer to adopt an attitude of passive observation rather than that of active opposition in relation to corruption. According to the survey findings, Slovakia is the country with the highest proportion of citizens who consider living with corruption as absolutely necessary to lead a normal life. Close to Slovakia in this respect came Hungary and Czech Republic. These findings refute a commonly held regional stereotype, "the further to the East the more essential to give bribes (GFK, Praha, 2001)."

The passive attitude of citizens of Central and Eastern Europe is very illustrative. To a considerable extent it stems from unfulfilled promises and numerous failures to contain corruption in these countries. One may suggest that unless this attitude is transformed into more active opposition, there is little chance for success of anti-corruption efforts in Central and Eastern Europe. Public apathy in Eastern Europe regarding anti-corruption policies, "... represents a formidable stumbling block" (Cirtautas, 2001). Therefore, it is essential to achieve even partial improvements in this area to encourage people, to raise their hopes and promote changes in their attitude so they feel more empowered to support fights against corruption. However, without significant state anti-corruption reform, such change in public attitudes and expectations will not come to pass.

CAUSALITY AND CONSTRAINS

Is there a line of causality between public management reform and reduction of corruption? If we proceed from a logical approach we may assume that a more professional, well motivated, better educated and trained, more transparent and accountable state administration should be less vulnerable to corruption than a corps of poorly educated, badly paid and poorly motivated administrators constrained by archaic rules and norms and working in an unstable and elite clientele-based environment. "Post-communist countries that have implemented less reform are generally perceived to be more corrupt than those that have introduced more reform" (Holmes, 1999). This assumption appears to be generally correct and it is reaffirmed by the findings of Transparency International and the World Bank. A report prepared by the World Bank based on the findings of detailed surveys conducted in Albania, Georgia and Latvia concludes that, "...anticorruption efforts should focus on reforming public policies and institutions" (World Bank, 1998, p. 54).

The examples of successful anti-corruption programs in Hong Kong and Singapore also highlight the crucial role of public administration reform in tackling corruption, even when it is deeply entrenched. We should bear in mind however that "allergy" to corruption may come from factors other than successful administrative or economic reform, e.g. peculiarities of historical development or well rooted democratic traditions, e.g. as in Estonia.

It is widely acknowledged that effective anti-corruption strategy should contain a comprehensive set of measures that go far beyond issues of organization, procedures, ethics and punishment. Recommendations advocated in particular by the World Bank are undoubtedly justified but, at the same time, as a rule are highly resources and time consuming, e.g. the WB states the need "... to target broader structural relationships, including the internal organization of the political system, relationships among core state institutions, the interactions between the state and firms, and the relationship between the state and civil society" (World Bank, 2000, p. 24).

Typically, the political leadership in the region, even if it is highly committed to changing the existing situation, does not have enough resources or sufficient support to implement a full-scale anticorruption program. As a body it is confronted with powerful resistance from vested interests. This is particularly true with regard to most CEE and CIS states. Therefore, identification of priorities in anticorruption strategy that are most likely to achieve progress in a few selected areas is crucial.

Remarkable in this respect are the recommendations of the World Bank Office in Poland, "... it is not always practical to tackle the worst areas first. It can be more important to identify committed leaders in areas where practical results can be achieved, creating demonstration effects and raising the credibility of the anti-corruption programme..." (World Bank, 2001, p. 56). Such an approach is more likely to enable hope and gain needed support in the broader society and, hence, more useful to build a sound platform for further resolute and comprehensive actions. Something needs be done to show even small but exemplary results in the short run, to generate confidence that change is possible, to convince citizens of good prospects for anticorruption efforts and to encourage their participation. In societies where the state has led in the past, some evidence of "frying even small fish" will be helpful.

Advocating a marginalist approach does not mean that larger initiatives are any less important. Rather, economic deregulation, reducing the discretionary power of the state, removal of excessive and non-value adding administrative rules, complemented by increased transparency and accountability and strengthened by attempts to build broad anti-corruption social and economic coalitions appear to be pivotal for achieving critical mass in the fight against corruption.

THE ROLE OF LEADERSHIP, DEREGULATION, TRANSPARENCY AND ACCOUNTABILITY

Managers of public management reform in CEE and CIS countries should focus on identification of "bad practices," and "vulnerable" arrangements that create administrative barriers and artificial deficits of services by the state and facilitate "administrative blackmail" and other corruptive behavior. The powers of officials to exercise control and impose possible sanctions should be reviewed to assess their vulnerability. Measures to reduce interference by the state in business affairs also should be considered. Particular attention should be paid to handling of public procurement and elimination of excessive administrative burdens, e.g. unnecessary licenses, permits, fees etc.

An interesting illustration is provided by Timothy Fry, who, after having studied the business environment in Poland and Russia, advocates public management reform as an effective instrument for reducing corruption. His main recommendation is to curtail the discretionary power of the state bureaucracy. He compares Polish and Russian experience and gives an example of an average shopkeeper, who in order to open his business needs to visit six different agencies in Moscow and four in Warsaw. After the start of business this businessman is inspected by various agencies on an average of nine times annually in Warsaw and nineteen times in Moscow. The key to the problem is apparent in Fry's view – get rid of monopoly and introduce strict and transparent rules for operation and inspection (Frye, 1998, p. 31).

On June 6, 2002 the Russian State Duma adopted amendments to the Criminal Code, which impose criminal responsibility for creating impediments to the legitimate entrepreneurial activities. From now on, unfounded refusal to register a legal entity or to grant license will be prosecuted by law (Rossijskaya Gazeta, 2002).

In another example, until recently Russian traffic policemen were empowered to determine on the spot the amount of fine (within a certain range – usually from $5 to $40) that should be imposed on drivers for virtually every type of traffic violation, depending on the "graveness" of misconduct. This created very favorable ground for graft. Recently the police have been largely deprived of this discretional power because precise levels of fines were fixed for almost every type of traffic violation. Still, some corrupt discretion still is present; only better training and hiring practices, increased professionalism and adoption of ethical standards of behavior will curb such practices in a comprehensive manner. And the importance of role of the public in objecting to fines that fall outside the rules cannot be understated.

In spite of some advances in the right direction made recently, the major anticorruption battles are still to come in CEE and CIS nations. In Moscow in May 2003, the issue of cutting redundant functions of individual ministries (assessed by a special commission to be approximately 500 functions) was discussed at a meeting of the Russian government. The event revealed that canceling even the 35 most obviously irrelevant functions turned out to be difficult as this measure met with strong opposition from state bureaucracts (Zvereva, 2003).

Deregulation and removal of administrative barriers should be complemented by measures enhancing transparency and accountability. These are directed above all at introducing a clear-cut and transparent mechanism of decision making, regular briefing of public on the results of all investigations in the field of corruption and organised crime, ensuring greater public oversight in particular over fiscal management and administration of public procurement, taking appropriate criminal, administrative and disciplinary measures against persons involved in embezzlement and graft.

In most CEE countries, punishments of officials convicted of corruption generally remain soft. For instance, out of the 70 sentences passed in 1996 on Polish officials accused of accepting bribes, the most severe was two years of imprisonment (Holmes, 1999). In the opinion of Holmes, it could be argued that if officials perform a crude cost-benefit analysis, for many of them it is economically rational to engage in corruption even if they get caught and are found guilty. Obviously, such situation can hardly be defined as optimal if the CEE and CIS governments are serious about combating corruption.

The role of media in strengthening transparency should not be underestimated. A major police corruption scandal in the city of Poznan, Poland erupted in March 1994 primarily as the result of a front-page article in the newspaper *Gazeta Wyborcza*. And a late-1996 scandal concerning the Hungarian privatization board broke with the publication of an article in the economic weekly *Figyelo* (Holmes, 1999).

Related to the role of the media, the accumulated experience of formation of broad coalitions in some of the post communist countries deserves special attention. A coalition of this type in the Ukraine called "The Freedom of Choice" was established by several hundred NGOs in 1999 to monitor and trace possible campaign violations during presidential elections. The coalition continued its activities after the elections and served as a good starting point for better coordinated support of country-wide anti-corruption measures (Sikora, 2002).

It is noteworthy that the basic elements of approaches advocated here have been tested in an environment similar to that of Central Eastern Europe at least with respect to the scale of corruption. Lessons may be drawn from the South Korean experience, where bureaucracy was once widely acknowledged to be exceptionally corrupt. It is not an exaggeration to state that Seoul civil servants had often regarded abuse of their official positions as part of their "job descriptions." A systematic approach to eradicate corruption adopted by the South Korean government brought about positive and relatively quick results. The basic elements of this approach consisted of: (a) radical deregulation that led to the abolishment and revision of 80% of regulations that were unduly confining; (b) introduction of internet based systems to monitor the real-time processing of citizen applications, accessible to everyone; (c) strengthening partnership with citizens and NGOs, in particular establishing direct dialogue between citizens and city mayors; and (d) regular evaluation of the level of integrity of each administrative unit against an Anti-Corruption Index and introducing competition between government units (Rekhviashvili, 2002a).

Hong Kong and Singapore provide other examples of effective anti-corruption strategy. According to Philip Segal, "Once among the world's most corrupt places, they have become two of its cleaner business centers." The keys to the success of anti-corruption measures among the "Asian tigers" consisted of strong commitment of top leadership, ensuring transparency, hard-edged law enforcement, exclusion of police from the reform process, and wide public participation and support (Segal, 1999).

SITUATIONS OF SYSTEMATIC CORRUPTION

Some clues to dealing with cases of embedded corruption have been described above. However, as Klitgaard notes, "When systems are so thoroughly corrupted, there may be little if any political will. Calling for better agents, improved incentives, better information, more competition, less official discretion, and higher moral costs is well and good. But who's going to listen? Who's going to act? When corruption reaches this point, the usual anti-corruption remedies may have little traction" (Klitgaard, 2000, p. 44).

Klitgaard argues that "... when corruption becomes systematic, coping with it must go beyond implementing liberal economic policies, enacting better laws, reducing the number and complexity of regulations and providing more training, helpful though these steps may be." He suggests that fighting systematic corruption requires administering a shock to disturb a corrupt equilibrium (Klitgaard, 1999). This may be appropriate provided there is strong support for the anti-corruption measures by the society and political opposition, which, as we know, is not always the case. Without this support the chances of failure are high and failure can move the whole process many years backwards.

Therefore, more relevant is another argument by Klitgaard, "If we cannot engineer incorruptible officials and citizens, we can nonetheless foster competition, change incentives and enhance accountability – in short fix the systems that breed corruption" (Klitgaard, 1998). Changing systemic and institutionalized practices in government and business that provide incentives which encourage and support corrupt behavior is essential.

Leadership is essential in fighting corruption. A recent World Bank publication emphasized that, "... where state institutions with weak administrative capacity co-exist with a high concentration of vested interests and a state highly susceptible to capture, the problem of corruption is particularly challenging ... in developing anticorruption strategy in the countries with systematic corruption it is critical to search for a feasible entry point to break the obstacles that prevent further reforms" (World Bank, 2000). Leaders in government and business can provide critical entry points if they are so inclined. The World Bank suggests further that, "... efforts to build up demonstration effects through intensive work with carefully selected organisations, sectors or regional authorities might provide a method of entry into broader anticorruption work" (World Bank, 2000). The approaches advocated by Klitgaard and the World Bank largely coincide with the views advocated in this chapter.

Finally, there is one rather obvious consideration that, however, continues to be neglected in practice. As stressed at a recent meeting of OECD Anti-Corruption Network, "Outsiders can never fundamentally root out corruption for others. Rather, people and societies must create their own integrity and incentive systems for achieving good governance and reducing corruption. On the other hand, because outside aid can either contribute to corruption or be a positive force for its eradication, it is important that donor agencies design their efforts to avoid negative impacts and maximize positive impacts" (Rekhviashvili, 2002b).

CONCLUSIONS

Based upon the description and analysis of corruption in post-communist nations provided in this chapter the following conclusions may be drawn:

(1) In 1990s public management reforms in CEE and CIS countries failed to achieve many of their proclaimed objectives. As a rule these reforms did not comprise a distinct anti-corruption component.
(2) CEE and CIS countries considered to be relatively more advanced in implementing public management reform are generally less affected by corruption than their neighbors with less advanced records of reform implementation.
(3) People in Central and Eastern Europe tend to adopt an attitude of passive observation rather than active opposition in relation to corruption. Unless this attitude is transformed into more active opposition there is little chance for success of anti-corruption efforts in Central and Eastern Europe. Therefore, it is essential to achieve even limited improvements in constraining corruption to encourage people to resist corrupt practices, to raise their hopes, and to promote changes in their attitudes.
(4) Leaders in post-communist countries who have committed themselves to resolute actions against corruption often face evident shortages of resources, little stakeholder support and powerful resistance by vested interests. In such cases, implementation of a full-scale comprehensive anti-corruption program is problematic. The situation necessitates elaboration of a more marginal strategy aimed at changing the existing patterns and norms of governance and achieving progress at least in separate selected areas, i.e. picking and hitting targets that are achievable and that will have high visibility in the media and

with average citizens. This is crucial for gaining much needed support of citizens and society in formation of a broad anti-corruption coalition.

(5) In most cases corruption is linked to opportunity. Reduction of opportunity, especially at grass root levels, as part of public management reform efforts may result in notable improvements and ensure greater public support and participation in anti-corruption programs. These improvements can be achieved through a focused policy of deregulation, reducing some types of discretionary bureaucratic power (e.g. that which permits petty rule enforcement without producing any value except to bureaucrats), removal of unnecessary administrative burdens on legitimate and legal free enterprise, all complemented by enhanced transparency and accountability supported by the media and anti-corruption interest groups and coalitions.

Alexander Kotchegura, Senior Analyst, Russian-European Center for Economic Policy (RECEP), and Adjunct Professor, People's Friendship University, Moscow, Russia: akotcheg@online.ru.

REFERENCES

Cirtautas, A. (2001). Corruption and the new ethical infrastructure of capitalism. *East European Constitutional Review 10/2/3*, 18–20.
Frye, T. (1998). Corruption: The Polish and Russian experiences. *Economic Perspectives*, *3*(5), 2.
Holmes, L. (1999, 26 October–6 November). Corruption, weak states and economic rationalism in Central and Eastern Europe. Melbourne: University of Melbourne. Paper Presented at the Princeton University – Central European University Joint Conference on Corruption, Budapest, pp. 1–5.
INDEM (1998). *Russia and corruption: Present and future*. Moscow: INDEM.
Klitgaard, R. (1998). International cooperation against corruption. *SPAN*, (Sept./Oct.), 38–39.
Klitgaard, R. (1999). Combatting corruption and promoting ethics in the public service in transition: enhancing its role, professionalism, ethical values and standards. Durban, SA: University of Natal.
Klitgaard, R. (2000). Subverting corruption. *Finance and Development*, *37*(2), 2–3.
Miller, W. (2002). Corruption and poverty in post-communist Europe. *Transition*, *3*, 30–32.
Rekhviashvili, I. (2002a). Anti-corruption. *Local Government Brief*, (Winter, Budapest), 63–64.
Rekhviashvili, I. (2002b). Annual meeting of the OECD anti-corruption network. *Local Government Brief*, (Summer, Budapest), 61–62.
Rose-Ackerman, S. (1999). Corruption and government: Causes, consequences and reform. Cambridge: Cambridge University Press.
Rossijskaya Gazeta (2002). News in brief. *Rossijskaya Gazeta*, *7*(6), 1.
Segal P. (1999). Hell of corruption, IFC, Impact, Spring 1999, Washington DC, p. 5.
Sikora, I. (Ed.) (2002). Anticorruption strategies for transitional economies. Kiev: Vizkom.
Transparency International (2001). *Global corruption report*. Available from the Transparency International, www.globalcorruptionreport.com.

Ustinov, V. (2001). Meeting of representatives of law enforcement agencies. *Rossijskaya Gazeta, 62*, 2.
World Bank (1998). New frontiers in diagnosing and combating corruption. *PREM notes*, p. 7. Washington, DC: World Bank.
World Bank (2000). *Anticorruption in transition. A contribution to the policy debate*. Washington, DC: World Bank.
World Bank (2001). *Review of priority areas and proposals for action 2001*. Available from the World Bank – www.worldbank.org.pl.
Zvereva, E. (2003). The ministries do not give up. *Moskovsky Komsomolets, 102*, 5.

APPENDIX A

The Transparency International Corruption Perception Index

The 2000 C P Index Score relates perceptions of the degree of corruption by business people, risk analysts and the general public. Scoring ranges between 10 (highly clean) and 0 (highly corrupt). Surveys Used – refers to the number of surveys that assessed country performance. Sixteen surveys were used and at least three surveys were required for a country to be included in the CPI. Standard Deviation indicates differences in the values of the sources: the greater the standard deviation, the greater the differences of perceptions of a country among the sources. High-Low Range provides the largest and smallest values of the sources. And, because of statistical factors it is possible, as with the three cases in the CPI, that the highest value exceeds 10.0.

Country Rank	Country	2001 CPI Score	Surveys Used	Standard Deviation	High-Low Range
1	Finland	9.9	7	0.6	9.2–10.6
2	Denmark	9.5	7	0.7	8.8–10.6
3	New Zealand	9.4	7	0.6	8.6–10.2
4	Iceland	9.2	6	1.1	7.4–10.1
	Singapore	9.2	12	0.5	8.5–9.9
6	Sweden	9.0	8	0.5	8.2–9.7
7	Canada	8.9	8	0.5	8.2–9.7
8	Netherlands	8.8	7	0.3	8.4–9.2
9	Luxembourg	8.7	6	0.5	8.1–9.5
10	Norway	8.6	7	0.8	7.4–9.6
11	Australia	8.5	9	0.9	6.8–9.4
12	Switzerland	8.4	7	0.5	7.4–9.2
13	United Kingdom	8.3	9	0.5	7.4–8.8

Country Rank	Country	2001 CPI Score	Surveys Used	Standard Deviation	High-Low Range
14	Hong Kong	7.9	11	0.5	7.2–8.7
15	Austria	7.8	7	0.5	7.2–8.7
16	Israel	7.6	8	0.3	7.3–8.1
	USA	7.6	11	0.7	6.1–9.0
18	Chile	7.5	9	0.6	6.5–8.5
	Ireland	7.5	7	0.3	6.8–7.9
20	Germany	7.4	8	0.8	5.8–8.6
21	Japan	7.1	11	0.9	5.6–8.4
22	Spain	7.0	8	0.7	5.8–8.1
23	France	6.7	8	0.8	5.6–7.8
24	Belgium	6.6	7	0.7	5.7–7.6
25	Portugal	6.3	8	0.8	5.3–7.4
26	Botswana	6.0	3	0.5	5.6–6.6
27	Taiwan	5.9	11	1.0	4.6–7.3
28	Estonia	5.6	5	0.3	5.0–6.0
29	Italy	5.5	9	1.0	4.0–6.9
30	Namibia	5.4	3	1.4	3.8–6.7
31	Hungary	5.3	10	0.8	4.0–6.2
	Trinidad & Tobago	5.3	3	1.5	3.8–6.9
	Tunisia	5.3	3	1.3	3.8–6.5
34	Slovenia	5.2	7	1.0	4.1–7.1
35	Uruguay	5.1	4	0.7	4.4–5.8
36	Malaysia	5.0	11	0.7	3.8–5.9
37	Jordan	4.9	4	0.8	3.8–5.7
38	Lithuania	4.8	5	1.5	3.8–7.5
	South Africa	4.8	10	0.7	3.8–5.6
40	Costa Rica	4.5	5	0.7	3.7–5.6
	Mauritius	4.5	5	0.7	3.9–5.6
42	Greece	4.2	8	0.6	3.6–5.6
	South Korea	4.2	11	0.7	3.4–5.6
44	Peru	4.1	6	1.1	2.0–5.3
	Poland	4.1	10	0.9	2.9–5.6
46	Brazil	4.0	9	0.3	3.5–4.5
47	Bulgaria	3.9	6	0.6	3.2–5.0
	Croatia	3.9	3	0.6	3.4–4.6
	Czech Republic	3.9	10	0.9	2.6–5.6

Country Rank	Country	2001 CPI Score	Surveys Used	Standard Deviation	High-Low Range
50	Colombia	3.8	9	0.6	3.0–4.5
51	Mexico	3.7	9	0.6	2.5–5.0
	Panama	3.7	3	0.4	3.1–4.0
	Slovak Republic	3.7	7	0.9	2.1–4.9
54	Egypt	3.6	7	1.5	1.2–6.2
	El Salvador	3.6	5	0.9	2.0–4.3
	Turkey	3.6	9	0.8	2.0–4.5
57	Argentina	3.5	9	0.6	2.9–4.4
	China	3.5	10	0.4	2.7–3.9
59	Ghana	3.4	3	0.5	2.9–3.8
	Latvia	3.4	3	1.2	2.0–4.3
61	Malawi	3.2	3	1.0	2.0–3.9
	Thailand	3.2	12	0.9	0.6–4.0
63	Dominican Rep	3.1	3	0.9	2.0–3.9
	Moldova	3.1	3	0.9	2.1–3.8
65	Guatemala	2.9	4	0.9	2.0–4.2
	Philippines	2.9	11	0.9	1.6–4.8
	Senegal	2.9	3	0.8	2.2–3.8
	Zimbabwe	2.9	6	1.1	1.6–4.7
69	Romania	2.8	5	0.5	2.0–3.4
	Venezuela	2.8	9	0.4	2.0–3.6
71	Honduras	2.7	3	1.1	2.0–4.0
	India	2.7	12	0.5	2.1–3.8
	Kazakhstan	2.7	3	1.3	1.8–4.3
	Uzbekistan	2.7	3	1.1	2.0–4.0
75	Vietnam	2.6	7	0.7	1.5–3.8
	Zambia	2.6	3	0.5	2.0–3.0
77	Cote d'Ivoire	2.4	3	1.0	1.5–3.6
	Nicaragua	2.4	3	0.8	1.9–3.4
79	Ecuador	2.3	6	0.3	1.8–2.6
	Pakistan	2.3	3	1.7	0.8–4.2
	Russia	2.3	10	1.2	0.3–4.2
82	Tanzania	2.2	3	0.6	1.6–2.9
83	Ukraine	2.1	6	1.1	1.0–4.3
84	Azerbaijan	2.0	3	0.2	1.8–2.2
	Bolivia	2.0	5	0.6	1.5–3.0

Country Rank	Country	2001 CPI Score	Surveys Used	Standard Deviation	High-Low Range
	Cameroon	2.0	3	0.8	1.2–2.9
	Kenya	2.0	4	0.7	0.9–2.6
88	Indonesia	1.9	12	0.8	0.2–3.1
	Uganda	1.9	3	0.6	1.3–2.4
90	Nigeria	1.0	4	0.9	−0.1–2.0
91	Bangladesh	0.4	3	2.9	−1.7–3.8

Note: On the Bangladesh score, data for this country in 2001 was available from only three independent survey sources, and each of these yielded very different results. While the composite score is 0.4, the range of individual survey results is from −1.7 to +3.8. This is a greater range than for any other country. TI stresses, therefore, that this result needs to be viewed with caution.
Source: www.nobribes.org.

APPENDIX B

In June, July and August 2001 GFK Praha, a Czech Republic-based Institute for market research, carried out a sociological survey on corruption climates in eleven Central and Eastern European countries: Bulgaria, Czech Republic, Croatia, Hungary, Poland, Austria, Romania, Russia, Slovakia, Slovenia and Ukraine. Results of the survey are provided below in Plates 1 and 2.

The level of corruption in the Central and East European region is usually estimated as moderate to very high, which casts an unfavorable light on the countries of this region, linking them to the position of the developing countries in Africa, Asia or South America. This assumption is underpinned by data from the index of corruption perception (CPI) annually published by Transparency International.

The research project GfK does not conclude this assumption is untrue, but highlights major variances between the countries of this region. For example, corruption most affects everyday life of people in Slovakia. Almost half of the Slovak population feels that the problem of corruption is absolutely pressing, corruption is quite necessary to be able to manage private life −48% of respondents in this country answer that bribes are natural part of life in their country and this supports the view "those who want to live, must give." Their figure highly exceeds the average in the whole of the region and thus Slovakia, in perception of corruption as absolutely necessary for people to be able to live a normal life provides an exceptional position in the region. Surprisingly, among these countries where corruption is perceived as very high are the Czech Republic and Hungary.

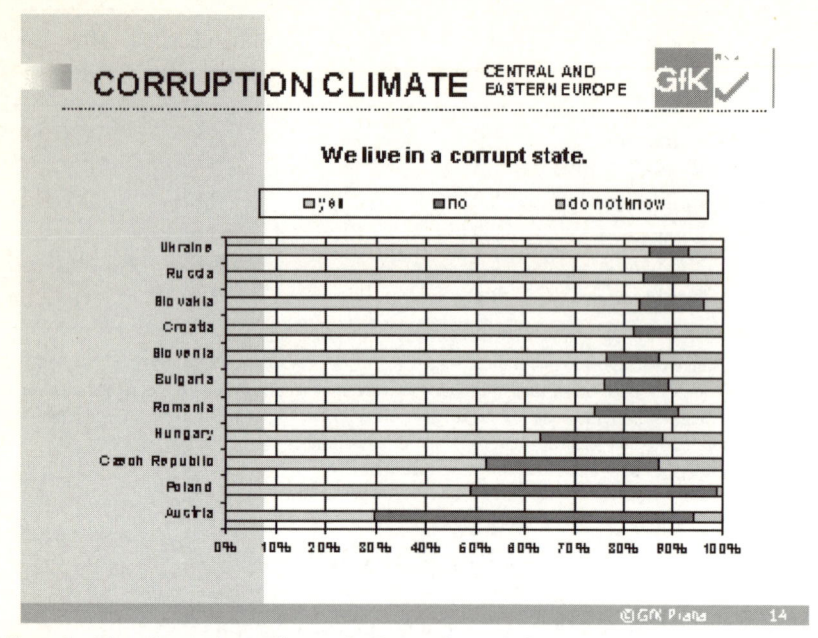

Plate 1. The Corruption Climate I: Perception of Corruption. *Source:* GfK Praha (2001).

A quarter of the population in these countries perceives corruption as absolutely essential in life. This finding contradicts the stereotype that the farther the East one moves in CEE and CIS nations, the more essential it is to engage in bribery.

If the people living in the Central and Eastern European countries tell us that they do not give bribes, how come they live in corrupt states? The answer is very simple, it is not enough to passively resist corruption, but it is necessary to actively fight against it. The passive corruption immunity of most people does not guarantee that the remaining minority would not make the state corrupt. However, the active resistance of individuals to corruption around them is pitifully low in the whole of the region.

The majority of the population living in the region do not perceive themselves as part of public control over adhering to generally accepted rules of state institutions functioning, and, speaking about a possible corruption behavior of clerks and politicians are more likely to take an attitude of passive observer than active initiator of their punishment. Obviously, the percentage of those determined to collectively fight against corruption is different between the individual countries. The greatest mobilization potential of anti corruption collective resistance exists in

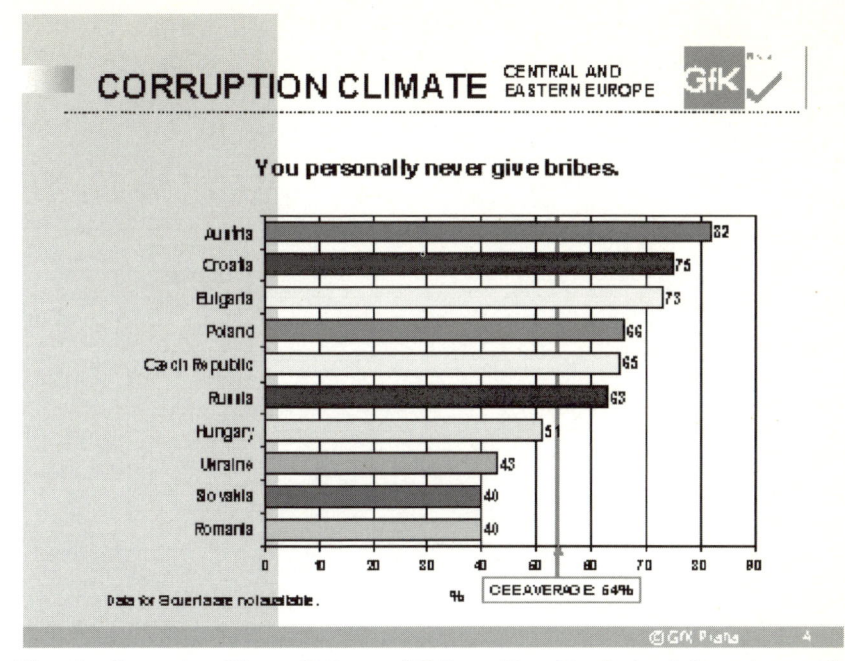

Plate 2. Corruption Climate II: Personal Bribery. *Note:* For further information see the GfK Praha website: www.gfk.cz/corruption. *Source:* GfK Praha (2001).

Romania and in Croatia, where the share of the respondents willing to demonstrate to support the fight against corruption comes close to two thirds of all respondents. Conversely, those least willing to get mobilized in the fight against corruption are the respondents from Austria, Ukraine and Poland.

PART IV:
PERFORMANCE ASSESSMENT AND MANAGEMENT STRATEGIES

14. A CONCEPTUAL FRAMEWORK AND METHODOLOGICAL GUIDE FOR RESEARCH ON PUBLIC MANAGEMENT POLICY CHANGE IN THE LATIN AMERICAN REGION

Michael Barzelay, Francisco Gaetani, Juan Carlos Cortázar Velarde and Guillermo Cejudo

INTRODUCTION

This chapter presents a conceptual framework and methodological guide for researching the process of public management policy change in the Latin America region. It provides an explicit the methodological approach for case study research on this topic. The focus on the Latin America region is due to the sponsorship of the Inter-American Development Bank, which desired an explicit methodological guide for conducting research on public sector management reform. While the chapter is specifically geared to this purpose, it also exhibits a distinctive general approach to a large class of case study research designs. This class includes instrumental case study research about processes, incorporating variants that are rich in narrative, explicit in their explanatory framework, and comparative (Barzelay, 2002).

Publication of this guide is appropriate since: (a) this class of case study research has not benefited from specialized methodological exposition; and (b) much public management research fits within this class. Accordingly, the chapter is addressed to both public management researchers interested in the specific research topic and those engaged in instrumental case-oriented research on processes more generally. The intention of the authors is to provide a practical guide for conducting case-oriented research on the process of public policy-making in the specific domain of public management policies.

Public management policy-making is related conceptually to administrative reform and state modernization, but has a narrower definition. Public management policies are government wide[1] institutional rules and routines[2] (Barzelay, 2001). These rules and routines relate not only to people, organization, and procedures, but also to planning, execution, auditing, and review of public expenditures. Public management policies fall into the following categories: expenditure planning and financial management, civil service and labor relations, procurement, organization and methods, and audit and evaluation.

The overall aim of the chapter, reflecting the intentions of its sponsor, is to gain insight into the process of public management policy change. Each case study is meant to provide such insight for a particular country. The common analytical treatment of each case provides a basis for comparison and thereby the formulation of plausible generalizations of an analytic and historical (as distinct from statistical) sort. The main objective of the chapter is to ensure that the country case studies receive such a common analytic treatment. Some specific techniques for accomplishing this objective are presented and illustrated in detail.

An understanding of the process of public management policy change cannot be attained without the successful execution of a carefully crafted research design. Formulating a satisfactory research design involves making coherent choices with respect to a large array of design issues, including the specification of the research goal (e.g. to understand the process of public management policy change in the Latin America region), selection of the cases to be studied (e.g. reform episodes within Brazil, Mexico, and Peru), the identification of case outcomes (e.g. public management policy choices), and selection of explanatory frameworks to be put into operation in explaining the case outcomes (e.g. the Kingdon (1983) and Baumgartner and Jones (1994) models). A successful case study provides satisfying answers to research questions about the experience studied and insightful statements about types of phenomena of scientific or practical interest. The likelihood that the answers are satisfying depends, in large measure, on how skillfully the researcher puts explanatory frameworks into operation in interpreting rich, appropriately ordered, evidence about the events to which the research questions concerning the experience studied. The likelihood that an understanding of the experience studied provides insight into a type of phenomenon depends, in part, on the conceptual relatedness between the research questions about the experience studied

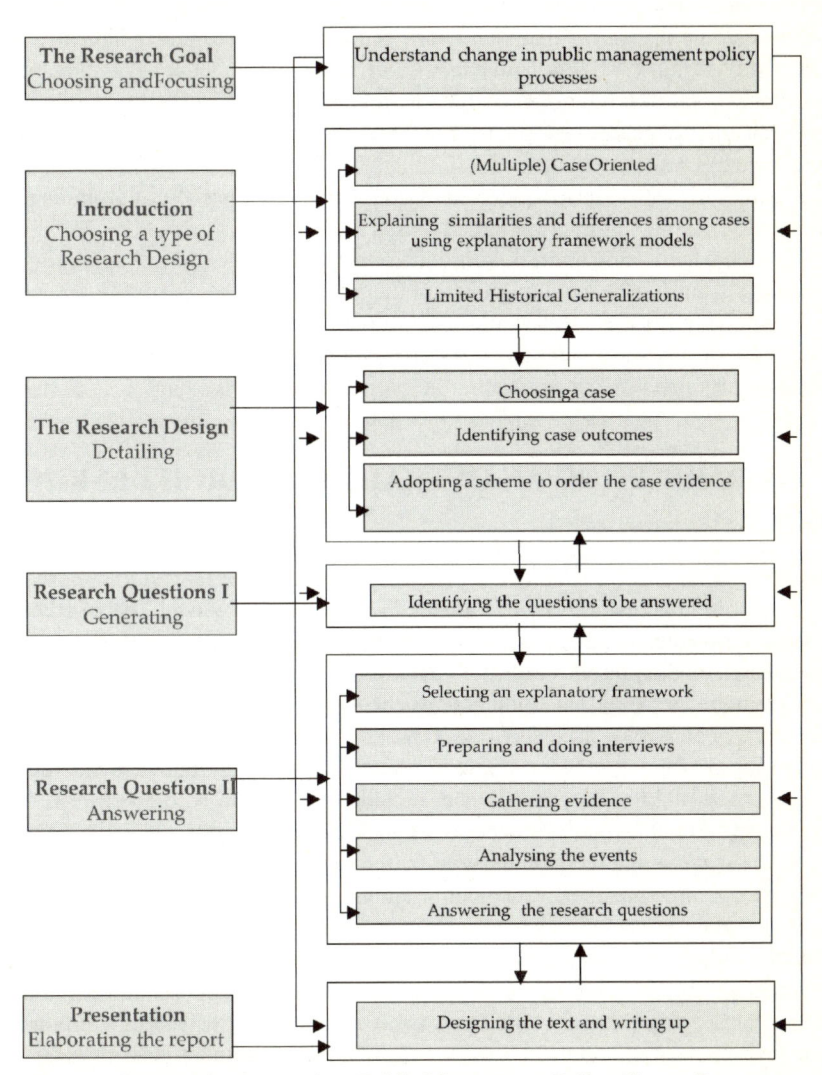

Fig. 1. Comparative Research on Public Management Policy Change Processes.

and broader questions of demonstrable interest to scientific and professional communities.

Case study research is admittedly improvised more than performed by formulating and executing a blueprint. In the words of the author of a well-regarded text on case-oriented research (Ragin, 1987), this style of work involves a dialogue between ideas and evidence. While case research is always improvised to a degree, we have come to believe that such work can be conducted more efficiently and effectively if improvisation is disciplined by a codified practice. This document codifies several of the most important aspects of the practice of conducting case research on the process of public management policy change, with particular reference to Latin America.

Figure 1 identifies these aspects and groups them by type of design issue and, notionally, by stage of the research process.

This chapter is not entirely self-sufficient, in that it calls for applying explanatory frameworks that are known in the political science literature on public policy-making. Researchers would need to read these guidelines in concert with that literature as well as texts on the methodology of case-oriented research – including Ragin (1987).

FORMULATING AN OVERALL RESEARCH DESIGN

Identifying Cases

The case oriented research style (Ragin, 1987) is appropriate to the task of creating formal knowledge about public management policy change in Latin America as elsewhere. In the present context, "cases" refer to experiences in which events involve policy making that could lead to changes in public management policies. Normally, a case refers to a network of events (or an episode) within a limited period, such as one defined by a single presidential administration. Cejudo's (2001) recent study of Mexico, for instance, included two cases, so defined. The first case analyzed public management policy-making events during the De la Madrid presidency, while the second analyzed public management policy-making events during the Zedillo presidency. Deliberate attempts of policymaking in various areas of public management policy occurred during both administrations: reforming expenditure planning and financial management, formulating civil service and labor relations policy, and fostering change in administrative methods and procedures. The Cejudo study compares the two cases (bounded by presidential administrations) to generalize about the process of public management policy change in Mexico.

When the research goal is to understand a process, such as public management policy change, the cases are usefully conceived as an array of parallel and/or serial events through which policy-making occurs. No matter how a reform episode is divided into events, the events comprising the case must individually and severally relate to the process of changing government-wide rules and routines in some or all of the five categories of public management policy mentioned earlier: expenditure planning and financial management, civil service and labor relations, procurement, organization and methods, and audit and evaluation.

Identifying Outcomes Within Cases

According to Ragin (1987)[3] a critical research design decision is to characterize case outcomes. The concept of *case outcome* is related to the more familiar concept of *dependent variable*: it is that which the analysis needs to explain. Generally speaking, the major research questions of a case oriented investigation are expressed in terms of explaining case outcomes. The researcher is accountable to readers, including academic peers, for providing satisfactory explanations of case outcomes. For this reason, the rationale for choosing a particular way to characterize case outcomes should be well considered and explained. In general, case outcomes need to be specified so that they help solve the co-ordination problem that is endemic to scholarly research. It is only by solving this problem that a research community, as a whole, can produce knowledge about such historically defined phenomena, as the process of public management policy change. Following this suggestion, Barzelay (2001) identified *comprehensive* public management policy change as a similarity of the New Public Management benchmark cases.

Given that reform is conceptualized as public management policy-making, a key property of any selected case outcome is that it refers to authoritative choices of government-wide institutional rules and routines within the public management policy domain (Barzelay, 2001, Chap. 3). This definition leaves room for interpretation, but it is meant to be different from other definitions evident in the literature, such as systemic organizational change in particular governmental systems (Aucoin, 1995). To reiterate, case outcomes should be instances of authoritative choices made by law-making power centers or central agencies that potentially affect expenditure planning processes, financial management, civil service and labor relations, procurement, organization and methods, and audit and evaluation across a given jurisdiction. Accordingly, administrative policy choices that have specific effect on a singular department cannot be considered a case of public management policy change.

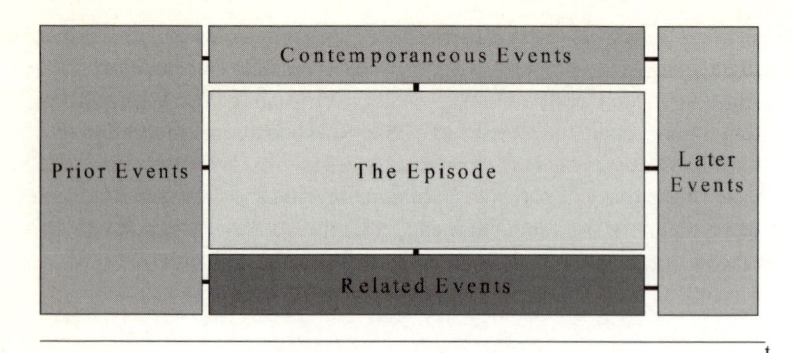

Fig. 2. Narrative Structure.

Ordering Case Evidence

To explain a particular policy choice requires employing an explanatory framework in to formulate a narrative explanation of the process by which the choice occurred. Policy processes are composed of parallel and serial events. To analyze how policy choices occurred, it is extremely helpful to identify and designate such events, and then explain how they began, progressed, and ended. We refer to the construct that defines the system of events constituting the experience studied as the "narrative structure" of the analysis.

The most generic form of a narrative structure is presented in Fig. 2. The basic element within an experience studied is an *event*. The set of events directly and intimately related to the process of substantive and analytic interest (e.g. public management policy making) constitutes the *episode*. The episode is situated within *surrounding events*. These events include *prior events* and *contemporaneous events*. Prior events occur before the episode, while contemporaneous events occur in the same time frame. Prior and contemporaneous events are locations of causal sources of aspects of the episode. A model of an experience can also include *related events* coincident with the episode but more affected by the episode's events than the other way around. *Later events* are sometimes included in the study frame for purposes of exploring the contemporary relevance of historical episodes.

An Illustration

In the Mexican study, the *experience studied* was public management policy change in the Mexican Federal Public Administration from 1982 to 2000 (see

A Conceptual Framework and Methodological Guide 355

PUBLIC MANAGEMENT POLICY CHANGE IN MEXICO

Case I
De la Madrid administration
1982-1988

Period a   (1982-1985)
Period b   (1985-1988)

Events
E1 (I) Combating corruption

E2 (Ia) Reforming expenditure planning and financial management

E3 (Ia) Formulating civil service/labour relations policy

E4 (Ia) Fostering change in administrative methods and procedures

Case II
Zedillo administration
1994-2000

Period a   (1994-1997)
Period b   (1997-2000)

Events
E2 (III) Reforming expenditure planning and financial management

E3 (III) Formulating civil service/labour relations policy

E4 Fostering change in administrative methods and procedures

Fig. 3. Comparing Two Cases of Public Management Policy Change in Mexico.

Fig. 3). The *periods* coincided with the three presidential administrations: Miguel De la Madrid (1982–1988), Carlos Salinas (1988–1994), and Ernesto Zedillo (1994–2000). Given the fact that during the Salinas period it was not possible to identify events of public management policymaking, only two *episodes* (De la Madrid and Salinas) were analyzed. These episodes were designated as the two *cases*.

Once the cases are identified, the next step is to enumerate the *events* that take place within each episode. In order to simplify this discussion, we focus exclusively on the first episode (the De la Madrid administration) (see Fig. 4). The *events* within the episode were:

- Combating corruption – an effort to reduce administrative corruption in the central government.
- Reforming expenditure planning and financial management – an attempt to restructure the planning and evaluation activities.
- Formulating civil service/labor relations policy – a failed attempt to create a career civil service.

Case 1

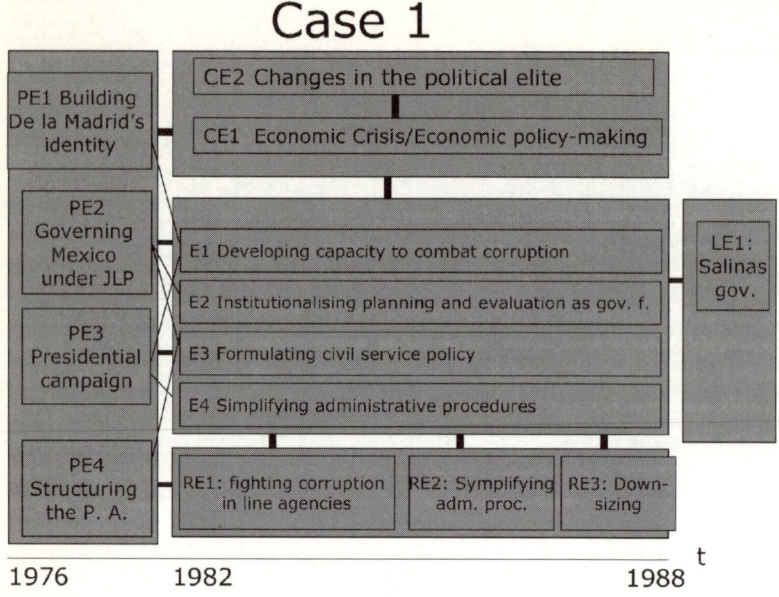

```
PE1 Building            CE2 Changes in the political elite
De la Madrid's
   identity             CE1 Economic Crisis/Economic policy-making

    PE2
 Governing                                                              LE1:
   Mexico         E1 Developing capacity to combat corruption          Salinas
  under JLP                                                             gov.
                  E2 Institutionalising planning and evaluation as gov. f.
    PE3
 Presidential     E3 Formulating civil service policy
  campaign
                  E4 Simplifying administrative procedures

    PE4
 Structuring     RE1: fighting corruption  RE2: Symplifying  RE3: Down-
  the P. A.         in line agencies          adm. proc.       sizing
                                                                                 t
   1976              1982                                     1988
```
Fig. 4. Narrative Structure of the De La Madrid Case.

- Fostering change in administrative methods and procedures – an administrative simplification program.

Each of these events is divided even further into a number of *component events*. For instance, combating corruption included, at least, two component events: (i) Developing institutional capacity to combat corruption; and (ii) Developing operational capacity to combat corruption.

Nonetheless, our main interest is in the identification and explanation of the event *outcomes*; that is, we have to identify what is the outcome of the event (for instance, following the same example, the creation of a new institutional venue for the fighting corruption policy), and to provide an explanation for it. To explain event outcomes, we look to other events as sources of change or stability in public management policy. Thus, we look into the *prior events*. They help us to understand the situation at the beginning of the period, including the factors that influence the agenda-setting process within the episode. For the De la Madrid episode, the prior events included: (i) building of De la Madrid's identity (his career and his political positions); (ii) governing of Mexico under López Portillo (both political and economic happenings during this administration); (iii) campaigning for the presidency (the De la Madrid's presidential campaign, focusing specially in the issues he raised concerning public management policy); (iv) structuring the Federal Public Administration (the situation inherited by the López Portillo government concerning the public sector organization). Accordingly, Fig. 4 defines several prior events within this case.

It is also typically necessary to analyze the concurrent events in the episode. As have been mentioned, *contemporaneous events* refer to events that are interpreted as sources of occurrences within the episode. During the De la Madrid period it is possible to identify two set of events that correspond to this definition: the economic crisis and the economic policy making performed as a response (which affected public management policy making by, for instance, reducing the public budget and, eventually, triggering the decision to downsize the public sector), and the changes in the political elite (as in many other Latin American countries, there was an evident transformation of the ruling elite, from old-styled politicians to new technocrats; this change produced more changes in the public management policy area). Accordingly, Fig. 4 defines several contemporaneous events within the episode.

ELABORATING THE RESEARCH DESIGN

Generating Candidate Research Questions

The formulation of the research questions to be answered is a key step in the design and refinement of any research project. A useful distinction is between type A research questions, related to broader policy debates, and type B research questions, related to specific reform episodes. Type A research questions require a high level of generality in order to capture the attention of the international academic and policy community. For instance: How do the processes of agenda setting and alternative generation work in this domain? What affects the generation and resolution of competition and conflict over institutional and policy choices in this domain? How can policy-makers learn from history in designing and improvising public management policy change? How do accepted doctrines of public management policymaking affect policy formulation? Why does comprehensive public management policy change sometimes occur?

Type B research questions structure inquiry about a particular case. One way of generating Type B research questions is to ask how designated events within the episode began and how their outcome was reached. In generating Type B research questions in this fashion, it is necessary to have completed a working version of the narrative structure. As discussed above, the narrative structure delineates the events that comprise the experience studied.

Illustration of Research Questions About Public Management Policy Change in the Latin American Region

The best way of understanding how to generate research questions is through a practical example. Therefore this subsection is about generating research questions in another concrete study: Peru. Public management policy making occurred in Peru in the past decade. Reforming the state was a broad policy issue that the government elected in 1990 perceived and tackled during the subsequent years in various ways. This policy-making process produced limited changes in the Peruvian public management policies (Cortázar & Carlos, 2002).

During a first period (1990–1995) some change in the public management policies happened, although exclusively focused on specific economy policy agencies that were created or reformed under the influence of the economic stabilization policy the government undertook. However, in a second period (1995–1997) governmental authorities became engaged in the implementation of a vast "State Modernization Program." This program aimed to develop a coherent and consistent public management policy change process. Nevertheless, after the program had generated a number of policy proposals and bills, President Fujimori terminated the process in 1997. This decision contributed to the very limited change in public management policies. Figure 5 shows the result of organizing the case evidence applying the proposed scheme.

The resulting scheme is useful for generating relevant research questions related to: (a) each singular event or sub event within the episode; (b) the whole episode; and (c) the comparison between different periods. Figure 6 presents an example of the route followed to generate the research questions, focusing on some of the events included in the episode presented in Fig. 5. Question 1, "Why were some institutions selected for being modernized?" is directly related to sub event E1-1 (I) "Creating or Reforming Agencies." In a similar way, Questions 2 and 3 are related to "Privatizing Employment Regime for Agencies" (sub-event E2-1 [I]) and "Developing a new Civil Service Regime for Executive Branch" (sub-event E2-2 [II]) respectively. Question 4 does not refer to a particular sub event but rather to all sub events that occurred in Period I, i.e. across the different public management policy areas. In a broader perspective Question 5 considered the whole event, comparing the changes occurred in both periods.

Let us now focus in some detail in the process that underlies this route. In the case of Event E2 ("Civil Service and Labor Relations") our aim is to explain why the outcome of this event occurred. Thus, we have to generate questions related to the particular outcomes the policy-making process of sub events in both periods, that is E2-1 (I) and E2-2 (II). In the first one, the outcome was the fact that special labor regulations – similar to the private sector ones – were approved for the

Applying the Schematics
Public Management Policy Events in Peruvian Case

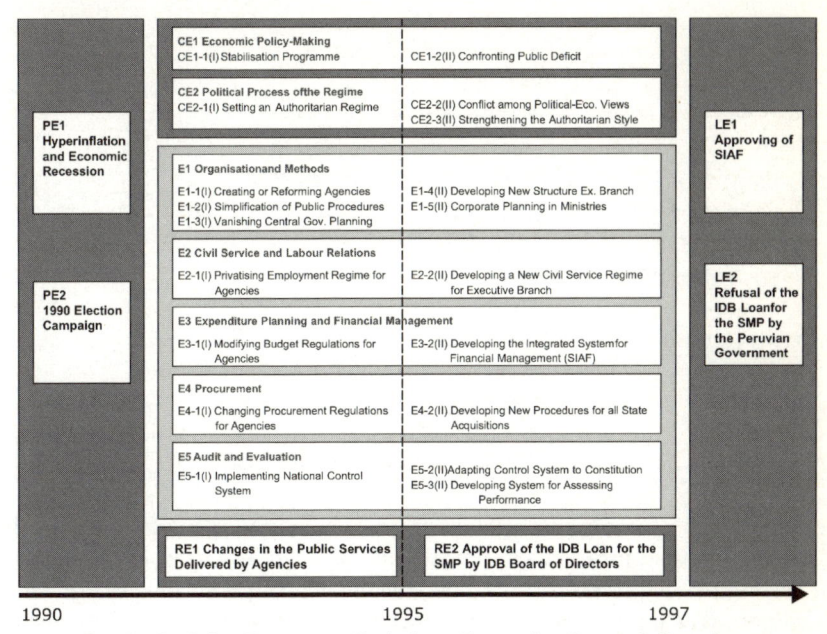

PE1 Hyperinflation and Economic Recession	**CE1 Economic Policy-Making** CE1-1(I) Stabilisation Programme	CE1-2(II) Confronting Public Deficit	
	CE2 Political Process of the Regime CE2-1(I) Setting an Authoritarian Regime	CE2-2(II) Conflict among Political-Eco. Views CE2-3(II) Strengthening the Authoritarian Style	**LE1** Approving of SIAF
	E1 Organisation and Methods E1-1(I) Creating or Reforming Agencies E1-2(I) Simplification of Public Procedures E1-3(I) Vanishing Central Gov. Planning	E1-4(II) Developing New Structure Ex. Branch E1-5(II) Corporate Planning in Ministries	
PE2 1990 Election Campaign	**E2 Civil Service and Labour Relations** E2-1(I) Privatising Employment Regime for Agencies	E2-2(II) Developing a New Civil Service Regime for Executive Branch	**LE2** Refusal of the IDB Loan for the SMP by the Peruvian Government
	E3 Expenditure Planning and Financial Management E3-1(I) Modifying Budget Regulations for Agencies	E3-2(II) Developing the Integrated System for Financial Management (SIAF)	
	E4 Procurement E4-1(I) Changing Procurement Regulations for Agencies	E4-2(II) Developing New Procedures for all State Acquisitions	
	E5 Audit and Evaluation E5-1(I) Implementing National Control System	E5-2(II) Adapting Control System to Constitution E5-3(II) Developing System for Assessing Performance	
	RE1 Changes in the Public Services Delivered by Agencies	**RE2 Approval of the IDB Loan for the SMP by IDB Board of Directors**	

1990   1995   1997

Fig. 5. Defining Events as a Prelude to Generating Research Questions.

new agencies. In the second one, the State Modernization Program furthered the privatization of labor relations, attempting to extend this policy to the entire executive branch through developing a new Civil Service Regime. As shown in Fig. 6, Questions 2 and 3 are keyed to sub events E2-1 (I) and E2-2 (II) respectively. Since these questions are analytically interesting to understand the dynamics of public management policy making in Peru, they are carried forward to the stages of data gathering and analysis.

Some questions are not keyed to particular events but to multiple events or even the entire episode. For example, Question 4 is keyed to all the events comprising Period I. This research question seeks to understand similarities among events during which policy-making teams worked to reform particular departments and agencies. Specifically, the similarity to be understood is the change in the employment regime in the direction of private, contractual practices. This change characterized each of several department or agency-specific interventions. Question 5 is another example of a research question keyed to multiple events.

```
┌─────────────────────────────────────────────────────────────────┐
│ E1 Organisation and Methods                                      │
│  E1-1(I) Creating or Reforming Agencies    E1-4(II) Developing New Structure Ex. Branch │
│  E1-2(I) Simplification of Public Procedures  E1-5(II) Corporate Planning in Ministries │
│  E1-3(I) Vanishing Central Gov. Planning                         │
├─────────────────────────────────────────────────────────────────┤
│ E2 Civil Service and Labour Relations                            │
│  E2-1(I) Privatising Employment Regime for  E2-2(II) Developing a New Civil Service Regime │
│    Agencies                                    for Executive Branch │
├─────────────────────────────────────────────────────────────────┤
│ E3 Expenditure Planning and Financial Management                 │
│  E3-1(I) Modifying Budget Regulations for   E3-2(II) Developing the Integrated System for │
│    Agencies                                    Financial Management (SIAF) │
├─────────────────────────────────────────────────────────────────┤
│ E4 Procurement                                                   │
│  E4-1(I) Changing Procurement Regulations   E4-2(II) Developing New Procedures for all State │
│    for Agencies                                Acquisitions      │
├─────────────────────────────────────────────────────────────────┤
│ E5 Audit and Evaluation                                          │
│  E5-1(I) Implementing National Control      E5-2(II) Adapting Control System to Constitution │
│    System                                   E5-3(II) Developing System for Assessing │
│                                                Performance      │
└─────────────────────────────────────────────────────────────────┘
```

(4) Why were the policy choices taken in reforming or creating agencies in Period I relatively similar despite the lack of explicit co ordination among the multiple teams working on this area?

(5) Why did little public management policy change occur in Period II compared to Period I?

(1) Why were some institutions selected for being modernised?

(2) Why was the employment regime for new agencies "privatised"?

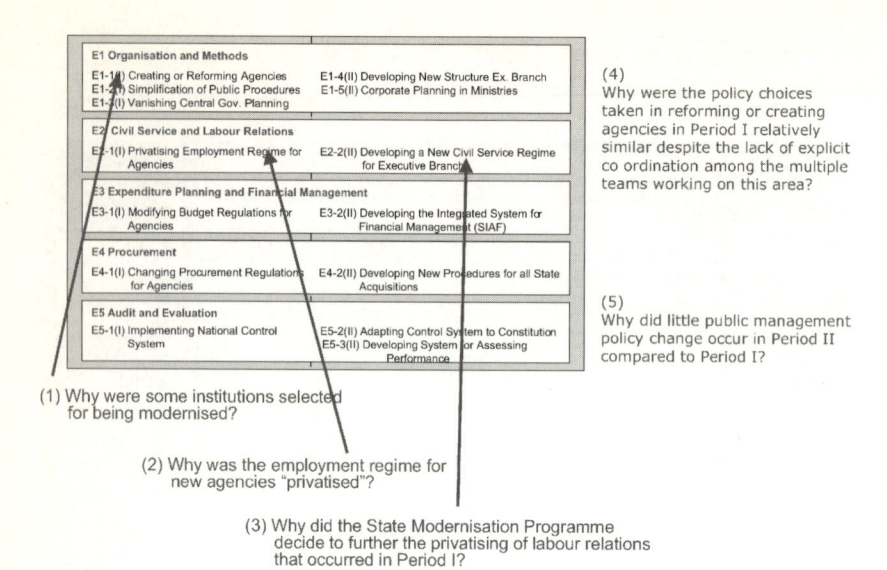

(3) Why did the State Modernisation Programme decide to further the privatising of labour relations that occurred in Period I?

Fig. 6. Generating Research Questions.

In this instance, the question asks for an explanation of differences between the outcomes of events in Period I (taken as a whole), on the one hand, an the outcome of events in Period II (taken as a whole), on the other. Specifically, the difference is conceived as the occurrence of significant public management policy choices in Period I and their absence in Period II.

However, considering event E2 outcomes we must recognize that in the first period important changes in the labor regulations were approved and implemented, while in the second period nothing really changed, as the Civil Service Bill proposed by the State Modernization Program was never approved. Thus, we need a question to pinpoint this difference and call for its explanation. Question 5 tried to do so, considering not only labor relations policies but all the public management policies in which changes occurred in period I.

It is important to take into account that the formulation of the research questions is not a linear process. In fact, we arrived to most of the questions presented trough a large number of different formulations, trying to take into account relevant outcomes and linkages among events. This required, as we will mention later, a continuous dialogue between the concerns that founded the questions and the outline of possible answers.

Following this procedure a vast set of research questions can be generated. Three general phases can be considered in this. The first phase is to identify the central questions that the research has to address. Five questions were identified as the core ones:

(A) Why did policy-making occur in the five areas of public management policies during the two periods?
(B) Why did the "state reform" issue maintain its presence in the governmental policy agenda between 1990 and 1997?
(C) Why did little public management policy change occur in Period II compared to Period I?
(D) Why were the policy choices taken in reforming or creating agencies in Period I relatively similar despite the lack of explicit coordination among the multiple teams working on this area?
(E) Why did the State Modernization Program produce changes in some Public Management Policy areas (Procurement) and not in others (Civil Service, Organization and Methods, etc.)?

Questions A, B, and C are related to the whole episode presented in Fig. 5. Thus, they are focused on the extent of public management changes and the presence of the State Reform issue in governmental agenda trough both periods. Question D, instead, is only referred to the events occurred in Period I, while Question E to those occurred in period II.

The second phase for generating the research questions was to organize all the secondary questions by means of relating them to one or more of the central questions. Figure 7 shows an example of how a central Question (E) served to organize several secondary and specific questions (the figure shows only three of a large number of secondary questions related to Question E). However, this is not

E. Why did the State Modernisation Programme produce changes in some public management policy areas (Procurement) but not in others (civil service, organisation and methods, etc.)?

E.1. Why was the State Modernisation Programme Created?

E.2. Why did the State Modernisation Programme have a negative assessment of the process that created agencies in Period I?

E.3. Why was the State Modernisation Programme aborted in the Cabinet?

E.1.1. Why did the Executive Branch ask the Congress for legislative powers for a comprehensive administrative reform?

E.1.2. Why was the SMP created eight months before the legislative powers were approved?

E.1.3. Why was the SMP created within central staff unit of the Cabinet of Ministers?

E.1.4. Why did the State Modernisation Programme ageda include all five areas of public management policy?

E.3.1. What facts originated the policy image of the State Reform issue as "minimal modernisation"?

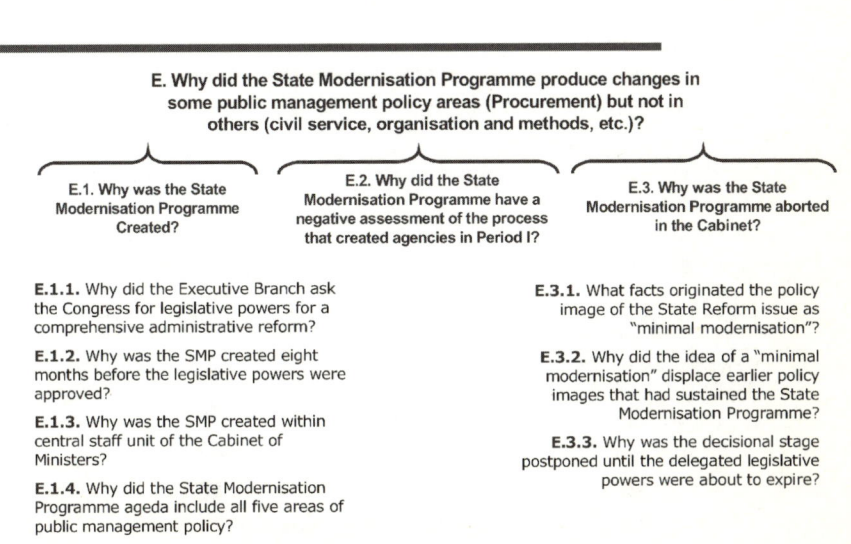

E.3.2. Why did the idea of a "minimal modernisation" displace earlier policy images that had sustained the State Modernisation Programme?

E.3.3. Why was the decisional stage postponed until the delegated legislative powers were about to expire?

Fig. 7. Organizing Secondary Questions.

a mechanical classification procedure. It required considering the possible answer to the questions and, by doing so, to identify which specific questions should be posed in order to provide relevant analysis for attaining adequate answers to the most important research questions.

In Fig. 7, for example, to answer the central Question (E) about why the State Modernization Program generated change in one public management area but not in others, requires examination of why the State Modernization Program was ultimately aborted by the President (Question E.3). But, for understanding why the program was terminated we must address Questions E.3.1, E.3.2 and E.3.3. Thus, generating adequate research questions involved establishing a dialogue between current questions and possible (provisional) answers.

Finally, the procedure reaches the stage of representing a body of questions, shown in Fig. 8. It is important to notice that not only the secondary questions are related to the principal ones (as shown in Fig. 7) but the central questions are also interrelated. Thus, Questions A, B and C – focused on the entire episode – are mutually connected and are also linked to Questions D and E – focused on each period.

Such a connection can be understood considering the process for generating answers to the research questions. In Fig. 8 the arrows indicate the direction this process has to follow. For answering Question B (comparing the extent of changes between period I and II), for example, we need to understand why did public management policy-making occur and why it affected all these policies (Question A). We also require understanding the progressive change of the policy image

(A) Why did policy-making occur in the five Public Management Policy areas during the two periods?

(B) Why did little public management policy change occur in Period II compared to Period I?

(C) Why did the "State Reform" maintain its presence in governmental agenda between 1990-97?

2 Specific Questions

2 Specific Questions

(D) Why were the policy choices taken in reforming or creating agencies in Period I relatively similar despite the lack of explicit co ordination among the multiple teams working on this area?

(E) Why did the State Modernisation Programme produced changes in some Public Management Policy areas (Procurement) but not in others (Civil Service, Organisation and Methods, etc.)?

12 Specific Questions

28 Specific Questions

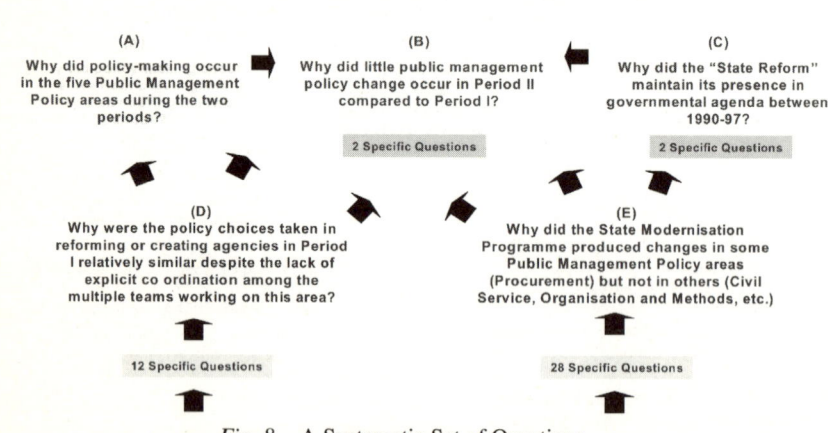

Fig. 8. A Systematic Set of Questions.

related to the State Reform issue (Question C). But, it is impossible to answer these three broad questions if we do not have previously a detailed account of what happened in Period I and Period II. This requires answering not only Questions D and E, but also all the specific questions related to them. Thus a systematic set of research questions as the one proposed above allows the researcher to interrelate the multiple answers he elaborates.

Selecting Explanatory Frameworks to Answer Research Questions

In order to answer research questions, theoretical frameworks for studying the policymaking process need to be applied to properly ordered case evidence. One example of a processual explanatory model of decision-making borrowed from political science is the multiple streams model of agenda setting and alternative specification of Kingdon (1984). See Fig. 9.

The Kingdon model is useful for several reasons. First, the career of an issue is an emergent phenomenon – a resultant of action – rather than action itself. It is therefore an attribute of the *process* to be understood. Second, an issue career is inherently dynamic, which draws attention to the temporal dimension of the policy-making process. Third, by explaining an issue's career, we can perceive the effects of many diverse influences leading to policy choices. However, Kingdon's model can usefully be complemented by other similar ones, including Baumgartner and Jones (1993).

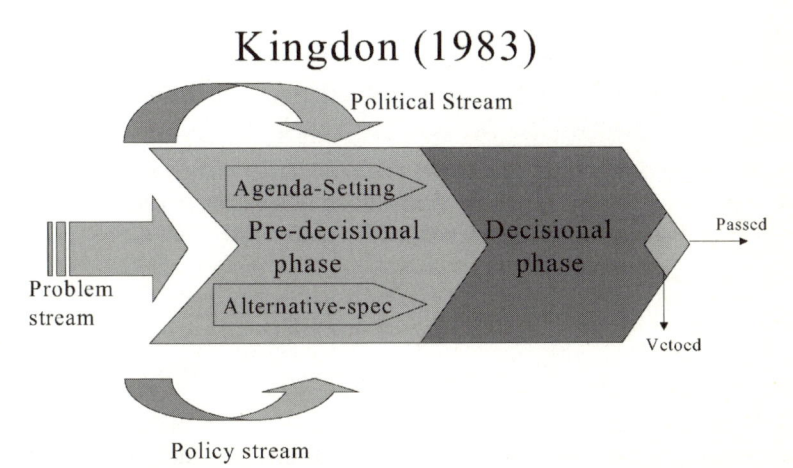

Fig. 9. Diagram of the Theoretical Framework Developed by Kingdon.

GATHERING CASE EVIDENCE

Identifying Sources

Applied research implies in gathering empirical evidence to support the analysis advanced by the reports. Researchers committed with the proposed methodology will need to make intensive use of interviews:

- Interviews help to get the facts straight, a central concern of an historic method.
- Interviews help to understand the dynamic of a policy process, including sequences of actions, changes in point of views, conflicts, and intermediate transient outcomes that will not be visible at the end of the process.
- Interviews contribute through the record of words to improve analytical descriptions of social phenomena and to fulfill blanks in an investigation. They are sense-making resources that help to provide a coherent account of what happened in the past.
- Interviews allow the researcher to get access to information stored at a personal level. Public management reforms are not usually well-documented experiences. They focus on gray areas of the public sector that do not beneficiate from the public exposure.
- Interviews are particularly suitable to refine descriptions of how and why situations evolved, although it is also useful to capture ideas, values, opinions and impressions of relevant protagonists.
- Interviews are not necessarily oriented to reveal subjective knowledge, in spite of their shortcomings. They can provide objective data as well as to indicate other hidden sources of neglected information.
- Interviews are appropriate to induce protagonists to retrieve past experiences from their memories in the search of discrepancies and holes in previously available descriptions.

Interviewing is especially critical in this research program because the bibliography of public management reforms in Latin America is unstructured, frequently insufficient, laudatory, superficial, and judgmental.

Preparing Interview Protocols

Interview protocols are a requirement for good interviews. The main reason is because they provide a systematized structure of the main questions that interviewers want to address. Putting them in writing is a prudent form of keeping the focus on the relevant research questions in order to avoid a diffuse interview.

There are at least five good cautions to be taken into account for elaborating an interview protocol.

- Interview protocols are primarily important to guarantee coherence between the interviewee answers and the research questions.
- Interviews need to be planned in advance. The researcher needs to know before what he is looking for, even if letting some room for the emergence of new questions.
- Interviews need to be managed. They do not flow naturally or if they do so they are not necessarily productive.
- Interview protocols provide guidance but also provide basis for comparability. The same questions addressed to different people facilitate triangulation and comparative deductions.
- Interview protocols minimize the sources of unreliability in the interviewing process: the interviewer, the person interviewed, and the chemistry of the relationship between them.

Interviewees should be selected on the basis of their potential contributions to answer the research questions. By the same token, interview protocols need to contain questions specifically oriented to answer the research questions. Respondents need to be questioned about how and why things turned out the way they did. Respondents need to be interrogated carefully about what accounts for the initiation, dynamics, and termination of key events of the episode. They can also explain the progression of the issue within the event as well as the occurrence of intermediate and final outcomes. In the absence of a reliable literature, they provide the most important source of evidence available.

Interview protocols can – and should – be modified along the way as part of a continuous dialogue between ideas and evidence. Intermediate findings eventually provoke re-orientations of angles and priorities. Therefore, interview protocols are inherently provisional tools, subject to change even at the moment of the interviews, depending on the dynamic of the meeting.

ANALYZING CASE EVIDENCE AND PREPARING TO WRITE

Analyzing the Events

The role of theory is to make sense of the process by which the case outcome happened. Explaining what led to an outcome is different from identifying factors *associated* with the outcome. Theory can illuminate the causal process that was at work in a case. Theoretically informed intra and cross event analysis of an experience is the key intermediate input to formulating causal explanations of cases outcomes. Intra-event analysis concentrates on how individual events progressed; cross-event analysis concentrates on analyzing how individual events were influenced by others within the larger experience. Explaining case outcomes within the research program on public management policy change requires a mix of intra-event and cross-event analysis, as previously mentioned.

Providing an Example of Event Analysis: The Brazilian 1967 Episode

In order to demonstrate how to proceed to analyze an event we will check at one example from a Brazilian episode, included in a dissertation in progress (Gaetani). The case selected refers to an episode that occurred between 1964 and 1967, when important public management policy changes took place. One influential package of public management reforms occurred at the sunset of the first military government of "authoritarian Brazil." It was a very turbulent period as we can observe in Fig. 10 (Gaetani, 2002).

Let us peruse an overview of the events that occurred during the episode beginning with the contemporaneous events. The coup d'etat (CE1-1) occurred at the beginning of 1964 and it was supposed to be a quick intervention in order to preserve democracy. A few months later the mandate of Castelo Branco was extended for one more year (CE1-2), until March 1967. Meanwhile Roberto Campos, the new Minister of Planning, institutionalized planning activities through several initiatives: the creation of the Ministry (CE2-1), the creation of a research governmental institute (RE-1), the launch of macro economic stabilization (CE2-2), the creation of National Council of Planning (CE2-3), and the elaboration of development plans (CE2-4). There was an administrative reform policy proposal available that had been sent to the Congress some months before (PE-4). The new president, who had participated in the previous initiative, decided to give the highest possible status to the treatment of the issue: the creation of a High Level Commission (E1-1) to review the available proposal. The importance the president attributed to the problem could be measured by the selection of participants in this commission (E1-2): the best cadre available at that times, ascendant figures of the new regime, and top governmental officials. It was established that the president of the Commission should be a well-known public administration champion, Beltrao, and the executive secretary, Dias, a technocrat that represented Campos because the Commission was located at the Ministry of Planning. There were not explicit decision mechanisms at the commission because the government expected that decisions through consensus would naturally emerge from the engagement of the selected experts in the field.

Brazilian 1967 Public Management Reform Episode

PE1 Governing Brazil	CE1 Implementing the Authoritarian Regime Coup- Extension of mandate Coup – Constitution		LE1 Consolidating Regime Change
	CE2 Institutionalizing Planning New Ministry - New Plan	Council- Ten Years Plan	
PE2 Generating the Military Project	E1-1 Assembling the reform machinary	E3-2 Resuming the issue	LE2 Consolidating Planning Policy Sub-system
		E1-2 Reformulating the reform machinary	
PE3 Attempting to institutionalize planning	E2-1 Generating policy alternatives	E2-2 Generating new policy proposal	
	E3-1 Frustrated Decision-Making	E3-3 Final Decision Making Process	LE3 Implementing Public Management Policy Change
PE4 Generating Admininstrative Reform Proposal	RE1 Creating a technical basis of planning experts	RE2 Submitting the proposal to international experts	
Period I 63	Period II 64-65	Period III 66-67	Period IV 67-69

Fig. 10. Brazilian 1967 Episode. *Source:* Authors (2002).

The event we will further explain as an example of how to precede to event analysis is the incapacity of this commission (COMESTRA) generating a policy proposal (E3-1), an impasse that took place after Beltrao took over the activities of the commission at the expense of Dias alienation. That event came as a surprise by all means. How did it happen? Why couldn't they achieve a consensus? Why didn't Campos stick with Beltrao's final proposal? What explains the impasse?

Part of the explanation can be found through a cross event analysis, at the previous event: generating policy proposals (E1-2). Beltrao and Dias successfully defeated the idea of resuming the proposal available at the Congress. That proposal was championed by the legendary Simoes Lopes and by the technocrats located at the once powerful central agency located at the presidency (the Department of Administration and Civil Service – DASP). However if they agreed about that common enemy, both did not share the same vision about the problems to be tacked and the way of doing it.

The impasse at E1-3 was derived from a clash of problem definition, in Kingdon's terms. An intra-event analysis revealed that while Beltrao defined the issue of the reform as de-bureaucratization, Dias was more concerned with public management problems. While the former suggested that the reform proposal should be resumed to a group of principles and general objectives, the latter was determined to detail specific measures and instruments related to all public management policies.

COMESTRA did not have decisional mechanisms capable of overcoming a conflict between its leading figures (E1-2). Beltrao was a public champion and an ascendant figure of the new regime. Dias was a key advisor of Campos and an experienced technocrat. When, finally, Beltrao's view prevailed, the Commission was not functional anymore. Dias had distanced himself from the process and the disputes over the control of the commission had undermined its credibility within the government.

Meanwhile, turbulence in the political stream had completely absorbed Castelo Branco and Roberto Campos attention. While the latter was facing the problems derived from a recessive economic policy, the president faced hardliners' reaction against the victory of opposition candidates in two key states at the governors' election of 1965 (CE1-3). The radicalization of the regime marked a compromise between the incumbent cabinet, dominated by the "Sorbonne" group, and the military hardliners. The leadership succession was solved at that moment with the unstoppable choice of Costa e Silva, the Minister of War, to become the successor president, almost fifteen months before the end of the Castelo Branco mandate.

The stabilization of the political stream (CE1-3) allowed Roberto Campos to resume the issue (E3-2) through a subtle solution: the creation of an advisory unit under his jurisdiction: *Assessoria de Estudos Tecnicos para a Reforma Administrativa* (ASESTRA). A new policy venue was created but centralized in only one person: Dias, his advisor E1-1 and E1-2 (period III). Dias had assembled public management policy solutions for areas like planning, civil service, auditing, financial expenditure, control, and procurement. But, moreover, Dias had provided a public management package of solutions consistent with Campos's broader objectives: creating the required conditions for the taking off of the developmental state. Dias proposal was instrumental to Campos's vision in a way that Beltrao's ideas could never be.

In short, to analyze E3-1 we had to dissect the event and its internal dynamics as well as to execute a cross event analysis in order to understand aspects of the problem located at other events "upstream" and "downstream," within the episode or at the level of contemporaneous events.

CONCLUSIONS

This guide has attracted attention among researchers setting out to conduct case studies about topics related to both policy and management change. Such interest indicates that well-established sources of advice on case study research design may not provide sufficient guidance on how to conduct research on such topics. One source of the problem is that prominent exponents of case study methods, such as Yin (1994), have played down commonalities between instrumental case studies on processes and narrative history. A particular contribution of the approach presented here is to provide *practical* methods for ordering and interpreting case evidence, once the similarities and differences between case studies on types of processes and narrative history are noted.

These analytical procedures include developing narrative structures and keying Type B research questions to events within the episode. Process theories, like Kingdon's analysis of policy change, are employed to structure a narrative explanation of the outcomes of analytically significant events within the episodes, lying at the center of the respective cases. The systematic use of process theories ensures that the analysis of case evidence is highly germane to the crafting of limited historical generalizations about types of social processes, like public policy and management change. This chapter has not examined all of the important issues of research design for instrumental case studies on types of processes, but does provide a base on which to build.

NOTES

1. Public management policies do not include ministries (departmental) or agency specific change processes.

2. An example of an institutional rule is one stipulating that an appointing official must choose among three candidates put forward by the personnel department (the so-called "rule of three"). An example of routines is the methods used by auditing bodies to conduct performance audits of program agencies.

3. Ragin (1987, p. 31) conceptualized limited historical generalizations as "modest empirical generalizations about historically-defined categories of social phenomena."

ACKNOWLEDGMENTS

We are deeply grateful to Dr Koldo Echebarria, Principal Public Sector Management Specialist at the Inter-American Development Bank, for commissioning this chapter as part of his office's technical support for the IADB Regional Dialogue on Management and Transparency. We also appreciate comments by Evelyn Levy, who presided over the Regional Dialogue while Secretary of Management within the Brazil Ministry of Planning, Budgeting, and Management.

REFERENCES

Aucoin, P. (1995). *The new public management: Canada in comparative perspective.* Montreal: IRPP.

Barzelay, M. (2001). *The new public management: Improving research and policy dialogue.* Berkeley: University of California Press.

Barzelay, M. (2002, November 14). Designing the process of public management policy change: Practical implications of case studies on Brazil and Peru. Chapter presented at the Regional Dialogue on Management and Transparency, Inter-American Development Bank, Washington, DC.

Baumgartner, F., & Jones, B. C. (1993). *Agendas and instability in American politics.* Chicago: University of Chicago Press.

Cejudo, G. (2001). *Public management policy change in Mexico.* MSc dissertation, Interdisciplinary Institute of Management, London School of Economics.

Cortázar, V., & Carlos, J. (2002, November). La reforma de la administración pública Peruana (1990–1997): Conflicto y estrategias divergentes en la elaboración de políticas. Chapter presented at the Regional Dialogue on Management and Transparency, Inter-American Development Bank, Washington, DC.

Gaetani, F. (2002, November 14). The Brazilian managerial reform of the state apparatus: The 1995–1998 policy cycle. Chapter presented at the Regional Dialogue on Management and Transparency, Inter-American Development Bank, Washington, DC.

Kingdon, J. (1983). *Agendas, alternatives, and public policies.* Boston: Little Brown.

Ragin, C. C. (1987). *The comparative method.* Berkeley: University of California Press.

Yin, R. K. (1994). *Case study research: Design and methods* (2nd ed.). Thousand Oaks, CA: Sage.

15. DEVELOPING PERFORMANCE INDICATORS AND MEASUREMENT SYSTEMS IN PUBLIC INSTITUTIONS

Kuno Schedler

INTRODUCTION

Performance measurement is a technique that has evolved in the European area only in recent times. Demands made on available information have changed primarily in line with the efforts to instill more management into the public sector (Buschor & Schedler, 1994). Whereas traditional administration has focused primarily on the financing of tasks, the question of efficient and effective performance has assumed more importance today. Performance measurement systems are a response to new requirements of decision making bodies.

This chapter is based on directions for action established in the course on consultancy and knowledge transfer projects at the Institute for Public Services and Tourism at the University of St. Gallen, and on the textbook on the subject by Schedler and Proeller (2000). The chapter examines the question as to how performance measurement systems can be developed in such a way that they will be able to furnish the correct information. Correct means as much as appropriate and relevant to a particular decision-making situation. The structure of the individual elements of performance measurement are outlined and explained on the basis of some practical examples. It is our intention to provide practitioners with directions that have as concrete a bearing as possible on the establishment of their own performance management systems. We do so mainly on the basis of experience gained in specific practical projects in Germany, Austria, and Switzerland.

PUBLIC MANAGEMENT AND PERFORMANCE MEASUREMENT

In recent decades, public administrations led largely through legislation and the allocation of resources. Administrations did not have to provide any clearly defined services but had to fulfil their tasks in compliance with the law and a detailed input budget. Thus it was accounting which furnished senior staff with the necessary, albeit rudimentary "controlling" information until in the early 1990s, New Public Management – which in Switzerland and Austria is known as Results-Oriented Public Management (Wirkungsorientierte Verwaltungsführung, WoV) and in Germany as the New Controlling Model (Neues Steuerungsmodell, NSM) – redirected the focus of administration management on effects and performance (Mäder & Schedler, 1994, p. 345).

The situation in the United States is different. Since the late 1940s, academics and practitioners have tried to develop management systems for the public sector based on performance measurement and performance control.

PERFORMANCE MEASUREMENT WITHIN NEW PUBLIC MANAGEMENT

Pioneers of New Public Management such as Dunlevay and Hood (1994, p. 9.9) attributed a great deal of importance to performance control on the basis of a well-developed performance measurement system. The Swiss model of NPM, Results-Oriented Public Management, adopted this approach and refined it into a controlling process which is cognitively divided up into four different levels of performance (Fig. 1). Outcome control plays a crucial role in Results-Oriented Public Management and calls for the measurement of effects and performance as a necessary element, thus making performance measurement an indispensable instrument for both political and public management.

When the target figures are planned, it is assumed that certain *political objectives* are defined in the state on the basis of *needs and values* of various groups of customers and people who are directly affected. These aims lead to a *product plan* that ideally enables the relevant people to reach the aims in question. When the product plan has been drawn up, then cost and result accounting will

Planned measures	Real measures	
Needs / Values	Real Impact	Benefit Accounting
Objectives	Real Outcomes	Outcome Accounting
Product Plan	Real Outputs	Output Accounting
Resources Plan	Consumption of Resources	Cost Accounting

Administrative Performance

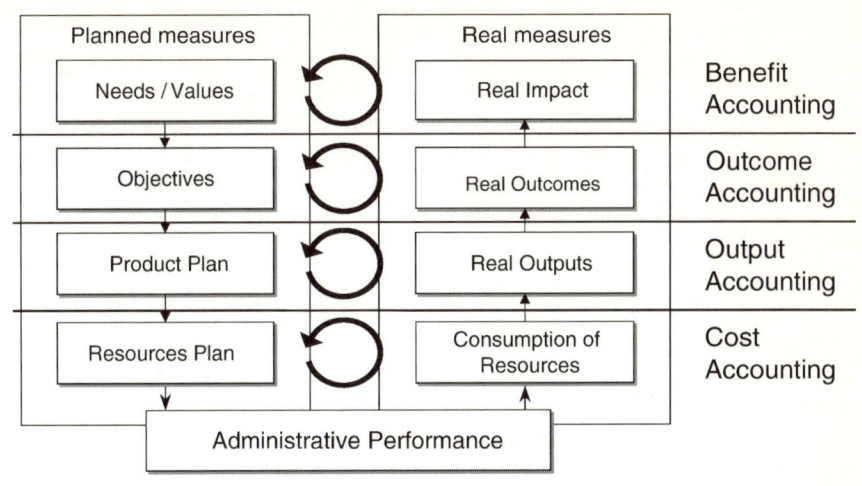

Fig. 1. The Controlling Levels of NPM with the Concomitant Accounts. *Source:* Schedler (1996).

serve to compute a *resources plan*, which should be sufficient for the production of the planned products; if the performance involved is of appropriate efficiency.

The performance achieved by the administration results in a *consumption of resources* that can and should be compared with the resources plan. The products that have actually been produced are the *real outputs* of this process, which as a rule is measured in quantitative terms, for instance as the number of products, and in terms of compliance with the set quality standards. As an example, a product called Road Snow Clearance might result in an output whereby x kilometers of first-class roads were cleared of snow on y days, with z percent of the roads being free of snow within 4 hours.

Products are often combined into a program whose outcome on the environment in general or on the environment of the administration can be determined and compared with the political aims. The outcome of Road Snow Clearance might be a decrease in traffic accidents, in the delays of public transport, or in road damage later detected in the spring.

The addressees of administrative performance, i.e. customers, experience such programs and their results against the backdrop of their needs and values. The *impact* of such programs can therefore differ from the outcome, which is easier to objectify. Particularly the latter two values – outcome and impact – are hardly recorded and distinguished between in practice but are of great importance as far as the general public's satisfaction with public administration is concerned.

The four levels of the political and administrative controlling process may be assigned to individual accounts (Fig. 1). In practical working life, this separation is apt to present problems; the levels often overlap so that the cost, output, the boundaries between result and benefit accounts become blurred. However, this concept is capable of representing the major elements of NPM performance measurement by way of a simplifying diagram.

Cost Accounting

Cost accounting is located on the resources level of the controlling process. It indicates the costs that the use of resources cause for every cost group and cost center, and how these costs are distributed. Yet even the most refined cost account is not capable of furnishing any essential management information unless it is used for the creation of historical, horizontal and vertical comparisons. However, valid comparisons can only be made with the help of a standard definition of cost units. For this reason, it is necessary to include a further level above and beyond the mere consideration of resources: the output level.

Output Accounting

At the second level of the controlling process, the output of the administration is described in terms of products, whose production is then recorded. Output accounting enables us to register the products throughout the administration, at least quantitatively, and to subject these data to a systematic evaluation. Thanks to the linkage between cost and output accounting, it can be worked out, for instance, what costs one particular product causes in comparison to another – a piece of information lacking in politics before.

Outcome Accounting

Outcome accounting registers the results of administrative activity, i.e. of the programs, and relates them to the political objectives that have been pursued with these programs. It provides information about the overall results created by the programs, including unintended side effects. The prerequisite for any expressive information with regard to outcome accounting is the existence of clear-cut objectives. Wherever results cannot be measured with the help of indicators, the methods of outcome accounting are frequently related to evaluation.

Benefit Accounting

Benefit accounting is the most interesting but also the most complex account in this system. It expresses the results of administrative action in the way in which the latter is subjectively apprehended by its addressees. Customer requirements serve as reference values here, and these are often as difficult to measure exactly as are the results themselves. Surveys conducted among the population and among customers serve as an aid in this context; through question focusing on satisfaction, they generate propositions about the relationship between the two blurred values that, in turn, can be compiled into quite reliable results.

In practice, it is revealed time and again that the qualitative differences of performance measures at the different levels of the controlling process are underestimated. The following nexus applies:

- The more closely a measured value is to the performance process proper, the more readily it can be recorded. Example: cost-and-output data can be measured routinely at justifiable expense.
- The further distant a measured value is from the performance process, the greater its interest and political importance. Example: the impact that a program to fight crime has on the population is considerably more interesting than the detailed description of the resources used for it.

The combination of these two propositions results in a trade-off of political controlling: here, we have data that are easy to measure but of little interest, and there, we have data that are interesting but can hardly be measured. Somewhere in between, there is the ideal level on which information can be recorded that can be reliably assessed and is of appropriate interest. Experience shows that a mixture of output and result data works best – or to put it differently, we often keep an eye on the outcome level and judge the output with regard to the intended results.

ACTIVITIES, OUTPUT AND RESULTS

Administrative activity cannot be directly compared with a service company. Even so, certain outputs are created in processes in public administration, too. In the terminology of Results-Oriented Public Management, the following connections apply as shown in Fig. 2.

The actual aim of administrative activity consists in the causation of certain results. Results-Oriented Public Management turns these results into the main object of political and administrative controlling by consistently asking for the results of each particular measure.

By means of a great number of usually internal *activities*, ⇨	an administration creates direct *outputs* for the benefit of its recipients ⇨	that trigger off indirect *results* among the recipients of these outputs or in their environment.
Activities are the daily actions in an administration which are not provided for third parties.	Output is the direct consequence of a bundle of activities; it is visible to third parties. As a rule, it is combined into products, which in turn serve as the basis for performance agreements, cost accounting, etc.	Results are the indirect consequence of the provision of one or several outputs by an administration.
Examples: ➢ Work on an appeal against the refusal of planning permission ➢ Work on reconstruction plan ➢ Procurement of teaching materials ➢ Preliminary examination of a patient ➢ Investigations in the environment of a social security case	Examples: ➢ Decision regarding the planning permission appeal ➢ Reconstruction of a road with regard to noise emissions ➢ Lesson given in class ➢ Therapy conducted in hospital ➢ Agreement reached with a social security case	Examples: ➢ The safety inside the building has been guaranteed ➢ Reduction of noise immission ➢ Success of a class in a test ➢ Recovery, change in the quality of life ➢ Reintegration, regular lifestyle

Fig. 2. Results-Oriented Public Management Connections. *Note:* Reading aid: Read top row from left to right. The boxes below serve as explanations for the top row and then list relevant examples. *Source:* Author (2002).

Results are the most interesting but at the same time the most elusive object of political controlling and public management. Many results can only be discerned after a great lapse of time. Moreover, the direct nexus between output and results is interfered with by environmental influences. Results-Oriented Public Management nonetheless systematically looks for suitable possibilities of sensibly integrating output and results into political issues. At the same time, however, the determination of the necessary activities should be left to the administration itself – always within the limits of legal provisions.

PRODUCTS

To register all government activities from the point of view of the state's customers, Results-Oriented Public Management avails itself of the *auxiliary construct* of the product. A product is the smallest independent output unit that provides its recipient with a benefit. Independent means that no additional output is necessary to achieve the desired benefit (e.g. waste disposal).

As a rule, products are combinations of several (partial) outputs that leave an organizational unit. They constitute the object of the performance agreement reached with an office. Since products are very detailed units, they are again combined into product groups, and these, in turn, into areas of responsibility. Thus the entire output of a state is ultimately represented as a number of areas of responsibility.

The new instruments, which are based on the product, serve to pursue a variety of objectives:

- citizens can be provided with information about the value for money they receive from the state;
- money flows can be recognized and controlled, and effectiveness and efficiency can be measured and rated;
- the controlling possibilities of political instances can be qualitatively improved, which in turn means that new scopes of action can be created for parliament and government and public management;
- the boundaries of the responsibilities of parliament and government, public management and administrative units can be clearly defined;
- Complete information can be furnished in time for strategic and operative planning in order to be able to respond to divergences at once.

Thus a product has four characteristics which can be used for its definition:

(1) It is made or refined in an output center, or a performance center is responsible for its provision or refinement in the sense of an office that is in charge.

(2) It satisfies the requirements of third parties (customers), i.e. the output center does not produce the output as an end in itself; rather, it creates a benefit for its customers.
(3) It is handed over to third parties; i.e. it leaves the output center.
(4) It is suitable for use as an auxiliary value for controlling purposes in a political and administrative system.

In practice, a distinction is made between internal and external products. Internal products are provided for customers inside the administration (but outside one's own administrative unit), whereas external products leave the administrative domain. A few consequences can be deduced from the four product characteristics.

Product Definition as a Process

Product definition is a strategic process to which administrations and politics are unaccustomed. For this reason, it is particularly important that this process is accompanied by an external consultant but is basically undergone by the people involved themselves. First, they know their areas of responsibility best, and second, product definition requires precisely that reorientation of thought that is the point of NPM as a whole. Moreover, an attempt should be made whenever possible to involve politicians in this product definition process. In this way, the situation whereby an administration resorts to a purely administrative rationality to create the basis on which political debates should be conducted can be avoided.

In a *pragmatic product definition*, the situation as it is serves as a basis for those involved to picture present output as clad in the mantle of the new controlling elements. Products, objectives and indicators are virtually indivisibly interconnected. At the same time, it is indispensable that participants in the definition process always bear in mind the desired result of this area of responsibility, i.e. the situation as it should be. Although the definition below may give the impression that this process can be systematized, a note of warning must be sounded against false expectations: only constant feedback, combined with improvement and learning processes, will lead to a product range capable of meeting exacting demands.

A product is defined in several cognitive steps:

(1) To begin with, the team asks itself the question as to who the customers of this particular institution are. This analysis will provide the basis that enables the team to alternate between an internal and an external view of things.
(2) Then, the team determines where the relevant organizational boundary is located, i.e. where an output "leaves its own administrative unit." In general, it is the entity that is subject to the performance contract in question.

(3) Subsequently, the team analyses contacts with third parties and records the output that these customers receive from their own administrative unit.
(4) Finally, the various outputs are bundled in such a way that they satisfy the demands made on a product as a measure for political control.

When these initial preparatory steps have been taken, the product definitions they have yielded must be subjected to a test. The most important questions in this respect are:

- Do the defined products create an independent benefit? (In particular, do we not have excessively detailed activities as products?) This question is predominantly asked by the service recipients, i.e. the customer point of view.
- Can the office's activities be sensibly controlled through the defined products; i.e. does a performance agreement for the office make sense on the basis of these products? The controllability question must primarily be asked against the background of a political perspective.

If these two questions do not yield satisfactory answers, the way in which the products are bundled must be discussed once more. There is no scientifically correct "flying altitude" for this process; rather, it is a matter of weighing things up, of applying tact and sensitivity as to the extent to which a condensation should take place.

Experience shows that it is easier to start with the definition of product groups before individual products are tackled. These groups can also be defined in

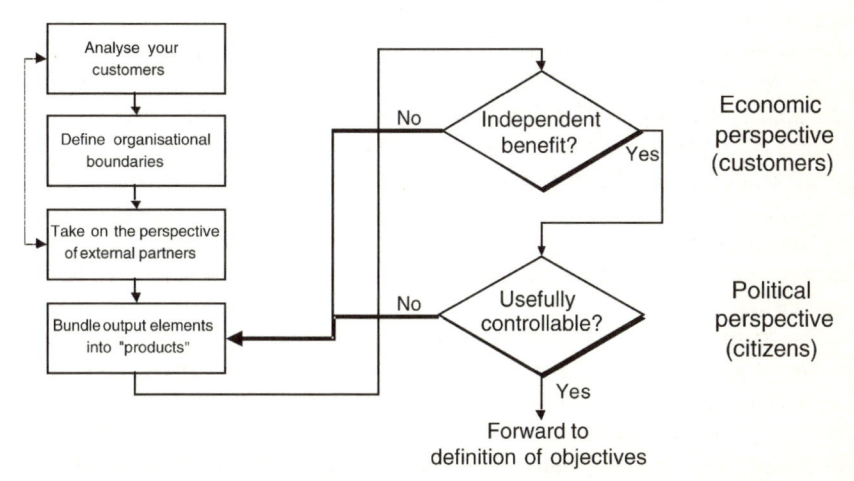

Fig. 3. How to Define Good Products? *Source:* Schedler and Proeller (2000).

terms of programs and are often closely connected with the organization of an administrative unit. Then, in a second step, the product groups can be subdivided into individual products. Finally, objectives and indicators can be defined for each product group and subsequently for each individual product (Fig. 3).

DEFINITION OF OBJECTIVES

The process of setting objectives in public administration has repeatedly been described as extremely difficult because the goal structures are "decisively more diffuse, more multi-dimensional, and heterogeneously controlled by interest groups" (Buschor, 1992, p. 210). It may well be for this reason that clear objectives are not set in all areas by any means, so that the administration depends on its own precepts. Administrative activities, however, which are not objective-oriented can easily become *ineffective*. This is why two different types of objective groups must be established for each product: the *generic factual objective (results-oriented objective) and the concrete (operative) objectives which must be pursued for this purpose* during the particular period under observation.

Where objectives exist (e.g. the reduction of the crime rate for a given city by *xy* percent), they are quite frequently measured even today. This also applies vice versa: where objectives are easy to measure they are regularly set even today. Consequentially, concrete objectives are often lacking in areas that are more difficult to measure, which means that their achievement is not measured and thus also not reviewed. Such areas are then declared to be *de facto* taboo zones for any result orientation. However, the results of an activity are among the most important success factors of both *output* and *intervention* management and must be consistently recorded even though this is not always easy. In this context, the *registration of output* is assigned a great deal of significance (Congressional Budget Office, 1993, p. 4). After all, it must be found out with regard to every project whether the efforts made by the administration really cover and satisfy its customers' actual requirements. This is based on the assumption that the administration is aware of these requirements, from which they infer what has to be done; this, in turn, provides the basis for the political decision of setting certain objectives for the administration.

The traditionally input-oriented view taken in administration is particularly persistent and disruptive in the process of objective definition. Even experienced consultants must always remind themselves that the object of the definition of objectives is not the resources or the question as to how an output is provided, but the concrete results of the endeavor. In this context, the following questions must be asked:

- For results-oriented objectives:
    What is the purpose of an activity?
    What is meant to be achieved in the long term with the creation of this product?
    What developments should be aimed at?
- For output-oriented objectives:
    What is supposed to be achieved in the period under observation?
    What quality standards are aimed at in the period under observation?
    What dimension of efficiency should be achieved in the period under observation?
    How many products are going to be delivered?

The differences in the two approaches to objective definition are evident. Although the definition of results-oriented objectives may occasionally present considerable difficulties, great weight must still be placed on a correct result. As will have to be shown later, these objectives are the basis for the creation of output indicators, which serve to register the success of the output provider and to control the contract.

Objectives are defined in an iterative process that again and again absorbs outside information and compares individual steps with previous results (Fig. 4). The process can be structured according to the following grid:

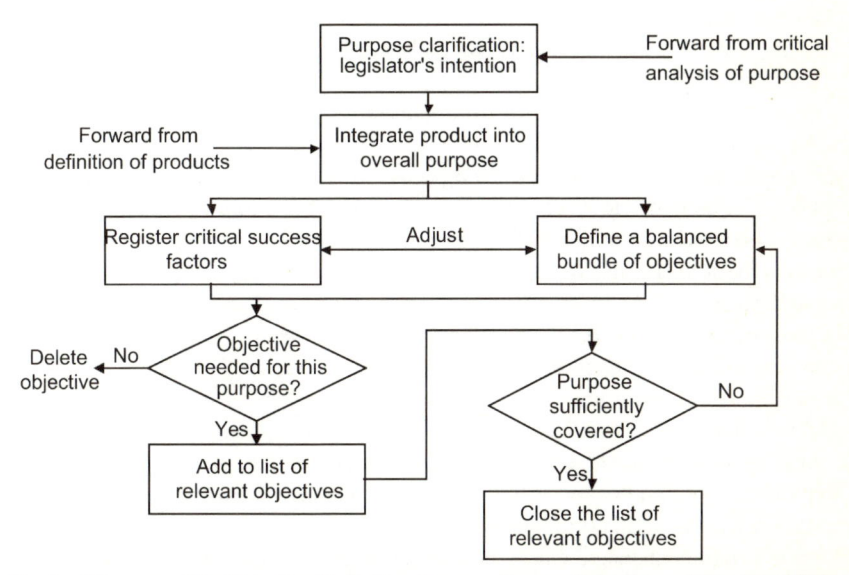

Fig. 4. Diagram of the Objective Definition Process. *Source:* Schedler and Proeller (2000).

(1) To establish the purpose of one's own activity ("mission statement"), reference can be made to the legislator's intention that is pursued with the task in hand. Many administrations can refer to the results written down in the criticism of the task (i.e. criticism of the purpose).
(2) The products defined in the product definition process are now viewed in connection with the overall purpose. What contributions will the products make towards the satisfaction of the purpose?
(3) Critical success factors are output elements that it is imperative to fulfil for the purpose to be attained. These critical success factors must be taken into consideration in order to define a first bundle of objectives.
(4) The bundle of objectives is checked for two questions: (a) is it necessary, i.e. can the objective not be attained unless each individual objective is attained? (b) Is it sufficient, i.e. has the purpose really been attained once all the individual objectives have been attained?
(5) The catalogue of objectives may be regarded as complete if the bundle of objectives satisfies these two conditions.

The definition of objectives also involves the establishment of the order of priorities. In the past, this has been done with a variety of methods, not all of which have subsequently been used in practice.

INDICATORS AND STANDARDS

Indicators

To check whether objectives are being pursued, administrative output and results must be measured and rated. In many cases, however, this is not simple; often, there is no sensible solution to this problem. In such cases, Result-Oriented Public Management makes use of an aid: *indicators*.

Indicators provide information about the state or development of part of an administrative output. As a rule, they are not sufficient to furnish a basis for a conclusive assessment. Indicators can often only point to a certain development. It is imperative that they are interpreted and placed in an overall context. One single indicator does not say anything about the actual quality of an administrative output. Indicators must be devised in such a way that they allow for comparisons between actual and desired values, since the analysis of divergences can serve to initiate a learning and correction process.

Good public management is not safeguarded or replaced by indicators. As always, it is the people in administration and politics who are responsible for

Developing Performance Indicators and Measurement Systems 383

success or failure. Yet in the same way that a pilot is in control of an aircraft, and would lose all bearings without instruments, so government and public management should base their decisions on the indicators in their own "cockpit," albeit not exclusively. Adjusted to a different level, this also applies to parliament.

Indicators that are noted frequently in the public sector include:

- the frequency of accidents as an indicator of safety on a certain road;
- the results of surveys among companies as an indicator of the reputation of a university in the economy and, in turn, as an indicator of the quality of its training;
- the average profitability of government investments in comparison to a reference profitability rate as an indicator of the quality of financial administration investment policies;
- the number of newly created jobs in innovative technology areas as an indicator of the success of Swiss cantonal promotion of trade and industry;
- The number of people returning to hospital subsequent to previous hospitalization as an indicator of the quality of hospital output.

These examples make clear that the formulation of good indicators is a tricky undertaking. Even with a suitable mixture of indicators, expert judgement remains the be-all and end-all of Results-Oriented Public Management.

Standards

If an output or result is assigned a target that is unlimited in duration and generally valid, then this is called a *standard*. Results-Oriented Public Management uses standards in order to make the expected quality clear to both customers and the administration itself. Standards often give a somewhat technical impression; however, a good mixture of suitable standards tends to describe an administrative output quite well.

Examples of standards include:

- maximum throughput times (known already as time limits placed on certain procedures);
- the limit of tolerance regarding delays of public transport;
- the response time of police, ambulance and fire service;
- The number of contacts with the administration within a certain proceeding.

Standards are very suitable for processes which can be organized routinely. They reach their limits if the processes that have to come into play are very different from each other. As a rule, however, their scope of applications is considerably wider than one tends to assume. In the UK, where so-called "charters" described people's legitimate claims on the quality of public output, these standards were capable of reinforcing customers' consciousness of their own position; however, they only yielded results in the sense of quality improvement where they also helped to establish a customer-oriented administrative culture. Once again it was revealed that new instruments must always be combined with strong leadership; if they are not, they will remain mere tools in reports, and will become bureaucratized (i.e. typically not used).

There is a logical connection between indicators and standards, which can be put to good use: sometimes, indicators deliberately refer to compliance with standards instead of average measures to ensure that very occasional mishaps will not falsify the overall result. This applies to time limits, in particular, such as in the following indicator for the fire service: In how many percent of the cases was the response time of ten minutes met?

Thus, the standard is the response time of ten minutes, and the indicator of the service's compliance with the standard. If the response time were registered as a mean value, a single mishap would result in a poor overall picture.

INSTALLING THE PERFORMANCE CONTROL SYSTEM

When the objectives, indicators and standards have been defined for each product, then this information must be integrated into the management process. In this context, it is helpful to proceed in circular processes, for only in this manner can corrections be made in time and the system thus is kept relevant to decision-making. Any information system whose results are not regularly used by the decision-making bodies will become a shambles and therefore lose its significance. At some stage, the cost/benefit ratio of such systems goes askew, and their value is basically suspect. This need not be the case, however: the use and maintenance of control systems is a management task that can be delegated only up to a certain point.

In a narrower circuit, products and objectives are first harmonized, with the desired result always firmly remaining center-stage. Once this has been done, the method of critical success factors can be used to define the indicators. Then, the data arising out of this are recorded and assessed. They can be tested for their suitability for the control of the political and administrative system by being fed into decision-making situations as processed information. This learning stage is eminently important since it is on the basis of such processes that the system of objectives and indicators is refined and/or adapted to new requirements (Fig. 5).

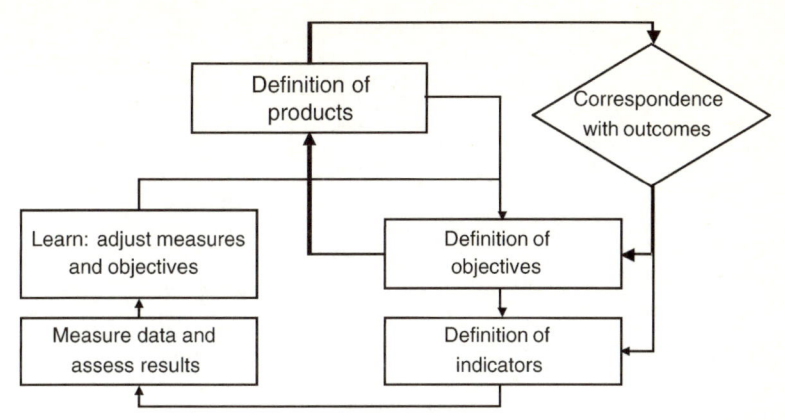

Fig. 5. The Circuit of Establishing and Maintaining Control Systems. *Source:* Schedler and Proeller (2000).

To learn from American experience, we must clarify the following correlation with a view to the design of performance measurement systems: politics and management constitute two worlds with their own cognitive patterns, terminology, and sanction and reward mechanisms. This creates rationalities of thought and action that are different for politics and management. Something that is politically rational may strike management as irrational. Management makes decisions based on facts as understood while politics depends on voting majorities. Majorities, in turn, are often the result of complex negotiation processes in which acceptance and rejection are bartered in relation to things that are frequently only tenuously connected. Politics and management are often equally objective-oriented; the ways they choose to reach the objectives, as well as the coherence of the objectives, may be fundamentally different.

Figure 6 makes clear that in the NPM model, different decision-making circuits apply to parliament, the government and administration; ideally, they interlock. At the same time, this separation of role assigns an area of responsibility to individual players, which ultimately delimits their system of objectives and thus the relevant performance measurement level. However, a so-called "translation function" is necessary: political precepts must be divided up into precepts that are relevant to management and, conversely, the result of administrative production must be ordered according to political aspects.

One example of typical NPM as executed by parliament is the control of secondary education in the Swiss Canton of Zurich. Parliament approves one single amount by way of a one-line budget. The use and allocation of this credit to individual schools and items of expenditure is the responsibility of the executives

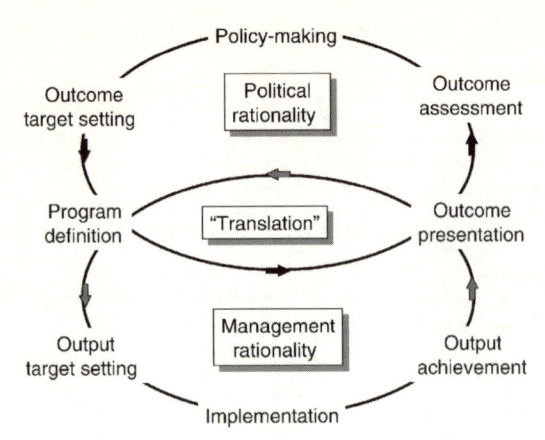

Fig. 6. Integration of Politics and Management in Control. *Source:* Schedler and Proeller (2000).

and the administrative units that report to them. The one-line budget is coupled with a performance agreement, which prescribes the results and the output to be attained by the executives. Result and output indicators enable the cantonal legislative to check whether the results and outputs defined in the performance agreement have been achieved. One of the results indicators that refers to the schools is the number of school leavers who are awarded a university degree within seven years of their final exams. It is now the task of the government, i.e. of the education ministry, to translate these precepts in individual schools, and to attain them with the schools in their entirety.

USING PERFORMANCE MEASUREMENT TECHNIQUE FOR STRATEGY

The balanced scorecard is by definition an instrument of strategic management. Kaplan and Norton (1997) its use presupposes that its users are willing to manage an organization strategically, i.e. to define a set of clear, rational objectives from which later operative decisions can and must take their bearings. This way of thinking is rooted in management theory; when the balanced scorecard is used in public institutions, it is transposed from its original habitat, the management system, into a new target area, the political and administrative system. This, however, is not merely by way of metaphor; rather, the people involved are also expected to adopt corresponding strategic behavior patterns. To begin with, the simplifying assumption is made that such a transposition can be conducted with success. Later on, the transposition will be subjected to some critical remarks.

The establishment of a balanced scorecard begins with the definition of consistent strategic objectives. The necessary process of determining these objectives is by far more layered and more complex in public administration than it is in private industry. Not only must political and legal precepts be taken into account, but also the requirements of various interest groups, such as stakeholders or even pressure groups, which as a rule are in competition with each other. The creation of transparency with regard to the objectives, as well as their prioritizing, is thus an evolutionary, time-consuming and eminently political process which, however, runs along exactly the same lines for the balanced scorecard as for any other performance measurement model.

NPM calls for the conception of a medium-term control model for politics and administration. This provides the cornerstone for planning work and the objectification of planning work in a longer term. In the Results-Oriented Public Management model for Switzerland, the instruments of medium-term planning in politics are the Legislative Plan, as well as the Integrated Task and Financial Plan. Whereas the government lays down the political focal points of the coming parliamentary term, the Integrated Task and Financial Plan constitutes an annually rolling overall plan. Both of them are also the platform for control and reporting in the context of political accountability. These instruments enable public management to derive its own strategic planning from, as it was, the cascade of superordinate political objectives, and to give these strategic plans a concrete shape. To this extent, concerns of the balanced scorecard are adopted.

The Multi-Dimensionality of the Balanced Scorecard

Occasionally, the public sector suffers from a somewhat one-dimensional view of control: as a rule, the financial perspective looms above everything else, while the customer perspective, the internal process perspective and the learning and development perspective is not given sufficient scope. NPM has been addressing these deficiencies ever since the 1980s and in the German-speaking area since the 1990s. To this extent, the concerns of the balanced scorecard are not new; however, the balanced scorecard furnishes a relatively simple picture, which is of great benefit in practical use. In particular, it forces management consistently to take its bearings from clearly defined strategic objectives – and thus to define such objectives in the first place. At first sight, however, the balanced scorecard suffers from the same deficiencies as the systems developed by NPM:

- problems with the absorption of delays;
- excessive complexity for "Joe Public";

- limited expressiveness of many parameters, particularly when they are supposed to represent complex correlation's between results.

It does not come as a surprise, then, that initial experiences in public institutions have revealed that the introduction of the balanced scorecard presents the same difficulties as, say, the establishment of a system of indicators in NPM.

PERFORMANCE MEASUREMENT ON THE BASIS OF THE BALANCED SCORECARD

In this section, the basic elements of performance measurement as conceived of by the Balance Scorecard are largely described at the level of administration, with political influences being taken into account. This is not a comprehensive depiction; rather, it focuses on the two elements: *dimensions of observation* and *objective orientation and strategy orientation*.

Dimensions of Observation in Performance Measurement

The balanced scorecard distinguishes between four dimensions of observation, that may be adopted as headings for public institutions without any modifications. In terms of substance, however, individual propositions may differ considerably from private industry.

Finances and Output

The central element of control in NPM is a shift from input orientation to output orientation: the yardstick of administrative action is no longer the resources available for production, but the output (products) to be produced. This only works with a well-designed system of recording and assessing public output and results. Whereas rather simple solutions are possible in the field of output administration, such as in road building, performance measurement with regard to sovereign authorities, such as the judiciary system, often creates difficulties. These are issues debated by performance measurement in the public sector, which now constitutes an international field of research of its own. In order to be able to generate information that is relevant to decision-making in public management, NPM propagates the introduction of cost-and-output accounting which assigns the consumption of resources to an output that has been produced (cost unit).

If cost and output account is used at all today, it is used in the context of operative controlling in public institutions and serves the short-term control and review of the provision of output. Administrative units hardly ever define output on the basis of the objectives and results to be attained, as is demanded by both NPM and the balanced scorecard. In order to be able to record the long-term effects of the production of output, the output must be derived from an administration's strategic objectives. This requires a functioning strategic management with which the office develops a manageable number of measurable objectives that reflect the state of affairs desired within three to five years. In a next step, strategies can be derived from this which reveal what outputs must be provided in what quality, and what initiatives for change must be launched in order to achieve these long-term objectives. This will be one of the major, but also most difficult, reform steps in the coming years.

Customer Orientation and Citizen Orientation

Particularly in administrations of sovereign authorities, the notion of the customer, along with the private-sector concepts suspected to lie behind it, have given rise to some bewilderment, as Mastronardi (1998, p. 99) states correctly. Customer orientation is accorded great significance in performance measurement, but it should only be understood as a *metaphor* for the opening-up of administration towards citizens' concerns. The literature treats customer orientation from the perspectives of product quality, service quality, and the measurement of customer satisfaction with corresponding generosity (Ösze, 2000, p. 106). Whereas the management of product and service quality in the public sector is comparable to that in the private sector, the measurement of customer satisfaction as the result of customer orientation looks different. When the customer satisfaction data are interpreted in the public sector, two peculiarities must be taken into particular account:

- Quality assessments by the customer are not feasible everywhere. The average hospital patient, for instance, is only able to assess the medical output he received to a limited extent.
- Realistic customer satisfaction cannot be recorded by means of survey results alone. If no price is charged for the required output, this will modify people's preferences and, in most cases, will lead to a distorted picture of the demand situation.

Public institutions differ from private sector ones in that their customers typically are not only consumers but are themselves involved in the production process: they are so-called "*prosumers*." This applies to students, patients, citizens, but also to many recipients of social security. In such cases, customer orientation is tantamount to providing "prosumers" with ideal conditions for self-help. Formally, this facet can easily be depicted in a balanced scorecard – in terms of substance, it is of eminent significance for organizational strategy.

Process Orientation

In the context of the process perspective of the balanced scorecard, management identifies the processes that are the most critical for the fulfillment of tasks and for the enhancement of customer satisfaction. Whereas private sector process parameters primarily take their bearings from the concept of the value-adding chain (Galbraith, 1987, p. 347), the literature only offers approaches to process models from which no specific process parameter for public administration can be derived yet. The "general process model of public administration" by Brenner and Horisberger (1998, p. 23) and the still rudimentary "mega-process model" by Ryf (1996, p. 31) are cases in point. For this reason, it is often only parameters regarding process time, process quality and rarely also process costs that are recorded; these data are hardly apt to help generate durable improvements in the sense of comprehensive process management. To bridge this gap, some in-depth theoretical work on process models in public administration remains to be done – in this context, NPM in the German-speaking area will have to accept some blame for having put insufficient emphasis on new process design. More recent work, such as Hunziker (1999), has paid better attention to this aspect.

Learning and Growth

Senior personnel in many administrative units notice that compliance with short-term financial budget objectives alone does not help them realize the potential of their staff. The long-term negative consequences of a systematic neglect of the realization of internal potential in an administration often do not become evident at once, but they are critical for an administration that is service-oriented and committed to a learning process. Whereas in their detailed analysis of the prerequisites for learning organizations, Reschenthaler and Thompson (1998, p. 83) are rather skeptical about the entire political and administrative system learning capacity. They regard the application of the model of a learning organization to the level of (public) management perfectly feasible and sensible. Finger and Uebelhart (1998, p. 18) come to the same conclusion. In future, the learning and development perspective in the public sector will have to be extended

Table 1. Measuring Performance in Theory and Practice.

	In Theory	In Practice
Measures of performance are	Answers, objective, neutral, interpretations, arguments	Facts, evidence, questions, slanted, weapons
Results are	Aggregated for everyone	For some but not others
Performance is	Long term	Short term
Policy is moved by	Data and analysis	Rhetoric
What to measure	The important	The measurable
Program domain	Comparable	Particular
Causal assertions can be	Demonstrated	Unclear

Source: Frederickson (2000, p. 8).

by the dimension of culture. Practical experiences have pointed to the importance of processes of cultural change; nonetheless, this aspect has so far been largely neglected in practice.

Discrepancy Between Theory and Practice

On the basis of a case study about the application of the U.S. Government Performance and Results Act (GPRA), Frederickson noticed a number of discrepancies between the theoretical claims of performance management and its practical implementation (Table 1). In particular, Frederickson criticized the fact that instead of the effects of entire programs, only the management objectives, such as adherence to deadlines or efficient output provision, are measured.

In the German-language reform debate, too, the discussion of objectives is still dominated by products. In more recent work, such as Hill (1996, p. 33), a shift can be recognized towards the actual results of administration activity; however, top administrative officials have fed such results into the political decision-making process before (Table 2). It must be assumed that under NPM, policies will largely continue to be drafted in the administration, which, on account of its higher

Table 2. Output and Results as Shown with an Environmental Example.

Measures and output	Direct results as intermediate objectives	Politically desired result
Restoration measures ordered	Number of miles of rivers and streams again made fit for fish to live in	Revival of mountain waters
Payment of incentive payments		Promotion of diversity
Agreements with farmers		

Source: Author (2002).

level of information, usually holds a dominating position in the preparation of certain policies. Output and results precepts therefore have their origin in the administration, which controls itself in this manner. At least – and this is a great step – it makes its own objectives transparent so that politics can exert an influence on them.

A further difficulty of result orientation is the provision of proof of valid cause-and-effect relationships. It is partially impossible, or possible only with an extraordinary amount of research work, to measure a certain result and trace it back to a certain government measure. Consequently, Results-Oriented Public Management concentrates on direct results that are easier to measure but can only be intermediate objectives on the way to the desired political result.

Performance measurement is not least controversial in the public sector because it is bound to base itself on indicators that refer to output or direct results. It will not be possible in the foreseeable future to define universally reliable and comprehensive indicators for major interrelations of results. In this way, however – and this criticism must be taken seriously – political interest will be focused on interrelations with too limited a scope. Fully aware of this weakness, we maintain that this imperfect solution must be preferred to today's zero solution, and that it must be further developed as best as possible.

CONCLUSIONS

Experts on political practice doubt whether politicians will ever let themselves be guided by measurement systems when they make political decisions. In strictly adversarial parliamentarian democracies such as the Westminster system, it is theoretically possible to develop and consistently pursue strategies; indeed, strong governments do so, the U.K. of the Thatcher era is a flagship example. The more complex the decision-making structures, i.e. the number of players and their possible influence on the decision-making process, the more difficult the formulation and pursuit of a consistent strategy. Clearly, hierarchical power structures favor strategic management; democratic participation makes it more difficult.

Thus, it hardly comes as a surprise that so far, no government in Switzerland – where a complex system of semi-direct democracy is prevalent, combined with a strong sense of federalism – has seriously considered the implementation of strategic management on the basis of a balanced scorecard. This does not mean that government should think and act strategically to a greater extent. It is supposed to show, however, that it is possible for government decisions to be dominated not only by the management rationality of strategic thinking, but also by the political rationality of the search for consensus and majorities. In such a case, performance measurement is only one decision-making basis among many – and often not even the most important.

Then again, a control system working along the lines of performance management furnishes a valuable basis for the management of the administration by the executive. This interface, and of course the administration itself, derives a demonstrable profit from a clarification of the expectations regarding output and results which are latent in politics and administration. The admission, too, that available resources will only allow for limited output, helps to prevent future disappointment.

REFERENCES

Brenner, W., & Horisberger, P. (1998). Von der input- zur outputorientierten Führung: Zur Einführung einer produkt- und prozessorientierten Organisation in der öffentlichen Verwaltung. *Io Management, 67th year, 12*, 18–26.

Buschor, E., & Schedler, K. (1994). *Perspectives on performance measurement and public sector accounting*. Berne; Stuttgart; Vienna.

Dunlevay, P., & Hood, C. (1994). From old public administration to new public management. *Public Money & Management, 3*, 9–16.

Finger, M., & Uebelhart, B. (1998). Public Management Qualifikationen für öffentliche Unternehmen und Verwaltungen. In: K. Schedler & C. Reichard (Eds), *Die Ausbildung zum Public Manager* (pp. 15–36). Berne; Stuttgart; Vienna.

Frederickson, G. (2000). Measuring performance in theory and practice. *PA Times, 23*(8), 8–10.

Galbraith, J. (1987). Organization design. In: J. Lorsch (Ed.), *Handbook of Organizational Behaviour* (pp. 343–357). Englewood-Cliffs.

Hill, H. (1996). Vom Ergebnis zur Wirkung des Verwaltungshandelns. In: H. Hill & H. Klages (Eds), *Modernisierungserfolge von Spitzenverwaltungen: Eine Dokumentation zum 3. Speyerer Qualitätswettbewerb* (pp. 33–39). Stuttgart.

Hunziker, A. (1999). Prozessorganisation in der öffentlichen Verwaltung: New Public Management und Business Reengineering in der Schweizerischen Bundesverwaltung. Berne: Stuttgart; Vienna.

Kaplan, R., & Norton, D. (1997). *Balanced scorecard: Strategien erfolgreich umsetzen*. Stuttgart.

Mäder, H., & Schedler, K. (1994). Performance measurement in the Swiss public sector – ready for take-off! In: E. Buschor & K. Schedler (Eds), *Perspectives on Performance Measurement and Public Sector Accounting* (pp. 345–364). Berne; Stuttgart; Vienna.

Mastronardi, P. (1998). New public management im Kontext unserer Staatsordnung, Staatspolitische, staatsrechtliche und verwaltungsrechtliche Aspekte der neuen Verwaltungsführung. In: P. Mastronardi & K. Schedler (Eds), *New Public Management in Staat und Recht: Ein Diskurs, mit einem Kommentar von Daniel Brühlmeier* (pp. 47–199). Berne; Stuttgart; Vienna.

Ösze, D. (2000). Managementinformationen im new public management – am Beispiel der Steuerverwaltung des Kantons Bern. Berne; Stuttgart; Vienna.

Reschenthaler, G., & Thompson, F. (1998). Public management and the learning organization. *International Public Management Journal, 1*(1), 59–106.

Ryf, B. (1996). Optimierung von Geschäftsprozessen im öffentlichen Bereich. *Praxis, Modernes Verwaltungsmanagement*, 2, 29–32.
Schedler, K. (1996). Ansätze einer wirkungsorientierten Verwaltungsführung: Von der Idee des New Public Management (NPM) zum konkreten Gestaltungsmodell: Fallbeispiel Schweiz. Berne; Stuttgart; Vienna.
Schedler, K., & Proeller, I. (2000). *New public management, UTB 2132*. Berne; Stuttgart; Vienna.

16. EVALUATION OF NEW PUBLIC MANAGEMENT REFORMS IN SWITZERLAND: EMPIRICAL RESULTS AND REFLECTIONS ON METHODOLOGY

Stefan Rieder and Luzia Lehmann

INTRODUCTION

The purpose of this chapter is to provide an overview of the empirical results of NPM evaluations in Switzerland. A number of evaluation studies are available to perform this task. Second, we compare the results of NPM reforms in Switzerland with those from abroad. For the purposes of the comparison we use the Pollitt and Bouckaert (2000) overview of the results of NPM projects in ten countries. We devote the third part of the chapter to methodological considerations for evaluation of public management reform.

Since the 1980s what has been termed New Public Management (NPM) has been a prominent part of the administrative reform agenda in most industrialized countries. One may distinguish two phases in the development of NPM. The first phase was characterized by the introduction of the reforms. The dialogue was about the goals, advantages and disadvantages of the introduction of NPM as well as the philosophy of the "NPM paradigm." The contents of NPM reforms and the arguments for their introduction became well known within administrations due to highly popular publications such as *Reinventing Government* (Osborne &

Gaebler, 1992).[1] During this phase, important questions were, "Shall we introduce NPM?" "How can we introduce NPM?" and "Is the new approach compatible with the political system?" (e.g. Naschold, 1997).

The second phase of the development of NPM is under way presently. The question is no longer "Shall we introduce NPM?" but "What have the results of the reform been so far and what are the consequences for its further development?" Since reforms have been implemented for some years, the first results of evaluation studies of NPM reforms are now available (for example Bulder et al., 1996; Holkeri & Summa, 1996; Pollitt, 1995). A comprehensive assessment is the provided by Pollitt and Bouckaert (2000).[2]

We can also identify the two phases in the NPM dialogue in Switzerland. The first phase included the conceptualization and the adoption of the NPM concept (Hablützel et al., 1995; Schedler, 1995). At the same time, discussion took place about the possible effects of NPM on the political system (see for example Hufty, 1998, or the debate in the *Swiss Political Science Review*, 1995). At issue were the theoretical considerations; the empirical base was slim.

Given more than five years of implementation of NPM reforms in Switzerland, a number of evaluation studies have been carried out and are available. The dialogue has therefore shifted to the question of whether the new model is a success and if it should be pursued. The purpose of this chapter is, first, to give an overview of the empirical results of NPM evaluations in Switzerland. With the number of evaluation studies available, a first general conclusion may be made. Second, we will compare the results of NPM reforms in Switzerland with those from abroad. For the purposes of comparison we use Pollitt and Bouckaert (2000) who provide an overview of the results of NPM projects in ten countries. We will devote the third part of the chapter to methodological considerations of evaluations of public management reform. We will deal with the methodological peculiarities of NPM evaluation and the challenges associated with carrying out evaluation research in this field.

NPM IN SWITZERLAND AND EVALUATION OF NPM PROJECTS

Provided below is a brief overview of the development of NPM in Switzerland and then, by means of a simple four-level model, a systematic overview of the results of NPM reforms in this country.

NPM reforms have been planned and implemented in Switzerland at the federal, the cantonal and communal levels since the early 1990s. As of today, 16 of 26 cantons have initiated NPM projects, and at the federal level, 12 agencies

Table 1. Overview of Elements of NPM Reforms in Switzerland.

Elements of the Reform	Differences	Examples
Scope	– Pure pilot projects with limited scope vs. – Incremental implementation of NPM in the administration as a whole	– Minimum of 6–8 units – Up to 50% of the administration with NPM reforms
Instruments	– Terms of performance contracts – Scope of action for government agencies concerning personnel and budgetary competences	– Valid for 1 to 4 years – Financial competence for the agencies between 50,000 and 250,000 SFR
Contracts	– Number of contracts between parliament, ministry and agencies	– Between 2 and 4 contracts per agency

Source: Authors, 2002.

have so far undergone NPM reforms. In this chapter, we will focus on the federal and cantonal levels exclusively.

The NPM reforms under way in 16 cantons are pilot projects, with the exception of the one in the canton of Zurich. Almost all the projects aim at testing new political instruments like global budgets and performance contracts. Some of them have made the step form a pilot to a definitive introduction. The projects differ with respect to the specific elements of the reforms introduced (Table 1).

Apart from the differences shown above, the Swiss NPM projects share a number of fundamental elements as follows:

- They distinguish between buyer (government), provider (agencies) and financier (parliament) of a public service;
- performance contracts are the main instrument for the three main actors (parliament, government, administration) to fix the performance objectives for (parts of) the administration;
- they define objectives and indicators to control the quality and quantity of services provided by a government agency and thus make public management more performance-oriented;
- they aim at improving customer orientation within agencies.

Since all the reform projects share the same basic philosophy, it is possible to compare some of the effects of the reforms. We will do this in the next section.

Evaluations of NPM reforms have been carried out for over four years. Most of these were done by private firms and commissioned by project management of the respective public management reform projects. Less often they are studies

Table 2. Four Levels of Possible Effects of NPM Reforms.

Levels	Possible Effects
Parliament	Change in the organization of parliamentary processes
	Change in parliamentary structures
	Change in the division of competences and power between parliament and government
	Change towards strategic decisions
Government and the ministries	Change in relationship between ministries and agencies (buyer and provider)
	Performance contracts as the main management instrument concerning agencies
	Change in culture toward performance orientation
Agencies affected by the reforms	– More scope of action in allocation of resources
	– Change in processes of the agencies
	– Change in structure of the agencies
	– Change in the culture of the agencies (customer and cost orientation)
Effects	– Change in output (quality, quantity)
	– Savings
	– Impact on the target groups of the agencies

Source: Authors, 2002.

by third parties such as universities. From a methodological point of view, the evaluations lack a common concept, method and structure. Every study has its own focus and methodological concept (for a list of evaluations, see Appendix). Some caution as far as comparability of the data is thus necessary. We adopt the model originally developed for the evaluation of the federal NPM projects (FLAG) to compare the evaluations for the purposes of the current chapter (Rieder & Ritz, 2000). The model defines four levels of effects that NPM reforms may have. The levels and the range of potential effects may be summarized as shown in Table 2.

The aim is to identify and present the similarities and differences in the reform projects, as they are made evident in the evaluations.

FINDINGS FROM EVALUATIONS OF NPM PROJECTS IN SWITZERLAND

For each level defined in the last section we review the results of the reforms.

Effects of NPM Reforms at the Level of Parliament

The different evaluation studies show that NPM reforms affect the work of parliament in three ways; we will discuss these effects below.

- NPM reforms lead to changes in the organization of parliamentary processes (new committees, change in communicative structures among committees etc.).
- NPM reforms lead to a change in the relationship between parliament and government agencies.
- NPM reforms lead to a change in the relationship between parliament and government.

Effects of NPM Reforms on the Organization of Parliament

NPM reforms lead parliaments to change their organizational structures. In almost all cantons as well as at the federal level, new committees have been established to deal with the new political instruments and the corresponding flow of information. The evaluations show that these committees help members of parliament to acquire the necessary know-how and subsequently the routine to discuss performance contracts and the new style "global budgets" effectively. In the process they have more contacts with the administration. This is generally a development in the right direction of the NPM spirit.

Furthermore, some parliaments have adopted changes in their internal structure for a more effective treatment of NPM issues. This includes new organizational procedures to deal with the new style performance contracts and budgets in order to ensure the coordination and cooperation between parliamentary committees and – at the federal level – between the two chambers of parliament.

The downside of this development is that those members of parliament that are not members of the relevant committees are insufficiently informed about NPM reforms and the workings of the political instruments associated with NPM. The result is a cleavage between on the one hand those members of parliament who are familiar with NPM processes and on the other hand a second group of less well informed members of parliament (MPs) largely indifferent to or ignorant about the reforms (e.g. canton of Soleure, FLAG). However, a cleavage between members and non-members of committees is not a new problem in Swiss parliaments. What is new and more crucial is the fact that the introduction of NPM has reinforced the cleavage.

This cleavage is a problem insofar as in the next few years' parliaments will have to decide about the future of NPM reforms. If a majority of parliament is not informed and has little or no experience with NPM reforms, the cleavage may jeopardize the reforms as a whole.

A second problem has to do with a peculiarity of the Swiss parliamentary system. Elected office in cantonal and federal legislatures is not institutionalized as a full-time job, neither in terms of time required for the office – although this varies considerably among the legislatures – nor in terms of income MPs derive from their seats in parliament. Hence the name "militia system" for the legislative level of politics in Switzerland. Now the semi-professional status of MPs is stretched seriously by NPM reforms because they require more time and work: MPs have to familiarize themselves with the concept of performance contracts requiring more in-depth study of individual government agencies than is necessary in the old style administration.

The same applies to the treatment of global budgets. In addition, global budgets make it necessary for MPs to acquire new financial know-how, especially those whose professional background is not equipped with any. Moreover, the reporting system associated with auditing procedures requires more expertise, too. It is thus increasingly difficult to be an effective MP in areas affected by NPM without having a serious background in financial affairs. NPM reforms have thus made the question of the professionalization of the legislatures an issue even though professional parliaments have little political support in Switzerland. Hence one cantonal NPM project explicitly stated as a goal the preservation of the militia system.

Effects of NPM on the Relationship Between Government and Parliament

Almost every evaluation study cites the fear of loss of power among a part of the MPs. The reason is the change in parliament's budgetary competences associated with the introduction of NPM: Global budgets put an end to traditional line item, incremental budgeting. This is in line with the idea of NPM, according to which the parliamentary budgetary process is more objective-oriented or performance-oriented: MPs are to focus more on the strategic level and leave the details of daily business to the administration. The question thus is whether global budgets constitute a loss of competence for MPs. The results of the evaluations on this issue are twofold:

- First, a part of parliament is convinced that their competences and power have been diminished. The same result emerges even in the few cantons where parliament's competences were explicitly increased, as in Soleure. It seems that those MPs with a more old style conception of politics that is antithetical to NPM reforms tend to see a loss in power when NPM reforms are implemented.

Their conception of and motivation for politics differs strongly from the basic assumption of NPM in that they conceive of politics as working on and influencing details as well as very concrete political decisions. They fail to see the NPM view of politics emphasising objectives and strategic guidelines.
- Second, parliament may indeed take an objective loss in competences as long as performance and financial indicators provided by the agencies and government are not in accordance with the objectives of the contracts, or if there are no indicators altogether. The evaluations in different cantons and the analysis of the reform situation at the federal level show that indicators are often criticized as problematic.

The problems with indicators are twofold: First, there is the confusion of concepts as to the different categories of performance and effect information (lack of conceptual clarity). Second, the reliability and technical validity of information including timely availability and accessibility may still be inadequate. Performance and effect indicators are in fact a weak point of the implementation of NPM reforms in Switzerland so far. Some reports of NPM agencies provide good indicators at the level of output (products produced and services provided). However, at the level of impact and outcome, i.e. the level of more indirect effects, the indicators are often poor or non-existent. When this is the case, budgetary processes lack transparency, hence parliament is unable to control goal achievement. The result is an administration with a broad scope of action on budgetary matters.

- Third, parliament may take a loss in competences as long as the reporting system is insufficiently developed. MPs rely on a sound reporting system if they are to judge performance and goal achievement as well as efficiency and effectiveness. Yet the reporting system suffers from two main shortcomings: The first is the problem of indicators discussed above; the second is a lack in standardization of the reports produced by government agencies, both in terms of content as well as availability.

Effects of NPM on the Relationship Between Parliament and Government Agencies

In general one can describe the relationship among parliament, government and government agencies as a triangle: The flow of information between parliament and the administration is channeled by the government. Parliament passes or revises laws, passes the budget and approves the annual account whereas government is obligated to implement parliament's decisions through the administration. In other words, the government is the head of the triangle; parliament and the administration are the corners at the base of the triangle. Of course there are direct contacts between MPs and the agencies; these take place when parliamentary committees do their auditing work of units of the administration or if representatives of agencies are invited to committee meetings as experts when bills are drafted.

The introduction of NPM affects the balance of the triangle. The evaluation in some cantons has shown (Soleure and Valais) that the number of contacts between certain committees and NPM agencies has increased. Moreover, NPM reforms tend to lead to an increase in the direct information flow from agencies to parliament. With NPM reforms, direct negotiations between parliamentary committees and representatives from the agencies have become the norm on account of discussions and negotiations about agencies' performance contracts and their global budgets. This development is critical from two angles.

- First, the necessary critical distance between parliament and the administration may be undermined. Committees may umwittingly make the administration's view their own. An essential function of ordinary parliamentary work – controlling the administration – may be diminished. This problem occurs especially at the cantonal level. The system at the federal level, institutionally different from cantonal legislatures insofar as it has two legislative chambers, does not seem to suffer from the problem of a diminishing "critical distance."
- Second, the government may be circumvented by the close connection between committees and agencies and thus potentially suffer a loss of power. This may lead to conflicts between the heads of government agencies and the government.

Based on the above we draw the following conclusions:

MPs are in the process of learning how to use the new NPM instruments. Some MPs have acquired the know-how to cope with global budgets and contracts, yet there is a long way to go before achievement of the following goals:

- a balance between the necessary information flow and a critical distance between parliament and the administration;
- appropriate indicators at the impact and outcome levels; a sound reporting system; and a strategic orientation on the part of members of parliament.

Effects of NPM Reforms at the Level of Government and the Ministries

In theory, government and the heads of the ministries negotiate with the agencies what services are to be provided and what they may cost. In reality, this system does function along NPM lines yet, neither at the cantonal nor at the federal level. The evaluations show that in most cases the government and especially the ministries do not conceive of themselves as buyers of products (yet). They fail to assume the leadership role that NPM assigns to them and remain in the old style role.

In pre-NPM times, the ministry and its administration formed more or less a unity. The ministries generally assumed the role of supporting the agencies in the political process and in the struggle for resources. NPM reforms have not been internalized sufficiently among the ministries. Especially at the federal level, but also in some cantons, the government and the ministries simply accept the contracts as drafted by the agencies without or with only minor modification. Although exceptions to this pattern do exist in some cantons, the members of the governments and the ministries generally fail to play the role assigned to them in the "NPM game" properly. There are different explanations for this:

- First, the ministries are often unable to negotiate and control the performance contracts due to a lack of personnel and know-how.
- Second, another peculiarity of the Swiss political system at the federal and cantonal levels exacerbates the situation. Governments in Switzerland – always multi-party coalition governments – consist of the various heads of the ministries ("departments") rather than a strong prime minister heading a cabinet. For the members of the government, the programs of their own ministries have priority; they often have no interest in arguing about the performance contracts of agencies in their colleagues' ministries. If their departmental administrations go uncriticized by the other members of government, they will also tend to be less critical.
- Third, the governments are not sure if NPM reforms have a future in public-policy making in Switzerland. Some parts of the government and the ministries look at the reforms with mixed feelings; they are the ones who will not invest a lot of their time discussing contracts.

Effects of the NPM Reforms at the Level of Government Agencies

We can distinguish between the effects NPM has on the one hand on the heads of the agencies and on the other hand on the workforce within NPM agencies. What are the effects of NPM for the top management of the agencies?

NPM: Benefits for Senior Management
For the heads of government agencies, NPM reforms are advantageous. They have benefited the most from the reforms. Surveys and interviews among the heads of the agencies give evidence for this.

- Agencies have more competences and expanded their scope of action in the budgetary process as well as on personnel issues.
- Motivation of top management at the agencies has risen. On the other hand, surveys at the federal level show that motivation at the lower echelons has changed very little. Sometimes job satisfaction at the level of lower management and the workforce has decreased with the introduction of NPM.
- The processes within the agencies have developed towards a product orientation. The new financial instruments help an agency's management to manage their unit.
- The structures within the agencies have changed. Especially at the federal level, the introduction of NPM has been accompanied by a change in structure. In the short run, this often led to conflicts, yet in the medium run, management and the workforce often turned out to be in favor of the changes.

These positive effects materialized after the first period of the introduction of NPM, that is four or five years into the reforms. It is important to remember that at first management was confronted with a series of problems: The definition of products was highly complex, the introduction of the accounting and budgeting system used in the private sector was entirely new for the administration, and the reorganization of work processes was accompanied by conflicts. In sum, the starting process of NPM was very labor-intensive. The first attempt to reorganize the agencies often ended in failure. However, in the long run the advantages of the NPM reforms for management where higher than the cost.

NPM: AMBIGUOUS BALANCE FOR EMPLOYEES

At the level of the staff in the agencies, the effects of NPM reform remain ambiguous. The positive effects observed in the evaluations are the following:

- The introduction of goal-oriented instruments has led to an increase in motivation among staff.
- Customer orientation and the awareness of costs have increased significantly.
- The definition of products and the introduction of product managers is seen as positive for the majority of the workforce. The output orientation has increased because of these effects.
- The scope of action at the lower levels of the hierarchy has increased.

On the other hand, some negative effects have also been identified:

- Stress and the pressure due to the workload are on the rise.

- The number of conflicts has increased in some agencies, especially where organizational changes were implemented.

In a survey among 22 agencies (11 of which participated in NPM projects, 11 did not), employee satisfaction was consistently lower in NPM agencies than in other agencies. The higher pressure in NPM agencies may well explain the difference.

NPM reforms have had the most obvious positive effects within the agencies: NPM principles have been implemented to a large degree here. Top management benefits most from the reforms, whereas there are both advantages and disadvantages for the workforce. NPM reforms, if consistently implemented, do indeed lead to changes in the administration. In one case study, a clear change was observed in the composition of the workforce. It was obvious that the people in favor of the reform remained at the agency whereas those who had problems with the NPM philosophy or its consequences in practice tended to quit at some point.

Although it is too early for definitive conclusions on NPM reforms, the balance, especially at the federal level, seems to tip toward the positive side. If we assume that some of the problems discussed above are typical for an early phase of reforms and will disappear over time, we may conclude the balance is positive also for the workforce.

Effects of NPM on the Output and Impact of the Administration

A goal of NPM reforms is to improve the quality of the services by changing the processes within the government. In two evaluations, the effects of the internal changes on the output (products) and impact (e.g. customer satisfaction) were studied.

Little Change Regarding Output

In general, the direct effect (change in products) at the output level was fairly small, i.e. there was a change in the composition and the quantity of the services in only a small number of the cases. Changes in some areas may be observed nonetheless, e.g. one agency cut the time for processing grants and applications in half. Another agency was able to change the product line or to add new products to the product line. This was made possible by the added competences in personnel matters and the allocation of financial resources.

We may observe some indirect effects at the level of output. The first element is the importance of information and marketing. NPM has enhanced activity in these areas. The agencies have increased their efforts both to improve the quality and user-friendliness of written documentation and to present themselves to the public etc. Furthermore, agency expanded scope of action has made it easier for them to react to changes in client needs. It takes less time than it did in pre-NPM times to modify products and services.

Cost Reductions
What can be said about cost reductions achieved with NPM? The adequate database necessary to give a clear answer is very often not available. But some indicators provide evidence that NPM may lead to financial savings: In one canton (Soleure), the average cost cuts at NPM agencies were higher than at non-NPM agencies. Although the financial indicators lack precision, it appears that NPM may make it easier for agencies to cut costs given their new competences in allocating resources. Another example confirming this is the federal NPM project: Every agency involved in the project had to cut costs by a certain percentage. Even before the entire contract periods were over, it became obvious that the NPM agencies may reach the goals. With regard to some products, the cost-coverage has been increased significantly with the implementation of NPM. A third example may be observed in the canton of Aargau: Average cost reductions in NPM agencies were higher than in the old style agencies.

Customer Satisfaction on the Way to Improvement?
At the level of customer satisfaction, positive developments can be observed. In the canton of Soleure and at the federal level, the effects of NPM on customer satisfaction were measured in evaluation studies by means of surveys. Positive effects for some products and customer groups were identified especially for agencies at the federal level. One agency was able to create a marketing strategy from scratch, a development positively received by its customers. The agency was able to do this due to an increase in the scope of action on the part of senior management. In other cases the services provided increased in quality, which was honored by a higher consumer satisfaction rate.

RESULTS IN COMPARATIVE PERSPECTIVE

In this section, we compare the results of NPM reforms in Switzerland with those gathered from studies in the ten countries included in Pollitt and Bouckaert (2000).[3] Table 3 provides an overview of the main results identified by Pollitt and Bouckaert that enable some rough comparability of data.

Although the comparison is very general and the data sets not fully compatible, we can formulate three conclusions:

Table 3. Evaluation of NPM Projects in Switzerland in Comparative Perspective.

Level	Results in Switzerland	Results by Pollitt/Bouckaert
Level of parliament	– Cleavage among MPs – Fear of loss of competences In part reduced distance between parliament and agencies Lack of good indicators for impact measurement results in difficult audit function of parliament	No change in competences or strategic orientation of MPs
Level of government and ministries	Lack of strategic orientation at the level of government/ministries Negotiation of contracts between government and agencies not established yet	Government not trained for nor interested in strategic leadership
Level of agencies	Increased scope of action for heads of agencies and top management, higher satisfaction among management – Increased cost and client orientation – Changes in structure and processes – More output orientation – More stress – Conflicts due to organizational changes	More output orientation Increased cost and client orientation – Changes in structure, a positive effect for management – Distinct cultural changes for management and workforce
Output/Impact	Small data base and problems of causality – Small increase in quantity and quality of products – Small increase in consumer satisfaction Some data, no indicators for increases in efficiency and savings in NPM agencies	Small data base and problems of attribution and causality – Some indicators at macro level point to higher efficiency, but no uniform pattern in results

Source: Authors, 2002.

- First, at the level of the agencies (management and workforce), there are some similar results. There is an increase in output, cost and client orientation. Nevertheless, Pollitt and Bouckaert relativise such findings by pointing, first, to the unclear attribution of results to NPM reforms and second, to the ambiguity of output and cost figures. Moreover, they find that in the "Anglo-Saxon regimes" – U.S., U.K., Australia and New Zealand – the greater freedom of public service managers to deploy their inputs was in part accompanied by closer scrutiny as far as their results were concerned than before. The latter development is largely absent in Switzerland, which is not surprising given the lack of good indicators at the level or impact and outcome to determine goal achievement. The similarities between Switzerland and the countries surveyed by Pollitt and Bouckaert extend to the fact that the introduction of NPM has led to a change in structure and processes (whereas the link with final outcome is less than certain). As far as Switzerland is concerned, we consider this the most important and best evaluated aspect of NPM reforms to date.
- Second, MPs in Switzerland tend to fear a loss of competences as far as NPM agencies are concerned, which is not the case in the countries Pollitt and Bouckaert studied. The political system and political culture in Switzerland may have contributed to this result. There is a pronounced aversion in Switzerland to any growth in competences or power of the administration or government. One reason is that the government level in the Swiss political system – unlike in parliamentary systems (the "Westminster model") – is constituted by multi-party coalition governments. The result is a type of "consensus politics" atypical of parliamentary systems: The links between political parties and their representatives in the government are thus weaker in Switzerland than in other countries, hence the reflex of fearing a loss in competences and power.
- Thirdly, there is not a great deal of in-depth knowledge about the effects of NPM on efficiency and savings. In Switzerland, some attempts at establishing these effects have been undertaken at the product level at the level of agencies. Pollitt and Bouckaert use a different approach. They compare select macro data (such as changes in government spending or debt as a percentage of gross national product, direct and indirect government expenditures etc.) in an attempt to identify the effects of NPM. It is difficult to compare data compiled with such different methods. This leads us to the last section on methodological considerations, where we will argue that micro level data seems methodologically sounder than macro-level data for such issues.

METHODOLOGICAL REFLECTIONS ON THE EVALUATION OF NPM REFORMS

Effects of NPM reforms are not easy to observe. The above analysis represents a first step. If we look at the positive aspects of thus far in Switzerland we may draw the following conclusions:

- The people in charge of NPM programs accept that evaluations are a necessary part of the implementation of NPM reforms. A good part of the larger reform processes at the federal and cantonal levels have been or are being evaluated. In that sense evaluation is an established instrument in the reform debate.
- There is an interest in and curiosity about evaluation results within the administration as well as at the political level. Apart from the usual exceptions there are thus no problems as to the acceptance of surveys, interviews and data collection.

The situation in Switzerland also points to shortcoming in NPM evaluations. If we compare evaluations of NPM reforms with evaluations of other policy programs or policy measures, some differences become evident. The differences have to do on the one hand with the object of the evaluations per se and on the other with the methodological approach to measuring the effects of NPM. The following reflections go beyond the methodological challenges typical of social science research, such as issues of causality or the difficulties of interpreting data, and pertain specifically to evaluations of NPM.

Ongoing NPM Reform Processes as an Object of Evaluation

NPM reforms are a moving target for an evaluation: In most cases the implementation of the reforms is still in progress when the evaluation is carried out. The goal of the evaluation is to provide a first or second impression about the effects of the reforms. In such a situation it is reasonable to carry out formative evaluations so that the reform program can be improved in the process through an external review. In many cases in Switzerland, there was a need for summary evaluations because governments and parliaments needed a basis for their decisions about whether or not to expand or introduce NPM across the administration. We can identify several problems associated with doing summary evaluations in an ongoing process:

- NPM reforms affect all levels of policy-making and produce a dynamic process as soon as the evaluation begins. Because of limited resources and the high complexity of the reforms, it is impossible to evaluate all aspects and potential effects of the reforms. There is a need for selection. Therefore, if the evaluation

comes to critical results which the NPM project managers do not agree with, it is always possible for them to say, "the results were ok, but in the last few months the situation has changed and the evaluation is not up to date." Another reaction to bad evaluation results is, "Oh yes, you're right, but this aspect of the reform is not that important. The aspects of the reforms that are highly relevant were unfortunately not the focus of the evaluation." In practice, there are of course always new developments and elements which where not a part of the evaluation. Sometimes evaluators feel a bit as if the reforms were a fish they cannot hold on to as it keeps slipping out of their hands.
- Another problem is the design of many reforms in Switzerland, namely the "pilot project." The idea of running reforms as a pilot project is to try out the idea of NPM with a small number of agencies first and only then to decide whether the reforms should be definitively introduced or not. Yet "pilot projects" may slowly and inconspicuously turn into "definitive facts." The point of no return may then be reached before the evaluation is finished. In such circumstances the sense of a summary evaluation is questionable. In fact such evaluations may even be instrumentalized as a subsequent legitimization.
- NPM reforms have an effect on the administration. The reforms are supposed to lead to improved performance. Nevertheless, very often it is not clear what effects the evaluation focuses on. Is the change in the administration per se the effect of the reform and the focus of the evaluation? What are the criteria for a successful reform? Is the reform seen as successful if the satisfaction of the workforce in the administration is raised? Or is the improvement of the output a criterion for the success? How important are cost reductions? In theory, we will answer: All effects were important.

In general, NPM is supposed to lead to performance management or results-oriented management, more efficiency, higher customer satisfaction and a better working environment within the administration. In practice, we may observe considerable changes within the administration but only weak effects at the output, impact and outcome levels. This may not only be due to the short period of time NPM reforms have been implemented. Very often, the output of an agency is fixed in legislation that is older than the reform. In such a situation, a change in the product line is difficult. The question now is whether the reform is defined as a success if we get a better administration but no change in output (or changes in output and outcome that are difficult to attribute to NPM). One may answer affirmatively because of the advantages for the workforce in the administration (higher motivation and transparency, better working environment etc.). Yet one may also deny the success and argue that reducing costs is a more important goal than improving the working situation of the administration. The view of what constitutes a successful NPM reform may thus vary according to the political agenda.

CONCLUSIONS: PROBLEMS IN EVALUATING NPM REFORMS

Every evaluation provided in this chapter has some methodological weak points. Some of the major problems include:

- How many agencies should the evaluation take into account? You can focus on a small number and get a very detailed description of the processes and effects for a limited part of the administration (for example the evaluation of the federal reform project FLAG). Or you can investigate all the agencies affected by the reform but not go into detail (for example the evaluation of reform in Lucerne). Because of limited resources one or the other decision always has to be made. Therefore, the results of the evaluations are bound to be limited in scope.
- From a methodological point of view, cross-comparisons between NPM agencies and non-NPM agencies would be the best approach to evaluate the effects. In practice, only one such study was carried out. And it was not by accident that this study's primary focus was not on evaluation-type questions but it was "only" a survey to measure employee satisfaction in the administration. In other words, NPM program managers fail to spend money on studying control groups. In (at least) two cases the issue of control groups was discussed, and in both cases the NPM program manager renounced a control group in the evaluation for two reasons: First they insisted on a maximum of information from those parts of the administration affected by the reform. The willingness to pay for a control group was correspondingly low. Second, it is difficult to communicate to an agency not part of the reform process that research is necessary not to improve their agency but to check if the reform works. The acceptance for such an approach is low in the control agency.
- In general, reforms need time for effects to ensue. Change in administrations is not easily realized. Hence evaluations should take place over a fairly long period of time. Apart from the evaluations in the canton of Berne and of the federal program FLAG, no reform project has been willing to spend the money on a long-term evaluation. In practice, evaluations had to be finished in a year or less. This makes it impossible to get any longitudinal "before-after-research." Hence second-best solutions are resorted to, as can be seen in surveys with questions asking about the development in the past, so-called "quasi-longitudinal

sections." Needless to say, effects at the level of impact are very hard to find with such a design.

The most critical point is the measurement of savings. As the table in this chapter shows, there are two ways to evaluate the savings effect. The first attempt starts from the micro level and tries to identify the costs for a single product or group of products. Observation over time may allow the observer to see changes in costs and link them to NPM reforms. The other approach is the comparison at the macro level: Comparing a canton or a country with another canton or country on the basis of macro-level data. In our opinion only the first method provides reliable results. It is impossible to identify the effects of reforms by means of macro-level data, as there are too many other variables influencing macro-level data. The same problem emerges in other policy evaluations (for example, when evaluating energy savings programs by means of consumer statistics, see Balthasar, 2000). Macro-level data may be highly relevant for political debates, yet they are not useful for cause-and-effect investigations concerning reforms and savings.

NOTES

1. For an overview of the early development of NPM reforms in Switzerland, see Haldemann (1995, p. 23).
2. Pollitt and Bouckaert (2000). *Public management reform. A comparative analysis.* Oxford, Oxford University Press.
3. The Pollitt and Bouckaert study includes ten countries across three continents: Australia, Canada, Finland, France, Germany, the Netherlands, New Zealand, Sweden, the U.K., and the U.S.A.

REFERENCES

Balthasar, A. (2000). *Energie 2000. Programmwirkungen und folgerungen aus der evaluation.* Rüegger, Chur and Zurich.
Bulder, F., Leeuw, F., & Flap, F. (1996). Networks and evaluation public-sector reforms. *Evaluation*, 2(3), London.
Hablützel, P., Haldemann, T., Schedler, K., & Schwaar, K. (Eds) (1995). *Umbruch in politik und verwaltung.* Bern.
Haldemann, T. (1995). *New public management: Ein neues konzept für die verwaltungsführung des bundes, schriftenreihe eidgenössisches personalamt, Band 1,* Bern.
Holkeri, K., & Summa, H. (1996). Contemporary developments in performance management: Evaluation of public management reforms in Finland: From ad-hoc studies to a programmatic approach. Chapter presented to PUMA/OECD, 4–5 November 1996, Paris.

Hufty, J. (1998). La pensée comptable, état, néolibéralisme, nouvelle gestion public. *Nouveaux Cahiers de l'IUED, 8,* Genève.

Naschold, F. (1997). Binnenmodernisierung, wettbewerb, haushaltskonsolidierung internationale erfahrungen zur verwaltungsreform. *KGSt, 15,* Coulogne.

Osborne, D., & Gaebler, T. (1992). *Reinventing government: How the entrepreneurial spirit is transforming the public sector.* Reading, MA: Addison-Wesley.

Pollitt, C. (1995, 2, October). Justification by works or by faith? Evaluating new public managament. *Evaluation, 1,* 133–154.

Pollitt, C., & Bouckaert, G. (2000). *Public management reform. A comparative analysis.* Oxford: Oxford University Press.

Rieder, S., & Ritz, A. (2000). Evaluation FLAG: Konzept und ergebnisse im bereich des betrieblichen wandels. *LeGes, 1,* Bern.

Schedler, K. (1995). *Ansätze einer wirkungsorientierten verwaltungsführung.* Bern.

Swiss Political Science Review (1995). *Debate on new public management, 1*(1), Zurich.

APPENDIX

Published Empirical Evaluations of NPM Reforms in Switzerland (in Order of Publication)

Title	Level	Type of Study	Year
Marek D.: Evaluation des Projektes "Neue Verwaltungsführung NEF," Bericht über die erste Etappe	Canton	Evaluation study commissioned by project management	1997
Balthasar, A.; Thom, N., Rieder, S., Zinsli Charlot, S., Ritz, A.: Konzept zur Beurteilung von FLAG und erste Beurteilung. Bericht zuhanden der Steuergruppe FLAG, Luzern und Bern	Federation	Evaluation study commissioned by project management	1998
Balthasar, A., Thom, N., Rieder, St., Furrer C., Ritz A.: Evaluation FLAG Phase eins – Analyse des betrieblichen Wandels, Luzern und Bern	Federation	Evaluation study commissioned by project management	1999
Ehrensperger M.: Erfolgsfaktoren von Verwaltungsreformen, Cahier de l'IDHEAP 183/1999, Chavannes près Rennens	Canton	Master study	1999

Title	Level	Type of Study	Year
Zürcher M.: Wider ein betriebswirtschaftlich verkürztes Public Management: Über Produkte, Indikatoren und die Wirksamkeit, LeGes 1999/2	Canton	Master study, focus on the use of indicators in NPM projects	1999
Rieder S., Bächtiger C.: Beurteilung der Einführung von Administration 2000 im Kanton Wallis, Luzern	Canton	Short evaluation study commissioned by project management	2000
Rieder S., Furrer C.: Evaluation des Pilotprojektes Leistungsauftrag und Globalbudget im Kanton Solothurn, Luzern	Canton	Evaluation study commissioned by project management	2000
Concept: Evaluation des WOV-Versuchs Kanton Luzern, Zürich	Canton	Evaluation study commissioned by project management	2000
Concept: Evaluation WOV Kanton Aargau, Zürich	Canton	Evaluation study commissioned by project management	2000
Reeder S., Farrago P.: Vergleichende Evaluation der NPM-Versuche in den Kantonen Aargau, Luzern, Solothurn, Wallis und Zürich	Canton	Evaluation study commissioned by project management in each of 5 cantons	2000
Balthasar, A.; Thom, N.; Rieder, St.; Lehmann L., Ritz, A.: Evaluation FLAG Phase zwei – Analyse der Prozesse im Parlament und Wirkungen von FLAG bei den Zielgruppen, Luzern und Bern	Federation	Evaluation study commissioned by project management	2001

17. MEASURING AND MANAGING FOR PERFORMANCE: LESSONS FROM AUSTRALIA

Bill Ryan

INTRODUCTION

Many Australasian-Anglo-American jurisdictions including Queensland, other Australian states, the Australian Commonwealth, central government in Britain, the U.S., Canada and New Zealand (Department of Finance and Administration, 2000; NZ Treasury/State Services Commission, 2002; Queensland Treasury, 1997; Treasury Board of Canada, 2000), are presently debating over "managing for outcomes." Throughout this chapter, the acronym MFO is used to stand for this whole movement even though it implies greater coherence than exists. There is a definite movement in this direction in Australasian public services with the emergence of widespread rethinking about its purposes and characteristics. It is driven in some jurisdictions by ministers wanting to know about actual policy outcomes and less about the shiny-chrome management systems behind them and, in other jurisdictions, by senior managers in central agencies and some line agencies who are rediscovering the real purposes constituting public management. There is also some back-pedaling in relation to some aspects of the economic reform agenda that was applied too hard during the late 1980s and 1990s in this part of the world. There are also some that claim that MFO is a logical extension of the first stage of reform undertaken during the 1980s and 1990s – one in which outputs rather than outcomes was the primary focus.

The alleged strength of MFO is that it promises to bring public management to where it ought to be. An economic approach to public management, its ascendancy now waning in Australia, makes public management a corporate means for improving economy and efficiency ("economic rationality"). Likewise, a technical approach converts public management into a collection of tools, the mechanics and aesthetics of which occupy managers' hearts, minds and time ("technocratic rationality"). Under MFO, public management might once again become "managing means for policy ends"; managing public organizations and the resources put at their disposal in such a way as to achieve the policy goals and objectives of the government of the day.

Some jurisdictions have talked about "outcomes" for some years (TFMI, 1992) but, this time, the managers tasked with progressing reform seem more willing and able to confront major issues previously glossed over. There is presently much thinking going on. There is also much doing. Some public managers working in some policy fields, in some agencies, in some jurisdictions are already managing for outcomes in the most astonishing and effective ways. Some public sectors organizations, too, while an overall mixture of bureaucratize, economism and managerialism; idealism, pragmatics and Machiavellianism; routines, inertia and bungling (as complex organizations often are) display flashes of MFO know-how. Their actions seem to reveal a "practical knowing" that appears several steps ahead of some of the more conservative central agency guidelines for MFO.

These individuals and agencies have inspired this study. Momentum in developing MFO is picking up in Australia with interesting fragments emerging here and there, but, overall, it still seems immature with much work still to be done: models emerging elsewhere seem much the same (Treasury Board of Canada, 2000; see also Radin, 2000).

Clearly, some kind of overall framework, a "model" of some forms, perhaps are more coherent and systematic than yet appears in practice, had to be developed. It made sense then to pull these fragments together, filling in any gaps and to represent them as an "MFO framework for the 21st century" designed to function as a heuristic. It would sketch where MFO might be heading over the next 3–5 years (all other things being equal). As such it would also serve to challenge those charged with leading MFO in the various jurisdictions and take some different types of public management thinking "Down Under" to an international audience.

A final introductory point should be made. This chapter makes great play of the idea that emerging conditions of governance in the 21st century bring new challenges to which public management must respond – to which traditional and recent forms of practice might not be particularly adaptable. Describing those conditions is a large task that cannot be accommodated in this paper. Drawing on the work of authors such as Giddens (e.g. 1984, 1990), Harvey (1989) and the OECD (2000a, b, 2001a, b, c), these arguments are laid out in some detail in Ryan (2002a, b). In essence, the argument is that Australasian-Anglo-American societies are becoming more complex, contextual, inexplicable, intractable, and paradoxical. They are marked by political trends towards plurality, participation, and devolution, and are moving away from bounded organizational forms towards networks and strategic alliances, and that these trends dramatically alter current practices in public management, particularly as they might develop under MFO. It is also important to note that this analysis is more "ideal-type" than "empirical." It focuses solely on these trends, identifies their essential features, fills in gaps and represents them as a descriptive and sometimes prescriptive heuristic – the notion of "should," however, must be understood in the sense of apparently logically and pragmatically necessary rather than in any sense of command. The practical reasoning that underpins this chapter does the same thing.

ELEMENTS OF MFO

Planning for outcomes is one element of MFO that is moving in clear and useful directions. Outcomes – or rather, goals and objectives – can be thought of in terms of overlapping layers and the participants engaged in their formulation (see Table 1). While the relationship between high and low level goals and objectives is often described as a "cascade" (higher level goals disaggregate into lower level ones), this should not imply that they must be formulated at the top first and fed down the line.

Goals and objectives that are emerging at any level will probably be a product of reiterative and recursive learning up, down, and across the governance system as a whole societal visions.

A wide range of activities and processes in society contribute to articulating those overarching visions that are held dear (e.g. a "fair go for all," an "egalitarian" society, and a "multi-cultural" society). Of course, "politics" is supposed to be a primary means of identifying and elaborating such visions; it is fundamental to party formation, platform development, consensus-building and electoral politics. In theory – and possibly in practice – elections provide citizens with a means to debate and select their preferred visions and aspirations by electing particular parties to power. And elected governments usually regard themselves as having a mandate to realize their particular vision.

However, once in power, there may be little that any government can do directly to alter societal states of affairs, certainly not simply or within a specifiable time frame. The complexity of societies in the 21st century seems such that states, trends and what are taken to be problems seem barely explicable, much less

Table 1. Outcomes Layers by Level.

Level	Features	Period	Participants
Societal visions	Vague, philosophical, societal end states	Eternal	Society, citizens, parliament, competing parties
Government priorities	Abstract policy aspirations but potentially and increasingly broken up into contributing specific goals and objectives	Mixture of eternal and continuous parliamentary terms	Party, caucus, electorate, ministers, senior officials
Policy and program goals and objectives	Specific statements about changed end states sought by particular policies and programs	Planning period, 1–5 years and 1–2 terms	Ministers, agency or agencies, managers, participants in policy community
Operational targets	Specific, precise and objective (empirically verifiable)	Milestones or regularity	Managers, staff

Source: Author, 2001.

tractable. They are altogether too complex for the normal range of incremental policies having much direct or immediate impact on them, so the contribution of policy may be a matter of conjecture. State action might seek to indirectly influence them by working on lower-level preconditions over time (i.e. policy and program goals) to change the conditions of their combination, but that is all. Wishful thinking aside, there is limits to state power.

GOVERNMENT PRIORITIES

Government priorities are usually particular actions promised in relation to a perceived problem that is high on the public agenda – often a state of affairs that runs counter to some aspect of a particular societal vision. MFO cannot work without the government of the day stating its priorities ("what this government stands for") and its aims ("what this government will achieve"). Yet recent Australasian governments have not always done so. The dynamics of politics and parliaments Westminster conventions have made ambiguity a positive electoral value. Too much detail, too much commitment, risks attack by the opposition if the result is anything less than unambiguous success, something that is fairly unlikely.

Governments are learning to articulate their hopes increasingly, however, albeit reluctantly. Typically, they appear as little more than sketchy desiderata intended to guide policy development and co-ordination at the whole-of-government level ("Reduce unemployment," "Maximize economic growth," "Give our children a good education"). Once made known, advisers and analysts can pull them apart and develop lower-level detailed, strategic policy and program goals and objectives ("Increase economic growth through exports at a rate greater than the national average," "Increase the percentage of students completing Year 12 or the equivalent to 88% by the year 2010," "Reduce disadvantage in indigenous communities and increase self-development through collaboration and partnership").

Policy and Program Goals and Objectives

Policy and program goals and objectives are the more-or-less precise and time-limited hopes expressed and agreed by ministers, managers and participants in the policy community that are put up for cabinet approval, have budgets allocated, and are managed by and through public services and associated organizations in the private and community sectors. These include single agency, cross-agency, and sectoral and whole-of-government initiatives (a.k.a. strategies, programs, schemes, task forces, and so on).

If MFO is to develop and mature in the foreseeable future, government priorities and policy and program goals and objectives must be articulated and the relationship between them elaborated and posited. This might seem obvious but is not always so in practice. In and of themselves, government priorities expressed in the form of headlines like "high, sustained economic growth" or "declining unemployment" or "improved population health" but, like societal visions, these are not much help to the practicalities of public management. An enormous amount of work is required from ministers, advisors, and officials in drawing out the combination of lower-level policy goals and objectives that are believed to constitute the end-states that governments seek. If MFO is to work, there is no alternative but for all those in the policy process – including ministers – to recognize the tortuousness, difficulty, time, and resource-dependence of this work.

This work might be done in the agencies and policy communities but ministerial accountability demands that ministers, individually and collectively, are at their centre and sign them off. One or more portfolios and/or departments will commit to these goals and objectives for a strategic planning period and/or a budgetary cycle. Forged jointly in a series of meetings, discussions and drafts, some objectives will be "vertical" and relate to a single policy field usually covered by one organizational unit (e.g. portfolio, department, and agency). Others will be "horizontal" covering several policy fields (e.g. "strategy," "initiative," "program") and several organizational units. Goals and objectives might involve multiple ministers, agencies, and policy communities and be sectoral or even cross-sectoral. As more emphasis is placed on "joined-up solutions to cross-cutting problems" (U.K. terminology), especially at the whole-of-government level, more outcome planning processes will be of this type.

PROCESS AND OUTPUTS: STRATEGIC DIALOGUE, RECURSIVE LEARNING, PLANS AND PROMISES

The process of planning for outcomes is equally if not more important than the outputs. Developing and strategizing goals and objectives at all levels must be based on ongoing strategic dialogue and collective and recursive learning within the political executive and policy community. New learnings will come from ongoing implementation, monitoring, and evaluation.

Strategic dialogue should occur in a wide range of settings and be continuous: it is hard to imagine how MFO can grow and mature if it does not. Cabinet ministers and senior officials should formally review whole-of-government goals and objectives at least once or twice a term, with much discussion in private offices and cabinet or caucus committee meetings throughout the year. Ministerial task forces can be effective in creating and furthering strategic dialogue, so can select parliamentary committees, so can cabinet committees, especially if they are connected to parallel groups of senior officials that focus on specific sectoral or cross-sectoral policies – particularly connections are made between the deliberations of ministers and officials.

The case for "strategic dialogue" seems incontrovertible – notwithstanding the political and parliamentary dynamics of Westminster-derived polities that militate against it. Whilst governance as a whole is inevitably a mix of passion and intellect, intention, direction, muddle and spin – from ministers and officials – strategic dialogue is should be underpinning by technical rather than political rationality, something for which few ministers have strong motives. It should also be based on collaboration, synergy and considerations of the collective good ("public value") rather than agency interest or individual good – even partisan good. It must occur at least within the political executive (in Westminster-based systems, the cabinet plus the public service) but should probably, increasingly, also involve policy communities – if for no other reason than civil demands for greater participation are increasing as the 21st century settles into place.

Promissory documents in the budget process and the puzzle of outputs and outcomes. There is fairly widespread agreement on some points regarding the outputs of planning for outcomes.

- Outcome-oriented strategic plans are essential at the agency and policy levels. Generally, these should be substantive and detailed.
- Promissory outcome-oriented planning documents are also required for the budget process and most jurisdictions have created a variant that each believes suits its purposes (e.g. in New Zealand, Statements of Intent; in Queensland, Ministerial Portfolio Statements; in the Australian Commonwealth, Portfolio Budget Statements; in the UK, Public Service Agreements).
- These budget documents should flow out of and, in some sense, concentrate the strategy documents produced by agencies over the course of any year.

They should be outcome-oriented and, as such, have a strong policy flavor (although they may validly point to organizational capacity-building as preconditions of achieving policy and programmed outcomes).

There is less agreement over the appropriate contents, comprehensiveness, and detail of these documents. For example, should these documents include both output targets and policy goals and objectives and the "linkages" between them (as indicated typically in Fig. 1) as most treasuries are presently arguing?

This sounds like a perfectly reasonable and logical proposition. But is it actually realistic? Here we strike the first of several major issues that will be explored in this article. Explicating the relationship between particular outputs and particular outcomes is probably empirically impossible – ex-ante or ex-post.

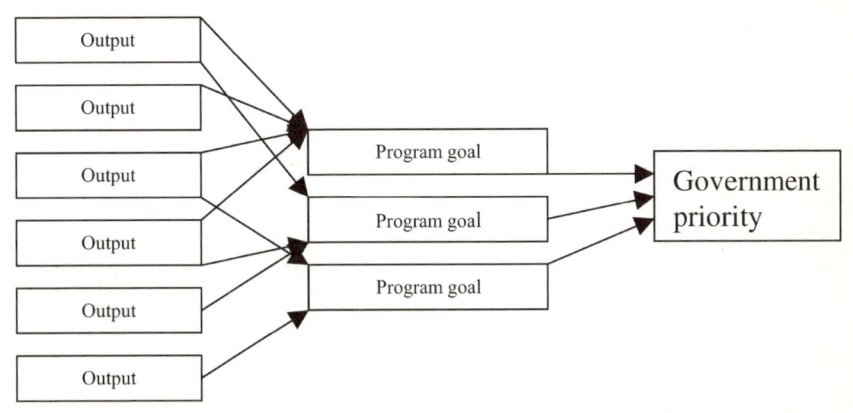

Fig. 1. Typical Prescribed Linkages Between Outputs and Outcomes. *Source:* Author, 2001.

There seem to be at least two reasons why this might be so. No matter how much sophisticated social science is put into figuring out how societies work, it is increasingly apparent that, at a detailed level, social reality is probably too complex and too open to be entirely and precisely explicable. The same applies to high-level policy outcomes (social visions and some government priorities). If so, there is no prospect that empirical analysis could discern with any degree of certainty which outputs contributed to which societal or government outcomes. It may also be the case that outputs and outcomes represent different and incommensurate paradigms (Kuhn, 1970) of public management, one based on a production/systems approach and the other policy/governance, but this possibility will not be explored here. Accordingly, trying to assert ex-ante connections would be essentially quixotic. Contiguous or imputed connections (e.g. "alignment" but not "equation") between outputs and outcomes could be asserted, recognizing that the relationship is hypothetical and symbolic rather than empirical and literal ("correspondence") – which is, perhaps how Fig. 1 should be interpreted.

The complexity, however, is not an excuse for evading the difficult work of explicating connections in the logic model; it merely qualifies the certainty, the directness, the literalness, and the degree of "reality" of the output-outcome relationship that can be claimed. An agency can make a "rough 'n ready" connection, knowing that it has to produce particular outputs to achieve any kind of effect at all (e.g. running schools is presumably a precondition for increasing levels of education across the population; trade negotiations and international marketing by governments will presumably pave the way for achieving increased exports) and may even be able to plausibly suggest that some outputs are more influential than others. A relationship can be posited. Arrows can be drawn. But each would be indicative at best. Each would represent a judgement, a "rule of thumb," rather than precise calculation. In other words, it would be a rough-'n ready claim that relies heavily on experienced and shrewd management judgement and expresses both the craft and art of governance.

The upshot of this argument would be that "outcomes" are not an extension or development of "outputs." They are two different but complementary approaches to public management, such as, in the future; outputs will probably remain the unit of analysis for budgetary and financial management and outcomes the unit for policy and program management. It suggests that outputs and outcomes represent different logic within public management. As such, two different types of promissory documents should go to the budget process; one focused on financial/outputs information (appropriations, output plans) and the other on policy/outcomes information (policy and program objectives and strategies). This would allow both types of document to speak to their own concerns and not have one dominate and skew the other. Practical reasoning points in this direction. Subsequent learning over coming years will confirm it or otherwise. Grasping this somewhat complex point is actually important in avoiding unrealistic expectation, wasted effort and unnecessary tension between central and line agencies in developing MFO.

LOGIC MODELS AND IMMEDIATE/ INTERMEDIATE OUTCOMES

Within MFO, there is growing interest in several new strategic management heuristics – although they are only "new" in the sense of being formalized since they are just labels for systematic types of thinking and acting that purposive, results-focused, action-oriented managers do anyway, albeit sub-consciously. In that sense they are codified versions of methods that constitute the "practical knowing" (Argyris & Schön, 1974; Schön, 1983) of strategic and effective public managers. Generally, their introduction makes sense as long as they are used as "heuristics" (general guides for thinking and doing) and not "tools" (specific, step-by-step instructions) (Ryan, 2002a).

Logic Models

Logic models are heuristics for explicating and enacting how, what, why and when strategies proposed and pursued will lead to the desired outcomes (cf. also "logical framework," Saldanha and Whittle 1998; "intervention logic" in New Zealand and "program logic" in Australia). In other words, it is a causal model presumed to underpin a policy or program, and is often represented figuratively or in a matrix, list or as a narrative. Figure 2 is an example using a "box and arrow" format to represent a management development program; other proponents (e.g. Baehler, 2002) prefer to use an "outcome hierarchies" approach (Baehler's approach is applied in Steering Group 2002).

When represented thus, (causal) logic models have similarities to flow charts, system maps, but they also have one major difference: they are supposed to be causal in character (Fig. 1 unwisely treats the policy as a closed if cybernetic system – there is no reason in principle why external determinants cannot be added; e.g. regional development policies that increase investment and jobs; subsidies to employers to take on previously unemployed applicants). They represents putative, ex-ante logics-of-action; in effect, the "road maps" whereby a strategy is hoped will change an existing states of affairs, as opposed to an explanatory, post-hoc model based on empirical research. They should therefore typically identify actors, strategies/practices/resources and the immediate, intermediate and ultimate outcomes

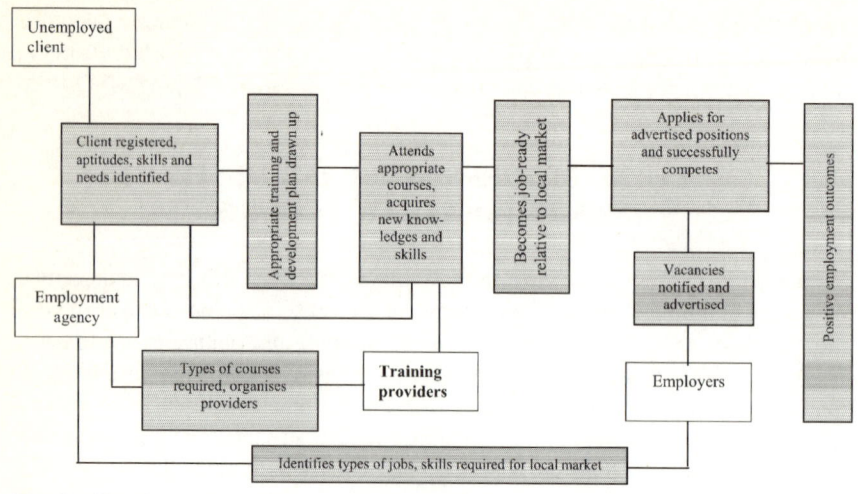

Fig. 2. Simple Logic Model for a Conventional Labor Market Program. *Source:* Author, 2001.

that each is considered to generate and the relationships between them. It is also worth noting that logic models seem most applicable in a "single agency/single policy" context but there is no theoretical reason why they cannot and should not be applied in multi-agency settings (e.g. whole-of-government policies), notwithstanding the probability that the strategy/outcome logic may get very complex – impossibly complex – to the point where its practical value declines very quickly.

Logic modeling should be regarded as a recursive process of goal identification, strategizing, and reviewing and the model as a heuristic – definitely not a "thing" – constantly revisited during planning, implementation, and review. Employed thus, logic modeling can bring benefits such as identification of usually tacit and sometimes unrecognized assumptions (in theory and practice) underpinning problem definition and option development; the various pathways whereby the policy is assumed to generate or enable the desired outcomes; the strategies required to do so; the immediate and intermediate outcomes required to achieve the ultimate policy outcomes; the outcome indicators to be developed to monitor and evaluate performance, and so on. And if treated as emergent, understandings of the program, objectives and strategies will start as a logic-in-theory that will inevitably re-emerge, modified, as a logic-in-practice, and change again as the determining conditions change. In other words, within MFO, heuristics such as logic models must be understood as practical as well as analytical means – as methods that reintegrate theory and action. They must also be understood as management heuristics without which MFO is likely to fail.

Table 2. Illustrative Immediate and Intermediate Objectives for Participation in a Typical Active Labor Market Program.

Immediate Objectives of Training Participation	Intermediate Objectives of Training Participation
Participation that stimulate and motivates	Increased "job-readiness"; i.e. improved skills and capabilities in relation to job vacancies in the local job market; improved capability to compete for job vacancies; realized in successful applications for notified and advertised vacancies
New and ongoing short and medium-term learning in relation to skills and capabilities	Increasing commitment to successfully complete the training and development plan

Source: Author, 2001.

Immediate and Intermediate Objectives and Outcomes

Immediate and intermediate outcomes are the lower-level objectives achieved "along the way" to achieving higher-level, ultimate outcomes (i.e. government priorities, program and policy goals and objectives). Thought of in process terms they are temporally or structurally necessary preconditions for the ultimate objectives of a program or policy; in that sense they must emerge "first." Typically, immediate and intermediate outcomes are the proximate effects generated in implementation and service delivery for direct and indirect users; and the higher-level effects at the population, group, or institutional level.

Immediate and intermediate outcomes for a generic active labor market program (as represented in Fig. 2) are illustrated in Table 2. The immediate objectives of participation in appropriate training (relative to the unemployed client's experience, aptitude, and preferences) should be something like increased knowledge's and capabilities, increased motivation, increased sense of personal salience, and so on. Over time and at a more abstract level, this can be described in terms of progressive increases in "job-readiness."

As with the logic model from whence they are derived, identifying key immediate and intermediate objectives can be hard and challenging work – and the work that is done in the planning stage can and must be subsequently modified by the logic-in-action of the program and the actual immediate and intermediate outcomes achieved (although practical knowing from implementation should also feed into planning and development). However, the benefits of doing so are considerable. With them, agencies are more able to: (a) develop relevant and realistic objectives for the current planning period; (b) develop meaningful indicators to monitor and evaluate progress; (c) use that information to improve management; and (d) report on short and medium-term achievements to ministers and parliament.

MOTIVATION, DOUBTS AND MESSINESS

Ministers in Westminster-derived polities have little motivation to sign off on outcomes. Electoral and parliamentary politics seem to militate against it. Signing up to goals and objectives that prove unachievable is one way of giving the opposition a free kick. However, management and electoral moods might be forcing their hand. Modernizing officials and some ministers are moving beyond the search for efficiency to the search for effectiveness.

MFO is one expression of this trend. But citizens are also seeking more from government than they have so far received. In countries such as Australia and New Zealand, fewer now accept the adversarial, rhetorical, opposition-for-opposition's sake style of politics and parliamentary practice than previously. Variegated interests have been voted into parliaments resulting in minority or coalition governments, and stronger demands for participation and policy that works. Some ministers and parliamentarians sense this mood change and are anxiously if slowly shifting their ground. Substantive shifts in parliamentary and ministerial practice are a pre-condition for MFO achieving maturity, but that still seems a long way off.

The approaches to MFO discussed here have a deliberate inconclusiveness and mutability to them, more like those emerging in practice rather than the mechanical and technocratic prescriptions appearing in some official versions. This is essential given the complexity and paradoxes that constitute the conditions of governance in the 21st century. In this context, goals and objectives are no more than visions, strategies no more than hypotheses and implementation always a journey of recursive collective learning. Public management needs to become something altogether unbureaucratic and un-Westminster. The formal, more-or-less linear, more-or-less top-down, more-or-less rationalistic approaches to planning represented by "corporate" or "design" or "formal" models of planning processes that some MFO frameworks still seem to presuppose, are inappropriate for the times.

Alternatives that appeared on the margins in the 1970s and 1980s such as logical instrumentalism (Mintzberg, 1994), more recently, organizational learning (Argyris & Schön, 1978; Senge, 1990), and emergent planning and management (Mintzberg, 1994, Mintzberg & Waters, 1985), seem much more appropriate. Nor can it be taken for granted that the promissory documents presented to the budget process can specify ex-ante the matters for which an agency can be held accountable one year later, come hell, or high water. MFO in the future may require more adaptable plans and parliament will need to treat them accordingly.

ISSUES IN IMPLEMENTING OUTCOME MANAGEMENT

Relearning Required: Implementation Counts

The theory of public management still needs to (re)learn a lesson arising out of 1970s and 1980s implementation research. Implementation counts. Policy design is often good enough; implementation and service delivery are often not. Policy failure is not infrequent, even where design and development appear to be appropriate. The explanations often lie with inadequate implementation. Particular shortfalls can include a poorly explicated model, under-resourcing relative to the task to hand, insufficient time, too many mediating variables between development and implementation, complex contexts of implementation with various competing interests, and so on (Pressman & Wildavsky, 1984; Sabatier, 1986; see also Hogwood & Gunn, 1994; Lane, 1993).

Several implications are immediately apparent for MFO.

- Implementation is not the easy phase of public management following the more difficult stage of development. The challenges are different but they need as much ongoing strategic, outcome-oriented management – maybe even more. Moreover, development should not proceed without full understanding of the conditions of implementation and service delivery.
- The 1990s separation of development and implementation via the purchaser/provider (cf. also policy/delivery) split may have created more problems than it solved and significant levels of reintegration (non-structural as well as structural) are required if the effectiveness of implementation and delivery are to be improved under MFO.
- Heuristics such as logic models are still under-utilized in implementation both in understanding existing conditions of implementation and ex-ante modeling of emerging goals, objectives and strategies. Given their potential contribution to effectiveness they should be inherent elements of any MFO framework.
- MFO cannot and must not treat implementation as a black box. A huge amount of developmental work within MFO is required in this respect.

Do existing MFO frameworks recognize the point adequately? Official prescriptions originating in central agencies do not always seem to although many managers in implementation do particularly bureaucratic entrepreneurs and their networked collaborators.

Reintegration Required: Development and Implementation

The 21st century conditions of governance are having major effects on implementation. Complexity, contextuality, inexplicability, intractability, and paradox are fast becoming the norm. Polities are pluralizing. New interests are emerging, organizing, and entering legislatures. Alliances and networks are forming, reforming, and metamorphosing. Demands are increasing for participation, devolution, and localism.

If implementation is a journey based on collective, recursive learning, it can no longer occur in a time and space that is alienated from development. Development and implementation are not a dichotomy but connected and interdependent stages in a process (program management in the 1980s argued a similar point). Moreover, where design and delivery occur in one discrete process (e.g. consultation, diagnosis, and treatment) and involve co-production by the client effects development and implementation become increasingly simultaneous and recursive. The more clients participate in the policy process and the more implementation and delivery are devolved and localized, the more this will be the case. Any disconnection becomes a problem – contra public choice theory – and the development of MFO must assume vertical and horizontal reintegration.

In policy fields such as justice and corrections, education and schooling, health care provision and so on, even more in relation to obstinate, multi-causal problems that stretch across agencies, programs, or sectors, the case for some level of structural reintegration in fragmented governance systems is strong. Here the desirable relationship between development and implementation is inherent and intricate but separation has made strangers or competitors out of those who should be colleagues and collaborators (less of a problem, perhaps, in those jurisdictions that built a portfolio-based system and were cautious in applying a purchaser/provider split).

The case for non-structural reintegration is probably even stronger and applies even more widely. Reconnecting development and implementation vertically within one portfolio and horizontally across several, depends largely on an emerging but well-recognized approach. This is the idea of "collaboration through networks"; transforming otherwise independent but related agencies into formal networks and creating synergies around a set of common goals that make the final result more than the sum of its parts (cf. Rhodes & Marsh, 1992; also OECD, 2001b, c). The collaborative network exists only for as long as is needed to produce the desired results, and participants may be members of more than one network. Considered in some circles to represent a 21st century organizational ideal (cf. "bureaucracy") (Clegg, 1990; Limerick & Cunnington, 1993; Thompson et al., 1991), it is being promoted in many jurisdictions; horizontally in policy development and service delivery (discussed further below), and vertically between policy "ministries" and delivery (or single-purpose) "agencies" or "departments."

The constraints are fairly obvious; including ensuring that the agencies involved, when required, work to collective rather than individual goals, and are prepared to collaborate rather than compete or protect their turf. Another is the manner and style of leadership in a network of equals – a special, collaborative style of leadership that is not widely distributed. Another is how to construct budgets and financial management rules so that dollars can flow across silos. Knowledge management for networks also imposes demands on information systems and the people expected to use them. These are significant challenges but they are well recognized and many jurisdictions are apparently moving to deal with them.

There can be little doubt that they are right to do so. The logic of MFO demands substantial reintegration across most public sectors, both structural and non-structural but particularly the latter. The reintegration must also be horizontal and vertical; including up, down and across different levels of government. Coordination may well be an administrative utopia (Hood & Jackson, 1991; Peters, 1998) and not all coordination might be a good thing, but the general case under MFO seems incontrovertible.

The greatest challenge for agencies however might be accepting that the time has come. These ideas have been talked about for some time and half-hearted attempts to achieve these objectives have been made at many levels on many occasions. Some have worked well. Others have not. There are no "tools" for successful network collaboration. Good will and transcendent commitment are essential, as are pragmatics and an outcome orientation. It calls out capacities such as the ability to compromise strategically, to exercise collectively-responsible autonomy, the verbal and intellectual skills to persuade and to influence, and the personal integrity and personality to carry others, characteristics normally associated with (collaborative) "leadership" rather than "management." It is why, perhaps, there is a perceived need now for "leaders" in public sectors and not just "managers" (Hesselbein et al., 1996; OECD, 2001d; PIU, 2002a, b). These and related issues have been recognized for some time. Like MFO more generally, managers have been able to walk away from the really difficult challenges up to this point, or the circumstances were not right to tackle them. If the time for MFO has finally come, so has the need to create the ways and means. The exciting thing about the present is that there are many managers who seem to share the will to do so.

UTILIZATION AND DELIVERY

Practical reasoning based on emerging practice, suggests that there are several heuristics that can be used to develop MFO in the implementation phase.

Models of Client Behavior

Public management tends to treat as a "black box" the process that occurs between clients accessing organizational outputs (goods and services) and the creation of the desired effect; i.e. what happens as, when and after clients use the program outputs. There is talk of "causing" or "influencing" or "shaping" outcomes but these are top-down assumptions that mask what is actually an important and little-understood process (an exception is Rose (1989) on "ordinary people" in the policy process).

Between access, take-up and effect is a process of "consumption" or "utilization," wherein the client "uses" or "consumes" the agency output in some way. The important point to recognize is the client's use of the output shapes the consequences of implementation; whether or not they use it in the manner sought and realize the outcome sought for the policy in the first place, or something else. This is particularly important where co-production by the client is a recognized aspect of delivering many types of services. In other words, there is a strong apparent case for developing models of client behavior as a necessary aspect of learning to manage for outcomes (Ryan, 2001; cf. also Giddens, 1984, on "agency").

The theory and research of public management contains little codified or detailed knowledge of the motivations, conditions, processes and effects of client behavior in relation to outputs (historically, of course, theory, research and prescription in public administration and management have been top-down in their orientation), unlike private sector marketing where a large amount of research goes into "consumer behavior." On the other hand many practitioners in the field, especially those most skilled at being effective with clients, know plenty, although their knowledge may be fragmentary and non-systematic – and often written off as anecdotal and unscientific. If models of utilization are to have a place in MFO, as they probably should, then their construction needs to start with the accumulated experience of practitioners in the field.

Program life cycles in delivery to state the obvious, policies and programs have a beginning, a period of growth, then reach maturity from whence they continue, for a while until discontinued (perhaps subject to a "problem shift" or change of government). This can be represented as a "program life cycle" as represented in

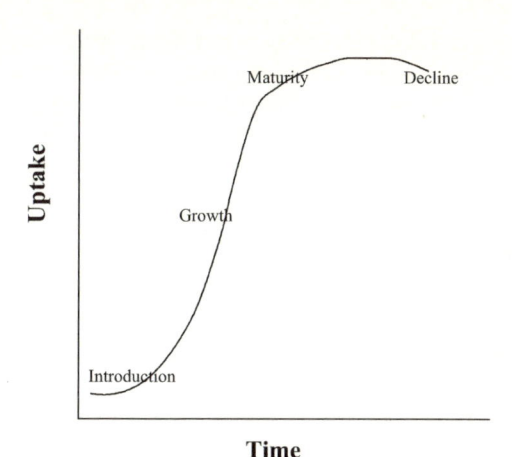

Fig. 3. Ideal Type Representation of a Program Life Cycle. *Source:* Author, 2001.

Fig. 3 (a figure obviously derived from the marketing notion of the "product life cycle").

This is another heuristic for designing, targeting and implementing efficacious and appropriate service delivery strategies. For example, it gives a basis for deciding when, how, where and why to introduce packaging and presentation strategies designed to introduce the program to clients, and targeting strategies that represent its value and benefits to them. Efficacious communication strategies can be developed; introductory strategies first, then more explanatory and differentiation strategies later. Leaders and followers in the client growth can also be targeted at different stages of the life cycle, as can different segments, and so on. A similar point applies to the planning of distribution strategies.

Using such heuristics in an MFO framework opens up new strategic possibilities, new ways of managing means to achieve the policy goals and objectives of the government of the day. The issues are: (a) whether MFO frameworks are advocating such approaches; (b) how are agencies using them; and (c) whether learnings are being derived and shared.

Delivery Strategies

MFO draws attention to effectiveness. There are many things that public managers can do to improve effectiveness in the delivery of services (e.g. Controller and Auditor-General, 1999a, b; Deputy Minister Task Force, 1996), all of which extend the idea of strategy into implementation and delivery and focus attention on initiating purposive activities that will have causal effects in realizing immediate, intermediate and ultimate objectives. One formulation (Ryan, 1991) identifies the following factors as contributing to effectiveness.

Client Access Needs

The substantive needs of clients (e.g. for a transfer payment while unemployed; provision of health care services while ill) are met through policy and program design. Clients also have a range of physical, financial, and socio-emotional needs that must be met so they can access services and outputs (e.g. travelling to outlets; the psychic and monetary costs of accessing services; brochures and forms they can understand and complete). Understanding the access needs of targeted clients is a precondition for effectiveness in delivery.

The Delivery Mix

Marketing has its "4Ps," product, price, promotion, placement all of which are designed to maximize sales and market share over time. The public sector equivalents are packaging, pricing, communication and distribution all of which can be mixed in various ways depending on the point reached in the program life cycle.

- Packaging: The ostensive benefits of policies and programs are rarely self-evident to clients. The possible meaning or value of a particular group of outputs needs to be made clear, achieved by representing the service through a package of symbols meaningful to the targeted client group. Typical packaging strategies include the use of logos, slogans, color, and design of clothing, buildings, and the like.
- Pricing: There are two primary methods of pricing: the "production cost plus (a margin)" method and the "premium/loss leader pricing" method. Production cost plus is probably appropriate although there are significant issues associated with calculating the "true and fair cost" of producing outputs in the public sector (an issue touched on in the next section of this paper). Premium pricing or loss-leader methods are probably inappropriate in the public sector except in unusual circumstances (e.g. licensing the use of publicly-produced outputs for commercial gain) – unless the notion of cross-subsidization was again to be regarded as acceptable. Another issue arises in the public sector when there is a "public good" associated with an output (a.k.a. community service obligations). In many instances, user charges should be kept to an absolute minimum so as not to limit access.

- Communication: Effective communication strategies demand that appropriate information is conveyed to clients' via media to which they have access and in a form, time, and place that they understand. Perhaps one of the biggest weaknesses of communication strategies in the public sector is that little attention is paid to this point yet it is crucial to effectiveness.

In managing delivery, most public organizations now conduct a wide range of communication strategies (more or less effectively), including public relations, promotions, press conferences, information products, advertisements, brochures and provision of web-based materials. Many organizations also now recognize sub-groups or segments ("sub-cultures") with a client group and their specific languages, ethnic and cultural. Effective communication depends on fluency. The potential of the new communication technologies in service delivery – mainly for communication but increasingly for transactions – is also on the increase. Issues associated with the "digital divide," however, remain a constraint in this respect.

- Distribution: Distribution entails ensuring clients are able to access outputs, by allocating outlets in places and spaces where targeted clients can access them. An important aspect in relation to effectiveness involves taking outputs to clients, reversing the traditional bureaucratic approach of expecting clients to come to the outputs or outlets. The design of appropriate distribution strategies entails recognizing access needs especially in relation to physical access, and a wide range of strategies are now regularly used including aspects of physical access to the built environment, decentralization, co-location, one-stop-shops, case/account management, intermediaries' telephone and visiting and mobile services and so on.

Other tools and methods introduced into the management of implementation at various points over the last decade or two of reform are worth noting for their potential contribution to effectiveness and should be part of any comprehensive MFO package. They include:

- "Total Quality Service": when "quality" is defined terms of standards that are known to signal efficacious qualities of the output to clients, then they have an effectiveness value.
- Service standards and charters: "satisfied" clients may be more inclined to use the outputs of a policy or program in the manner sought, thus bringing about the desired immediate, intermediate, and perhaps ultimate outcomes.
- Managing stakeholders: managing service delivery must involve maintaining the legitimacy and value of a policy or program in the eyes of clients and stakeholders, including those who oppose it.

- Risk management: like other heuristics, the application of risk management frameworks can remind managers to deal with threatening as well as supporting aspects of the environment. It can also serve to temper the blind enthusiasm that managers and staff can build up in relation to the strategies they are presently involved in.

Coordination in Delivery

There is no aspect that better illustrates the collective learning occurring in public management than the number and extent of present efforts being undertaken to coordinate service delivery (e.g. Home and Community Care, Strengthening Families, Oceans Policy, various kinds of case management and coordinated care trials and pilots and various types of regional coordinating groups). This applies particularly in Australia where the Federal system has forced public managers to look for ways and means to harmonies Commonwealth and State government activities. Moreover, many of these initiatives emerged out of experiments and work-around that bureaucratic and policy entrepreneurs previously created as an informal part of their delivery work (e.g. referrals between professionals and related agencies).

The aim has been "coordination and integration of otherwise fragmented services according to the holistic needs of clients." It has been about providing "seamless service" across a range of service types, regardless of which portfolio or department or agency they come from or even which level of government. Much of the drive towards coordination has also been associated with demands for devolution and localism (dealt with below).

There can be little doubt of the importance of such developments. They are fundamentally all about effectiveness. Typically, they involve developing processes of holistic needs assessment, the development of a care or service plan across a range of appropriate services – in which the client participates and is a co-producer – the ongoing coordination of delivery, periodic review, and replanning in the light of immediate and intermediate client outcomes by a designated person or agency. In some cases, funds have even been pooled prior to delivery in order to enable the service mix to be entirely shaped according to clients' needs. Every aspect of service coordination is predicated on creating the conditions for effectiveness.

Devolution and Localism

These developments are equally part of accumulated learning about effectiveness and strategic, outcome-oriented management. They also reflect tacit recognition of the changing conditions of governance and public management – again, pioneered through innovations in policy networks but drawing on older ideas of community development and newer ideas regarding social capital (PIU, 2002a, b).

The principle of "local solutions to local problems" are now well accepted. It assumes an overall national framework of agreed goals and objectives but with discretions at the local level to identify the mix of outcomes sought in any locality or community (noting that "communities" are no longer understood only in geographic terms) and the mix of services required to achieve them. This may involve community consultations that shape individual and collective agency responses in a region, or it may involve devolution of budget holding such that a community is given the authority to decide priorities and allocate resources. Once again, the focus is effectiveness; finding a governance process that will best meet the agreed goals and objectives of government of the day and the policy community.

As with many developments in enacted practice identified throughout this analysis, coordination of delivery and devolution and localism represent important and accumulated learnings about managing means for policy ends. To a significant degree, they have already become emerging norms within public management in both New Zealand and Australia and are fundamental to implementing for outcomes.

MONITORING FOR OUTCOMES

Learning to Monitor Outcomes and Monitoring Outcomes to Learn

Monitoring the right things in the right way for the right reasons is crucial to the success of MFO especially given the recent prevalence in Australasian jurisdictions of monitoring for control ("of agents by principals") – that has its place but which must be balanced.

The public managerial reform agenda has always argued that monitoring is crucial to effective management (see Fig. 4) and, even in its early formulations; the idea that its primary purpose is improving management was strong. If 21st century public management is moving towards a learning model, then monitoring for the purposes of learning about what does and does not work and hence improving management in relation to achieving outcomes becomes even more important – for all members of the political executive, ministers as well as officials.

Actual Outcomes: Immediate and Intermediate

Too much monitoring to date has focused on matters of process, resource-use, and output. Even quality, when combined with quantity, cost, timeliness, and location, is an output measure, usually whether the output conforms to specified technical

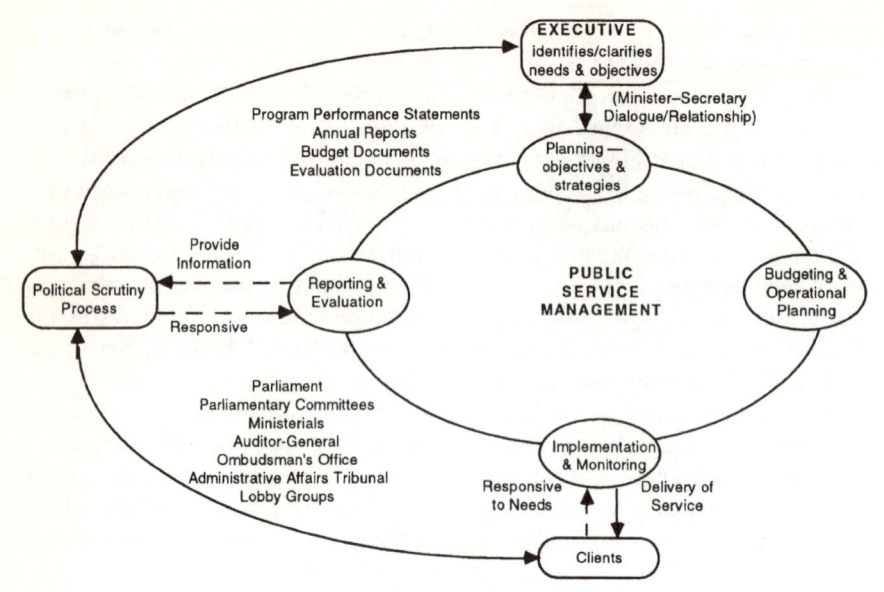

Fig. 4. The Management Cycle. *Source:* Barrett, 1992, p. 3.

or process standards. Monitoring outcomes under an MFO framework demands that outcomes – actual outcomes – are the focus of attention. Other information is certainly required by managers to manage organizational processes but, in relation to outcomes, is of little use.

In other cases, too much attention is paid to high-level outcomes. Ultimate outcomes (e.g. societal states) are usually complex effects of myriad events and activities and usually cannot simply or directly be attributed to government action and certainly not within a specifiable timeframe. MFO has more to gain from monitoring immediate and intermediate outcomes – which can then be interpreted against the logic model driving management to assess progress. Moreover, the immediate outcomes of implementation and service delivery are clearly identifiable and readily measured.

This last statement might cause surprise since it is often said outcomes are difficult to measure. In one respect, of course, this is true. They are difficult to "measure." The difficulties arise only if "measurement" is assumed to be exclusively quantitative or if the search for indicators is restricted to formal, validated indicators used in "scientific" research. Freed of those bounds, indicators are easier to find or create. Professionals have been doing it for decades via complex qualitative and quantitative (often non-positivist) assessments that they use to: (a) diagnose and prescribe; and (b) review and (re)prescribe as required. They also use the same methods to weigh up progress. And their indicators are quite objective; they are legitimated by acceptance as the "rules of thumb," the "know-how" that professionals in those fields use as a matter of course. Bureaucratic entrepreneurs do something similar. MFO frameworks should point managers' attention in these directions. The task ahead is not to ignore or derogate non-positivist approaches based on professional judgement but to make them objective through collective codification and criteria for their use (Ryan, 1996, 2002a, b).

Recursive Learning and Strategic Dialogue

Monitoring outcomes in this way is crucial for management improvement. It is also crucial for the ongoing strategic dialogue that should be conducted in (re)planning. To ensure this occurs, managers must shift their monitoring to actual immediate and intermediate outcomes and regard it as learning. So should ministers and cabinet. The ongoing strategic dialogue that is essential to effective MFO should be based on recursive policy and management learning. Monitoring information on actual immediate and intermediate outcomes will and should cause ministers and managers to rethink their goals, objectives, and strategies in the light of these new conditions of implementation. And so the management cycle will continue.

Outputs or Process? Performance Reports and Performance Culture

In relation to building and establishing MFO, a performance culture is equally important as performance reports. The former will automatically lead to the latter but not vice versa. Public management frameworks tend to emphasis documents and their standardization thereby over-emphasizing formal accountabilities but, like many other aspects of management, the process itself is where the important things happen. It is worth noting that, despite their apparent organizational informality, bureaucratic entrepreneurs invariably monitor; they always ask what is required to meet the objectives and whether these are being achieved, they look constantly for signs of success and not always the same ones. They do record the evidence but only in optimal forms, valuing informal as much as formal means. Again, there is a lesson here – although necessarily mediated by the requirements of public accountability. MFO prescriptions should focus as much on ways of working as the production of formal documents – certainly not standardized pro formas that do not relate to policy outcomes.

Concerns are often expressed that performance reports are sometimes produced by agencies out of compliance and not used by ministers and parliaments in the manner intended. When given over to information for one type of purpose and little of it policy-related information, this is not surprising. Their production and use will change if the knowledge (not just information and certainly not just data) brought to ministerial and parliamentary considerations is relevant, timely and useful. They will be if the performance indicators are developed from the logic model and/or from the middle-outwards. Collated, analyzed, and interpreted, they will provide useful knowledge for providers, managers, and ministers, ongoing learnings about progress towards policy goals and objectives.

MFO EVOLUTION: MEANS AND ISSUES

MFO refocuses attention on issues regarding the types and use of indicators that arise periodically. These include the following.

Simple or Complex

Most performance information currently reported by agencies is based on simple indicators. Nominal and ordinal measures abound and they are overwhelmingly quantitative (they are also often process oriented). Occasional reports will contain more complex indicators such as a qualitative matrix or typology or a quantitative index – and the benefits of creating and using them are immediately apparent. If MFO is to mature, several developments have to occur, one of which is systematic development of more complex indicators – whilst acknowledging the volume of work usually required developing, testing and conventionalizing them. Outcomes in all their complexity require explication. Forms of performance indication that are up to this task must become sufficiently sophisticated to deal with the realities they are supposed to signify.

Direct or Proxy

It is often said that if a direct indicator is not readily available then use a proxy; i.e. one that that does not directly or validly address the outcome sought but that, for example, focuses on another or contiguous factor that is correlated with the presence of the desired state of affairs. In practice, though, proxies are commonplace – selected too often because of intellectual defeat in the face of complexity. If the outcomes to be monitored are complex then a complex but direct indicator, qualitative or quantitative (e.g. a matrix/typology or index) should be constructed.

Managing for outcomes is complex and creating appropriate means is taxing. Wistful attempts to keep it simple are little help and sometimes damaging.

Standardized or Bespoke

Standardization and comparability are not always desirable or even possible when monitoring outcomes. Each policy field has its own specific circumstances, its own conditions. As strategies are developed for each in the light of its particular conditions, so must the indicators of progress be custom-made to deal with those specifics. There is every reason to believe that agencies working in sectoral contexts and/or in similar circumstances to their international counterparts can collaborate and use similar or related indicators to enable some level of comparison and collective learning. But, by and large, policy fields are not all apples or oranges.

Qualitative or Quantitative

This is probably one of the most important issues in evaluation and monitoring and one most likely to have a significant influence on the development of MFO in coming years (about which more will be said in the section on evaluation).

The quantitative fixation within public management has been a constraint on its development. There is now cautious growing acceptance of the possibilities of qualitative methods and a willingness to use them properly and rigorously in monitoring (e.g. in social policies, where they are particularly appropriate). The case for doing so derives partly from the capacity of qualitative methods to pull together large amounts of data in a manner that enables objective, plausible, and adequate judgements on performance. Monitoring, like other forms of knowledge management in the 21st century, must be founded on post-positivist epistemologies and methodologies.

EVALUATION IN MFO

The significance of evaluation in an MFO framework is apparent from its definition. Evaluation uses the methods of social science to assess the value and significance of an enacted policy or process and its outcomes. It describes the actual outcomes of policy and/or management, compares them with the original goals and objectives, describes any variation, explains any variation, assesses the achieved state of affairs relative to the original need or problem (including whether the need or problem is still defined as such) and recommends future actions. The information thus generated can be interpreted by managers and ministers to improve the policy and/or its management, add, or subtract resources as required, and to account to parliament and the public for what has or has not been achieved.

If learning is becoming a sine qua non of public management in the 21st century, the formative approach to evaluation comes into its own. This proposes that evaluation is best undertaken during development and implementation to provide an ongoing flow of clarification, assessment, and advice, to help managers and participants find paths to their objectives (even to engage in revisiting their substance). In that respect the evaluator is a disinterested but engaged participant in the policy and management process. This approach differs radically from the traditional "summative" evaluation traditionally carried out after the program has reached maturity, usually conducted by an expert perceived to be independent and expected to derive an objective truth.

Monitoring and evaluation also contribute to the strategic learning that must occur within the political executive and the accountability of the executive to parliament and society. Trends towards devolution include increasing participation by a wider range of voices (including attentive publics) who are increasingly involved in evaluation and monitoring (e.g. stakeholder and client evaluation). The collective and collaborative creation and brokerage of knowledge ("knowledge management") is increasingly significant at all stages of the policy and management process. MFO initiatives should promote evaluation in that context and manner. Key issues are linking evaluation and strategy.

MFO and Types of Evaluation

The search for effectiveness and appropriateness, reviewing actual outcomes against those intended, is crucial under MFO. This means evaluating ultimate, intermediate, and immediate outcomes, the program or policy logic model and the manner in which it is materialized and managed by those responsible. Different types of evaluation can be timed relative to strategy so that relevant knowledge is created at a useful time.

Impact evaluation, the classic form of evaluation, the evaluation approach that identifies actual outcomes (as well as unintended, unacknowledged and unknown outcomes), can be applied prior to the achievement of ultimate outcomes. Immediate and intermediate outcomes being achieved during implementation can be explored, to check whether reality is holding together in the manner anticipated in the logic model. If not, remedial action can be taken in relation to policy objectives, design or management or all of the above. An MFO framework could and probably should propose regular intermediate impact evaluation, especially if based on "4th generation" (Guba & Lincoln, 1989) or "formative" designs (e.g. action research) to enable ongoing learning during policy (re)implementation and (re)design (see also Patton, 1990).

Process evaluation sets out to examine whether the program or service processes are working as expected and, if not, provide restorative or progressive recommendations. Process evaluation is primarily interested in the activities wherein outputs are produced, and whether the outputs have the characteristics anticipated in the logic model such that, if they are, there is a reasonable expectation that the ultimate outcomes will be achieved. The learnings provided by this type of evaluation can feed recursively into the logic model itself and the policy goals and objectives. In fact, a well-designed process evaluation is likely to combine an impact evaluation of immediate and intermediate outcomes with a process evaluation of implementation and management. MFO frameworks can and should strongly promote this type of evaluation.

Effective MFO can and should also rely on ex-ante evaluation. As with logic modeling (to which it is closely related), this type of evaluation is unfamiliar by name to many public managers but not by enacted practice. It involves evaluation of an option or proposal before it is implemented – something that effective strategic managers are inclined to do anyway, whether formally or informally. Ex-ante evaluation attempts to answer the question, "What if?" by modeling, or simulating the effects of changing a key factor in the policy or its management or the policy and management environment. Social and environmental impact assessments are well known, as are econometric and sociometric modeling; less well-known is the idea of a hypothetical run-through of a policy design or management plan: i.e. a conceptual test of the program model based on accepted concepts, models, and theories. In this sense, ex-ante evaluation is a powerful MFO heuristic that should be recommended for wide use.

Evaluation and the Program Life Cycle

How to connect evaluation and strategy? The program life cycle can help answer the question.

The program life cycle gives a clue to what types of evaluation should be undertaken when (see Fig. 5). Ex-ante evaluation should be conducted at the design stage and prior to introduction. Process evaluation during growth can be focused on understanding the actual (immediate, intermediate) outcomes of the program relative to those sought, and the meaning of the emerging outcomes relative to the stated objectives, strategies, policy design and program management – any of which could be modified in the light of recursive learning. Impact evaluation should be conducted from the time the program or policy approaches maturity.

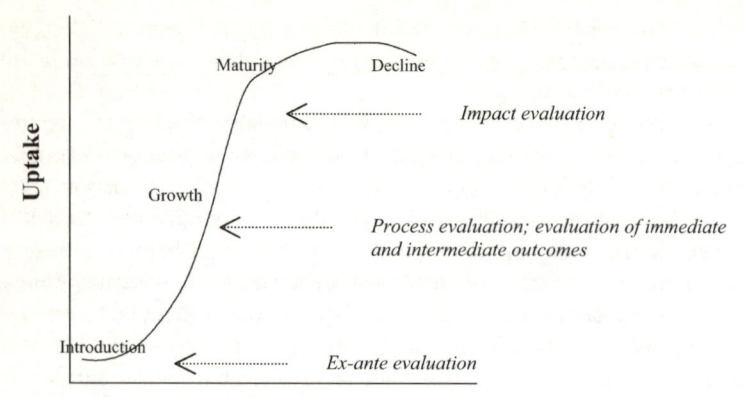

Fig. 5. Types of Evaluation in Relation to the Program Life Cycle. *Source:* Author, 2001.

Positivist, Non-Positivist and Post-Positivist Evaluation

Not only must MFO frameworks promote evaluation, they should also promote the full range of evaluation designs and methodologies and the context-dependence of their application. Evaluation, unfortunately, has been dominated by positivist methodologies (sometimes referred to incorrectly as "quantitative approaches") in the belief that this represented "proper" scientific method: quasi-experimental methodology was regarded and still is by some as the gold standard evaluation design. More recently, non-positivist approaches (sometimes called "qualitative") and post-positivist approaches have been advocated and widely accepted within the evaluation and research community (see especially Patton, 1990; and Fischer, 1998 respectively; also Guba & Lincoln, 1989).

What is meant by the idea of post-positivism? There is no standard definition of "post positivism." Most fundamentally, it is grounded in the idea that reality exists, but can never be fully understood or explained, given both the multiplicity of causes and effects and the problem of social meaning. Objectivity can serve as an ideal, but requires a critical community of interpreters. Critical of empiricism, it emphasizes the social construction of theory and concepts, and qualitative approaches the discovery of knowledge...McCarthy...has defined the task of developing a post positivist methodology of social inquiry as figuring out how to combine the practice of political and social theory with the methodological rigor of modern science (Fischer, 1998, footnote 2).

A particular point to make is that post-positivism is not at all opposed to the appropriate use of quantitative methods, nor does it repeat the positivist error in reverse by privileging particular methods (e.g. qualitative methods – see also

Shaw, 1999). Generally, post-positivist approaches to research and knowledge promote context-dependence and relativism in relation to epistemology (theories of knowledge) and methodology (ways of creating knowledge) and are willing to use a range of quantitative and qualitative methods (tools for collecting and analyzing evidence) – if for no other reason than the complexity, contextually and paradoxes of contemporary realities and a learning approach to public management make this essential. The wisdom in play here reflects a very old rule of research design. The question asked determines the types of information needed to answer it. The types of information required determines the types of data needed to construct it; the types of data require determine the methods needed to capture it; and the methods will be drawn from a certain selection of research methodologies. For this reason, some authors prefer to talk of "mixed method" approaches to analysis and evaluation rather than locate their discussion in the complexities of the philosophy of science (Greene & Caracelli, 1997).

Unfortunately, public management reformers in many jurisdictions seem unaware of these developments and continue promoting older and much less appropriate conventional wisdom. Even worse, non-positivist or post-positivist designs are often frowned upon or not regarded as legitimate or, prima facie, not rigorous. This is bad advice from my view. Rigor should no longer be an issue given recent improvements in qualitative methods (e.g. Miles & Huberman, 1994; see also Blaikie, 2000). The real benefit of non-positivist and post-positivist approaches to evaluation though is that they make no claims to independent scientific authority, are self-reflexive of their weaknesses and the crucial role of human judgement in assessing the value or otherwise in policy processes and outcomes. In that respect alone, post-positivist approaches to evaluation are more appropriate for the conditions of governance in the 21st century. Its recommendation should figure strongly in MFO.

FUTURE APPROACHES FOR EVALUATION UNDER MFO

Technical Capacity or Evaluative Culture?

MFO removes any place for agencies to hide in relation to evaluation. Australian agencies are generally thought to have an adequate evaluation capacity (which may or may not be correct) but the same does not apply on the other side of the Tasman Sea. So, should New Zealand agencies commence immediately building their technical evaluation capacity and should the central agencies with oversight of MFO be helping them to do so?

Technocratic and scientific approaches retain a legitimate place in the evaluation armory so some level of technical capacity building over the long term is required (for a fuller account, see Ryan, 2003a, b). Demand should also be strengthened; ministers and agencies are requesting and commissioning more evaluation, as they should do within MFO. Supply needs to be cranked up via professional and university training. More evaluators and evaluation houses are needed as well as evaluation units within agencies. One or more central and/or line agencies should become a sector wide consultant or resource in relation to evaluation, brokering advice, consultancy services and training.

However, the spirit of 21st century public management under MFO views technique and science as only one set of means amongst many. This analysis has stressed the conditional and contingent character of practice, the hypothetical character of strategy ("strategic groping" – see also Behn, 1988 on "managing by groping along") and the open learning approach that must sit under it. Post-modern public management admires technocracy and science but puts them in their place and reinstates heuristics, practical knowing, experience, and judgement alongside them. On that basis, it is equally inclined to focus on everyday practice, values and culture as the basis for organizational and management development. Accordingly, the success of MFO in coming years must depend on building evaluative management and evaluative cultures within and between organizations over the short and medium term. This means that certain questions will constantly drive management, such as "How are we doing?," "How close are we getting to our goals and objectives?," "Will these actions and activities take us closer – if so, how, can we improve, and, if not, why are we doing it?" Doing so presupposes an organization with the commitment and courage to confront the answers, even if negative. Creating an evaluative culture of this type in organizational that are managing for outcomes is as important as developing a technical evaluation capacity.

Rigorous and Costly or Rough-'n-Ready?

The case for "rough-'n-ready but valid, timely, shrewd and efficient evaluation" is based on an argument regarding "appropriate" knowledge, and the degree of fit between management need and evaluation provision. If management is learning how to act strategically without full or certain knowledge, aware that strategy is provisional and subject to recursive learning, then any choice of strategy is a hypothesis about its impact. It is an 80/20 and perhaps even 60/40 game where optimality is the goal. By extension, monitoring and evaluation of progress is therefore essential to maintain direction and purpose, but the type and quality of the knowledge required to strategies and act must be fit for purpose and at an equivalent level of confidence.

Managers need a type of knowledge that is strategic, effect-oriented, timely, conditional, and cost-effective: they need appropriate knowledge, knowledge of a type, level, and rigor that matches the task at hand. This will sometimes be knowledge constructed from precise, extensive, and artful methods. More often than not it will be useful knowledge, timely, context-specific, and strategically valid – the types of knowledge more likely to come from evaluative organizational cultures and internal evaluation than specialist, external evaluation units. What exactly constitutes rough-'n-ready evaluation is not clear but it would have something to do with allowing accumulated, tacit experience and/or consensus formation to validate strategic choices from within uncertain knowledge. It would also involve a fair amount of "evaluation by walking around" (to paraphrase an old management axiom), using the powers of observation, listening, interpretation and judgement.

Internal or External?

The classic argument is that evaluation should be external and independent, so as to avoid bias and vested interest distorting the "truth" created by the evaluation.

From the last decades of the 20th century, partly because of the rise of relativism, but also because of the new conditions of governance, learning approaches to strategy, delivery and evaluation have come to the fore. This modifies traditional understandings of the form and content of evaluation. If management is learning – as it must be under MFO – it is probable that internal evaluations will take on greater importance (without taking away from those circumstances in which external evaluation is essential). With internal evaluations, managers, staff, clients and stakeholders, often combined with specialist evaluators, is all involved in ongoing evaluation over time, constantly questioning and constantly learning. Nor need objectivity be compromised. Honesty and disinterest can be achieved via an independent chair of the steering group, or balanced participation in all aspects of design and implementation, or peer oversight and meta-evaluation. Undertaken in this way, internal evaluations can become extraordinarily useful and able to generate more accepted and feasible recommendations than many an external evaluation. As such they have a definite role in the future of MFO.

CONCLUSIONS

The types of analysis outlined here highlight the many incompatibilities between a full-blown "managing for outcomes" framework applied to governance and public management, and the historical conventions that underpin Australasian polities and their current accepted management practices – notwithstanding the significant departures including that of the Australian Commonwealth, especially in relation to reform of the Australian Senate (Chapman, 2000). The MFO model developed here emphasizes a proactive public sector focused on the purposes and outcomes of policy, a collective public manager who stands as a partner with the minister and less of the classic subordinate public servant (actually, a genuinely "public" servant as opposed to the "ministerial" servant that has been (re)institutionalized in some jurisdictions in recent years). But in some respects, the ideal-type or model of MFO elaborated here looks unrealistic. Political rationality runs strong in Australasian polities with traditions of strong political executives and subordinate and anxious public servants. "Macho" manners in the House, a competitive and adversarial party system and an unforgiving media allow few subtleties. Public servants, senior managers in particular, play the odds conservatively. Few risk "having their heads shot off." Survival depends on "staying behind the line of fire" and not being "courageous." The prospect of a heuristic/entrepreneurial rationality permeating one half of the executive with learning and strategic dialogue at its core seems like too un-Westminsterian a flower to survive.

The truth is though that the model of MFO in the 21st century has been created at least in part from observation. Some of the elements explored in this article are already established and are acquiring a level of legitimacy – because they work or seem to. They represent learnings derived from almost two decades of public management. And there seems to be a new determination across all the liberal democracies (e.g. Australia, New Zealand, Britain, Canada, the U.S.) to grapple with the difficulties. Change is occurring across many fronts that take time and distance to register. Who would have predicted 25 years ago the enormous changes that have taken place in our systems of governance since the early 1980s? My guess is that current trends will continue, some more quickly than others but few at a transformational rate, reaching a new stage of maturity in around a decade.

In Australasia, this must include reconstituting accountability relationships between the two arms of the executive, between the executive and parliament and the executive and economic and civil societies – probably forgetting "Westminster" and, as John Dawkins (1985) has argued, identifying what we mean by our own systems of government. If governments do mean to "manage for outcomes," then explicating the issue of accountability in a context of partnership, alliance and interdependency will need to be worked through. For the moment, any MFO framework needs to recognize: (a) collaborative and multiple responsibilities and accountabilities for governance-level outcomes; (b) ensure that ministers, agencies and managers think, talk and act in that manner; and (c) that the internal, external and parliamentary discourses surrounding accountability account for the subtleties involved. The timing is probably better now than at any time since the 1990s. An

MFO framework that retreats into reductionism will engender cynicism and disengagement. An MFO framework that is courageous will become a self-fulfilling prophecy.

REFERENCES

Argyris, C., & Schön, D. (1978). *Organizational learning: A theory of action perspective*. Reading, MA: Addison Wesley.
DOFA, Australian Commonwealth. Department of Finance and Administration (2000). *The outcomes and outputs framework: Guidance document*. Canberra.
Baehler, K. (2002). Intervention logic: A user's guide. *Public Sector*, 25(3, September), 14–20.
Behn, R. (1988). Management by groping along. *Journal of Policy Analysis and Management*, 7(4, Fall), 643–663.
Chapman, R. (2000). Accountability: Is Westminster the problem? *Australian Journal of Public Administration*, 59(4), 116–123.
Clegg, S. (1990). *Modern organizations: Organization studies in the postmodern world*. London: Sage.
Controller and Auditor General (1999a). The accountability of executive government to parliament, third report for 1999. Office of the Auditor-General, Wellington.
Controller and Auditor General (1999b). Towards service excellence: The responsiveness of government agencies to their clients. Office of the Auditor-General, Wellington.
Deputy Minister Task Force (1996). Discussion paper on service delivery models. Ottawa.
Giddens, A. (1984). *The constitution of society: Outline of the theory of structuration*. Cambridge: Polity Press.
Giddens, A. (1990). *The consequences of modernity*. Cambridge: Polity Press.
Greene, C., & Caracelli, V. (Eds) (1997). New directions for evaluation, advances in mixed-method evaluation: The challenges and benefits of integrating diverse paradigms, No. 74. San Francisco: Jossey-Bass.
Guba, E., & Lincoln, Y. (1989). *Fourth generation evaluation*. Newbury Park: Sage.
Harvey, D. (1989). *The condition of postmodernity*. Oxford: Blackwell.
Hesselbein, F., Goldsmith, M., & Beckhard, R. (Eds) (1996). *The leader of the future: New visions, strategies and practices for the next era*. San Francisco: Jossey Bass.
Hogwood, C., & Gunn, C. (1994). *Policy analysis for the real world*. Oxford: Oxford University Press.
Hood, C., & Jackson, M. (1991). *Administrative argument*. Aldershot: Dartmouth Publishing.
Kuhn, T. (1970). *The structure of scientific revolutions enlarged* (2nd ed.). Chicago: University of Chicago Press.
Lane, J.-E. (1993). *The public sector: concepts, models and approaches*. London: Sage.
Limerick, D., & Cunnington, B. (1993). *Managing the new organisation: A blueprint for networks and strategic alliances*. Chatswood: Business and Professional Publishing.
Miles, M., & Huberman, A. (1994). *Qualitative data analysis: An expanded sourcebook*. Thousand Oaks: Sage.
Mintzberg, H. (1994). *The rise and fall of strategic planning*. New York: Free Press.
Mintzberg, H., & Waters, J. A. (1985). Of strategies, deliberate and emergent. *Strategic Management Journal*, 6, 257–272.
OECD, Organization for Economic Co-operation and Development (2000a). *Government of the future*. Paris: OECD.

OECD, Organization for Economic Co-operation and Development (2000b). *Trust in government: Ethics measures in OECD countries*. Paris: OECD.
OECD, Organization for Economic Co-operation and Development (2001a). *Devolution and globalisation: Implications for local decision-makers*. Paris: OECD.
OECD, Organization for Economic Co-operation and Development (2001b). *Governance in the 21st century*. Paris: OECD.
OECD, Organization for Economic Co-operation and Development (2001c). *Citizens as partners: Information, consultation and public participation in policy-making*. Paris: OECD.
OECD, Organization for Economic Co-operation and Development (2001d). *Public Sector leadership for the 21st century*. Paris: OECD.
Patton, M. (1990). *Qualitative evaluation and research methods* (2nd ed.). Newbury Park: Sage.
Peters, B. G. (1998). *Managing horizontal government: The politics of coordination*. Research Paper No. 21. Canadian Centre for Management Development.
PIU, Performance and Innovation Unit (2002a). Social capital: A discussion paper. London, UK: Cabinet Office.
PIU, Performance and Innovation Unit (2002b). Strengthening leadership in the public sector: A research study by the PIU. London, UK: Cabinet Office.
Pressman, J., & Wildavsky, A. (1984). *Implementation: How great expectations in Washington are dashed in Oakland; Or why it's amazing that federal programs work at all this being a saga of the economic development administration as told by two sympathetic observers who seek to build morals on a foundation of ruined hopes* (3rd ed.). Berkley: University of California Press.
Queensland Treasury (1997). *Managing for outcomes in Queensland*. Brisbane: Treasury.
Radin, B. (2000). The Government Performance and Results Act and the tradition of federal management reform: Square pegs in round holes? *Journal of Public Administration Research and Theory, 10*(1), 111–135.
Rhodes, R., & Marsh, D. (1992). New directions in the study of policy networks. *European Journal of Political Research, 21*, 181–205.
Rose, R. (1989). *Ordinary people in public policy: A behavioural analysis*. London: Sage.
Ryan, B. (1991). Towards a model of public sector marketing. In: C. O'Faircheallaigh, P. Graham & J. Warburton (Eds), *Service Delivery and Public Sector Marketing*. South Melbourne: Macmillan.
Ryan, B. (2001). A missing link? Effective public management and the idea of utilization. In: *Essays in Implementation and Service Delivery 1990–1993*. Unpublished manuscript, Victoria University of Wellington.
Ryan, B. (2002a, November). Beyond intervention logic? A public management heuristic for the 21st century. Paper presented to the association for public policy analysis and management 24th annual research conference, asking "what if...": assessing the public policy and management implications of social science research. Dallas, TX, 7–9.
Ryan, B. (2002b). Managing for outcomes in the 21st century: A discussion paper. Brisbane, Institute of Public Administration Australia, available from http://www.ipaa.org.au.
Ryan, B. (2003a, April). From technocracy to learning: Analysing and evaluating in the 21st century. Paper presented to the Ministry of Social Development Social Policy Research and Evaluation Conference, Wellington, 28–29, available at http://www.msp.govt.nz/keyinitiatives/conference/abstracts/index.html#Parallel1.
Ryan, B. (2003b, July). Hard yards ahead: The second stage of public sector reform in New Zealand, 1996–2003. *International Review of Public Administration, 8*(1).

Sabatier, P. (1986). Top-down and bottom-up approaches to implementation research: A critical analysis and suggested synthesis. *Journal of Public Policy*, 6(1), 21–48.

Saldanha, C., & Whittle, J. (1998). *Using the logical framework for sector analysis and project design: A user's guide*. New York: Asian Development Bank International.

Schön, D. (1983). *The reflective practitioner. How professionals think in action*. London: Temple Smith.

Senge, P. (1990). *The fifth discipline: The art and practice of the learning organization*. New York: Random House.

Shaw, I. (1999). *Qualitative evaluation*. London: Sage.

TBC, Treasury Board of Canada (2000). *Managing for results 2000*. Treasury Board of Canada, Ontario.

Thompson, G., Frances, J., Levaˇci'c, R., & Mitchell, J. (Eds) (1991). *Markets, hierarchies and networks: The coordination of social life*. London: Sage (in association with the Open University).

TFMI, Task Force on Management Improvement (1992). *The Australian public service reformed: An evaluation of a decade of management reform*. Canberra: AGPS.

Tsy/SSC, New Zealand. Treasury/State Services Commission (2002). *Pathfinder: Guidance on outcomes based management*. http://www.io.ssc.govt.nz/pathfinder accessed August 2002.

PART V:
TRENDS IN REFORM STRATEGY

18. ASSESSING PUBLIC MANAGEMENT REFORM STRATEGY IN AN INTERNATIONAL CONTEXT

Lawrence R. Jones and Donald F. Kettl

INTRODUCTION

This concluding chapter attempts to capture and extend the lessons rendered in the previous chapters in this book. In overview we may observe that over the past three decades, criticisms about government performance have surfaced across the world from all points of the political spectrum. Critics have alleged that governments are inefficient, ineffective, too large, too costly, overly bureaucratic, overburdened by unnecessary rules, unresponsive to public wants and needs, secretive, undemocratic, invasive into the private rights of citizens, self-serving, and failing in the provision of either the quantity or quality of services deserved by the taxpaying public (see, for example, Barzelay & Armajani, 1992; Jones & Thompson, 1999; Osborne & Gaebler, 1993). Fiscal stress has also plagued many governments and has increased the cry for less costly or less expansive government, for greater efficiency, and for increased responsiveness. High profile members of the business community, financial institutions, the media, management consultants, academic scholars and the general public all have pressured politicians and public managers to reform. So, too have many supranational organizations, including OECD, the World Bank, the European Commission. Accompanying the demand and many of the recommendations for change has been support for the application of market-based logic and private sector management methods to government (see, for example, Harr & Godfrey, 1991; Jones & Thompson, 1999; Milgrom & Roberts, 1992; Moe, 1984; Olson et al., 1998). Application of market-driven solutions and business techniques to the public sector has undoubtedly been encouraged by the growing ranks of public sector managers and analysts educated in business schools and public management programs (Pusey, 1991).

Driving the managerial reform movement has been a notion that the public sector builds on the wrong principles and needs reinvention and institutional renewal (Barzelay & Armajani, 1992; Jones & Thompson, 1999; Osborne & Gaebler, 1993). The strategies have included caps on public spending, tax cuts, selling off of public assets, contracting out of many services previously provided by government, development of performance measurement, output- and outcomes-based budgeting, and business-type accounting (Guthrie et al., 1997). The reforms produced all sorts of promises: a smaller, less interventionist and more decentralized government; improved public sector efficiency and effectiveness; greater public service responsiveness and accountability to citizens; increased choice between public and private providers of public services; an "entrepreneurial" public sector more willing and able to work with business; and better economic performance, among others.

The potential has lured many elected officials to what has become known as the "new public management" (NPM). However, academic observers, citizens, and public managers alike have wondered how many of these promises will produce genuine results – and how long any such results will endure. Some principles have already well established themselves. The financial management and accounting reforms have already proven successful. So, too, is the notion that public organizations should be better managed, more responsive, and held more accountable for results. Almost everything else about the new public management, though, is open for debate.

In both practice and study, NPM is an international phenomenon (see, for example, Borins, 1997; Gray & Jenkins, 1995; Hood, 1995, 2000; Jones & Schedler, 1997; Kettl, 2000a; Olsen & Peters, 1996). The OECD continues to monitor NPM developments across a range of countries (OECD, 1997; PUMA, 1999), and researchers report on developments in particular countries, especially New Zealand, which have drawn international attention (Boston et al., 1996; Guthrie & Parker, 1998; Jones & Schedler, 1997; Pallot, 1998). In its early days in the 1980s, NPM was mostly strongly associated with right-leaning governments, like Thatcher in the U.K., Reagan in the U.S., and Hawke in Australia. Since then, however, it has lost its ideological stripes. Left-leaning governments like Clinton in the U.S. and Blair in the U.K. have embraced it as well, along with a democratic Swedish parliament and a conservative British parliament (Olson et al., 1998).

Despite the rapid spread of these reforms, they have produced wide diversity in practice, even across countries widely regarded as active reformers (Guthrie et al., 1997; Olson et al., 1998). If financial management and accounting changes have been perhaps the most universal reforms, there has been little detailed analysis of the practical application and results of these techniques (Hood, 1995; March & Olsen, 1995). Indeed, analysts have found that the new public financial management has not been so much a uniform, global movement as a "reforming spirit" focused on instilling private sector financial practices into public sector decision making. It has emphasized new standards in financial reporting, accrual accounting, debt and surplus management, and capital investment strategy that had previously been missing from much government decision making. It there has been broad application of these techniques, however, there has been little research about what results these strategies are likely to produce.

Attempts to understand the global public management reform movement suggest two general implications for research. First, there is a glaring need to understand the short- and long-term outcomes of the reforms where they have been implemented. Second, despite the importance of conducting this research, doing so is almost impossible in the short term and exceedingly difficult in the long term. It is hard enough simply to keep pace with management changes in each nation. It is even harder to make sound multi-country comparisons. Efforts to solve this problem sometimes have led researchers to use a particular nation's reforms – often New Zealand's – as a benchmark, but the particular problems facing each nation weaken the value of such comparisons (see, for example, Barton, 2000; Olson, Humphrey & Guthrie, 2000; Riley & Watling, 1999). The paucity of "results about reforms" – and the need to assess whether management reforms have helped each nation solve its particular problems – should motivate researchers to press ahead.

LESSONS FROM REFORM IN AUSTRALIA AND NEW ZEALAND

Scholars have perhaps focused most on the Australian and New Zealand reforms. They were the vanguard of the NPM. Their strategies and tactics heavily influenced the broader scholarly debate as well as the practice in many other nations. Any understanding of the NPM, therefore, must begin there.

English and Guthrie, for example, have analysed the NPM in Victoria, Australia's second largest state, between 1992 and 1999 (English & Guthrie, 2001). The reforms were far-reaching and aimed at a major shift in the role and accountability of government. The Victorian model grew on a well-articulated theoretical framework from classical economic theory, and it was well supported by a series of specific government directives and manuals. The reforms attempted to be comprehensive, tackling all components of the public sector and its subsystems. The output-management model developed to determine and report on expenditure, planning, financial management, control and evaluation were comprehensive in both scope and implementation. The reforms, however, promised more than they delivered. In particular, the speed and massive scale of contracting out and privatisation proved difficult to implement.

In fact, Hughes and O'Neill (2001) argue, the public management reforms introduced in Victoria by the Kennett government led to somewhat contradictory consequences. While the government implemented arguably successful reforms, particularly in sale of government assets and privatization of services and balanced the budget after serious deficits, cuts in social services also appear to have contributed to Kennett's electoral defeat. The new public management may have some payoffs, but the political consequences can be significant and unanticipated.

Carlin and Guthrie have examined recent efforts in Australian and New Zealand public sectors to implement accrual output-based budgeting (Carlin & Guthrie, 2001). While agreeing on the need for public sector accounting reform, the authors use two detailed case studies – Queensland, Australia and the New Zealand national government – to show that the reforms have not accomplished all that their governments had hoped. For example, there is little real difference between the old cash-based and the new accrual budgets. That led the authors to wonder about the effectiveness of management reforms if decision making was unchanged. Carlin and Guthrie identify three conditions to be met if reforms in public sector accounting are to succeed. First, carefully defined and appropriately specified outputs that relate directly to the activities of the agency are needed. Second, appropriately specified and measurable outcomes must be identified to provide accountability as to the degree to which public resources are achieving public goals. Third, performance indicators and performance measures should provide a link between outputs and outcomes.

In New Zealand, Jonathan Boston (2001) has examined the hard questions of that nation's cutting-edge reforms. For example, at what stage of reform in the public sector does it become possible to conduct a thorough appraisal of results and how does one know when this stage has been reached? How should such an assessment be undertaken? Boston argues that most assessments have focused upon specific changes in management practice, including the introduction of performance pay, the move to accrual accounting, the growth of contracting-out, the separation of policy and operations or the devolution of human resource management responsibilities. Some studies have dealt instead with management changes in particular policy domains – such as health care, education, community services or criminal justice – or within a particular organization (department, agency or private provider). By contrast, there have been relatively few macro evaluations: comprehensive assessments of the impact of root-and-branch changes to the system. Boston provides broad reflections on the limitations to policy evaluation in the field of public management, and more particularly explores the obstacles confronted when assessing the consequences of systemic management reforms. Given his foundation in New Zealand's reforms, perhaps the most systematic and far-reaching in the world, his warnings underline the importance of the evaluation problem.

In his own study of New Zealand, Laking (2001) agrees that serious debate about the New Zealand reform is bedevilled by the limited evaluation. In fact, he concludes, the assessments of the successes and failures of reform in New Zealand to date seem not to be particularly concerned about the absence of comprehensive evaluation. Laking finds that most evaluations tend to assert that there have been overall gains in efficiency as a result of reform, but they are far less certain or negative about the consequences for effectiveness.

Despite the lack of clear evidence about the New Zealand reforms' impact, the elegant simplicity of the reforms has had a seductive quality for analysts. Gill (2001) finds that much of the elegance has been obscured in the intervening years, but that the yield from the reforms has been significant. The trick in evaluating the New Zealand experience with public management reform, he argues, is to compare it with real world alternatives. In using the existing reforms to guide future questions, Gill attempts to unravel the disparate threads about "what remains to be done" by distinguishing four categories of problems: (a) Political – problems that are inherent to the political arena, and are evident under a range of public management regimes; (b) Incompleteness – problems that provide evidence the system is incomplete in some areas, but do not suggest inherent difficulties; (c) Implementation – problems the stem from the way the system has been implemented; and (d) Inherent – problems that flow directly from the nature of the New Zealand regime, which might be different in other systems (Gill, 2001, p. 144).

Few observers write about the New Zealand reforms with more authority than Graham Scott, one of the movement's chief architects for more than twenty years. In looking carefully at the New Zealand experience and comparing it with reforms around the world, Scott has identified important lessons (2001). Among other things, he concludes, the success of management reform depends on: (a) the clarity of roles, responsibilities and accountability in the implementation of management reform; (b) the importance of matching decision capacity to responsibility; (c) the significance of ministerial commitment and clarity of expectations; (d) the structural innovations within the New Zealand cabinet; (e) the need to analyse disasters carefully for what they teach; (f) approaches to embrace and foibles to avoid in implementing performance management; (g) problems caused by confusion over ownership and improper assessment of organizational capability; (h) the fact that actually doing strategic management in the public sector is hugely complicated; (i) that it is time to put an end to the notion that there is an "extreme model" of public management applied in New Zealand; and (j) that public management, government and governance innovations in New Zealand are no longer novel compared to those advanced in other nations. Scott concludes with an admonition to avoid too quickly drawing the conclusion from New Zealand's change in government that past reforms must be quickly and radically changed – or that the New Zealand model has failed.

A senior public servant in the New Zealand Treasury, Andrew Kibblewhite, agrees with Scott on the need for detailed analysis of results and a careful consolidation of the lessons (2001). He suggests that much of the initial energy for reform has faded, that it is time to assess what has and has not been achieved, and that it is important now to search for ways to move forward. The election of a new government in November 1999 stirred a sense of anticipation, as well as some apprehension, across the New Zealand public sector. As New Zealand moves into a new phase of reform, one of the key challenges is to take advantage of what has already been achieved to make government even more effective. Kibblewhite argues further that central agencies can sharpen the specification of outputs by being clearer about the basic management framework by being more flexible about how that framework is applied. Outcome measures should be refined and used along with outputs where feasible. However, he suggests, some outcome measures should be abandoned where they do not provide useful information.

The New Zealand reforms, however, have certainly drawn critics. Robert Gregory (2001) contents that a price has been paid for the overly narrow theoretical framework used to design state sector reforms. According to Gregory, the way ahead must be informed both by more eclectic theoretical input, as well as by closer dialogue between theory and practice. He argues that the state sector reforms in New Zealand, especially in their application to the public services, have been too "mechanistic" and too blind to the important "organic" dimensions of public organizations. They have focused too much on physical restructuring and they have tried too hard to reduce complex government practices to artificial dualities, such as "outputs" and "outcomes," "owner" and "purchaser," "founder" and "provider." They have tended to ignore the less quantifiable and more holistic elements that underpinned a strong culture of public service trusteeship in New Zealand prior to reform. Gregory argues that it is difficult to conclude that reform has all been for the good. There is too much evidence to the contrary, he asserts.

Tooley's analysis of the New Zealand school system (2001) helps identify those tensions. Despite the rhetoric about decentralization and democratization through devolution of governance and decision making to the level of the individual school and principals as chief executives, there has been a concomitant strengthening of central control over curriculum and tighter monitoring by the Education Review Office. These changes have reduced citizen choice in school education, turned principals into managers instead of skilled leaders and, ultimately, wrested control over education from educators and into the control politicians. Tooley suggests that the educational "experiment" in New Zealand is being reversed because of its inability to deliver the outcomes promised from reform. Recent changes proposed by the government suggest its intent to rein back some of the more "market-oriented" elements of the educational reforms and, in particular, to soften some of the key features of the managerialist approach to education administration. Tooley concludes that the reforms failed almost completely, and that the coalition government elected in November 2000 has or will reverse many of the changes made under previous governments.

Newberry's study of the operation during 1996 of a public hospital emergency department (2001) likewise revealed serious problems. Hostility between the hospital's clinical staff and management escalated to the point that the hospital's Medical Staff Association released a report to the public titled, "Patients are Dying: A Record of System Failure and Unsafe Healthcare Practice at Christchurch Hospital." The report detailed the story of four patient deaths and alleged that deteriorating conditions within the hospital contributed to those deaths. The Medical Staff Association sought a public inquiry, but the Health and Disability Commissioner announced a more-narrow consumers' rights inquiry. Newberry revisits that inquiry and recast its findings in the context of the NPM. She finds that, although the hospital-based reforms were structurally sound and had real value, they did not address the broader issues of performance and accountability. She concludes that NPM as applied in New Zealand needed to create better structures, involve customers more directly in evaluation and decision making, and be more accountable to the public for results.

Putterill and Speer (2001) likewise found problems in information technology. New Zealand benchmarked its IT innovation and development against its own policy aims and the achievements of a set of peer countries, chosen for similar size and technical sophistication. They concluded that peers nations have significantly outperformed New Zealand. The Zealand government maintained a "hands off" stance, while most of the peer countries actively promoted IT involvement. Putterill and Speer question past policy direction, call for more active industry involvement by the New Zealand government, and argue for more industry-friendly policies to advance competitiveness in the region.

In sum, the Australia and New Zealand reforms are the benchmarks by which reforms around the world have been judged. A careful look at those reforms – or, at least, at what analysts have written about them – reveals how much we have yet to learn about what truly has worked and why. Moreover, as the work of some analysts show, serious issues, both managerial and political, lurk just below the surface. Only more careful analysis and comparison can sort out the claims and counterclaims.

LESSONS FROM REFORM IN ASIA

Many Asian nations have worked energetically to reform their public management systems, but comparing their results has been handicapped by the relatively small collection of studies written in English. Moreover, since many of these reforms have occurred in developing nations, they present very different issues and require a different kind of analysis. Clay Goodloe Wescott (2001) poses a number of important questions concerning these Asian reforms. Is it possible, he asks, to measure the quality of overall governance in a developing Asian country? Are present measures robust enough to allow the ranking of countries along a continuum from well-governed to poorly-governed? Should these rankings be used by donor agencies and private investors in making investment decisions? Wescott reflect on these questions and concludes that, despite the complexity and diversity of approaches of governance systems, qualitative and quantitative tools are being used reasonably well in the region.

In Hong Kong, for example, Kevin Yuk-fai Au, Ilan Vertinsky and Denis Yu-long Wang chart a paradigm shift in New Public Management (2001). They argue that contemporary reform has its roots in the late 1960s and early 1970s, with periods of lull and renewal characterized by shifting powers and expectations among stakeholders. Early reforms, especially in the colonial period, sought social legitimacy. The transfer to sovereignty, adjustment of a both the economy and society, and diffusion of new ideas into public management all shaped Hong Kong. The authors investigate the conditions that shaped the reform process in each of Hong Kong's key episodes, the triggers that accelerated it, and the forces that emerged to dampen it. They conclude that, as with many nations, it is simply too early to determine whether reforms now under implementation will be successful.

Yu-Ying Kuo (2001) has explored public management reform in Taiwan in the 1990s. The apex of the movement was government reinvention. In 1998, Premier Vincent C. Siew announced, "the Executive Yuan is energetically planning for and promoting the national development plan for entering the next century, of which the Asia-Pacific Regional Operations Center (APROC) plan and the Taiwan Technology Island Initiative comprise the core." The author argues that NPM developments are likely to determine the direction of Taiwan's government modernization over the next several decades. The government has launched an across-the-board reinvention to create a new, flexible and adaptable government and to raise national competitiveness. At this point there is no way to tell what the new government that took office in 2001 will do with these developments or where they may lead.

Roberts's work (2001) has explored the strategies that public officials use to cope with "wicked problems," especially in Afghanistan. Three coping strategies – authoritative, competitive, and collaborative – have been especially important. The strategies derive from a model based on the level of conflict present in the problem solving process, the distribution of power among the stakeholders, and the degree to which power is contested. Collaborative strategies, she believes, offer the most promise, as illustrated in a case study of the relief and recovery efforts in Afghanistan. Her paper, a revised version of the contribution that won the Frieder Naschold Best Paper Award at the International Public Management Network conference held in Sydney, Australia in March 2000, explores the implications of using collaborative strategies to deal with wicked problems around the world.

The imperatives of management reform have deeply affected the institutions working with Asian nations as well as the nations themselves. David Shand, a senior official at the World Bank working in the East Asian region, has examined World Bank experience in public sector management reform in Asia (2001). He argues that public sector management reform has stimulated a "new wave" of activity in his institution since the 1970s. Many of the World Bank's strategies to reinvigorate state institutions reflect the thinking of the new institutional economics – the importance of structures, incentives, rules and restraints, norms, and best practices. Recent public sector work has focused on three of the "East Asia five" – Thailand, Indonesia, and the Philippines (the other two of the five are Korea and Malaysia). The World Bank has also focused on smaller countries including Cambodia and Laos. It has made preliminary efforts in the transition economies of China (including Mongolia) and Vietnam. Shand concludes that recent fiscal and economic crises in Asia have created urgent pressures for public sector management reform.

Less clear, however, is how the broader lessons of the Asian experience add up. Research has been scanty and far less systematic than the admittedly rudimentary work on the Australian and New Zealand reforms. Moreover, the experiences of developing Asian nations are bound to be different from highly developed governments with rich administrative traditions, like Hong Kong. Research into these questions, however, is in its infancy, and we consequently know relatively little about the central questions.

LESSONS FROM TWO DECADES OF PUBLIC MANAGEMENT REFORM

What lessons spin from the two decades of reforms and transformations flying loosely under the banner of "the new public management?" A careful review of the experiences of nations around the globe suggests a series of propositions (Jones, 2000).

Public Management Reform is Never Done

Analysts and practitioners alike have sometimes been tempted to view the reforms with cynicism. For some, the lack of clear or full success led to the conclusion that the reforms had failed. For others, the evolution of new strategies led to the conclusion that earlier efforts had been abandoned. In fact, history shows that public management reforms recur, with each new piece woven – sometimes seamlessly – into the next. There are several reasons for this. First, no reform can ever fully solve the problems that led to its creation. Lingering issues tend to breed the next generation of reforms. Second, public management is not so much a problem-solving activity as a problem-balancing enterprise. Any reform strategy requires making choices at the margin that focus on some problems more than others and that emphasize some values more than others. Because no solution can ever be complete, each reform necessarily leaves problems unaddressed and under-addressed and every reform therefore breeds the next. Third, because management problems tend to recur and the bag of management tricks is relatively limited, reforms tend to cycle between accepted strategies – periods of centralization followed by episodes of decentralization, deregulation replacing bureaucratisation. Careful observers of administrative reform can detect the recurring patterns.

The "New Public Management" has Proven a Fundamentally Different Approach to Reform

Some critics have therefore dismissed the new public management as worthless nostrums or old ideas dressed up in new clothes. The experience over the last two decades, however, shows that there truly has been something new in the "new" public management. To the dismay of some detractors and to the hopes of some reformers, the new public management has introduced a heavy dose of economic models and tactics into public management. From privatisation to performance contracts, the new public management has sought to replace bureaucratic authority with economic incentives. Contracting out and other market-based strategies, of course, have been around for decades, if not centuries. But the new public management pursued them with a single-mindedness unseen previously. Moreover, the new public management reforms spread around the world with an energy and simultaneity never seen before with any kind of management reform. The rise of the internet and relatively inexpensive international air travel helped drive this movement. So too did the near-universal rise of citizen discontent over the cost and performance of government. Never before have so many governments tried such similar things in such short order.

Political Reality Drives Management Reform More Than Management Concerns

Scholars in particular have examined the new public management and other management reforms, like America's reinventing government, for theoretical insights. Enduring analytical conclusions have proven elusive because the reforms have been so different. Different nations have gone down different paths because their high-level officials have been trying to solve different problems and cope with different political realities. Even relatively similar nations, such as the United Kingdom, Canada, Australia, and New Zealand, have produced markedly different strategies. Finding common ground with other nations' experiments has often proven difficult. In large part, this is because top officials launched the management reforms for fundamentally political reasons: to cope with budget crises, to sustain public services without increasing taxes, and to signal concern about citizens' disaffection with government. Top officials sustained the reforms as long as they had political value; they transformed them or backed away when political pressures demanded. When asked to comment on the New Zealand reforms, one careful observer immediately began discussing the proportional representation plan for the parliament – not the fifteen years of management reforms that preceded it. A New Zealand official tells audiences of his mother's constant question about the management reforms: "Why does it still take so long to get a gall bladder operation?"[1] Politics lies at the core of management reform, not vice versa. Management reforms have their genesis and sustenance in the degree to which they help solve political problems.

The Political Clout of the New Public Management has been Negligible

After the new public management's first twenty years, it has become clear that the effort provided little political clout in any nation. In the U.S., President Bill Clinton significantly downsized the bureaucracy and proudly proclaimed the smallest bureaucracy in 30 years, only to have Republicans win control of both houses of

Congress for the first time in 40 years. Vice President Al Gore barely mentioned his reinventing government effort on the presidential campaign trail in 2000 and got no political credit for having led it. Prime Minister Tony Blair made little of his own management reforms in the 2001 elections. There simply is little evidence that management reforms have translated into electoral victories or, even, into modest political gains.

Despite the Lack of Traction from Management Reform as a Political Issue, it is a Puzzle with Which Elected Officials Nevertheless Feel Obliged to Wrestle

Even if public management builds little political capital, management problems do have the potential to cause enormous headaches. Prime Minister Blair found himself struggling with the management of the foot-and-mouth outbreak as he geared up election campaign, and these struggles in fact shifted the timing of the elections. In the language of political consultants, management reform has little upside potential but can pose a tremendous downside threat. In other words, it might not help, but it certainly can hurt. Management problems have a recurring tendency to develop, and elected officials must deal with them effectively or risk serious political damage. Thus, management reform springs eternal.

With the New Public Management, Reforms are Moving Increasingly from Restructuring to Process Re-Engineering

In most countries, public management for generations had built on the traditions of hierarchy and authority. The Prussian influence was especially strong in European nations and in other countries, like the United States, that borrowed heavily on these ideas. As these nations developed their empire, the traditions spread as well. When these approaches encountered problems – as inevitably they did – the instinct was to reorganize the structure and reorient the authority. The launch of the new public management movement was a frank recognition that hierarchy and authority, in all their variations and reforms, had reached their limits. The new public management emphasized market incentives and contract-based approaches. The reforms, in short, sought either to supplement or replace traditional structure-based approaches with process-based reforms.

Despite Wide Variation in Reform Strategies, There is a Convergence of Reforms Around General Themes

The enormous variation in reforms has long frustrated analysts, who have struggled to define what "the new public management" actually is. Assessing whether the new public management actually constitutes an identifiable set of ideas, let alone whether nations are increasingly pursuing more-similar ideas, is a daunting problem. No less an authority than Graham Scott, however, has observed, "For most of the world, the late twentieth century has been about reducing the scope of government. But this process must inevitably slow down." In time, he suggested, the pace of downsizing will inevitably slow and governments will face the task of managing the programs that remain. That, in turn, will likely turn more governments to the American reform strategy of making government "work better and cost less." As Scott concluded, "Over time, the rest of us will look more and more like the United States, as the problems of what the government is going to do become less urgent and we deal with them by marginal adjustments rather than sudden and radical change, and focus more on the steady processes of improvement around the organizations that will persist" (Scott, 1999).

Developing Nations have Different Management Reform Problems than Developed Nations

For at least some observers, the convergence argument suggests that nations that are serious about performance pursue management reform and that most reforms are moving in at least loose synchronization. However, Allen Schick bluntly warns (1998) that "most developing countries should not try New Zealand reforms" or other "new public management" strategies. Indeed, facing a huge need to grow their economies and shrink their governments, many developing countries have found the reforms irresistible. Schick contends that the new public management-style reforms require a foundation of governmental rules, vigorous markets, and broadly accepted dispute-resolution processes that many developing countries lack. Seeking short cuts, Schick concludes, risks sending developing nations into dead ends. Different nations in different positions with different traditions, structures, and capacities need different strategies, even if they attempt to follow the new public management course.

The Pursuit of the New Public Management Strategy has Revealed a Mismatch Among Practice, Theory, and Instruction

Unlike some previous reforms around the world, where scholars charted at least some of the course, the new public management has evolved with only modest theoretical foundation. Formal theory has suggested concepts like moral hazard and adverse selection, but most of the hard work has come from pragmatic officials cobbling together approaches to very hard problems. Theorists have struggled to determine just what the new public management is, how it differs from country to country, whether it has succeeded, how it might transform itself, and whether it will prove a lasting phenomenon. Public officials, pressed with high public demands and limited resources, have rarely stopped to ask such questions. Meanwhile, in public policy programs around the world, academic leaders have struggled to assess whether they need to transform their curricula to prepare students for the new public management. For the most part, these leaders have understandably taken a cautious approach. However, this has left public officials with an even greater problem of finding young managers with the skills to operate effectively in the new program strategies. Of all the options, the one sure bet probably lies in forecasting rapid change. The tensions at the core of the practice, theory, and instruction dilemma thus will only increase.

What Role will National Governments Play?

Osborne and Gaebler inspired some officials and enraged others by suggesting that the government of the future ought to steer, not row (1993). Central governments around the world have found themselves in the midst of a fundamental transformation, with simultaneously more globalization and devolution of power (Kettl, 2000b). What role can and should central governments play in a world where their traditional roles have become more marginal yet their importance has only increased? Managers of central government agencies have sought greater leverage in the management of networks and the creation of information systems, among other tools. How to weave these new tools together into a freshly defined role, however, proved anything but clear.

CONCLUSIONS

Learning from the experience of public management reform strategy within and across national boundaries is daunting. The tendency is to say that context dominates all lessons. However, the lessons reviewed here and elsewhere suggest some interdependence. In many regions of the world, cross-national organizations, like OECD, the Asian Development Bank, the World Bank, the International Monetary Fund, have encouraged management reform and have stimulated reform networks across national borders. There are elements of isomorphic transference in the reform experiences of some countries: in Hong Kong, in Taiwan, and from New Zealand to almost everywhere.

One nation's copying the reforms of others can help improve the effectiveness of public services and attract greater investment. Information technology has spurred the spread of reform ideas. The internet reveals, at least to the computer literate, the success or failure of policy adventures in different countries and analyses of reforms by academics and others. The media play an important role in identifying policy problems and comparing solutions among nations. Consultants have spread many ideas among their clients. As a result, nations engage in far more rapid policy reproduction and perhaps even learning than has been evident in the past.

Public management reform invites evaluation of convergence: how much, of what kind, and in what directions. Boston's assessment of New Zealand invites questions about the degree of unisonance in reform. He finds clear benefits, but the dearth of "before and after" studies, or even thoughtful quasi-experimental designs, prevent genuine evaluation of the effectiveness of public management reforms. Boston terms the broad nature of evaluations about reform as "counter-factual," because gauging the impact is difficult without greater specificity. Similarly, Wescott's analysis reinforces this picture of diversity with his analysis of methodological problems in defining and introducing reforms. In Gregory's account, the "mechanistic" adoption of reform in New Zealand created long-term implementation problems, which proved especially notable compared with the enthusiasm that first greeted the reform process.

Convergence vs. divergence is a long-standing debate in public administration and management. Principles of economic efficiency and effectiveness, or choice and market forces would suggest that rhetorically one would expect to see a more consistent picture of reform in the past decade or so. There is ample evidence of a convergence in rhetoric. Reformers speak eagerly of "reinvention," "entrepreneurial management," and "results-based approaches." Indeed, the work reviewed here suggests that there indeed in some convergence. However, there clearly are instances of divergence as well, because of the special circumstances of nations, regions, and the developed-developing nations contrast. On balance, there appears to be a convergence in the reform agendas and implementation efforts in the U.K., in most British Commonwealth nations, in selected OECD nations, and the United States. The convergence emerges among developed nations. The experience of developing nations is more diverse.

Even assessing the convergence/divergence question, however, requires far greater precision in defining the problem and developing a useful language for exploring it. Roberts' analysis of the inability to define "problems" accurately shows the underlying problems affecting both the formulation and implementation of management reform. That, she suggests, is why cooperative strategies can prove useful. Similarly, both Wescott and Shand suggest that while diversity exists, cooperative tools can assist in the reform process and are applicable across borders.

Nevertheless, application of the same or similar approaches in different nations may succeed or fail in different ways. Reform is about building capacity to do the old things in different ways and to discover new things that need doing. Reforming public organizations may provide institutional remedies, but traditional restructuring cannot eliminate the changes of retrograde tendencies or prevent problems from recurring. This comparison, moreover, suggests the need for more careful analysis about what constitutes "good reform." Is it merely locating the definition of a "problem" in the standard NPM lineup and finding the relevant "solution?" Is there greater need for refinement of interpretive and epistemological skills before nations embark to mimic what is done elsewhere? A significant lesson, thus, is this clear definition of the problems to be solved is the first step towards successful change.

From there nations need to move toward experimenting with various methods, and carefully gauging results, until the combination that best solves their problems emerges. This experimentation takes time, energy, patience and a commitment to careful, unbiased, and unvarnished evaluation. It requires the will to ask questions when the answers could prove inconvenient or embarrassing. Then there is the question of building the political will to move in the direction the evaluation points. Politics plays the crucial role throughout this cycle in determining how the problem is to be defined, what methods may be tried, whether evaluation is to be done and by whom, and whether the results are to be heeded and followed.

Other lessons apply to the role of the state. English and Guthrie, and Hughes and O'Neill emphasize the importance of strengthening the institutions of governance. Accountability is a paramount virtue in governance. Reform *per se* is not sufficient to ensure greater accountability; it is necessary to strengthen the institutions of governance *and* management. Shand and Wescott concur in this observation. Neale and Anderson outline the challenges for the New Zealand performance reporting process with respect to parliamentary utility. Jones and Mussari suggest (2001) that the U.S. Congress and the Italian Parliament may not benefit from the accountability mechanisms they have enacted. Conversely, Schedler (2001) demonstrates the value of performance budgeting in Switzerland to result from a unique balance between freedom and regulation, between the rigidities of the law and the needs of politicians.

Institution building is not likely to be achieved by enlarging the role of the state, but by *rediscovering* the tasks and roles that governments are best suited – and most needed – to perform. Those tasks can include building critical capacity for planning and evaluation. Reform might well produce more effective service delivery institutions as well as governments that work more effectively with the private sector. It might also produce new forms of regulation that more productively shape market behavior.

The manifestations of public management reform are many and varied. Debate about its variations can be awkward because of widespread differences in governance problems, political cultures, and reform language. This reinforces the need for a conceptual framework and language for public management reform, allowing for contribution from different disciplines. Barzelay (2001) argues that without a common frame of reference and language, meaningful dialogue on public management reform cannot occur.

The public management reform movement has also framed new questions. What role should the nation-state play as but one player in a new architecture of governance where networks of organizations comprise more effective problem solving entities than single governments? How can public bureaucracy effectively solve complex governance problems without sacrificing the public interest? New organizational forms such as hyperarchies, flatter and more decentralized entities with greater delegation of authority and responsibility and faster learning-adaptation-action cycles (Jones & Thompson, 1999, pp. 3–4, 174–176; see also Evans & Wurster, 1997, p. 75), appear likely to be more effective than traditional bureaucratic organizations to manage networked programs.

It is simply too early to tell whether NPM is or is not a new "paradigm," in the Kuhnian sense. Indeed, it is not clear whether the question has meaning and it certainly is clear that not enough information is available to try to answer it. Management reform, in fact, has proven a far more subtle enterprise that extends over the medium and long-term in order for any political or managerial regime to succeed relative to the ambitious agendas proposed and the need for assessment and feedback using an appropriately broad set of evaluative measures. The survival of governments, politicians and managers advocating reform and attempting to implement comprehensive change appears to depend upon relatively slow and careful implementation. Moreover, any theory of public management by necessity is highly contingent.

Nevertheless, it is also clear that the "new public management" is no longer new. Many of the reforms labeled as NPM have been under implementation for ten, twenty or more years. Although academics can claim to have defined the techniques and terminology of the "new public management" with a reasonable degree of precision (see Borins, 1997; Jones & Schedler, 1997), much of the dialogue about NPM, pro and con, is confusing, disconnected and, in effect, a distraction that inhibits sincere attempts to determine the outcomes of change.

Out of this decades-long tradition have emerged criticisms by academics from a variety of social science disciplines. Indeed, NPM critics appear to out-number advocates in academe, if not in the practitioner environment. Some of this may be related to the fact that academics face professional and career incentives to find fault rather than to extol success. Additionally, some criticism of NPM may derive from the fact that it is perceived to draw conceptually too strongly from a business-driven perspective. This approach threatens the traditions of public administration and public policy programs, which build on the primacy of government aggressively pursuing the public interest. The NPM debate will – and should – continue, and as it does it should move toward a better structured and more informed dialogue about reform more generally. Recently published works on NPM and public management reform attempt to clarify this dialogue (see, for example, Barzelay, 2001; Jones & Thompson, 1999; Kettl, 2000a).

At the core of the reforms lurk the issue of equity, which neither academics nor practitioners have considered carefully enough. In particular, public officials have not sufficiently addressed equity goals while pursuing managerial efficiency. It is surely the case that those who support increased public sector efficiency will (or wish to) ignore the risk of greater income disparity, impaired earning capability for many citizens, increased poverty, and worsening of health, social, and educational services. Much reform appears to be directed with a high degree of insularity of purpose to change governments internally without much attention to distributional consequences. Any careful review of the implications of management reform must address those linkages. As Frieder Naschold would warn (Naschold & Daley, 1999), unless better government and improved services result from reform, why should change be undertaken?

NOTE

1. Interview with the author.

REFERENCES

Barzelay, M. (2001). *The new public management*. Berkeley, CA: University of California Press.
Barzelay, M., & Armajani, B. J. (1992). *Breaking through bureaucracy: A new vision for managing in government*. Berkeley, CA: University of California Press.
Borins, S. (1997). What the new public management is achieving: A survey of Commonwealth experience. In: L. R. Jones & K. Schedler (Eds), *International Perspectives on the New Public Management* (pp. 49–70). Stamford, CT: JAI Press.
Boston, J. (2001). The challenge of evaluating systemic change: The case of public management reform in New Zealand. In: L. R. Jones, J. Guthrie & P. Steane (Eds), *Learning from International Public Management Reform* (Vol. 11A, pp. 103–132). Oxford: JAI Press/Elsevier.
Boston, J., Martin, J., Pallot, J., & Walsh, P. (1996). *Public management: The New Zealand model*. Auckland: Oxford University Press.
Carlin, T., & Guthrie, J. (2001). Lessons from Australian and New Zealand experiences with accrual output-based budgeting. In: L. R. Jones, J. Guthrie & P. Steane (Eds), *Learning from International Public Management Reform* (Vol. 11A, pp. 89–100). Oxford: JAI Press/Elsevier.

English, L., & Guthrie, J. (2001). The challenge of evaluating systemic change: The case of public management reform in New Zealand. In: L. R. Jones, J. Guthrie & P. Steane (Eds), *Learning from International Public Management Reform* (Vol. 11A, pp. 45–60). Oxford: JAI Press/Elsevier.

Evans, P. B., & Wurster, T. S. (1997). Strategy and the new economics of information. *Harvard Business Review* (September–October), 71–82.

Gill, D. (2001). New Zealand experience with public management reform. In: L. R. Jones, J. Guthrie & P. Steane (Eds), *Learning from International Public Management Reform* (Vol. 11A, pp. 143–160). Oxford: JAI Press/Elsevier.

Gray, A., & Jenkins, B. (1995, Spring). From public administration to public management: Reassessing a revolution? *Public Administration, 73*, 75–99.

Gregory, R. (2001). Getting better but feeling worse? Public sector reform in New Zealand. In: L. R. Jones, J. Guthrie & P. Steane (Eds), *Learning from International Public Management Reform* (Vol. 11A, pp. 211–231). Oxford: JAI Press/Elsevier.

Guthrie, J., Olson, O., & Humphrey, C. (1997). Debating developments in new public financial management: The limits of global theorising and some new ways forward. *Financial Accountability and Management 15, 3*(4), 209–228.

Guthrie, J., & Parker, L. (1998). Managerialism and marketisation in financial management change in Australia. In: O. Olson, J. Guthrie & C. Humphrey (Eds), *Global Warning – Debating International Developments in New Public Financial Management* (pp. 49–75). Bergen, Norway: Cappelen Akademisk Forlag.

Harr, D. J., & Godfrey, J. T. (1991). *Private sector financial performance measures and their applicability to government operations*. Montvale, NJ: National Association of Accountants.

Hood, C. (1995, Spring). Emerging issues in public administration. *Public Administration, 73*, 165–183.

Hood, C. (2000). Paradoxes of public sector managerialism, old public management and public service bargains. *International Public Management Journal, 3*(1), 1–20.

Hughes, O., & O'Neill, D. (2001). Public sector management in the state of Victoria: 1992–1999: Genesis of the transformation. In: L. R. Jones, J. Guthrie & P. Steane (Eds), *Learning from International Public Management Reform* (Vol. 11A, pp. 61–76). Oxford: JAI Press/Elsevier.

Jones, L. R. (2000). IPMN Newsletter No. 2, IPMN website www.inpuma.net.

Jones, L. R., & Mussari, R. (2001). Management control reform within a responsibility framework in the U.S. and Italy. In: L. R. Jones, J. Guthrie & P. Steane (Eds), *Learning from International Public Management Reform* (Vol. 11B, pp. 499–530). Oxford: JAI Press/Elsevier.

Jones, L. R., & Schedler, K. (Eds) (1997). *International perspectives on the new public management*. Stamford, CT: JAI Press.

Jones, L. R., & Thompson, F. (1999). *Public management: Institutional renewal for the 21st century*. Stamford, CT: JAI Press/Elsevier.

Kettl, D. (2000a). *The global public management revolution: A report on the transformation of governance*. Washington, DC: Brookings Institution.

Kettl, D. (2000b). The transformation of governance: Globalization, devolution, and the role of government. *Public Administration Review* (November/December), 488–497.

Kibblewhite, A. (2001). Effectiveness: The next frontier in New Zealand. In: L. R. Jones, J. Guthrie & P. Steane (Eds), *Learning from International Public Management Reform* (Vol. 11A, pp. 177–192). Oxford: JAI Press/Elsevier.

Laking, R. (2001). Reflections on public sector reform in New Zealand. In: L. R. Jones, J. Guthrie & P. Steane (Eds), *Learning from International Public Management Reform* (Vol. 11A, pp. 133–142). Oxford: JAI Press/Elsevier.

March, J. G., & Olsen, J. P. (1995). *Democratic governance*. New York: Free Press.

Milgrom, P., & Roberts, J. (1992). *Economics, organization, and management*. Englewood Cliffs, NJ: Prentice-Hall.
Moe, T. M. (1984). The new economics of organization. *American Journal of Political Science, 28*(4), 739–777.
Naschold, F., & Daley, G. (1999). Modernizing local governments. *International Public Management Journal, 2*(1), 25–98.
Newberry, S. (2001). Network structures, consumers and accountability in New Zealand. In: L. R. Jones, J. Guthrie & P. Steane (Eds), *Learning from International Public Management Reform* (Vol. 11A, pp. 257–278). Oxford: JAI Press/Elsevier.
OECD (1997). *In search of results: Performance management practices*. Paris: OECD.
Olsen, J. P., & Peters, G. (1996). *Lessons from experience: Experiential learning in adminstrative reforms in eight democracies*. Oslo: Scandanavian University Press.
Olson, O., Guthrie, J., & Humphrey, C. (Eds) (1998). *Global warning – Debating international developments in new public financial management*. Bergen, Norway: Cappelen Akademisk Forlag.
Osborne, D., & Gaebler, T. (1993). *Reinventing government: How the entrepreneurial spirit is transforming the public sector*. New York: Penguin.
Pallot, J. (1998). The New Zealand revolution. In: O. Olson, J. Guthrie & C. Humphrey (Eds), *Global Warning – Debating International Developments in New Public Financial Management* (pp. 156–184). Bergen, Norway: Cappelen Akademisk Forlag.
PUMA, OECD (1999). *Performance contracting: Lessons from performance contracting case studies*. Paris: OECD.
Pusey, M. (1991). *Economics rationalism in Canberra: A nation-building state changes its mind*. London: Cambridge University Press.
Putterill, M., & Speer, D. (2001). Information policy in New Zealand. In: L. R. Jones, J. Guthrie & P. Steane (Eds), *Learning from International Public Management Reform* (Vol. 11A, pp. 279–290). Oxford: JAI Press/Elsevier.
Riley, K., & Watling, R. (1999). Education action zones: An initiative in the making. *Public Money and Management* (July–September), 51–58.
Roberts, N. (2001). Coping with wicked problems: The case of Afghanistan. In: L. R. Jones, J. Guthrie & P. Steane (Eds), *Learning from International Public Management Reform* (Vol. 11B, pp. 353–376). Oxford: JAI Press/Elsevier.
Schedler, K. (2001). Performance budgeting in Switzerland: Implications for political control. In: L. R. Jones, J. Guthrie & P. Steane (Eds), *Learning from International Public Management Reform* (Vol. 11B, pp. 455–477). Oxford: JAI Press/Elsevier.
Schick, A. (1998). Why most developing countries should not try New Zealand reforms. *The World Bank Research Observer* (February), 123–131.
Scott, G. (1999, January 14). Presentation at the global forum on reinventing government. Plenary Session 1, Washington, DC.
Scott, G. (2001). Public management reform and lessons from experience in New Zealand. In: L. R. Jones, J. Guthrie & P. Steane (Eds), *Learning from International Public Management Reform* (Vol. 11A, pp. 133–142). Oxford: JAI Press/Elsevier.
Shand, D. (2001). The world bank and public sector management reform. In: L. R. Jones, J. Guthrie & P. Steane (Eds), *Learning from International Public Management Reform* (Vol. 11B, pp. 377–390). Oxford: JAI Press/Elsevier.
Tooley, S. (2001). Observations on the imposition of new public management in the New Zealand state education system. In: L. R. Jones, J. Guthrie & P. Steane (Eds), *Learning from International Public Management Reform* (Vol. 11A, pp. 233–255). Oxford: JAI Press/Elsevier.

Wescott, C. (2001). Measuring governance in developing Asia. In: L. R. Jones, J. Guthrie & P. Steane (Eds), *Learning from International Public Management Reform* (Vol. 11B, pp. 295–310). Oxford: JAI Press/Elsevier.

Yuk-fai, A. K., Vertinsky, I., & Wang, D. Y. (2001). New public management in Hong Kong: The long march toward reform. In: L. R. Jones, J. Guthrie & P. Steane (Eds), *Learning from International Public Management Reform* (Vol. 11B, pp. 311–336). Oxford: JAI Press/Elsevier.

Yu-Ying, K. (2001). New public management in Taiwan: Government reinvention. In: L. R. Jones, J. Guthrie & P. Steane (Eds), *Learning from International Public Management Reform* (Vol. 11B, pp. 337–351). Oxford: JAI Press/Elsevier.

SUBJECT INDEX

A compact of mutual, collective responsibility, 40, 41, 43, 44, 49
A model for stakeholding, 96
Absence of boundaries, 120
Acceptability in principle, 299
Accountability, 1, 2, 8–11, 19–36, 38–49, 57, 86, 106, 114, 119, 128, 153–157, 160, 162, 166, 167, 180, 197, 230, 232, 235, 237, 239, 249, 251, 253, 269, 270, 274, 276, 279, 288, 290, 293, 298, 327, 329, 331, 334, 335, 337, 339, 387, 419, 437, 440, 446, 454–457, 459, 468
Accounting reform, 214, 454, 456
Activities, 21, 36, 38, 39, 42, 69, 92, 97, 98, 117, 121, 127, 135, 137, 138, 141, 144, 145, 147–149, 152, 162, 166, 168, 170, 179, 183, 194, 206, 209, 219–222, 230, 233, 235, 238, 239, 246, 247, 251, 270, 289, 298, 303, 305–307, 311, 315, 327, 335, 336, 355, 366, 367, 375, 377, 379, 380, 417, 432, 434, 436, 441, 444, 456
Actual outcomes, 435, 436, 439, 440
Algorithm, 329
Ambiguous balance, 404
Analyzing the events, 365
Anti-corruption plan, 286, 293, 305, 306, 308, 310, 312, 314–316
Anti-corruption strategy in Albania, 286, 305, 319
Anti-money Laundering Office, 161, 162, 165
Asian Development Bank, 466
Asia, 13, 233, 343, 460, 461
Australia, 3, 10, 12, 13, 138, 211, 224, 268, 277, 340, 408, 415, 416, 423, 426, 434, 435, 446, 447, 454–456, 459, 461, 463

Balanced scorecard, 386–390, 392
Benefit accounting, 375
Blueprints, 195
Breaking the accountability mindset, 42
BundOnline 2005 e-government initiative, 141

Capital allocation in the NHS, 57
Carrot-and-stick theory of motivation, 25, 26
Case evidence, 354, 358, 363–365, 369
Case outcomes, 353, 350, 366
Causality, 265, 333, 407, 409
CDU, 245, 246, 250, 251, 253
CEE and CIS Countries, 328, 330, 331, 334, 335, 338, 344
Cheating, 30, 31, 47
Citizen attitudes, 332
Citizen orientation, 389
Client access needs, 432
Communication and management, 159
Comparative perspective, 107, 406, 407
Complexity in contractual relationships, 69
Conceptual framework, 3, 10, 109, 134, 261, 349, 469
Constrains, 333
Construction of the hospital and trust relationship, 72
Contracts and control, 59
Contract complexity, 70
Control of risk, 76
Coordination in delivery, 434
Corporate governance, 262, 264, 274–276, 278, 279,
Correlation, 135, 147, 148, 152, 262, 264, 265, 283, 303, 385
Corrupt practices, 259, 260, 263, 265, 280, 299–301, 303, 329, 338
Corruption expectations, 302

475

Corruption pressure, 300
Cost accounting, 187, 206, 239, 374
Customer orientation, 140, 159, 170, 389, 390, 397, 404

Delivery mix, 432
Delivery strategies, 431
Dependent variable, 144, 146, 147, 353
Developed nations, 230, 231, 465, 467
Developing nations, 4, 9, 12, 229, 230, 233, 234, 460, 465, 467
Development and implementation, 428
Devolution and localism, 434
Dimensions of observation, 388
Direct or proxy, 438
Document Processing System (DPS), 188, 191, 192

Educational accountability, 21, 23–28, 35, 43, 46, 47
Effect of the FCPA, 267
Effectiveness of corruption, 301
Effects of NPM Reform, 398, 399, 402, 404, 409
e-Government, 2, 9, 133–135, 137–141, 143–149, 152–156, 159–164, 166–172
Elements of MFO, 417
Empirical findings, 140
Evaluation in MFO, 439, 440
Evolution of excellence, 124
Externals, 139, 140, 144, 147, 152

Facilities management, 59, 72, 74, 75
FCPA, 260, 262, 265–270, 275, 279, 280
Financial rewards, 27, 28, 46

German Federal Administration, 138–140, 144, 147, 148
Goals of transparency and accountability, 166
Government agencies, 141, 142, 151, 164, 165, 186, 191, 400–403, 466
Government priorities, 418, 419, 422, 425
Government reform, 10, 119, 138, 153, 155, 295, 355

ICT policy, 161, 162, 166, 171, 172
IMF, 466
Immediate and intermediate objectives, 424, 425, 434–437, 440, 441,
Impact, 5, 9, 26, 29, 30, 46, 56, 69, 80, 92, 95, 96, 103, 105, 106, 112, 114, 135, 139, 148, 154, 158, 159, 161, 162, 192, 202, 216, 260, 267, 292, 295–298, 302, 304, 305, 308, 316, 325, 326, 331, 373, 375, 398, 401, 402, 405, 407, 408, 410, 412, 418, 440, 441, 444, 457, 467,
Implementation counts, 427
Increases in Public Information, 315
Increase of transparency, 313, 314
Independent variables, 144, 146, 147
Indicators, 1, 3, 7, 10, 46, 75, 106, 110, 157, 219, 289, 290, 313, 371, 374, 378, 380, 381–384, 386, 388, 392, 397, 401, 402, 406, 407, 408, 414, 424, 436–439, 456
Industrial model, 34, 35
Informal networks, 105–108, 110, 117, 120, 123, 125
Interest focus, 100
Internal control, 260, 262, 268–274, 278–280, 314
Interview protocols, 364, 365
Introduction of PFI, 64, 80
IRS, 175–177, 179, 182, 183–201,
IT modernization, 179, 190, 194, 196, 197, 198
IT renewal, 184, 185, 189, 193, 194, 199

Learning and growth, 390
Level of government and ministries, 402, 407
Logic models, 423, 424, 427

Mangement activties, 135, 137, 144, 147, 149, 152
Management control organization, 218
Management control reform, 205, 206, 222, 225
Management fraud, 272, 273
Management reform strategy, 453, 466
Managerial reform, 13, 105, 106, 116, 127, 158, 171, 202, 435, 454

Measures of corruption, 262
Measuring corruption, 297
Methodological reflections, 409
Methodology, 3, 32, 111, 114, 118, 143, 213, 263, 312, 314, 352, 364, 395, 442, 443
MFO evolution, 438
MFO, 415–420, 423, 424, 426–431, 433, 436, 437–447
Models of client behaviour, 430
Modernization, 2, 3, 9, 109, 119, 122, 123, 127, 151, 153, 155, 158, 175–177, 179, 181, 183–186, 188, 190, 191, 194–198, 201, 214, 317, 350, 358–362, 461
Monitor outcomes, 435
Motivation, doubts, and messiness, 426

New Zealand, 12, 13, 49, 138, 211, 212, 224, 252, 253, 268, 340, 408, 415, 421, 423, 426, 435, 443, 446, 447, 454–459, 461, 463, 465–468, 455,
National Health Care System (NHS), 116
Non-positivist, 436, 437, 442, 443
NPM in Switzerland, 396
NPM reforms, 5, 155, 235, 249, 395–406, 408–413
New public management (NPM), 85, 86, 214, 230, 395, 403, 454

OECD Principles, 275
Organizational risk, 175, 178, 179, 181
Organization, network relationships, behaviour and innovation, 122
Outcome accounting, 374
Output accounting, 374, 388
Output, 35, 70, 74, 87, 166, 206, 208, 209, 373–375, 377–384, 386–389, 391–393, 398, 401, 404, 405, 407, 408, 410, 421, 422, 430, 432, 433, 435, 447, 454, 456

Paradoxes of NPM, 89, 102
Parliament, 98, 100, 102, 218, 222, 223, 314, 317, 377, 383, 385, 397–402, 407, 418, 426, 427, 440, 446, 454, 463, 468
Performance control system, 384

Performance measurement technique for strategy, 386
Performance measurement, 1, 3, 4, 11, 24, 159, 206, 209, 371, 372, 374, 387–389, 392, 393, 454
Performance reports, 437
Policy and Program goals and objectives, 419
Political corruption in France, 240, 246, 248
Political corruption, 229–232, 235, 240, 245, 246–254
Political involvement, 135, 136, 138, 144, 147, 152
Positivist, 442
Post-positivist, 439, 442, 443
Post-TSM, 179, 194
Process and outputs, 420
Process orientation, 390
Product definition, 378, 379, 382
Products, 35, 48, 171, 183, 216, 373, 374, 377–382, 384, 388, 391, 401, 403, 404, 405, 406, 407, 412, 433
Program life cycle, 430–432, 441, 442
Public administration in Albania, 294
Public administration reform, 156, 314
Public finances management and audit mechanism, 314
Public management policy change, 3, 105, 108, 349–355, 357, 358, 361, 366,
Public sector reform, 12, 108, 155, 156, 158, 161, 170, 171, 326

Quantitative, 143, 271, 373, 436, 438, 439, 442, 443, 460

Reform of public management, 3, 153, 330
Reform strategies, 7, 9, 12, 159, 464,
Reforming the reform, 13
Regulatory and political environments, 277
Prevalence of corruption, 302, 327
Renewal, 7, 153, 155, 177, 183, 184, 185, 189, 193, 194, 199, 201, 214, 460
Research approach and organization, 178
Research design, 111, 143, 350, 352, 353, 357, 369, 443
Research questions, 106, 350, 351, 353, 357–365, 369

Resources and assistance for schools, 22
Responsibility budgeting, 206–208, 210, 211–214, 222–224
Responsibility framework, 205, 208
Responsibility structure formulation, 207
Return rate, 142, 143, 151
Risk culture, 176–179, 181, 188, 191, 193, 198
Risk-taking, 175–181
Role of auditors, 276
Role of leadership, 334
Rough-'n-ready, 422, 444, 445

Senior management, 223, 224, 403, 406
Simple or complex, 438
Soft factors, 135, 136, 138, 144, 147–149, 152
Spread of corruption, 301
Stakeholder literature, 91
Stakeholding in health, 93
Standards, 11, 19, 22–26, 29–31, 45–47, 63, 87, 90, 122, 127, 136, 141, 157, 164, 182, 196, 209, 212–214, 234, 243, 253, 264, 270, 272, 273, 277, 278, 291, 293, 306, 307, 312, 317, 318, 326, 331, 335, 339, 373, 381–384, 433, 436, 455
Strategic approaches to reform, 1
Strategic dialogue, 420, 437, 446
Susceptibility to corruption, 300
Switzerland, 3, 4, 10, 13, 140, 268, 340, 372, 387, 392, 395–398, 400, 401, 403, 406–410, 412, 413, 468

System trust, 63–68, 72, 73, 78–80
Systematic corruption, 337

Technical capacity, 443, 444
The Brazilian 1967 Episode, 366
The nature of stakeholder power, 97
Theoretical framework, 108, 285, 287, 363, 455, 458
Theory and practice, 391, 424, 458
Transition countries, 291–293, 297, 298, 327
Transparency, 2, 9, 10, 12, 32, 107, 122, 145, 153–158, 160–162, 164, 166, 167, 223, 229, 235, 237, 239, 246, 253, 254, 259, 263–265, 275, 276, 279, 280, 293, 307, 308, 311, 313, 314, 315, 318, 327, 329, 330, 332–337, 339, 343, 369, 387, 401, 410
Travelgate, 240, 241, 244, 250
Trust and PFI contracts, 69
TSM, 177–179, 181–184, 186–190, 192–195, 199, 239
Types of evaluation, 440–442

Underpinnings of new public management, 235, 253

Value of learning models, 5

World Bank, 230, 235, 260, 261, 280, 286–288, 291, 297, 298, 302, 309, 310, 326, 333, 334, 337, 338, 453, 461, 466

Set up a Continuation Order Today!

Did you know you can set up a continuation order on all JAI series and have each new volume sent directly to you upon publication. For details on how to set up a continuation order contact your nearest regional sales office listed below.

To view related Business, Management and Accounting series, please visit

www.ElsevierBusinessandManagement.com

30% Discount for Authors on all Books!

A 30% discount is available to Elsevier book and journal contributors ON ALL BOOKS plus standalone CD-ROMS except multi-volume reference works.

To claim your discount, full payment is required with your order, which must be sent directly to the publisher at the nearest regional sales office listed below.

Elsevier Regional Sales Offices

For customers in the Americas:
Customer Service Department
11830 Westline Industrial Drive
St. Louis, MO 63146
USA
For US customers:
Tel: +1 800 545 2522
Fax: +1 800 535 9935
For customers outside the US:
Tel: +1 800 460 3110
Fax: +1 314 453 7095
Email: usbkinfo@elsevier.com

For customers in Europe, Middle East and Africa:
Elsevier
Customer Services Department
Linacre House, Jordan Hill
Oxford OX2 8DP
United Kingdom
Tel: +44 (0) 1865 474140
Fax: +44 (0) 1865 474141
Email: amstbkinfo@elsevier.com

For customers in the Far East:
Elsevier
Customer Support Department
3 Killiney Road, #08-01/09
Winsland House I,
Singapore 239519
Tel: +(65) 63490200
Fax: + (65) 67331817/67331276
Email: asiainfo@elsevier.com.sg

For customers in Australasia:
Elsevier
Customer Service Department
30-52 Smidmore Street
Marrickville, New South Wales 2204
Australia
Tel: +61 (02) 9517 8999
Fax: +61 (02) 9517 2249
Email: service@elsevier.com.au